# Empiriomonism

# Historical Materialism Book Series

The Historical Materialism Book Series is a major publishing initiative of the radical left. The capitalist crisis of the twenty-first century has been met by a resurgence of interest in critical Marxist theory. At the same time, the publishing institutions committed to Marxism have contracted markedly since the high point of the 1970s. The Historical Materialism Book Series is dedicated to addressing this situation by making available important works of Marxist theory. The aim of the series is to publish important theoretical contributions as the basis for vigorous intellectual debate and exchange on the left.

The peer-reviewed series publishes original monographs, translated texts, and reprints of classics across the bounds of academic disciplinary agendas and across the divisions of the left. The series is particularly concerned to encourage the internationalization of Marxist debate and aims to translate significant studies from beyond the English-speaking world.

*For a full list of titles in the Historical Materialism Book Series available in paperback from Haymarket Books, visit:*
https://www.haymarketbooks.org/series_collections/1-historical-materialism

# Empiriomonism

*Essays in Philosophy, Books 1–3*

Alexander Bogdanov

Appreciation of Bogdanov's intellectual achievements by
V.A. Bazarov

Edited and translated by
David G. Rowley

Haymarket Books
Chicago, IL

First published in 2019 by Brill Academic Publishers, The Netherlands
© 2019 Koninklijke Brill NV, Leiden, The Netherlands

Published in paperback in 2020 by
Haymarket Books
P.O. Box 180165
Chicago, IL 60618
773-583-7884
www.haymarketbooks.org

ISBN: 978-1-64259-348-8

Distributed to the trade in the US through Consortium Book Sales and Distribution (www.cbsd.com) and internationally through Ingram Publisher Services International (www.ingramcontent.com).

This book was published with the generous support of Lannan Foundation and Wallace Action Fund.

Special discounts are available for bulk purchases by organizations and institutions. Please call 773-583-7884 or email info@haymarketbooks.org for more information.

Cover design by Jamie Kerry and Ragina Johnson.

Printed in the United States.

10 9 8 7 6 5 4 3 2 1

Library of Congress Cataloging-in-Publication data is available.

# Contents

Editor's Introduction on Text and Translation   VII
Bogdanov's Autobiography   XII
Bogdanov as a Thinker   XVII
   V.A. Bazarov

## Book One

1   The Ideal of Cognition (Empiriomonism of the Physical and the Psychical)   3

2   Life and the Psyche   44
   1   The Realm of Experiences   44
   2   Psychoenergetics   66
   3   The Monist Conception of Life   87

3   *Universum* (Empiriomonism of the Separate and the Continuous)   103

   Conclusion to Book One   130

## Book Two

4   The 'Thing-in-Itself' from the Perspective of Empiriomonism   133

5   Psychical Selection (Empiriomonism in the Theory of the Psyche)   162
   1   Foundations of the Method   162
      1.1   *The Model of Psychoenergetics*   162
      1.2   *The Model of Psychical Selection*   167
      1.3   *The Model of Association*   181
   2   Applications of the Method (Illustrations)   198

6   Two Theories of the Vital-Differential   249

## *Book Three*

7   **Preface to Book Three**   267
    1   Three Materialisms   268
    2   Energetics and Empiriocriticism   278
    3   The Path of Empiriomonism   283
    4   Regarding Eclecticism and Monism   295

8   **Social Selection (Foundations of the Method)**   303

9   **Historical Monism**   324
    1   Main Lines of Development   324
    2   Classes and Groups   362

10  **Self-Awareness of Philosophy (The Origin of Empiriomonism)**   403

    **Bibliography**   415
    **Name Index**   418
    **Subject Index**   419

# Editor's Introduction on Text and Translation

Instead of an editor's introduction, I am including a brief autobiography of Alexander Bogdanov, an appreciation of Bogdanov's intellectual achievements by V.A. Bazarov, one of his closest friends and associates and a philosopher in his own right, and a brief discussion of the original text and my translation of it.

The history of the text is as follows:

Bogdanov's first two philosophical works, *Osnovnye elementy istoricheskogo vzgliada na prirodu*, and *Poznanie s istoricheskogo tochki zreniia*, had been written for a popular audience. As Bogdanov suggested in his autobiography, he wanted to provide a whole worldview for workers who had accepted the principles of historical materialism and Marx's critique of capitalism. He was sharply criticised, however, by certain Russian revisionist Marxists for writing too simply; they accused him of philosophical ignorance and for glossing over profound issues of epistemology and ontology.[1]

Bogdanov responded with two philosophically sophisticated articles laying out the foundations of his neutral monist philosophy of knowing and being, 'Ideal poznaniia (Empiriokrititsizm i empiriomonism)' ['The Ideal of Cognition (Empiriocriticism and Empiriomonism)'][2] and 'Zhizn' i psikhika. (Empiriomonizm v uchenii o zhini)' ['Life and the Psyche. (Empiriomonism in the theory of life)'],[3] both of which were published in 1903 in Russia's leading philosophical journal, *Voprosy filosofii i psikhologii* [*Problems of Philosophy and Psychology*]. They became the first two chapters of Volume One of *Empiriomonism* to which he added a third chapter 'Universum', which was written specifically to complete Volume One, published in 1904.

Book One has considerable inner unity. Its task, according to Bogdanov, was 'to find that path along which it would be possible to systematically reduce all the gaps in our experience to the principle of continuity' (p. 130), and he identifies three gaps: the gap between 'spirit' and 'matter', the gap between 'consciousness' and 'physiology', and the gap in the field of experiences that separates the individual from the universal and individuals from one another. The three chapters deal with these gaps in succession.

Book Two (published in 1905) was less unified. The first chapter (4 in the present volume), 'The "Thing-in-Itself" from the Perspective of Empiriomon-

---

1 Peter Struve wrote a highly critical and dismissive review of *Osnovnye elementy* (G-d [P.B. Struve] 1899), and Nikolai Berdiaev treated *Poznanie* with similar disdain (Berdiaev 1902).
2 Bogdanov 1903a.
3 Bogdanov 1903b and 1903c.

ism', was a response to the charge from the camp of the 'orthodox' Marxists that Bogdanov was an idealist. The second chapter (5), 'Psychical Selection (Empiriomonism in the Theory of the Psyche)', which had been published in *Voprosy filosofii i psikhologii* in 1904,[4] deals with the problem of how a physical brain can acquire knowledge of the external world through purely physical processes. In the third chapter (6), 'Two Theories of the Vital-Differential', Bogdanov criticises Avenarius's concept of the 'vital-differential' and defends his own understanding of it.

All the chapters of Book Three were written specifically for it and had not previously been published elsewhere. It was published in 1906, after the relaxation of censorship after the Revolution of 1905, and this permitted Bogdanov to write much more openly about issues connected with Marxism. In the 'Preface to Book Three' (Chapter 7 in the present volume) Bogdanov recounts how his philosophical thought developed and criticises Plekhanov's metaphysical materialism. In the second chapter (8), 'Social Selection (Foundations of the Method)', Bogdanov takes up the question of causation in social change, applying the same energetical principles to social forms that he had applied to mental forms in 'Psychical Selection'. In the third chapter (9), 'Historical Monism', Bogdanov demonstrates how his conception of social selection applies to the relationship between base and superstructure. What Marx refers to as 'the material forces of production', Bogdanov calls 'the technology of productive labour', and what Marx refers to as 'the production of material life', Bogdanov calls 'assimilation of energy from the environment'. But for both Marx and Bogdanov, the process is the same: the mode of production conditions social, political, and intellectual life. The fourth chapter (10), 'The Self-Awareness of Philosophy (The Origin of Empiriomonism)', provides what Bogdanov terms a 'social-genetic', empiriomonistic explanation of empiriomonism itself. That is, he analyses the social basis of his own philosophy in order to understand how it is ideologically derivative of deeper-lying social conditions. He concludes that 'point of view, while not being "materialist" in the narrow sense of this word, belongs to the same order as "materialist" systems, and it is consequently the ideology of the "productive forces" of the technological process' (p. 407).

Book One of *Empiriomonism* was first published in 1904.[5] A second edition was published in 1905[6] and a third in 1908.[7] Book Two was published in 1905,[8]

---

4  Bogdanov 1904a. Incidentally, a detailed summary of this article was published in one of America's leading philosophical journals, *The Journal of Philosophy, Psychology, and Scientific Methods*. Bogdanoff 1906.
5  Bogdanov 1904b.
6  Bogdanov 1905a.
7  Bogdanov 1908.
8  Bogdanov 1905b.

and a second edition was published in 1906.[9] Book Three was published in 1906.[10] This translation is based on the 1905 editions of Books One and Two and the 1906 edition of Book Three. I compared these editions with the 2003 edition edited by V.N. Sadovskii,[11] based on the latest editions of each volume, and, with the exception of the omission of five paragraphs from Chapter Five, Part A, Section Two (which I have included in my translation), I found only minor stylistic changes and typographical corrections.

Any attempt at a word-for-word translation of one language into another is out of the question, and this is certainly true for Russian and English. The Russian language is gendered and highly inflected, and word order is not as important to meaning as it is in English. Bogdanov takes full advantage of this feature of Russian, and native English speakers who are ingrained with the patterns of English word order can find his prose very hard going. In the process of reproducing Bogdanov's ideas in idiomatic English, I have reordered and reformulated his sentences, and I have freely divided his sometimes very long and complex sentences into shorter ones. In addition, where Bogdanov uses nouns to indicate action, I generally use verbs. Where his repeated use of pronouns might be confusing, I substitute the noun to which the pronoun refers. If this is not a 'word-for-word' translation, however, I have done my best to make it an 'idea-for-idea' translation.

The editors of the Bogdanov Library have decided not to interrupt the flow of the text by inserting transliterated Russian words in brackets after problematic terms, and I will therefore discuss problems in terminology here.

Bogdanov does not employ arcane or idiosyncratic philosophical terminology. Regarding the basic empiriocriticist/empiriomonist understanding of human cognition, he adopts Ernst Mach's vocabulary. Thus, 'bodies' (*tela* in Russian, *Körper* in German) that make up physical reality are decomposed into 'elements' (*elementy, Elemente*), that is, separate 'sensations' (*oshchushcheniia, Empfindungen*), which are also often referred to as 'psychical images' (*predstavleniia, Vorstellungen*). It has been easy to maintain a one-to-one translation of terms associated with perception: 'perception' (*vospriatie*), 'impression' (*vpechatlenie*), 'sense' (*chuvstvo*), 'feeling' (*chuvstvovanie*), 'sensation' (*oshchushchenie*).

The greatest difficulty presented by Bogdanov's terminology is not that he uses terms in idiosyncratic ways, but that he often uses the same term to mean

---

9     Bogdanov 1906a.
10    Bogdanov 1906b.
11    Bogdanov 2003.

a number of different things, sometimes in a philosophical sense and sometimes in an everyday sense. A case in point is *predstavlenie*. When he discusses perception as it relates to empiriocriticism, Bogdanov uses *predstavlenie* as a translation of Mach's *Vorstellung*. 'Presentation' was the English term that was used to translate *Vorstellung* at the time, but it has fallen out of use, and I have chosen to translate *predstavlenie* – when used to mean *Vorstellung* – as 'psychical image'. However, Bogdanov often also uses *predstavlenie* simply to mean 'conception' and 'representation', and in those cases I translate it accordingly. Thus, when 'psychical image' appears in the text it is *always* a translation of *predstavlenie*, but it is not the *only* translation of *predstavlenie*.

*Sviaz'* presents the same problem. In everyday language, it can mean 'tie', 'bond', 'connection', 'link', 'relationship', etc., while as a technical term in Russian philosophy, *sviaz'* means the interdependent and mutually-conditioned interrelationships of physical phenomena. When Bogdanov uses *sviaz'* in a non-technical sense, I translate it as either 'tie' or 'connection'. When Bogdanov discusses the concept of causality, he employs the expression *prichinnaia sviaz'*, which I translate as 'causal relationship' (the standard English expression), and, therefore, whenever Bogdanov uses *sviaz'* in relation to the idea of causation, I translate it as 'relationship'. But when it is clear that Bogdanov has the technical philosophical usage of *sviaz'* in mind, I translate it as 'interconnectedness'.

Bogdanov's use of concepts drawn from Mach and Avenarius causes some ambiguity for translating German (and Russian) terms for 'experience'. In German, *Erlebnis* refers to a single event of consciousness and Bogdanov translated it as *perezhivanie* (which can also connote feeling, worry, anxiety, tribulation), while *Erfahrung* refers to the totality of a person's conscious past and Bogdanov translated it as *opyt* (which can also connote experiment, trial, practice). English, however, uses 'experience' for both concepts. Works of psychology in English typically avoid this problem by using the word 'sensation' to mean a single event of consciousness, but I have reserved 'sensation' as the exclusive translation of *oshchushchenie*. Moreover, Bogdanov uses *perezhivanie* in three separate meanings: (1) a single sensory event; (2) a single conscious event (a necessary distinction, since some *perezhivaniia* occur outside of consciousness); and (3) a single episode in someone's life. I have found no satisfactory terms to translate these separate meanings (and, indeed, some usages are ambiguous), so I have translated *opyt* and *perezhivanie* as 'experience' and rely on the reader to understand the meaning from the context.

The term *zakonomernost'* also has an everyday and a technical meaning. In ordinary usage, it means regularity, conformity to a pattern, obeying rules, etc. Dictionaries of philosophy, however, take *zakonomernost'* to mean 'conformity to the laws of nature' consistent with the conception that physical reality is governed by cause and effect. This is indeed what Bogdanov had in mind, except that, whereas he conceived of the processes of the universe as invariably subject to cause and effect, he understood 'laws of nature' to be human formulations, the truth of which is relative to its time. Consequently, although I translate *zakonomernost'* with the word 'regularity', the reader should keep in mind that what Bogdanov has in mind is the invariable regularity of the natural world in which nothing occurs without a cause and all occurrences have consequences. At the same time that Bogdanov was developing the philosophy of empiriomonism, Russia's revisionist, neo-Kantian Marxists used the word *zakonomernost'* to mean 'determinism'.[12]

The same sort of caution to the reader is necessary for the term *obshcheznachimost'* (for which the standard dictionary definition is 'validity' or 'general validity'). I translate it as 'social validity' because of the explanation that Bogdanov himself provides in *The Philosophy of Living Experience*, where he says that *obshcheznachimost'* is what Karl Marx meant by the phrase *gesellschaftlich gültig* in his discussion of commodity fetishism in *Capital*,[13] and the standard English definition of *gesellschaftlich gültig* is 'socially valid'. However, readers should keep in mind that 'socially valid' does not mean that the objective world is somehow *created* by social agreement but that it is only *received* and *understood* by social agreement. In 'Bogdanov as a Thinker' above, V.A. Bazarov defines *obshcheznachimost'* as 'objectivity' and indicates that Bogdanov considers 'the regularities of nature' to have 'universal meaning'. James D. White, one of the foremost authorities on Bogdanov's thought, translates *obshcheznachimost'* as 'universal validity'.[14]

It is a pleasure, once again, to thank Evgeni Pavlov for his continued encouragement and advice. He reviewed the entire manuscript and has been an invaluable reference for problems of translation. I am very grateful, as well, for Georgii Gloveli's expert editing of 'Bogdanov as a Thinker' and for sharing it with me.

---

12   The question of determinism versus free will was a central point of contention between revolutionary Marxists (who stood behind historical materialism) and the neo-Kantian revisionists (who believed in free will and transcendent values). Thus, in his translation of the contributions of Marxist revisionists to the symposium, *Problems of Idealism*, Randall A. Poole has translated *zakonomernost'* as 'determinism'. Poole 2003.
13   Bogdanov 2016, p. 215.
14   White 2018.

# Bogdanov's Autobiography

This autobiographical sketch was written by Bogdanov in 1924 in response to a request from the Lenin Institute sent out to a multitude of people who had been a part of the revolutionary movement in Russia. The autobiographies became part of a multi-volume project.[1] However, I have used the version reprinted in *Neizvestnyi Bogdanov* [*The Unknown Bogdanov*],[2] since it comes from Bogdanov's original manuscript, which is held in the Rossiiskii Tsentr Khraneniia i Izucheniia Dokumentov Noveishei Istorii (RTsKhIDNI) [The Russian Centre for the Preservation and Study of Documents in Contemporary History]. (Bogdanov's arrest by the GPU in 1923 was not mentioned in the published version.)

∴

Bogdanov (Malinovskii), Alexander Alexandrovich, the second of six children, was born on 10 August 1873,[3] the son of a village schoolteacher. My father quickly rose to the position of teacher-inspector in a city higher school, and because of this I had access to the library of the school for six or seven years and later also to its small physics laboratory. I was awarded a scholarship to study at the Tula Gymnasium[4] and lived in its dormitory, which was very much like a military barracks or prison. The malicious and narrow-minded authorities there taught me to fear and hate the powerful and to repudiate all authorities.

Having graduated with a gold medal,[5] I enrolled in Moscow University as a natural scientist. In December 1894, I was arrested for membership in the Union Council of *Zemliachestva*[6] and was exiled to Tula. I was drawn into work as a propagandist in workers' study circles by I.I. Saveliev, a worker in an armaments factory, and soon afterwards V. Bazarov and I. Stepanov[7] began to

---

1 Nevskii 1931.
2 Bordiugov 1995.
3 Russia at that time still used the Julian calendar. According to the Gregorian calendar, to which Russia converted in 1918, it was 22 August.
4 *Gimnaziia* was the term for university-preparatory high schools in imperial Russia. The government charged fees to attend, in order to restrict university attendance to the wealthy, but scholarships were available for particularly bright young men. (Women could not attend.)
5 The equivalent of an honours diploma.
6 *Zemliachestva* were student self-help organisations whose purpose was to help students from the provinces to cope with life in large metropolitan universities.
7 V.A. Bazarov (Rudnev) (1874–1939) and I.I. Stepanov (Skvortsov) (1870–1928).

participate. In 1896, in the course of this work, I moved from the outlook of the 'People's Will'[8] to Social Democracy. I gathered my lectures for those study circles into *Kratkii kurs ekonomicheskoi nauki* [*A Short Course of Economic Science*],[9] which came out – maimed by the censors – at the end of 1897. (It was warmly reviewed by Lenin.)

Beginning in autumn 1895, I spent part of my time in Khar'kov, studying in the Medical Institute of Khar'kov University. I was involved in Social-Democratic, intelligentsia circles there, the leader of which was Cherevanin,[10] but I broke with them over the question of morality, to which they attributed independent significance.[11] In 1898, striving to answer the broad needs of our workers for an overall worldview, I wrote my first philosophical work, *Osnovnye elementy istoricheskogo vzgliada na prirodu* [*Basic Elements of an Historical View of Nature*].[12] I graduated from the University of Khar'kov in the fall of 1899 and was subsequently arrested for propaganda.[13]

After six months in prison in Moscow, I was exiled to Kaluga, and then from there for three years in Vologda. I studied and wrote a great deal. In 1902, I organised and edited a collection of articles against the idealists, *Ocherki realisticheskogo mirovozzreniia* [*Outlines of a Realist Worldview*].[14] I served for a year and a half as a physician in a psychiatric hospital. At the end of 1903 I began to edit a Marxist journal, *Pravda* [*Truth*], which was published in Moscow.

---

8   The original *Narodnaia Volia* [The People's Will] had been created in 1879 by populists who were disillusioned by the failure of a widespread peasant revolution against the autocracy to occur. They decided that the only alternative was to use terror to force reform from above, and it was the executive committee of this party that assassinated Tsar Alexander II in 1881. The party was suppressed by the police in the aftermath of the assassination, but the name was adopted by various local populist groups in the 1880s and '90s to indicate their concern for the peasantry and their hatred of the tsarist regime.
9   Bogdanov 1897.
10  F.A. Cherevanin (1869–1938) went on to become a Menshevik.
11  i.e. they treated moral values as absolute and not relative.
12  Bogdanov 1898.
13  The official charge was disseminating 'social propaganda among workers' (Biggart 1998, p. 462).
14  *Ocherki realisticheskogo mirovozzreniia* (Bogdanov 1904c) was specifically a reaction to *Problems of Idealism* (Poole 2003), published in 1902 by the Moscow Psychological Society. *Problems of Idealism*, which was a landmark in Russian culture, signifying the blossoming of the 'New Religious Consciousness' of the Russian intelligentsia. It was especially galling to Russian Revolutionary Social Democrats, since the leading Russian Marxist revisionists – including P. Struve, N. Berdiaev, S. Bulgakov, and S. Frank – were contributors.

In the autumn of 1903, I took the side of the Bolsheviks, and, my exile having come to an end, I shortly thereafter (in the spring of 1904) travelled to Switzerland where I connected with Lenin. At the 'Meeting of the Twenty-Two',[15] I was elected to the Bureau of Committees of the Majority (BKB), the first Bolshevik Centre. It was around that time that I was first declared a heretic from Marxism by the Menshevik journal *Iskra* [*The Spark*]. (An article by Ortodoks[16] in issue no. 70 accused me of philosophical idealism.)

In the autumn I returned to Russia and, starting in December 1904, I worked in St. Petersburg in the BKB and the Petersburg Committee. I wrote the tactical leaflets of the BKB regarding armed uprising and the summoning of a Party Congress, and I wrote the majority of the other leaflets of the BKB. In the autumn of 1905 I reported on the question of an armed uprising at the Party Congress in London – the Third (Bolshevik) Congress – and on the question of party organisation as well. I was also elected to the first Bolshevik Central Committee, I worked in Petrograd and served on the editorial board of the Bolshevik journal, *Novaia zhizn'* [*New Life*], and I was the representative of the Central Committee on the St. Petersburg Soviet of Workers' Deputies, where I was arrested on 2 December 1905.[17]

In May I was freed on bail, and I was sent by the Bolsheviks to be a member of the now Menshevik-dominated Central Committee. I was exiled abroad, but I returned illegally[18] and lived in Kuokkala, Finland[19] with Lenin, working on the editorial boards of Bolshevik journals and also with the Duma fractions of the First, Second, and Third Dumas.[20] In regard to the question of elections to the Third Duma, I was a 'boycotter',[21] but after a Party Conference

---

15   This was the meeting, 30 July–1 August 1904, which formally created the Bolshevik fraction of the Russian Social-Democratic Labour Party (RSDLP).
16   Liubov' Akselrod (1868–1946) was a close associate of G.V. Plekhanov, second to him in prestige as a philosopher in the Menshevik fraction.
17   This was the beginning of the suppression of the 1905 Russian Revolution.
18   This may not be accurate. It appears that the Minister of Internal Affairs actually granted him permission to travel abroad (Biggart 1998, p. 467). Perhaps the illegality was his return to Finland and not to Russia.
19   Although Finland was part of the Russian Empire, it was a 'Grand Duchy' with a high degree of legal autonomy and resentment of interference by Russia. Russian revolutionaries in Finland were safe from arrest.
20   The Duma was the legislative body provided for in the constitution promulgated by Tsar Nicholas II in 1905.
21   After the First and Second Dumas were dissolved by the Tsar because they were too radical, Prime Minister Peter Stolypin changed the voting laws (in violation of the constitution) to increase the representation of the wealthy. In protest, the 'boycotters' called for a boycott of elections to the Third Duma.

decided against the boycott, I contributed to the electoral campaign to the Third Duma in *Vpered* [*Forward*], the underground workers' newspaper that I edited.

At the end of 1907 I was sent abroad by my comrades in a troika (with Lenin and Innokentii) to edit the Bolshevik organ *Proletarii*. In the fall of 1909 I, along with L.B. Krasin, was removed from the Bolshevik Centre for being a Left-Bolshevik, and in January 1910, when the Bolsheviks and Mensheviks merged, I was removed from the Central Committee of the Party as well. In the autumn of 1909, I participated in organising the First Party School for Workers on the Isle of Capri, and in the fall of 1910 the Second Party School in Bologna. In December 1909 I reported on behalf of the platform of the 'Group of Bolsheviks', which soon after adopted the name 'the Literary Group "*Vpered*"'. Their platform – 'The Present Moment and the Tasks of the Party' – formulated the slogan of Proletarian Culture for the first time.

In the autumn of 1911, when the group '*Vpered*' began to move from cultural-propagandistic work to émigré-style politics, I left the group and left politics as well. From then on, until the Revolution of 1917, I only wrote propagandistic articles in *Pravda* and other workers' organs. I returned to Russia in 1913, and in 1914 was sent to the front as a doctor. The Revolution of 1917 found me in Moscow, and it was there that I began to write political-propagandistic articles. In one of them, in January 1918, I made a diagnosis of War Communism, and I subsequently switched over entirely to cultural and scientific work – in the Proletkult, the Proletarian University, etc. In the fall of 1921 I ceased my work on proletarian culture,[22] and I devoted myself entirely to science. But even though I decisively left politics alone, it did not completely leave me alone, as shown by my arrest in September to October 1923.[23]

Since 1918 I have been a member of the Communist (formerly Socialist) Academy.

---

22  Lenin had been an enemy of Bogdanov ever since his expulsion from the Bolshevik Centre. He was alarmed at the great success of the Proletarian Culture movement, and in 1920 he forced Bogdanov out of his leadership position in the Proletkult and encouraged a campaign of vilifying him as a Marxist 'heretic'.

23  Bogdanov was arrested by the GPU (State Political Directorate) on 8 September 1923 on trumped up charges of having links with anarcho-syndicalists and collaboration with émigrés and foreign intelligence agencies. However, Bogdanov was able to convince Felix Dzerzhinsky, head of the GPU, that he was innocent, and he was released on 13 October (Biggart 1998, pp. 379–83).

[Editor's Postscript]

Bogdanov devoted the last years of his life to the science of blood transfusion, and he became the Director of The Institute of Haematology and Blood Transfusion. He died in 1928 as a result of a transfusion experiment in which he himself was one of the subjects.[24]

---

24  See Krementsov 2011 and White 2018.

# Bogdanov as a Thinker[1]

*V.A. Bazarov*

V.A. Bazarov (Vladimir Alexandrovich Rudnev, 1874–1939) was a Social-Democratic activist, philosopher, and economist. Bazarov and Bogdanov first met when they were students in high school in Tula, and, following graduation, they both enrolled in the natural sciences faculty of Moscow University. After being expelled from the university for student activism (Bogdanov in 1894, Bazarov in 1895), they found themselves together in exile in Tula, and it was there, while leading workers' study circles, that they took up a serious study of Marxism and began to identify themselves as historical materialists.

The two friends worked closely together for the next decade and a half. Bazarov edited Bogdanov's first work, *Kratkii kurs ekonomicheskoi nauki*, and Bogdanov edited Bazarov's translation of Marx's *Capital*. They were both committed to seeking a modern, scientific foundation for historical materialism, and to this end they adopted the radical empiricism of Ernst Mach and Richard Avenarius. They joined the Bolshevik fraction of the Russian Social-Democratic Labour Party at its inception, and in the era of the Revolution of 1905 they contributed to the Social-Democratic press, defending Bolshevism and criticising the neo-Kantian Russian Marxist revisionists.

Their political collaboration came to an end during the period of counter-revolution following the suppression of the Revolution of 1905. Bogdanov emigrated to Europe, broke with Lenin, and engaged in factional politics, even as he was developing the idea that cultural revolution was a necessary prerequisite for socialism. Meanwhile, Bazarov remained a Bolshevik and stayed in Russia, carrying on propagandistic and educational work with workers in St. Petersburg. He was arrested in 1911 and exiled to Siberia for three years. Bazarov continued to follow Bogdanov's work, adopting his theory of cultural revolution and applying the principles of tektology to problems of economic development.

---

[1] Bazarov wrote this article in 1928 as a memorial to his life and work. However, because Bogdanov's work had been declared ideologically anathema by the Soviet establishment, it could not be published at the time. The manuscript was discovered in the Central Party Archive of the Communist Party of the Soviet Union by a research assistant of Dr Georgii D. Gloveli, Professor of Theoretical Economics in the Higher School of Economics, National Research University (Russia), and it was published for the first time in 2002 (Bazarov 2002). This translation is of a version of the article that was further edited by Dr Gloveli, who kindly shared it with me.

Bazarov was in Petrograd in 1917, and, following the February Revolution, he worked in the economic section of the Petrograd Soviet. At the same time, he contributed to Maxim Gorky's journal, *Novaia Zhizn'*, and joined with likeminded activists in attempting to unify Russia's revolutionary and democratic forces and overcome the Bolshevik-Menshevik divide. He left the Bolshevik fraction in the summer of 1917 and, after the Bolshevik seizure of power in October, he became active in the left-Menshevik fraction, the RSDRP-Internationalists.

Despite his opposition to the Bolshevik seizure of power, Bazarov supported the new Soviet government, and in 1921 he began work as an economist for Gosplan – the government organ responsible for economic planning – and applied tektological concepts and mathematical models to economic planning. Bazarov believed that a planned economy could achieve unprecedented growth, but when Stalin called on the development of a Five-Year Plan for the economy in 1928, Bazarov was one of a group of former Menshevik economists within Gosplan who argued that the goals of the First Five-Year Plan were too ambitious and could not be realised. In the summer of 1930, those economists – including Bazarov – were arrested and charged with forming an underground Menshevik organisation that sought to 'wreck' Soviet industry by setting unnecessarily low targets. In a public show trial, most of the accused economists confessed their guilt. Bazarov, however, was tried in secret (probably because he would not confess) and imprisoned. After his release, he lived in Moscow until his death in 1939.

The most complete coverage of Bazarov in English is by Naum Jasny.[2]

∴

In A.A. Bogdanov, the Soviet Union has lost one of the greatest revolutionary figures and thinkers of the last three decades.

Possessing an extraordinary power of organisational thought as well as an incomparable gift as a populariser, A. Bogdanov educated several generations of Marxists. His youthful work, *Kratkii kurs ekonomicheskoi nauki*[3] – rigorously steadfast in the spirit of Marx's teachings and striking in the architectural symmetry of its design and the crystal clarity of its exposition – immediately brought general attention to the young author and became the essential handbook of every worker or student embarking on the study of Marxism.

---

2  Jasny 1972.
3  Bogdanov 1897.

*Kratkii kurs* underwent nine editions before the Revolution of 1917 and has been repeatedly republished in the Soviet period.

A. Bogdanov did not work on economics within the four walls of his study but in living communication with the revolutionary workers among whom he carried on propaganda. *Kratkii kurs* consisted of the lectures that Bogdanov gave over the course of several years to secret workers' organisations in the city of Tula, which he revised and adapted to the conditions of censorship of that time. The needs of the worker-students not only determined the author's external manner of exposition, but they also had a huge influence on the responsive propagandist's own internal development. The worker-students posed more and more questions and compelled him to consider certain aspects of the Marxian idea ever more deeply, boldly, and independently. Already in these years it became clear to Bogdanov that the theory and practice of Marxism must not be limited to a revolutionary critique of the economic contradictions of the society that existed, but that Marxism signified the initiation of a new social consciousness and a new culture in the broadest sense of the word.

Bogdanov began to fix his attention predominantly on general questions of worldview.

The more clearly he became aware of the universality of the socialist revolution that was being born in the contemporary workers' movement, the more persistently he raised the question of what the world that would be renewed by this all-embracing revolution would look like. What kind of 'organisation of things, people, and ideas' did the Marxian worldview aim at? Marx and his closest comrades-in-arms had not succeeded in illuminating all aspects of this problem, and Bogdanov made this his life's work. This is how he himself described his first steps directed toward the construction of a picture of the world in the spirit of Marxian *historical* materialism:

> At the time when life, in the form of comrade-workers, prompted me to become familiar with Marx's historical materialism, I was occupied principally with the natural sciences and was an enthusiastic supporter of the worldview that could be designated as the 'materialism of natural scientists'. This somewhat primitive philosophy was once, for good reason, the ideological banner of strict democrats – the 'nihilists'. There was a great deal of distinctive radicalism in it and a great deal that was kindred to all 'extreme' ideologies.
>
> Attempting to arrive at a strict *monism* in cognition, this worldview constructs its picture of the world entirely out of one material – out of 'matter' as the object of physical sciences. The whole content of the world and the essence of all experience – both physical and psychical – is

formed by matter conceived in the form of atoms in their various combinations and continuous movement. The invariable laws of the movement of matter in space and time are the ultimate instantiation of all explanations that are possible ...

But the social materialism of Marx made demands on my worldview that the old materialism could not satisfy. And, meanwhile, these were demands whose validity could not be denied and which, in addition, completely correspond to the objective and monist tendency of the old materialism itself, except that those demands took that tendency even further. It was necessary to *cognise one's own cognition*, to explain one's own worldview. And, according to the idea of Marxism, it was possible and obligatory to do this on the ground of social-genetic investigation. It was obvious that the fundamental concepts of the old materialism – both 'matter' and 'invariable laws' – were worked out in the course of the *social* development of humanity, and it was necessary to find the 'material basis' for those concepts as 'ideological forms'. But since the 'material basis' has the property of changing as society develops, it became clear that all given ideological forms can have only historically-transient and not objectively-suprahistorical meaning; they can be 'truth for their times' (*objective* truth, but only within a certain era) and in no way 'truth for eternity' ('objective' in the absolute meaning of the word).

pp. 268–269 in this volume

In his book, *Osnovnye elementy istoricheskogo vzgliada na prirodu*, published in 1899, Bogdanov provided the first outline of the resolution of the task set down in the passage just cited.

Already in this work, notwithstanding an insufficient development of a number of important details, Bogdanov presented his worldview fully formed in general and as a whole. A series of further works published immediately after and completed in the three volumes of *Empiriomonism* (1906) provided no more than a development and expansion of the philosophical ideas that were formulated in *Osnovnye elementy*.

Bogdanov's philosophical works did not meet the same unanimous recognition in Russian Social Democracy that his work on political economy enjoyed. It is true that Lenin, who was in Siberia when *Osnovnye elementy* was published, responded very positively to the book and recommended it warmly to his co-exiles. But, on the other hand, Plekhanov, who at that time was held in very high esteem as an authority on philosophy by the great majority of Russian revolutionary Marxists, immediately pointed out the fundamental differences between his own understanding of Marx's theory and Bogdanov's interpretation of historical materialism. And since Bogdanov continued to develop his conception of Marxism in print with great persistence, Plekhanov entered into a polemic with him that took on increasingly harsh forms.[4]

In the first years of the twentieth century, when differences appeared in Russian Social Democracy that quickly led to the organisational division of the party into two fractions, Bogdanov adhered to the fraction of Bolsheviks led by Lenin and immediately became one of its most influential figures. Lenin, regardless of all the bitterness of the political struggle with Plekhanov and his Menshevik supporters, continued to relate to Plekhanov as a student to a teacher in the realm of theory (and especially of philosophical theory), and he took Plekhanov's side in the latter's philosophical feud with Bogdanov. However, as long as Bogdanov remained a close comrade-in-arms with Lenin in the arena of revolutionary practice and while he – to use the expression of M.N. Pokrovskii – played the role of 'vice-leader' of Bolshevism, the theoretical disagreement between leader and vice-leader did not become embittered, did not break out into the open, and was manifested only in facetious altercations in private conversations.

This *modus vivendi* changed fundamentally in the second half of the first decade of the twentieth century – in the era of reaction that arrived after the revolution of 1905–06 – when Bogdanov fell out with Lenin on a great number of political questions and became the leader of a separate grouping within the Bolshevik fraction.

Starting from that moment, Lenin thought it necessary to completely dissociate himself from all Russian Social Democrats who did not accept his views entirely and fully, to dissociate himself not only in the realm of politics but also in the realm of philosophical theory. In 1909, in his famous work, *Materialism and Empirio-criticism*,[5] Lenin came out with harsh criticism against all Marxists who understood historical materialism differently from Plekhanov, and the sharpest of this criticism was aimed most of all against Bogdanov.[6]

The polemics of the second decade of the twentieth century led to more distinct contrasting of the various philosophical positions within our revolutionary Marxism, but it did not arouse a further in-depth development of them. Among them, Bogdanov arrived at the conviction in those years that purely philosophical arguments were pointless and that, in any event, the very pretensions of 'philosophy' were illusory at their *foundation*. Previously, 'philosophy' had been for him only a temporary surrogate for exact science, and, proposing

---

4  Evgeni Pavlov covers this well. Pavlov 2017. [Trans.]
5  Lenin 1927.
6  Bazarov himself was criticised by Lenin in this work [trans.].

that science – at the level of development that it had attained – was still incapable of constructing a whole, monistic picture of the world, he acknowledged the necessity of anticipating future scientific conclusions in the form of philosophical 'hypotheses'. Now, in evaluating the soundness even of this temporary service of philosophy, he was filled with ever greater scepticism.

Along with this, the conviction was born in him and grew stronger that at the present time it was fully possible to embark on the construction of a monistic science and to develop methods of scientific cognition that possessed universal meaning. Bogdanov dedicated all his powers to this grandiose problem, and it was no longer necessary for him to divide his energy between theoretical work and practical political struggle. In 1911–12, on the basis of a great number of considerations that I cannot touch on here, he once and for all gave up active participation in party activity. The lessons of the amazing events of the great Revolution of 1917–18 did not cause him to waver; indeed, on the contrary, they merely strengthened his resolve. The result of the intense work in this final and especially productive period of Bogdanov's life was *Vseobshchaia organizatsionnaia nauka* [*Universal Organisational Science*] or *Tektologiia* [*Tektology*][7] – a work that was extremely original, mature, and, if it may be put this way, very appropriate to the characteristics of A. Bogdanov's creative talents.

In this article I will not undertake to provide any kind of detailed presentation of Bogdanov's views, and, by the same token, I do not intend to subject to any kind of critical evaluation the polemics through which Bogdanov forged his worldview. My intentions are much more modest. I want only to cursorily point out to the reader the main theoretical positions that Bogdanov successively defended.

One can note three basic stages in the development of Bogdanovian theory: 'an historical view on nature', 'empiriomonism', and 'tektology'.

To begin, I will dwell for a moment on the first stage, on *Osnovnye elementy istoricheskogo vzgliada na prirodu*. I provided above a citation in which the frame of mind in which Bogdanov embarked on this work is evident. In light of Marxian *historical* materialism he became aware of the limitedness of the *static* 'materialism of natural scientists' that he had shared up until then.

But what does it mean to replace the static view of nature with an historical view? It means, first and foremost, to reject the interpretation of nature as the totality of unchanging 'things' that are sharply distinguished from one another.

---

7   For the numerous editions and versions of this work consult Biggart 1998. For English translations see Gorelik 1980 and Dudley 1996.

It means to consider nature as a continuous flow of transformations in which one can single out not static 'things' but only relatively stable 'forms of movement' that are in a process of continuous interaction with the environment that surrounds them.

Further, the historical nature and the dynamism of this view of nature are not compatible with categorical distinctions in the methods of construction of the separate sciences. A dynamic interconnectedness among all the phenomena of nature signifies not only monism of the object of cognition but of the methods of cognition as well.

The regularity of the processes of nature finds it most precise and rigorous formulation in a mechanics based on the 'axioms' or 'laws of movement' (Axiomata sive leges motus) established by Isaac Newton: (1) the law of inertia; (2) the law of direct proportionality between a change in the amount of movement and the magnitude of effective force; and (3) the law of the equality of action and reaction. Analysing these basic principles of classical mechanics, Bogdanov posed two questions: (1) are not Newton's 'axioms' partial applications of universal principles that are applicable not only to mechanical movement but also to all processes of inorganic and organic nature in general? And (2) may they not be viewed as three stages of the discovery of a single and universal foundation of regularity in cognition, a foundation of the causal interconnectedness of phenomena?

Bogdanov answered 'yes' to both these questions. The law of inertia in a generalised form says 'if in a given system of external actions the form of a process is unchanging, then, in order for it to change, a new external action is necessary'. More succinctly: 'any change comes from the outside'. Thus, the maintenance of a body not under the influence of any forces (that is at rest or is moving uniformly in a straight line) is a partial case of the application of the universal principle of cognition that contradicts absolute freedom, such as 'the capability to begin a series of actions from within oneself'.

The second foundation of Newtonian mechanics is generalised in the 'law of specific action': 'identical forms of processes under identical actions undergo identical changes'.

Bogdanov developed the law of the equality of action and reaction in the following formula, which has general significance: 'when two processes interact, the change of the form of movement characteristic of one of them is accompanied by an equal and opposite change of the form of the other. Replacing two processes with one process in its entire external environment – i.e. the totality of the processes acting on it – we arrive at this formula: every change of the form of a process is accompanied by equal and opposite changes in its external environment'. That is, as a result of interaction, a given 'form of a process' acquires exactly as much as the environment that surrounds it loses, and vice versa. We thus see that this proposition, in essence, is nothing other than the 'law of the conservation of energy'.

The law of inertia provides the least developed and, moreover, *negative* formulation of the principle of causality: *ex nihilo nihil fit*, without external influence one or another balanced forms of a process cannot change. In the vestments of Newton's second law, causality becomes more meaningful and definite. It obtains here a *positive* distinctness, but only qualitatively: identical causes in the presence of other equal conditions produce identical effects. The law of conservation of energy is the third and highest stage. It establishes not only a qualitative, but also a quantitative specificity of the causal connection of phenomena: the measurability and commensurability of cause and effect.

Thus, the substance of causality in contemporary cognition is exposed in a series of propositions that can be arranged according to levels of growing complexity, such that each higher formulation includes the lower level and at the same time substantially enriches it. This means that causality is not at all an elementary 'category of pure reason' that is invariably inherent in everyone's cognition as Kant asserted. Just the opposite, there is every reason to think that causality, like all other ideological categories and forms, takes shape gradually in the process of historical development, and at each given level of this development causality has a content that responds to the social relationships of the era that are, in turn, determined by the level of material productive forces.

In this way a new task arises: to illuminate from the point of view of historical materialism the origin and development of the basic categories of cognition and the scientific structures that are built with their help, along with metaphysical and religious structures and, in general, the whole sum of ideological forms.

The resolution of this task was basically outlined already by Bogdanov in the book *Poznanie s istoricheskoi tochki zreniia* [*Cognition from an Historical Point of View*][8] (1901) and elaborated in detail in a great many subsequent works.

But let us return to *Osnovnye elementy*. The law of the conservation of energy – an expanded form of the law of causality – is identically applicable to all processes; it permits us to establish a quantitative measure of all qualitative changes observable in the world, but it tells us nothing about the *direction*

---

8  Bogdanov 1901.

in which these qualitative changes occur. What are the outcomes of the historical process? Are they expressed in the predominant preservation of some forms and disappearance of others or do we see a kaleidoscopic play of transformations without any kind of clearly expressed tendencies of development in a definite direction?

It is well known that such tendencies do exist among *living* forms. Biological species develop in definite directions, and in the theory of 'natural selection' contemporary science reveals the mechanism that regulates this development. One must ask if there is not an analogous universal regulator also in the development of social forms of human life when definite tendencies of development are manifested no less sharply than in biology and the speed of change of forms is even more significant? And, from another perspective, different 'forms of movement' of inorganic nature reveal far from an identical capacity to resist the destructive actions of the external environment, and, as a result, one can expect a kind of 'survival' of the most adapted forms here as well.

Subjecting the conditions of development of various spheres of life to analysis, Bogdanov showed which modifications acquire the principle of 'selection' when applied to the individual psyche, to social forms, to technology, etc. The law of selection comes into force everywhere that 'with an equal expenditure of energy one form of life produces changes in its external environment that are more favourable to its preservation and more useful for itself than another form does'. And since this prerequisite is present in almost every bit of life, and since the formula that has just been adduced is also broadly applicable with very small changes to inorganic nature, then the 'law of selection' turns out to be really universal.

Enough has been said to characterise the basic aspiration of Bogdanov's theoretical thought in the work under consideration in the following way: it is the extension of the most precise and most developed methods of the separate sciences into neighbouring realms by introducing corresponding modifications into these proven tools of cognition. As a result, a cognitive apparatus is obtained that is reduced to internal unity, that is whole, and that is also universal – a monistic methodology of cognition.

But all this is purely the scientific – or at least a science-like – theoretical-cognitive side of the concept under examination. What is its 'philosophical' content in the proper use of the word? How did Bogdanov conceive of the correlation between 'thought' and 'being', between 'cognition' and the 'world' as it is 'in itself'? In *Osnovnye elementy* this problem is touched on only in passing. Developing a consistently energetical point of view applicable to all phenomena and processes of the external and internal world alike, Bogdanov stipulated that energy could not at all be thought of as some kind of 'unchanging essence' or 'substance' of any being. He conceived of the very concept of substance as a legacy of the era of static thinking. 'If the word "energy" could impart any kind of meaning', he wrote, 'then it is exclusively that this term expresses the *commensurability* of all the changes that occur in nature, the reduction of them to one quantitative measure'. This is exactly the meaning of the proposition 'energy is uniform and eternal'. 'Heat, light, electricity, mechanical movement, etc. ... are only different means by which human consciousness perceives energy'. But since 'energy is manifested *only in changes* and in nothing more, since it is measured *only by means of them*, and since it is only known through them, then it is obvious that for cognition energy is absolutely the same as the changes that occur in nature'.

What is energy 'in itself'? *Osnovnye elementy* does not give a completely precise answer, but from the context it is clear that the very posing of such a question seems to the author to be false and unnecessary and leads thought into the blind alley of empty metaphysical abstractions.

Before long, however, Bogdanov had to take up this 'philosophical' problem in earnest, since it was precisely along this line that all the bitterness of his polemic with Plekhanov and the Plekhanovites – and subsequently with Lenin – was directed.

As is well known, Plekhanov asserted that it is impossible to be a materialist and not recognise a 'substance' that is hidden behind the flow of the phenomena that we observe, and that matter is just such a substance. He agreed with Kant that we do not have immediate knowledge of either substance or 'things-in-themselves' but only their 'appearances', but, contrary to Kant, he thought that a certain indirect knowledge of a thing-in-itself was attainable. To be more precise, the point here was not about *knowledge* but about a certain hypothetical assumption that although it did not yield to factual verification, nevertheless was absolutely necessary to us for the substantiation of the objectivity of our science. That is, according to Plekhanov, any realist – and even more a materialist – must admit that any change that we immediately observe in experience completely corresponds to a specific change in the world of 'things-in-themselves'. And, in addition, changes in this hypothetical realm are independent of our knowledge of 'being' and are *primary*, while changes in what we are aware of in our experience are *secondary*; the first are causes, the second are effects. 'The thing-in-itself, or matter, acts on our organs of feeling and cause sensation in us' – this is the brief formula in which Plekhanov summarised his understanding of the materialist point of view.

As is evident from the preceding, Bogdanov did not share this point of view. He developed his understanding of the connection between 'thinking' and 'being' more thoroughly in a series of philosophical studies published from 1904–06 under the general title *Empiriomonism* (three volumes). The author of *Empiriomonism* did not see the necessity of assuming that the evidence of our feelings gives us distorted, or, as Plekhanov put it, 'hieroglyphic' representation of the real qualities of things. And the very idea of the division of the world into two (noumena and phenomena), breaking it down into 'external' realities and their reflection 'in us', seemed to Bogdanov to be internally inconsistent and contradictory. In reality we see, touch, and, in general, perceive qualities of 'things' not 'in us' but *outside us*, outside our body, in those very points of space where those very things that we perceive are located. The localisation of sensation 'in us' is not given in experience but in theory and, moreover, unsuccessful theory. In the opinion of Bogdanov, the failure of this theory was revealed by R. Avenarius in his theory of 'introjection' in a completely convincing way. Along with Avenarius and Mach, Bogdanov considered that the most acceptable and at the same time the simplest point of view was 'naïve realism', which held that objective realities, or, at least, their simplest composite parts – their elements – existed 'in themselves' exactly as we perceive them, whereby in one combination – in one interrelationship – complexes of these elements form a physical body, and in another interrelationship they form the phenomena of our consciousness.

This is not yet 'empirio-*monism*'. In this starting point, Bogdanov's philosophy is not fundamentally distinguishable from 'empirio-*criticism*'. But already the subsequent step of 'empiriocriticism' – its understanding of the link between physiological and psychical processes – compelled Bogdanov to introduce his own *monistic* correction, in the light of which the entire problem acquired an essentially new and extremely original approach.

Empiriocriticists were satisfied by the establishment of a *functional* relationship between processes in the central nervous system (Avenarius's system 'C') and the psychical 'experiences' that correspond to them without determining – and not considering it necessary to determine – the form of this functional relationship. Avenarius stated only that it was impermissible to think of it as a causal relationship. This position definitely did not satisfy Bogdanov. In his opinion, it was acceptable to be satisfied by a purely formal mathematical concept of a function only to the level of abstract analysis that deals only with *magnitudes* – only with quantitative correlations – independently of exactly what realities these correlations applied to. If the investigation touches on real elements and complexes of elements, then the interaction of these elements and complexes must have a real and not a formally-mathematical nature. But causality in the given case does not decide the question. According to Bogdanov, the mistake of the empiriocriticists consisted in that they came to a stop at the parallelism of the psychical and physiological series – i.e. in the final analysis, at a dualistic conception – instead of taking a monistic point of view that considers the physical and the psychical as two forms of the perception of the same real process.

Let us recall that Bogdanov defines any 'experience' – any psychical process – as a specific organised complex of elements that are, in themselves, neutral – neither physical nor psychical – but that form the bricks, so to speak, from which all the phenomena of our world – both 'external' and 'internal' – are constructed. When a psychical complex that is experienced by a given individual comes up against the psyche of another individual – i.e. with 'elements' that are organised differently – a real interaction according to the law of causality occurs between these two complexes. The first complex produces a change in the second and leaves its imprint on it; the first 'is reflected', so to speak, in the second. But since the organisation of the first and the organisation of the second complex are different, the reflection is essentially different from the reflected. The physiological process that is immediately connected with the act of consciousness is just such a distorted *reflection* of the psychical process in another psyche. We do not perceive the experiences of other people directly; we do not perceive them as they themselves flow in in actuality but only indirectly, in the form of changes of the organism that 'correspond' to them, and, guided by our own experience, we only mentally *substitute* psychical processes in place of these physiological processes. '*Universal substitution*' follows from this as the necessary basis of communication among conscious individuals.

Why do we immediately perceive the external phenomena of inorganic nature as they are, while the psyche of someone else, acting on us, gives a 'reflection' that does not correspond to the original? This is because the psyche is an organisation (complicated and adapted to the needs of the individual) of the same primary complexes that, in their immediately given disconnectedness, form the content of the external world. 'Immediate complexes' thus enter into the flow of psychical experiences as a whole. As regards the psyche of another person – presenting in its complexity the formation of the same kind of order as our own psyche – has a different form of organisation from ours, since it is an adaptation to the needs of a different individual with a different heredity and with a different historical fate. Therefore, the immediate entry of one psyche into another or the mutual interpenetration of two psyches is impossible – the action of one on the other is realisable only through an indirect route in the form of indirect imprints that are the immediately perceivable physiological correlates of the experiences of others.

Thus, in contrast to the materialism of Plekhanov-Lenin, 'empiriomonism' does not recognise a transcendent boundary between the world as it exists in itself and our cognition of the world. Being 'in itself' and being 'for us' are identical in their basic elements and in their simplest combinations. We perceive the real, actual qualities of things and not a reflection of them, not more or less distorted copies of them. But in our consciousness, 'immediate complexes' appear in new interrelationships among themselves, organised into a complex unity, answering the specific peculiarities of a given individual. We call this 'individually organised experience' our psyche.

The interactions between different psyches, communication between people, according to Bogdanov, is by means of 'universal substitution', i.e. by substituting the psychical complexes that we know from personal experience for the physical changes that we immediately observe in the organisms of other people. In thus denying that the consciousness of a given individual can directly perceive the experiences of other conscious beings, empiriomonism nevertheless does not tear the kind of chasm between individual consciousnesses that has been postulated by idealistic philosophy since the time of Leibniz's monadology. According to Leibniz, no real action of one monad on another is possible, since monads are absolutely enclosed in themselves and 'have no windows' through which to communicate with one another. According to Bogdanov, cognition of the psyche of another person, although mediated, is, at the same time, a completely real interaction, and the more accurately it reproduces its object, the closer the organisation of the perceiving psyche is to the organisation of perceived psyche. If the organisations of both psyches were completely identical, then there would be space for fully equivalent cognition of the experiences of other people. Consequently, the nature of the distinction here is relative-empirical and not absolute-metaphysical. The more harmoniously society is constructed, the more homogenous the fundamental orientations of the individuals that compose it and the deeper, the more many-sided, and the more precise the mutual understanding of people. In an ideally harmonious society where there is no basis for fundamentally different organisation of individual experience, the boundaries between the consciousnesses of different people will be completely overcome in practice and the so-called 'Du-Problem' will cease to exist.

It obviously follows from the preceding that, from the point of view of empiriomonism, human consciousness is connected with the 'external' physical world more closely and with a more intimate link than with the consciousness of surrounding people. Physical phenomena are perceived in their immediate, authentic reality; psychical phenomena are perceived only through an indirect route. And this is the reality, if one means by 'physical world' what

Bogdanov calls 'immediate complexes', i.e. material processes. The latter are simpler combinations of the same elements of which psychical life is made; in the action of cognition they enter into the content of the psyche as its constitutive parts.

But a completely different correlation results if by 'physical world' one means the picture of the world that is drawn by natural science. Science unifies the immediate complexes of the external world by means of the complex interconnectedness of the regularities of nature that has universal meaning. This 'social validity' or 'objectivity' of the physical world of science is the product of the *collective organisation* of experience. Bogdanov demonstrates that it is only on the basis of cognitive collaboration among people that such universal forms of the scientific picture of the world as abstract, evenly flowing time and 'isotropic' endless space can emerge. In our psychical 'individually organised experience', the flow of time is fantastically variable and space is finite and heterogeneous. In the process of the social organisation of experience, all other scientific concepts and laws of nature are also established. 'Laws', Bogdanov writes,

> do not belong to the sphere of experience – to the sphere of immediate experiences – at all. Laws are the result of the cognitive processing of experience. Laws are not given in experience but are created by thought as a means of organising experience in order to harmoniously reconcile it into an orderly unity. Laws are *cognitive abstractions*, and physical laws no more possess physical qualities than psychological laws possess psychical qualities. One cannot relate them to one or the other series of experience, and therefore if they themselves form a socially-organised system, it does not follow that there is a realm of experience that is socially organised and embraced by them ... *The difference between the physical and psychical orders boils down to the difference between experience that is socially organised and experience that is organised individually.*
> p. 28

Thus, the empiriomonistic picture of the world unfolds before us like a staircase of forms of organisation that are continuously becoming more complex: the gradation of immediate complexes from the almost complete chaos of some astral nebula to the orderly unity of millions of elements in a cell of living tissue, the historical development of individually organised experience from the elementary perceptions of simple organisms to the infinitely differentiated psyches of contemporary civilised human beings, and, finally, the socially organised experience of monistic science that completes the edifice.

In the final synthesis of 'socially organised experience', the contraposition of 'physical' and 'psychical' loses its meaning. Experience that is organised individually enters the system of experience that is organised socially as an inseparable part and ceases to constitute a special world for cognition. What is 'psychical' disappears in the unifying forms that are created by cognition for 'the physical', but what is physical also ceases to be 'physical' as soon as it no longer has the continual antithesis of the psychical. An integrated world of experience appears as the content of an integrated cognition. This is empiriomonism.

The empiriomonist conception, the basic architectural lines of which we have cursorily traced here, was richly illustrated by the author by a great many applications in the most varied realms of our cognition. These illustrations were frequently very important to an understanding of the basic ideas of the author, but unfortunately we are not able to touch on them. We note only that in this period Bogdanov's social-historical analysis of the origin and development of ideologies was the most perfected of his theoretical works.

Empiriomonism was not cast by the author in a strictly orderly philosophical system. We do not get exhaustive answers to a great many theoretical-cognitive questions. Thus, for example, according to Bogdanov, the social validity of forms of scientific cognition is *genetically* created by the collective organisation of experience; does this also mean that *logically* the concept 'universal validity' or 'objectivity' is equivalent in its very content to social organisation? And further, as we have just seen, Bogdanov did not relate scientific laws either to the realm of the physical or to the realm of the psychical. The temptation might arise from this of declaring forms of social organisation of experience to be a special sphere of being – the being of the 'logical', let us say. Formally, such an attempt to inject Husserlianism into empiriomonism is easily feasible, except, of course, that it would contradict the frame of mind of the author of empiriomonism at its root.

A.A. Bogdanov absolutely consciously declined to theoretically-cognitively polish the philosophical propositions that he defended. As we have already noted above, philosophy never had self-sufficient value for Bogdanov. Like Engels, he saw in philosophical constructions only hypothetically conditional anticipation of scientific constructions. The significance of philosophy, as far as he was concerned, was exclusively to play a purely auxiliary role – the role of a temporary tool that clears the ground for scientific work. It is therefore completely understandable why Bogdanov did not see any need to spend years imparting a form to his philosophical propositions that would be correct and irreproachable in the eyes of professional philosophers.

It is curious to note that G.V. Plekhanov – Bogdanov's main theoretical opponent, who apparently proceeded from a completely different evaluation of philosophy – worried even less about the theoretical-cognitive consistency of his constructions. The very word 'epistemology' put him in a sarcastic mood and in private conversations he often called this venerable discipline 'gnusiology'.[9] In order to show the kind of sovereign contempt he had for epistemology and how he abused it in his philosophical works, it is sufficient to recall the following episode. Defining the 'thing-in-itself' or 'matter' as 'that which, acting on our organs of sensation causes sensations in us', Plekhanov, in his earlier articles, objected to the Kantian theory of cognition that considers space and time to be 'subjective forms of our contemplation'. (Thus, for example, on page 172 of *Kritika nashikh kritikov* [*Critique of Our Critics*][10] we read, 'Likewise, he [Kant] also badly contradicts himself in regard to the problem of time. The thing-in-itself can obviously only act upon us in time, but meanwhile Kant considers time to be a subjective form of our contemplation'.)

Plekhanov subsequently adopted the Kantian interpretation of space and time as subjective forms and only supplemented it with his hypothetical thesis that these forms of consciousness 'correspond' to certain 'forms or relationships of real things themselves', but he did not think about how to consistently adapt the bases of his philosophy to this new point of view – for example, to replace the causal connection between things and sensations (which is obviously impossible in light of the subjectivity of space and time) with any other correlation. Plekhanov presented his readers and admirers with a radical change of his epistemological conception – the transition from an immanent to a transcendent theory of cognition in the form of a purely *editorial correction* of the formulations that he had used up until then but whose 'inconvenience' had gradually become clear to him.

Thus, neither Bogdanov nor the most prominent of his opponents had a particular taste for a deep, purely philosophical theoretical-cognitive elaboration of the views that they defended. Meanwhile, Bogdanov's scornful attitude toward epistemological 'scholasticism' was, as we have seen, a completely deliberate and thought-out conclusion from his view of philosophy as the totality of hypotheses that anticipated scientific theories.

What is the difference between philosophical 'anticipations' and the foundations of one or another theory that are really scientific? Philosophy formulates its propositions in such a way that they cannot be either proven or disproven

---

9 This is a play on words. In Russian, *gnosiologiia* (the cognate of 'gnosiology') is preferred to *epistemologiia* (the cognate of 'epistemology') to denote the philosophy of knowledge. '*Gnusiologiia*', however, takes as its root, '*gnus*', which is a generic term for blood-sucking insects like mosquitoes and horseflies [trans.].
10 Plekhanov 1906.

by experience, while, just the opposite, scientific theories are always subject to empirical verification. The task of philosophy is to theoretically connect a series of principles in a logically faultless system; the task of science is to subordinate one or another unexamined realm of nature to the power of the human collective in practice.

Approaching 'empiriomonism' with this criterion, we find that the part of it that is purely philosophical and not subject to practical verification is the theory of 'immediate complexes' and their connection with our experience – with subjective or 'individually-organised' experience on the one hand and with objective or socially-organised experience on the other. This aspect of the philosophy of empiriomonism cannot be transformed into science. In the debate with his opponents, Bogdanov could not appeal to actual reality and was forced to limit himself to purely logical argumentation. He proved that his immanent realism is the simplest and most cognitively expedient of all the conceptions of materialism that had been conceived of and that specifically it agreed better with Marx's social theory than the transcendental materialism of Plekhanov. Just the opposite – according to Plekhanov, Lenin, and other philosophical opponents of Bogdanov – in order not to fall into a contradiction, matter could only be thought of as a transcendental being, and any immanent theory of cognition inevitably led to idealism, to 'solipsism', and was absolutely inconsistent with Marxism. The problem of thought and being in this approach is not scientific but purely philosophical, and both resolutions of the problem can be disputed only from the point of view of the inner consistency of their separate elements, but cannot be proven or disproven by confronting them with the facts of experience.

But in empiriomonism there is also another *scientific* side. This is the theory of the unity of the elements of experience, an attempt to reduce the differences that are observed in experience to different forms of organisation of similar elements and on this basis to construct a monistic methodology that embraces not only all spheres of cognition but also all forms of people's practical activity. It is in the posing of this latter problem that empiriomonism reveals its scientific aspect; it is here that it is a real philosophical anticipation of scientific theory, i.e. a theory that is subject to empirical verification.

The further he advanced in working out the problems contained within in the broad bounds of 'empiriomonism', the more exclusively Bogdanov's attention was fixed on the part of these problems that were scientific and operative in practice and the more it seemed to him that the philosophical debates about being and thinking were fruitless and 'scholastical'. As has already been pointed out, in the course of the last fifteen years of his life, Bogdanov entirely ceased to occupy himself with philosophy and devoted all his powers to working on the scientific mission to which empiriomonism had led him. The result of these efforts was an attempt to construct a 'universal organisational science' or 'tektology', i.e. a science that reveals and systematises all the basic principles that have a place in the 'organisation of things, people, and ideas'.

The concept of *organisation* lies at the basis of tektology. All sorts of 'actions-reactions' can be elements of organisation, beginning with such complex processes as the psychophysiological efforts of people who work consciously and systematically and ending with the simplest quanta of physical energy in the vibrations of light.

No matter what elements have joined together in an organised interrelationship, the basic content of that interrelationship is always the same: 'organisation' was the term Bogdanov gave to a combination of elements that created more significant aggregate activity or, what is the same thing, more significant resistance to external actions than the arithmetical sum of 'actions-reactions' of all the elements taken separately. Consequently, in an organised complex *the whole is more than the arithmetical sum of its parts*. If the whole is less than the sum of its parts, then we have a process not of organisation but of *disorganisation*. Finally, if a whole is precisely equal to the sum of its components, then we have a *neutral* complex. In practice, neutral complexes are the result of an equilibrium between organising and disorganising processes. And since there is a countless multitude of actions-reactions chaotically colliding with one another, the odds of obtaining an organising or a disorganising effect as a result are approximately equal, and so neutral complexes – or, more precisely, systems of dynamic equilibrium close to neutral – are a very common phenomenon in the world of our experience. Mathematics in which the whole is always equal to the sum of its parts turns out from this point of view to be a 'tektology of neutral complexes'.

Mathematics is applicable without particular reservations or explanations to a neutral complex – and only to neutral complexes; however, even here its truth is proven not with complete precision but only approximately: a dynamic equilibrium is never precise but is always a succession of insignificant deviations from a neutral level to one side or the other. Consequently, even in the realm of neutral complexes, 2 + 2 is never exactly equal to 4, but usually is very close to that magnitude. This does not mean, however, that the method of mathematical analysis is not applicable where there are pronounced processes of disorganisation or organisation. To the extent that we are in need of precise quantitative accounting in all spheres of our cognition and practice, mathematics is universally applicable, and now tektology, in establishing a unity of methods in the most varied realms of theory and practice, broadly expands the field of application of mathematics. But, in the great majority of cases, in order to apply mathematical analysis it is now necessary to abstract oneself from the specifically qualitative peculiarities of elements and complexes that manifest themselves as organising or disorganising phases. As objects of mathematics, elements and complexes are non-qualitative, and are always in themselves equal 'magnitudes'. Mathematics is an extremely powerful theoretical tool for any organising activity, even though the essence of organisation, as such, is not expressible mathematically, and in attempting to formulate it in mathematical terms we arrive at an absurdity: 'the whole is greater than the sum of its parts', etc.

In *Tektologiia*, Bogdanov formulated the interrelationships and regularities that are inherent in all aspects of an organisation and consequently have universal cognitive value, but I will not undertake a systematic exposition of the content of universal organisational science. It would of course not be very difficult to extract from Bogdanov's works the concepts that he takes as the basis of his construction and the definitions that he provides, to blend them with the logical links that unify them, and thereby to demonstrate the *system of tektological categories* to the reader. But such a dogmatic formulation of the bases of tektology at the current level of its development would not be a real 'systematisation' of it at all. In reality, to provide a systematic valuation of tektological principles would mean to prove that, speaking mathematically, they are 'necessary and sufficient' for attaining that goal for which the author advanced them. In other words, it is necessary to prove, on the one hand, that each principle formulated by Bogdanov in *Tektologiia* has universal-organisational significance and, on the other hand, that only the principles stated by Bogdanov can pretend to universal application. It is obviously impossible to resolve such a task by means of abstract logical analysis of concepts. For this, massive concrete-critical work is necessary: it is necessary to test in reality whether or not tektological formulas are applicable to the main spheres of human knowledge and human practice. And only after such a comprehensive verification would it be possible to construct an exposition of universal organisational science that is 'systematic', in the strict meaning of the word.

I will limit myself, therefore, to a pair of illustrations that provide a conception not so much of the content of tektology as a special discipline as much as the methodology of tektological investigation.

The fundamental task of tektology is to smash the scholastic insularity of the specialised sciences, to connect separate, partial methods through the unity of a universal methodology of cognition. It is natural that the elaboration of tektology must run into huge resistance from contemporary scientists who are thoroughly imbued with the psychology of scientific specialisation. In order to critically evaluate the possibility of applying one or another generalising method in various scientific disciplines, it is necessary to have sufficient knowledge in all those disciplines. Meanwhile, at the present time a huge majority of scientists are narrow specialists who have neither the ability nor the desire to broaden their scientific horizon beyond the bounds of the specialty they have chosen. In such a situation, tektology's practical critique is seldom encountered, and aspirations for a monistic methodology are denied or, more accurately, discredited a priori. Such scientists point, for example, to the fact that the boundaries that have been established by contemporary faculties between scientific disciplines are not accidental but rest on profound fundamental differences: realms of knowledge such as social science, psychology, biology, and physics are so qualitatively distinctive that there can be no talk of any scientific unification of their methods and all attempts in this direction can be based only on amateur, scientifically impermissible 'superficial analogies'.

It is curious that in this argumentation against the tektological project, one observes complete unanimity among bourgeois and a majority of communist scholars; tektology faces a united front. This forces me to dwell in a little more detail on how universal organisational science understands the 'method of analogy'. One must admit that in the *history* of attempts to bring different sciences together, superficial analogies have played a really important role. Take, for example, the so-called 'organic theory of society' that enjoyed significant popularity among bourgeois scholars 30–40 years ago.[11] This theory was based on extremely shaky analogies and was used for extremely reactionary goals. (One must consider Menenius Agrippa to have been its first proponent, provided the legend that attributes the famous fable to him is true.)[12] But this approach to the problem directly contradicts the tektological approach. The basis for the convergence of the sciences in the 'organic theory' approach is that there is a *qualitative similarity* in the various realms of being. It goes without saying that this 'similarity', which is not precisely definable or quantifiable, can lead only to capricious dilettantish constructions. Just the opposite, from the point of view of tektology the transfer of a given method to a new realm is legitimate when and only when the organisational structure is *identical* in both cases, i.e. when

---

[11] The most notable of these scholars was the English philosopher and sociologist Herbert Spencer (1820–1903) whose works were widely read in Russia in the late nineteenth century [trans.].

[12] The Roman historian Livy wrote that when the plebeians protested their oppression by the patrician class by seceding from Rome in 493 B.C.E., the Senate sent former consul Agrippa Menenius Lanatus to convince them to return. Menenius told them a fable about how each part of the human body has its own role to play, and the body could no more do without a stomach than Rome could do without the patrician class. [trans.]

there is complete *uniformity* of correlations between the elements of what is subject to investigation, although the elements can be very different qualitatively. Qualitative differences of elements must be taken into account only to the extent that they modify to one degree or another organisational interrelationships. In such an approach to the question, all talk of ignoring 'qualitative specificity' or of 'superficial analogies' disappears of its own accord. What we see is an attempt to broaden the application of methodology established in a great many *classical* sciences. Such, in particular, is the abstract-analytical method that is applied in political economy by classical economists and by Marx. Analysing the structure of exchange in commodity-producing society, Marx arrived at the conclusion that the correlation of value between commodities absolutely did not depend on 'qualitative specificity' of the commodities but was entirely determined by the quantity of 'abstract' socially-necessary labour expended on the production of any commodity. If such an operation is permissible – and for a Marxist there can be no doubt that it is permissible – then why is it not permissible to abstract from qualitative specificity and investigate the parallel dynamic interrelationships of two processes such as, for example, the dissolution of an alkali in acidified water and the absorption of merchandise in a market. There can only be one objection *in principle*: in the first case the unity of method is sanctioned by the centuries-old tradition of science, in the second case the attempt is made to unite what in all well-structured bourgeois universities from time immemorial has been spread across various departments. But this argument can hardly be particularly convincing for revolutionaries.

A completely different question is to what extent, from the point of view of the criteria of tektology itself, the merging of sciences indicated above is attainable *in practice*. In order to answer this, it is necessary to carry out a most thorough and detailed analysis of the complexes being compared. It is necessary first of all to determine to which of the types of equilibrium studied in physics and chemistry are related to the equilibrium of a commodity market. Investigation shows that this is a so-called *dynamic* equilibrium, which is also characteristic of a chemical reaction. It is further necessary to determine with which type of reaction (multi-molecular or mono-molecular) the structure of the absorption of commodities by the market is identical to, and many other questions touching on the *interrelationships* among elements. In conclusion, the question arises of whether the qualitative particularities of the elements (molecules in one case, commodity owners in the other) cause any modifications in the application of the theorems of probability theory to the dynamics of both processes? And only after such an exhaustive analysis has given a satisfactory result can we apply a formula to the study of the speed of market processes that depicts the dynamic regularity of a specific kind of chemical reaction.

This is not inference by *analogy* at all. A scholar who is not familiar with physics or chemistry but who is capable of mathematical analysis could have arrived at the very same formula by investigating market processes alone, since it proceeds with compulsory logical necessity from the identical organisational structure of both processes. Analogy does not give arguments to tektologists; it only stimulates them to pose problems and spares them the necessity of reinventing the wheel in those cases when exhaustive analysis of a given case shows that the problem is posed correctly.

In the example that I adduced, the question had to do with transferring from the realm of exact science into social science the kind of formula that permits one to detect the quantitative, algebraic regularity of the processes being studied. In the contemporary state of organisational science we are comparatively rarely able to apply tektological principles in practice with such precision and specificity. In the great majority of cases, Bogdanov provides not quantitative regularity but basic guidelines of thought. There is colossal orienting significance in such generalised guidelines, nevertheless, and I will explain this with an example. In physics and chemistry a major role is played by the so-called law of Henri Louis Le Chatelier,[13] according to which an established system of organised equilibrium is resistant to actions that strive to destroy that equilibrium. Thus, for example, if you bring a magnet near a metallic loop, an inductive current will spring up in the latter that obstructs this movement. When the magnet moves away, the current springs up in the opposite direction. When the temperature of soil drops below zero, the freezing of water is held back by the escaping 'latent warmth of melting', and when snow thaws the warmth of melting is absorbed so that again the process is slowed. Bogdanov posed the question of whether Le Chatelier's law had universal applicability, and there can be no doubt that the formulation is completely valid. In fact, it is natural to expect that the destruction of an equilibrium causes the additional resistance in all such cases when there is a 'positive complex', i.e. the kind of combinations of elements in which the effectiveness of the whole is greater than the sum of the effectiveness of its component parts. This consideration suggests that Le Chatelier's Law must play no less an important role in biology, in sociology, and, in particular, in a planned economy than it plays in physics. Actually, it would not be difficult to show that a great many errors of judgement in the work of economic reconstruction in the Soviet Union were caused by ignoring the supplemental resistance of organisations that were being reconstructed.

---

13   Le Chatelier's Law states that if a chemical system in a state of dynamic equilibrium undergoes a change in the factors that determine it (concentration, temperature, or total pressure), the position of the equilibrium will move in order to minimise the change [trans.].

In estimating the magnitude of the expenditures necessary for the restructuring of our economy and the effectiveness expected from these expenditures, we naively view all economic complexes as neutral. This results in a great many errors that could be avoided if the organisational problems were subjected to a more thorough analysis, and if the applicability of Le Chatelier's law was not ignored in this analysis.

In conclusion, I will point out one tektological principle that has now become a lasting property of the planning methodology of Soviet economists. I have in mind the law of the chain of interrelationships between elements of an organised whole and the law of the minimum (the strength of the entire chain is determined by the strength of its weakest link; the speed of movement of a complex is determined by the speed of the slowest moving element, etc.). When A. Bogdanov first applied the law of the minimum to certain phenomena of our community, his attempt was harshly rebuffed; it seemed to the majority of our activists to be not only untenable but anti-revolutionary. 'We are building our economic policy in such a way', his critics wrote, 'that the leading link was industry that developed with maximal speed, while Bogdanov wanted to hold us back to be level with the most backward link'. And only a small group of planning workers, with V.G. Groman[14] in the lead, from the very beginning placed the principle of the chain of relationships and the law of the minimum at the basis of the methodology of the economic plan. In the Soviet Union at the present time there is not one economist or one important scientific worker who in drawing up economic perspectives could manage without the analysis of the 'chain of relationships' of phenomena and without the establishment of 'limits' (i.e. minimums).

But even the practical use of tektological methods is not always accompanied by a conscious recognition of them. It is often said, for example, that the principle of limits and a chain of relationships is something that is elementary and clear, that goes without saying, and that does not need any special organisational science to justify it. And this is said by the very same people who several years ago met this 'self-evident' idea of chain-like causality with indignant protests. Thus we see that the old story of Columbus's egg remains forever new.

---

14   Vladimir Gustavovich Groman (1874–1940) was a Russian economist affiliated with the Menshevik fraction. He was a leading figure in Gosplan (the agency responsible for economic planning in the Soviet Union) in the 1920s, but because he argued that the targets for Stalin's first five-year plan were unrealistic, he – along with Bazarov – was arrested and accused of counter-revolutionary activity. Groman publicly admitted his guilt, while Bazarov did not [trans.].

Down to the present, tektology has had considerably more opponents than supporters in our literature. A great many articles and a few thick books have been written against tektology. Nevertheless, there still has been no real, practical criticism of it. The failure of Bogdanov's opponents consists in the fact that the majority of them are professional philosophers, i.e. people who are capable of working with abstractions but lack competence in the concrete fields of knowledge to which Bogdanov applied his principles. Meanwhile, tektology is absolutely invulnerable to abstract-philosophical criticism.

The first and principal philosophical accusation against Bogdanov is 'idealism', and various modifications of the old polemical articles by Plekhanov are usually used to prove the justice of this accusation. But after all, Plekhanov was denouncing the ideological essence of *empiriomonism*. The principles of universal organisational science are not tied to the *philosophy* of empiriomonism at all. The applicability of those principles depends in no way upon the model according to which the 'thing-in-itself' acts upon us – an empiriomonistic model, a Plekhanovite model, or any other. Tektology has to do only with the facts of experience and is absolutely uninterested in things-in-themselves.

Further, in recent years Bogdanov has frequently been reproached because his worldview is mechanistic and not dialectical. First and foremost, this is factually untrue. The basic mark of 'dialectical-ness' is considered, as is well known, to be the recognition of the idea that different realms of being have unique qualities that are not reducible to quantity. But the foundation of tektology – the idea of organisation – is exactly the recognition of such qualities. Besides that, from Bogdanov's point of view mechanics itself is not 'mechanistic' but dialectical, since the same qualitative characteristics are characteristic as in the sphere of the processes of the simplest mechanical phenomena as in the sphere of the complex phenomena of individual or social life. The dialectical-ness of tektology appears with particular clarity in the theory of crises that according to Bogdanov have, yet again, universal significance.

But even if the accusation of mechanistic-ness were justified, it would not be enough to discredit tektological constructions – as is true of all *operational*-scientific constructions. Bogdanov repeatedly emphasised that the concepts of organisational science do not have the goal of 'explaining' phenomena but of preparing humankind for practical struggle, to help it 'master' nature. This is a substantial distinction.

The passively explanatory function of cognition is to place new facts under old, habitual general concepts that have been sanctioned for one reason or another. This calms the mind and facilitates a purely theoretical orientation for it, but in itself it still does not elevate the practical power of humanity over nature. For this latter goal more perfected cognitive instruments are necessary that provide not only a qualitative description but also quantitative measurement, and, in addition, that that allow one to predict the approach of an event being studied or to purposefully cause it. If a tool that successfully carries out this practical task does not correspond in form to the established and sanctioned model of any 'philosophical' theory – for example, appears mechanistic to a dialectician – then the simple statement of that fact is still not sufficient to critically destroy a scientific construction that one does not like. Critics must devise the kind of dialectical construction to replace the mechanistic construction that they do not like that would carry out the cognitively operative work of the latter and, moreover, carry it out better and not worse. Only then can critics hope for a successful performance. As far as the abstract philosophical reprimands that are conventionally given to scientists under the guise of criticism are concerned, they deserve only compassionate smiles.

The time has not yet come for an evaluation of the scientific legacy bequeathed to us by A. Bogdanov. That the legacy is huge is already clear to any impartial person. This is also admitted by the most thoughtful of Bogdanov's theoretical opponents. In the speech that N.I. Bukharin[15] gave at Bogdanov's grave, he did not conceal his disagreements with the deceased in the least, but he emphasised that Communists will learn a great deal from him for a long time.

I end my essay with the hope that Bogdanov's ideas will promote – among both his supporters and his critics – that serious and profound work of scientific thought without which it will be impossible either to adequately continue Bogdanov's work or to introduce valid corrections into it.

---

15   Nikolai Ivanovich Bukharin (1888–1938) was a Marxist theorist, Bolshevik revolutionary, and Soviet politician. At the time he gave this speech, Bukharin was a member of the Politburo of the Communist Party, its highest policy-making organ. For a discussion of Bukharin's relationship with Bogdanov and a translation of Bukharin's speech, see Pavlov 2013 [trans.].

*Book One*

∴

CHAPTER 1

# The Ideal of Cognition (Empiriomonism of the Physical and the Psychical)

Our age is predominantly an age of criticism.[1] Beginning in the era of the Renaissance, the great liberating progression of the human spirit has been gradually clearing the way for the continual, unimpeded progress of human powers, both individual and social ... This liberating work appears in the sphere of *thought* in the form of criticism, smashing countless fetishes that stand in the way of knowledge and tearing asunder countless fetters that hold back the development of knowledge. But the decisive dominance of criticism began at the end of the eighteenth century. The French Revolution made criticism the all-pervasive principle of human social being, while Kant made it the all-pervasive principle of thought. All limits to criticism were removed in principle, and ever since the only limits to criticism are those it must set for itself.

Since that time, criticism has been the slogan of all that is progressive in life and thought. First, the Utopian Socialists in their assaults on the social order marched under its banner, and now the great class struggle is being carried on under its banner. In science the power of criticism led to the elaboration of precise methods, and in philosophy it has led to consistent positivism.

Of course, there have been many instances of authoritarian reaction in life and of dogmatic reaction in thought. But here also the power of criticism has made itself felt. It has made an impact not only because it finally won out, but also because reaction usually tried to dress in its clothing and pass itself off as criticism. This tendency of reactionary forces to transport its historical contraband under the flag of criticism was the best proof of the power and the respect that this noble flag enjoyed in all the seas and bays of the stormy ocean of modernity.

How can the huge and seemingly ever-growing vital importance of criticism be explained? It signifies the struggle between two different forms of life (those that are dying out and those that are being born), the accumulation of forces that are kept in tight restraints, and the thirst for space and freedom. As we know, there are organic eras and critical eras in the development of peoples.

---

1 It would appear that Bogdanov is referring to a line from the preface to the first edition of Kant's *Critique of Pure Reason*: 'Our age is, in every sense of the word, the age of criticism, and everything must submit to it' (Kant 1922, p. xix) [trans.].

There are eras when life peacefully flows along its accustomed channel, slowly broadening and deepening and not needing new paths, since the old ones do not yet constrain them. And there are eras when life violently rushes through rapids and cliffs, clearing a new course in place of the old one that is too narrow and cramped. Heavy moss-covered rocks are rolled along and carried to the sea; age-old mountains are undermined and washed away. This is the critical work of life, and it is in such an era that we live.

But the river does not flow just in order to remove stones and mountains; criticism cannot be the final goal, the end product at which life can come to a stop. Human feelings, will, and even knowledge cannot be satisfied by criticism alone. The life that is growing and the forces that are building up must necessarily take shape in new forms; they must be organised into a new unity. The task of criticism is to provide space for these forms, to prevent them from developing abnormally and inharmoniously, but it cannot create those forms. Criticism is a gardener who carefully clears the ground for a tree and prunes superfluous and crooked branches, but the gardener is not what causes the tree to grow and bear luxuriant fruit. Life develops from life, and life defines its own goal. And this goal is not criticism but creativity.

The content that is seeking new forms for itself in our times is truly huge. In its struggle with external nature over the preceding centuries, the collective forces of humanity have grown a hundredfold and have been applied in infinitely varied directions. The field of scientific practice has broadened even more significantly, so much so that the sphere of production is only a fraction of it. The profusion of ideas and worldviews has increased immeasurably, intertwining and colliding in the contemporary world. We need forms that are infinitely broader and stronger and suppler so that this content, as it continually develops, can be embraced and freely combined. We need forms that are infinitely complex but that at the same time are infinitely harmonious so that all the diversity of this boundlessly progressing life can be arranged within them without contradictions. Our imagination cannot conceive how incomparably magnificent and grandiose, how incomparably elegant and orderly, these new forms must be.

The rough, general contours of these forms are already taking shape in the distance. As consciousness develops, it dimly discerns them and passionately strives toward them. The ideal of practical life in our times emerges more clearly; it expresses the striving to harmoniously unite all of humanity for struggle with the elemental world and for the uninterrupted development of its powers. The ideal of cognition is not so clear; it is not formulated in words that are alive and understandable for everyone, and it is even alien to a large majority of those who are committed to the ideal of practical life. And at the same time, the living, indivisible unity of practice and cognition tells us that both goals must be inseparably connected with one another and must remain in strict harmony. Therefore, any attempt to delineate the ideal of cognition is also legitimate – if only in the sort of general model in which we conceive of the ideal of life.

Setting such a task for ourselves, we already know in advance that the path to resolve it passes through the realm of criticism – not that passionate criticism that transforms the forms of practical life, but the cold and rigorous criticism of experience and abstract thought.

I

If we strive to base our investigation on all the attainments of the great era of criticism, then our starting point in regard to our cognitive relationship to reality must be to ever more rationally work with the most perfected and rigorous expression of the spirit of criticism. *Empiriocriticism* represents just such an expression of the critical tendency of our times; it is a critique of all cognition from the point of view of experience and a critique of experience itself from the point of view of the interconnectedness and regularity of experience.

Empiriocriticism is a contemporary form of positivism that has developed on the basis of the modern methods of natural science, on the one hand, and of modern forms of philosophical criticism, on the other. This philosophical current found its most prominent exponents in Ernst Mach and Richard Avenarius, the first of whom formulated it with particular clarity and lucidity, and the second of whom formulated it with particular completeness and precision.[2] It has attracted most of its adherents from among young scientists and philosophers, both inside and outside of universities. It increasingly influences the scientific and philosophical development of our times. Even its opponents recognise the growing force and influence of empiriocriticism.

It is not necessary to present the philosophical foundations of empiriocriticism with any degree of completeness. As far as our task is concerned, it is sufficient to describe this school's most general cognitive relationship to reality, to the world of experience.

The task of cognition, according to Mach and Avenarius, consists in systematising the content of experience in such a way that experience is both the natural basis and the natural boundary of cognition. In its objective meaning, this

---

2 The term 'empiriocriticism' applies specifically to Avenarius, but it also characterises Mach well, although in a few details Mach's views differ from those of Avenarius.

systematisation of the content of experience is a powerful vital adaptation, a tool for preserving and developing life. The view of cognition as an adaptation – having arisen in evolutionary thought considerably earlier than empiriocriticism, of course – found the broadest and most comprehensive development in works of this school and became the basis of a consistent *critique* of cognition. On the one hand, Mach's *Die Analyse der Empfindungen* [*The Analysis of the Sensations*] and his scientific-critical works, particularly *Der Wärmelehre* [*Thermodynamics*], and, on the other hand, Avenarius's *Kritik der reinen Erfahrung* [*Critique of Pure Experience*] give a full picture of a critical-evolutionary theory of cognition that is the same in all essentials.[3]

But in this picture, cognition is not only an adaptation in general; it is also a *social* adaptation. The social genesis of cognition – its dependence on social experience, its continual social coordination, and the fundamental equal worth of the thought of different people – clearly comes out and is deliberately emphasised by both thinkers. And here we must recognise the great founders of historical monism as their predecessors, even though it is unlikely that either philosopher had any clear understanding of them.[4]

In the places where Mach delineates the connection between cognition and the process of social labour, the coincidence of his views with the ideas of Marx is from time to time quite striking. In several philosophical reflections in his *Der*

---

3   In the development of their views, Mach started from a position of philosophical *idealism*, while Avenarius's position had a *realistic* colouration from the beginning. It is all the more remarkable that their philosophical conclusions – reforming the theory of cognition on the basis of advanced scientific methods – are identical. The completely inconsequential differences of opinion between these philosophers bears, however, the obvious imprint of the difference between the starting points of their development (especially in relation to the concept of Mach's 'elements (sensations)', and it will be necessary to speak of this later). Avenarius's *Der menschliche Weltbegriff* [*The Human World Concept*] (his theory of introjection) occupies a rather special position in the series of basic works of empiriocriticism, but we will also return to this again.

4   Alois Riehl stands nearer in time to Mach and Avenarius, and he also recognises the social nature of cognition and its biological role as an adaptation, but he insufficiently substantiated it in his analysis of cognition (*Der philosophische Kritizismus* [*The Critical Philosophy*] II B. 2 T.). In general in past decades one often comes upon these ideas in philosophical and social-philosophical literature. The development of comparative philology greatly facilitated their consolidation, clarifying the organic link between thought and speech, the social form of communication. (Ludwig Noiré and Max Müller are particularly important). But, as a rule, neither philosophers nor scholars have taken this social-genetic perspective on thought to its ultimate conclusion with strict methodological consistency. [Alois Adolf Riehl (1844–1924) was an Austrian neo-Kantian philosopher. Ludwig Noiré (1829–89) was a German philosopher of language. Max Müller (1823–1900) was a German-born philologist and orientalist who taught at Oxford University (trans.).]

*Wärmelehre* we meet such propositions as, for example, the following: 'science arose from the needs of practical life ... from technology' (p. 451), a formulation that strictly conforms to the principle of historical materialism. This is additional proof for us of the profound progressiveness of empiriocriticism as a trend that is capable of organically apprehending all that is most vital in its ideological environment.

In investigating cognition as a social adaptation, empiriocriticism does not find any fundamental difference between ordinary, uncritical cognition and scientific-philosophical, critical cognition. The tasks and the methods in both cases are essentially the same, and the difference is only in the degree of elaboration of the adaptations. Scientific and critical methods perform the tasks of cognition with relatively greater thoroughness and with less expenditure of energy; they are characterised by the *economisation* of time and effort. Thus, ordinary and inexact cognition, as it progresses, striving to embrace all the increasing profusion and variety of experience, must necessarily transform, step by step, into critical and precise cognition. Accordingly, cognition approaches, to an ever greater degree, a *pure description* of what is in experience – and, needless to say, a description that generalises and systematises. Here the problem arises of the content of experience, of the interconnectedness and regularity of experience, and of the vital significance of the various parts of its content. This is the problem of the critique of experience.

The endless flow of experience, from which knowledge crystallises, presents in its whole not only a very grandiose but also a very variegated picture. In breaking down this whole, step by step, analysis moves from its more major parts to increasingly minor parts and arrives in the end at a certain boundary beyond which the flow of experience cannot be further broken down. The *elements* of experience lie at this boundary. What exactly are these elements?

Mach calls them 'elements (sensations)'. The experience that we have relative to the 'external world' is reducible to 'bodies' as combinations of various 'specifiers' – locations, times, colours, forms, dimensions, and so forth. Decomposing these 'specifiers' brings us to elementary sensations of space, time, colour, sound and sensations that are stimulative, tactile, savoury, etc. In the so-called 'internal world' we have perceptions, psychical images, desires, and emotions. Further analysis yields, in part, the very same elements as for external experience (for example, in the 'perception' of any body there are also sensations of extension, colour, stimulation, etc.) and, in part, elements that are by all appearances different – elements of will and emotion ...[5] Elements

---

5  Avenarius distinguishes 'elements' from 'feelings' so that for 'elements' he has in mind col-

can properly be called 'sensations' with complete accuracy only in regard to the 'psychical' world, since 'sensation' is a psychological term that is inapplicable to the physical realm of experience,[6] but it is of the utmost importance that the exact same elements can both belong to 'bodies' as their 'specifiers' ('red', 'green', 'cold', 'hot', 'hard', etc.) and can also be part of the composition of 'perceptions' and 'psychical images' as 'sensations' proper (the sensation of red, green, cold, etc.). 'Red' in bodies and 'the sensation of red' in the perception of those bodies are *identical* elements of experience, which we only designate differently.

Bodies are complexes of the elements that we call 'sensations' when we 'perceive' them. This proposition is so extremely important that it is necessary to dwell upon it.

The human organism exists for us as a body in a series of other bodies. What are the elements from which this body is assembled? First and foremost, we find a series of elements perceived with the aid of sight: a series of (form). Then there is a series of completely different elements, perceived with the aid of the sense of pressure and the sense of temperature: elements of form and space that are given to us by means of palpation of the body, elements of warmth and coolness that appear along with them, etc. Further, there is a series of elements accessible by hearing: sounds and noises that constitute speech, singing, crying, laughing, and so on ... The material of each of these series is completely different; they are *qualitatively different*, even though

---

ours, sounds, hardness and softness, sweet and bitter, etc., and for 'dispositions' he has in mind tones of happiness and suffering, beauty and ugliness, reality and illusion, clarity and obscurity, etc. For my goals, this distinction is not significant, and therefore I prefer to follow Mach in my presentation.

6  Mach, himself, repeatedly pointed out this difference in order to eliminate the possibility of an idealist interpretation of his views. His Russian translator (Engel'meier, *Ocherki po teorii poznaniia E. Makha* [*Outlines of E. Mach's Theory of Cognition*], 1901) is somewhat guilty in this regard, since he pays little attention to this aspect of the matter. In translating Mach's views, he even goes so far as to make statements such as the following: 'our sensations are not produced by the world but we produce the world from our sensations' (Introduction, p. 17). Mach would never consent to this way of putting it. He would point out, first, that elements are only properly called sensations when we speak of them from a psychological point of view and that this term is not permissible in relation to the 'physical' world, and second, that elements are not what we make the world out of but are *products of the cognitive decomposition* of experience, so that experience, in toto, is *primary* and not secondary in relation to them. Perhaps in the future it will be possible to decompose today's 'elements' further – they are, after all, not atoms. Then they will be replaced by elements that are simpler but even more 'derivative', in the sense of the length of the path that cognition travels to arrive at them.

they all unite into one complex that is signified by the word 'human'. The visual series (elements of colour and visible forms) cannot conceivably be compared in its immediacy with the tactile series (elements of tangible forms of solidity and warmth) or with the acoustic series (sounds and noises). In this sense, it is impossible even to compare discrete elements within one series – to compare 'red' with 'green', for example. But a 'body' is something that is unified. What gives it this unity? The stable interconnectedness of the parts of the complex.

In our experience, this stable interconnectedness is far from absolute. In most cases we only see people who pass by us, but we do not hear them or touch them. The visual series is given, the other series are not given, yet we still do not doubt that what we see are 'bodies', 'people'. In other cases, we only hear or only touch, or we see and hear, etc. Nevertheless, the individual series of elements of experience are securely associated among themselves, We know from experience that if we see a person then, in order to be palpably aware of them, it is sufficient for us to walk up and to touch them and probably also to hear them. From each series of elements, only one insignificant part of the elements might be available, but still the whole complex – the whole 'body' – enters the sphere of our experience. We can see one finger of a person, or touch only their hand, or hear only their step, but still we have no doubt that it is a person in front of us. If the question is of a given person, Mr A., then the whole composition of the complex can change greatly. He can, for example, put on different clothing, the colour of his face and physique can be affected by illness, his voice can become hoarse, etc. We, however, will recognise exactly that person, exactly that complex. In general, the relative stability of a complex of elements is sufficient in order to make a 'body' of it.[7]

One aspect of the matter at hand that neither Mach nor Avenarius dwelt on is very important for us. The visual, tactile, and acoustic series that have become part of the composition of one 'body' are qualitatively differenti-

---

7  The very idea of the absolute in philosophy – 'substance' or 'thing-in-itself' – emerged from this relativity. Every given part of a complex cannot be grasped by our experience at a given moment, but we still recognise a 'thing' as being *the same* as the whole complex that appears to us. Does this not mean that it is possible to throw out all 'elements', all 'signs' of things, and nevertheless the thing remains – now not as a phenomenon but as a 'substance'? This is, of course, only an old logical mistake: one single hair can be pulled out and the person is not bald, but if you pull them all out together, then a person will be bald; the same is true of the process by which a 'substance' is created, which Hegel justifiably called the *'caput mortuum* [worthless residue] of an abstraction'. If all elements of a complex are thrown out, then the complex will not exist; all that will remain is the *word* that signifies it. A word – this is what the 'thing-in-itself' is.

ated according to their elements. They are completely incommensurable in regard to material – compare, for example, 'red' with 'hard' or with 'bitter' – and yet the various series present themselves as inseparably connected. Why do they not form independent complexes for cognition? Does not cognition strive to unite the homogeneous and separate the heterogeneous? Why is our experience made up of complexes that are so dissimilar in their composition? The answer to these questions is obtained very easily if we stick to the basic fact of experience – to the *parallelism of the several series* that form a body.

If we simultaneously see, hear, and touch a person, then the *mutual relationships* of elements in all three series of experience are situated in a certain correlation among themselves. A change in the visual series corresponds to a specific change in the tactile series, and vice versa. When we see that a person raises his hand (a change in the combination of elements of colour and space), then, if we wish, we also are always able simultaneously feel it with the aid of the sense of touch (a change in the combination of tactile elements). The relationships of both elements change in a specific interrelationship that cannot be replaced by another. If we see a specific movement of lips and thorax, then we usually hear specific sounds of speech, and, yet again, the relationships of the two elements change in specific mutual correspondence. Suppose that you have a visual series of elements but no tactile ones at all, and you are unable to obtain any – i.e. you see a person but upon touching them you do not obtain any tactile sensation, either resistance or temperature. In such a case it is not a person at all but an apparition or some kind of optical illusion. Suppose you hear a person speaking, but, despite the presence of all the usual conditions for perceiving a corresponding visual series, you do not obtain it or you obtain a series with completely different relationships. In such a case, this is, yet again, not a person but an auditory hallucination or perhaps a recording. Wherever the habitual parallelism of such-and-such a given series breaks down, then the recognition in experience of such-and-such a given 'body' that is usually perceived is also eliminated, and the necessity arises of uniting the facts of experience differently – of recognising not such-and-such a 'body', as usual, but another one, or of completely denying the presence of a 'body' at all.

The parallelism of a number of dissimilar series of experience, united in one 'body', gives these series a certain uniformity, but it is a uniformity of *relationships* and not of elements. It is precisely this uniformity of relationships, observed for the various series of experience, that is the immediate basis for the unity of a *body*. The spatial and temporal unity of a body is only a particular form of that uniformity of relationships, of that parallelism of the various series. Visual space, for example, is coordinated with tactile space precisely by virtue of the parallelism between the different series of elements, and the unity of time is really another name for the parallel flow of all these series amid the general stream of immediate experiences.

Let us note that one of these series usually plays a special *organising* role in a complex. When we think to ourselves of a human body, it appears to us either *predominantly* as a tangible object or predominantly as a visual object. That is, one series – for the most part the tactile series, to be precise, and less often the visual series – lies at the foundation of the complex, and it is the central part of the complex around which the other series are united. It is not difficult to understand the reason why the tactile series plays such a special role: the reason is connected to the special significance of the tactile series in the biological struggle to survive. It is usually only when the tactile series is involved that objects can turn out to be very useful or very harmful for life. All objects of 'production' in the economic sense – materials of labour, tools, objects of consumption – represent 'tangible' objects. Bodies that lack a tactile series – shadows, reflections, clouds, for example – are not vitally important (at any rate, not immediately important; indirectly they might acquire great importance, such as, let us say, rain clouds). Besides this, the great completeness and distinctness of the tactile series (in the palpation of objects) has considerable significance and is closely connected with this biological role. However, in this respect it easily gives way to the visual series, which can also appear as an organising series, instead of the tactile series, when the latter is not present and sometimes even when it *is* present.

Let us now return to the presentation of Mach's views. As has already been said, the exact same elements can enter the content of both 'physical bodies' and 'psychical processes'. If the 'body' that is called a human organism is a complex of such-and-such elements of colour, space, touch, etc., then what are the elements that make up the complex of the *perception* of this body? That complex is obviously made up of all those very same elements of colour, space, touch, etc., only here these elements are called 'sensations'. These same elements also make up the 'psychical image' of the body when that body is not being immediately perceived. But what kind of difference is there between a 'body' and the 'perception' of a body or the 'psychical image' of it? After all, these are unquestionably far from being the same thing as far as our experience is concerned.

A body in a series of other bodies belongs to a specific system of things that is characterised by specific relationships and that is called the 'physical' or 'external' world. A perception or psychical image of a body belongs to a different system in which the relationships are different and that is called the 'psychical' or 'internal' world. The question consequently boils down to the difference between two realms of experience: the physical and the psychical, the 'external' and the 'internal'.

In the world of physical complexes, bodies are characterised by a definite and stable regularity of their external and internal relationships. A table is in front of you. Your perception of the table changes with each varying position of your head. It disappears if you turn away from it or leave the room. But the table, as a body, does not change under these circumstances and remains in its place. You can arbitrarily, by the effort of concentration alone, recall the psychical image of the table and place it in a series of other psychical images in the most varied associations of forms, but you cannot, in the same way, arbitrarily, by an act of will, make that table appear in a series of other bodies or in a new correlation with other bodies. The interconnectedness of phenomena in both cases is different. In the physical world, it has a much more specific nature; it is exempt from any wilful caprice and is *independent of fortuitous changes in the state of our organism*. In the psychical world, phenomena appear *as specifically dependent precisely on the state of the organism* and proximally on the nervous system.

Perceptions are formed when the stimulation of various organs of sensation is transmitted to the central nervous system, and those perceptions change in conformity with the form of this stimulation, on the one hand, and with the state of the neural conductors and nerve cells, on the other. If the two optic nerves are severed, the whole world of visual perceptions disappears for a given psyche. If the nervous system is poisoned with santonin,[8] all objects will be perceived in a different hue than before. If an organism is subjected to the action of a sufficient dose of narcotic toxin, not only will perceptions disappear but psychical images and even emotions and desires will disappear as well. Disrupt the nourishment of the cortex of the brain, and the entire psychical world seems confused and disordered; all its relationships change dramatically. But the physical world, regardless of this, remains as before.

All these correlations – and they could made without end – lead to the following formulation: to the extent that the data of experience appear *as dependent on the state of a given nervous system*, they form *the psychical world* of a given individual, and to the extent that the data of experience are taken *outside such dependency*, we are confronted by the *physical world*. Avenarius therefore designates these two domains of experience as the *dependent series* and the *independent series* of experience.

---

8  Santonin is a drug that was widely used in Bogdanov's day as a cure for intestinal parasites. One of its side effects was to cause the patient to have yellow vision [trans.].

The intermediary cases where the two series of experience are temporarily confused are especially important for understanding the real difference between them. At first, people attribute their dreams and hallucinations to the external world, but subsequent experience convinces them that these phenomena depend entirely on a particular, transient state of his nervous system, and then they attribute them to the psychical world. If people are not sufficiently educated to establish this form of correlation, as often happens with uncultivated people in regard to hallucinations, then they would attribute the phenomenon to the 'external' world, no matter how unstable the hallucination is. They would understand it as a 'ghost' or 'spirit' – in general, as a *body*, although one with special properties. (The word 'spirit' need not lead to confusion here; for an animist, 'spirit' is certainly not 'psychical' in the scientific sense.)

Besides those complexes that can appear equally in the physical series (as bodies) and also in the psychical series (as perceptions or psychical images), complexes of another kind nevertheless also exist that pertain entirely to the psychical world and that we never attribute to the physical realm of experience. These are emotional and volitional complexes: sensations, passions, desires, and so forth. Joy, anger, longing, love, etc. never present themselves to us as 'bodies' but always as only psychical processes. At the same time, complexes of this kind are sometimes extremely stable; many are more stable than some fleeting phenomena of the physical world. What is more, what we signify by the word 'I' is a complex that is also notable for being exclusively 'psychical', and it is the most stable complex in the series of our experiences. How can we understand *this* particular grouping of experiences?

The specifically-psychical character of this entire group of experiences is determined by the fact that it is particularly and immediately dependent on the state of a given nervous system and cannot be conceived of outside of that dependence – outside of the regular interconnectedness that characterises the physical sphere of experience. At this point the desire to sharply distinguish the specifically-psychical series from the general system of experience tends to arise – the desire to separate it out as something independent of all psychophysical experiences. But such a view cannot be accepted as correct.

Emotional and volitional complexes and the complex 'I' can be broken down by analysis into elements, and these elements are *exactly the same sort of* elements that appear in any other psychophysical combination. Thus, in accord with experimental research, even if we do not accept the general theory of James and Lange,[9] it is unquestionable that innervational and tactile

---

9  William James (1842–1910) and Carl Lange (1834–1900) arrived independently at one of the

elements – elements that in other combinations enter the makeup of 'perceptions' and the makeup of 'bodies' – play a huge role in the emotions. In exactly the same way, volitional complexes represent complex combinations of various elements with specific 'feelings' (in the terminology of Avenarius), and innervational elements have a special significance here.[10] In regard to 'I', the 'I' is a most complicated complex of vitally important combinations, predominantly innervational and volitional – in general, those combinations that are most closely connected with the self-preservation of the organism.[11] Thus, specifically-psychical complexes are not distinguishable in their elements and their material from other groupings in the sphere of experience; they are not distinguishable from psychical-physical combinations.

II

I have outlined the most general relationship of empiriocriticism to reality as a system of experience to the extent that is necessary for the task we have set. What we have here is a worldview that is deeply grounded on the achievements of contemporary science, on the one hand, and that is captivating in its simplicity and clarity, on the other. It does not fit comfortably within the confines of customary philosophical definitions. It is clearly different from naïve realism because of its profoundly analytical and strictly critical relationship to the whole content of experience. But it is no less distant from any kind of idealism. It is far from transcendental idealism because it does not accept any higher reality of super-sensory ideas and because it considers any idea that is thought to be the product of the elaboration and processing of experience. And it is far from immanent idealism because it absolutely does not locate reality and experience entirely within the confines of the psyche and of 'psychical images'. Instead, it treats the 'psychical' as only one specific realm of experience. Empiriocriticism has nothing to do with either materialism or spiritualism or with any kind of metaphysics in general; for empiriocriticism both matter and spirit are only complexes of elements, and any 'essence' or supra-experiential knowledge

---

first theories of emotion in modern psychology. This theory holds that emotions are caused by a physiological reaction to a stimulus [trans.].

10  See R. Avenarius *Kritik der reinen Erfahrung*, II, p. 206 and following. See also G. Simmel, 'Skizze einer Willenstheorie [Sketch of a Theory of Will]', *Zeitschrift für Psychologie und Physiologie der Sinnesorgane* [*Journal of Psychology and Physiology of the Sense Organs*], 1895, for the innervation theory of volition.

11  See R. Avenarius, *Kritik der reinen Erfahrung*, II, pp. 335 and 275 (about the 'dominant'); also E. Mach, *Analyse der Erfahrung*, pp. 13–20.

are terms without content, empty abstractions. To characterise empiriocriticism as critical, evolutionary, and sociologically-coloured positivism would be to immediately indicate the main currents of philosophical thought which flow into it.

By breaking down all that is physical and all that is psychical into identical elements, empiriocriticism does not permit the possibility of any kind of dualism. But at this point a new critical question arises: if dualism is disproved and eliminated, does that mean that monism has been achieved? Has the point of view of Mach and Avenarius liberated all our thinking from its dualist character *in reality*? This question must be answered in the negative.

The critique of experience makes dualism impossible, but dualism nevertheless remains, only taking on a new form. In relation to content, there is only one experience, but *why does it contain two types of regularity*? The interconnectedness of the physical series and the interconnectedness of the psychical series are fundamentally different. They are not reducible to one another, and they are not susceptible of being unified into any third, higher regularity.[12] This is not dualism of reality, but dualism of *methods of cognition*, and Avenarius believes that '*diese Dualität ist kein Dualismus*' (this duality is not dualism). But it is difficult to accept this point of view as correct, no matter how reassuring it is.

The fact of the matter is that, as far as wholeness and coherence of cognition is concerned, *regularities* that are fundamentally different and irreducible to unity are only slightly better than *realities* that are fundamentally different and irreducible to unity. When the realm of experience is broken into two series and cognition must operate completely differently with each of them, then cognition cannot feel itself to be integrated and harmonious. A series of questions inevitably arise that are directed toward removing the duality and replacing it with a higher unity. How is it possible for there to be two fundamentally different regularities in a single flow of human experience? And why are there precisely two of them? Why is the dependent series, the 'psychical', situated in close functional correlation with just the nervous system and not with some other kind of 'body', and why does experience not contain an infinite number of dependent series, connected with 'bodies' of other types? Why do some complexes of elements appear in both series of experience – both as 'bodies' and as 'psychical images' – and others never appear as bodies but always belong to one series, etc.?

---

12   It is possible, of course, to reduce them both to an abstraction that generalises them, but this would only be an empty concept of relationships in general that would be incapable of organically uniting the two basic forms of regularity of experience.

Empiriocriticists will, of course, be correct – from their point of view – to reject the very posing of these questions. For them, the task of cognition is to describe what is in experience, and if there is a duality in it then this must be stated, but there is no point in asking 'why'. However, in this case, the question 'why' expresses an obvious, completely real need for a truly harmonious, logical unity in the description of experience – a need which the critique of experience generally acknowledges as completely legitimate, and the rejection of the question leaves this need completely unsatisfied.

There is no sharp boundary between 'duality' and 'dualism' in cognition. Duality becomes dualism to the extent that a more intense striving toward harmony and unity in cognition is present and to the extent that the developing psyche becomes more sensitive to any dualisation – that is, when elements of both aspects of the duality present themselves simultaneously to the consciousness with increasing frequency, causing a feeling of contradiction to build up. For Spinoza, the duality of the cognitive attributes of a single substance – thought and extension – did not contradict the monism of the system in the least, but for us people of the twentieth century it is an unquestionable dualism. And this must happen with any fundamental duality of the means of cognition.

This is why our striving toward the ideal of cognition must take on the task of overcoming this duality.

III

Let us examine relationship of the two orders of experience – the physical and the psychical – a little more closely and attentively. We must, as much as possible, *describe* their differences more precisely and, if possible, figure out the origin of these differences. The question of the *origin* might appear irrelevant, but let us try to get rid of any preconceived judgements about it and see if a rigorous critique of these very differences does not lead to this question.

The invariable element of all characterisations of anything that is 'physical' is the latter's *objectivity*. No one can conceive of a physical body or process which could be designated as something 'subjective'. There are no exceptions whatever. But what does 'objective' mean?

The first and the simplest answer to that question that presents itself would be this: we call objective what is durable and stable in our experience. But we must immediately reject such a view. One observes extremely fleeting and almost imperceptible events in the physical world, but this still does not prevent them from being characterised as 'objective'. On the other hand, extremely durable and stable things – constantly returning combinations – are encountered in the psychical world to which this characterisation of 'objective' unquestionably does not apply. The form of a given cloud at a given moment is something completely objective, even though in a tenth of a second it will already be completely different. On the other hand, the perception that the sun revolves around the earth is an extremely stable, often repeated psychical combination, and yet we cannot accept this movement as an objective fact. Obviously, it is necessary to seek another definition of objective.

We could take a position like this: what is objective for us in phenomena – what we can successfully rely on in our actions – is what does not lead us to contradictions in practice. Physical bodies and their properties present something objective because when we accept these bodies as reality and utilise their evident properties we do not arrive at contradictions between them and ourselves. This, in essence, is a modification of the previous view, only embracing experience within broader bounds. But this point of view must also be rejected precisely inasmuch as it relates to *individual and not to collective experience*. In the course of their lives, separate individuals often go around with extremely subjective views in practice, but, due to the narrow confines of their experience, they do not arrive at appreciable contradictions. Peasants who never leave the country for their entire lives can consider the earth to be a flat circle, the sky to be a blue, crystal dome, and the sun to be a shining disk, yet the harmony of their practical lives will not suffer in the least. But are these data of their experience objective? Certain pathological cases can clarify the question even more. There are people suffering from paranoia who remain completely in their own unreal world inhabited by people who do not exist and who are usually pursuing them. Believing in these pursuers and struggling against them, sometimes in a highly organised delirium, such paranoids do not arrive at any cognitional contradictions in their experience. But if they should try to treat their enemies objectively (in our sense) even for a short time (which, of course, is hardly possible) – i.e. to recognise that they are not real and not take measures against their malicious intentions – very soon new persecutions from the imagined enemies would bring them to a practical contradiction. Here in *private* experience 'objective' cannot serve as a reliable foundation for practice, while 'subjective' experience can.[13]

---

13  An excellent example of this sort is cited by S. Korsakov (*A Course in Psychology*, vol. 1, p. 198 ff.) – a systematic delirium with a detailed description of the appearance, manner, and characteristics of members of a criminal secret society, which persecuted the patient. The whole life of the patient was reduced to a variety of relationships with these nonexistent people.

We arrive at the following conclusion: the characterisation of 'objectivity' altogether cannot be based on individual experience – neither the stability of its compositions nor the harmony between the results of activity and the data of experience that is the starting point of that activity. The basis of 'objectivity' must lie in the sphere of *collective* experience.

We call those data of experience 'objective' that have the same vital significance for us as for other people – those data on which not only we construct our activity without contradiction but on which other people should, in our opinion, also base their actions in order not to arrive at a contradiction. The objective character of the physical world consists in that it exists not only for me alone but for everyone, and it has a specific meaning for everyone that I am convinced is exactly the same as it has for me. The objectivity of the physical series consists in its *social validity*.[14] What is 'subjective' in experience is what does not possess social validity, what has meaning only for one or a few individuals.

This point of view does not contain anything new; it is widespread and applies to a great variety of philosophical doctrines. But if it is understood in terms of its sequential generation, then it presents itself to us in a new light.

Social validity is nothing other than the *coordination* of the experience of different people, the *mutual correspondence* of their experiences. From where does this coordination, this mutual correspondence, come? Is it proper to consider it as 'predetermined harmony' or as the result of development?

We can find the data for an answer in how the forms of space and time developed.

IV

In the theory of space it is necessary to strictly distinguish between the space of sensory perception and abstract space – between visual and conceptual space as Ewald Hering[15] puts it, or between physiological and geometrical space in Mach's terms. Although the two kinds of space are inseparably connected, they nevertheless play different roles in the system of experience.

Physiological space is what our immediate experience gives us in the act of seeing or the act of touching. It is what we directly perceive in the form of the optical and tactile series of elements. Abstract space is the space of our

---

14   In our literature the term 'generally obligatory' is often used, but it is less precise since it carries an unnecessarily normative connotation.
15   Karl Hering (1834–1918) was a German physiologist best known for his research into colour vision and binocular perception [trans.].

thought. It is all-embracing and is not connected with any particular perception; it is space that is presented to us as a 'universal' or 'pure' form of contemplation. The characteristics of these two kinds of space are very different in many ways.

Physiological space possesses neither uniformity, nor continuity, nor permanency of relationships, or, to be more exact, it possesses all these things but only in part. Things appear to be different in different parts of physiological space. The same thing becomes bigger or smaller depending on its distance, and it takes on one or another form depending on its position relative to the eye. When located nearby, objects seem textured, when they are far away they lose their vividness and become flat, and beyond a certain limit they disappear. This relates to space in regard to sight. Space in regard to the sense of touch is more stable but in general it is the same as for the eye. In tactile space, the size and form of objects also change depending on conditions of touch: one or another position of the hand when palpating something, touching one or another parts of a tactile surface in general, and also the ordinary or unusual condition of that surface. The same object seems larger when touching it in one's mouth with one's tongue than when touching it with one's hands. Things that feel smooth when touched by the cheek seem rough to the fingers. Something that is felt to be two objects by the skin of the fingers – the two sharp points of a compass, for example – can seem to be one object to the skin of the forehead or the shoulder. And so on. In general, we are so accustomed to the heterogeneity of physiological space and the fluctuation of its relationships that they do not even attract our attention, despite the sometimes extremely fantastic nature of the transformations that occur in it. In the end, physiological space is always limited; it is what we call the 'field' of vision or touch.

This is not true of abstract space. It is strictly uniform in all its parts. Everything happens in it without interruption, and all relationships are regular. Things in it do not change either form or size without external influence. They do not appear or disappear without sufficient reason. And they do not change their qualities by virtue only of their position in one or another of its regions. It is infinite space.

In physiological space stars appear as small shining points with variable streaks of light issuing from them – rays with constant modulations of colour. These points exist during the course of the night and disappear at the approach of day. Their distance from the eye is no greater than the distance of forests or mountains seen from afar. In abstract space, they are depicted for us by astronomy in pictures that would overwhelm any imagination …

What is the mutual relationship between the two forms of space? Physiological space is the result of development. In the life of a child it only gradually crystallises from the chaos of visual and tactile elements, and this development continues even beyond the first years of life. In the perception of an adult, the distance, size, and form of objects are more stable than in the perception of a child. I clearly remember that as a child of about five years of age I perceived the distance between the earth and the sky as a dimension two or three times greater than the height of a two-storey house, and, having gotten onto the roof, I was very surprised to find that I had not gotten noticeably closer to the heavens. Thus I became familiar with one of the *contradictions* of physiological space. In the perception of an adult these contradictions grow less but they always remain.

Abstract space is *free of contradictions*. In it the same object (that is not subject to sufficient influence) does not seem to be both bigger and smaller than a certain other object or to be of two different forms, etc. Abstract space is strictly regular and is completely uniform everywhere. Some people are of the opinion that abstract space is completely identical for everyone and it is unchangeable. Apriorists assert that throughout the entire history of humanity, as far as we know, 'pure space' (space as a form of intuition) has not changed.

But this last assertion is *factually* incorrect. History shows that abstract space is indeed the result of development. In order to be convinced of this, there is no need even to go to a child, to a pre-civilised person, or to a primordial human (to whom apriorists so readily attribute their most abstract conceptions). It is sufficient to turn to philosophers of ancient and modern times.

Aristotle rejected the possibility of empty space and simultaneously asserted that the universe is spatially limited. Thus for him space did not appear as infinite, although he did recognise the infinity of time. For Epicurus, space contained an up and a down, which he used to explain the movement of the flow of atoms; thus absolute space was not uniform. In effect, it seems that only Kant clearly represented absolute space as strictly uniform; only he established the *relativity of all movement* for the first time, and this relativity is precisely a straightforward expression of the universal uniformity of space. If space possesses absolute uniformity, then movement A in the direction of B and the movement of B in the direction of A are obviously completely identical. In the kind of space in which all parts are completely identical, the position of a given body cannot be distinguished except in relationship to another body. But since the relativity of all movements was not recognised before Kant, we are completely justified in asserting that the abstract space of the people of ancient times still preserved certain traces of non-uniformity.[16] All this should

---

16    The history of geometry also points to a different degree of abstraction of space between

convince us that abstract space is in fact the result of the cognitive development of humanity.

The relationship of physiological and abstract time is altogether the same as the relationship of the forms of space that we have examined. Physiological time is different in comparison with abstract time. It flows unevenly – sometimes quickly, sometimes slowly – and sometimes it seems to disappear from consciousness – during deep sleep or fainting, to be precise. Moreover, physiological time confines itself to objects of personal life. In accordance with all this, the 'temporal magnitude' of the very same phenomena taken in physiological time is also variable: the very same process, not being subjected to any influence, can flow quickly or slowly for us and can sometimes appears to be outside our physiological time.[17] This is not true of abstract time ('the pure form of contemplation'). Abstract time is strictly uniform and continuous in its flow, and phenomena occur in it with strict regularity. It is infinite in both of its directions – in the past and in the future.

It is unquestionable that time is not only a more general form of experience than space but it also originated earlier.[18] Therefore, to detect the signs of historical changes in regard to this form is considerably more difficult than to detect it in regard to space – even abstract time appears everywhere in historical memory as having been already roughly established. However, one can with good reason assert that in the undeveloped thought of children or of primitive people pure time still does not possess the character of *eternity*. Moreover, the question of the *beginning* of time still existed for Greek philosophy, and it later played a well-known role in patristics. But if the question of the beginning of time could enter into the consciousness of a thinker, then it is obvious that this very 'form of contemplation' did yet not possess the definiteness and distinctness that it does in our day.

---

Greek and Indian geometers. The exact same pair of figures represented equality for the Greeks, while it represented symmetry for Indian geometers. A similar difference also obtains in their theories regarding the similarity of figures.

17  In this regard, it is curious that the universally known fact that the passage of time that is boring drags out extremely slowly in an immediate experience, while later on, in memory, it seems to be very short. For an attempt to explain this fact, see Mach's *Die Analyse der Empfindungen*, Chapter XII, where a general analysis of the sensation of time is given.

18  Rudolph Willy considered physiological time to be identical *with the flow of experience* – with the succession of emotional experiences of different breadths and intensities. ('Time is experience itself as it flows ...'. See the chapter in *Krisis der Psychologies* devoted to a critique of Mach.) For my purpose the question of the *elements* of physiological time is not significant.

We arrive at the following conclusions. Abstract space and time are products of development. At their lowest stages of development, they partly preserve certain traits of physiological space and time, which they completely or almost completely lose at their highest levels of development. It is obvious that pure 'forms of contemplation' arise *out of* physiological space and time. But how? This can be explained by comparing the two forms.

Abstract space and time are characterised by the *removal of all contradictions* of physiological space and time from them in order to *harmonise* experience, to coordinate its different parts. This is achieved by removing the heterogeneity of physiological space and time, by bringing continuity into them, and by mentally broadening them beyond the boundaries of any given experience.

Further, abstract space and time are *objective*, i.e. they exist not only for a particular individual in his particular experiences but possess *social validity* for all people who experience cognition. They also represent a contradiction to physiological space and time, which have a subjective colouration – an individual, limited meaning.

All these differences are very profound and important, but on the basis of the preceding we do not need to assume them to be absolute. If abstract forms of space and time take shape in the process of development, then their specific characteristics at each given level of development apply to them only to the extent that these forms have really already taken shape. Thus, as we have seen, the thinking of the ancients did not attain the same level as our thinking in regard to either the uniformity or the limitlessness of space. Therefore, the objectivity – i.e. the social validity – of our 'forms of contemplation' is not absolute in relation to ancient forms, and also the other way around.

This leads us to the following important proposition: the objectivity, or social validity, of given forms of space and time applies in reality only to beings that are significantly close in the level of their cognitive development.[19] Along with this, the question of the origin of this objectivity inevitably arises. It is inseparably connected with the origin of other traits of abstract space and time.

---

19  I understand that this proposition might cause an intense feeling of contradiction in the reader's soul. We habitually suppose that all other people – and even animals – of the past, present, and future live 'in the same space and time as we do'. But habit is not proof. It is undeniable that *we* conceive of these people and animals in *our* space and time, but it does not follow that *they* think of themselves and us in *the exact same* space and time. Of course, to the extent that their organisations are in general similar to ours and to the extent that their utterances are understandable to us, we can suppose that they also have 'forms of contemplation' that are similar but not identical to ours.

How is it possible for a cognising individual to make the transition from *perceptions* that are persistently heterogeneous, devoid of continuity, and always limited in space and time to *abstract forms* of space and time that are uniform, continuous, and limitlessly unfolding? There is only one way – *through communication with other people.*

In individual experience, time flows sometimes faster and sometimes slower, and it sometimes seems to stop. If the temporal measure of experience changes, then all experiences change their tempos. What could cognising individuals who are completely separate from other people – those eternal Robinson Crusoes of philosophy – create from this? Anything they like, except what we are looking for: the uniformity and continuity of abstract time. The memories of the aforesaid Robinson Crusoe are cut short at a certain limit. What could he conclude from this? Anything he likes, except the limitlessness of time. But the countless utterances of other people, filling in the gaps and smoothing over the irregularities of his personal experience convince him that the discontinuities in the flow of the processes of nature that exist for him do not exist for other people, and those gaps and irregularities could be replaced by other people's experience so that the slowing down or speeding up of time is also 'not objective' – i.e. it is not consistent with the experience of other people, and it would be useful to adjust it to conform with the experience of others. *People create an abstract form of time by coordinating their experiences with the experiences of other people.*

The idea shared by a majority of psychologists that the simple observation of the recurrence of natural processes – the movement of the sun, for example – would be sufficient to create the idea of the uniform flow of time is utterly wrong. The periodic processes of nature also flow unevenly in the perception of a pre-civilised person. During pleasant times, the sun moves more quickly and everything around occurs at a livelier tempo; when things are boring, the sun moves more slowly and everything around slows its tempo. And this would make complete sense to pre-civilised people; after all, they are animists and conceive of all of nature according to the form and likeness of themselves. They know that sometimes they travel quickly and sometimes slowly depending on their mood, and, from their point of view, the sun also changes its celestial gait depending on its mood. Only the utterances of other people, for whom time often passes quickly just when it is passing slowly for another and vice versa – only these utterances lead to the production of the idea of uniform time.

In regard to space, in which up and down are permanently different in personal experience, all bodies change their features and nature of movement depending on whether they happen to be moving upwards or downwards. The possibility of assuming that all directions in space are fundamentally uniform only results after collective experience has conceived of the earth as a sphere and of bodies as falling toward its centre. Space was obviously not uniform for all the people of the past who thought that it was impossible for people to live on opposite sides of the earth because it is impossible for people to walk with their feet in the air.

It is also obviously impossible to speak of the infinity of space in individual experience.

Consequently it is necessary to draw the same conclusion regarding space as regarding time: it is a form of social coordination of the experience of different people.

All this also resolves the question of the origin of the objectivity of space and time. Spatial and temporal relationships attain social validity – i.e. objectivity – to the extent that they turn out to be *coordinated* in the experience of different people.

So, in the end, what do abstract forms of space and time in fact signify? They express the *social organisation of experience*. In exchanging countless utterances with others, people constantly mutually remove contradictions from their social experience, harmonise it, and organise it into forms that have universal meaning, i.e. that are objective. The further development of experience then proceeds on the basis of these forms and necessarily keeps within their confines.

In our times, economists and sociologists now make difficulties for themselves by applying the absurd figure of Robinson Crusoe in their analysis. But for all that, the economic Robinson Crusoe is more possible than a cognitive Robinson Crusoe – that improbable solipsist, who more often than not appears as the hero of epistemological analysis. Such individuals arrive at knowledge completely independently of other people, and it is only with the help of various subtle subterfuges that they succeed in crossing over beyond the bounds of their 'internal world' to a more spacious world – the 'external' world – where they usually begin to create various fetishes such as 'matter' (which exists independently of experience) and other 'substances' as well. Who could have intellectually lived and developed outside social experience, outside the milieu of 'utterances'? And when? It is not to be doubted that in our times people obtain abstract forms of experience almost ready-made in their inherited psychical organisation. But from this it only follows that, after a long series of generations, socially composed forms can attain a stability similar to the stability of other biological formations, a stability that is expressed in organic inheritance. In so doing, socially composed forms actually appear to be 'a priori' individual experience; and it is completely possible to find this socially-evolved apriorism conceivable. But one must remember that people's experience cannot be entirely and unconditionally kept within the confines of these socially composed forms: it can gradually change them, which, as we have seen, has happened in reality.

V

We now have the starting point for the resolution of a more general question about the physical and the psychical world.

The general characteristic of the 'physical' realm of experience is, as we have pointed out, objectivity or social validity. We attribute what we consider to be objective exclusively to the physical world, and if it turns out later on that an experience that we have so attributed is only subjective – i.e. that it does not possess real social validity – then we immediately transfer such an experience to the sphere of the psychical, under the designation, for example, of hallucination, illusion, or dream. And if our habits of thought are insufficiently scientific, then we can simply accept this experience as incomprehensible, a miracle, etc. In other words, we cease to relate to it cognitively.

In light of the preceding, the question of the origin of the objectivity of the physical world need not present any great difficulty. The coordination of collective experience which is expressed in this 'objectivity' can only appear as the result of the progressive coordination of the experience of various people with the help of mutual utterances. In the final analysis, the objectivity of the physical bodies that we encounter in our experience can only be established on the basis of the mutual verification and coordination of the utterances of different people. In general, the physical world is socially-coordinated, socially-harmonised, in a word, *socially-organised experience*. This is why we find abstract space and time – these fundamental forms in which the social organisation of experience is expressed – to be inseparable from the physical world.

At this point, the following objection is possible. In the huge number of events we experience, we are convinced – and with complete justification – in the objectivity of various external objects without utterances of other people. If I stub my toe on a rock, is it possible that I could doubt the objectivity of that rock, while I await the utterances of other people in regard to that rock? But such an argument is based on a misunderstanding.

In the final analysis, the objectivity of external objects always boils down to an exchange of utterances, but it is far from always *immediately* based on such an exchange. In the process of social experience certain general relationships and general regularities (abstract space and time among them) take shape that characterise the physical world. These general relationships, which are socially put together and consolidated, are pre-eminently connected with the social coordination of experience; they are pre-eminently *objective*. We accept any new experience that entirely coordinates with them, that entirely fits within their confines, as objective, without waiting for utterances from anyone else. New experience naturally obtains the characteristics of the form of the old experience in which it is crystallised.

In our example with the rock, the criterion of the objectivity of the rock is the fact that it fits into the spatial and temporal consecutiveness of the physical world, as a body among other bodies, and it fits into a causal relationship with other phenomena of the physical series.[20] The rock appears in the 'objective' realm of experience, and it therefore stands out for us as something objective. But the monitoring of social experience as it develops always stands above that objectivity and sometimes cancels it. The house elf that smothers me at night is perhaps no less objective than the rock I stub my toe on. But the utterances of other people cancel out that objectivity. If one forgets about this higher criterion of objectivity, then systematic hallucinations could form an objective world that normal people could hardly agree with.

---

20   The causal relationship is a product of social-cognitive development that came later than abstract space and time. In historical memory, the causal relationship gradually changed from an animistic form (the cause of a phenomenon is the action of a will or a soul that is hidden behind it) to a form of energetics (the cause of a phenomenon is another phenomenon commensurable with it and quantitatively equivalent to it, without any losses in the transformation). Regarding the various stages of this development, see my works, *Osnovnye elementy istoricheskogo vzgliada na prirodu* and *Poznanie s istoricheskoi tochki zreniia*. See W. Ostwald, *Naturphilosophie*.

In its modern, 'energetical' phase, causality attains the same uniformity of relationships among the phenomena of experience that was produced earlier in the 'objective' forms of space and time. Regarding continuity and infinity, these traits were already long ago common to the causal series and to the temporal and spatial series (although not always included in them).

In any event, the causal relationship is a more complex formation than abstract space and time, and it presupposes them. There is, therefore, no need to especially dwell on its particular origin. Hume, who reduced the causal relationship to merely the habitual consecutiveness of experience, was, of course, wrong, while Kant was correct in pointing out that it is impossible to obtain general obligatoriness (social validity) of the causal relationship from habitual succession. Nevertheless, Hume was fully justified in rejecting the *absolute general obligatoriness* of the causal relationship – in this regard the mistake was in Kant's 'epistemology'. Neither Hume nor Kant could resolve this question, since they stood on the ground of individualism in experience and cognition, and the social-genetic point of view was foreign to them both.

Thus, we are fully justified in characterising the physical world as socially-organised experience. In that case, how must we characterise 'psychical' experience?

The realm of the psyche is characterised first and foremost by the fact that the psychical experiences of one individual do not possess social validity in relation to other people. My perceptions and psychical images, taken in their immediacy, exist only for me, and they acquire cognitive significance for other people only indirectly, and, moreover, only in part. The very same thing applies to my emotions and desires. All these facts of 'internal experience' are distinguished by their extreme certainty, but it is certainty only for me – only for the person who experiences them. They are 'subjective', i.e. they are not coordinated with the experiences of other people or brought into harmony with the experience of other people and therefore are not 'objective' for other people. They lack the social organisation that is characteristic of physical experience.

This does not in the least contradict the fact that what is psychical can also be socially communicated from some people to others with the help of utterances – body language, speech, art. To communicate one's experiences to others still does not mean to coordinate and harmonise them with the experiences of others. Such communication still does not make the psychical experience of an individual person an integral, organic, constituent part of collective experience; it remains personal experience.[21]

However, psychical experience is not simply unorganised and chaotic. It still possesses a certain coherence and coordination, although to a lesser degree than physical experience. Its elements are *associated with one another* – this is its special form of organisation. Perceptions, psychical images, and desires are grouped in specific chains and complexes. In the end, all this is united around one extremely solid and durable complex of memories, feelings, and desires – the complex that is signified by the word 'I'. To put it differently, the psychical is organised, but it is organised individually and not socially. It is individually-organised experience.

In order to avoid a confusion of terms, I note both that individual experience can be organised socially and that social experience can be organised indi-

---

21   The difference between simple social experience (expressed in its transmission from people to people) and the social organisation of experience (coinciding with 'objectivity') can be explained by an analogy with the world of economics. In exchange society, labour is unquestionably social, because some people work for others – and vice versa – as is revealed in the exchange of commodities. But this still does not mean that labour is socially organised, i.e. that people's labour activities are socially coordinated and harmonised. Just the opposite, exchange production always has an unorganised and 'anarchistic' character.

vidually. For an astronomer, who has just discovered a comet, the comet still remains only an individual complex of elements of experience. But inasmuch as the astronomer immediately places it in the domain of socially-organised experience, situates it in the common interconnectedness of this experience, and coordinates it with other data, then his individual experience immediately becomes a constituent part of socially-organised experience – in this case, the world of astronomy. On the other hand, people can acquire a significant part of social experience through the utterances of other people, but to the extent that they associatively combine this social experience with other experiences around their own 'I', they organise it individually. In that case, their experience is entirely psychical and refers, for example, to the sphere of individual memory.

Yet another terminological misunderstanding is possible. It might be said that the psychical is cognised just like the physical, that the science of psychology and psychological laws exist, that this science and these laws are socially produced and organically enter into the system of social knowledge, and, consequently, that psychical experience is socially organised in the form of these laws, and it is not only individually-organised experience. But this objection can easily be eliminated by an explanation of the concepts of 'law' and 'experience'.

Laws do not belong to the sphere of experience – to the sphere of immediate experiences – at all. Laws are the result of the cognitive processing of experience. Laws are not given in experience, but are created by thought as a means of organising experience, of harmoniously coordinating it into a coherent whole. Laws are *cognitive abstractions*, and physical laws are just as lacking in physical properties as psychological laws are lacking in psychical properties. Laws must not be attributed to either one of the series of experience. This is why, even though laws, themselves, form a socially-organised system, it still does not follow from this that there is a realm of experience that is socially organised and embraced by them. They result from experience by abstraction, and, by the way, they can be abstracted precisely because the given realm of experience is *not* socially organised. This is exactly how the matter stands regarding psychology and its laws. Psychology is abstracted from a *given* concrete individual, from his given, separate 'I', and has to do with psychical individuality in general. But the given, separate 'I' – the concreteness of a given separate individual – is also precisely experience that is individually, and not socially, organised.

To summarise: the contrast between the physical and the psychical series of experiences boils down to the difference between experience that is socially-organised and experience that is individually organised.

## VI

On the basis of the preceding, we can no longer be satisfied with the way in which Mach and Avenarius formulated the difference between the physical and the psychical. I will not talk about the 'independent' series and the series that is dependent on system C.[22] Keeping to Avenarius's terms, I would need to talk about the series that is dependent on the 'congregated (social) system' and about the series that is dependent on the individual system C.[23] But such a characterisation of the two series still does not sufficiently express the idea of their *type of organisation*, and it is precisely the type of organisation that is the essence of the matter.

Those 'questions of dualism' that we would have to pose to empiriocritical monism no longer present any particular difficulties for us. While we find two fundamentally different regularities in a single stream of human experience, nevertheless both of them have their source in our own organisation. They express two biologically-organising tendencies by virtue of which we enter into experience simultaneously as individuals and as elements of a social whole. To the question of why there are only two of these types of organisation of experience, we say that the answer is to be sought in the biological and social history of humanity. History relates how the tribal life of humanity arose in the struggle for survival, how the individual person was separated out of humanity and, at the same time, an ever broader social interconnectedness unfolded, and, finally, how human forms of thinking, with their real duality, developed and adapted to that very struggle for survival. In so doing, the question is answered of why some complexes of elements of experience are present sometimes in the physical series and sometimes in the psychical series, while others are present only in the psychical series. Emotional and volitional complexes are exclusively psychical, i.e. they are those experiences that, according to the conditions of the social and intra-social struggle, are most differently directed in different people.

---

22   Avenarius used the term 'R-values' to refer to the parts of the environment that are available to experience. This is the physical series that Bogdanov refers to here as 'the independent series'. Avenarius used 'System C' to refer to the physiology of the central nervous system – which is part of the set of R-values, since it is physical [trans.].

23   Avenarius argued that factual validity as being based on social agreement, and he referred to it, from the psychophysical point of view, as the cooperation of different nervous systems (multiple Systems C), he referred to this as the 'Congregal System' and signified it as ΣC. Hence, the dualism that Bogdanov is discussing here is not the psychical and the physical, but the individual and the social [trans.].

But if the questions of dualism posed earlier thus lose their keenness and appear to be fundamentally resolved, then a new question – issuing from this resolution of them – demands our attention all the more urgently. What is the relative meaning of the two types of organisation of experience? How are they to be evaluated from the point of view of development? What fate must be expected for each of them as regards the subsequent progress of human life? The question is very complex, and, for the present, it is possible to hope only for a very approximate resolution of it. But certain data do exist for answering it.

In a great number of cases one can observe the mutual correspondence and harmony of both series of experience – the physical and the psychical – and in a great number of cases one can observe the mutual contention and even contradiction of the two series. Harmony and correspondence are revealed in the most immediate form in cases where perceptions and psychical images can be said to be 'true' or to 'correspond to the things themselves' such that a physical body and the psychical image of that body 'coincide' sufficiently enough so that practical and theoretical misunderstandings do not result. Conversely, when perceptions and psychical images are 'wrong' or 'do not correspond to things', there is mutual lack of correspondence and disharmony between socially-organised and individually-organised experience (the physical and the psychical series). People might experience an 'illusion' (accepting one 'thing' for another), suffer from 'hallucinations' or 'false memories', or simply 'not understand' the thing they are dealing with. The consequences can be that, on the one hand, they respond by failing in practice because they obtain various harmful influences from a given 'thing', and, on the other hand, they fail in theory because their utterances produce contradictions in other people and also in themselves, to the extent that they have assimilated collective experience.

The harmony and the contradictions of both series of experience are less immediately evident in the process of cognising them and systematising them by means of generalisation and differentiation. Here harmony boils down to the fact that both the physical and the psychical are placed under the very same generalising forms – 'categories' or 'laws' – and a contradiction arises where this is not successful. For example, to the extent that cognising people subordinates both the physical and the psychical to a single law of causality, both series are harmoniously united in cognition, but to the extent that the cognising people place the physical under the category of causality and the psychical under the category of 'freedom' (i.e. a state that is not conditional on something else) or to the extent that they represent the causal chain of both series as absolutely separate and not merging at any point, what results is a contradiction between the physical and the psychical series in the form of 'dualism' – i.e. it is impossible for cognition to complete its unifying and generalising tendency.

Sometimes the contradiction between the physical and the psychical takes the form of competition between them. This is observed either directly, in which case people – as happens under certain pathological states – consider what is 'real' to be 'apparent', consider reality to be an illusion, or, just the opposite, take the images of dreams, hallucinations, and so forth to be physical reality. In these cases, either the realm of the 'physical' expands at the expense of the 'psychical' in individual experience or the other way around. Later, in cognition – especially in philosophy – the contention between the two series appears in the form of materialist or spiritualist monism. In the first case, cognition simply includes the psychical in the physical series, and in the second case, it is the other way around, and the physical is packed into the confines of the psychical series. In both cases, one series supplants the other, so to speak, taking its place in cognition.

Physiological space, and all that it contains, presents an example of how the physical (experience that is organised socially) and the psychical (experience that is organised individually) are really combined. We are very seldom subject to illusions of physiological space, and our perception of one object or another is usually not in fact exactly the same as – indeed, it is usually considerably more than – the image given to the retina. When seeing some kind of object in part and only from one side, we immediately conceive of it to ourselves as a whole and from all sides – as it would only appear, in fact, in geometrical space. And this augmented psychical image flows together with the immediate perceptions so continuously that a special effort of the psyche is necessary in order to distinguish them, in order to see no more than is in the optical image. And even this is very seldom completely successful. Along with this, certain parts of an immediate perception are subjected to a certain correction. For example, not only do our two eyes not generally duplicate objects in our vision, but even when the images in both eyes do not completely correlate with one another, they are not for the most part noticeably duplicated for us. When we look at close objects, distant objects are often not duplicated and vice versa. The psyche constantly strives to make its 'psychical' experience and 'physical' experience agree. It augments and corrects the former with the latter, and, as a result, forms of experience such as physiological space result – forms that are coloured partly with 'subjective' and partly with 'objective' hues.

We have also obtained here a biological assessment of both types of organisation of experience. Everywhere they compete or conflict with one another, the socially-organised or objective type turns out to be of supreme importance for life, and the individually-organised or subjective type must be coordinated with it, in order not to result in unadaptedness to life. And this makes perfect sense, since the basis of objective experience is incomparably broader than subjective experience. The basis of objective experience is social development – the life of millions of people in thousands of generations – while subjective experience has an organic basis – only the individual process of development of a particular person in any given case. This is the essence of what we meant when we characterised one series of experience as 'socially valid' and the other as only 'of individual significance'.[24]

But if one of the two types of organisation of experience is biologically superior, then it is obvious that the process of development must lead to the growing domination of precisely that type of experience; it must lead to the continuous crystallisation of all the content of experience precisely in its form. Does this mean that the other type must simply disappear? We cannot draw such a conclusion from what has just been said. We saw only that in all cases when a clash or direct contradiction arises between the two types, then one of them must be subordinated to the other, must be confined within its bounds, and must be coordinated with it, but it is definitely not simply destroyed. Where 'perceptions' do not correspond to 'things which are perceived', they must be corrected to correspond to these 'things', but they do not disappear altogether and cease to be 'perceptions' – i.e. they are 'psychical facts' and not 'physical phenomena'. The psychical series must progressively adapt to the physical series and harmonise with it, but it is not eliminated by it.

---

24   I once again remind the reader that 'objective' experience is not at all the same as 'social' experience, and subjective experience is not the same as 'individual' experience. Social experience is far from completely socially organised and always contains various contradictions, such that one of its parts does not agree with others. Woods goblins and house sprites can exist in the sphere of the social experience of a given people or a given group within a people – for example, the peasantry. But it is not appropriate to include such things in socially-organised or objective experience because of this, since they are not in harmony with the rest of collective experience, and they do not fit into its organising forms – into the chain of causality, for example. Just the opposite, in other cases, even while it is still individual and partly refutes old facts, experience can factually harmonise to the highest degree with all the totality of collective experience and be in full agreement with its general organising forms – such as, for example, the experience of any researcher who discovers and verifies new facts. Besides, in cases of the first kind, disharmonious elements of social experience are gradually removed in the process of development, and they retain their meaning at first for fewer and fewer groups in society and subsequently only for individual people. In cases of the second kind, individual experience attains a social character gradually and is spread ever more broadly in society. Precisely on this is based, on the one hand, the continual harmonisation of social experience by the removal of its contradictions and, on the other hand, the broadening of social experience by bringing ever newer elements of the individual experience of separate, developing individuals into it.

There is no contradiction here. Individual organisation does not at all exclude social organisation, but, on the contrary, it easily becomes an element of the latter, just as in the processes of labour the harmonious unity of the will of an individual does not at all exclude the harmonious unity of the will of the collective but, on the contrary, under certain circumstances permits the latter to attain a higher level. There can be no doubt that a lower unity can be an integral part of a higher unity, so long as it is sufficiently coordinated with the other lower unities that compose the higher one.

VII

Dualism of experience and cognition does not originate where two types of organisation exist, but where the two types are not situated in an organised correlation, i.e. where they are not harmoniously united. The organisation of a cell, on the one hand, and the organism to which it, together with other cells, belongs, on the other hand, still does not form a vital dualism. Dualism appears only where the cell begins to live an independent life that is not adapted to its whole. In that case, the absence of harmony between the part and the whole leads to a lowering of vital capacity of the part, of the whole, or of both together. This is the dualist contradiction.

Dualism is obtained in experience and cognition if individually-organised experience ceases to be an inseparable part of socially-organised experience, if individually-organised experience takes shape in self-contained forms, independent of the socially-organised form and not harmoniously adapted to it, in a word, if the 'psychical' transforms into a special world with its own categories and laws, not forming an organic unity with the categories and laws of the 'physical'. Then the world of experience, lacking wholeness, transforms into a world of contradictions and struggle. Individuals turns out to be incapable of coordinating their experiences, in general, and their actions, in particular, with the experiences and actions of other people who then appear in their experience as units that are organised differently. Consciousness is then tangled up in the hopeless contradictions of animism and metaphysics. This is exactly the contemporary situation of the human psyche.

The way out of this dualist situation can occur only if individually-organised experience is systematically adapted to socially-organised experience is such a way that the former finds a place in the unified forms of the latter, like a cell in the system of tissues of an organism. That this is the only way that is theoretically permissible becomes clear by a process of elimination. If adaptation occurred in the reverse direction, if the socially-organised type adapted to the individually-organised type, then this would obviously mean simply the destruction – the systematic decomposition – of the socially-organised type; it would be impossible to speak of any kind of harmony of social experience. And we cannot propose that they harmoniously merge into some kind of other third and higher type, if we do not want to depart from the realm of experience, in which there is altogether no indication of such a third type.[25] There remains only one way to harmonise experience, and it is precisely the way that I have just now indicated.

In reality, such a tendency of development is directly revealed in all those cases where immediate practical needs compel people to seek to reconcile contradictory data of experience. In such cases, they usually subject their 'psychical' and 'subjective' experience to verification by 'physical' and 'objective' experience without a moment's hesitation; they verify their perceptions and 'psychical images' with the help of the latter and remove everything from 'subjective' experience that does not fit in the confines and forms of 'objective' experience. They would then express themselves in approximately this way: 'It seems to me that such-and-such (this is experience as "psychical"), but this is impossible for such-and-such reasons (this is verification by means of causality – forms of "objective" experience and facts that are also established from "objective" experience). I obviously erred (this is the removal of those elements of "the subjective" that are not adapted to "the objective"). No doubt in reality such-and-such exist; I think this for such-and-such a reason (this is the approximate harmonisation of "the subjective" and "the objective" by adapting the first to the second)'. There also exists, it is true, an opposite route to adaptation: 'although everyone speaks in favour of this, I cannot concede that it is so, and I believe that it is not this, but that (this is the adaptation of the "objective" to the "subjective")', but this is a regressive path of adaptation. Along this route, contradictions can only grow, and the system of experience and cognition can only become disorganised.

In a system of cognition which entirely represents the progressive harmonisation of experience, the subordination of the 'subjective' to the 'objective' in experience is the basic organising principle, outside of which cognition itself is inconceivable. Therefore, cognition deals with the 'subjective' only to the extent that it strives to bring it into agreement with forms of the 'objective' – for example, to place it in a causal relationship with objectively specified and established data of experience. Only in the sphere of cognition is the definitive

---

25  Philosophy has sought many times to harmonise experience in this way – outside the confines of experience, in higher knowledge. But it is, of course, factually impossible to leave the confines of experience, and philosophy has arrived only at empty abstractions and contradictory forms, all the elements of which were nevertheless taken from experience.

and general harmonisation of experience – the all-embracing monist organisation of experience – possible. Immediate experience, constantly bringing in more and more experiences, inevitably brings along with them new particular contradictions which cognition must subsequently reconcile.

The question is how cognition is capable of realising this monist organisation of experience and of generally reconciling its dualist contradictions. In order to find the answer to this question, we must examine the connection of 'the physical' and 'the psychical' at the point where both these realms of experience impinge on one another most closely.

## VIII

In their research, most psychologists accept in practice (and many of them also in accept in theory) the principle of so-called 'psychophysical parallelism'. This is the idea regarding a certain constant correlation between psychical phenomena and the 'physiological processes of the nervous system'. To be precise, it posits a correlation whereby each given act of consciousness corresponds to a definite change in the nervous system, so that a series of facts of consciousness unfolds parallel to a series of simultaneous physiological nervous processes and in a continual and constant connection with them. As a method of research, this point of view has turned out to be useful to the highest degree and has not met a single contradiction that would fundamentally undermine it. It has proven itself to an altogether sufficient degree.

It must be noted that several philosophers – chiefly of the neo-Kantian persuasion – have tried to construct an original form of 'monist worldview' on the idea of parallelism. To be precise, they consider the physical and the psychical to be 'two aspects of a single reality' – the inner and the outer. According to this view, what appears as physical to 'external' perception appears as psychical to 'internal' perception, just as the arc of a circle viewed from within seems to be a convex line and viewed from without seems to be a concave line. This view, obviously, does not have a necessary, logical connection with the scientific-psychological theory of parallelism. It includes something that is not there: so-called 'introjection', the placement of the psychical world *inside* the nervous system, a hypothesis that is completely unnecessary for our goals and that is more than debatable. Since we are striving not to distance ourselves unnecessarily from what is in experience, there is no need to accept introjection, but this does not in the least prevent us from preserving the *methodological* idea of parallelism.[26]

---

26   The term 'introjection' was introduced by Avenarius, who devoted his remarkable work

The position of Avenarius on the 'functional correlation' of the psychical or 'Series E', as he expresses it, with physiological changes of the central nervous system or 'series C', is, in essence, only a different formulation of *scientific* psychophysical parallelism. In reality, it recognises a constant, specific connection between the corresponding members of both series, and to understand parallelism in a different, narrower sense – such as geometrical parallelism, for example – is, of course, inappropriate since phenomena of both series are insufficiently analogous to allow the possibility of the same kind of parallelism as the parallelism of isotropic lines or planes.

The term 'psychophysical parallelism' is also used by Mach, but now in a different sense, when he speaks of the repetition of the same complexes in the sphere of the physical and the sphere of the psychical: what appears as a 'body' in the interconnectedness of physical experience becomes a 'perception' or 'psychical image' in the interconnectedness of psychical experience. But this parallelism[27] does not contradict the psychophysical parallelism we are now dealing with and relates to a completely different realm of relationships – not to the narrower relationship between individual consciousness and the nervous

---

    *Der menschliche Weltbegriff* to the theory of introjection. In that work he gave both a general history of introjection (more from the point of view of its logical development than of its cultural-historical development), and a general critique of it (an explanation of the logical contradictions of introjection that revealed its philosophical bankruptcy).

    Introjection absolutely predominates in contemporary thought. In ordinary psychology, it is expressed in the assertion that the 'body' is the external shell of the 'soul', which is its internal essence. In scientific psychology and philosophy, introjection is revealed in the conceptions of 'external experiences' by which the physical world is perceived and of 'internal experiences' by which the psychical world is perceived. The physiological organism is conceived of like a box with opaque sides, within which the 'mind' is placed.

    The fundamental consideration that disproves introjection is as follows.

    The organism itself is a specific complex of visual, tactile, and similar elements in their specific relationships, and only homogenous (but lesser) complexes – organs, tissues, fibres, cells – can be placed 'inside' this complex, and it makes no sense to place in it complexes of a different type that are not homogenous with it. It would be exactly the same as to place the melody, perceived by hearing, inside a musical instrument that is perceived by sight and touch. Spatial relations are in themselves essentially *visual-tactile*, and it is therefore impossible to place complexes of a different, non-visual-tactile type in the purely spatial relationship of 'inside' and 'outside'.

27    Mach also calls this 'identity', which, however, is not completely true. The elements are really the same but the 'perception of a body', taken separately, is considerably poorer in those elements than the 'body' itself. A 'body' is a complex that is considerably more definite and considerably more complex because it is formed by the social harmonisation of countless 'perceptions'. In a 'perception' of it, a body never appears fully, as a whole, but always appears only in part. For example, the 'perception' of a body can never include all sides of it at the same time.

system but to the broader relationship between individual consciousness and the physical world in general. At present, only the first of these relationships is important for us.

If we recall what was said earlier about the parallelism of the series of experience that form the 'bodies' or 'processes' of the physical world then we immediately see that psychophysical parallelism unquestionably has to do with exactly that type. In reality, the physical 'body' or 'process' is formed through the organic merging of different series of experience – series that are different precisely *in their elements*. The visual, tactile, and acoustic series are united in a complex called the 'human body', and basis of this unification is precisely the *parallelism* of these series, i.e. the specific correspondence between the elements of one and the elements of the other two series. The difference between the series themselves is not quantitative but qualitative, i.e. their elements are completely incompatible with one another, but on the basis of mutual parallelism they all are united around one (usually the tactile) series in the whole complex with which cognition operates.

In essence, this is absolutely the relationship between the psychical series and the neural-physiological series in the issue that we are dealing with. They are *qualitatively different in their elements, but they are connected by parallelism* – parallelism like that, for example, between the visual and tactile series in the complex that is called the 'human organism'. It is a strictly specific functional correlation of the two series, but it is not at all a direct quantitative and qualitative correspondence. There exists a specific perception, emotion, desire, which is a complex of such-and-such and such-and-such innervational, tactile, visual, aural, etc. elements. Corresponding to such a 'psychical' phenomenon, we either observe (if observation is possible) or we conceive of (if observation is impossible) a certain definite 'physiological process' that is a complex of completely different elements (also visual, tactile, etc.) but that are not at all the ones that form a 'psychical' complex. If, for example, elements of 'green' exist in a perception, then it does not follow that the corresponding 'physiological fact' possesses the same elements of 'green'. Those elements might not even be in our conceptions of neural processes at all, and there might only be the chromatic elements 'white', 'black', and 'red'. For all its correspondence with the psychical series, the physiological series turns out to consist of absolutely different material, in exactly the same way as the visual-innervational series in any 'physical body' consists of material that is different from the tactile-innervational series, and so on.

All of this leads to the following conclusion. If cognition, in its striving to harmonise experience, is to be consistent and faithful to the method it has worked out, then it must connect the psychical and the neural-physiological series in one 'process', one that is perceived differently but that is holistic. It must not be psychical nor physiological but psychophysiological, just as the human body is not visual and not tactile but visual-tactile. In both cases, the matter has to do with whole complexes that are not immediately given but that are formed from a manifold of elements of experience. The difference is only that this task was accomplished for physical complexes far back in the history of humanity while it still remains to be done for psycho-physiological complexes.

Precisely this sort of actively-organising activity of cognition can, in our opinion, remove dualist contradictions and lead to a really harmonious worldview. This will not be a monism of 'essence' or of 'reality'. Empty concepts such as these cannot satisfy critically-monist thinking. It will be a monism of a type of organisation that will systematise experience, a monism of cognitional method. Let us see what, in reality, this method provides the cognising person in the pursuit of a unified worldview.

In our times, the method of cognition of the physical world is already highly monist. Physical phenomena, in all their endless complexity and variety, are fit into all-embracing formulas that are gradually acquiring ever more definite content, ever more fully harmonised experience, and that provide the ever greater possibility of practical action and adaptation. At the same time, the immediate elements of experience, in their succession and differences, do not have direct significance for such formulas and especially for the basis of those formulas – the law of the conservation of energy. The same 'body' or 'process' – no matter it is perceived in the visual, tactile, or auditory series – presents the same energetical magnitudes and combinations. Cognition is drawn away from the methods of immediate perception, and the world of 'elements' is replaced by the world of relationships. Coherence in the world of relationships is achieved by grouping complexes rationally – by differentiating them and uniting them to satisfy the demand for the fewest contradictions and the greatest harmony. This very grouping is carried out and registered with the help of symbols, and the elaboration and collation of these symbols originates in the social process of communication. All collective scientific and philosophical creativity is based on this process of communication.

What cognition does in relation to physical experience, it also strives to achieve in regard to psychical experience. But here it encounters a huge number of special difficulties and contradictions that cannot be eliminated as long as cognition does not follow the same path in the psychical realm as it followed in the physical realm of experience. Ultimately, these difficulties and contradictions are summed up in one word – 'dualism' – and the essence of these difficulties and contradictions consists in the fact that the different methods by which cognition operates in the two realms of experience are unavoidably encountered over and over again in one field of consciousness, and they create a bifurcation in psychical activity, which is sensed as cognitive unadaptedness, as a disharmony of thought. But this disharmony disappears when what is psychical presents itself to cognition as one of the parallel series of a complex in which the other series (the visual, the tactile) are able to form a 'physical body' (the nervous system).

In reality, cognition does not need to create a special method for each of the parallel series that flow together in one or another complex; cognition deals with whole complexes. The psychophysiological process, cognised as one whole, must fit within the confines of the same method by which the physiological process is cognised from its several series. This is the method of physical science for our times – the method of *energetics*. And, by the way, it makes absolutely no difference whether we take elements from the 'physiological' series or from the 'psychical' series to analyse. Each case has to do with one or another energetical magnitude, since energetical cognition is abstracted from the means of perception and does not take the visual series and the tactile series, for example, to be separate energetical complexes. Just as in an ordinary physical complex (called a 'body') one of the series of experience (for example, the tactile series) serves to organise the other series, so in a psychophysiological complex one of its series turns out to be the organising, principal series for cognition, and we suggest that this will be precisely the physiological series – as the series that is more definite and more stable in its relationships. But all the same, this difference here is not as significant for cognition as the difference between the organising, tactile series and the visual, auditory, etc. series that are grouped around it. The same cognitive whole – the psychophysiological process – can be perceived by different means, but as far as cognition is concerned it is all the same. Differences of the *elements* disappear in the unity of *relationships*, and the unity of cognition is restored.

But in so doing, the very contraposition of the 'physical' and the 'psychical' will lose its meaning. Experience that is organised individually will enter the system of experience that is organised collectively as an indivisible part of the latter and will cease to constitute a special world for cognition. The 'psychical' will disappear into the unifying forms created by cognition for the 'physical', but the physical will also cease to be 'physical' as soon as it no longer has a constant antithesis – the psychical. A common world of experience will emerge as content for a common cognition. This is empiriomonism.

Empiriomonism is possible only because cognition actively harmonises experience, removing its innumerable contradictions, creating universal organising forms for experience, and replacing the primary, chaotic world of elements with the derivative, orderly world of relationships. It goes without saying that it can be admitted that empiriomonism is not now being realised in the forms in which we have presented it, but it must be realised in the future, and if there is an inability to do so, then it will mean the eventual failure of cognition.

∴

It would be wrong to think that, in arriving at the model of empiriomonism, we have attained a monist worldview. This model formulates the highest cognitive tendency, but a whole worldview can be obtained only through the systematic implementation of this tendency. A cognitive picture of the world – an organised system of sciences and philosophy – cannot be provided by one formula. A monist model is only the harmonising principle behind this picture, and a huge amount of work is necessary in order to bring this principle into all parts of the picture. And as long as this is not done, as long as parts remain that are not subordinated to the harmonising model – whether they contradict it or simply are not imbued with it – it is impossible to speak of real empiriomonism.

Considering the colossal amount of collective labour that humanity has dedicated to the elaboration of systems of sciences and philosophy and the long period of time in which the tendency toward cognitive monism has been actively displayed, it is natural to ask the question: why has this monism, regardless of everything else, not succeeded in taking form before now? Why has it been impossible for such a long time to precisely formulate even the model of cognitive monism?

It would, of course, be possible not to dwell on this question and simply to assume that the harmonisation of experience is so complex and difficult that, despite the huge amount of time and energy expended on it, humanity has so far fulfilled only part of it and be satisfied with that. But it seems to us that there is good reason to mention a few specific obstacles that, precisely in our times, set limits on the tendency toward monism. This will allow us to come to several rough conclusions regarding the further development of cognition in that direction.

Contemporary society is broken up into classes and is full of antagonism. People who belong to the same social system often differ very greatly from one another and clash harshly in life because of a difference of interests. Competition, on the one hand, and the relationships of the division of labour and especially relationships of domination and subordination, on the other hand, colour all the social life of our times. These dominating forms of life cannot help but also put their imprint on the realm of cognition.

The essence of the matter is that people are opposed to one another both practically and cognitively. In practice, their desires clash in a struggle of interests, in the form of competition between the representatives of one class or group as well as between classes and groups. They do not understand one another theoretically, since their experience is different and they have different types of thinking. This struggle and lack of understanding does not occupy their entire life but exists only within limited confines. The same is true of cooperation and mutual understanding, which is also partial. But to the extent that struggle and lack of understanding exist, the monist organisation of experience runs into the greatest difficulties.

In reality, if individuals fight with other individuals, they cannot pass on their own experience to them with sufficient completeness. It is well known that the point has arrived where people involved in struggle frequently find it necessary to conceal their experiences or even to convey them in a distorted form. This explains all the 'lies' in contemporary society – lies that are frequently necessary and that are an integral part of the very system of relationships. This is already sufficient to produce mutual misunderstanding, but the division of labour makes the sphere of this misunderstanding even wider than the sphere of struggle. Specialists do not understand one another insofar as the material of their experience is different (for example, an artist does not understand a scholar, a philologist does not understand a natural scientist, and so on). Subordinates do not understand their superiors, and vice versa, insofar as not only is the material of their experiences different but their factual relationship to the same data of experience is also different (for example, what is a tool of labour for one is a tool of exploitation for the other, and so on). But what does 'misunderstanding' mean?

It means that the experiences of other people that are accessible to us (through social communication) do not conform to the regularity of our experience, and we therefore cannot correctly evaluate their psychical states and predict their actions. And it is obvious that, to the extent that the experience of certain people lies outside the regularity – i.e. organisation – for other people, their experience necessarily appears as socially unorganised or 'subjective' or 'psychical'. Just the opposite, the part of experience for which general – or, more precisely, socially valid – regularity has been produced in the social process stands out as socially-organised; it has the attribute of 'objectivity' and the characterisation as 'physical'. Here is the starting point of the antithesis; here is the basis for determining its historical boundaries.

Let us note that the aspects that appear as predominantly 'psychical' in our experience are those for which social unity is least achieved. People's emotions and desires diverge in life most sharply, and it is precisely these complexes of elements that never find a place for themselves in the physical series, whereas other complexes in various people that are in less contradictory relationships can appear both in the psychical series as 'perceptions' or 'psychical images' and in the physical series as 'bodies'. Therefore, the more individual the nature of a psychical event, the more it appears to be 'psychical'.

In a naïve, undeveloped consciousness the emotions are often 'objectified' – transferred to the physical world. For example, beauty, ugliness, happiness, etc., are considered to be characteristics of the objects themselves (and not phenomena of the perceiving consciousness). This happens precisely when the emotional utterances of people are in such great agreement that people seldom contradict one another in a multitude of cases of the given kind. People are accustomed to considering these emotions to be *socially valid*, socially agreed upon – what, from our point of view, is the basis of the characterisation of 'objective' or 'physical' experience.

The individual 'I' is the organising centre for all that is psychical, contrasted with the 'I' of others. When the 'I' disappears from the field of consciousness, the antithesis between the psychical and the physical also ceases, and this happens not only in moments of loss of consciousness but also in moments of the most intense activity. As Schopenhauer noted, a deep aesthetic affect eliminates 'individuation' – i.e. the contradistinction between our 'I' and the external world and between the psychical and the physical. In the rapturous contemplation of a beautiful scene in nature or of a truly artistic work, we cease experiencing a bifurcation in our experience. But the same thing relates also to moments of cognitive creativity and to moments of intense manifestation of collective will; people 'forget themselves' and then their experiences are most harmonious.

The adaptation called 'I' stands out all the more clearly wherever disharmony in experience is displayed – disharmony that disrupts individual existence. This happens when we feel hunger, cold, fear, sadness, unhappiness … This is an adaptation for the *individual* struggle for life, and therefore only in *individualistic* society, such as the present one, does it become the centre of experience for each individual, sharply separating the individual's 'psychical world' from the psychical world of other people. It was not so in primordial society, which was communistic and was devoid of internal struggle and contradictions. In primordial society, individuals were unable to separate themselves from their group. Their experience flowed immediately together with the experience of other people, and the word 'I' signified only their own body with its immediate needs. 'I' did not in any way signify a complex of emotions and desires that is sharply distinguished from the emotions and desires of other people, such as occurs in contemporary society. In an advanced society,[28] with collectively-organised labour and with the elimination of internal contradictions and sharp differences between individuals, it would be as impossible for the human 'I' to serve as the centre of a singular world – the world of an individual psyche – as it was in primordial society. Any tendency to counterpose one's own 'psyche' to the psyche of other people would disappear in close mutual communication and deep mutual understanding among people. Harmoniously organised collective experience would give people the kind of grandiose fullness of life that we people of an era of contradictions cannot conceive.

In such a world as this, it would also be easy for cognition to unite the whole sum of human experiences in harmoniously-whole, infinitely-plastic forms, in which the experience of each person flows organically together with the experience of everyone else. Of course there will be contradictions in experience and in cognition, but they will not be the irreparable contradictions of petrified fetishes of thought that do not accept any higher authority. They will be only temporary disagreements among creatively thinking people who are consciously striving to reconcile and unify their experiences, who are consciously seeking out the best and most expedient forms for such coordination and unity. Free striving toward social harmony of cognition together with deep confidence in the possibility and necessity of attaining it will constantly govern all manifestations of individual consciousness. Human thought, liberated from internal disorder, obscured by nothing, pure and clear, will build for itself a path to infinity with an energy that we cannot imagine. There they will attain true empiriomonism, which seems to me to be the ideal of cognition.

If we compare this ideal of cognition with the contemporary ideal of people's life of practical labour, then we are struck by their deep inner parallelism, by the general organising tendency that is common to them both. This is not an accidental similarity. Cognition arises from practice; the harmony of practice and the harmony of cognition mean the same thing.

---

28   Bogdanov is referring to socialism, but this was published in *Voprosy Filosofii I Psikhologii* in 1902 and that journal would not have wanted to risk falling foul of government censorships [trans.].

CHAPTER 2

# Life and the Psyche

## 1  The Realm of Experiences

I

The stream of experiences that forms what we call psychical life does not always constitute a real object of cognition or material suitable for cognition. It becomes such an object or such material only where it appears in a more or less organised form, in the form of experience. Even within the bounds of immediate experience there are many unclear, vague experiences that disappear, hardly having sprung up in the field of the psyche at all, and which are so indefinite and fleeting that they escape cognition, almost not existing as far as cognition is concerned. But the question still remains of what lies outside the bounds of immediate psychical experience, although not outside the boundaries of possible experience in general.

Are there sufficient grounds to deny that there is psychical life in a foetus or in a person who sleeps deeply and cannot recall having dreamt? The more completely our entire cognition is filled with the idea of *continuity*, the less capable it is of accepting any divergence from that idea and the more decisively it makes continuity its universal premise. Moreover, to deny such psychical life would mean to accept the idea that psychical life springs up from nothing, as an epiphenomenon of continuously developing physiological life that can completely cease for several hours and then be resurrected anew from psychical 'nothing' at the moment of waking. However, neither foetal life nor dreamless sleep gives us immediate psychical experience, and they therefore can serve only indirectly as material for psychological cognition. This is the dark chaos of experiences, in which there is no 'soul', no organising unity that is characteristic of the world of experience.

The psychical world of a child during the first years of life and also the world of dreams and delirium present a series of intermediate phenomena of life – the bordering realm between psychical chaos and psychical experience. There is organisation here, but it is only fragmentary: fluctuating images and unstable combinations. It is the germination of order amid the formless material of life and the intrusion of formless life into the order of experience. Naturally, these experiences are indefinitely and variably related to the system of experience. In the sphere of memory, we find only fragments of impressions of the first years of life mixed with illusions of memory and implanted memories, and in the life of sleep we find only isolated scenes that disappear in a mass of unclear sensations of haziness and disharmony. At the dawn of the life of a person and of humanity, this realm of semi-organised psychical life still dominates the germinating coherence of experience, and it retreats extremely slowly in the face of that development. Down to the present day, the traces of the domination of this realm are preserved in the form of superstitions, premonitions, and mysticism. But for a long time the victory of experience, with its growing harmony and wholeness, has been unquestionable.

Let us look a little closer at these different levels of the psychical unity of life and try to understand their vital interconnectedness and the objective conditions of their transition back and forth.

In comparing the condition of a person in deep sleep with the condition of a foetus, it is impossible not to find a great similarity between them. In both cases, external impressions are removed and the manifestations of life boil down to vegetative processes. Tissues of the organism gain more nourishment than they expend, and, aside from certain reflexes, there are no reactions to the external world. In general, deep sleep is like a temporary return to the type of life which is characteristic of people before birth, and in constructive significance for the organism it could hardly be less similar to death and its invariable companion, the destruction of the organism. However, there is a deep and fundamental difference between sleep and foetal life. Sleepers can wake up to find themselves in the world of experience, in the sphere of conscious life, but the unborn child must wait to be born and to develop for this to happen. In one case, the system of experience has not yet been able to unfold and become organised, in the other, it is as if it is temporarily dismantled and disorganised.

The sum total of experience, the profusion of experiences, is determined in both its quantitative and qualitative aspects by the relationship of the organism to its environment. Wherever there is full equilibrium between an organism and the environment, where there is no difference in potential energy between the organism and the environment it is in contact with, there is no basis for experiences. It would be as if the organism did not exist and flowed together with its environment without any distinction between them. Any experience is a distinction, and life is not present where nothing is distinguished. But as soon as the environment and the organism stand out as unequal energetical combinations, as soon as there is a difference in the level of energy, as soon as a definite flow of energy springs up between two complexes, then there is something for the organism to experience, and insensibility is replaced by life.

But when we attempt to take this point of view, we run up against a large number of prejudices that are caused by superficial analogies and insufficient analysis. These prejudices can be formulated thus: *the belief that there can be real life without experiences* and the idea that experiences are only epiphenomena, phenomena that are incidental to life.

II

Until now a dualistic understanding of life has prevailed; the physiological life of an organism and its 'psychical experiences' are taken to be two completely different realms, never having anything to do with one another directly, even though they are connected by a definite correlation. This correlation, most frequently designated as 'parallelism', seems in individual experience, however, to be incomplete and interrupted. In a large number of cases, changes in the nervous system occur without any noticeable reflections in the psyche, in the sphere of consciousness. Only an insignificant part of the minor stimuli that are continually acting on the nervous system produce noticeable 'impressions', and in periods of temporary cessation of psychical work, physiological life remains, completely freed, apparently, from a connection with 'psychical experiences'. Thus, it is as if these experiences are only 'epiphenomena' of life; there is no telling where these additions to life's physiological manifestations come from or where they disappear to. One has every reason to consider the bounds of this epiphenomenon to be very narrow in comparison with the huge dimensions of the biological world in general.

It is natural to suppose that the complexity of the experiences of a psychical organism that are associated with the states of a neural-cerebral apparatus corresponds to the complexity of that neural-cerebral apparatus. And, at the same time, it would seem self-evident that such experiences are lacking entirely where there is no neural-cerebral system – i.e. for example, with all protozoa and many of the lower metazoa. As it is, even for human beings, with their unusually complex nervous system, these experiences are not always observable – and then only subject to a large number of conditions – and they are very easily interrupted. Thus it is obviously possible to assume that the existence of a complex nervous system, speaking in general, still does not constitute a sufficient basis for conclusions about whether 'experiences' are present. As a result, it cannot be said that a very coherent and harmonious picture has been obtained. We see two types of vital processes that are completely different in content; one of them appears everywhere, and the other appears only in certain comparatively few cases, as a distinctive supplement to the first, and that is connected with it in a correlation that is specific to each particular case but that in general is often interrupted.

However, even if the lack of orderliness of this picture offends our aesthetic sense, this obviously does not tell against its objective truth. It is based on completely indubitable facts and completely warrantable analogies that cognition cannot in general do without.

The critique of any cognitive conception boils down to two points: a critique of generalisations and conclusions from the point of view of experience and a critique of the very experience that lies at their basis from the point of view of its interconnectedness and regularity. Plainly, it is necessary to begin with the latter point, since only experience that is tried and true and free from errors and illusions is a reliable basis for a critique of cognition. This point is especially important for the issue that we are examining.

First and foremost it is necessary to establish the most direct and immediate form of correlation between an organism's 'experiences' and its 'physiological processes' – a task that is very difficult to accomplish. It would be mistaken, for example, to assume that this correlation is a connection between the complexity of the neural-cortical apparatus, on the one hand, and the multiplicity and fullness of experiences, on the other. It would be mistaken because in the most developed neural organisation (a human's) one can observe not only complex experiences but also extremely simple and elementary ones, not only intense experiences but also very weak ones, and not only specific experiences but also very vague ones. It would therefore be pointless to attempt to establish by deduction the extent to which a complex and developed central apparatus is necessary in order for the life of an organism to become complex by means of 'experiences' and at what step on the ladder of living beings experiences in general appear. More precise and more direct correspondences are necessary in order to resolve the issue of psychophysical parallelism.

Beyond the confines of our immediate psychical experience, all experiences – that is to say, all experiences in general that are not our own – become accessible to our cognition only through an indirect route, by means of utterances. The definite and constant connection of our own 'psychical experiences' (our perceptions, psychical images, desires, emotions) with our motor reactions serves as the basis for associating our psychical life with the life of other beings; it is the basis for 'mutual understanding' of what we and other people experience. The critique of psychical experience must begin with the analysis of utterances in their connection with immediate experiences.

Here, at the very start, the question can be asked: in general, how legitimate and accurate is it to associate the utterances of other organisms that we observe with experiences that are similar to our own? This question can be answered very easily. The largest part of our experience is given to us through the utterances of others (through our 'understanding' them), and our understanding serves as the means of verifying and regulating our immediate experience through the experience of other people. Thus, the whole system of objective cognition is based on the understanding of utterances, and since, as a whole, this system does not contradict itself or life in general, and, since we can successfully base our practical activity on it, then we have no choice but to adopt it. And, along with it, we must also make it our continual practice to 'understand' utterances by attaching to them – as their necessary supplement – perceptions, psychical images, desires, emotions that are completely analogous to our own.[1]

Utterances include far more than just specialised 'forms of expression', such as speech, body language, and art; they also include all motor reactions of an organism in general that we can 'understand' in connection with psychical experiences.[2] If, for example, we see people who are carrying out some kind of work, we can find a large number of utterances in their actions. Those utterances clearly express the presence, first of the *perception* of all the objects and tools of their labour, second, of the *psychical image* of a certain desirable transformation of these objects as a 'goal', third, the *desire* to attain this 'goal' and the *decision* to do so. All *practical* utterances of such a kind not only have no less significance than 'theoretical' utterances (verbal utterances, for example), but they are even of fundamental significance in relation to such utterances. Speech, body language, and other special forms of expression arise on the basis of the practical unification of human actions. People's social labour is the primary realm of their communication and consequently also of utterances. The socio-technological process gives rise to the necessity of harmoniously *unifying the experience of different people*. Cooperation, in its various manifestations, is the basis of social experience.[3]

---

1  It stands to reason that any individual utterance of one organism might be 'incorrectly understood' by others as a result, for example, of differences in their experience, in their physiological makeup, etc. But in this case, all that is needed to restore cognitive harmony and remove practical contradictions is to substitute some experiences for others, i.e. one must still 'understand' utterances, only differently from how they were first understood.

2  I think there is no need to explain that at the foundation of an 'expressive' reaction – even pronounced words – lies a definite complex of muscle contractions, a *motor* reaction.

3  It is not possible to provide detailed substantiation here of the idea of the primary character of practical utterances, nor is it necessary. This idea proceeds from the historico-monistic conception of the social process and is sufficiently corroborated in contemporary scientific views in general (for example, in Noiré's theory regarding the origin of the roots of words, in Ernst Mach's analysis of the connection between technology and cognition, etc.). [Noiré argued that words originated in the shouts and cries of primordial people that served to coordinate the work of a labour collective. (trans.)]

   We note that Avenarius, having based his theory of cognition on the analysis of utterances, understands 'utterances' predominantly or exclusively to be in the form of words, gestures,

But can we assume that there is a corresponding experience behind every motor reaction of an organism and that every experience is expressed in a motor reaction? Each of these questions requires particular and careful examination.

III

We know from immediate experience that many of our experiences – a huge majority of them – pass by without any 'utterances', without any noticeable motor reactions. From this it is obvious that the sphere of experiences is broader than the sphere of utterances. But how much broader *is* the former than the latter and what is the immediate correlation of the two? Psychophysiology can explain this.

Any muscular reaction, and consequently also any utterance, assumes that the *equilibrium* of the central nervous system *is disturbed*, because *innervation* (a flow of neural energy from the centre to the peripheral motor apparatus) occurs, and if the system were in equilibrium this flow, obviously, could not arise. Equilibrium depends on a continuous and comprehensive correspondence between the 'nourishment' of the system and its 'work', i.e. correspondence between the assimilation of energy (taken from the surrounding environment) and the expenditure of energy (its transfer to the surrounding environment). Thus, an utterance is conditioned by what Avenarius calls the 'vital-differential', i.e. the difference between 'nourishment' and 'work' – in part or in general – of the system. A vital-differential is the preponderance of assimilation over expenditure or vice versa – the fluctuation of the energy of the system above or below the given level of its vital equilibrium and psychical insensibility.

But not every 'vital-differential' leads directly to utterances, and the only ones that do are those that are sufficiently significant to be able to cause a flow of innervation capable of leading to noticeable movements of the organism. A huge mass of small and tiny vital-differentials – as long as they do not add up to an amount sufficient to be expressed in physical movements – remain without external manifestation before they disappear into the internal equilibrium of the system. But the major vital-differentials that are vitally important

---

and such, while overlooking utterances of a practical significance, which he looks at only from the perspective of their immediate practical significance (*'ectosystematische Anderungen'* [extra-systemic changes], *'appetitives Verhalten'* [appetitive behaviour], etc.). Incidentally, in the *Kritik der reinen Erfahrung* he does not altogether directly explain exactly what he means by 'utterances'.

also might not engender utterances. First, it is well known that this happens in pathological cases when the neural conductors that transmit innervation are damaged or disrupted or when muscles are atrophied or injured, etc. – in general when parts of the organism are subject to various paralytic and unconscious states. Second, and what is still more important, this also happens in cases of normal physiology as a consequence of a blocking influence of some centres on others, when an incipient flow of innervation is continually suppressed so that it does not transform into real motor reactions. In such cases, the experience is not immediately connected with an utterance. People can, for example, experience pain (which corresponds to a rapidly advancing preponderance of the expenditure over the assimilation of energy by the system) but not express the pain because it is too insignificant, because they cannot express it due to an abnormal condition, or because they want to hide it and suppress its external manifestations.

In the present state of psychology, the following view seems to be the most likely: everywhere that experience gives us experiences without utterances, it is possible, after sufficient investigation, to discover a vital-differential in the central apparatus. If it is not, in fact, always successfully discovered in such cases, then this is a result of the crudity of our methods, and, as those methods progress, research will produce unsatisfactory results with decreasing frequency.

Keeping this in mind, it is natural to assume that *the realm of vital-differentials and the realm of experiences altogether coincide*. Such a point of view would immediately give us the ability to present the relationship of psychical life and physiological life in a harmonious picture, but various difficulties immediately present themselves.

First and foremost, if it is not always possible to observe vital-differentials in our experience when experiences are present, is this really a consequence only of limitations in our methods of investigation, or might there be – at least sometimes – some cases in which it results from the fact that there is no vital-differential at all? In general, can we consider it to be proven that a complete equilibrium of a system is accompanied by psychical indifference and the absence of experiences? It hardly need be said that it is impossible to consider this to be absolutely proven in the present state of science, but a great many facts of experience support this conclusion over any other.

Within the confines of the existing material that has been observed, we can consider it established that a weak vital-differential corresponds to a weak experience and that, as the former decreases, the intensity of the latter also declines. Judging from this, the reduction of a vital-differential to zero must also mean the cessation of the experience. This is especially obvious in those cases where the causes that produce a vital-differential are easily subjected to objective observation and even measurement – for example, in the case of external irritations apprehended by organs of sensation. No matter how complicated the correlation between the irritation and the corresponding experience, as the magnitude of the irritation approaches zero, the magnitude of experience will also approach zero, and the absence of vital-differentials of a given type is linked with the absence of the corresponding experiences.[4] Then, when causes that stimulate a certain kind of vital-differential are removed from the life of an organism, not only are the experiences that are directly stimulated by these causes removed, but those experiences that are indirectly caused by them are also gradually removed. If, for example, a person goes blind – i.e. if the path of light stimulation is obstructed – then, first of all, visual perception is cut off, and this corresponds to the removal of the vital-differential received from the retina. But visual *psychical images* are temporarily preserved, obviously, precisely because reflected vital-differentials continue to spring up in the optical centres that still retain a certain unstable equilibrium. These vital-differentials are caused by the influence of other centres and also by fluctuations in the vigour of the circulatory system – the system of nourishment. Over the course of time, however, as a result of the absence of specific stimulation, a relatively durable, stable equilibrium must be established in the visual centres, the vital-differentials of the *former type* must disappear, and, corresponding to this, the last remnants of visual experiences will be lost.

Other very important biological considerations also argue that there can be no experiences if no vital-differentials are present in the central nervous system. From the point of view of contemporary biology, psychical experiences represent *adaptations* of the system. At the same time, in an 'ideal' equilibrium of the nervous system, the nervous system is 'ideally' adapted (at that moment); there is nothing for it to adapt to and psychical activity is unnecessary. In general, in the present state of biology and psychology, there is virtually no one who would especially defend the idea that psychical experiences are not connected with fluctuations in the physiological life of the nervous system. Therefore, what is considerably more important for us is another aspect of the issue.

There are a large number of cases when we can confidently assume the presence of definite vital-differentials in our nervous system while, at the same

---

4 I note that irritation only *excites* a vital-differential, and it therefore cannot be simply proportional to it, since it still depends on the status of the nervous system (on the presence of potential energy that has accumulated in it), and it is discharged by the external impulse. But this is not important for the question that I am now dealing with, and I will return to it in the future.

time, we are not aware of corresponding experiences in our psychical experience. Such conditions include, for example, all vital-differentials that arise during sleep, anaesthesia, etc. It also often happens when one is awake – especially during intense concentration of attention on one thought or object – that many external influences that are sufficiently strong to reach the brain and cause a vital-differential in it remain 'unnoticed', i.e. outside psychical experience. Sometimes it even happens that people who are 'deeply engrossed in thought' react appropriately to an external influence, completely 'unaware' of it – straightening their clothing or moving from an open window, for example – while 'not noticing' their actions. In this case, there is not only a vital-differential but also an 'utterance' based on it, while there are no experiences in the field of psychical experience that are connected with it. Obviously, all such facts lead to a completely definite conclusion: vital-differentials are not always connected with corresponding experiences. But if we stop at this conclusion, we again lose the possibility of a generalised, coherent – in a word, monist – depiction of life in its psychical and physical manifestations.

To resolve this issue, a *critique of psychical experience* – i.e. an explanation of the boundaries and the objective cognitive significance of psychical experience – is necessary.

IV

The world of the psychical experience of an individual is a very complex but coherent system of experiences. Each experience is more or less firmly joined with others in a so-called 'associative' connection and is a part of psychical experience only in this connection. What is outside of this connection is outside of psychical experience; what falls outside the limits of this connection, falls outside the limits of psychical experience. These are the countless 'unremembered' experiences that at one time entered a given system but lost their connection with it. People would themselves never know anything about them if they did not again enter the sphere of their experience by an indirect route – the utterances of other people informing them of their previous utterances with which the corresponding psychical experiences must have been joined. This is how, for example, a people learn about a large part of their experiences related to the first years of their life.

We thus see that the boundaries of psychical experience coincide with the boundaries of the specific interconnection of experiences that psychology calls an 'interconnection of associations'. This connection is not at all constant and uniform in all parts of the system of experience but appears in the most varied degrees of stability and durability. There are complexes of experiences that are so durably connected with all the others that their destruction or disappearance would immediately disorganise the entire system. The complicated complex of organic sensations, recollections, and strivings that is called 'I' is such a complex. There are other complexes that are not so durably connected with others and that are not so essential for the preservation of the system, and which in fact are not specifically preserved in the system for very long but which come to the surface from time to time under the most varied circumstances. These complexes consist for the most part in what customary speech calls a person's 'life experience' (in psychology, the realm of 'habitual associations'). There are other such complexes whose connection with the rest of the system is weak and fleeting; they spring up, coming to the surface in the field of consciousness on several occasions, and then they disappear without a trace, filling a whole realm of what is experienced: that which is forgotten. There are experiences of yet another kind whose joining with the system of experience is so unstable and imperceptible that they only enter the field of psychical life for a moment and absolutely do not enter the realm of memory – even temporarily – so that their existence can be established only indirectly. And this, as we shall see, is still not the end of it, but before we go further let us dwell a little on this latter group of experiences.

In the great majority of cases, our perception of the surrounding environment is extremely incomplete. Certain parts of the environment 'attract our attention', stand out distinctly in our field of consciousness in a definite coordination with other experiences that we are conscious of, and thus enter into our system of psychical experience. Other parts of the environment 'escape our attention' and do not enter into a general coordination with other experiences, and, as far as psychical experience is concerned, it is as if they had not been sensed at all ('*todte Werte* [dead values]', according to Avenarius). However, we cannot say that they are altogether not perceived, and we cannot even assume that perceptions that correspond to them are absolutely absent from psychical experience. It sometimes happens that, after a certain amount of time, people who have been in some sort of unusual conditions – in a state of abnormal agitation, for example – will, when remembering a given occurrence and its circumstances, recall not only the facts that had occupied their consciousness at the moment of that occurrence but also certain details that at the time had eluded them, and these formerly 'dead' experiences are brought back to life with great clarity. However, if the unusual conditions had not arisen that led to the resurrection of 'dead quantities', they would have remained as if dead and would never have entered the sphere of psychical experience. This is what mostly happens. If, for example, you take a walk along an unfamiliar street with a great bustle of people, masses of merchandise in shop windows, and bright signboards, you will obtain millions of impressions. But how many of them will you yourself 'notice' during that time, and how many of them will you ever 'remember'?

Now suppose that you are walking down such a street, but you are in deep thought, entirely absorbed in the resolution of a difficult mathematical problem. You 'could not care less' about your surroundings; they do not exist for you. Nevertheless, you behave as if you see and hear all that is going on around you; you step aside for ladies, you avoid cabbies driving by, you excuse yourself if you bump into someone ... For a nearby observer, these are all utterances behind which experiences must be hidden. But these utterances are, as they say, 'mechanical'; there is 'no soul' in them. Does this mean that they are empty, that they appear without any experiences? Of course not. But the experiences that are expressed in the utterances remain outside the organised system of psychical life. They are isolated experiences, and we cannot know anything about them from immediate psychical experience.

In many pathological cases, whole broad complexes and sequences of experiences appear in this kind of isolated situation, and sometimes they are not altogether weak but are very intense, if judged according to the energy of the utterances. You observe individuals who are mentally ill and see that they undertake a series of complex and well-coordinated actions that are apparently aimed at a definite goal; in a word, their actions proceed with the kind of harmony and consecutiveness as would happen in normal circumstances on the basis of the broad associative interconnectedness of psychical experiences. From subsequent utterances of such patients, after they wake up, you discover that their entire dreamt life absolutely does not exist for their psychical experience. Can you draw the conclusion from this that all the manifestations of psychical illness are 'completely mechanical' and that no kind of experiences are connected with them? But how do we reconcile this with the fact that in their movements such mentally ill individuals carefully distinguish the most minor conditions in their surroundings, and that when walking onto a ledge where they would never go when awake they can balance their bodies very skilfully and can set their feet as precisely as the unevenness of this dangerous path demands. Some people who are mentally ill can, in their strange dreams, write letters, i.e. enter into communication with other people with the goal of arousing specific experiences in them. Can we really conceive of all this as simply automatism? But then there would be no grounds for relating any differently to all the usual, normal utterances of other people; you would have to see in everyone besides yourself a uniquely made machine with varied and complex movements. If this were the case, communication among people would lose all meaning, and the grounds for objective cognition would altogether disappear along with it. There is no need to create such pointless and hopeless cognitive contradictions. One need only grant that certain groupings of experiences proceed outside of a connection with psychical experience, forming isolated, particular coordinations, in the same way that the psychical experiences of other people are alien to the main system of coordinations of the psychical experiences of a given person.[5]

Psycho-epileptic seizures are a clear example of the extent to which there can be cases of intense experiences that lie beyond the bounds of psychical experience. Instead of falling to the ground in terrible convulsions that are completely devoid of purposefulness, an epileptic sometimes performs a series of actions that appear to be conscious and spontaneously energetic and that are often directed at the immediate destruction of his surroundings and are appallingly horrible in their wild lack of control. The force of these 'utterances' reveals the enormous intensity of the experiences that are hidden behind them; but no traces at all of this remain in the field of psychical experience – provided we do not count the subsequent feelings of fatigue and perhaps exhaustion of the epileptic person's organism.

In certain cases, extensive groupings of experiences that are separated from the main system of psychical experience form complex and stable coordinations of the same type as the main system, which they are not a part of. This is what psychopathology calls a 'split personality'. This peculiar phenomenon – the presence of two and sometimes even more individuals combined in what is obviously one physiological individual – still remains a mystery in many ways and has given rise to a large number of mutually contradictory scientific explanations. As far as a critique of psychical experience in concerned, however, only the factual aspect of the split personality is significant, regardless of how it might be explained by one or another hypotheses. There are a sufficient number of precise observations and completely substantiated facts in which there is a clear appearance of the phenomenon of a broad and complex organisation of experiences beyond the confines of a given system of *psychical experience* but connected with the *same nervous system* with which that system of psychical experience is functionally connected.

---

5 Sometimes the dream life of people who are mentally ill is not entirely isolated from their psychical experience. People have unclear memories later on of certain of their sleepwalking activities and experiences that they have had similar to a dream. Such intermediate, transitional cases are, of course, only an additional confirmation of the point of view that I am taking. The fluctuation of the limits of immediate psychical experience indicates that similar experiences also exist outside its boundaries.

In the most typical and advanced cases of this type – such cases as are often cited by doctors Azam, Camuset, and MacNish,[6] for example – the matter proceeds in the following way. The entire psyche of such a patient periodically changes, passing from one state to another and back again – sometimes there are even more than two different states – whereby it is evident that the former associative interconnectedness of the psyche is infringed upon or even interrupted and replaced by a new one. Sometimes patients then completely lose all recollection of what they thought, said, and did in their previous state. This was what happened, for example, in a case described by MacNish regarding one of the two states of Felida, a patient of Dr Azam. Sometimes her memories of the other state of Felida were preserved, but the patient felt herself to be so mentally transformed that she could not accept herself as being the same person as the previous one. The whole 'character' – attitudes and manners – of such people changes, and they not only consider themselves to be 'another person', but the people around them, based on the general picture of their utterances, also think so. If a memory of the previous psychical phase is preserved, then the patient refers to it as 'the other one', 'the other I', and so forth. A patient named Dufay characterised her primary (normal) state with the words 'quand moi est bête' [when I am stupid]. If the former phase is completely forgotten, and if it is the basic, 'normal' phase, corresponding to the period before falling ill, then it can come to the point where such patients must learn to write, read, do math, and, in part, even to speak all over again and must become acquainted with their surroundings all over again as well. This happened to an American woman whom MacNish writes about. When she entered into her 'second state', she knew only what she had learned while in that state. The change from one phase to another usually occurs more or less abruptly – sometimes immediately and unexpectedly, sometimes after deep sleep, and sometimes after a peculiar liminal condition.

No matter how we interpret facts like these – whether we see a real 'multiplicity of consciousness' in them or, following another hypothesis, broad, protracted hysteria with significant amnesia and with a change of the general state of organic health, etc. – it is possible to confidently draw one conclusion from them: the psychical experience of an individual does not include the whole sum of 'experiences' that are connected with that individual's physiological processes. A great number of different experiences can exist beyond the bounds of that psychical experience, which are usually comparatively isolated

---

6  Étienne Eugène Azam (1822–99) was a French physician; Léon Camuset (dates unknown) was a French physician; Robert MacNish (1802–37) was a Scottish physician [trans.].

and diffuse but which can sometimes be grouped in complex unities that are in many ways analogous to the main system of psychical experience. These ancillary psychical groupings can even temporarily displace the main grouping and govern, in its place, over the realm of utterances. This is what gives rise to the conception of a 'change of personality' in the observations of specialists that I have pointed out. The same kind of picture is also presented by insanity and psycho-epilepsy. In other cases, the utterances of ancillary psychical groupings can be observed *simultaneously and side-by-side* with utterances of the main 'consciousness'. Facts of this kind also are very important for a critique of psychical experience, and it is necessary to dwell a little on them.

In experiments that have been carried out many times on hysterical subjects, it has been possible to obtain complex, coordinated, strictly reasonable utterances in response to stimuli which in no case could have been able to reach the 'main' consciousness of the individual. The following are the most typical examples (from the experiments of Janet, Binet, Babinski,[7] and others). A female patient undergoing local anaesthesia – specifically, full anaesthesia of her right hand – is situated in such a way that a screen hides that hand from her. A pencil is placed in her hand, her fingers are arranged as required for writing, and paper is put beneath her hand. Since the patient cannot see it and her hand is *insensible* to her, she herself knows nothing about it. Next, a metal letter or some kind of embossed image is placed on the back of her hand, and the insensible hand, by itself, uses the pencil to write the letter or draw the image with fair accuracy. In doing so, the details of the depiction that are produced are sometimes so precise as to suggest a real tactile hyperesthesia in the anaesthetised hand. In other cases, the experimenter, located behind the patient, asked her questions in a very quiet voice at the very same time that her attention was completely distracted by a lively conversation with other people. These questions could not in any event have reached the 'consciousness' of the patient, nevertheless, her insensible hand used the pencil to write answers to the questions at the same time that she 'herself' did not even know that a pencil had been placed in her hand.

Similar experiments were successfully carried out in the most diverse variations – for example, by replacing the usual hysterical anaesthesia with an induced state of hypnosis.[8] It is evident from the very performance of the exper-

---

7    Pierre-Marie-Félix Janet (1859–1947), Alfred Binet (1857–1911), and Jules François Félix Babinski (1857–1932) were French physicians and neuro-psychologists [trans.].
8    In changing the conditions of the experiment one can succeed in establishing quite a close connection between 'consciousness' and extra-conscious coordinations. By acting on the anaesthetised surface of the skin, the experimenter can instil the 'consciousness' of various

iment that the utterances that are thereby obtained correspond neither to the 'consciousness' of the individual nor to the main psychical coordination of that consciousness but to another grouping of experiences that 'subconsciously' exist alongside the main 'consciousness' and independent of it to a certain degree.

In essence, all 'mechanical' or 'unconscious' utterances of normal people that we spoke of earlier – the reasonable reactions of people who are lost in thought or otherwise preoccupied to outside stimuli that they were not aware of – are completely consistent with the facts just related. These phenomena are only clearer and more complex for subjects who are hysterical and are obviously connected with the usual narrowing of the field of main consciousness that comprises the basic characteristic of hysteria. The 'subconscious' of hysterical people, like a 'second consciousness' in the cyclical change of dual personalities, presents a system of experiences that *is separately organised* and that remains beyond the threshold of normal psychical experience. Indeed, in the majority of cases, such a separate organisation does not form and experiences flow outside the main system in isolated groupings, while sometimes *indirectly* entering into a connection with this system by means of utterances that are observed by other people or by material traces that remain behind such as written words, drawings, broken objects, and so forth.

We thus see that a critique of psychical experience, based on comparing it with objective experience, shows that the realm of 'immediate experiences' that are connected with physiological processes is much wider than the realm of psychical experience that embraces only one system of such experiences and does not include ancillary groupings that are to a certain degree independently organised systems, partially isolated groupings, or particular isolated experiences. In consequence of this, the conception of 'immediate experiences' must be broadened in order to resolve the question of their connection with physiological life.

Exactly how much should this conception be broadened? First and foremost, it is obvious that it is necessary to assume that experiences are present everywhere there are utterances, even if they remain outside any connection with

---

presentations and even hallucinations. For example, unnoticed by him, the insensible skin of a patient was pricked several times with a pin; he was then asked to think of any number, and he gave exactly the number of pricks he had received. An embossed metal image was placed on the anaesthetised skin on the back of a patient's head, and he obtained a visually-hallucinated form from that image. And so on. This connection of 'consciousness' and 'extra-conscious impressions' corresponds, obviously, to the vital unity of the organism, although it is not the kind of immediate associative connection that stands out in the field of consciousness.

personal psychical experience. But behind these utterances *vital-differentials* are hidden – to be precise, vital-differentials that are sufficient to disrupt the equilibrium of motor centres to a significance degree and to elicit from them a significantly strong current of energy (in the form of innervation) that is directed toward the periphery. Meanwhile, psychical experience informs us of a great number of such experiences that are not expressed in utterances because they are connected to weaker vital-differentials that are incapable of eliciting external movement. If this is so, then we must assume that 'immediate experiences' exist beyond the bounds of psychical experience not only where they are expressed in noticeable movements but also where the vital-differentials that are joined with them are not significant enough to be expressed in movement. Thus we arrive at the conclusion that *the realm of a person's 'immediate experiences' – in the sphere of psychical experience and also beyond it – coincides with the realm of vital-differentials of the central nervous system.*

Having taken this position, we cannot avoid the question of when experiences enter the sphere of psychical experience and when they do not. Which vital-differentials have an immediate relationship with psychical experience and which do not? The answer can only be based on an analysis of the basic psychophysiological data that touch on this question.

V

The basic characteristic of psychical experience is that it is a system of specific connections – associative connections, to be precise. Therefore, the experiences that exist 'outside experience' are those that do not make it into the given system of connections, those that remain isolated from the main current of experiences. The associated chain of memories, psychical images, and desires that are excited by any given experience expresses itself, from the physiological point of view, as vital-differentials that are reflected and derivative, that are produced as the initial disruption of the equilibrium spreads through the nervous system, producing fluctuations of varying intensity and varying form in the various parts of that system. If a vital-differential flows in isolation in certain elements of the nervous system, not provoking a response in the remaining elements, then the experience that corresponds to it also must seem to be unconnected with psychical life, because there are no intermediate (associative) links that could connect it. These general considerations are corroborated even more if we look at typical cases of vital-differentials that are not connected with psychical experience.

The great majority of the very weak stimuli that act on the human organism go absolutely 'unnoticed' in the sphere of consciousness and do not cause sensations that are accessible to psychical experience. This makes perfect sense: very weak vital-differentials do not leave the confines of a limited number of immediately affected elements since neural conductors present a significance resistance to the transmission of energetical fluctuations. But in certain special cases such weak stimuli do have an effect in the field of consciousness, and, physiologically, this also makes perfect sense. Nerve cells, as accumulators, contain a supply of potential neural energy that sometimes can be sufficiently stimulated by a very weak vital-differential from outside, and this stimulus can itself form a considerably more powerful vital-differential with a wider circle of successive fluctuations in other parts of the nervous system.

It is well known that a person becomes more perceptive to a specific, weak stimulus precisely when his 'attention' is directed toward that perception. From the perspective of the most accepted theories of attention (arteriomotor-muscle theories) the act of attention is always connected with an elevated supply of nourishment to the elements of the central system that are in an active condition. Let us suppose that you wish to examine the details of a particular object and you peer at it attentively. This means that your circulatory system widens the small vessels that nourish the active parts of the brain and directs the greatest amount of nourishment to those parts at the expense of others. In this way, potential energy quickly builds up in the corresponding optical brain cells. They turn into charged apparatuses, and at the slightest external input they are stimulated as if by a burst of energy, causing derivative fluctuations at many points of the central system. It is also natural that the nourishment of the remaining parts of the brain is lowered in comparison with its usual conditions. The energy of those parts is lessened and more significant vital-differentials are required in order to cause the transmission of fluctuations in various directions in the comprehensive realm of the central system. Consequently, such stimuli as would affect touch and hearing, for example, and that would be immediately 'noticed' if 'attention' had not been 'diverted' from them, remain 'imperceptible' to consciousness because they are not included in the act of attention to visual sensations.

During deep sleep, anaesthesia, or fainting, a reduction in the nourishment of the brain is always observable – anaemia, weak blood pressure, slowing of the flow of blood (as a consequence of a decrease in the work of the heart). Therefore, obviously, the level of energy in the cortical accumulator-cells is in fact greatly reduced, and the stimuli that reach them produce only minor vital-differentials that are incapable of flowing broadly in the brain core. Additionally, in the normal sleep that follows the fatigue of the day, the connections of the central apparatus are disrupted as the result, to all appearances, of yet another cause: during wakefulness various products of the breakdown of tissue that is active in the processes of life accumulate in the cells and conductors, so that, as the result of a change in chemical composition, the excitability of cells and conductivity of the conductors weakens very significantly. The vital-differentials that spring up thus remain isolated, and this also applies to the corresponding experiences.

Incidentally, during sleep, due to the uneven distribution of nourishment and also to the comparatively strong stimuli and other incidental combinations of conditions that readily arise in such a complex system, some vital-differentials turn out to be sufficiently great to cause a series of derivative fluctuations. This produces dreams. In so doing, it is also possible that the derivative fluctuations can bypass their ordinary paths and instead pass along those conductors that are the least obstructed, so to speak, by the products of the vital functions of tissues. It is this which probably causes the typical disjointedness of dreams, the incongruous transitions that appear in them, and so on.[9] In regard to insanity, the matter obviously has to do with a derivative, particular system of physiological connections that do not function in a normal state but that appear during sleep when the main system is suppressed by the fatigue of the day. In terms of the psyche, this must be expressed in a second, narrower coordination similar to the system of psychical experience. In a comparatively more developed form this second system appears as a 'split consciousness'. In that state, it can attain such a complexity and adaptedness that it can replace the primary, main system in governing the vital activity of the organism for a long time, and, in some cases, it gradually supplants the main system so that the latter atrophies (as in the case of the patient of Dr Azam).

There is an unquestionable connection between the phenomena of hypnosis and an unusual state of nourishment of the brain: a weak pulse, a certain pallor of the face, and a headache if the subject is abruptly awakened all point to an anaemic condition of the brain due to a lowered blood pressure. The field of 'consciousness' is extremely narrowed, but since 'consciousness' is preserved, one might suppose that the nourishment of the core is not decreased equally throughout it – as in deep sleep, for example. This unevenness is expressed especially clearly in cases of hypnotic suggestion. When repeated

---

9 Under anaesthesia there are completely analogous phenomena. On the one hand, there is the poisoning of neural elements, the diminishment of their excitability and conductivity, and, on the other hand, there is the lowering of blood pressure and also, it would seem, of nourishment. The less the anaesthetic agent lowers the blood pressure, the less constant and infallible its sleep-inducing action – to the point where it is not sufficient to eliminate the connectedness of neural-physiological life. The attempts of pharmacologists to create a reliably acting narcotic that would not repress the circulatory system more than is consistent with normal sleep have so far been unsuccessful.

external influences – the utterances of the hypnotist, for example – cause the general weakening and disorganisation of the life of the brain, the work of *some* elements of the brain is supported, and then this work proceeds in precisely the kind of interconnectedness that is caused by those influences, i.e. the hypnotic suggestions.

There is much that is unclear and unexplored here, but everything points to the possibility of 'psychical' groupings outside the main system of psychical experience. Experimenters have been able to induce a complete lack of memory of what a patient experienced during a hypnotic dream, and they have artificially removed entire complex series of experiences from the sphere of psychical experience. They have succeeded in using hypnotic suggestion so that the subject does not see or hear something in a post-hypnotic state. This has been carried out with great precision, and it demonstrates that an organism can distinguish and pick out 'invisible' objects and 'inaudible' sounds very well, but the corresponding perceptions remain outside the interconnectedness of psychical life and its utterances. Hypnotic suggestion can induce a subject to do something at a specific time after awakening, and that hypnotic suggestion, which has been forgotten, will enter the field of psychical experience with irresistible force at the designated moment. In a word, the arbitrary isolation of some groups of experiences from their general and main system can be achieved by hypnotic suggestion, and they can be inserted arbitrarily back into that system again. It is unquestionable that all this corresponds to significant changes in the nourishment of the brain in its entirety and of its separate parts; it consequently corresponds to fluctuations in both the potential energy of nerve cells and the conductivity of nerve fibres. It corresponds, in general, to conditions that change the system of connections in the nervous system and that change the boundaries and the direction of transmission of the vital-differentials that spring up in it. Consequently, it is completely justifiable to propose that groupings of experiences correspond to groupings of vital-differentials and the reverse.

In any event, the nervous system represents one vital whole, and therefore it is hardly possible for there to be *absolutely* isolated groupings of connections in it. This means that absolutely isolated groupings of experiences are also impossible. The combinations of experiences which do not enter the main system of experiences consist of parts which themselves enter that system in other combinations. If this did not happen, we would not be able to understand utterances connected with such 'extra-conscious' groupings of experiences. When, for example, individuals who are mentally ill perform various actions that are quite usual for them when they are functioning normally, then it is perfectly clear that behind these actions are hidden entire quite complex associations of experiences which in other correlations appear in the main field of psychical experience, in 'the field of consciousness'. In other cases – in minor 'unconscious' reactions, when a person is pondering something deeply, for example – the matter has to do with narrower groupings of experiences and with comparatively simple psychical combinations which under other conditions would appear wholly in the 'field of consciousness'. And, finally, even those experiences that are outside experience and that are so extremely uncomplicated and weak that they are altogether not expressed in outward form – even they, corresponding, as they do, to the vital-differentials of various particular organs and cells of the nervous system, are formed from those same *elements* of which all the experiences in psychical experience are composed.

We have arrived here at what is essentially a tautological proposition. As modern positive philosophy has established, the elements of psychical experience are identical with the elements of all experience in general, and therefore they are also identical with elements of physical experience. Elements of experience (chromatic, innervative, tactile, acoustic, etc.) – elements of red and green, elements of extension, elements of hard and soft, warm and cold, elementary tones, etc. – all equally form both the 'bodies' of the objective, physical world and the perceptions, forms, and psychical images of the psychical world. The difference is only in the type of grouping – in the nature of the interconnectedness which appears in one case as the interconnectedness of objective regularity and in the other case as the interconnectedness of associations. Thus, it is altogether impossible to speak of 'extra-psychical' experiences that correspond to isolated neural processes in the human organism that are different in their elementary composition from the experiences that enter the system of psychical experience. It is necessary only to add that the *type of grouping of elements in both experiences is also identical – that is to say, it is associative* – as we can confidently conclude from the utterances that correspond to both psychical and physical experience.

It is completely clear that from this point of view there is no fundamental difference between 'centres of consciousness' and 'centres of unconscious reactions'. If the area of diffusion of any vital-differential does not extend beyond the bounds of the spinal cord or of a separate neural node of the sympathetic nervous system, for example, then the corresponding experiences remain 'unconscious' precisely in the sense that they do not belong to the coordination of experiences which form our 'psychical experience'. And, since vital-differentials of the central system are made up of vital-differentials of separate cells, we are then fully justified in assuming that everywhere a neural cell is present and where a vital-differential springs up, there also exists something that is completely analogous to our 'immediate experiences' although very simple and weak in comparison with the usual content of the field of our consciousness.

But there is more to it. A nerve cell in the process of its individual evolution is the result of the development and differentiation of embryonic cells, and the entire psychophysiological organism in the biological process is the result of the evolution of independent cells like protozoa. Development cannot create anything essentially new but creates only newer and more complicated combinations of what was present earlier in the form of elements. Therefore, if we acknowledge the law of the uniformity of nature, we must assume that everywhere there is a living cell there is something that is fundamentally the same as our psychical experiences. There is no life without experiences, no 'purely physiological life'. And so we must do away with the impossible, astounding leap in the form of a 'first sensation' that sprang up on the stairway of the biological process that has been created by thinkers like Du Bois-Reymond.[10]

But on the other hand, must there not necessarily have been such a leap when *life* sprang up from non-organic processes? Of course not. No other nature exists for us besides the one that is made up of *elements*, and these elements, despite their diversity, are identical in physical and psychical experience, and that holds true in inorganic and organic nature. Life is a particular *organisation* of these elements, and the non-organic world is another combination of them that possesses no or a very low level of organisation. Only our talent for abstraction makes non-organic nature 'lifeless', but this absolutely does not correspond to the entire meaning of our experience, since this non-organic nature is a necessary part of *our own life*. The continual transformation of non-organic material by living organisms to become a constituent part of those very organisms and the possibility of continual renovation of life from lifeless matter clearly tell us that in this whole process there are only different combinations and changing relationships; there are none of the absolute differences that are so dear to metaphysicians. The material of life and all of nature is the same everywhere; it is the groupings of that material that are different. The development of life always signifies the same thing: the *growth of organisation* in the grouping of elements.

Have we not arrived at panpsychism – at the conception of all of nature according to the model of human consciousness? Hardly. Nature is not something 'psychical', and this becomes clear when one fully understands what exactly is meant by 'psychical'. The psychical is not a 'substance' at all but only a

---

10   Emil du Bois-Reymond (1818–96) was a German physician and neuro-physiologist [trans.].

*relationship*. That is, it is a specific *interconnectedness* of phenomena, a specific *regularity* of experience. When 'elements' of experience present themselves to us in an objective, socially valid regularity, we call complexes of these elements 'physical' bodies, and when the regularity is the other, non-objective, non-socially valid type of regularity (associative, to be precise), we call those complexes 'psychical'. *Elements* have neither a physical nor a psychical character; they are *outside* these definitions. Panpsychism, for which all nature is made up of psychical complexes and which 'explains' the physical by means of the psychical, consequently expresses a tendency to reduce the objective regularity of phenomena to a subjective interconnectedness. This desire is anti-scientific to the highest degree. The ideal of science is diametrically opposite to it; science reduces all subjective interconnectedness to objective regularity. In this sense, materialism was always incomparably closer to the progressive tendencies of science, but it strayed too far afield in the analysis of reality, and instead of direct elements of experience – physical and psychical – it substituted complicated complexes called 'matter'. Because materialism considered these complexes exclusively from the point of view of objective regularity, it was true to the spirit of scientific cognition and therefore presented the closest step up to a scientific worldview. It was more objective and positive than the spiritualistic tendency, but it was still not sufficiently objective and positive. The truth in this case, as usual, was not in a 'golden mean' between conflicting tendencies but something outside them both. Progressive thinking of our time relates to the struggle between materialism and spiritualism in approximately the same way it did to the struggle that once occurred between Protestantism and Catholicism: progressive thought could not be satisfied by considering either one of those two tendencies to be 'more true' than the other.

Now let us return to the main theme. On the basis of all that has been presented, we take it that experiences are present everywhere vital-differentials in organic processes exist. We also assert that the connection between experiences and vital-differentials is constant and uniform. We shall attempt to define the nature of this connection more precisely.

## 2   Psychoenergetics

I

It is necessary, first and foremost, to establish the meaning of the very concept of 'vital-differential'. The fact of the matter is that Avenarius, who created the concept, formulated it in a way that, in our view, is completely unsatisfactory from a biological perspective. One senses in his formulation the remnants of a conservative, static understanding of life – remnants that have gradually been removed as evolutionary thought has developed. To explain these remnants is sufficient to reject them.

At the basis of the phenomena of life lies a fluid equilibrium of energy, a two-way flow between a living system and its environment. Assimilation, the intake of energy from the external environment goes side by side with disassimilation, the expenditure of energy, its dissipation in that same environment. A complete equilibrium of both flows in all parts of the system would be a case of ideal conservation.[11] Such conservation cannot be found in reality, but it is a convenient abstraction that can serve as the best starting point for investigation. Any real process of life presents a series of continual disturbances of ideal conservation, now on one side, now on the other.

The norm of the ideal conservation of life is itself a *continually changing magnitude*. Each moment brings some change – no matter how insignificant – in the inner relationships of the system; in each successive moment the system is already not completely what it was in the preceding moment. This is completely obvious if one considers whole, broad periods of the life cycle: the equilibrium of life for a child is not the same as for an old person, it is not the same for a youth as for an adult. And since the transformation is continually going on, there must be infinitely small changes at each moment that are not noticeable but that undoubtedly occur.

Imagine that the equilibrium of life in the course of a certain amount of time is disturbed for the purpose of assimilation – that is, assimilation prevails over the expenditure of energy. Then, at a certain moment, both sides of the vital process level out. The ideal equilibrium is restored, but now it is not the same equilibrium as it was before it was disturbed. The general sum of energy which the system presents is greater than before – the organism grew, the child

---

11   Bogdanov uses the terms *sokhranenie* and *konservatizm* to correspond to Richard Avenarius's *Erhaltung*. *Erhaltung* has been variably translated as 'maintenance', 'preservation', or 'conservation'. When used in the sense of *Erhaltung*, I translate both *sokhranenie* and *konservatizm* as 'conservation' [trans.].

became a youth. If the system had returned to the former equilibrium, that would signify a reduction or degradation of life. Therefore the ideal (conceivable) equilibrium of a system is not at all the *ideal* of life; or, more accurately, it is an ideal of life, but it is one that is static and stagnant not one that is dynamic and progressive. In the analysis of vital fluctuations, one must not lose sight of the difference between the growth and the reduction of the energy of the system; one must not consider both cases to be fundamentally the same. But this is exactly what Avenarius does.

For Avenarius, the situation seems to be as follows. In a living system,[12] in the course of sleep, let us say, a surplus of 'nourishment' builds up as the result of the preponderance of 'nourishment' over 'work'. The person enters the active life of wakefulness with this surplus, and the *vital task* of the organism is to establish an equilibrium through an increase of 'work'. Avenarius does not use the term 'vital task', but this is precisely his understanding of this process, because he considers that the preponderance of 'nourishment' continually diminishes 'vital-conservation' ('*Vital-Erhaltungswert*'), and only by a corresponding increase of 'work' can this diminishment of 'vital-conservation' be kept to a minimum. In this sense, both cases are completely the same for him – both the preponderance of 'nourishment' over 'work' and the preponderance of 'work' over 'nourishment'.

First and foremost, we must remove the crudely materialistic and imprecise term 'nourishment' ('*Ernährung*') from our analysis. The process of nourishment is only the main path of assimilation of external energy into the system, but it is not the only path. There is every reason to believe that energy – for example, the minor stimuli that reach the central system along neural conductors – can be assimilated by neural cells, elevating their store of potential energy. The term 'nourishment' needlessly muddies the waters, forcing us to always conceive of the process of vital assimilation as the intake of material particles, when the reality is a flow of energy for which such particles are only one of the usual forms. The second term, 'work', is less unsatisfactory, but it also forces us not to think of all possible types of disassimilation but mainly of one – of the process of innervation. In any case, it is really difficult to connect disassimilation with, for example, the continual expenditure of the energy of cells

---

12   Avenarius is concerned in his account only with 'System C', the central nervous system, and, for the most part, even only with the 'partial systems' ('*Partialsystem*') of which it is composed. System C is also of the greatest interest to me, but, because I treat life processes as fundamentally homogenous, I broaden my task and take up more general formulations.

that is expressed in the dissipation of heat, but we cannot ignore such paths of disassimilation. We cannot ignore them entirely because the vital process is first and foremost the process of an integral, dynamic whole.

The excess of 'nourishment' over 'work' can easily be understood in the sense that a living system receives supplies of energy from outside that the system cannot assimilate. It is as if the system is overloaded and the flow of its vital functions is disrupted, which gives rise to intensified expenditures of its energy. In this interpretation, the 'vital-differential' that accompanies an excess of 'nourishment' turns out, of course, to be harmful to life, and it must be removed for the sake of 'vital-conservation'. But it is clear that the concept of 'vital-differential' is applied incorrectly in this case. A 'vital-differential' is the difference between two vital magnitudes, but these magnitudes must be strictly homogenous – only then will the operation of subtraction have scientific value. If one makes the quantity of energy that is attained from outside the system (that is still in the process of being assimilated and that is consequently still *alien and extraneous* to its vital process) the minuend of the equation, and if one makes the quantity of energy that is expended by the system (that already *belongs* to the system as its *own* energy) the subtrahend, then the process of subtraction is a comparison of two heterogeneous vital magnitudes, and the expression 'vital-differential' has no scientific value. It is necessary to compare the system's actually-occurring assimilation of energy with its actually-occurring disassimilation of energy, and only then is the concept of 'vital-differential' suitable for analysis. In his definitions, Avenarius undoubtedly tended toward the latter, more scientific conception of vital-differential, but in his conclusions, he continually switches over to the first, imprecise conception, and the picture of the life of System C appears in an inaccurate light.

For Avenarius it seemed unquestionable that the excess of assimilation over disassimilation (this is called a 'positive' vital-differential) and the excess of disassimilation (a negative vital-differential) have fundamentally the same meaning. To be precise, they bring the system closer to death or degradation. In a word, they signify *unadaptedness*. From a biological perspective, this view, although it is still very widely spread among physiologists, seems to be completely invalid; it contradicts both the general conception of the progress of life and the concrete facts of development.

In any event, a positive vital-equilibrium, the predominance of assimilation, signifies the growth of energy of a system – potential energy, to be precise – that can then be expended in the vital process. It is obvious that, all other things being equal, the more energy than a system can expend in the struggle for life – i.e. the greater the sum of potential energy that is available in the system – the longer it will be preserved and the more surely it will prevail. Therefore it is precisely positive vital-differentials that are the *quantitative aspect of biological progress*. Just the opposite, a negative vital-differential – a preponderance of the expenditure of energy – leads to the lowering of the potential energy of the system and to the lowering of its forces in the struggle for life. This is the *quantitative degradation of a system*. The two types of phenomena are mutually contradictory in their vital significance, and they must not be put in the same bracket.

One is fully justified in considering the entire first half of the life cycle of an organism, from birth to full maturity, to be progressive evolution – the growth of the vital capacity of the organism and of the power of resistance in the struggle of life with external nature. Meanwhile, this entire half of the organism's evolution is based on *positive vital-differentials* – an excess of assimilation, the accumulation of energy that is known as the 'process of growth' of the organism. When negative vital-differentials begin to predominate, the second half of the life cycle begins; the energy of the system gradually declines and the system degrades.

In order to remove a few doubts that still remain regarding the question of how to interpret these basic facts of life, I will permit myself to quote a few lines that I wrote several years ago in another work.[13]

> The period of comparative equilibrium – maturity – is also the period of the greatest adaptedness of the system. Should we not conclude from this that the equilibrium of the system also must be called its 'ideal condition'?
>
> In order to realise how false this idea is, one need only recall those cases where the vital equilibrium is attained prematurely. If the process of growth is arrested in childhood and does not reach the norm then the equilibrium of the system is associated with very low vital-conservation. This vital-conservation is significantly less than what is observed in other people under the same conditions but with the normal excess of 'nourishment' over 'work'.
>
> However, it is doubtful whether someone can assert that the high degree of adaptedness of the stage of maturity depends precisely on the elimination of the normal vital-differentials of childhood and youth – the excess of 'nourishment' over 'work'. Surely everyone agrees that the high degree of adaptedness of maturity is attained to a significant degree pre-

---

13  *Poznanie s istoricheskoi tochki zreniia*, p. 19. I dealt with this question (regarding the meaning of vital-differentials) there in passing and in a comparatively cursory and brief way.

cisely *because of* these vital-differentials, *because of* the growth of energy of the system that they create.

All this seems quite elementary and incontestable. But is this the point of view of Avenarius? Here is what he says in his *Kritik der reinen Erfahrung* (Book I, pp. 63–64):

> Aus dem Mutterschoss, diesem Sanktuarium der Erhaltung, wird das Kind vertrieben: ausgestossen in eine fast absolut andere, neue, ungewohnte, nur zum Teil noch erhaltungsfreundliche Umgebung. Nun ist es ausgesetzt den Änderungen, die ihm aus der Umgebung und deren Wandlungen erwachsen; und ausgesetzt wird es alsbald sein den Schicksalen, weiche ihm die typischen Änderungen des eigenen Entwicklungsganges aufdrängen.
> Und das heisst: das System C ist durch die Geburt aus einer annähernd idealen Umgebung in eine nichtideale Umgebung versetzt worden …
> Und unsere Aufgabe wird somit zunächst darauf gerichtet sein, bei Änderungen des Systems C zu analysieren: sofern sie als *Verminderung* des vitalen Erhaltungswertes des Systems C oder aber als Behauptungen, dieses Systems unter solchen Verminderungen zu denken sind.

> A baby is violently expelled from its mother's womb – that sanctuary for preserving life – and is thrust into a new, almost absolutely different and unaccustomed environment that is only partly favourable for sustaining its life. Here the baby is subject to changes caused by the conditions of the environment and the changes in those conditions. Then it has to endure the fates that are imposed on it in the typical sequence of changes in its cycle of maturation.
> In other words: System C, through the act of maturation, is relocated from an environment that approximately corresponds to the ideal to an environment that is not ideal …
> Our immediate task is to analyse the changes in the system to determine the precise extent to which they must be considered to be either decreases in the vital-conservation of System C or to be acts to maintain that system in the presence of (among) such decreases.

Thus, for Avenarius 'decreases of vital-conservation' begin with the very birth of the infant and continue right up until the arrival of death, and, fortuitously, they are brought to an end by death. But from this point of view, what is to be done with the whole period of the progressive evolution of the individual?¹⁴ The essence of the matter consists in the *absolute nature* of Avenarius's very concept of vital-conservation.

> Da, wie das ganze System C, so auch seine Bestandteile, bez. seine Formelemente, entstehend und vergehend gedacht werden, so muss – wenn für irgend einen Zeitpunkt der verlangte denkbar grösste vitale Erhaltungswert des Systems C angenommen wird, mit demselben eine *absolute* Erhaltung aller *zentralen* Partialsysteme, bez. Formelemente, angenommen werden; d. h. der denkbar grösste vitale Erhaltungswert des Systems C ist als die Summe der denkbar grössten Erhaltung aller seiner Bestandteile, bez. Formelemente, zu denken.
> *Kritik der reinen Erfahrung*, Vol. 1, p. 66

We posit that, just as System C, as a whole, springs up and is destroyed, so do the constituent parts that correspond to the whole and the elements (cells – A.B.) that form it. Therefore *if* for any moment in time we assume the greatest conceivable magnitude of vital-conservation for System C, then we thereby also assume the *absolute* conservation of *all* partial systems of the central system and all the forming elements that correspond to it. In other words, the ideal of the greatest vital-conservation of System C must be thought of as the sum of the ideally greatest vital-conservation of all its composite parts – of all the elements that form it.

Operating with such 'absolute' magnitudes, it goes without saying, makes it impossible to give a true picture of the progressive development of life. Any change in the system – even a change that is most practical for life's struggle – seems to be a disruption, a 'diminishment' ('*Verminderung*') of the absolute conservation of life, something that is seen nowhere in nature. In its essence,

---

14    'Is it not appropriate to accept that the life-conservation of the child is greater than the life-conservation of the adult, since the child might still have 70 years to live while the adult, if he is 30, has hardly more than 40 years left? But here it is necessary to pay attention to the following: the odds that a child will live to 70 are very low, for example, 1 out of 50 to 60, while the chances that an adult of 40 will live that long are considerable higher, for example 1 out of 5 or 6. The generalising tendencies of science do not permit us to count the first magnitude of life-conservation as greater than the second – that would mean giving more significance to a separate case than to a general rule. It is possible to draw only one conclusion from this comparison: that the life-conservation of the child *might still grow* in the process of its development but for the adult it is already close to the maximum and can hardly become greater. Therefore *under favourable conditions* the child will live longer'. (*Poznanie s istoricheskoi tochki zreniia*, p. 18, footnote.)

this conception is very doubtful even from a logical perspective. Where there is absolute conservation, there *is no life*, since life is inconceivable without the conception of activity, of struggle with the external environment, and where there is no life it is incorrect to talk about any kind of 'magnitude of conservation of life'. But even leaving logic to one side, the conception of ideal conservation is completely groundless from a biological point of view.

Ever since the evolutionary idea permeated the entire realm of the life sciences, the static conception of unchanging, absolutely fixed forms of life became more and more unsuitable, and with every passing day it was further eliminated from scientific thinking. Finally, Darwinism finished off this conception by showing that, generally speaking, the way that life is preserved is actually by *changing* its forms. Only progressive adaptation to the environment, with its continually changing influences, guarantees the preservation of any given form of life, and this preservation means, of course, not absolute but only relative conservation. But it also can mean something greater than any kind of conservation – the growth and progress of life, to be precise. The task of biomechanics is to understand this progress and to give an accurate and coherent depiction of it. If such a task is posed, formulas constructed on the idea of absolute conservation become cognitively useless.

Because the 'absolute conservation of the system' was an untenable abstraction, it proved to be difficult for Avenarius himself to rigorously sustain the point of view that he had arrived at. Meanwhile, in almost all his work he sees only 'diminishments of vital-conservation' and 'support (*Behauptungen*) of the system amid such diminishments' in the course of vital fluctuations. In a chapter about 'congregational systems' (collectivities such as the family or society, for example) he unexpectedly discovered an 'increase of vital-conservation' (*Kritik der reinen Erfahrung*, Vol. 1, p. 165):

> Je mehr sich die Teilsysteme im Sinne gegenseitiger Vermehrung des vitalen Erhaltungswertes behaupten, desto günstiger sind die Bedingungen für die Erhaltung des Gesamtsystems.

> The more the self-conservation of partial systems (separate individuals, for example – A.B.) is carried out in the sense that they mutually enhance their maintainability, the more favourable are the conditions for the conservation of the entire system.[15]

---

15   It is necessary to note that the chapter on 'congregational systems' in *Kritik der reinen Erfahrung* stands out to a certain extent: while the other parts of the work have a strongly

In justifying his idea that *every* vital-differential signifies the immediate unadaptedness of the system, Avenarius points to several concrete facts. But these facts are partly interpreted inaccurately and partly tell against Avenarius's opinion.

All those cases in which too much nourishment is *delivered* to a vital system under conditions of comparatively normal 'work' and in which the system is disturbed and becomes maladjusted as a result of this are not directly related to the question. I have already pointed out that the delivery of nourishment is not at all the same as the assimilation of nourishment, and it cannot be considered as one of the two sides of the vital equilibrium. When nourishment that has been delivered from without is not assimilated by tissues, it remains in them as a foreign body – in the form, for example, of fatty accumulations – that hamper the vital-activity of tissues and that can easily cause those tissues to atrophy and degenerate. Thus, what is going on in this situation is precisely the excessive expenditure of energy of living tissues due to the chronic, harmful influence of the fatty accumulations and not because of excessive assimilation. But when *assimilation* – and not merely delivery – of increased nourishment occurs and is not used up by increased expenditures, one observes only the phenomenon of *growth*, and this cannot be considered to be unadaptedness.

Avenarius offers a psychiatric example as a particular case of just such a kind – manic excitement and mania. In its main physiological manifestation, mania is the congestion of the brain, '*also ein zu viel an Ernährung*' ('hence a surplus of nourishment') in the words of Avenarius. But the fact of the matter is that congestion signifies only an intensified *delivery* of nourishment and not the elevated assimilation of it, and the term 'nourishment' taken in its vulgar meaning has apparently confused the philosopher. Has that mass of raw material that is delivered by the circulatory system to the brain that is in a manic state really been assimilated? Or, on the contrary, did nerve cells have to expend a mass of energy only in order to be freed from overloaded tissue and from the undigested material that is hampering vital-activity? There can hardly be any doubt as to the answer to this question. Any living cell can assimilate nourishment only within limited parameters, and this is particularly true of a delicate ganglionic brain cell in such an unfavourable state as protracted, elevated intracranial pressure.

But under closer analysis this example tells against Avenarius in an even more obvious way. At the beginning of the development of manic excitement,

expressed neo-Lamarckian tinge, in this chapter a Darwinian point of view predominates. Unfortunately the ideas that are outlined in this chapter are applied too seldom in the rest of the work.

while congestion is not yet strong and cells succeed in assimilating surplus nourishment, the organism displays a temporary increase of life, and the pathological nature of the increase is only revealed later on. At first, there is only a certain pleasant stimulation that is accompanied by the elevation rather than the diminution of physical health; vital resilience of tissues grows and muscular power increases, giving evidence that there is a certain *growth of immediate adaptedness* and not a decrease of adaptedness. Meanwhile the question consists in the *immediate*, direct meaning of the given vital-differential. If, subsequently, clear phenomena of an actual disease (unadaptedness) appear, then, after all, the vital-differential also changes its character, turning from positive to negative. Nerve tissue then cannot cope with the mass of material brought by the blood, and that material entirely disrupts the vital-activity of the nerve tissue. Besides that, a huge quantity of energy is spent on countless impulsive movements which cause the entire system to be further poisoned by the appearance of the products of the vital disintegration of functioning tissues in extremely elevated amounts. In a word, while assimilation dominates, life is immediately elevated, and, when disassimilation becomes preponderant, life declines. It is absolutely impossible to explain the condition of the patient in the first stages of manic excitement from Avenarius's point of view.

Avenarius attaches the greatest significance to the general fact that a *lack of work* leads to the degeneration and loss of formative elements. But very little analysis is required to discover the basic error here. Tissues that do not do enough work *atrophy*, as Avenarius himself has pointed out, i.e. at least they lose their energy. They are insufficiently 'nourished' and assimilate less than they disassimilate (the very word 'atrophy' means a lack of nourishment). And this makes perfect sense: work is a necessary *physiological stimulus* of nourishment and, in general, of assimilation. Tissue that works very little is even less nourished, and it therefore does not grow (as it would if there were an actual preponderance of 'nourishment'), and it diminishes and becomes flaccid. Deposits of fat, which are obtained for the most part in this way, do not at all signify an excess of assimilation. A fat deposit is a foreign body as far as tissue is concerned.

There is no doubt that there are cases where a prolonged preponderance of assimilation leads to a crisis and even to the destruction of the vital system, but under closer examination these facts also do not support Avenarius's view. The fact of the matter is that as long as assimilation actually predominates, the organism thrives. A turnabout in the condition of the organism coincides with a turnabout in vital-differentials. After a number of years of a free and easy life, satiety or depression arrives. A chronic contraction of minute blood vessels appears; the vasomotor system becomes spasmodic. A huge amount of nervous energy is expended on the increased innervation of countless annular muscle fibres that surround the minute blood vessels, and, at the same time, the surface area through which the nourishment of tissues takes place is diminished. Positive vital-differentials are replaced with negative ones; 'good turns into bad'. But as long as that transformation has not happened, it is 'good', all the same, and not 'bad'.[16]

We must therefore strictly distinguish a positive vital-differential, which has an immediately progressive significance for life, from a 'negative' vital-differential, which has an immediately regressive significance. The *indirect* and at the same time *ultimate* significance of either of them can be different. The elevation of the energy of a system can bring with it the destruction of the harmony of its functions, and a decrease of energy can bring the renewal of that harmony. But then, in cases of the first kind, this is expressed as a subsequent lowering of the energy of the system, and, in cases of the second kind, it is just the opposite. But in these *fluctuations* of adaptedness, the immediate significance of vital-differentials for life remains the same. They are either positive or negative, and they are correspondingly marked 'plus' or 'minus'.

II

The problem of positive and negative vital-differentials is of interest at the present moment only to the extent that it is possible to establish a definite and necessary connection between them and 'immediate experiences'. Although for the time being, of course, it is possible to deal only with the most general expressions of how they correlate with one another.

All experiences without exception are characterised by what psychophysiologists usually call 'sensory tone' and what Avenarius designates with the term 'Affectional' – a colouration of pleasure or of pain.[17] This colouration has a

---

16   Here, consequently, positive vital-differentials are not directly the cause of the crisis. In the end, it is the gradually changing structure of the system on the basis of those vital-differentials that turns out to be disharmonious. This 'phenomenon is completely analogous to the general crisis of capitalist production. The growth of productive forces is a fact, generally speaking, that is beneficial for the life-conservation of society, just as the growth of energy of the central nervous system is beneficial for its life-conservation. But, being carried out in an inharmonious way … the growth of productive forces can produce a change in the internal relationships of the system that subsequently causes a huge expenditure of social-labour-related energy – expenditure that is absolutely counterproductive. The same thing can sometimes happen with the accumulation of energy in an individual psychical system' (*Poznanie s istoricheskoi tochki zreniia*, pp. 20–2, footnote).

17   So-called 'neutral sensory colouration' is, obviously, only a threshold magnitude where

clearly quantitative nature: there can be 'more' or 'less' pleasure or pain in a given experience, and the difference between 'pleasure' and 'pain' is the difference between the algebraic signs of 'plus' and 'minus'. When pleasure and pain, as magnitudes that are positive and negative, come together in the field of psychical experience, they mutually decrease or eliminate one another.

The 'qualitative' tones of pleasure and pain are very different, but this does not prevent all 'pleasures' and all 'pains', as quantities, from being mutually comparable and commensurable,[18] although, of course, for an observer the more different the 'qualitative' tones, the more difficult it is to compare them. Fortunately, our task is not to make such comparisons but to explain the general correlation between the algebra of the *Affectional* and the algebra of vital-differentials.

The question of the biological meaning of sensory tone should not cause any particular problems. Since pleasure is what an organism strives for and pain is what it avoids, then, from an evolutionary point of view, pleasure must signify a certain enhancement of life and pain a diminishment of life. If things were arranged differently, then an organism's desires would be a false guide, and it would inevitably quickly perish. Of course, in reality, this guide is not ideally reliable – pleasure sometimes has harmful results and pain sometimes has positive results, but, in general, there can be no disagreement that what is pleasant coincides to a significance degree with what is useful for life and what is unpleasant coincides with what is harmful for life.

In conceiving of the *immediate* characteristics of experiences, pleasure and pain obviously signify what is immediately useful and immediately harmful precisely for the central nervous system – what *immediately* elevates or lowers

---

pleasure diminishes and turns into the beginning of pain and vice versa (Wundt's '*Indifferenzpunkt*').

18  I will take the liberty of adducing an explanation from one of my previous works: 'Not everyone agrees with this proposition. Based on the evidence of their own immediate consciousness, some people find that there are also types of phenomena of feeling that are not comparable because they are heterogeneous. Thus, they take elevated versus base pleasures – such as, for example, the pleasure that comes from a good deed and the pleasure that comes from a glass of vodka – as being impossible to compare. However, experience shows that even for such different forms of feeling as these a quantitative comparison is possible inasmuch as, in regard to above case for example, many people are capable of considering both sides of the question and of determining which pleasure is greater'. (*Poznanie s istoricheskoi tochki zreniia*, p. 220).

It is possible, of course, not to approve of such 'commensurations' of heterogeneous forms of feeling, especially if it is done from a practical point of view (30 pieces of silver or the life of a teacher), but they are an unquestionable fact that theory must take account of.

its life. Positive and negative vital-differentials have precisely the same immediate meaning in physiological life, and that is why it could not be more natural to assume that a positive sensory tone – pleasure – corresponds to a positive vital-differential (an elevation of the energy of the system), while a negative sensory tone – pain – corresponds to a negative vital-differential (a reduction of the energy of the system). And this conclusion can be affirmed by a plenitude of facts.

In summing up these facts into a concise formula, one can say from one's own experience that pain exhausts the nervous system and lowers the energy of its vital functions, just as pleasure enhances it powers and increases the energy of its vital functions. In regard to those incomparably less numerous cases when the opposite relationship is apparently observed, they can be entirely explained by the fact that *subsequent results* of certain vital-differentials do not correspond to their *immediate, direct* significance. As the result of a specific sum of conditions, a given increase of energy can lead to a considerably greater subsequent decrease, and vice versa. But the immediate meaning of any *Affectional* does not change because of this.[19]

Since my conception of the *Affectional* issues from the view that I have taken regarding the vital-differential, then it is completely natural that a different understanding of vital-differentials must lead to a different point of view regarding the *Affectional*. For Avenarius, any vital-differential signifies an immediate unadaptedness, and therefore pleasure signifies for him the lessening or cessation of any kind of vital-differential whatever, while suffering signifies the appearance or increase of a vital-differential. This is a completely logical conclusion, but it comes from an incorrect premise, and, as such, it cannot but contradict reality.

At first glance, it is already easy to notice a certain biological absurdity in this conclusion. If a specific vital-differential is established in a system – let us

---

19   Not all experiences but only a small part of them fall within the field of psychical experience – in the sphere of introspection. It is, therefore, extremely rare for the factual elevation of the energy of the nervous system to be accomplished without a noticeable sensation of pleasure or the factual lowering of the energy of the nervous system without a sensation of pain. This is exactly the meaning of those cases in which a person, after a long series of pleasures, changes without noticing it into a state of deep enervation or in which a person emerges from great and seemingly hopeless suffering even stronger and more energetic than before. The most important processes of building up and expending life take place in the depths of elemental organic phenomena, in the realm of indefinite isolated experiences, which psychical experience subsequently adds up, adding its own summands. The fundamental homogeneity of 'consciousness' and 'the unconscious' is clearly expressed in this.

say a negative vital-differential that remains at one level for a long time or that fluctuates very little in either direction – then an *Affectional* must be absent. Meanwhile, it is clear that the system is thereby headed for destruction, and if the vital-differential is great, this will happen very quickly. The *Affectional* does not give the organism any directives, but it is precisely upon the *Affectional* that the direction of further vital development of the system depends; the *Affectional* stimulates the system to struggle against unfavourable conditions. Avenarius's *Affectional* clearly turns out to be biologically untenable – or at least a result that is quite improbable.

There are a large number of cases where the colouration of happiness is combined with an unquestioned disruption of the relative equilibrium present in the system. These are all the cases of 'pleasant surprises'. One is in a calm, neutral mood and suddenly the mail brings one news that one did not at all expect but that turns out to be excellent. Or, a chance combination of minor circumstances prompts one to a discover something that one was not in the least looking for but that turns out to be valuable. In these cases, what vital-differentials are being removed? It is absolutely the opposite: vital-differentials spring up, but they are positive. And on top of that, the picture of physiological manifestations of joy, in comparison with the calm state of the organism, provides still more evidence that vital-differentials are not being eliminated – that the ideal equilibrium is not being approached. The expansion of the small blood vessels and capillaries in the brain – the basic symptom of pleasant emotions – provides obvious evidence of an increase of assimilation in the central system, and the subsequent growth and also the expenditure of energy both appear only as a derivative manifestation in the form of the elevation of voluntary innervation (movements that express joy).

From the outside, a state of manic excitement very much resembles the external manifestations of the emotion of joy. Avenarius himself, as we have seen, pointed out manic excitement as an example of the negative value of the vital-differential which is involved in the preponderance of 'nourishment'. It is strange – and Avenarius did not make note of this – that this example directly undermines the theory of the *Affectional* that he embraces. After all, the general state of the patient, especially at the beginning of the disease when congestion of the brain and a positive vital-differential has only just appeared, *is pleasant*. According to Avenarius it ought to seem unpleasant.

It is particularly difficult, from the point of view of Avenarius's theory, to understand the action of narcotic poisons on the psychical system. The first stage of this action is characterised by a pleasant stimulation. Does this mean that when morphine or alcohol, for example, poisons the nervous system that it brings it to the ideal equilibrium of assimilation and disassimilation? But if this is the case, one would have to assume that such poisons have two contradictory physiological actions: a relative increase in assimilation when disassimilation preponderates and a decrease of assimilation when disassimilation preponderates. This is more than a far-fetched interpretation of the facts. It is more probable that the matter boils down simply to a temporary elevation of the energy of the system (needless to say *only* temporary).

There can be no doubt that a negative emotion must have a negative vital-differential at its basis. Sadness, for example, in its physiological manifestations, unarguably indicates insufficient assimilation: the basic trait of that emotion consists in the constriction of small arteries and capillaries with the consequent amplification of innervational expenditures in the vasomotor system and with the decrease of the surface area of tissues for nourishment. The exhausting action of sadness on the nervous system also proceeds from this. Should one now propose that the emotion of sadness arises in the presence of a general preponderance of assimilation? In such a case, the beginning of the emotion, as long as it only removes this inequality and brings the system to equilibrium, must have a *pleasant* colouration. Reality, of course, does not produce such a psychophysiological absurdity.

It is easy to see that all the difficulties we have pointed out do not exist for the point of view that I am taking: the facts fit entirely within the confines of my approach. Therefore, if Avenarius considered his views on the vital significance of the vital-differential – and consequently also on the nature of the *Affectional* – to be the '*wissenschaftliches Gemeingut*' (the general scientific consensus), then he erred. It would be more accurate to characterise this not as a general consensus but as an extremely widespread preconception among physiologists, such as are often held in science.[20] This preconception can be eliminated by adopting the most simple and natural point of view – the point of view that Spinoza[21] already clearly formulated in his *Ethics* (of course, in terms

---

20   Most of the material aggregated in *Kritik der reinen Erfahrung* relates to negative vital-differentials, which have exactly the biological significance as Avenarius ascribes to vital-differentials in general. It is therefore understandable that contradictions in his descriptions turn out to be far fewer that one might expect in light of the mistaken starting point of his investigation.

     I note that I am dealing far from exhaustively with Avenarius's views on the question of the sensory colouration of experiences; I deal with them only from the one angle that is most important for my task.

21   Spinoza was a naturalist in philosophy and psychology, as were Avenarius and Bogdanov. In Part III of the *Ethics*, Spinoza treated humans as part of the natural world and considered the human mind to follow the laws of nature. An 'affect' (*affectus*, often translated

of 'power' and not energy) and which can, to a significant degree, be associated with Meynert's point of view.[22] This point of view can be concisely expressed thus:

*The Affectional sign of experiences corresponds to the algebraic sign of the vital-differentials.*

Experiences are magnitudes in the full meaning of the word. They possess not only a 'sign' (of the *Affectional* – positive or negative), but they also have what corresponds to the algebraic concept of absolute magnitude, to be precise, *intensity*. It is true that the accurate measurement of their intensity presents great difficulties, but this does not change the significance of their measurability in principle. Vital-differentials are also magnitudes; they are measurable in terms of *energetics*. Assuming that there is a constant connection between experiences and vital-differentials, we arrive, consequently, at the task of explaining the connection of two series of magnitudes – the series of the intensities of experiences and the series of the energetical levels of vital-differentials. Because of the lack of accurate means of measurement, experience provides only approximate and very imprecise correlations. As we move to a more accurate formulation, it is necessary beforehand to keep the necessarily hypothetical nature of these correlations in mind – with a greater or lesser degree of probability and reliability, of course.

From the data of psychophysiology, it undoubtedly follows that, generally speaking, the greater the intensity of experiences the greater the vital-differentials and vice versa, but this still does not provide the precise formula of the interrelationship between them. What remains unknown is whether certain magnitudes grow proportionally with others or grow slower than others or grow in some variable relationship – in short, whether the growth of some occurs along with the growth of others precisely according to some law. The first and most natural conjecture is the idea that experiences and vital-differentials are *proportional* to one another. Since we cannot conceive of any mediating links between them, then the idea automatically arises that there is a most immediate and direct connection, a mutually proportional change of the two magnitudes.

---

as 'emotion') is the change produced in the human body or mind by interacting with another body that increases or diminishes the body's active power. Spinoza conceived of three fundamental affects – desire, pleasure, and pain – in a variety of permutations [trans.].

22  Theodor Hermann Meynert (1833–92) was a German-Austrian neuropathologist and anatomist. He theorised that ideas and memories were attached to specific cells in the brain [trans.].

But we can adopt this position only as long as there are no facts in our experience which would directly contradict it, and, moreover, psychophysics *apparently* provides such facts, and it is apparently easy to interpret the Weber-Fechner[23] law in such a way.

The Weber-Fechner law of psychophysics states *that sensation increases in proportion to the logarithm of the stimulation* – in other words, that an external influence on the peripheral apparatus of the nervous system causes an experience in psychical experience that is *not proportional* to the influence itself but is proportional only to the logarithm of the influence (on some specified basis). In a simpler form, this correlation is expressed in this way: when a stimulus increases in a geometrical progression, sensation grows in an arithmetical progression. For example, if the series of stimuli presents the magnitudes 1, 2, 4, 16, 32 ..., then the series of sensations is expressed in the corresponding magnitudes 0, 1, 2, 3, 4, 5 ... This is the approximate expression of this law, which also has a very approximate nature.

The Weber-Fechner law easily leads to a dualist conception of experience and cognition. It would seem to indicate that the regularity in psychical experience is *fundamentally* different from the regularity in objective, 'physical' experience; the geometrical relationships of one realm correspond to arithmetical relationships of the other. But such conclusions are, in essence, very hasty and superficial.

A stimulus is not situated in an *immediate* connection with a sensation. What is connected with a sensation is a *vital-differential* that is elicited by the transmission of the stimulus through the neural conductors of the central system. And are there sufficient grounds for thinking that the vital-differential is proportional to the stimulus that causes it? The grounds for such an idea are shaky to say the least.

The transmission of external influences into a living organism does not have a crudely mechanical character at all; it is an extremely complex series of physico-chemical processes, and these processes do not produce changes of the central organ that stand in *direct* and *simple* correlation – either qualitatively or quantitatively – with changes of the peripheral apparatus. On the contrary, from the point of view of the biological struggle for the vital stability of the system, it is to its advantage that powerful influences of the environment are transmitted in a weaker form – otherwise they might shock the system and very quickly damage it. For the organism, consequently, the arrangement

---

23 Ernst Heinrich Weber (1795–1878) was a German physician and one of the founders of experimental psychology; Gustav Theodor Fechner (1801–87) was a student of Weber and the founder of psychophysics [trans.].

whereby vital-differentials increase more slowly than their external stimuli – in a logarithmic relationship, for example – is vitally expedient.

From another perspective, the logarithmic function is extremely widespread in the sphere of *physical* and *chemical* processes. It is present in all those cases where a phenomenon occurs in such a way that the speed of the change that expresses its magnitude is proportional to the magnitude itself. Such, for example, is the formula that is applied to 'physical' and 'chemical' reactions of dissolution where the speed of the reaction diminishes with the decrease of the quantity of the substance that has not yet dissolved or the formula that is applied to the cooling of a body in an environment with a constant temperature where the speed of the cooling diminishes as the difference between the temperature of the body and its environment diminishes, and so on. In all such cases the interval of time between two specific phases of a process turns out to be proportional to the logarithm of the magnitude that expresses the geometrical relationship of these phases.[24] And, in the problem that we are concerned with, it is important to figure out whether there are any indications that the logarithmic relationship reflects a correlation between different *physiological* processes and not directly between physiological and *psychical* processes.

It is easy to see that there are serious grounds for such an idea. First, let us look closely at the sum total of the experimental data that is abstracted in the Weber-Fechner law.

The researchers' experiments were set up in the following way. A certain magnitude of stimulus is applied to a specific sensory surface. For example, a given limited area of skin is subjected to the pressure of a plate on which a weight of a given size is placed. In so doing, the person on whom the experiment is being carried out feels, of course, a certain specific sensation. Then the force of the stimulus (the magnitude of the weight, in this example) is increased to such a degree that the change in the magnitude of the acting force (the external pressure, that is to say) would be sensible (but only just barely sensible) to the subject of the experiment. A large number of experiments such as this are carried out with various magnitudes of stimulus in relation to various organs of external sensation. For more or less ordinary stimuli of average force, it is universally observed that the minimal difference in sensations that is accessible to consciousness is obtained when the stimulus increases by a specific fraction of its magnitude, which is approximately the same for every given organ. For example, for touch, the sense of temperature, and also hearing,

---

24  See, for example, the chapters on 'Exponential function' and 'Verlauf der unvolständigen Reactionen', etc. in Nernst and Schönflies, *Einfürung in die mathematische Behandlung der Naturwissenschaften*.

the minimal noticeable difference in sensation is obtained when the stimulus increases by 1/3. For muscular sensation the minimal noticeable difference is 1/17, and for sight it is 1/100. (All these are approximate, since experiments, obviously, cannot be particularly exact.) If one considers the minimum of sensation that is registered by the consciousness as *unit* of sensation and if one expresses the connection that is found between the series of stimuli and the series of sensations in algebraic terms, then precisely the Weber-Fechner law is obtained.

This is what happens, as we have said, with more or less ordinary stimuli of average force. For the weakest and the strongest stimuli, the formulation of the law turns out to be not at all precise. The denominator of the progression changes with each step – that is, it increases in both directions – so that to obtain a minimal difference in sensations a stimulus must grow stronger than according to the formula. In the end, below a certain boundary a stimulus is completely unable to cause a sensation, and above another boundary a sensation, having attained the maximum, ceases to grow noticeably for consciousness.

Just because this picture does not sustain a correlation between the physical and the psychical with sufficient completeness and rigour, it does not support the idea that the physical and psychical worlds have different types of regularity. Rather, this picture leads to the idea that the central apparatus possesses only limited sensitivity to stimuli transmitted by nerves. The central apparatus is too crude to be able to react to the very weakest stimuli, and it evidently possesses only one threshold reaction for the strongest stimuli that exhausts its reserve of specific energy of a given kind. For the remaining stimuli, there are sufficient inner resistances so that the energy of a stimulus is impeded or dissipated to the same degree as the magnitude of this energy. This disposes of any need to assume indirect and awkwardly fluctuating interrelationships between the 'psychical' and the 'physical'.

From the point of view of contemporary physiology and histology of the nervous system, it is possible to provide a purely energetical picture of the correlation between external stimuli and the vital-differentials of the central organ that can accommodate not only the Weber-Fechner law but also all principal and secondary deviations from it. We stipulated earlier that, for the sake of simplicity and clarity in this article, one must severely schematise complex histological and physiological relationships, but a competent reader can easily supplement what is missing.

It is well known that the energy of an external stimulus, converted in the terminal apparatus of a nerve into a 'telegraphic' neural current (that is still insufficiently studied but is devoid of any mysticism), first of all reaches neurons situated in the so called 'lower' – ganglionic, spinal, subcortical – centres. The neurons are connected, first, with contiguous neurons by means of the adjoining ramuli of their dendrites (bifurcated protoplasmic processes), second, with neurons of higher cortical centres with the aid, yet again, of 'telegraphic' fibres of the projective system (Meynert's), whereby this connection in some cases is direct and in other cases indirect (by means of still other centres). According to contemporary views, the main part of neurons – the neural cell – are distinctive accumulators of built-up neural energy, which, arriving along conductors from outside, can discharge and be released like the discharge of the chemical energy of gunpowder. We now make one minimal and, by now most probable, a priori assumption. We assume that the vital-differential in a cell of the higher centres ('centres of consciousness') is caused precisely by the transmission of the discharging energy of a spinal or subcortical cell, but the projective conductors between the higher and lower centres are not adapted to the transmission of discharging energy (the energy of an external stimulus) so that this latter is passed on only by contiguous neurons. And we now have almost all that is needed to explain this mysterious law.

In reality, although we do not know the specific form in which the energy of an external stimulus is transmitted from neuron to neuron by contiguity, it is still unquestionable that this is kinetic energy and that its dissipation and absorption – in general, its expenditure – must occur in the conductor-dendrites. We naturally take the law of dissipation and absorption of this energy to be the same as that of the most typical forms of kinetic energy: loss is proportional to time and to the relative intensity of the energy. That is the way it is, for example, for the dissipation of temperature (when there is not too great a difference between a body and its environment), for the absorption of light in a not fully transparent environment, and so on.[25] It then turns out that *the number of neurons that are excited by a stimulus approximately corresponds to the logarithm of the force of the stimulus.* This is readily seen in randomly chosen numerical examples.

In order to exhaust the intrinsic potential energy of a neuron, a certain sum of energy transmitted from the periphery that corresponds to the specific magnitude of stimulus is necessary. Let us take the magnitude of this stimulus to be 1. Then let 1/2 the transmitted energy be lost in transmission along each dendrite. Thus, for one neuron to receive stimulation from the periphery, a stimulus of 1 is sufficient, but for two neurons to be stimulated, a stimulus of not 2 but 3 is necessary. One unit of energy is expended on the first neuron, but only one

---

25   The principle of entropy, as well as the general character of physiological processes, permits us to think that the dissipation of energy in neural conductors occurs exclusively or mainly in the way that heat does.

of the remaining 2 units arrives at the second contiguous neuron (the remaining unit is dissipated on the way). This unit of arriving energy stimulates the second neuron, but nothing or almost nothing reaches the third contiguous neuron. For the stimulation of three neurons a stimulus of 7 is necessary. (In the first neuron, one is expended in the discharge of its potential energy, 3 of the remaining 6 make it to the second, and, of them, one is again spent in the exhaustion of the neuron, and nothing further happens). Four neurons can only be affected by a stimulus of 15, five by a stimulus of 31, and so on. Two series result.

The energy of the stimulus: ... 1, 3, 7, 15, 31, 63, 127, 255 ...

The number of number of contiguous neurons affected: ... 1, 2, 3, 4, 5, 6, 7, 8 ...

We see that the connection of the two series is only minimally different from the 'logarithmic' relationship of the series ... 2, 4, 6, 16, 32 ... and the series ... 1, 2, 3, 4, 5 ... Each of the lower neurons, transmitting its freed energy along a projective fibre to a cortical neuron, causes – by means of this same cortical neuron – a particular vital-differential with a particular starting point in the higher centres. It then turns out that each such particular vital-differential corresponds to a minimal sensation, and thus the direct and full parallelism between vital-differentials and experiences is revealed. The mysterious character of the psychophysical law disappears – along with the dualist interpretation of it.

In my example, I took a completely arbitrary coefficient of the loss of energy in its transmission between contiguous neurons. But it is easy to calculate the real magnitude, once the denominator of the progression of stimuli is discovered by experiment – a number that is revealed by how many times a given stimulus must be multiplied in order to obtain a noticeable difference in sensation. This denominator, as we have pointed out, is different for different 'external feelings' – for the sense of touch, the feeling of temperature, and hearing, it is approximately $1^{1}/_{3}$, for muscular feeling (the innervation of ocular muscles) it is approximately $1^{1}/_{17}$, and for the sensation of light it is approximately $1^{1}/_{100}$. The coefficient of loss in each transmission then turns out to be $1/4$ for the first group of sensations, $1/_{18}$ for the second, and about $1/_{100} - 1/_{101}$ for the third. Such diversity of coefficients must, obviously, depend on the different construction of individual psychical centres, their neurons and conductors.[26]

---

[26] It is very possible that this difference in construction and arrangement of neurons will not be too delicate for the methods of contemporary histology. Then the point of view that I am presenting could serve as the starting point – a 'working hypothesis' – for research.

If we now take the minimal perceptible stimulus as 1, as before, and compile a parallel series of magnitudes of stimulus and sensation – regarding the sense of touch, for example – we obtain the following:

A.  The forces of stimulation: 1 – 2.33 – 4.11 – 6.48 – 9.64 – 13.85 – 19.45 – 26.9 – 36.8 – 50 ...
B.  The number of lower neurons that are activated: 1 – 2 – 3 – 4 – 5 – 6 – 7 – 8 – 9 – 10 ...

(In the numbers of the first series the decimals are rounded off for brevity.)

We now see the extent to which the relationships of these series correspond to the actual relationships of 'stimulation' and 'sensation'.

The correspondence breaks down for the very highest units of the series – for the strongest stimuli. Sensation increases there more slowly than would accord with the formula of the series, and, beyond a certain boundary, it completely ceases to noticeably grow. But this divergence between the pure formula and experience could already have been predicted a priori on the basis of our assumptions. Individual neural centres are of limited size, and there are a limited number of neurons which are accessible to a given form of stimulus. And, besides that, some neurons lie to the side of the usual paths of simulation, and they present greater resistance to the stimulus than do the other neurons. With maximum stimuli, the neurons that are more difficult to activate are, initially brought into the chain reaction following the others and then the reaction increases more slowly than for average stimuli. But subsequently, if the stimulus increases even more, there are no more free neurons in that particular special centre, and sensation does not noticeably change.

The middle members of the series also present divergences between the formula and experience, but those divergences are insignificant and indeterminate – now in one direction, now in the other. They are naturally explained, first, by the non-identical structure of separate neurons – differences in their length and in the conductivity of the paths between them, and, second, simply by inaccuracies in experimentation, which, in this field, is still not very precise.

Finally, the lowest terms of the series, the first two and maybe three, must be acknowledged as deviating quite markedly from the data of experience. In a series of calculated stimuli, the first, minimal stimulus must be bigger than the second in order to obtain a noticeable difference in sensation; it actually must be 1½ times greater or a little more. How can this be explained? The question is answered very simply if it is assumed that the terminal perceptive structures of nerve fibres possess a certain constant charge of energy (as has been established with complete certainty in a number of cases) that can resist external stimulation. Thus, for example, it has been definitely ascertained that the retina of the eye possesses a weak 'intrinsic light'. A certain part of the energy of a stimulus can be spent in neutralising the charge of the terminal structures. The magnitude of this unnecessary expense of energy must be added to all the members of our first series in order to obtain the actual energy of a stimulus sufficient for the minimal increment of sensations. If this peripheral loss of energy is 1, then the relationship of the two series presents itself in the following form: A = 2 – 3.33 – 5.11 – 7.48 – 10.65 ... and B = 1 – 2 – 3 – 4 – 5 ... and this accords fully and sufficiently with the data of experience.[27]

Even though, as has been pointed out, it was necessary to severely schematise the physiological and histological relationships of the nervous system to facilitate this presentation, nevertheless, a reader who is familiar with the subject and who makes all the appropriate additions can easily see that they do not change the conclusion in the least. And the essence of the conclusion is this: based on the data of psychophysics, one can with the greatest justification assume that *sensations are proportional to those vital-differentials with which they are directly connected.*

Once this is acknowledged, all reasons for asserting that there is, in general, a complex, dualist connection between vital-differentials and the experiences that correspond to them disappear. It is necessary to recognise that in terms of quantitative assessment *the most straightforward correlation of direct proportionality* exists between the two.[28]

## 3  The Monist Conception of Life

I

The conclusions that I have drawn regarding the quantitative interconnectedness between vital-differentials and experiences seem to be very important for psychoenergetics, but important precisely in the sense that they show *how* psychoenergetics *is to be understood* and *how it is to be used* in research, but

---

[27] This full agreement of the formula with experience is also obtained in cases in which the terminal structure of the sensory nerve is assumed to be an altered neuron, only one that does not have an independent connection with the higher centres. It is not unreasonable to assume that such a neuron is a peripheral, sensory cell with its axon.

[28] Several years ago, I presented the psychophysical formulations regarding the Weber-Fechner law that are presented here in a popular and comparatively cursory form (*Osnovnye elementy istoricheskogo vzgliada na prirodu*, pp. 245–9).

not in the sense that these conclusions prove that psychoenergetics is a law of nature or is the 'truth'. It is possible and appropriate *to accept* psychoenergetics – to acknowledge the validity of the application of the energetical method to 'psychical phenomena' – completely independently of our conclusions, i.e. even if one considers these conclusions to be groundless and wrong. To accept psychoenergetics in principle it is sufficient only to acknowledge a *constant connection* between physiological processes and experiences – any connection as long as it is completely specific and has one meaning for each given case. In Chapter 1, 'The Ideal of Cognition', I showed that, from the point of view of energetics, provided such a correlation exists, a physiological phenomenon and the psychical phenomenon that is connected with it present *the same* magnitude, the same energetical total; they are only perceived by different means. This is similar to how the human body as it is 'seen' (a visual complex) and as it is 'felt' (a tactile complex) are also the same in energetical terms and differ only according to the means of perception. In general, mathematical proportionality between the combinations of the elements of the psychical and physiological series is not necessary in order to acknowledge them to be one body, just as no such proportionality between visual and tactile combinations is required.[29]

But I am not limited to an overall recognition of the energetical nature of psychical experience. In addition to that, I found a direct proportionality between the energetical magnitude of vital-differentials and the magnitude of the intensity of experiences, while the sign of both of them also turns out to be relatively the same.[30] So this has established the definitive form for the energetics of experiences. It is a form which is very broad and very general

---

29  And that is why W. Ostwald, for example, acknowledged the energetical nature of 'consciousness', even though he did not see a qualitative proportionality between the energetics of the nervous system and the magnitudes of experiences that I have established. For him the relationship between these two realms was quite complex, and it cannot be said that he formulated it very clearly (see the chapter on consciousness in his *Natural Philosophy*).

The usual, old objection to the energetical nature of consciousness is that to accept it would mean to contradict the law of the conservation of energy. In being added to the energy of physical processes, psychical energy would change its total and that total – in accord with the principle of the indestructibility of 'mechanical' energy – is unchangeable (see A. Lange, A. Riehl, and others). This objection comes from a *mechanical* understanding of energy and does not have any significance for the *methodological* understanding that I (following R. Mayer, Mach, Ostwald, and others) have adopted. This is why I consider it unnecessary to dwell on this objection.

30  'Relatively' because it depends on considering pleasure to be a positive magnitude and pain to be a negative magnitude in this analysis and not the other way around.

and which must have a definite scientific and philosophical significance. What exactly *does* this significance consist in?

In regard to the possible scientific significance of my conclusions, no special explanation is required. It is altogether the same as the significance of any generalised formula that concisely summarises the interconnectedness of facts and that thereby directly organises experience. Here, once again, the question can arise whether a given formula is useful while it is hypothetical and while it has not been decisively proven by the facts – whether it is useful as the starting point for further investigation as a 'working hypothesis' or whether its significance might be only very ephemeral. But it is easy to see that my formula, having to do with fundamental, measurable relationships (the energy of neural processes, the intensity of experiences) provides a definite guiding thread (even if only provisional) and opens the widest expanse for attempts at experimental verification and detailed investigation.

The question of the philosophical significance of the formula is of a different sort. It depends entirely on the extent to which the formula is in harmony with all the other conclusions of cognition and on the extent to which it organically merges with them as identical or homogenous – in a word, to the degree to which it manifests that *universal tendency to monism* which comprises the philosophical soul of cognition. We must apply this criterion to our psychoenergetical conclusions.

II

First and foremost, it is obvious that if there is a direct proportionality between vital-differentials and immediate experiences then it is impossible to conceive of vital-differentials without corresponding experiences or, the other way around, of experiences without vital-differentials. A magnitude of zero of one corresponds to a magnitude of zero of the other; the maximum magnitude of the one corresponds to the maximum magnitude of the other. We see that this is again the same conclusion to which the critique of psychical experience led us earlier by a different route – by juxtaposing experiences and utterances. It has, then, already become clear to us that it would be contradictory to limit the realm of experiences connected with a given organism to the sphere of psychical experience of a given individual. We saw that it is necessary to acknowledge a multitude of experiences and groupings of experiences beyond the bounds of psychical experience that are not fundamentally coordinated and therefore are not accessible to immediate observation – just as the psychical experience of other people is inaccessible to such observation. We arrived at the idea that immediate experiences must exist everywhere there are living cells and their vital-differentials – everywhere there is 'physiological' life. Now we are again convinced that this idea is the unavoidable assumption of a conception of life that is free from contradictions.

However, have we not arrived at the philosophical doctrine that says that the physical and the psychical are 'two parallel aspects of one essence which is not knowable in itself', or, in a more positive variation, 'one reality' which is known precisely in its 'two aspects'? This is one of the forms of 'monism' that is still very widespread in our times. But we can by no means come to a halt at this point of view. We cannot do so if only because we consider it not monist but dualist. The uniting of the two 'aspects' and the two methods of cognition of them in the one word 'reality' does not seem to us to be a real unification at all. From our perspective, two methods of cognition can mean only dualist cognition, and two 'parallel aspects' is only a poor metaphor from geometry. This is not a resolution of the question we are dealing with, but at best it only poses the question. And it is not particularly successful since, when experience is analysed, it turns out that there are not two 'aspects' but more.

Let us pose the following question: what is a 'living being' – a 'human being', for example? And let us try to answer this question on the basis of the data of experience, on the one hand, and on the basis of the generalised propositions (of the connection between vital-differentials and experiences) that we have thus far arrived at, on the other.

A 'living being' – a 'person', for example – is, first and foremost, a definite complex of 'immediate experiences'. Some of them are a part of one basic coordination ('psychical experience') and some of them, as we have recognised, are not directly a part of this coordination, but are situated in a certain connection with it (that so far has not been subject to close scrutiny). This is a 'person' in its 'immediate existence', 'a person *an sich* [in itself]', so to speak. But that is not now a person appears in the experience of *someone else*.

For someone else, the 'living essence' of a person presents itself first and foremost as a *perception* in a series of other perceptions, as a specific visual-tactile-acoustic complex in a series of other complexes. This complex appears and disappears and once again manifests itself in the same interconnectedness as other 'perceptions'. Sometimes it is called to mind as a 'conception' in a rather different interconnectedness and with a different colouration. This is the *primary psychical form* of a person in the experience of another person.

A person also presents to himself the same kind of complex (although different in many particulars) to the extent that he 'apprehends' his 'body' through vision, hearing, touch, etc. – in the same way that other people 'apprehend' his 'body'.

Subsequently, in the further development of experience, a 'person' turns out – both for himself and for other people – to be a physical body in a series of other physical bodies. This body is connected with the others and with the entire 'physical world' in general according to an *objective regularity*. Under specific conditions, this body appears and exists for a certain time, it is subject to a specific, objectively conditioned cycle of changes, and it finally completes this cycle by being obliterated. It is also a complex of visual, tactile, and other elements that is very similar to the two previous phases (as a perception by other people and as apprehended by himself) and is completely 'parallel' to them (in the expression of Mach), but it is a complex that stands out in a different interconnectedness of experience: a person as an objective physiological process.

Finally, due to the fact that people mutually 'understand' one another in their 'utterances', a person becomes a coordination of immediate experiences for other people as well through a 'psychical process'. Such a conception, united together with the previous one makes up the usual dualist form of person which is completed by means of 'introjection', that is, experiences are inserted into the physiological organism. The result is the most widespread, commonplace, synthetic conception of a 'person'. A person then appears to himself and to other people as the combination of a 'body' and a 'soul' that is located inside the body – a combination that is not particularly harmonious, to say the least.

Such is the series of the different conceptions of a 'person' that cognition deals with. The task arises of bringing all these concepts together into a cognitive unity while remaining entirely on the ground of experience. In other words, it is necessary to reduce their mutual interconnectedness to simple, constant, and universal relationships of experience. This is how the question must be posed from the perspective of empiriomonism.

The starting point of investigation, naturally, is to take the first of the stated concepts – a 'person' as a complex of immediate experiences or, speaking more generally, 'life' in its immediate realisation. Each individual experience is now a more or less complex grouping of elements of experience into which that individual experience can be broken down; the vital process is the organised unity of a large number of such groupings mutually connected in coordinations that are sometimes more solid and stable and sometimes less so. The development of life, in this understanding of it, is conceived of as a progressive organisation of experiences in an ever wider and more harmonious unity.

In its various stages, this organising process forms vital complexes of the most varied types of structure, varying according to the number of elements and how harmoniously those elements are united. But for cognition – the monist organisation of experience – *fundamental* or *essential* differences among all complexes are inconceivable, and relationships among those complexes cannot be fundamentally different from relationships among any complexes of experience in general. Thus vital complexes and complexes of experiences mutually act on each other directly or indirectly, mutually change each other, and are mutually reflected in one another, just like any of the combinations of elements that cognition deals with.

But how, in general, are some complexes of experience 'reflected' in other complexes? Despite all the diversity of these relationships, they are substantially the same for all realms of life – both 'physical' and 'psychical' – and can easily be generalised in one formulation. In regard to the 'physical' world, for example, we know how the form of objects is 'reflected' in the physical-chemical structure of the light-sensitive plate of a camera, how the fluctuation of air pressure is 'reflected' in the movement of the pointer of an aneroid barometer, how changes in the natural environment of a plant or animal organism are 'reflected' in changes of the structures of its tissues and organs, etc. It is exactly the same with 'psychical' complexes. The form that arises in the psyche with a particularly strong Affectional colouration of pleasure or pain is 'reflected' in all other forms that it runs into in the field of consciousness, putting its impress on them, making them vivid, lively, and bright or (the opposite) dim, pale, and dismal. A new idea that arises in consciousness is usually 'reflected' in many particular conceptions that appear in connection with it. Thus, from the moment when a person learns the general conception of the construction and function of living organisms, all his particular conceptions of one or another person, animal, or plant which enter the field of his experience gradually change. The general biological idea is 'reflected' in all these conceptions, making their content richer and more complex because of the new relationships and elements. A new philosophical conception, as it permeates a person's worldview, can be 'reflected' in all the particular combinations of which that worldview is made. For example, the idea of monism substantially transforms the makeup of all forms of consciousness that were previously formed on the basis of dualism, smoothing out sharp edges and creating transitions and connections between groupings that were previously absent.

An endless number of similar illustrations could be cited, but quite enough have been cited in order to produce the following general formulation that must be approximately this: if complex A is directly or indirectly reflected in complex B, then complex A is reproduced in complex B not in its direct form but in the form of a definite series of changes in complex B, changes that are connected with the content and structure of the first complex by a functional correlation.

It is obvious that this formula expresses all cases of *mutual influence* ('interaction') of the complexes of experience. In its various modifications, this formulation corresponds to various historically developed forms of how the 'causality' of phenomena is understood.[31] And this formula is also completely sufficient to express monistically the connection of various 'parallel aspects' of life or, what is the same thing, to 'explain' their parallelism.

The first concept of 'life' – the concept to which our critique of psychical experience brought us, as we have shown – boils down to the following. The vital process, taken in its immediate content ('life *an sich*'), is a complex of experiences united in varying degrees into one whole by an organising interconnectedness. This complex can be directly or indirectly 'reflected' in other, similar complexes, but, in accordance with the universal formulation of the relationships of experience, it is 'reflected' in them *not* as it is in its immediate form but in the form of one or another series of changes of these complexes, in the form of a new grouping of elements that enter those complexes and that complicate their 'inner' relationships. *This new grouping is the 'perception' of a given vital process by another similar process of life* – for example, the perception of a 'person' (as an organism) that emerges in a series of experiences of another person. This 'perception', like any 'reflection' in general, is not at all a direct copy of what is 'reflected' but is connected with it in a definite – but different in different cases – *functional* correlation. And, as we know, such a functional correlation between the experiences of one living being and the perception of this being in the experience of another person exists in reality. Any communication between living beings, any mutual 'understanding' between them, is based on this functional correlation.

Now there is one more very important thing. The mutual interaction of 'living beings' is not accomplished directly and immediately: the experiences of one being do not lie in the field of experience of another being. One vital process 'is reflected' in another only indirectly and precisely by means of the 'environment'. But what is the 'environment'?

The concept of 'environment' has meaning only in contrast with what it is that has that 'environment' – in this case, a vital process. If we view a vital process as a complex of immediate experiences, then the 'environment' is everything that is not a part of that complex. But if it is indeed by means of that 'environment' that some vital processes are 'reflected' in others, then the 'environment' must be the sum total of elements that do not enter into the organised complexes of experiences – the sum total of unorganised elements,

---

31   I use the term 'reflection' here exclusively in view of its illustrative value. Using the expression more accurately, we would have to speak about 'the results of the influence of one complex on another', about their functional correlation with the content of the 'influencing' complex. This would be very abstract and very ponderous.

a chaos of elements in the precise meaning of that word. The 'environment' is what presents itself to us in perception and cognition as the 'inorganic world'.

At this point I must remove unnecessary misunderstandings. *In our experience*, the inorganic world is not a chaos of elements but a series of specific groupings in space and time; *in our cognition* the inorganic world is even transformed into a harmonious system, united by the continuous regularity of relationships. But 'in experience' and 'in cognition' means somebody's *experiences*. The terms unity and harmony, continuity and regularity apply precisely to experiences as organised complexes of elements. The inorganic world, taken independently from this organisation, taken '*an sich*', is precisely a chaos of elements, completely or almost completely undifferentiated. This is not metaphysics at all; this is only an expression of the fact that the inorganic world is not life and an expression of the basic idea of monism that the inorganic world is distinguished from living nature not in its material (the same 'elements' as the elements of experience) but by its lack of organisation (to be more accurate, presumably, a *lower* organisation).

If an unorganised 'environment' is the intermediary link in the mutual interaction of vital processes, if it is by means of that 'environment' that complexes of experiences are 'reflected' in one another, then the fact that a given living complex 'is reflected' *in itself* by means of the environment does not present anything new and strange. Complex A, acting on complex B, can by means of B turn out to have an influence on complex C, but also on complex A – that is, on its own self. Thus, by means of the light in the environment the retina of the eye obtains not only a depiction of other objects – someone else's eye, for example – but also, under specific combinations of conditions, it can obtain the depiction of its own eye. In changing the environment in which it lives, a living organism indirectly changes itself, since that changing environment acts, in its turn, upon the organism. From this perspective, it is absolutely understandable that a living being can have an 'external perception' of its own self. It can see, touch, hear itself, etc. That is, it can find in a series of its own experiences some experiences that present an indirect reflection (by means of the 'environment') of this very series of experiences. It is natural, also, that this 'perception' seems to a significant measure to be consistent with the 'perception' of a given vital process of other similarly organised living beings, but the first 'perception' will also partly differ from the second, since it does not have the identical relationships to the 'environment' that constitute the intermediary link between the vital process and the 'perception' of that process. For example, the visual perception of person A is in many ways different for him than for other people around him – person B, person C, etc. But this difference is of the same order as the difference of perception A in the psyche of another person B depending on the distance, the mutual position of the two, the lighting, the place occupied by various objects in the environment, and so on. In a word, the relationship of 'life' and its 'external perception' here is in no way fundamentally distinguishable from the usual relationships between any complex of experience and its 'reflection'.

Finally, there still remains one final conception from the basic phases of an understanding of 'life', and that is the *objective* conception of life – life as an objectively regular process in a series of other processes of the objective, 'physical' world. From the point of view of individual psychology, this stage is entirely inferred from the associations of personal experience. In coordinating its perceptions and psychical images, the psyche elaborates a spatio-temporal order for them. By tightly uniting perceptions and psychical images that are mutually consistent in their elements, structure, and relationship with other complexes into this system, the psyche forms from them the 'bodies' and 'processes' of the objective world.

Thus, from this point of view, the objectively existing 'body' of a person appears in the experience of that body by each and every other person as the result of simple individual coordination (in the spatio-temporal order) of various 'perceptions' of that 'body' in a given psyche. But such an understanding of the matter seems to us to be extremely inadequate.

We will not present our views on this question in detail here, since we did this in Chapter 1, 'The Ideal of Cognition'. We will limit ourselves to concisely summarising our point of view, which is as follows. The 'physical' world and all the 'bodies' in it are characterised by 'objectivity', i.e. social validity. By accepting 'objective' experience with its interconnectedness and regularity, a person thereby assumes that this experience – the interconnectedness and regularity – exists not only for himself at a given point in time, but that it also has the same cognitive meaning for any cognising being and at any given point in time. Such a relationship to experience cannot take shape exclusively on the ground of individual experience; it is the result of the mutual understanding of living beings and their utterances, and the mutual agreement – mutual harmonisation – of 'uttered' experiences; in a word, such a relationship to experience emerges through the collective organisation of experience.

This can be shown even more easily and clearly in the universal forms of 'objectivity' of experience, such as 'pure' or 'arithmetic' time and 'pure' or 'geometric' space and causality. Arithmetical time and geometric space are characterised by their complete *uniformity, continuity, and limitlessness*; there is no basis for all these basic traits in individual experience, in which only 'physiological' time and 'physiological' space – heterogeneous in their particulars, lacking continuity, and finite in magnitude – is produced. In exactly the same way, there is no basis in individual experience for universal objective relationships of causality – only *habitual relationships of the consecutiveness of phenomena* (relationships of a private nature) – can take shape.

Thus, forms of the 'objectivity' of experience are forms of the social coordination of experience, and 'objective experience', in general, is socially-organised experience.[32] All 'objectively existing' bodies and processes are the product of the social agreement of perceptions and psychical images that are 'felt' by separate people and 'expressed' by utterances. The same is also true of the physiological processes that are 'living bodies' – what is called the 'physiological' aspect of life. As you can see, this is not any particular 'aspect' of the vital process, but only a special type of grouping of the same material which is present in the previous two phases of the understanding of life (life in its 'external perceptions' of various living beings and, of course, in the 'psychical images' that correspond to those perceptions). This is the result of the collective harmonisation of those countless 'reflections' that are engendered by some living complexes in other living complexes.

Due to this harmonisation, an 'objective' conception of life (as a physiological process) is attained which begins to increasingly correspond to its actual *immediate* content. Psychoenergetics first of all creates a real *cognitive parallelism* between life as a complex of experiences and the reflection of life in socially-organised experience[33] – at the same time, the relationship between life in its immediate content and life that is objectified for cognition turns out to be fundamentally the same as the relationship between absolutely any complex of experience and the reflection of that complex in another complex. No room remains here for any kind of dualism. This is the point of view of *empiriomonism*.

From this point of view, it cannot be clearer and more understandable how all people realise both their own immediate psychical experience and also the psychical experience of other people and of other living beings, in general. The experience of other people, as we know, is constructed on the basis of utterances. In reproducing the 'consciousness' of other people, the psyche functions like a kind of phonograph. Our perceptions of the utterances of other people

---

32  Although the content of 'experience' in each case is still only individual, it is socially-organised or objective experience if it fully takes shape in the form of 'objectivity' of experience, in the form of social agreement. See Chapter 1.

33  There is no need to dwell on the usual (always essentially dualist) 'psychophysical' conceptions of life (life as the sum total of the series of psychical experience and the series of physiological processes that are parallel or not parallel to it). This is a historically necessary and transitory combination.

represent a distinctive 'reflection' of their experiences, a reflection that is highly 'un-similar' but that is functionally dependent on 'the reflected' – exactly the same as the groove on the cylinder of a phonograph is 'un-similar' to the melody that is reproduced in it but is functionally dependent on the structure of that melody. And when the phonograph is running, this groove serves as the starting point for the 'reproduction' of the melody, which is, as a matter of fact, *the second reflection* of the melody and which is more similar to it than the first reflection. In the same way, the utterances of someone else, under the associational activity of consciousness, serves as the starting point for 'reproducing' the experiences of someone else, i.e. a second reflection of them that is more similar to them than the first reflection. In our cognition, our psychical experience of someone else is the *reflection of the reflection* of the immediate experiences of other beings.

We have shown above that an orderly and harmonious conception of experience is possible only if we assume an 'associative' organisation of experiences for each physiological organisation of life, that is, if we assume the full parallelism of life in its 'objective' and 'subjective' manifestations. In other words, every 'physiological' process must be considered as a disclosure – an 'utterance' – of associative, immediate complexes (we would call them 'psychical' complexes, if it were not for the fact that this term is usually coupled with the conception of a certain complexity of experiences).

Does it not follow that this principle should be extended beyond living nature to all 'dead', inorganic nature as well? For consistent monist thinking this is unavoidable, but only as a *cognitive tendency*. This is not yet something that we can realise in concrete terms. A phonograph can only accurately reproduce a melody when its needle is activated in an environment that is sufficiently similar to that in which the melody was captured (i.e. in the atmosphere). If you put the phonograph in water or in the vacuum of outer space, the reproduction of melodies recorded by a phonograph cannot possibly be achieved in their previous form. The same is true of the 'phonograph-like' activity of the psyche. The less our psyche accurately reconstitutes the experience of another being, the less akin it is with the psyche of that being. The dissimilarity of the psychical environment of experiences is an obstacle to the 'understanding' of the utterances of other people. We are able to reproduce the various experiences of the higher animals in our psyche to a certain degree, and this is cognitively useful since it helps us to predict their actions. But in regard to the lower animals it is comparatively rare for us to successfully know what is going on in their psyches; we usually do not 'understand' their utterances to the extent that we can predict anything on this basis. Hence, in this case it is often necessary to substitute the 'physiological' in place of the 'psychical' rather than the other way around.

In regard to plants, the very idea of 'utterances' becomes almost useless, and it is even more useless in regard to the inorganic world. Associative complexes are complexes that are *organised* in a definite form; how can we substitute them for nonorganic phenomena, in which we do not find any organisation altogether? The chaos of elements – this is the kind of form in which we must conceive of the non-organic world 'in itself'.

A primitive animist and a contemporary poet do not go beyond the bounds of legitimate methods of cognitive creativity in the least when they 'animate' all of nature. But scientific cognition takes from the countless applications of these methods only what can serve to the broadening of human 'foresight' – i.e. in the final analysis, to the growth of human power over nature.

III

The ultimately simple and understandable conception of life that we have adopted must inevitably meet a number of objections, which we also must take into account, as far as possible, beforehand. We are not obliged, of course, to pay attention to those countless perplexities and contradictions which will issue from the usual dualist conceptions or from metaphysical sources. We ignore the first because our point is precisely to remove any dualism and the second because our task is not to go beyond the boundaries of the harmonisation of possible experience and, consequently, not to deal with any kind of meta-empiricism. But there are objections that will stand entirely on empirical grounds, and it is easy to anticipate which of them must present themselves as the most obvious and natural.

First and foremost, it might appear strange how great the discrepancy is between 'the reflection and the reflected' in our conceptions. If a 'perception' of living being A in the consciousness of another being B is the reflection of the entire complex of experiences A in complex B, then this would seem to be an insignificant and dissimilar reflection. On the one hand, there is the colossal complex of experiences that encompass the whole world of an individual's experience, and on the other hand, there is the insignificant visual-tactile-acoustic combination of elements. What do they have in common? It is easy to answer this. What is common here is what is always in common between 'the reflection' and 'the reflected' (to the extent that we know the interconnectedness of experience). This commonality is the functional correlation of the 'reflection' with the 'reflected'. This correlation is sufficiently definite and complete so that being B, on the basis of his perception A, can 'understand' A. That is, B can imagine to himself A's immediate experiences and their changes – often even very insignificant changes – with rough certainty. We cannot expect any other 'similarity'. What kind of 'similarity' is there between a change in weather and the movement of a column of mercury in a barometer or thermometer? And yet, for a meteorologist these are quite clear 'reflections'. And besides, in this case we might more readily expect a certain immediate similarity between what is reflected and the reflection of it, because it has to do with the influence of one *unorganised* complex of elements – the atmosphere – on another, also *unorganised*, complex – the column of mercury. Unorganised complexes must 'reflect' one another with the least resistance, so to speak. Organised complexes, on the contrary – i.e. complexes that are harmonious, stable, and that maintain themselves under various influences – must 'reflect' these influences in the least 'changed' form. A complex organisation of life is not at all a simple mirror of its environment.

But, the reader says, too little is provided here for even a purely functional correlation. Let us take a person who lives an extremely intense life. Over a very short period of time his psyche undergoes whole revolutions, and all the activity of his consciousness changes its direction and character. Yet, the 'perception' of this person – i.e. the reflection of his experiences in the psyche of someone else – remains approximately the same as before. Why does it not change as radically as what it is the 'reflection' of?

But such an argument is based on a misunderstanding. The organised complex of experiences that makes up a given 'being' is not at all subjected *in its whole* to the kinds of 'revolutions' that take place in the sphere of that being's 'consciousness'. It is not *ever* subjected to them, except perhaps in the case of disorganisation, i.e. death. It has already become sufficiently clear that the real sum of experiences that corresponds to a given physiological organism is far broader than what is present in the field of consciousness at a given moment. Even the realm of one's own 'psychical experience' (considered in the entire totality of experiences that are preserved in the sphere of 'memory' and that are revived in the consciousness under certain circumstances) is almost infinitely larger than any given field of consciousness. In the field of consciousness there appear, for the most part, current vitally important changes in the system of psychological experience. No matter how rapidly and intensely the work of consciousness is accomplished, it cannot introduce big turnabouts in the vast realm of experience itself (the realm of the past) and in the main groupings of experience (the general forms of coordination that are produced by this past experience). In addition, the whole sphere of psychical experience makes up only part – and, one may surmise, an insignificant part – of that sum of experiences that in reality corresponds to a given 'organism'. Psychical experience is only the main coordination of these experiences, but besides that coordination, as we have seen, there are still a multitude of collateral experiences that are connected with that main coordination but that are at the same time narrower and less organised coordinations that are relatively independent. In my view, any living cell corresponds to a certain complex of experiences (no matter how insignificant) and only a trifling number of these countless complexes enter the sphere of immediate psychical experience. A living being, such as a person, is a whole world of experiences, and every time a 'revolution' occurs in his consciousness it transforms only a trifling part of that world. Therefore there is nothing strange in the fact that an 'external perception', which appears as a 'reflection' of this world in another similar world, is only insignificantly changed by apparent revolutions of the psyche.[34] And, all the same, that perception *is* changed so that in a majority of cases it 'expresses' such revolutions, otherwise those revolutions could not be noticed and understood by other living beings by means of utterances.

But the simple 'perception' of one living being in the experience of another (or in its own self) is only the lowest phase of the 'reflection' of a living complex in other such complexes (or in its own self). At further stages of development, 'bodies' and 'processes' are made up of these 'perceptions'. This occurs through the accumulation of individual experience, on the one hand, and through social communication, on the other. In personal experience similar perceptions and psychical images are united in stable complexes, and the mutual transmission of experiences by the exchange of individual utterances leads to the fact that similar complexes, put together in the experience of various individuals and being mutually supplemented and harmonised, attain the character of social validity or objectivity and become complexes of socially-organised experience. This is how 'physical bodies' and 'processes' are obtained. 'Living organisms' – objective physiological coordinations – also appear in the series of physical bodies and processes. They are a reflection of individual life in socially-organised experience, a reflection that is immeasurably more complex and complete than the separate 'perception' of a living organism in the experience of another.

Endlessly expanding collective experience, assuming the form of scientific experience in the life of cultured humanity, introduces more and more traits into the concept of the physiological process and enriches the conception of

---

34  Thus, from my point of view, a dual consciousness in one 'physiological organism' is completely conceivable. It would signify only a partial disorganisation in the sphere of psychical experience, i.e. yet again, in one particular realm of a given complex of experiences – a 'living being'.

the organism with more and more elements. As a result, the 'reflection' begins to correspond ever more accurately to 'the reflected'; the functional connection of reflection and reflected becomes ever more direct and clear. In being presented with various 'immediate experiences', people consciously seek a physiological process that directly corresponds to them, and vice versa. In this process, all the various degrees and forms of organisation of immediate experiences are objectively reflected in various degrees and forms of physiological organisation. This is the *psychophysiological parallelism of life*, but in a strictly monist – and not a dualist – sense. It is a parallelism not of two attributes of one substance or of two sides of one reality, but rather the parallelism of the reflected and its reflection – the exact same thing as is observable in the mutual interaction of all possible complexes of experience when some complexes are 'reflected' in others and vice versa.

These are the basic traits of the path taken in adopting this point of view. Following the majority of contemporary psychologists, we acknowledge the psychophysiological parallelism of life – or, speaking more generally, the functional correlation between physiological life and immediate experiences – as a fact. We believe it is possible to seek an explanation of this connection only in the real correlations of experience without attempting to go beyond its boundaries. This parallelism – or unequivocal functional correlation in experience – stands out as a constant relationship precisely where the question is of a 'reflection' of one complex in another, or, expressing it more precisely and clearly, of the result of the effect of one complex on another. Of course, it is not only 'the reflection and the reflected' that are parallel, but also the two 'reflections' of the same third thing. However, since we do not find in experience any third thing whose 'reflection' could simultaneously be both a physiological process and a flow of immediate experiences, and since we cannot and do not want to go beyond the boundaries of experience, then we must acknowledge that, of the two complexes, one is the 'the reflected' and the other is the 'reflection'. But since the history of psychical development shows that objective experience with its continuous interconnectedness and harmonious regularity is the result of a long development and only gradually crystallises from the flow of immediate experiences, then we must acknowledge that the *objective* physiological process is a 'reflection' of the complex of immediate experiences and not the other way around. The question that further remains is: if the physiological process is a 'reflection' then what, exactly, is it reflected in? The answer we have given conforms to the socially-monist conception of life that we have adopted. Acknowledging the social validity of objective experience behind the expression of the social organisation of experience, we have arrived at the following empiriomonist conclusion: physiological life is the result of the collective harmonisation of the 'external perceptions' of a living organism, in which each perception is the reflection of one complex of experiences in another organism (or in its own self). In other words: *physiological life is the reflection of immediate life in the socially-organised experience of living beings.*

CHAPTER 3

# *Universum* (Empiriomonism of the Separate and the Continuous)

The point of view of empiriomonism regarding life and the world forces us to face a new question, a new mystery. If various coordinations of an associative nature can be 'reflected' in one another – i.e. can cause changes in one another that fit the pattern of the causal relationship – then they must be situated in a certain 'common field' and not be completely 'separate' from one another. As far as dualism is concerned, there is no particular difficulty *on this point*. Dualism assumes that all 'bodies' are located in one continuous, common field – 'physical nature' – and, plainly, that they can 'exert influence' on one another there. A psyche 'exerts influence' on another psyche *by means* of bodies and not directly, and therefore there is no need for an immediate 'common field' for two psyches (although, of course, another 'common field' is necessary for each psyche and the 'body' that corresponds to it). But we take 'physical nature' itself to be a *derivative* of complexes of an immediate nature (among which 'psychical' coordinations are also included), and we take it to be a reflection of such immediate complexes in other coordinations that are analogous to those coordinations, only of a most complex type (i.e. coordinations that are the socially-organised experience of living beings). Thus, it turns out to be impossible to make the 'physical universe' the mediator between separate immediate coordinations – the psyches of person A and person B, for example. Those psyches require another universal field – another system of continuous connections that immediate experience does not provide. How can the consciousness of another person, being unquestionably situated *outside* of my consciousness, cause changes in my consciousness that express correlations of a *continuous* character that accord with the pattern of cause and effect? How do my own 'unconscious experiences' simultaneously appear to be vitally connected with both the main coordination ('consciousness' as part of the same 'psychical system') and with coordinations that are separate from the main coordination ('inaccessible to consciousness')? In general, if cognition strives to establish the *continuity* of everything that is cognised, then how can it acknowledge the *separateness* of different phenomena? How can cognition be reconciled to the fact that various complexes do *not* appear in *one field* and do not flow together in one immediate *pan-complex*?

This question can be expressed as a problem of the 'individual' and the 'universal' – as the demand to embrace the independence of the 'particular' and the unity of the 'general' in one harmonious cognitive conception. Philosophy's fatal question of 'I' and 'not-I' presents itself as only part – only a certain aspect – of this problem, and it will be decided along with it.

Cognition cannot create an accurate picture of experience if it cannot accommodate all the various *discontinuities* in experience. But the picture will not be monist if these discontinuities remain as simple *disruptions of continuity*. The question, consequently, consists in attempting to reduce those discontinuities to the same uniting forms that in general create the cognitive continuity of 'reality', similar to how we reduce the discontinuity between the 'organism' and the 'psyche' to the unifying continuity of the causal relationship. If this cannot be achieved, then we would arrive only at a new form of dualism or, perhaps, to a pluralism of 'continuities divided by discontinuities'. Here is a decisive test for the empiriomonist point of view.

I

It is most convenient to begin the investigation of our problem with the question of the real unity of the psychical system – of the living connection between 'consciousness' and the 'unconscious' within the confines of the psychical system.

By acknowledging the full parallelism of physical processes and immediate experiences and by acknowledging that the former represents a definite 'reflection' of the latter, we obtained a huge methodological advantage for our analysis: the possibility of substituting one 'aspect' of life for the other, as necessary. Some features of vital complexes are easier to trace and systematise from the 'physiological' point of view, and others are easier to trace and systematise from the 'psychical' point of view. It is obvious that the problem of the real unity of a living being is most reasonably considered first in physiological terms, since physiology provides us this unity in the most obvious and most understandable form as the unity of a 'living body'. Relying on all the attainments of physiological analysis makes it much easier to overcome the difficulty of analysing 'immediate experiences'.

Physiologically, a living being presents itself as a continuous, three-dimensional, finite complex of physico-chemical processes. These processes can be understood energetically as the assimilation and expenditure of energy by an organism in one 'place' or another. 'Immediate experiences' correspond to those cases when assimilation and expenditure are not mutually balanced, when a 'vital-differential' springs up. Only those immediate experiences that correspond to vital-differentials of the central nervous system – the most well-developed and the most *coherent* of the physiological systems of the organism – enter the sphere of 'psychical experience'. But not nearly all experiences penetrate into the confines of psychical experience. When 'vital-differentials' percolate in isolation in various corners of the central nervous system and do not merge into the general current of vital-differentials of the unifying, 'higher' centres, then the experiences that correspond to them remain 'outside of consciousness'. Where the interconnectedness of vital-differentials is interrupted, the interconnectedness of immediate experiences is also interrupted.[1]

Thus, a 'general field of consciousness' exists to the extent that vital-differentials of the central organ are mutually connected together in an unbroken series. We obviously do not have any reason to suppose that the situation is different for other extra-conscious coordinations. The following conclusion is obtained: immediate experiences emerge in the same field (i.e. in an immediate interconnectedness) in precisely those cases when physiological vital-differentials are immediately united with one another, but when vital-differentials are physiologically disconnected and do not form a continuous chain in the physiological system, immediate experiences flow into a different fields.

Let us suppose that vital-differentials spring up in two parts of the physiological system, A and C. Both these parts are vitally connected together by means of a complex of cells and tissues B. If B is in a state in which a vital-differential exists, then that vital-differential immediately passes on to vital-differentials A and C, and then the experiences that correspond to all these vital-differentials appear in one coordination, on one field. But if B is in a state of vital equilibrium, so that vital-differentials A and C are disconnected from one another, then immediate experiences that correspond to both vital-differentials, flow into different, mutually separate coordinations and appear in different 'fields of experiences'. For example, one of them is 'conscious' and the other remains 'outside consciousness'.

---

1 The conception apparently held by R. Avenarius that vital-differentials that flow in separate *'Partialsysteme'* [*'partial systems'*] that are united with 'facts of consciousness' (*E-Werte* [*E-values*]) is absolutely unsatisfactory. It is contradicted by all those cases where the *'Partialsystem'* is unquestionably affected by a stimulus and even reacts to it, but the subject is not conscious of it (for example, complex automatic actions while attention is directed in another direction). Of course, *'Partialsysteme'* exist – this is proven by studies of brain localisation – but their special vital-differentials are connected with 'consciousness' only to the extent that these *'Partialsysteme'* are the *starting points of common coordinated* vital-differentials of the higher centres and to the extent that their vital-differentials enter into the continuous current of the vital-differentials of the central nervous system.

The vital assimilation and vital expenditure of energy are *continuous* and *mutually-opposite* processes. In conditions of vital equilibrium both these processes do not cease but only mutually neutralise one another. Considered separately, the process of assimilation is a continuous positive vital-differential, and the process of expenditure is a continuous negative vital-differential. Consequently, a vital equilibrium presents itself as a specific case of the *interference of vital-differentials* – a case of the mutual elimination of opposite vital-differentials.

As we already know, a vital equilibrium corresponds to a 'null' experience – the absence of immediate experiences. If a vital-differential is replaced by an equilibrium, then the experience disappears – it is cut short. Thus, we arrive at the following conclusion, which is very important for our analysis: *discontinuities of experiences correspond to the complete interference of opposing vital-differentials*.[2]

Now we will attempt to explain what implications for the empiriomonist conception of psychical life follow from this position.

II

A vital-differential is not a simply an algebraic magnitude. It is an energetical magnitude of *vital processes*. It possesses a specific 'form', more or less complex, and this form corresponds to a specific type and combination of elements of 'what is immediately experienced'.[3]

Let us suppose that there is a vital-differential +A in certain neural centres, the 'form' and sign ('plus') of which is given to us, i.e. assimilation preponderates over the expenditure of energy. In the sphere of 'immediate experiences', this vital-differential corresponds to a completely specific complex of elements that we will designate as E. A contrary vital-differential is completely conceivable in those very same centres, but one with a form that is completely 'symmetrical' to the first – that is, reproducing the first vital-differential only with the opposite sign. This second vital-differential can be signified as –A, because, when combined with the first one, it must completely interfere with it, producing a vital equilibrium. But, taken separately, it, in turn, corresponds to a

---

2  For convenience of presentation, I earlier arranged with the reader that I would use the term 'interference' in this broader meaning – the mutual elimination of magnitudes that are equal but are mutually opposite in their algebraic sign ('plus' or 'minus'). In physics, as is well known, this term also serves to signify other cases, such as the interference of waves relating to those combinations when one wave, joining with another, amplifies it.
3  See Richard Avenarius, *Kritik der Reinen Erfahrung*, vol. 1, pp. 73–6 ff. and vol. 2, pp. 16–18 ff.

specific 'immediately experienced' complex, which we will provisionally designate X, since we do not know in advance what it is exactly.

If both vital-differentials appear together and at the same time, then due to the parallelism that we assume, we can be completely justified in expecting that both complexes will also have an 'immediate' nature in common. However, what results from this? Both vital-differentials *interfere*, forming a vital equilibrium, and it signifies the absence of immediate experiences. Consequently, complexes E and X, combined, produce a null result, *mutually cancelling* one another, i.e. they interfere in the same way as the vital-differentials do.

$E + X = 0$ or $X = -E$

The necessary conclusion is that *the interference of vital-differentials corresponds to the interference of immediate experiences*. According to empiriomonism, the first is obviously the reflection of the second.

III

An abstract and deductively derived formula that deals with the interference of experiences cannot say anything really significant about those experiences as long as we do not know what its concrete contents are. It is necessary to clarify the question of what the interference of experiences consist in and what sort of experiences interfere with one another, mutually cancelling each other out. The answer must obviously be sought in the realm of psychical experience.

As we know, psychical experience presents itself as a continuous series of *changes* in which various complexes appear and disappear, being replaced with new ones. Some kind of complex springs up, is conserved, and leaves. All the immediate experiences that we know of boil down to these three phases and, at the same time, to these three *types*. Logically, it is obvious that the first and third points are mutually contradictory, and if they occur at the same time and mutually correspond to one another, then they must eliminate one another. This would be interference, producing a 'null' experience.

But at this point, a rigorous critic might say that such a conclusion is a purely formal deduction for which it is impossible to offer actual observations. If, in reality, such interference occurs, then it would be impossible observe it, would it not? A 'null' experience that is interfered with is completely imperceptible, and it is all the more impossible to establish that it arose from two parallel experiences: the appearance and elimination of some complex. Of course, it is impossible to prove the idea that any complex is eliminated in a consciousness exactly to the extent that it arises, so that, as a result, the consciousness receives nothing. But is this a *false* idea, an empty tautology from which it is impossible to draw any conclusions?

We can answer this question with an extremely simple experiment that also will simultaneously prove to us that there is an empirical basis for our conclusion and explain the relationship of all three phases of an 'experience'.

Suppose that there is an opaque, black screen in front of us that closes off our field of vision. In this screen there is only one small opening through which we see a limited part of a completely even and uniform surface that is coloured, let us say, blue. Leaving to one side our impressions of the screen, we can say that there is a completely specific complex of elements 'of blueness' in our visual field of experience (to simplify things, we will speak only of the elements of colour without touching on the visual-innervational elements of 'form'). Suppose that the entire blue surface is moving constantly and evenly in some direction but in its own plane. We do not *observe* this movement. In our 'perception' – in our psychical experience – only the exact same complex of elements of 'blueness' remain that does not change no matter how great the speed of the 'physical' movement of the plane.[4]

What does this mean? The movement of the plane continuously removes elements of 'blueness' from the field of visual experience, one after another, but that same movement introduces a new, identical element in the place of each element that disappears. Identical series of elements appear and disappear in strict correlation with one another and completely parallel to each other and the result is precisely what the concept of interference expects: no new experience arises.

As we see, the idea of the interference of experiences is necessary here in order to remove the contradiction in experience between the 'subjective' (the unchanging perception) and the 'objective' (the moving plane). The necessity of such a concept becomes especially obvious when we take into consideration the usual variations of observations of such a kind.

Suppose that the blue plane has a limited size and after it moves for a certain amount of time its 'border' comes into the field of vision of the observer. Now the disappearing elements of 'blueness' are not replaced in perception with reappearing elements that are exactly the same, and the 'blue' complex shrinks and then disappears (usually being replaced by something else). Here the movement of the plane is 'noticed', or, speaking more precisely, movement appears as an immediate, necessary, and directly arising hypothesis that harmoniously unifies a series of changing perceptions. The hypothesis regarding the interference of the elements of what is experienced is, although it is consid-

---

4  We ignore changes that occur due to fatigue of the eye and similar conditions, since they have no effect on the meaning of the experiment.

erably more complex, no less necessary for harmoniously uniting all the data of experience on the basis of which we 'know' that the blue plane is moving (for example, from other people's communications about it) with the 'perception' of the plane as being relatively invariable. And everyone must 'acknowledge' this hypothesis, expressing it, for example, in this form: I know that the plane moves but it *seems* stationary because what is moving away is identical to what is arriving.

But this is not enough. The further harmonisation of experience requires the broadening of the sphere in which the hypothesis is extended, expanding it to other series of facts. Suppose that the blue plane is not moving. One 'sees' it as long as one's eyes are open; if one closes one's eyes, the perception disappears; it is sufficient to open them and the plane appears again. Combining a great many similar observations, one 'acknowledges' the existence of 'bodies' or 'things' as constant 'sources' of sensations. On the basis of scientific synthesis, one accepts that one's 'perception' of a blue plane is 'conditional' on rays of light constantly issuing from it that cause a change in the retina of one's eye, neural conductors, and neural centres. But now a new contradiction arises: the action of the rays of light that cause the change continues without interruption, while the corresponding 'perception', having quickly increased to the maximum, does not noticeably change with the passage of time. It would seem that the perception, continually appearing over and over again under the prolonged actions of the conditions that produced the perception, would necessarily continue to increase, just as what occurred *at the very beginning* of its development when it was still only 'taking form'. The contradiction disappears if we recognise that, beyond a certain limit, the perception is 'eliminated' to the same extent that it 'appears' – i.e. that beyond this limit the interference of elements does not allow the perception to grow. Physiologically, this is expressed in the fact that changes of the neural elements – their 'vital-differentials' – do not grow endlessly but, depending on the whole sum of conditions, stop at a specific level, because their further growth is balanced by new vital-differentials that spring up in the central apparatus *reactively*.

If the action of a ray of light on the retina ceases because the eye is closed, for example, then the visual perception disappears. This occurs very quickly, but with a well-known continuous consecutiveness. The disappearing elements of the complex are not replaced by newly arising ones. Physiologically, the removal of the prior vital-differential corresponds to this. The conditions that repeatedly caused the vital-differential no longer exist, and the 'reactive' vital-differential that also repeatedly sprang up in these conditions, preserving the first vital-differential up to a certain limit, now finally comes into equilibrium with it and is extinguished. At this point, the second vital-differential itself disappears, since the extinguishing of the first vital-differential cuts off what had caused it to arise.

We arrive at the following conclusion: the interference of experiences is not only altogether possible, but must necessarily be acknowledged for all such cases when a psychical complex is maintained in the field of consciousness. In order to harmoniously connect the data of 'subjective' and 'objective' experience, one must inevitably acknowledge that the 'conservation' of psychical complexes is a *fluid*, dynamic equilibrium, based on the uninterrupted entry of elements into the field of consciousness and their uninterrupted exit. It is an equilibrium similar to the way the form of a waterfall is preserved.

Contemporary cognition, by the way, *cannot* conceive of psychical life otherwise than in the form of a flow of experiences. Cognition cannot but reduce the regularity of the movement of this flow to the causal relationship, and the interference of experiences that we have spoken about *is one of the typical forms of the causal relationship of phenomena*. We constantly use this form of causality for physical experience, and the task now is to show what it can provide for psychical experience and for a monist conception of any experience in general. To resolve the question of whether this idea is cognitively useful is to resolve the question of whether it is true ...

IV

The interconnectedness of immediate experiences that we find in our psychical experience is an associative interconnectedness that possesses a distinctive, *chain-like* character. Only a very limited number of other similar complexes are always *immediately* joined to each experience, but *by means of* these others a considerably greater quantity of yet other complexes are now joined, and by means of *them* a further series of experiences are joined, and so on without end. Complex Z can stand outside of any direct relationship to complex A but nevertheless can belong to one of the chains associated with A and connecting with it through a series of intermediary complexes Y, X, V, U ... E, D, C, B. Only in this way does the system of psychical experience attain the huge dimensions that are observed in reality.

But it is perfectly obvious that with such a structure of the associative system all that is necessary for the connection to be destroyed and the chain to be broken is for one of the mediating links to drop out. If experiences A and C are connected by means of B, then they cannot be *in the same field* while B is absent. And complex B, when A is present, will not be in the field of psychical experience if conditions are such that it is *subject to full interference*, i.e. that it is balanced by a diametrically opposed experience. Thus, *the interference of experiences causes an interruption in the psychical field*. Both A and C, as immediate experiences, can then exist simultaneously but not together – one, for example, in the field of consciousness and the other 'outside of consciousness'.

At each step one can observe how an associative connection is broken off and then renewed again. A pupil answers a lesson he has learned; it seems to him that he knows it perfectly and suddenly he comes to a standstill. The pupil has 'forgotten' everything further. The teacher utters only a few words and everything left unsaid immediately floods into the psyche of the pupil. These few words were the connecting link that had temporarily fallen out of the associative chain. The student 'forgot' them; however, if he were given time to 'think a little', he, himself, would 'recall' them. It is obvious that a missing link had not simply been destroyed; it 'existed', but it was not 'experienced'. In order that such a combination of concepts would not be a flat contradiction, it is absolutely necessary to assume what we have acknowledged: the missing experience, which ruptures the associative chain, is in a state of full interference, i.e. it is combined with a directly opposite experience. The entry of elements into the field of consciousness goes hand-in-hand with the exit of completely identical elements, and vice versa.[5]

No matter how insignificant the size of a complex that is 'interfered' with, whatever would have been connected to the field of consciousness *by means* of this complex turns out to be outside the field of consciousness. The size of the gap makes no difference at all here; a pupil can 'forget' one letter and cannot recall either the name which starts with that letter or the whole history with which this name is associated. It is enough to remember this letter, and the pupil immediately remembers everything else. In so doing, that 'everything else' usually enters the field of consciousness with a speed and in an amount that far surpasses the antecedent current of associations of that same person. We cannot help but suppose that all these complexes are already 'possessed ready-made' and have already 'been experienced', only in another field that was separated by a gap from the field of consciousness. Once the gap disappears, both spheres of experiences flow together.

In any given case such a supposition might seem unsubstantiated. But in a large number of other cases that are very close to this in their basic meaning, it turns out to be a necessary supposition and the only possible supposition.

---

5 It is impossible to assume here that the missing link of the associative series 'is experienced' in another field, since it is precisely a link that is *directly* and *immediately* associated with existent links in the field of experience, so that a gap between it and these latter links would seem to be inexplicable.

We already know these cases: all phenomena of 'unconscious utterances' and in general 'extra-conscious experiences'. We must dwell on them once again, since the idea of the interference of experiences sheds new light on the matter that does away with all their fundamental mystery.

V

As we have seen, 'unconscious utterances' correspond to isolated coordinations of experiences that do not directly adjoin the main coordination – consciousness. But, at the same time, they are vitally connected with it, and we have so far not attempted to determine more exactly how they are connected. So far, we have only hints concerning the nature of this connection, and these hints were given to us by the parallelism between experiences and their physiological reflections – vital-differentials. Not all vital-differentials merge directly with the main stream of vital-differentials of the central apparatus; those vital-differentials that are isolated from the central apparatus must correspond to experiences that are 'isolated' from consciousness along with their 'unconscious' utterances. We can now understand both the origin of this isolation and the kind of vital interconnectedness that are associated with it.

All the various coordinations of immediate experiences that belong to the same 'living being' are connected to one another by essentially the same connection that is observed inside coordinations – the *associative* connection. If, nevertheless, they appear in 'a different field' – if they do not immediately merge together – then this *is not because there are absolute gaps* between them. If this were so, we could not speak of any kind of vital unity. The gaps are only links in a continuous associative chain that are interfered with – experiences that are neutralised by opposing experiences that are flowing in parallel. Once these intermediary links exit from their dynamic equilibrium, the various coordinations merge together and appear 'in a common field'. This often, indeed, happens in reality.

I will clarify this with an example. Your 'consciousness' is entirely engrossed in deep thought regarding a difficult and complex undertaking that you preparing for. You walk down a street 'unconsciously', carefully avoiding all the obstacles that you encounter. But all of a sudden you run into an acquaintance who stops you and asks where you are going. You immediately 'return to reality' and begin to notice your surroundings. At the same time, the former thread of thoughts is not broken but is only a little confused and begins to progress more slowly. In this way, two formerly isolated coordinations merge into one field. What has caused this turnabout? A new complex (the greeting of an acquaintance) enters one of the associative series with great force and upsets the equilibrium of associatively adjacent complexes. Among these complexes, one complex turns up that can associatively connect one given series with the other, and, exiting a state of complete interference, it actually connects them.

In this illustration it is easy to see how such an interference of experiences can be vitally expedient. As long as two associative series are separate, each of them unfolds independently and neither of them 'disturbs' the other. But as soon as they meet in one field they would immediately begin to affect one another so that if they were very different it would lead to disharmonious combinations. One's relationship to one's surroundings would cease to be 'automatic' and spontaneously resolved and would become 'conscious' and also more complex and more unsettled; it would require a greater expenditure of energy than before.[6] From the opposite perspective, 'cogitation' is impeded by 'extraneous circumstances' that 'distract attention'. Cogitation would not only require a greater expenditure (extra effort), but it also would advance less successfully because new complexes, having arisen in consciousness, would be disharmonious with the complexes that are grouped together in the process of 'cogitation' and would reduce their energy.

The realm of psychological and psychiatric 'miracles' – hypnotism, suggestion, and hysteria – are much clearer illustrations of my point of view and are much more convincing proof of its validity.

VI

This is not the place to survey the rich material from the realm of psychiatry, neuropathology, and hypnology that bears directly on our idea. This material can be found in textbooks and specialised studies. Due to the aura of mystery that is still quite characteristic of this material, it has even entered popular literature. Our task will be to note the *general traits* of this material that cannot be made fundamentally understandable in any other way than from *my* point of view.

Hysterical paralysis and anaesthesia have a purely 'functional' character: no 'organic' changes such as are present in other cases of paralysis and anaesthesia can be established. There is no damage or degeneration in the neural centres nor is there a disturbance in the histology of the conductors. More than this, the fundamental instability of these phenomena – the possibility that abrupt

---

6   The transition from 'automatic' to 'conscious' reactions always signifies an immediate elevation of the expenditure of energy, since conscious reactions are always a process of 'production' (see the chapters about habitual and malleable reactions in my work, *Poznanie s istoricheskoi tochki zreniia*).

changes in their course can almost instantaneously appear (transference, various effects of hypnosis, unexpected recovery, and so forth) – clearly proves that there are in reality no significant or at all profound changes in the vital system. And, obviously, all this applies to an even greater degree to paralysis and anaesthesia resulting from hypnotic suggestion.

How then, considering the vital wholeness of the neural centres and conductors, are such massive and serious breakdowns of their function possible?

Various experiences and observations of people suffering from hysteria show that 'anaesthetised' parts of the body cannot only 'feel' external stimuli but often even 'feel' considerably more sensitively than under normal conditions, so that a real 'hyperaesthesia' must be acknowledged.[7] This 'sensitivity that cannot sense' can be expressed in complex utterances, and this has compelled many researchers to assume a special 'subconsciousness' that directs the reactions of the anaesthetised parts of the organism and that also emerges in certain other cases.[8] We have seen that it is even simpler and more rational to consider all these things as particular cases of the vital isolation of psychical coordinations from the main grouping of experiences – from consciousness. The question consists precisely in what it is that isolates them, what 'walls' or 'barriers' spring up in these cases between groups of experiences belonging to one being.

Take any of the remarkable facts that excite the popular imagination when successful hypnosis eliminates those mysterious 'barriers' and the patient feels 'miraculously healed'. It makes no difference if this occurs in the clinic of a specialist physician, in the office of a charlatan hypnotist, in the Lourdes caves, etc. What can one person impart to another in the act of 'hypnotic suggestion'? 'Hypnotic suggestion' is only the specific utterance of a hypnotist that occurs under specific conditions. Physiologically, the person who undergoes this act can only obtain one thing through it – one *vital-differential* or another. But this vital-differential can under certain conditions have to do with precisely those parts of the system that, being in a fluid equilibrium, *divide* two currents of vital-differentials that have been flowing in other parts of the system. Then both currents merge together into one, the disunited systems of

---

7   Some of these experiments and observations are pointed out in the first section of Chapter 2, 'Life and the Psyche'. It is important to note that objective and reliable criteria exist in the form of various methods of investigating sensitivity and detecting minute mechanical movements with accurate instruments – criteria that make it possible to exclude the possibility of deception and simulation.

8   For example, when 'attention is distracted' and normal consciousness does not perceive weaker stimulations – such as questions given from behind in an undertone, and so forth.

utterances are united, and the coordination that had broken away becomes attached to the main system. Mentally, the person obtains a new experience, that, joining the associative chain ('consciousness'), simultaneously turns out to be directly associated with the other and heretofore separate chain of experiences. It is obvious that this is the same thing as the 'forgotten word' with which the teacher prompts the pupil and without which the entire end of a poem escapes from the realm of the pupil's psychical experience. And just like this forgotten word, the 'new experience', which permits the patient to 'remember' how volitional movement is accomplished before the moment his legs were paralysed, cannot be an *actually new* complex. How could this 'new experience' have turned out to be then associated with a coordination that has 'broken away', when it is directly introduced not into that coordination but into the main coordination?

Obviously, what is going on here is an experience that is *interfered* with. (In psychological terms, it is the vital-differential that is interfered with). The 'suggester' cannot provide the missing associative link directly, in the way that a teacher directly prompts the forgotten phrase; the 'suggester' provides it indirectly, provoking the available links that are closest to it so that they stand out with exceptional, unusual energy. The suggester says in a decisive tone, 'stand up and walk'. No doubt the psychical images and desires connected with these words are precisely those which are connected, for the person who was paralysed, in the closest and most intimate manner with the missing complex that is interfered with (probably one that is innervated). Appearing with sharply elevated energy, the words disrupt the dynamic equilibrium of this missing complex, and it becomes an 'immediate experience' and links the ends of the broken associative chain.

It is common knowledge that 'hypnotic suggestion' is not the only cause of such cures. All strong shocks to the psychical system possess this characteristic to a certain degree. Quite often (comparatively often, it goes without saying) simple fright helps a hysterical subject 'remember' how to use the paralysed parts of his body. The path here turns out to be even more indirect than in the case of hypnotic suggestion, but the essence of the matter is the same. A series of experiences that burst with great energy into the chain of 'consciousness' cause sharp oscillations in the intensity and force of other complexes in this chain. Among the other complexes that experience such an oscillation are those complexes which most closely adjoin the links that are interfered with. These links are drawn into the general shock to the psychical system and introduce whole new coordinations into it.

*Suggested* paralysis or anaesthesia provides us another example of these phenomena – the formation of an interruption of coordinations by way of a vital interference. Here the mechanism of the phenomena presents itself even more obviously. The hypnotist directly tries to summon and fix in the psyche of the patient experiences that are directly contradictory to those that correspond to the normal function of the given organ ('your hand cannot feel anything ... it is powerless ... you cannot move it ... it is beyond your control' ... and so on). If the hypnotist succeeds in this way to produce the appropriate interference at only one minimal point in the series of experiences that connects the given particular coordination with the rest, then the task is done, and the interruption between groups of experiences is accomplished. It is very clear that it is possible to remove this interruption by a path that is completely analogous to how it was created.

Through hypnotic suggestion, under conditions that are particularly favourable for it and that produce certain hypnotic states, experimenters achieve results that at first glance are not only psychologically but even logically contradictory. For example, when people are hypnotised 'not to see' such-and-such a thing after waking up from hypnosis, they carry out exactly what the various controlling techniques have convinced them of without the slightest simulation. Such subjects are sincerely amazed, for example, when an 'unseen' person picks up and carries a certain object, since it seems that the object hangs in the air. In order 'not to see' the person in such a way it is obviously necessary to *distinguish* it among all the surroundings, to clearly single it out – in a word, clearly *to see*. The only possible resolution of this formal contradiction, which demonstrably contradicts the absolute apriorism of logic, is this: the given 'unseen' person continues all the time to exist for the hypnotised subject as a complex of elements that either is interfered with as a whole or is separated from the main chain of experiences by interfering associative links.[9]

Various experiments with induced forgetfulness and the like are also completely analogous to this, but I think that there have been enough illustrations for now. In essence, all these facts are not any more mysterious than the constant phenomenon of discontinuities. There are discontinuities in all the complexes of consciousness that exist in our psychical experience, and there are discontinuities in all our motor reactions in the sphere of physical experience. Cognition cannot be reconciled with the rupture of continuity; it creatively

---

9   These phenomena are often designated as induced 'negative hallucinations'. From our point of view, this term is particularly apt; it is not fundamentally different from an induced positive hallucination. If in the presence of complex A (the perception of a given person) a supplementary complex $-A$ is induced, which neutralises it, so to speak, then how is this essentially different from the hypnotic suggestion of a given complex B which is not present so that it appears as a positive hallucination?

completes them on the basis of that same experience, creating models that transform discontinuities into particular cases of continuity. Cognition uses the model of the interference of experiences for discontinuities in consciousness, and it uses the model of the interference of vital-differentials for motor reactions.

VII

One part of my task can be considered complete: I have shown how the vital interconnectedness of the complexes that form one 'living being' can be divided into the 'fields' in which these complexes appear. From the point of view I have arrived at, it would appear at first glance that the other part of my task – the question of how the disunity of the psychical fields of different living beings is possible – would be perfectly easy. But, upon closer analysis, what seems very easy sometimes turns out to be even more difficult. The matter at hand is not only about how the complexes of the experience of different living beings are *disconnected* but also about how they *interconnect* – in what common field their separate psychical fields are situated. Interference can only disunite what is already connected.

I have assumed, on the basis of many considerations, that any physiological complex corresponds to the complex of immediate experiences which it reflects. Take a physiological complex such as the retina of the eye. Since it is basically *nerve* tissue, one can suppose that the corresponding complex of immediate experiences is very highly differentiated and in general is distinguished by a high degree of development. It is situated in a continuous vital connection with the rest of the system of experiences and this connection is expressed in the presence of the visual nerve that joins the vital-differential of the retina with the vital-differentials of the brain. If we cut one of the visual nerves, the connection of one of the retinas with the brain is destroyed. All 'immediate complexes' that correspond to its vital-differentials are separated from the main associative chain, and they no longer elicit those combinations that are called 'visual impressions'. This is visual anaesthesia, but it is not similar to any hysterical or hypnotic blindness; it is not subject to the action of any hypnotic suggestion. This is not the interference of associative links, but something else.

And yet the connection is not absolutely lost. The *other* eye can see and with the help of a quite simple combination of optical mirrors and lenses it can be arranged for that person to see with his other eye the *retina* and the optical nerve that was cut. But 'to see' – to 'perceive' – the retina means, as we know, to obtain a *reflection* of those 'immediate complexes' which correspond to the retina as a physiological phenomenon. In other words, these complexes are isolated from the main chain of experiences because the nerve was destroyed and the connecting links were disorganised, and these complexes are left in a different 'indirect' connection with this chain. They are indirectly 'reflected' in it, but do not directly enter it. It is plain that this 'reflection' is immeasurably inferior to the intrinsic content of these complexes, and this is infinitely less than 'to see by means' of this retina.[10]

The severing of the visual nerve destroys it and disorganises it, and the disorganised part of it acquires the same significance both in regard to the brain and in regard to the still living retina as any part of the 'unorganised environment'. The discontinuity here is not absolute; we are completely justified in thinking that the physico-chemical changes that light still continues to elicit in the retina do not disappear but are now not sensed by the brain. Those changes are now 'conveyed' through the discontinuity of the nerve but absolutely not in the same form and to the same degree as before; they do not elicit those 'visual' changes in the brain as before, but different, incomparably less significant and incomparably less complex changes, and – what is of chief importance – changes of another type. In a word, only a weak 'reflection' of the processes that are going on in the retina is obtained across the discontinuity, in just the same way that the other retina obtains only an insignificant 'reflection' of the physiological life of that same first retina by means of waves of light, mirrors, and lenses and the unorganised environment in general. From these two cases of 'reflection' it is only the latter that, for completely understandable reasons, we are well familiar with and have studied. But this does not change the essence of the matter. It does not change the fact that, from the point of view of contemporary science, everywhere an organised vital connection does not exist or is destroyed, unorganised complexes – of the internal or external environment – can serve as the intermediary connection for the *indirect reflection* of some vital processes in others.

This kind of reflection of some vital complexes in others also easily comes into being when there is an immediate and direct vital connection between them. People can 'see' their own retina 'with the help' of that very retina (very simple optical devices are required for this); people can 'perceive' their own bodies, and under certain circumstances (circumstances that are completely exceptional, it is true, yet fundamentally practicable) they can also perceive

---

10   This last expression regarding our conception must be considered imprecise: the retina, a physiological phenomenon, is not a 'tool' of sight but a 'reflection' of a series of immediate complexes that proximally condition the visual series of experiences.

certain of their 'neural centres'. All such cases are absolutely the same as those cases when, in general, one living being 'is perceived' by others.

We define the 'environment' of living beings that is not 'reflected' in their perceptions and psychical images but taken *'an sich'* as a chain of unorganised complexes.[11] The problem that arises from all the facts of experience presented above consists in the following: *to explain in causal terms the dual relationship of the environment to vital coordinations. It is characteristic of the environment that it both disunites these coordinations (making the consciousness of one being immediately inaccessible to another, for example) and at the same time indirectly unites them, conditioning the mutual 'reflection' of one coordination in another.*

VIII

First and foremost, we have data for certain negative characteristics that are of interest to us in the realm of 'unorganised complexes'.

In any case, their 'unorganisedness' cannot be complete and absolute. They cannot present themselves as absolute chaos – otherwise they would not be complexes and would not make up any kind of environment at all. Not possessing any kind of organisation or any distinctness, they could not be 'reflected' in our experience in the form of *fully defined* 'external perceptions' and 'physical bodies'. They could not turn out to have any definite, stable influence on the course of our experience. Obviously, the matter has to do only with *relative lack of organisation* or, what is the same thing, about extremely low or insignificant organisation that is indefinite and unstable in comparison with the complexes of well-developed experience.

Further, these complexes also must not be considered as being in a state of complete interference, since interference signifies a *complete interruption*

---

11   Let us remember the sense – not metaphysical in the least – in which we use the expression *'an sich'*. We substitute 'immediate complexes' – consciousness – for a certain physiological process in other people; the critique of psychical experience forces us to broaden the realm of this substitution and we view all 'physiological life' as the 'reflection' of immediate organised complexes. But *inorganic processes* are fundamentally indistinguishable from physiological processes that present only their organised combination. Being situated in one continuous series with physiological processes, inorganic processes also must obviously be viewed as a 'reflection' – but as a reflection of what? Of immediate, *unorganised* processes. We have *so far been unable* to carry out this substitution concretely in our consciousness, but, after all, we also often are not able to accomplish this in regard to animals (the experiences of amoebae) and even of other people (the inability to 'comprehend' their psyches). But instead of a concrete substitution we can formulate a *relationship* of these cases ('life *an sich*' consists of immediate, organised complexes; 'the surroundings *an sich*' are unorganised).

of the connection between two associative series. And even though the 'environment' separates associative groupings (for example the psyches of different people), it nevertheless still leaves a certain connection between those associative groupings and allows the possibility of their indirect communication, the possibility of one psyche to be reflected in another.

But, on the other hand, in any chain of complexes (it makes no difference whether organised or not organised) *an interruption of their common field is attained only through complete interference*, otherwise it would be uncaused. If consciousness A and consciousness B are connected by a chain of unorganised complexes in which there was not any complete interference, then this chain could not be distinguished from any associative chain except for a very unstable content, and the chain would form one common field that included both consciousness A and B, only it would contain a mass of indefinite and unstable combinations in addition to the two series of specific combinations. In reality, this is never observed.

Thus, interference in a series of complexes in the environment is both complete (but the kind of interference that does not completely interrupt the connecting chain) and, at the same time, produces a relative interruption (by which, for example, two systems of consciousness that form two different fields of experiences but that are 'reflected' in each other). Once again we apparently have a complex of contradictions and outright contradictions at that.

But this is only apparent. Let us look at the matter a little more closely.

In an organised associative chain, separate complexes possess a certain definiteness and stability. If they undergo interference then the interference also presents itself as something definite and stable. Under the continuing succession of experiences in both parts of the associative chain, both of them are disconnected in that current of events for a certain amount of time – they live really separate lives. Unorganised complexes are not like this: they are indefinite and unstable, they do not possess a structured and steady composition, and they change continually and spontaneously – otherwise we would not conceive of their 'unorganisedness'. But if this is so, then complete interference for each such complex can only be *momentary and not its permanent state*: it is a fleeting, unstable interference.

Assuming that great simplicity and indeterminacy are the most probable characteristics of unorganised complexes and that they constantly disintegrate and only combine weakly, and assuming that various associative systems – psychical systems, for example – are connected by means of *a very great number* of such small unorganised complexes, we can – on the basis of the principle of probability – already draw one important a priori conclusion. That conclusion will be this: in each such chain of unorganised complexes that adjoin two different organised series there must be, at any given moment, points of complete interference (and, moreover, we can suppose there are *many* such points).

Since this is so, and since separate groupings always exist in an intermediary series of complexes in the 'environment', then it cannot be clearer to us why the field of psyche A and the field of psyche B turn out to be different. But, it must be asked, why is the connection between A and B not therefore absolutely destroyed?

The question is answered by the fact that the issue here has to do with an *unstable* interference that momentarily springs up and just as quickly disappears at every given point of it. As long as the interference continues, it interrupts not only the 'field' of complexes but also the mutual influence – the mutual interaction – of those complexes that are disunited by the interfering groupings. But as soon as the interference of a given grouping ceases, the formerly disunited complexes appear in the same field and begin to mutually change one another – the more intensively they change one another, the less organised and the more unstable they are. In this way, interruptions that continually arise in a chain do not prevent the various links of that chain from acting on one another and being 'reflected' in one another in a certain way. And if this chain connects two associative systems, then this series of consequent 'changes' or 'reflections' leads to the fact that each of these systems will change the other – not directly but, as we have seen, quite indirectly. Each will be 'reflected' in the other and will engender in it the 'perception' of a vital complex.

For example, let living being A and living being Z be connected by a chain of unorganised complexes in the environment $b, c, d, e \ldots k, l, m \ldots v, w, x, y$. Let us suppose that at a given moment groupings $d, l$, and $x$ are in a state of complete interference. In such a case, (1) A and Z are in *different* fields, (2) $b$ and l are in the same field as system A and are changed under its influence, and $y$ is in the same field as Z and is also influenced by Z; (3) $d$ acts upon $l$, v acts upon $w$, and vice versa, but, as long as $d, l$, and $x$ are interfered with, no influence and no change is transmitted through them – no influence or change is 'reflected'. But suppose that the following moment, through the action of various adjoining complexes, groupings $d, l$, and $x$ are brought out of a state of interference and cross over to a new form – d', l', and x' – and suppose that the complexes $b$, $m$, and $v$ are brought into a state of interference – also, of course, through the action of adjoining complexes. Now complex $c$ turns out to be in the same field as d' and e', and since in the preceding moment it was changed by influences $B$ and $A$, this change is now 'reflected' through it in both d' and $e$ – in a word, it is 'transmitted' further along the chain. But at some point further it is 'arrested' by other interfering groupings. In the following moment these groupings leave their equilibrium and change is reflected through them on the links that follow, etc. By this path – not direct, but indirect – 'communication' of living beings – their 'perception' of one another – is accomplished.

In providing a picture of this transmission, we have unwillingly had recourse to spatial symbols ('chain', 'adjoining groupings', and so on), but they have the same figurative meaning here as is imparted to them in the expressions: 'associative chain', 'association by contiguity' and so on. We perceive our 'environment' spatially, but this is already a *reflection* of the unorganised complexes of the environment in our psyche and not those very complexes in their immediacy. This is completely analogous to the case when we perceive people as 'bodies', in a spatial form, but their 'consciousness' does not seem to be something spatial.[12] The contiguity of all 'immediate' complexes in general is bound to present itself according to the model of the contiguity of psychical groupings in our experience.[13]

I would like to continue to present my conception, but at this point a misgiving arises that forces me to digress a little. It is very probable that my conception will bring other positivists to such great bewilderment that they will exclaim 'this is metaphysics!' and even, perhaps, slam the book shut with indignation. And what about metaphysicians? They, of course, will not read my book at all, and, speaking candidly, this would not upset me very much. But I beg the positivists' attention for only a few more minutes. I would not want there to be a misunderstanding between us that, I sincerely believe, would not benefit either of us.

IX

Metaphysics arises where thinking attempts to venture beyond the confines of *possible experience*. Since any real thinking is the harmonisation of experi-

---

12  We are usually inconsistent here – we 'pack' consciousness into the body of a living being and, consequently, represent consciousness partly in a spatial form. This is so-called 'introjection'. Avenarius provided a logical analysis of it in *Der menschliche Weltbegriff*, and I investigate its socio-psychological origins in my article '*Aftoritarnoe Myshlenie* [Authoritarian Thinking]' in *Iz psikhologii obshchestva* [*Essays on the Psychology of Society*].

13  But without its distinctness and stability, this contiguity is not an 'associative' connection that already presumes a significant level of permanency in the combinations of elements and complexes according to which A, as a whole, has the tendency to bring into the field of experiences complexes B, C, etc., also as whole systems. The connection of unorganised complexes is itself distinguished by lack of organisation, but it is just as *immediate* as the psychical connection of associated complexes. [This footnote was added in the second edition of Volume I (1905). trans.]

ence, and, consequently, it has experience as its content, then metaphysics is *false thinking*. Metaphysics is possible because the realm of the use of words is broader than the realm of thinking; metaphysics consists of verbal combinations without positive content. Metaphysics is subordinate not to the laws of logic but to the laws of grammar, although in its enthusiasm it nevertheless sometimes also violates them.

Departure beyond the confines of *possible* experience is accomplished in two directions:

1. It is assumed that there are *elements* of a kind other than exist in experience – such as the basic idea of an uncognisable 'thing-in-itself' which has no content (i.e. no elements) in common with a 'phenomenon'.
2. It is assumed that there are *relationships* that are different from those that unite the elements of experience – such as 'absolute', 'indisputable', 'timeless', etc.

Metaphysics is characterised by these two characteristics.

Departure beyond the bounds of *actual* experience into the realm of *possible* experience is not metaphysics but *hypothesis*. A hypothesis is a necessary element of all cognition; one might even say it is the soul of cognition. All cognition strives to construct possible experience on the basis of actual experience; it strives toward a reliable hypothesis that provides a solid basis for practice.

A hypothesis that has to do with the actual elements of experience and the actual relationships of experience and that only makes new combinations from them – such a hypothesis, of course, might be *incorrect*, but it is not metaphysical. It does not have the 'prerequisites' of metaphysics.

Such is our hypothesis. Its 'immediate complexes' are complexes of those same elements as are discovered through the analysis of experience. And the internal and external relationships of these complexes are fundamentally the same as those by which elements and complexes are connected in experience.

But is there perhaps in this hypothesis a third (although derivative but still a very important) characteristic of metaphysics – the verbal emptiness of abstraction? This would be sufficient. After all, we cannot conceive of 'immediate complexes' that in this hypothesis are 'reflected' in plants and inorganic bodies. Does this mean that they are only words?

But a word is not empty when it expresses a *definite tendency* in the grouping of facts of experience even though it is not successfully realised at a particular time. We cannot imagine 'inhabitants of Mars', but this is not an empty word when one is considering the question of the origin of canals on Mars.[14]

---

14   In 1877, the Italian astronomer Giovanni Schiaparelli observed straight lines along the

The given term for such a person expresses a definite cognitive tendency: to conceive of certain peculiarities of the planet Mars according to the form of cultural changes on the surface of the earth. 'Martian' completes the analogical sequence: 'canals on earth' are to 'humans' as 'canals on Mars' are to ... The task is accomplished. To determine an 'unknown' that relates (not in the algebraic sense, it goes without saying) to canals on Mars as human beings relate to canals on Earth. It is highly probable that the task is poorly posed, but that does not matter. The point is that the 'X' in the analogy is not an empty word but a function of given magnitudes, although even the form of this function is not completely definite.

My task is this: to determine an unknown that stands in the same relationship to non-organic processes and any lower form of life as psychical experiences stand toward the physiological processes of the nervous system. Given three data of experience, a fourth is sought in order to connect it with these three in a harmonious formula. The form of the connection cannot be established any more closely than this, and most positivists propose that the unknown is approximately zero. I arrive at a different resolution, and I point out the directions in which, on the strength of the given data, it is appropriate to seek the unknown. (The elements are the same as in experience; the relationships are fundamentally indistinguishable from those that we are familiar with in experience but are only far less complex, far less definite, far less stable, etc.). It is possible to criticise this resolution, it might be found that the hypothesis is untrue and ineffective, but it is impossible to assert that it is empty and metaphysical.

X

Thus, my hypothesis considers the 'physical' environment of life as a 'reflection' (in the socially-organised experience of living beings) of the 'immediate' environment which is decomposed into a series of unorganised (minimally organised, to be precise) complexes. And the 'world' – i.e. the sum of vital processes and their environment – appears in this conception as an *infinitely unfolding series of groupings in which the interconnectedness of elements presents the most varied levels of organisation, from the very lowest, which are characteristic of the complexes of the environment, to the highest, which are characteristic of the psyche of a human being.* Finally, 'physical nature', also including the 'bodies' of

---

equator of Mars that he called 'canali'. It was not realised until much later that these lines were actually optical illusions caused by telescope lenses of the day. In Bogdanov's day, the idea that there were 'canals' on Mars was still current. [trans.]

living beings, appears as a 'reflection' of this world in certain of its parts – in the highest 'psychical' groupings that are organised in the human psyche under the influence of its 'communication' with other psyches.

From this point of view, many of the basic puzzles of human experience lose all their mysteriousness.

First, it makes understandable the fact that material for the highest 'conscious' forms of life is continuously brought out of 'dead nature' and that 'living life' continuously passes on into 'dead nature'. What is going on here is the grouping of less organised complexes in more organised, associative combinations and also the disorganisation of these latter again into less organised complexes.

Second, it is also understandable that 'life' is subject to all the general laws of the 'inorganic world' without creating any exceptions. This only means that the highest levels of organisation, arising through the increasing complexity and development of the lowest levels, naturally *includes* these latter levels as the greater contains the lesser.

Third, it turns out that there is nothing mysterious not only in the communication of 'psychical' beings by means of the 'physical' environment but also in the *limitedness* of this communication – that communication is possible only under a considerable number of conditions, that it is easily cut off, and even when it exists it remains highly incomplete. One need only keep in mind how indirect the path is through which this communication is accomplished, how many intermediary links (each of which only influences the adjacent links) there might be, how the influence of the beginning links necessarily becomes weak as the general number of them grows, and how often interfering combinations must spring up in the path of their transmission that undoubtedly cut them short. It becomes clear how in every given case the chance that vital complexes will be isolated is greater than the chance that they will be communicated.[15] But isolation creates nothing, while communication produces an organising process, the results of which progressively accumulate and increase.

My conception of the role of unorganised complexes in the environment naturally leads to this question: is it not possible that for the entire chain of these complexes that are connecting two living beings there is a point at which interference *is not* complete so that the 'experiences' of both beings turn out to be *directly in the same field* and so that the two associative chains are directly united? This would be a real joining of souls ... The answer to

---

15   'Communication' in the broadest meaning of the world, including even the simple 'perception' of one living being by another.

this question is that *in our* experience, evidently, this does not happen, but with other living beings it evidently does happen. I have in mind the *conjugation* of one-celled organisms and of reproductive cells. The merging of two cells into is one can hardly be expressed as anything other than the uniting of two previously independent series of experiences into one series. Such a method of merging of souls, obviously, does not work for people, although Greek mythology has found one such case (the story of Hermaphroditos and the nymph).

The question of whether in the future humans will discover methods and means of directly uniting their psychical organisations is a question that there is no point in discussing here.

XI

One of the most plausible and, it seems to me, strongest objection to the conception that I have been expounded is the following. Since we are not able to imagine the lowest 'immediate complexes', then why introduce them into a system of scientific thought? Do they broaden the realm of our ability to make *predictions* – which is the real meaning of cognitive activity?

It would be simplest of all to reject this objection in the following way. If a given point of view really removes certain chronic cognitive contradictions and does not create new contradictions that are equally strong, then it broadens the sphere of prediction because it saves some of the energy of the cognising person for the creative activity of cognition. But I, personally, am not inclined to stop here. I am inclined to suggest that a conception that is really true must more directly increase the possibility of prediction, even if this is not immediately evident.

It is perfectly obvious that my point of view permits us to constantly substitute, as required, 'the reflections' in place of the combinations that 'are reflected' and 'physical things' in place of 'immediate' complexes and vice versa. In fact, we do this everywhere we acknowledge these two 'sides' of reality. When we must predict a person's actions, it is most useful to begin with a conception of his 'immediate experiences'. When we must predict the trajectory of his fall or the influence of his opaqueness on our field of vision, then we take him as a 'physical' body.

The very same thing is practiced in all realms of biological experience; but this point of view regarding immediate experiences becomes increasingly less useful as we approach the lowest forms of life. But even here, our point of view need not be given up entirely. When, for example, we see a creeping plasmodium and we know that there is a place in its path that is lightly moistened with sulphuric acid, we 'predict' that the plasmodium will roll to one side, even though we do not know the nature of the physico-chemical reaction that is taking place in this process. In exactly the same way, we predict that plants that we have planted in the shade will 'reach out for light', even though we are not completely clear about the mechanism of this process. And we are not even talking of insect-eating plants and similar biological facts. We strive to 'explain' all this from a 'physical' point of view because then our prediction becomes more precise, more specific, and broader. However, after the explanation it will sometimes be more economical for us to use the old method of prediction.

But science also often provides the kind of formulae for prediction in the sphere of inorganic phenomena so that, in applying them, we must take the point of view of the anthropomorphic analogy. Such, for example, are all the laws in which the ideas of *minimum* and *maximum*[16] are involved ('the path of least resistance', 'the principle of minimum surface', and so on). Various metaphysical philosophers, such as Wundt,[17] draw conclusions from this anthropomorphism that imply a teleological worldview. Our point of view puts all these nuances of cognitive activity in their proper place. It does not permit teleological conclusions because it *causally* explains the vital idea and meaning of this anthropomorphism. If anthropomorphism is appropriate for making predictions in regard to the inorganic world, it is precisely because our psyche retains the general features of the inorganic complexes from which it arose and developed. At the same time, our point of view obviously explains the limited significance of this anthropomorphism; it shows that the confines of its usefulness become narrower the further we depart from our own type of organisation of experiences. By realising the limits of anthropomorphism, the many false predictions that are possible from the point of view of panpsychism and similar doctrines are averted.

A wide field opens up here for investigating the methods and possibilities of human prediction in general.

∴

---

16   'Minimum' and 'maximum' are printed in Latin characters whenever they appear in Bogdanov's text [trans.].

17   Wilhelm Wundt (1832–1920), a German physician and scientist, was the founder of experimental psychology. However, as Bogdanov indicates here, Wundt did not believe that human subjective experience could be studied with the methods by which the natural sciences study the physical world [trans.].

From the point of view of my conception, the idea of *universal* progress obtains a specific meaning. With any dualist worldview the concept of progress is applicable only in the realm of *life*, and what is more, strictly speaking, not to all of that realm. Under dualism it is a real stretch to speak of the progress of life that is 'devoid of consciousness'. But if, as we acknowledge, the kingdom of the inorganic and the kingdom of life, the life of reflexes and the life of consciousness only represent different levels of organisation of 'immediate complexes' then the concept of progress become identically valid in all these realms. Progress, then, is the *growth of the organisation* of complexes.

The law of entropy which speaks of the movement of the content of the universe toward more stable, more balanced groupings must not by any means be viewed as a law of *progress*. Stability, equilibrium are, generally speaking, not the same thing as organisation. Entropy has a *static* tendency; the growth of organisation has a *dynamic* tendency.

The growth of organisation goes in two directions: first, the broadening of the material – the content – that a given complex embraces (the increase in the sum of its elements), and, second, the growth of the strength of the interconnectedness that unites the parts of that complex (such that an ever more powerful external influence is required to break that interconnectedness, to 'disorganise' the complex). For example, the passage from a lower psychological type to a higher one signifies both the progressive growth of the quantity of experiences and the progressive harmonisation of those experiences. This is the *biological* characterisation of progress, but it is clear that for the conception that we have adopted it is completely natural that the concept of increasing organisation also applies to the 'inorganic world' – looking at it not from the perspective of its reflection in our psyche and in our social cognition but from the perspective of its 'immediate' existence.

Thus, the universal idea of progress puts into words the same ideal that, in the biological and social sphere that is closest to us, is expressed with the words: the endless growth of fullness and harmony of life.

The same tendency in a still more particular realm – cognitive life – is embodied in the ideal of *empiriomonism*.

Every step forward on the path of cognition, or, what is the same thing, any *true cognition* is empiriomonist: it either broadens content that is contained in given forms of cognition – that is, broadens its *empirical* material – or creates more integral and solid forms for this material – that is, transforms it *monistically*. In the final analysis, true cognition realises them both.

The progress of cognition cannot have any other meaning. Metaphysical, extra-empirical cognition is an empty fiction; cognition that is devoid of unity and that is non-monist means only that there is a blank in cognition. Neither of them is 'truth'.

We consider our point of view to be one of the necessary stages of empiriomonism.[18] If we are not mistaken, our view is the *truth of our times*.[19]

---

18   It seems to me that the concept of empiriocriticism is a necessary but passing stage of this journey. I have in mind, of course, not the principle of the critique of experience itself – such a critique is always necessary – but the totality of the views of that school. I will not undertake here to differentiate my point of view from these views – that will be very easy for a competent reader. But in order to illustrate the difference of our approaches, I invite the reader to compare how the question regarding the interconnectedness between living beings is treated in *Kritik der reinen Erfahrung* by Avenarius (Ch. 11) and in his *Der menschliche Weltbegriff* or in the book by his student Holzapfel, *Panideal*, with how it is treated in my work.

19   This sentence appeared in the second edition of the first volume of *Empiriomonism* but was deleted from the third edition [trans.].

# Conclusion to Book One

All three basic issues that are examined in this work boil down to one general task: *to find that path along which it would be possible to systematically reduce all the gaps in our experience to the principle of continuity.*

Among the basic gaps in experience, the first – the most common for contemporary consciousness – is the chasm between 'spirit' and 'matter'.

Modern positivism has shown that the *elements* into which the content of both of these realms of experience is broken down are identical; the gap is thus reduced to two fundamentally different types of interconnectedness of elements – the physical and the psychical.

My analysis has led to the conclusion that these two types of interconnectedness are not fundamentally different in any way, that they are two sequential phases of the organisation of experience: *the psychical is experience that is organised individually and the physical is experience that is organised socially.* The second type is one of the results of the development of the first.

Another of the basic gaps presents, properly speaking, a partial case of the first: this is the gap between 'consciousness' and 'physiology' in the sphere of life. But it acquires a particular significance and is felt with particular sharpness precisely because it runs through the realm of the real that is closest to us and because it requires us to unite in one conception – 'life' – a group of phenomena that by all appearances are absolutely different in nature and content.

My analysis asserts a *causal relationship* between the realm of 'immediate experiences' and the realm of 'physiological processes'. The second is considered as a reflection of the first (in the socially-organised experience of living beings).

This conclusion is inseparably connected with the conception of the *strict parallelism* of both orders of phenomena and of the identical applicability to them both of the *principle of energetics.*

In the end, the third basic gap is the one that is expressed in the antithesis of the individual and the universal and also of one individual with another. This is the gap in the field of experiences.

My analysis has reduced that gap to the law of causality, to a specific form of causality – *interference* (to be precise, the interference of 'immediate' experiences and 'immediate' complexes in general).

It goes without saying that all these remarks do not completely satisfy our task: the resolution of some issues poses other issues. But these further issues are of a less general character, and the place for them is in a more particular, more specialised work.

*Book Two*

CHAPTER 4

# The 'Thing-in-Itself' from the Perspective of Empiriomonism

When refuting any widely prevailing and influential misconception, a philosophy that stands on a strictly historical point of view can never limit itself to arguments that prove that the misconception is utterly unsound. For a philosophy that takes a historical perspective, there is neither absolute truth nor absolute error. Such a philosophy is obligated to find in every error that portion of relative truth which justified belief in it, just as it strives to find in every truth that portion of error that requires us to move on from this truth to another, higher truth.

In the history of errors, the historical perspective must reserve an honourable place for the problem of the 'thing-in-itself'. When Kant brought the idea of the 'thing-in-itself' to the highest degree of philosophical purity, the collapse of that idea became inevitable. The logical emptiness and the real meaninglessness of the 'thing-in-itself' could no longer be hidden from the knife of criticism behind the protection of a formal lack of clarity. It turned out that the idea of the 'thing-in-itself' expressed nothing other than reality taken to such a degree that nothing remained of it. In this idea, there is nothing that can be thought – this is its main deficiency. And Kant *almost* discovered this deficiency, having placed his 'thing-in-itself' outside the categories of human thought, i.e. essentially outside the sphere of the very thinking that operates with these categories.

Attempts to restore the destroyed 'thing' by 'critical' interpretation and discussion did not lead to anything. In these attempts the pitiful 'thing' invariably had to play the degrading role of an absolutely unnecessary term for philosophical concepts which already had completely satisfactory designations without it – as, for example, the idea of the limitless progress of knowledge. Since, on top of everything, this unnecessary term has turned out to still be most capable of engendering lengthy philosophical arguments and treatises and all sorts of confusion, it is obvious that it would be desirable to do away with it as soon as possible.

And now, in order to accomplish the necessary liquidation of the untenable 'thing', it is necessary to clearly separate its immortal soul – that portion of truth that lives in it – from the mortal body that has been in the process of decomposing since the time of Kant, from the scholastic concept which died and will not be resurrected.

I

The dualism of 'phenomena' and 'things-in-themselves' is nothing other than the pale, burnt-out gleam of another bright and vital dualism that spiritualised all of nature and that found a soul hiding behind all physical reality and governing it – in a word, the dualism of the animists. For animists, a 'thing-in-itself' and a phenomenon are in a very simple and completely real relationship – in the very same relationship as exists between their own psyche and the functioning of their body. This relationship was conceived of as universal and was the first form of the development of the 'category' of causality.

I will not consider here the social genesis of this form of causality.[1] What is sufficient here is the undoubted fact that it exists, and for a certain stage of cultural development it is universal. I also will not describe the process of its subsequent transformation from its primeval, crudely realistic forms to the most highly refined 'idealism' of our times.[2] It is sufficient to turn our attention to the following facts. The progress of the labour-related experience led to the differentiation between dead and living nature, and in so doing the soul was taken from most phenomena and remained only for living beings as a necessary assumption for understanding and predicting their reactions. But the striving to think of all reality as dualistic did not disappear and could not disappear as long as the closest and more important realities – people and living beings in general – were necessarily thought of according to this type. This striving only took on new forms as it adapted to the new content of expanding experience. Thus metaphysical 'forces' are conceived of as none other than the depersonalised souls of things. 'Things-in-themselves' are one of the results of the further depersonalisation and emptying out of 'souls'. This result is the product pre-eminently of the *philosophical* treatment of experience.

Philosophy arose as the desire to think about the entire content of experience in *homogeneous* and *coherent* forms, and it acquired independent meaning precisely as a reaction against the extreme disunity and contradiction of experience that appeared at a specific stage of cultural development.[3] The division of nature into the animate and the inanimate created many difficulties for

---

1 I have done this in another of my works, the chapter on 'authoritarian thinking' in *Essays in Social Psychology* (St. Petersburg, 1904) that was previously published in *Obrazovanie* in 1903.
2 From a logical perspective this process was traced by R. Avenarius in his work *Human Understanding of the World*.
3 It was precisely at that stage when specialisation developed and the authoritarian-tribal commune broke down, yielding to the anarchy of the commercial economy. See my article, '*Sobiranie cheloveka*' ['The Gathering of Humanity'] (*Pravda*, 1904, no. 4).

philosophy: how could such heterogeneous things be connected in homogeneous forms of thinking? The 'thing-in-itself' arose on the basis of these difficulties and as a means to resolve them.

The original, animistic understanding of the causal relationship is characterised by the fact that in it the chain of causes is *limited* and is cut short at a specific link – to be precise, at the spirit, which thus is the *final* cause of a given series of facts. The 'spirit' or 'soul' is something that is 'free', taking action on its own account and not in need of any further 'explanation'. In the era of universal animism the whole chain of causality was thus reduced in every given case entirely to *two links*: the phenomenon and the spirit that was hidden behind it. This spirit could act according to goals, like a person, but there was no thought *of the causes* of its actions and goals.

The progress of technological experience – the struggle with nature – caused this chain to lengthen, but its fundamental nature did not change. First, the relationship of any cause to its effect continued to be thought of anthropomorphically, just like the relationship between a person's will and the actions that it summons. Second, the chain necessarily ended at the 'final cause' – a free soul, either a supreme creative spirit or a 'force' that was active of itself, and so forth.

As it became more difficult to retain a 'soul' in the phenomena of inorganic nature, the need to replace it with something different, with a 'final cause', became more pressing. Otherwise, the series of causes would become infinite, and this would be a harsh, painful contradiction for all static and dualist thinking, which was accustomed to operating (and capable of operating) only with limited causal series and short chains of cause and effect.

'Force' – a depersonalised soul – only partly provided such a replacement, since force, like a 'soul', expressed *activity* and appeared as a cause of changes. Meanwhile, in the process of people's successful struggle with nature it became ever more evident that things are 'passive' and that active influence on them is necessary to discover the 'forces' hidden in them.

Integral thinking required 'final causes' of things in regard both to their activity and their passivity – causes both of the 'actions' and of the simple 'existence' of things. These 'final causes' acquired the name 'thing-in-itself'.

The development of the 'thing-in-itself' followed exactly the same path as the development of the 'soul' – from crude realism to the most refined idealism. It is well known that in the early stages of animism the 'soul' was the simple *doubling* of a human being – its exact likeness enclosed inside its body. Then the soul increasingly lost its physical characteristics, becoming ever more ethereal and delicate, until it was transformed into a pure abstraction. Similarly, the 'thing-in-itself' was at first an exact repetition of the thing-phenomenon, and even among the ancient Greeks, for example, the view was still widely held that we see things because they give out tiny and insubstantial exact likenesses of them which strike the eye. But in the course of the discovery that perceptions of external objects are correlated with the state of the organs of feeling and of the nervous system, the difference between the 'thing-in-itself' and the 'phenomenon' began to grow. It became clear, for example, that the colour of things could not be attributed to the properties of a 'thing-in-itself' because the exact same things could appear to different people in different hues: our 'red' and 'green' seem to many colour-blind people to be the same colour, and for blind people those colours do not exist at all. Similarly, the characteristics of 'warm' and 'cold' turn out to be 'subjective'; the very same water can be felt as 'cold' to warm hands and as 'warm' to cold hands. The same thing applies to the odour of 'things', to their taste, etc.

Thus arose the distinction between the properties of things that are 'apparent' or that 'subjectively exist for us' and the properties that are 'completely real' and 'objective'. The former properties depend on our organisation, so to speak, properties that are added by our organisation to the 'phenomenon'. The latter properties are independent of our organisation and apply to 'things-in-themselves'. This is how the matter was still viewed by the sensualists and materialists of the seventeenth and eighteenth centuries. The qualities of extension (form) and impenetrability were attributed to the 'objective' properties of 'things-in-themselves' for even longer.

Kant made the final step in the cleansing of all reality from the 'thing-in-itself'. He took all 'sensory' properties from it, even spatiality. His transcendental aesthetics teaches that the perception of things in space, just as in time, is the result of our cognitive organisation; they are properties of the 'subject'. Thus, the 'thing-in-itself' lost all *experiential* content and became unknowable.

And here, just as happened with the concept of 'soul', development led to a naked, empty abstraction, whereby both abstractions united together – the 'free' and 'immortal' soul fell into the world of 'noumena' or 'things-in-themselves'. This unification confirms and elucidates the idea that they have a common origin.

II

After it was emptied out by Kant, the 'thing-in-itself' became cognitively useless. Did this mean that it was only an 'error'?

Of course not. True, it was predominantly a *philosophical* product; practical consciousness managed for the most part without it by considering all things to be things that exist *for it* and not distinguishing them in any way from things that exist *in themselves*. But cognition has a *legitimate* need for philosophy, and satisfying that need is neither an amusement nor a luxury.

This philosophical need is the striving to think monistically. The 'thing-in-itself' was the result of extending throughout all of nature the dualism that had developed from animistic views. It is the 'transformed soul' of a phenomenon, and the 'soul' is not in any way a simple error of cognition.

In order to understand and predict the actions of humans and other living beings, a person *must* assume that they have perceptions and psychical images, emotions and desires that are just like one's own. The error begins when one places all this *inside* bodies. The error broadens and develops when one also places *the very same* psychical complexes into unorganised bodies, thereby 'animating' inanimate nature.

The 'thing-in-itself' does not suffer from this second mistake. It is not anthropomorphic. Before Kant, the 'thing-in-itself' suffered from the first mistake. It was 'introjected'; it was imagined to be hidden *spatially* underneath a phenomenon. In this regard, Kant corrected the mistake by making the 'thing-in-itself' extra-spatial.[4] I am inclined to think that Avenarius is partially indebted, consciously or unconsciously, to this particular feature of Kant's teaching for his idea of the needlessness of introjection – 'placing' the psyche in the body. Taken from Kant's idea regarding the illogic of the spatial conception of the 'thing-in-itself', introjection – this homologue of the 'soul' – was easily (psychologically easy, it goes without saying) transferred to the idea that it is invalid to conceive of the psyche as spatially related to the body.

In one way or another, since the 'thing-in-itself' is historically derivative from the 'soul' and since, as the result of philosophical aspiration, it originally sprang up as an addition and in parallel to what was accepted as the 'soul' of a living body in order to create something similar for all the other phenomena of nature, then an objective critique of the 'thing-in-itself' and an explanation of its positive elements must begin with its prototype – the 'soul'.

One of the fashionable doctrines of our times is *panpsychism*, the idea that every 'physical' process also corresponds to a 'psychical' process that is hidden behind it, in the way that the processes of nerve centres correspond to the 'consciousness' that is hidden behind them. This contemporary restoration of universal animism undoubtedly has a metaphysical character. It has no scientific *application*, even though it is accepted by some scientists. It does not eliminate that fundamental dualism of spirit and body, and it poetically gen-

---

4  By the way, he also made it extra-temporal. This made it completely metaphysical and completely 'unknowable', which is what absolutely empty abstractions must be.

eralises that dualism. Nevertheless, this theory expresses the same legitimate demand – to think monistically, to make recognised forms of cognition *necessary* – to make them universal and not limit them to a separate, private realm of phenomena.

At this point the question arises: is it really absolutely necessary to substitute the 'psychical' for the 'physical' even in a few cases? Cannot a person consider other living beings to be only 'bodies' that move around among other bodies like complex, self-operating machines? Cannot a person manage without the 'hypothesis' that those bodies 'feel', 'think', 'desire' – that their actions are dependent on 'psychical experiences'? Even if no one can manage without this 'hypothesis' in practice, is it not possible to renounce it at least in the realm of pure *theory*? Does not such a point of view turn out to be the most strictly positivistic, the most 'critical', and the most foreign to compromise between knowledge and faith? If there is any dualism in this hypothesis, then critical analysis must do away with it ...

This question is not as complicated and difficult as it might appear. It is easily eliminated by the fact of the *social nature of cognition*. Thinking is inseparable from the conception of *proving* what is true and *refuting* what is false, and both presuppose the *social communication* of people. The subjective nature of 'truth' for anyone who thinks that they have found it consists in his ability to prove to any other sufficiently rational being that this truth is 'universally obligatory' – i.e. that it has meaning not only for the given observer of it but also for their fellow human beings. Thus, psychical solipsists, by not accepting the presence of a psyche in other people, not only fall into a practical contradiction when they explain their views to other people, but they also fall into a theoretical contradiction when they consider their views to be 'true', i.e. demonstrable, i.e. having meaning not for the solipsist alone.

We see that the 'hypothesis' that other people have psyches is, in reality, not a hypothesis at all but a necessary element of cognition. When I substitute such-and-such feelings and thoughts for such-and-such utterances of other people, then this is only hypothetically the *given content* of what is substituted. The content not infrequently turns out to be wrong; I can 'fail to understand' other people. But the substitution itself is not a hypothesis at all but a 'constitutive criterion' of cognition as the struggle for truth, a struggle that is social both in its origin and in its goal.

The 'substitution' that we are talking about does not in any way represent a departure beyond the bounds of possible experience. Its validity in every case is proven by practice. In relying on the 'substitution' of our feelings for the utterances of others, we predict the actions of other living beings, and we calculate our own acts correspondingly. If we are thereby deceived in our expectations, but we do not find any inconsistency in those calculations, then we must correct the substitution: 'a person deceived me', 'I did not exactly understand someone', and so on.

Successful 'substitution' becomes a more difficult matter the further removed it is from the mode and tendencies of the life of the other being. It is more difficult to 'understand' a friend than an enemy, a foreigner than a compatriot, a cat than a person, an amoeba than a cat, etc. The more difficult the 'substitution', the more one has occasion to formulate unsuccessful hypotheses in particular cases that must subsequently be rejected or corrected. Each concrete substitution must tolerate failure. This does not shake the principle of substitution, which remains inseparably connected with all our cognition.

To the extent that experience progresses, the nature of substitution changes. At first it leads to naïve anthropomorphism: all people, all living beings, and even all objects of inanimate nature are 'understood' according to a direct and immediate analogy with the psyche of the cogniser. But, gradually, corrections are introduced into the analogy. In part, the realm of the application of the analogy is diminished. For example, people stop animating inorganic nature; they stop considering the rustling of leaves to be a particular form of speech. In part, the application of substitution is individualised consistent with the sum total of conditions – different content is accepted for similar utterances. With animals it is simpler than with people, with a person of one nature it is different than with a person of another nature, etc. *Substitution takes on the colouration of relativity and conditionality.*

What causes such changes? The development of another type of cognition – let us say 'abstract' cognition – which boils down to a generalised description of phenomena as they immediately enter into experience. In the struggle with nature, substitution frequently turns out to be of poor service to people and leads to unpleasant errors and the uneconomical expenditure of energy. In these cases, people find it necessary to completely abandon the usual association of the observed 'physical' with the supposed 'psychical' and limit themselves to the recollection of the consecutiveness of acts as they flowed in their experience. 'Naturalistic' knowledge develops from such a recollection in which what is repeated the most in phenomena is preserved the best in memory, and this 'naturalistic' knowledge is what makes up the basic content of contemporary science and the contemporary worldview in general.

This knowledge is interlaced everywhere with the old 'substitution', frequently acquiring an anthropomorphic, 'fetishistic' colouration from it. Thus, the functional connection between conditions and what is conditioned – 'causality' – is conceived, in general, in the form of a cause 'summoning' a consequence in just the same way that our will summons action. Examples of this include: 'nature abhors a vacuum', 'the force of gravity strives to bring bodies with mass together', 'plants struggle for existence', and so on. But at the same time, this cognition corrects the old substitution, marking out its boundaries everywhere and pointing out how it is necessary to change it in these or other cases in order not to run into contradictions. 'Naturalistic' cognition states that the organisation of external feelings, the intellectual abilities, and the nature of different living beings are not the same and that under such-and-such conditions it is necessary to 'substitute' precisely such-and-such perceptions, ideas, strivings, even though – under other, equal conditions – the interconnectedness and relationship of experiences of the 'thing that is substituted' itself are different. People who possess normal vision and who are required to give directions to a colour-blind person must remember that instructions regarding the colour of houses and other objects can seriously confuse the person they are talking to. People who want to teach a child something must not explain the interconnectedness of facts exactly in the form that they customarily appear to themselves but with changes and conversions that are adapted to the 'understanding' of the pupil. Phlegmatic people who argue with sanguine people must keep in mind that their opponent can be made terribly angry by a contradiction that would only cause a mild irritation in themselves, and so on.

Generally speaking, these corrections become more significant the further the organisation of the cogniser stands from the organisation of the being that it is necessary to 'understand'. For example, it is established that other organisms lack 'senses' that we possess (of which I do not think it is necessary to provide examples) and that they possess senses that we lack (for example, the 'sensation of distance' by bats, the visual perception of ultra-violet rays by ants, and so on). It is established that there are instincts and reflexes that are not similar to ours ('heliotaxis' and 'chemotaxis' of many lower organisms, for example), and so on. At a certain point, these corrections of phenomena are transformed (at the current state of knowledge) in a decisive leap in cognition. *One* universal correction is given for the inorganic world and for the vegetable kingdom, and, to be precise, the substitution in question is done away with (but, as we shall see, only apparently done away with).

It is assumed that the series of immediate experiences, just like our psychical experiences, is completely missing from lower animals and that there is an *absolute emptiness* – nothing goes on in this sense. In regard to the vegetable kingdom, however, this is not unconditionally recognised. For independently living plant cells and also for plants with clearly expressed reflexes (for example, insect-eaters) substitution is still permissible – although to the most minimal degree. But now the inorganic world is considered decisively 'dead'.

Here, as a matter of fact, the real dominion of 'pure description', free of any anthropomorphism, begins. The very idea of 'pure description' expresses precisely the desire to absolutely set naturalistic cognition apart from interwoven elements of substitution. If Mach and others attack the concept of 'causality' – the idea of the 'explanation' of phenomena – then it is precisely to the extent that they find the old anthropomorphism in these forms of thinking, that is, the invalid *substitution* of needless subjective content in place of the objective data of experience. It is true that adherents of 'pure description' do not oppose substitution in those cases where it is obviously useful and necessary – in relation to people and other living beings whose actions we would not be able to predict without the aid of substitution. But these thinkers strive to keep substitution within the bounds of strictly naturalistic cognition. For this, on the one hand, they purify it of 'introjection' – i.e. the spatial location of feelings, ideas, wishes, etc. within a living organism – and, on the other hand, they try to introduce substitution into strictly scientific expressions of the 'functional correlation of the facts of experience'. They assume that a specific state of a living organism (for higher beings, the central nervous system, specifically) 'functionally corresponds' to strictly specified, completely simultaneous 'psychical experiences' whereby any attempt to represent one or the other side of this correlation (the 'physiological series' and the 'psychical series') as the cause of the other, is a priori recognised as invalid – as the introduction of unnecessary and contradictory elements into description.

This is the extreme limit of the reaction of 'pure' naturalistic cognition against the 'animistic' substitution. We must investigate whether cognition can stop at this point, whether it can unconditionally accept the method of 'pure description' in *this* form and if 'pure description' really completely eliminates substitution beyond the boundaries of living nature.

III

Cognition has practice as its foundation and its goal, and, drawing its material from practice, cognition supports practice by *predicting* the future. Precisely for this reason, the centre of cognitive life, toward which every one of its countless particular manifestations has gravitated, has been until now the *causal connection of facts* – the interconnectedness of their *necessary and constant consecutiveness*. One must predict what does not yet exist on the basis of what does exist and did exist in the past. Therefore, it is precisely this correlation that connects the *non-simultaneous* – that connects what precedes from what follows – that is vitally important. This is the universal causality of phenomena.

In its struggle against the 'fetishism' of causality, modern positivism replaces causality with the pure 'functional correlation' of the facts of experience. And, actually, in removing all anthropomorphism from the idea of causality, we obtain only a strict functional correlation of facts – but precisely of *facts that precede and facts that follow*. I will subsequently designate this correlation simply as 'causality', seeing no necessity to reject a good, old word that is familiar to everyone for the sake of the clumsy, descriptive formula, 'functional correlation of consecutiveness'.

But contemporary positivism recognises causality not only in this sense of the word but as still another kind of regularity – that is, *the functional correlation of simultaneity*. The main field of this correlation is the relationship of 'physiology' and 'psyche'. Positivists acknowledge that if there is a certain state of nerve centres then there is simultaneously a specific complex of 'facts of consciousness' and also vice versa. I will designate this formula of functional correlation as 'parallelism' in order not to resort to complex expressions like 'regular interconnectedness of the simultaneous' and so on.

It is obvious, in itself, that parallelism is a completely different cognitive form to causality, even though they are united in the generalised, imprecise concept of 'functional correlation'. It is also obvious that it would be a huge gain for cognition – making it more harmonious and monist – if one of these categories were brought into the other or both of them into a third completely specific category instead of the simple, diffuse idea of the causal relationship in general. Complete independence of both categories would signify two *completely different worlds of relationships*, i.e. a strict dualism of cognition. From the point of view of the positivist, the only possible form of cognitive monism is a single basic type of grouping of the data of experience; and here we have *two* basic types that are mutually irreducible.

'But what is to be done?' the reader asks. 'Since a strictly scientific and critical relationship to experience does not permit cognitive monism, in the sense of a single universal type of systematisation of experience, then dualism it will be!'

But are things really so hopeless?

In the natural sciences the relationship of parallelism plays a completely specific and quite important role. In very many cases, the following formula appears: if such-and such traits are found in an object being studied, then one must assume yet other such-and-such traits that accompany them everywhere, even though in the given case they cannot be directly ascertained. For example, the external attributes of a species of animal correspond to a specific internal anatomical and histological structure. Or specific genera of animal and plant remains correspond to a given arrangement of geological layers that they are found in. And so on and so on. In all 'natural history', i.e. the concretely-described part of the natural sciences, the formula of 'parallelism' decisively prevails. Every species, genus, class, etc., is characterised precisely as a combination of attributes and of their groupings that exist *in parallel* and are encountered *simultaneously*. It would therefore seem that the model of 'parallelism', and its independent significance must be accepted without question as a cognitive necessity.

This is how things were before the idea of evolution appeared on the scene. The parallel existence of different forms in organic and non-organic nature and parallelism in the internal correlations of one or another given form were taken as a fact established by experience and not requiring any particular scientific *causal* explanation. Instead of such an explanation, reference was made either to an act of creation or to the purposefulness of the given parallelism. But all this did was merely to attach two non-scientific forms borrowed from the realm of 'substitution' to two scientific forms of grouping: the freedom of a creating will and teleology (most frequently combined in the idea of 'teleological creation').

However, the fact that these surrogates of causality are now applied as 'explanations' of parallelism precisely points out the need for a causal explanation; it points out that thinking *organically* cannot stop at the simple assertion of one parallelism or another. Evolutionary thought has already specifically posed the problem of *causes* of the development of the world and of life. Evolutionary thought has taken up the goal of *causally* explaining why organic forms present such-and-such complexes of traits, why the solar system has such-and-such a structure, etc. In so doing, the parallelism of phenomena has attained an absolutely new scientific significance: if in specific forms the traits A, B, C ... are found everywhere to be 'parallel' with traits X, Y, Z ... then this has its *cause* in the preceding phases of development of these forms and in the conditions of the environment in which they developed. In so doing, parallelism boils down to causality.

Biology knows many so-called 'correlative deviations' that appear side-by-side and simultaneously in development, even though it is not possible to detect any causal connection between them. Why, for example, do blue eyes and deafness run in parallel in cats? We still do not know this, but it never enters anyone's mind to refuse the question 'why?' or to announce that, having ascertained a functional correlation of the simultaneous existence in cats of being deaf and having blue eyes, there is nothing further to seek, and the desire to find a cause of this fact is radically mistaken. Such a point of view would be recognised as unscientific.

The problem of the correlation of physiological and psychical life is the only case in which contemporary positivism behaves in this way. It this case, positivism declares that it acknowledges – partly as an assertion and partly as a hypothesis – a functional correlation of the simultaneous existence of specific neural processes and specific 'psychical' complexes. In principle there is nowhere further to go, and it is possible only to investigate particular cases of the given correlation. Positivism concludes that the desire to 'explain' it by reducing it to a causal relationship is groundless and unscientific; it goes beyond the bounds of pure description of the data of experience.

This point of view is naturally not satisfying. Recognising two fundamentally different forms of functional correlation – causality and parallelism – and recognising the legitimacy of the subordination of the second of these forms to the first in all cases save only for one – the relationship of physiology and psyche – we obtain an extremely disharmonious system of cognition: a grandiose world of continuous causal relationships to one side of which is stuck a limited realm of relationships of pure parallelism, and, in order to preserve the complete independence of this realm, the angel of strict positivism stands on its border with a flaming sword and does not permit any aggression on the part of causal cognition. By comparison with such a picture, even complete dualism in cognition would be harmonious and whole.

As has become clear, the parallelism that creates this disharmony is the result of the scientific purification of the old substitution of the 'psychical' for the 'physical', and the problem of a single type of cognitive grouping of the facts of experience boils down to the problem of introducing 'substitution' into the model of scientific causality.

IV

This is a strictly scientific form of 'substitution': specific facts of consciousness correspond to specific physiological states of neural centres.

The first question that arises here is the following. From the point of view of experience, what is the precise 'physiological process' that corresponds to the psychical process?

For one person, another person is first and foremost a perception made up of visual, tactile, acoustic, and other elements. In a series of multiple repetitions, this complex acquires stability and distinctness. Due to its similarity to other such complexes – through the perception of one's own body by a cognising person – this complex is amplified by means of 'substitution', and 'communication' among people appears. Collective experience, transmitted in 'utterances' creates the idea of the *continuous* existence of this complex – as also of other, similarly stable complexes. These complexes 'exist' in collective experience independently of whether they are 'apprehended' at a given moment by a given individual or not. They exist as 'bodies'.[5]

Thus, a 'physical body' is the result of the grouping and systematisation of *perceptions* that are at first individual and later collective. The same thing obviously also relates to the 'physiological process of the nervous system', whereby a complex of such a kind now develops to a still higher level of the organisation of collective experience – to the stage of scientific treatment of it. In view of this, the problem of the parallelism of the physiological process with the psychical process boils down to another problem: the parallelism between the psychical process and the perception of the corresponding physiological process in the psyche of other beings.

I will explain this with a concrete example. In one of the usual experiments related to explaining the nature of emotions, a dog, which has had a part of its cranium removed, is severely startled. The brain instantly becomes pale and is reduced in size (due to the constriction of blood vessels, especially small arteries and capillaries). From the point of view of the *psychical* experience of the patient and the experimenter, the following seems to be the case. In the consciousness of the dog there appears a distinctive, complicated, indefinite, and fluctuating complex of innervated elements of a general organic feeling of distress that is designated by the word 'fear'. In the psyche of the observer, there is a definite change of the complex that represents the 'perception of the brain of the dog' – to be precise, the quickly diminishing sum of spatial and tactile elements (the diminishment of volume) and the even more quickly diminishing sum of elements of 'redness' (the brain becoming pale), etc. For the dog, the 'immediate experience' is fear, and for the observer it is the perception of changes in the brain of the dog – an experience that is absolutely dissimilar and completely specific and that is functionally connected with the first experience. The 'parallelism' of these two experiences by two different beings also presents a task the resolution of which will provide the key to understanding psychophysiological parallelism, since the 'physiological process' is the result of the systematic unification and harmonisation of corresponding perceptions.

We will now return for a moment to the general model of causality, and, for comparison with the functional correlation described above, we will take up several typical cases of functional correlation that have a *causal* nature.

---

5   For greater detail about this, see my article 'The Ideal of cognition' (Chapter 1 of the present work).

If the density of air decreases, then the mercury in a barometer falls. This is the functional correlation of a specific consecutiveness. What do the successively appearing complexes – the sum total of atmospheric changes of a given kind and the change in the level of mercury – have in common? *Qualitatively* it is impossible to find the slightest similarity between them. This does not prevent them from being situated in a relationship of 'cause' and 'effect'. However, in order to grasp the entirety of this causal relationship, one must keep in mind the construction of the barometer. It is a necessary condition of the given result and makes up part of its 'cause'. In order to make my presentation simpler and clearer, I will designate this kind of connection of facts by the term 'reflection'. Our example then can be expressed thus: the lowering of the density of the air 'is reflected' in the mechanism of the barometer in the form of the downward movement of the column of mercury.

Thus, in their strictly functional correlation, it is possible for there to be the most complete qualitative dissimilarity between the 'reflection' and the 'reflected'. Such a dissimilarity is actually more the rule than the exception. There is nothing mysterious in this. We know that the 'reflection' is proximally determined precisely by the *environment that reflects it* – by those complexes *in which* a given phenomenon is reflected – and to a lesser degree by the phenomenon that is 'reflected'.

Let us look at a few more examples that are similar. A melody that is heard next to a phonograph is reflected on its cylinder in the form of a series of little grooves that are absolutely dissimilar to the melody. A colossal physical complex – a planet with all the huge diversity of its composition – is reflected in the retina of a person living on earth in the form of minimal chemical changes on an area of several microns. An appropriate modification of this latter example brings us nearer to the basic problem regarding the relationship of the physical and the psychical. A whole world of physical complexes – including, perhaps, a huge mass of intense life – is reflected in the psyche of an earthly observer as the perception of a small bright point that is disseminating short rays of light on a dark blue background.

It is easy to establish the same relationships in the sphere of psychical experience. When one psychical complex is 'reflected' in another, it causes a functionally specific change that can turn out to be absolutely dissimilar to the 'reflecting' complex. Let us say, for example, that you have composed a completely specific conception of person A as an intellectual and moral individual. A 'perception' of several lines written by him or several phrases uttered by him enters your consciousness, and your entire conception of him quickly changes. At the same time, the new combinations, having entered your conception of A's characteristics, are in no way similar to those visual or auditory perceptions that caused the change – that are 'reflected' in it. In exactly the same way, any new 'idea' entering your worldview and gradually transforming it is 'reflected' in a huge number of your conceptions, but the changes that the idea causes in each of them is qualitatively far from similar to the idea, itself. The changes are far from representing the simple inclusion of the idea in the psychical forms in question.

In summing up relationships like this, it must be said that if complex A is reflected in some complex B, then the reflection is only functionally defined by what is reflected, and it appears, generally speaking, to be qualitatively different from it. This applies to all possible complexes of experience and presents a partial characterisation of the causal relationship of the facts of experience.

The psychical life of every person is an extremely complicated and extensive complex, but, all the same, it is only a complex of elements of experience. Take two such complexes – the psyche of person A and the psyche of person B. The question arises, in what form can one of them (let us say A) be reflected in the other (complex B), supposing, of course, that the former *can*, in general, be reflected in the second because they both belong to the same 'nature'? On the basis of the preceding it must be considered completely credible that the 'reflection' turns out to be absolutely different from 'the reflected', but it is connected with it by a definite functional correlation.

Now recall that when we previously spoke of the connection of the psychical and physiological processes, we found that in formulating their relationship it is possible to substitute the *perception* of the physiological process by other living beings for the physiological process *itself*, without changing the basic nature of the formulation ('parallelism').

If we juxtapose the model just obtained, we obtain two correlations that, for clarity, I write side-by-side:

| | |
|---|---|
| 1. The psychical process of person A. *Functionally connected with it:* | 1. The psychical process of person A. *Functionally connected with it:* |
| 2. The perception of the corresponding physiological process in the psyche of another person B. | 2. The reflection of A (as close as can be determined) in the psyche of another person B. |
| *The functional correlation (is taken to be) parallelism.* | *The functional correlation is causality.* |
| 1 and 2 are absolutely different in qualitative terms. | 1 and 2 can be absolutely different in qualitative terms. |

Comparing both correlations, we find a striking similarity. At first glance, the main difference consists in that one correlation is parallelism (i.e. simultaneity) and the other is causality (i.e. consecutiveness). But is there really complete simultaneity in the first case? Of course not. The perception of the physiological process in the psyche of another person *inevitably lags behind* the psychical process to which it corresponds. Thus what is indeed going on here is not exact simultaneity but *consecutiveness*, and there are no differences between the two relationships.

Considering the coincidence of our two series, the most likely hypothesis is that they are identical. The as yet unknown second member of the second relationship is identical with the second member of the first relationship, just as the first members are identical. In other words: the reflection of the psychical processes of person A in psyche B is 'the perception of the corresponding physiological processes'.

This conclusion creates a point of view that is far from usual and apparently paradoxical. We will treat it with all the doubt that is appropriate when encountering an unexpected hypothesis, and we will see whether or not it contradicts experience.

V

First and foremost, it is obvious that this point of view cannot essentially remain within the confines of the case that we have examined. It must be applied to the perception of any living being by any other living being. The following conclusion is obtained: any living being, as a complex of immediate experiences, 'is reflected' in another living being (and even in its own self) as the 'perception of a body'.

If this is so, then it seems apparent that the *full* parallelism of physiological and psychical processes must be acknowledged. To every 'perception' of a physiological process – and therefore to the physiological process itself – there must correspond a psychical process that is 'reflected' in that perception. This would appear to be an absolutely obligatory conclusion due to the fact that it is impossible to show that there is any fundamental difference between the physiological processes of the nervous system and other physiological processes.

There is more. Physiological processes are also not fundamentally distinguishable from the non-organic processes that they spring from and change into. The 'perception' of a living body and the 'perception' of a body that is not alive exist in one continuous chain. It is apparently necessary to extend our parallelism to all of nature and to assume that something 'psychical' is 'reflected' in our 'perceptions' of non-organic nature.

Thus, it would appear that our point of view leads to *panpsychism*. However, it is already obvious that if this really does turn out to be 'panpsychism', then it would not be the dualist panpsychism that *inserts* the psychical into the physical everywhere, but something completely different. It would be a strictly monist panpsychism for which the 'physical' is not a shell enclosing the 'psychical' but is a distinctive reflection of the 'psychical' – its real 'other form of being'. For this kind of panpsychism, the physical body would be the result of a specific grouping and coordination; it would be the result of a process of 'organisation' of homogenous perceptions that present themselves as a reflection of one 'psychical' thing in another 'psychical' thing. In a word, it would all seem to boil down to a strict pan-psychical monism.

In reality, however, this is not the case. 'Panpsychism' is inescapably connected with a false idea about the *structure* of the various complexes that form nature. In order to understand the falsity of panpsychism, it is necessary first and foremost to get a complete grasp of what 'the psychical' is.

VI

In investigating the various complexes of the elements of experience, it is easy to establish *three* different types of interconnectedness of elements.

First, various images pass through our experience, and each of them presents itself as a certain immediate combination of elements. As long as this combination is simply *data* for us and as long as we do not in any way break it down, transform it, or give it any kind of specific characterisation, then we are dealing with the primary, basic, and *immediate* form of the interconnectedness of elements of experience in complexes.

However, we break the various complexes of our experience down into other, lesser complexes and then into elements. Such a breaking down presupposes certain conditions. In order that a whole complex A is broken down into its parts x, y, z, it is necessary that these parts enter experience not only together but also individually, so that both these and other events are preserved in the memory of the cogniser and so that it would be possible to compare them. Otherwise, complex A would always be only an immediately-given A and nothing more. The idea of the possibility of breaking it down would not even arise.

Second, the sum total of the stated conditions characterises the *associative* – in other words, the *psychical* – interconnectedness of experience. If complexes x, y, z sometimes appear together and sometimes not, and, moreover, this is *ascertained* and noted, then they are 'associated' among themselves and 'associated' with a mass of other complexes that form the system of 'memory' and 'consciousness' – the *psychical* system, in other words. I do not believe that these elementary psychological considerations require any particular proof;

they delineate the 'psychical' part of experience in a completely satisfactory manner. This is associative interconnectedness in an associative system.

Third, in 'physical' experience, the interconnectedness of complexes presents other particulars that are expressed by the terms 'continuity' and 'necessity'. This is the objectively-regular interconnectedness of experience. Complexes that are united by such an interconnectedness – 'bodies' or 'processes' of the physical world – cannot be taken now as a whole, now in parts, now in one combination, now in another combination in the way that associative complexes are. At any given moment, 'physical' complexes represent a completely specific system, and they change only through continuous transitions from one combination to another that are connected with them in a necessary correlation. This is an 'objective' correlation that does not change with the individual cogniser and that remains the same – is 'socially valid'[6] – for the most varied individuals. This is the most specific form of interconnectedness of the elements and the complexes of experience.

The three types of interconnectedness of experience correspond to the three Kantian categories of reality, possibility, and necessity.[7] The immediate interconnectedness is at the same time also the primary interconnectedness, and it is universal because it is precisely the least specific and it *is contained* in both associative, psychical interconnectedness and also in objective, physical interconnectedness; it consequently embraces all experience, all 'reality'. Just the opposite, the associative interconnectedness, let us say of complexes A and B, is expressed in the fact that sometimes they are together and sometimes not together, i.e. this interconnectedness has the colouration of *possibility*. Possibility is altogether only a 'psychical' combination. In the present case, it is a combination of the conceptions of those cases when A appears together with B and of those cases when A appears outside of a connection with B. For example, 'it is possible' that 'X' (such-and-such a person) is located 'at home' or 'not at home'. Both are still only my conceptions situated in an associative interconnectedness between themselves and other conceptions, and they both, consequently, are *psychical reality*. 'Necessary' or 'objective' reality is narrower than this psychical reality; in the present case it boils down to one definite fact of *physical* experience, for example, 'X' (in reality) 'is at home'. And it is obvious that the psychical, associative interconnectedness is already contained in this

---

6  This supra-individual 'social validity' of relationships of the given type is the result and expression of the supra-individual – i.e. *social* – organisation of experience. (See my article 'The Ideal of Cognition' in the present volume.)

7  Kant's terms are usually translated in English as 'possibility, existence, necessity'. They are the three categories of the class of 'modality' [trans.].

necessary interconnectedness. An indefinite and fluid combination of complexes here is only transformed into a definite, as if crystallised, combination that could be changed only by other combinations of the same order ('objective forces').

Thus the three types of interconnectedness of the elements and complexes of experience are, at the same time, three phases of its progressive organisation. Each lower type is the starting point for the development of the higher type that is necessarily contained within it. Each higher type has its particular preconditions that are not possessed by the lower type. For the *psychical* type of interconnectedness (which it is important that we now clearly present in order to resolve the issue of 'panpsychism') these preconditions are the presence of an organised, 'associative' system (memory, consciousness) and a limited variability of combinations (such as are characteristic of associations of images, concepts, and such). Where these preconditions are not present, one cannot speak of the 'psychical'.

VII

If, as we have assumed, the psychical process and its physiological equivalent relate to one another as 'the reflection and the reflected', then to make an inference from the second to the first is just as valid as the other way around. But does it follow from this that we can infer from every physiological process precisely a 'psychical' process that might be expressed in it?

The 'psychical' is an associative combination in an associative system, i.e. an organised part of an organised whole. We also identify the corresponding 'neural process' as an organised change in an organised system. This is completely understandable: the organisation of what is reflected appears in the organisation of its reflection. But the conclusion that is obtained from this is that we have the right to *presuppose* the first only when the second *is present*. Thus, pursuant to the 'parallelism' of physiological and psychical process, in scientific terms, we can only assume that a psychical complex is behind any physiological complex to the extent that the *organisation* of the first permits us to assume the associative character of the second. In other words, we must assume the 'psychical' behind one or another datum in the experience of 'physiological life' only to the extent and to the degree that the organisation of the former corresponds to the organisation of the processes of the nervous system.

Thus, to fully accord with experience one must first and foremost assume that the lower forms of the nervous system correspond to lower forms of 'psychical' associative life. And where there is no nervous system? As far as we can tell, any living cell is capable of 'accumulating' the energy of stimuli and 'becoming accustomed' to having specific reactions to repeated combinations of conditions. This forces us to surmise the existence of elementary forms of *memory*, i.e. of associative, psychical groupings. This proposition is supported by the fact that any organism with a complex nervous system developed *from one undifferentiated cell*, so that it is necessary to seek in the life of this embryonic cell the starting point of all the unfolding richness of associative combinations. In a word, one must acknowledge it to be most likely that organised living protein is the physical expression (or 'reflection') of immediate experiences of a *psychical* nature – of course, the more elementary the experiences, the more elementary the organisation of this living protein in every given case.

What should we surmise beyond the confines of organised proteinaceous bodies where we meet with all sorts of other considerably less complex 'material' combinations, both chemical and physical? It is obvious that there is no basis for assuming anything 'psychical', i.e. associatively organised groupings, behind these *unorganised* bodies. But to assume *nothing* would be an abrupt leap in cognition – the violation of its fundamental principle of *continuity*. It would mean to assume that something *in itself* (outside our consciousness) is *nothing* and nevertheless causes something positive in our consciousness ('the perception of a physical body') and causes it regularly and necessarily. Then, as in other cases, what is caused is the completely analogous result (the 'perception of a physiological process') of 'something' and *in itself represents something positive* (another psyche that indeed exists outside our consciousness). I suggest that readers reflect a little about what is necessarily (in consequence of the lack in our language of terms that exactly correspond to the ideas) a confusedly and awkwardly expressed comparison, and they will understand that to see in a physical complex *only* this immediately given complex in perception would mean to assume that sometimes something arises from nothing, i.e. to assume a continual act of miraculous creation.

However, what indeed must we assume to be behind this 'purely physical complex', if, as has been pointed out, it is impossible (because associative organisation is expressed in physiological organisation) to assume the 'psychical'? Where there are no prerequisites of a psychical interconnectedness of elements and groupings, there remains only an *immediate* interconnectedness – the lowest form of interconnectedness. From the point of view of a strict scientific analogy, this is something what we must assume in this case.

We thus arrive at the conclusion that the 'substitution' of psychical complexes for all sorts of physical complexes is impossible, but that substitution in general is necessary if cognition is to remain true to the principle of continuity. For inorganic nature, 'substituted' complexes must be unorganised. Not absolutely unorganised, it goes without saying, but only relatively unorganised (i.e. joined only by the lowest form of interconnectedness that I have termed 'immediate').

My point of view is not panpsychism, but a rigorously scientific substitution of organised psychical complexes for organised physiological complexes. My point of view presents nature as an infinite series of complexes, broken down into the same elements as the elements of our experience, possessing the most varied degrees of organisation and 'being reflected' in one another just as this occurs in our experience.

VIII

All right, the reader observes, your point of view is monist, but it requires 'substitutions' and that is where scientific cognition is not allowed to go or, at least, what until now it has managed to do without. Is not such a point of view just unnecessary ballast for cognition? Is it not contradicted by the demand of the principle for the economy of effort in thinking that you have acknowledged? And, besides that, in requiring substitution, your point of view does not at all indicate *what precisely* should be substituted, for example, for one or another specific inorganic process of the physical world, and what substitution is useful for cognition in each case. Does this not mean departing into the mists of self-contained philosophising, i.e. simply metaphysics?

All these objections are very serious and must be very rigorously considered, and the answer to them must be as precise as possible. Otherwise, our 'empiriomonism' will inevitably collapse at its first steps.

The first thing that I will point out in the analysis of these objections is the *incorrectness* of the main premise – as if scientific cognition has managed until now without 'substitution' in the realm of cognition of inorganic nature. No, substitution has been practiced constantly, except that it was the substitution of the *psychical* for the *physical*.

What are the mechanical theory of heat, the theory of light waves in ether, and other similar theories that are of great service to science, if not theories of substitution from the perspective of which our perceptions of heat, light, etc. represent only *reflections* in our psyche of other 'immediate complexes' that are conceived in the form of molecular-mechanical vibrations, waves in the ether, etc. Fundamentally, this is absolutely the same as the substitution of a 'thing-in-itself' for a 'phenomenon', and, in the final analysis, it is the same as the substitution of the psychical for the physical. The only question is the extent to which one or another substitution is successful, the extent to which it is expedient for cognition.

From this point of view, the substitution of the 'physical' for the 'physical' contains huge defects.

In reality, 'physical' signifies a specific interconnectedness of experience that is very harmonious, very organised, and is the most developed form of this interconnectedness (objective regularity). This is what the physical *is* in our experience; it is a reflection of immediate complexes that affect the psyches of different living beings that are socially-connected by means of communication. But the organisation of a given *reflection* belongs precisely to *what it reflects* – to the socio-psychical environment provided by it and worked out in it. The *reflection* cannot, by itself, present such a level of organisation. And, as we showed in relation to the inorganic processes of nature, it is even necessary to assume a very low level of organisation of the 'reflection'. When 'mechanical' complexes are substituted for complexes of heat and light, then this means that the high organisation of experience is transferred beyond the boundaries of the realm in which it really exists – the collectively-cognitive organising process – and is applied independently of its real living basis. This mistake is the same as attributing a soul to a stone like the soul of a human being. Progress in cognition must eliminate this mistake.

Contemporary science also displays a tendency to improve 'substitution' by freeing it from the mistake that has just been pointed out. This tendency is not realised very clearly and is not always properly conducted, but it definitely appears in the *newest* scientific theories, such as, for example, the electromagnetic theory of light, the electron theory of mass, and so on. In these theories there already are neither molecules nor atoms as particular, stable realities that are hidden beneath the flowing reality of experience. In these theories, apparently, there are only naked formulas and models by which the direct data of experience are connected. However, in closely examining these formulas and models it is easy to see that behind them yet again is hidden a 'substitution' – merely a consciously indefinite, elusive transference of forms of higher organisation into the realm of the basis of phenomena of lower organisation. The concepts with which these theories operate – for example, 'voltage' at one or another point of an electrical or magnetic field, a positive or negative 'electron', and so on – express *no specific experiential content* ('perceptionally' specific). Instead, they express not the simple absence of content but an endless series of 'potentials' – the *possibility* of completely specific experience. All these possibilities do not have a subjective character at all, as in psychical experience, but are completely *objective*. Each of them need only be associated with specific conditions (particular to each one) to be transformed into 'necessity' – into objective (i.e. socially valid) reality. Under such-and-such supplementary conditions, depending on the given potential and voltage, such-and-such thermal phenomena (i.e. such-and-such perceptions in the psyche of every normally organised observer) are displayed. Under other conditions, such-and-such phenomena of light are displayed – the perception of a spark, for example. For a third set of conditions, such-and-such mechanical phenomena are displayed, etc. Each of these possibilities exists, consequently, not only for given individuals who receive these 'symbols' at a given moment for a specific field of observation, but they also exist independently from their limited personal experience. What does this mean?

It can mean only one thing – that 'something' corresponds to a given 'symbol' that does not depend on the individual experience of one or another individual. Reality is not bound by the limits of individual experience; it even lies outside *direct* personal experience and enters in *indirectly*. But this relationship to individual experience does not make reality metaphysical in the least, just as the consciousness of another person is not made a metaphysical reality. In exactly the same way, my or your direct personal experience is inaccessible but it constitutes the basis of various 'possibilities'. If the reality that we are speaking of cannot be more closely defined – only the 'possibilities' connected with it are defined – then in a given case this agrees most easily with the idea of its general 'indeterminacy' or unorganisedness. It would be absurd to conceive of this as fundamentally different from our experience in its content, material, or 'elements', since its very influence on our experience would then be inconceivable. Differences in essence and differences in substance exclude mutual interaction. Thus, everything forces us to assume that that the reality that we seek boils down to unorganised complexes of elements analogous to elements of experience.

What we see here is that the progress of science is essentially not the elimination but the improvement of substitution. Any scientific theory that asserts 'objective' regularity (i.e. regularity that is not significant only to an individual) for inorganic phenomena thereby effects a substitution – it assumes a 'reality' beyond the bounds of direct experience. The validity of substitution is verified by subsequent experience and on this path the forms and means of substitution are changed. The tendency toward 'pure description' signifies only a struggle against the substitution of phenomena of a lower type for complexes of a higher type – against the substitution of inorganic processes for 'physical' and 'psychical' complexes (in both cases highly organised complexes). But even the 'purest' description assumes substitution at the same moment that it recognises the 'objectivity' of its 'functional correlations'. This assumption contains the idea that reality is independent of the private experience of one, another, or a third individual but that it is 'reflected' in this experience and influences its flow.

In order to avoid misunderstandings, I note that the 'objectivity' that is under discussion has nothing in common with the *absolute* objectivity of Kantian epistemology. This 'objectivity' is only that 'social validity' of facts and relationships that is ascertained in the communication of living beings. This is not unconditional – and not even complete – social validity, but all the same it is *supra-individual*, and it is sufficient in order to acknowledge a supra-individual reality, i.e. one that stands outside direct individual experience as the 'cause' of organic and inorganic phenomena that relate to the 'objective' world. In principle, it is possible to 'substitute' this reality everywhere when the issue has to do with 'what objectively exists', but in practice it must be acted upon only to the extent that it is *cognitively useful* and broadens the realm of prediction. No one doubts the legitimacy of 'substitution' in regard to a living 'conscious' being. But when this being falls on us from a roof, it would be a terrible waste of time for us to substitute a psyche for the movement of the being in order to predict its important practical effects for us. It is sufficient to be aware that this fall is an *objective* fact and not a subjective form of our psyche, in which case it would be possible for us to avoid it by simply turning our thoughts to something else or closing our eyes. The recognition of the objectivity of facts is, as we have shown, the lowest level of 'substitution', its most indefinite form. In regard to physical complexes of the nonorganic world such a form of substitution is definitely predominant, but the question remains of whether it will be satisfactory as cognition develops further.

In the sciences of the inorganic world, a large number of highly useful formulas are applied that possess a nuance of another kind – of a more complex substitution. These are the formulas which involve the concepts 'striving to the maximum', to the 'minimum' or 'for preservation'. These formulas have led many thinkers (among the most recent, I would name Wundt) to various metaphysical conclusions, and in any event they speak as if they substitute *the psychical* for inorganic phenomena. They are the same type as the old formulas – 'nature abhors a vacuum' or 'bodies are attracted to the centre of the earth' – except that they are distinguished from the old formulas by their stability in scientific knowledge. They are preserved while the others have long since been rejected.

From our point of view, of course, such formulas do not present anything fundamentally mysterious. In empiriomonist terms, our psyches are distinguished from 'inanimate nature' only by a higher level of organisation, and the higher level *includes* and *encloses* the lower levels in it. It is therefore natural that models that correspond to certain features of complexes of a higher organisation can also correspond to relationships of lower complexes. There is no room for metaphysics here, but there is room for a methodological investigation of 'substitution'.

IX

We have seen that the realm of 'substitution' in contemporary cognition is *not the least bit narrower* than in the cognition of animists, except that animism's naïve forms are replaced by scientific ones. Historically, both seem to be extremely different.

1. Substitution of the *psychical* for the *physical*. The scientific form of this is where the psyche is substituted for the physiology of the nervous system, for the movement of animals and perhaps partly of plants, and also of free living cells ('protists'). It is scientific, of course, only to the extent that it is critically verifiable. Otherwise it crosses over into naïve substitution, such as, for example, in animal fables where a complex human psyche is applied to animals. Typical naïve forms of this substitution are universal animism, the poetic spiritualisation of nature, pantheism, and panpsychism.

2. Substitution of the *physical* for the *physical*. This includes 'mechanical' theories of light and heat, theories of electric and magnetic currents, and so on. In our times they are all considered to be 'naïve'.

3. Substitution of the *physical* for the *psychical* (we have not specifically spoken of this before now: it is sufficient to point it out). Primeval animism did this in part, and particularly to the extent that the soul is conceived of as 'material', appearing as if a simple duplication of the body. This is the materialism of Democritus, Epicurus, Büchner, and so on. These are naïve forms.

4. Substitution of the *metaphysically indefinite* for the *physical and psychical*. The 'thing-in-itself' is fundamentally distinguished from a phenomenon but constitutes its cause. It is 'unknowable' or 'vaguely knowable'. This is characteristic of sensualists, materialists of the type of Holbach, the Kantians, Spencer, and so on. These forms are contradictory and therefore naïve.

5. Substitution of the *empirically indefinite* for *physical and unorganised* processes. Theories that strive for 'pure description' in abstract-monist models and that accept the 'objective' character of the facts that are subject to description. This makes up the majority of the *modern* theories of natural science; they are forms of substitution that are scientific for our times. Empiriomonism negatively defines the 'indefinite' substituted complexes as unorganised (not absolutely, but relatively) and so places this substi-

tution in the same chain as the substitution of the 'psychical' for the 'physical'. In principle, this provides for the possibility of research into the origin of life, both physiological and psychical (the derivation of the more organised from the less organised).

Thus, the development of science and philosophy leads in reality not to the elimination of substitution, as many contemporary positivists are inclined to think, but to the critical correction if it. Substitution has been unconditionally removed from only one sphere – where we deal with psychical phenomena. It is not appropriate to substitute a 'thing-in-itself', unknowable or vaguely knowable, for psychical phenomena, since this is unhelpful for cognition, and downright unsuitable for monist cognition. The psychical is the starting point for substitution itself. The content of the initial substitution comes from the psychical, and its connection with the 'physiological' is the objective foundation and at the same time the stimulus for substitution. This kind of substitution can only be 'naïve'; it can only be the result of a mistaken analogy.

From the point of view of the systematic correction of substitution, all of nature presents itself as an endless series of 'immediate complexes', the *material* of which is identical with the 'elements' of experience, and the *form* of which is characterised by the most varied levels of organisation – from the lowest (corresponding to the 'inorganic world') to the highest (corresponding to human 'experience'). These complexes mutually influence one another and mutually 'reflect' one another. Each separate 'perception from the external world' is a reflection of any of these complexes in a specific, formed complex – in a living psyche – and 'physical experience' is the result of a collectively organising process that harmoniously unites such perceptions. 'Substitution' provides something like a reverse reflection – the reflection of a reflection, more similar to 'what is reflected' than the first reflection. It is like a melody *produced* by a phonograph which is the second reflection of the melody *perceived* by the phonograph, and it is incomparably more similar to the latter than to the first reflection – the little lines and dots on the cylinder of the phonograph.

In the empiriomonist picture of the world there is nothing that is above experience; in that picture there is only *immediate* experience and its sequel – the realm of the 'substituted' or *indirect* experience. The 'substituted' is simultaneously the basis and the condition of the 'objectivity' of immediate experience. Both of them equally lie in the sphere of *cognition*.

∴

We now have sufficient data in order to pronounce a just sentence – as severe as necessary and as merciful as necessary – on the 'thing-in-itself'. That the old 'thing-in-itself' is dead is unquestionable, but that is what makes the most impartial judgement of it possible.

The 'thing-in-itself' was the expression of a legitimate and just striving to supplement experience by means of substitution. Even the indefinite nature of this substitution did not present anything fundamentally wrong; it only expressed the insufficiency of experience and cognition. The mistake began where cognition attempted in one way or another to do away with that indefiniteness and created a hypothesis that was not susceptible to verification.

Such hypotheses went in two directions. Some, lapsing into a rough and ready analogy, substituted extreme distinctness in place of indefiniteness. These especially were animist and materialist hypotheses; panpsychism and panmaterialism are typical forms of this *naïve positivism*. Others replaced the indefinite with the unknowable, at the cost of exaggerating the indefiniteness but thereby saving themselves the trouble of attempting to create greater distinctness in its place. This was the typical point of view of Kant and Spencer (sceptical-metaphysical hypotheses).

The golden mean is adopted by materialists of a more critical hue, who, while renouncing the *absolute* unknowableness of the 'thing-in-itself', at the same time consider it to be *fundamentally* different from a 'phenomenon' and therefore only 'vaguely cognisable' in phenomena and extra-experiential in its content (i.e. apparently possessing 'elements' that are not the same as the elements of experience) but that lies within the confines of what are called the forms of experience, i.e. time, space, and causality. This was approximately the point of view of the French materialists of the eighteenth century and of the modern philosophers Engels and his Russian disciple, Bel'tov.[8] Like almost every golden mean, this point of view did not entirely remove the deficiencies of the extremes but rather actually combined them, although, of course, making them less extreme.

This kind of materialism assumes that the 'thing-in-itself' influences our 'feelings' (affects[9] them) and in this way engenders a 'phenomenon' or 'experience'. But A can affect B only in the event that they both are *similar* to a certain degree in regard to their material, their 'elements'. If they are *fundamentally different*, they cannot influence each other, just as a band of shadow cannot affect a bullet that flies through it. Consequently it is necessary here to assume that the 'thing-in-itself' is similar in regard to 'elements' with the 'feelings' that

---

8   'N. Bel'tov' was a pseudonym used by G.V. Plekhanov for his legal publications in Russia [trans.].
9   Bogdanov uses the term *affitsirovat'*, which is a cognate of the term, *affizieren*, that Kant uses to refer to the relationship between things-in-themselves and a subject [trans.].

it 'affects', i.e. with psychical experience, i.e. with *experience in general*. On the other hand, the simple and direct transference of the forms of space, time, and causality into the realm of 'things-in-themselves' in the same form and meaning as we accept them in physical experience is an insufficiently valid and even a partly contradictory hypothesis. Even for psychical experience, spatial relationships appear with immeasurably less distinctness than for physical experience, and many people suggest that psychical phenomena in general do not have a spatial nature. This is why we must acknowledge that the 'thing-in-itself' conceived from the point of view under discussion differs so greatly from experience that it sheds light on nothing at all. And, in general, the assertion that time, space, and causality, as we now conceive of them, have an absolute meaning is nothing other than a particular form of absolute apriorism – a metaphysical and static idea. In the memory of humanity, all these forms of experience developed from the finite to the infinite, from the heterogeneous to the homogeneous, from the discontinuous to the continuous.[10] So what gives us the right to assume that the current phase of their development has absolute meaning?

Incidentally, we must keep in mind from the outset that these considerations of ours are valid only if the 'thing-in-itself' is understood in the sense of an *empirical substitution*, but not in the sense that it is understood by all its contemporary advocates, including dialectical materialists as well. For them the issue has to do with *meta-empirical substitution* or, what is the same thing, metaphysical substitution. Their 'thing-in-itself' stands in place of what is provided by empirical substitution. For example, in place of psychical phenomena, they substitute a still hidden 'thing-in-itself' that must manifest itself in these phenomena. But we have shown that the very concept of 'thing-in-itself' arose from the substitution of the psychical for the physiological, so that no further substitution for the psychical is required.

If we use the term 'thing-in-itself' in the strictly positive meaning of empirical substitution, then our view must be summarised in the following way. The initial 'thing-in-itself' for every person is one's own experience; it is from this that one infers the experiences of other people and other beings – this is the series of substituted 'things-in-themselves' that is closest to a person. Being convinced that physiological life is fundamentally not distinguishable from other physical and chemical phenomena, a person carries out a similar substitution by various means in regard to all 'objective' processes. In the course

---

10   To be more specific regarding the variability and development of these forms, see Chapter 1, 'The Ideal of Cognition'.

of this, one makes many mistakes and corrects them through further knowledge. A further series of 'things-in-themselves' is obtained in this way, which are become less and less definite as their difference from the initial 'thing-in-itself' – the person's own psyche – increases. In principle, they are all completely cognisable; in practice the difficulties of precise cognition grow with the transition from higher forms of life to lower forms, from organic nature to inorganic nature, from more complicated complexes of inorganic nature to simpler complexes. But as the difficulty of such precise cognition of 'things-in-themselves' grows, the need for it also diminishes. 'Phenomena' become simpler and are cognised more easily so that in practice it is more and more possible to manage without precise substitution. Nevertheless, even here it is impossible to manage *completely* without substitution; substitution is already included, in an indefinite and hidden form, in the assumption of the *objectivity* of phenomena.

But the very use of the term 'thing-in-itself' in our positive meaning is now to a certain degree a philosophical misuse. Over the course of the centuries, too much that is metaphysical has accrued to this old concept. Consequently, it will be best if we avoid misunderstanding by simply saying that a 'thing-in-itself' is an obsolete philosophical idea. Everything that was alive in it boils down to *empirical substitution*. As cognition developed, it preserved empirical substitution, supplementing it on the basis of widening experience. Empiriomonism makes it a tool for working out a holistic worldview free from discontinuities.

CHAPTER 5

# Psychical Selection (Empiriomonism in the Theory of the Psyche)

## 1    Foundations of the Method

### 1.1    *The Model of Psychoenergetics*

I

I have set myself the task of showing in what direction investigation into the psyche must develop if one consciously places the idea of the *fundamental unity of experience* at the basis of that investigation. This task boils down in its entirety to *questions of method*, and therefore it will be completely natural to begin with an explanation and analysis of the most general methodological principle by which I will be led. This, as I have already explained more than once, is the principle of energetics, and in the sphere of specifically psychical experience, with which we are now dealing, this is the idea of a *psychoenergetical method*. So, what does this idea immediately signify?

The concept of 'energy' serves cognition by making it possible to conceive of all phenomena as *commensurable*. It is made up of two elements: first, a conception about the *measurability* of all phenomena – all phenomena are considered as 'magnitudes' – and, second, a conception about their universal *equivalence* – it is recognised that in the continuous change of phenomena some are replaced by others according to a specific and continuous quantitative relationship. This is the content of this concept as it has been worked out in the sphere of 'natural sciences' by scientific synthesis and scientific critique. It needs to be applied to 'psychical' phenomena.

First and foremost, it is necessary to pose the question: are psychical phenomena measurable? Although methods of measuring them might at present be very incompletely worked out, imperfect, approximate, and inadequate, it does not change the fundamental answer to the question. Psychical phenomena are measurable; they have magnitudes. To the extent that they appear in the field of the psyche with more or less 'force', they present magnitudes of 'intensity', and, to the extent that they can unite with one another and create a more or less complete life of consciousness, they present magnitudes of 'extensity'. Every 'objective' measurement of physical bodies and processes boils down to these two forms of quantitative comparison of the facts of consciousness. The act of 'measurement' is always *psychical* activity, and the material of that activity is the data of *psychical* experience. If these data did not have the nature of magnitudes then altogether no kind of measurement would be possible.

From this point of view, in a great many cases when cognition is unable to express a given psychical phenomenon as a completely specific magnitude of energy, the possibility nevertheless exists of determining its *relative* magnitude. It is possible to observe the 'increase' or 'decrease' of energy of that psychical phenomenon. The case is even simpler when the question has to do with 'the same' psychical phenomenon which, however, 'changes'. For example, if a given image pales in the consciousness, i.e. loses its intensity, or if it loses some of its elements, becoming less full, so to speak, then we are justified in speaking of the decrease of energy of this conception. In cases of the opposite kind, one must acknowledge the growth of energy, etc. But also when various images replace others in the psyche, consciousness usually registers their comparatively greater or comparatively lesser energy; it is obvious to people when the activity of their consciousness becomes more or less full of energy. These are not simple analogies, since the measurability and commensurability of psychical processes – i.e. traits that provide the basis for an energetical conception of these processes – are revealed with full clarity in such utterances.

It would be mistaken in the highest degree to attribute a particularly decisive significance to the fact that all immediate 'measurement' and 'commensuration' of psychical processes are distinguished by extreme approximateness and inexactitude and on this basis to reject an energetical understanding of the psyche. Whoever is familiar with the factual applications of energetics in the natural sciences knows very well that the scientific significance of energetics extends far beyond the confines of precise measurement to places where they are not technically feasible. The realm of really precise measurements is essentially very narrow, but even without such measurements, the energetical point of view leads to scientifically important conclusions in a huge number of cases. Frequently – maybe even in a majority of cases – it even *creates* the possibility of technically precise measurement of phenomena by permitting the substitution of other easily measurable things in place of those that are difficult to measure. This, as we will see, is the case in the sphere of psychical experience.

II

Even though the problem of the measurability of psychical processes does not present any fundamental difficulties, the problem of their *equivalency* is nevertheless considerably more complex. In this regard, it is necessary first and foremost to determine if it is appropriate to assume that psychical phenomena are only equivalent with psychical phenomena or if they are equivalent with physical phenomena as well. The latter might seem doubtful especially since the forms of the interconnectedness of phenomena in physical experience and in psychical experience are very different.

Energetical equivalence expresses the idea of the universal *continuity* of phenomena, which requires that, as one complex of elements is removed from experience, another complex appears that is connected with the first by a specific quantitative relationship. But psychical experience, taken in its immediate form, is the realm of *discontinuous* relationships. In deep sleep, fainting, or death the flow of psychical experience ceases temporarily or permanently, and in various phases of conscious life it changes sharply in the intensity as well as in the extensity of experiences. It is clear that applying the idea of equivalence to immediate psychical experience separately would create a large number of contradictions. Consequently, energetical equivalence can obtain a real meaning only in relation to a broader sphere of phenomena than one psychical experience – in relation to experience in its whole, the physical and psychical worlds together. Meanwhile, physical experience is *in itself* characterised by continuity; to join it together with processes of the psychical order – processes that are discontinuous – by equivalent replacement would apparently only mean to violate its inherent continuity. We arrive at this dilemma: either to reject psychoenergetics or to accept the violation of the continuity of physical experience. The majority of philosophers adopt the first resolution and arrive at a hopeless dualism of method.[1] To adopt the second means to transform physical experience into something fantastic, having taken from it its fundamental trait, its 'constitutive' sign – continuity. Neither resolution is very comforting.

Fortunately, empiriomonism is not bound to this dilemma – it is capable of removing it and leaving its confines. Empiriomonism provides the possibility of knowing the psyche energetically without violating the energetical continuity of physical experience. How does it arrive at this?

There is a definite parallelism – to be more precise, a definite functional correlation – between the 'psychical' and 'physical' phenomena of life. But where the same functional correlation exists between different series of elements of experience, these series do not present different objects to cognition, but *one*

---

1 This is what the so-called 'critical' arguments against psychoenergetics, based on the 'law of conservation of mechanical energy' (the expression of A. Riehl) boils down to, i.e. to the continuity of physical experience.

*object*.[2] A psychical phenomenon and the corresponding physiological process should be considered not as different energetical magnitudes but as one and the same magnitude. They are different means of perceiving the process of life, and they can no more be disconnected in terms of energetics than a body as it is perceived by vision can be disconnected from that same body as it is perceived by touch. The 'parallelism' of both 'sides' of the vital process here is the same as the parallelism of the optical and tactile series of elements that form a specific 'physical body', and in both places the law of conservation of energy is abstracted from the multiplicity of elements, based on the *unity of relationships*.

All this becomes especially simple and understandable from the point of view of the 'second empiriomonist proposition'. This proposition asserts the universal parallelism of 'immediate experiences' and 'physiological life' and reduces this parallelism to the relationship between the 'reflected' and the 'reflection'. If the physiological process is the reflection of 'immediate experiences' – their reflection in the socially-organised experience of living beings, to be precise – then it is obvious that it makes no sense for monist cognition to create separate objects from them. It would be the same as to consider a planet observed directly by the eye and the same planet observed by means of the concave mirror of a reflecting telescope as being separate objects of cognition.

Therefore, in energetical investigations we always have the right and the grounds to substitute the psychical process for its physiological reflection, and vice versa, depending on which of the two is most accessible and convenient. For example, when the physiological process has not been established but it is easy to observe the corresponding psychical process, it is better to substitute the second for the first, and when the psychical process cannot be measured, it is possible to attempt to measure its physiological process instead.

III[3]

I will now define the precise dimensions and boundaries of the realm that lies *outside* physical experience, on which we consider it possible to apply the cognitive methods of energetics.

---

2   It is not necessary to repeat the explanation of this proposition. It was given in Chapter 1, 'The Ideal of Cognition'.
3   This third section of Part One appeared in the 1906 edition but not in the 1908 edition [trans.].

For all people, in addition to their own immediate-psychical experience, there also exists the psychical experience of other people and of other living beings in general. This experience of others is constructed on the basis of utterances. In reproducing the 'consciousness' of another, the psyche acts like a phonograph. The utterances of other people that you perceive represent a distinctive 'reflection' of their experiences, a reflection that is very 'dissimilar' to what is 'reflected' but functionally dependent on it – exactly like the grooves on the cylinder of a phonograph are 'dissimilar' to the melody that is reproduced in them but is functionally dependent on the structure of the melody. And just as, when the phonograph is running, these grooves serve as the source for the 'reproduction' (i.e. actually the *second reflection*) of the melody which is more similar to the melody than the first reflection, so the utterances of other people under the associative activity of consciousness serve as the starting point for the 'reproduction' of the experiences of others, i.e. their second reflection, which is more similar to them than the first. The psychical experience of others in our cognition is the *reflected reflection* of the immediate experiences of other beings.

But the realm of the immediate experiences that are connected with the life of a given organism is not, as a matter of fact, limited to 'psychical experience' – i.e. to that *organised system* of experiences that is 'immediately known' to the given being. So-called 'unconscious utterances' reveal that countless minor coordinations exist outside this system – in some kind of connection with it – that take shape according to the same 'psychical' (i.e. associative) type. Further clarification of this issue leads to the conclusion that an orderly and harmonious conception of experience is possible only if we acknowledge an 'associative' organisation of experiences for any physiological organisation of life – if we acknowledge the full parallelism of life in its 'objective' and 'subjective' manifestations.[4] In other words, any 'physiological' process must be considered as the disclosure – the 'utterance' – of associative complexes (we would call them 'psychical' if this term were not usually connected with the conception of the well-known *complexity* of experiences).

Is it not appropriate to also extend this principle beyond living nature to all of 'dead' inorganic nature? For consistent monist thinking this is unavoidable, but only as a cognitive tendency; at the present time it is *not quite* in our powers to be able to realise this concretely. The phonograph is able to accurately reproduce a melody only when its needle operates in an environment that is sufficiently similar to the one in which the melody was recorded (i.e.

---

4   See Chapter 2, 'Life and the Psyche'.

with an atmosphere). If you place a phonograph in water or in a vacuum, the reproduction of the recorded melody in its previous form by the phonograph will be in no way possible. The same is true of the 'phonographic' activity of the psyche. The less similar our psyche is to the psyche of another being, the less accurately it will reconstruct the experiences of that being; the dissimilarity of the psychical environment of experiences obstructs the 'understanding' of the utterances of others. We are still able to reproduce various experiences of higher animals in our psyche to a certain degree, and this is cognitively useful since it helps us predict their actions. But in regard to lower animals it is comparatively rare that we can take the point of view of their psyche; we usually do not 'understand' their utterances to the extent that we can predict anything on that basis. Thus, it is now most often necessary to substitute here the 'physiological' for the 'psychical' rather than vice versa. In regard to plants, the very concept of 'utterance' becomes almost useless, and it is even more useless in regard to the inorganic world. Associative complexes are complexes that are *organised* in a specific form. How can we substitute them for inorganic phenomena in which there is no organisation? The chaos of elements – this is what the inorganic world presents 'in itself'.

The primeval animist and the contemporary poet do not at all leave the confines of legitimate techniques of cognitive creativity when they 'animate' all of nature. But scientific cognition chooses from the countless applications of these techniques only what can serve to broaden human 'prediction', i.e. in the final analysis to increase the power of humanity over nature.

## 1.2   *The Model of Psychical Selection*

I

The philosophical investigation of the psychical world takes on the task of elaborating a *unifying* point of view regarding all the different processes that occur in that realm. Thus, the breaking down of psychical experience into its elements here means only preparatory work and no more: philosophical investigation proper beings where the relationship of these elements to the psychical *whole* is explained and where the question of how they are coordinated in a psychical system – how the *psyche is organised* – is answered.

In subjecting the psychical world to the universal principle of energetics, we immediately obtain the first purely qualitative approach to the question that I have just formulated. In this approach, the question should be expressed in this way: taken as magnitudes – and, moreover, as energetical magnitudes – how do separate experiences and their elements relate to the psychical system as integral energetical magnitudes? And we immediately obtain the first and most general answer, which proceeds from the very concept of magnitude. This answer must be the following: for a psychical whole, separate experiences and their elements can appear as positive or negative magnitudes that increase or diminish the sum of energy of the whole.[5]

In this abstract formula, the data of biomechanics and psychology immediately permit the insertion of more concrete psychical content. The increase and decrease of the energy of a psychical system is identical with *the immediate increase and decrease of its vital capacity*, and the oscillations of immediate vital capacity are expressed mentally in sensations of pleasure and pain – in the so-called 'Affectional'. The energetical formula transforms into a psychological formula: a positive Affectional of an experience (pleasure) is cognitively identical with the increase in energy of the psychical system and a negative Affectional (suffering) is identical with the decrease of energy.[6]

Thus, for example, if it is 'pleasant' for a person to see individual A and 'unpleasant' to see individual B, this means that one experience – the perception of A – entering the system of psychical experience elevates the sum of the system's energy, just as the other experience – the perception of B – diminishes that sum. All experiences possess a positive or negative Affectional – an indifferent Affectional is only the bordering magnitude in between them. Therefore, *all experiences are energetically commensurable in their relationship to the psychical system*. Indeed, this special form of their commensurability serves as the basis for our investigation.

---

5   The reader who is familiar with mathematics will note, of course, that in this conception the latter elements of the mind play the role of differentials in relation to the whole as an integral. And this is not at all simply an analogy but a legitimate mathematical determination of the given processes as variable magnitudes of energy.

But readers should not fear that we are taking them into the realm of pseudo-mathematical fantasy in the spirit of Herbart's psychology. With its strict methodological requirements, energetics does not provide a space for such forms of creativity, even if we wished to engage in it. Energetics is first of all a method of quantitative *description* of what is given in *experience*.

6   I cannot repeat here the entire explanation of this proposition – it is given in my book, *Poznanie s istoricheskoi tochki zreniia* (pp. 13–23), and in Chapter 2 of the present work, 'Life and the Psyche'.

My point of view regarding the given question far from coincides with popular views, but in everything essential it conforms – with, of course, a huge difference in form of expression – to the views of B. Spinoza and T. Meynert. [Baruch Spinoza (1632–77) posited a strict parallelism of the physical and the mental, famously declaring that 'the order and connection of ideas is the same as the order and connection of things'. Theodor Meynert (1833–92) was an Austrian psychiatrist and neuropathologist who argued that ideas and memories were attached to particular cells. (Trans.)]

## II

'We seek what is pleasant and avoid what is unpleasant' – it is difficult to even call this a definite formula; it is almost a simple tautology. Nevertheless, its vital significance is huge. In the final analysis, this is what all the principles of applied psychology – pedagogy, politics, morals – and all methods of juridical and moral influence of some people on others boil down to.

Any psychical experience – whether it is a wilful act, a perception, or a psychical image – as soon as it is characterised by the colouration of pleasure displays a tendency to be consolidated in a given system, to force out those experiences that do not have such a colouration. That experience can be eliminated only with increasingly great resistance, and it is increasingly easy for it to be preserved and repeated. It is also reflected in all other experiences that are proximally connected with it in an associative way, and their energy and stability also grow. The colouration of pain causes the opposite tendency. The experiences that belong to that pain and everything that is closely connected with them all decrease in energy and stability, and it is increasingly easy for them to be removed them from the psychical system. The tendencies of pleasure and pain form a kind of 'psychical selection' of experiences. In the succession and in the repetition of experiences, those that are more 'pleasant' display a relatively much greater vital capacity, and those that are more 'unpleasant' are characterised by a much lesser vital capacity.

Accordingly, if politicians deliberately try to create an inseparable connection between the conception of their political programme and a pleasant conception of certain practical benefits in the psyche of the voters, they are applying the principle of psychical selection. If teachers deliberately strive to closely associate conceptions of mischief with the unpleasant conception of punishment, they are applying the principle of psychical selection. Here is a necessary 'a priori' for any systematic influence on people; this is the practical role of this principle. What is important for us at this moment is to explain its theoretical meaning.

The *fact* of psychical selection is unquestionable, or, to put it more accurately, it is unquestionable that a great number of psychical facts lie completely within the confines of the idea of 'psychical selection' as we have presented it here.[7] But I seek an *empiriomonist* point of view for psychology, and therefore

---

7   I used the term 'psychical selection' previously but in another meaning – in the idea of the *natural selection of psychical forms*. And no matter which path that selection followed, it was nevertheless unrelated to the Affectional. But the selection I am discussing here can also be called the natural selection of psychical forms. I propose my idea of 'psychical selection'

the question that arises is whether the entire realm of psychical experience or only part of it must be subordinated to this distinctive principle and whether that principle can or cannot become a universal 'a priori' for psychological investigation. This is a question of the methodological significance of the idea of psychical selection.

In order to answer this question it is necessary first and foremost to reduce the very idea of psychical selection to the empiriomonist concepts that have already been established. It is necessary, as it is usually expressed, to 'explain' psychical selection, to determine 'what' it is exactly and 'how' and 'why' it occurs.

So far we know the following: we have given the term 'psychical selection' to the tendency toward the vital strengthening or weakening of separate experiences depending on the their Affectional colouration in the field of consciousness – positive (pleasure) or negative (pain). Thus, the basic features of psychical selection boil down to two facts. First, it appears in the field of consciousness (immediate psychical experience), and, second, its direction depends on the Affectional. We already know what the Affectional itself represents from an empiriomonist point of view: for cognition, pleasure is identical with the immediate increase of energy of a psychical system, and pain is identical with the immediate decrease of energy. Now we must deal with another peculiarity of psychical selection – its relationship with the field of consciousness.

III

'Consciousness' and immediate psychical experience are identical concepts. Some people have the opinion that, since these concepts express what is 'immediately known' (and, consequently, best known) to us, they are altogether not subject to definition and 'explanation'. This, of course, is wrong. The task of cognition is to harmoniously organise experience, to establish the interconnection and correlation of its elements and their combinations. 'Definition' and 'explanation' of such combinations present an expression of precisely this interconnection and correlation. Nothing can be excluded from this task, and therefore everything is subject to definition and explanation. Thus, any realm of experience must be defined and explained through other realms of experience, i.e. realms of experience that are precisely distinguished from it and simultaneously inseparably connected with it by a common, established regularity.

---

because it seems to me necessary to single out this distinctive characteristic of the development of psychical processes. The reader will subsequently find out how reasonable this is.

So, what is 'consciousness' as immediate psychical experience? First and foremost, it is obvious that it is a certain combination of experiences that belong to a specific psychical system. But, as we know, this is not all there is to it. What combination exactly? The fundamental characteristic of consciousness is a specific temporal form. Here the content continually changes over time but it is not deployed in space. And since only changes provide content for purely temporal interconnectedness, 'immediate consciousness' is first and foremost the realm of changes. Changes of what? Obviously changes of the psychical system that appertains to consciousness. And, in reality, each experience that passes through the field of consciousness signifies a certain change in the psychical system and its subsequent vital reactions. This change can be more or less significant, or perhaps even minimal, but it is always there, and the continual adaptation of the system to its environment is accomplished through these changes. What is the relationship among these changes? They are mutually coordinated; they are mutually united by an *associative* connection that makes one 'field of consciousness' from a series of experiences and that makes one unbroken chain of psychical experience from these continuously changing fields. Consequently, in regard to the psychical system, consciousness can be defined thus: *it is the realm of coordinated changes of the psychical system* (and the associative connection is the form in which they are coordinated).

At present we do not need a further explanation and investigation of the nature of the associative coordination, of its particular forms, etc. For now, it is sufficient to simply state the following. Any given field of consciousness can be viewed as a complex of simultaneous, mutually connected changes of the psychical system. In experience, the 'field of consciousness' primarily appears as a certain undifferentiated whole and breaking it down into separate experiences and establishing the specific interconnectedness among them is a derivative act, an act of 'cognition'. Cognition transforms an undefined unity into a defined unity but does not in the least eliminate that unity.

Proceeding from this proposition, we can 'explain' to ourselves the process of psychical selection, i.e. we can represent it in a simple, monist formula.

IV

The 'field of consciousness' of a given moment reflects the sum total of coordinated changes that occur in the psychical system. In terms of energetics, all these changes are commensurable and, *taken as a sum, they form a specific increase or decrease of energy of the psychical system.* But precisely what significance does the *Affectional* have? Pleasure corresponds to the growth of energy of the system and pain corresponds to the decrease of energy. What follows from this?

Suppose that there is a series of images in the field of consciousness – visual, motional, etc. – and a general negative Affectional (pain). These visual, motional, etc. reactions signify specific psychical adaptations that exist in the psychical system *not only* at the moment when they appear in the field of consciousness. This is fully proven by the fact that the given images are reproduced from time to time in the consciousness, and consequently they do not disappear once and for all from the psyche when they disappear from immediate perception.[8] Since the field of consciousness is the realm of *changes* of the psyche, it is obvious that the appearance of any given images in the field of consciousness expresses a series of changes that occur precisely in the sphere of those continually existing psychical adaptations that correspond to these images. What kind of change? This is what the Affectional clarifies. If the Affectional is negative, then what is going on is the decrease of energy of the psychical system, i.e. obviously, the lowering of energy of the given psychical adaptations. The psychical adaptations make up the *realm of changes*, and, therefore, the proceeding diminishment of energy proceeds *at their expense*. But the decrease of the energy of psychical adaptations is at the same time a decrease of their vital capacity, and it also appears as 'negative psychical selection'. We have thus arrived at an almost tautological formula: under the conditions of a negative Affectional (pain), negative psychical selection exists because the negative Affectional expresses the lowering of energy, and consequently also of the immediate vital capacity of those psychical adaptations that are appearing in the given field of consciousness. And the same thing, with corresponding changes, of course, relates also to positive selection when the Affectional is positive.

The simplest and most typical example of psychical selection is when a child puts his hand in a fire and gets burned. What happens in the psychical system in this circumstance? In the field of consciousness there is at first a visual perception of fire and, along with it, the conception of a specific motor reaction ('I want to grab this'). This conception has a positive colouration (the characteristic of 'pleasant'), i.e. it is associated with the increase of energy of the psychical system. But this increase occurs in the sphere of the system's '*coordinated changes*', in the realm of adaptations that correspond to the field of consciousness. The energy of the visual perception of fire is elevated as also is the motor conception of the grasping reaction. The perception of fire becomes clearer, sharper, richer in elements – the force and clarity of perception increases. The

---

8 For more detail regarding this, see *Poznanie s istoricheskoi tochki zreniia*, pp. 35–6 (the terminology is somewhat different).

motional conception becomes more intense and definite and transforms into an 'act of will' in a complete psycho-motor reaction. But now an intense tactile-thermal stimulus enters the field of consciousness that acts destructively on the psyche – a significant negative Affectional ('it is very painful') is immediately revealed. The field of consciousness as a realm of coordinated changes makes up one whole, and its general negative Affectional signifies the decline of the energy of all psychical adaptations that are presented to it at a given moment. As a result, the visual perception of fire becomes dim and unclear (the subject is 'blinded by pain'), although the perception does not disappear, of course, since the action of its 'external cause' – light waves on the retina – continues. The motor reaction of 'grasping' *is interrupted*, but the tactile-thermal perception cannot disappear because of the continuing 'external irritation'. Just like the visual perception of fire, only to a greater degree, the tactile-thermal perception becomes dim and unclear as a 'perception' – no particularity or details can be distinguished in it other than its approximate localisation in the fingers of the hand. It is overwhelmed and disappears in chaotically rising waves of 'burning pain' – an imprecise, convulsive psychical reaction presented by the huge expenditure of energy of the psychical system.[9] Subsequently a new psycho-motor reaction appears – the reflex of 'withdrawal of the hand'. Of all that follows, only one thing is important for us: those psychical complexes that were in the field of consciousness at the moment of the negative Affectional are subsequently recalled to mind in a comparatively weak from and less often. Even the visual image of fire, springing up in the memory of the child, is suppressed by other actions more quickly than before – the child 'steers clear' of this memory. Subsequently, the motor reaction of 'grasping' that proximally preceded the appearance of the negative Affectional is absolutely not repeated in connection with the perception of fire as it was in this case. And in any other connection, the motor reaction of 'grasping' is reproduced less quickly and energetically and with greater hesitancy and 'carefulness'.

In the majority of cases, the action of psychical selection is less intense, especially when it is directed in a positive direction – in the direction of strengthening and consolidating psychical combinations that arise. But then in the final analysis, the action of psychical selection, repeating and accumulating, can seem even considerably more significant in its results. It is thus obvious that, from the point of view of my conception, *the entire field of consciousness*

---

9  It is easy to see how much clearer and more distinct tactile-thermal perceptions are when stimuli are weaker and the Affectional is not so negative (for example, when a child picks up and feels ordinary objects).

*continuously appears at the same time to be a field of psychical selection*, and the entire life of consciousness presents itself as the process of development and destruction of psychical forms, the tenor of which at any given moment is determined by the positive or negative sign of the Affectional.

V

The connection of psychical selection with the Affectional signifies a connection with specific types of vital-differentials of the nervous system. This would seem to provide another perspective on the issue of psychical selection. It is necessary to 'resolve' this issue; it is necessary to 'explain' the process of psychical selection on the basis of the physiology of the nervous system.

Suppose that there is a series of concurrent images in the consciousness and that the series is coloured with the feeling of 'pleasure', i.e. a series of vital-differentials of various 'forms' is flowing in the nervous system, and their total sum is positive (the energy of the central organ of the system is elevated). The very presence of 'consciousness' corresponds to the fact that the vital-differentials are not flowing in a few isolated cells of the system but are spread through it in various directions and at the same time are situated in mutual interconnection and correlation. But, at the same time, the presence of *specific* reactions of the psyche signify that these vital-differentials have their own centres that in the given case are the main field of the vital-differentials and their starting points – special organs, so to speak, of these reactions. Such organs at the present state of science can be conceived of only in the form of specific complexes of nerve cells that are mutually connected by neural conductors. The neural conductors are the means by which the cells easily bring one another into a state of 'functional vital-differential' – into a 'dynamic' state, as it is often expressed. In the given example, the nature of the vital-differential is positive, and the energy of the nerve cells that have become part of the functioning special organ increases. As a result, the intensity of their life is magnified, and, along with this, obviously, the capability for them to functionally energise one another and, in general, to arrive together at a 'dynamic' state is also magnified. Thus, first, the chances of the repetition of psychical reactions connected with this dynamic state are increased, and, second, the intensity of these reactions also grows. Both of them, in aggregate, are designated as positive psychical selection.

It is possible to conceive of the picture of negative psychical selection in a completely analogous way. Under conditions of decreasing energy of the cells of the special organ of reaction, the cells are less capable of energising one another to function. Because of the weakened transmitting current, the resistance of the conductors can no longer be overcome as it was under former conditions – and the reaction is repeated less frequently and intensively.

In such a 'physiological' conception of psychical selection, a new trait appears that would be difficult to notice under a purely 'psychological' method of depiction. As I have shown, during one or another psychical reaction, its special organ serves as the *main field* of vital-differentials, but not their only realm. They are spread out – in a reduced degree – also to various other realms of the central system, which – precisely as an integral whole – is the organ of consciousness in general. If this is so, then the process of psychical selection must embrace not only the reactions that exist in the field of consciousness under the conditions of a given Affectional, but also other reactions (only to a considerably lesser degree) and, of those reactions, predominantly those in the special organs that are most closely connected with the special organs of the first reactions. And there are many facts that support this deduction. Thus, after a series of transferred feelings of suffering, a general diminution of the sphere of memory and practical reactions becomes apparent. A great deal is 'forgotten' that apparently was not directly connected with the negative Affectional; a person often 'unlearns' or 'breaks the habit' of doing what was nevertheless not, in itself, the source of pain. And, just the opposite, a series of intensely-pleasurable experiences often resurrects in the psyche many long-forgotten images that apparently are not in any kind of close relationship with these experiences.[10] All of this expresses the real vital unity of the psyche in the continual succession of the contents of psychical experience.

But now how are we to think about the fact that we have obtained two explanations of psychical selection – one from the point of view of immediate psychical experiences and another from the point of view of the physiology of the nervous system? It is not difficult to see that, as energetical formulas, both 'explanations' are *identical*, with the only difference being that, in one, psychical reactions are under discussion and, in the other, it is the vital-differentials of the organs of these reactions that are discussed. We recognise that the physiological process is the *reflection* of complexes of immediate experiences in the socially-organised experience of living beings. In energetical formulas, the reflection and the reflected completely merge together because these formulas are abstracted from the method of perception – 'direct' or 'indirect' perception. Thus, two 'explanations' of psychical selection represent in reality *one*

---

10  In this case, the indication that these forgotten images spring up again due to an indirect associative connection cannot in itself explain anything. The matter at hand is precisely about how to explain this 'indirect associative connection' that presents is no more than a denotation of the facts under investigation.

explanation in two different forms of presentation, and, in any given case, we can choose the one of them that in precisely that case is more convenient for a clear description and harmonious grouping of the facts.[11]

VI

The idea of psychical selection is, as we have seen, the generalisation of a very broad series of facts. But I want to make something larger from it – a guiding point of view for further investigation of the psyche. And since I seek *monist* methods, whose application would be able to include the *entire* realm of psychical experience, it is natural to pose the following question: how broad is the realm in which it is possible – in which it is conceivable – to employ the idea of psychical selection for research? The data we already have is sufficient for a very general answer to this question.

Psychical selection, as I defined it at the outset, is the form of the selection of experiences that is associated with the Affectional of those experiences. The Affectional is a property of experiences that is located precisely in 'consciousness' – i.e. in the field of immediate psychical experience – and only in that field. But is this the boundary of the phenomena of psychical substitution?

In experience and in cognition a person is never a solipsist, except in his immediate, i.e. personal, experience. The psychical experience of other living beings does exist for him, and this incomparably wider sphere of psychical experience is constructed on the basis of the 'utterances' of other organisms. It is clear that the idea of psychical substitution not only can but must be transferred to this entire realm, and this is all the easier since the Affectional is also provided in 'utterances' – people and animals 'express' feelings of pleasure and pain.

Psychical experience is in general characterised by a special type of coordination of elements and their complexes – the associative connection, to be precise. This is how psychical experience is distinguished from physical experience

---

11  In my earlier works, *Osnovnye elementy istoricheskogo vzgliada na prirodu* and *Poznanie s istoricheskoi tochki zreniia*, I gave another 'explanation' of psychical selection – an explanation that was narrower and more purely physiological. In that explanation, I attributed particular significance to the functions of the vasculomotor system – the nourishment of the brain. I am now inclined to consider this posing of the question not as inaccurate but as not broad enough and not simple enough. The role of the system that regulates nourishment in the fluctuation of vital-differentials must, in reality, be huge, but, all the same, 'nourishment' is only one of two aspects of the vital process, and a *universal* explanation must simultaneously pay attention to both sides. Therefore my previous formula, proceeding from a more *particular* group of facts, turns out to be more *complex*.

with its higher, objective regularity. But the critique of psychical experience has led us to conclude that psychical experience is only a certain part – the most organised part, to be precise – of the realm over which the associative coordination governs and that we have designated as the realm of 'immediate experiences'. I arrived at the conviction that to any vital-differential of physiological processes there correspond (or, to express it better, in any vital-differential there are revealed to cognition) certain immediate experiences with their own associative connection of elements and complexes of those elements. From this point of view, the psychical experience of a given living being is only its main associative coordination with which other, less complex, relatively independent coordinations of a similar type are vitally connected. The question consists in whether it is possible to extend the idea of psychical selection to all *these* coordinations and, consequently, to the entire realm of immediate experiences in general. And this realm, according to our conception, coincides with the kingdom of *life* in nature.

This question can already be empirically determined to a certain degree. Many of the lower coordinations that remain on the threshold of psychical experience are accessible to us by means of utterances when we observe, for example, the 'automatic' actions of people, the behaviour of insane people, and the various movements of lower organisms that stand so far below us on the stairway of development that we cannot ascribe real 'experience' to them. An automatic action of people who are deep in thought ceases when they meet a 'harmful resistance' that would cause 'pain' if it were reflected in the sphere of consciousness. Someone who is mentally ill makes direct utterances of an Affectional nature – in facial expressions, for example – and there are changes in the form of that person's actions that correspond to them. A lower organism like an amoeba quickly ceases to move when that movement brings it up against a 'harmful' influence that lowers the energy of the cell, etc. Clearly, for all such events the principle of psychical selection is cognitively expedient.

But further? As we know, far from all immediate experiences are reflected in 'utterances'. It is obvious that this does not mean that there is a fundamental difference between immediate experiences that are reflected and those that are not, and this essentially changes nothing. In reality, the property of psychical selection that we have arrived at is this: it is selection that proceeds in the sphere of the coordinated changes of a system and that is based on the increase or decrease of the energy of the system. This means that everywhere there are such coordinated changes, the phenomena of psychical selection must be caused by the elevation or lowering of the energy of the system that is present in those changes. But this applies to the whole realm of immediate experiences.

Thus, from the formal perspective there are solid grounds for taking the idea of psychical selection as a *universal principle* for the investigation of life as a flow of immediate experiences. This, however, still does not mean that the application of this principle must always and everywhere be successful. It depends on whether there is sufficient concrete data for such an application – a limitation that applies to all principles of cognition.

VII

The term 'psychical selection' that we have used can, in itself, cause a certain misunderstanding, especially on the part of readers who are biologists. This term indicates that psychical selection is a certain partial aspect of that universal selection of forms of life that is usually signified as 'natural' selection. Meanwhile, the method of actions of psychical selection, evidently, is quite unique and not similar to the method of action of natural selection. The factors of the former are the simple increase or decrease of energy of a psychical system, perceived as pleasure or pain, and the factors of the latter are reproduction and the death of individuals, perceived as objective phenomena. What do they have in common, and is it valid to subordinate the former to the latter like a species to a genus?

First and foremost, the difference of the means of perception cannot have a fundamental significance for the method of cognition. What 'subjectively' exists as pleasure and pain appears 'objectively' as a physiological change – in the sense of the development or degradation of the system. What is perceived as 'objective', such as death or reproduction, proceeds 'subjectively' in the form of the disappearance of an earlier series of immediate experiences or the appearance of a new such series. The difference is only that in one case the material for investigation is provided more easily and fully by one type of perception, and in the other case it is provided more easily and fully by another type of perception; but this is not important for the question.

Further, it would be mistaken to reduce the whole process of 'natural selection' to only the moments of death and reproduction. The idea of selection expresses a continual correlation between a given form of life and its environment. Negative natural selection is only completed by death (i.e. the destruction of the vital coordination), but up until that moment it is expressed precisely in the lowering of energy of the given form, in the taking away of that energy by the environment. In exactly the same way, positive selection does not boil down to the preservation and reproduction of forms. It is instead the continual equilibrium or growth of its energy at the expense of the environment; it boils down to processes for which preservation and reproduction are only the most graphic expressions. The 'pains' that a mal-adapted being must undergo and that, by lowering its vital capacity, hasten its death, serve as a most real expression of 'natural selection'.

Thus, we must not assert any kind of fundamental difference between 'psychical' and 'natural' selection. These concepts are not to be understood in a crudely realistic sense as independent 'actors' in life but in that strictly methodological sense, devoid of any personification, in which we have taken them.[12]

But psychical selection must be viewed as a particular form of 'natural' selection because the former relates only to associative coordinations of experiences, while the second relates to all phenomena of life in all forms.

VIII

The continuous connection of psychical selection with the 'Affectional' poses a new question for us. The majority of psychophysiologists consider the Affectional, itself, as a distinctive psychological adaptation that is very important and especially necessary for the preservation of life but that is nevertheless only a *particular* psychical adaptation, one of many that are elaborated by development. If one took this point of view, it would be impossible to make the idea of psychical selection, itself, which enters psychical experience as an Affectional selection, into a universal method of investigation of the psyche. But is it possible to altogether agree with this point of view?

The Affectional means only pleasure or pain as immediate sensations or, more accurately, as a certain immediate colouration of experiences (their 'sensory tone'). Taken individually, this colouration in itself is not any kind of adaptation. But pleasure is what living beings strive for and pain is what they avoid, and both serve to aid the preservation and development of life. It is thus completely possible to consider them both to be 'adaptations'. What does this mean?

A child puts his hand out toward fire and experiences a well-known thermal sensation in the colouration of powerful pain and withdraws his hand. This is an adaptation. A child sees a monster and is very afraid; the emotion of fear is

---

12  In science, the methodological conception of *natural* selection is most precisely expressed, in our view, by Felix Le Dantec in his critical works about Darwinism and neo-Lamarckianism, except that he attaches too exclusive a significance to the *chemical* conditions of the equilibrium of a vital form with its environment, whereas it is doubtless that the matter has to do with a physical and mechanical equilibrium. Le Dantec does, however, mention this aspect of the question, only too superficially. [Félix-Alexandre Le Dantec (1869–1917) was a French biologist and philosopher of science (trans).]

characterised by powerful pain, but in this case the pain only deprives the child of the strength needed to run from the monster or fight with it. Clearly, there is no adaptation. Pain in both cases signifies the same thing – the destructive influence of the environment, the expense of energy of the psychical system. But the reactions of the system are different, and the result for the psychical system is different. In one case there is an adaptation; in the other there is unadaptedness. One conclusion follows from this: if we take the perspective of the system and distinguish the Affectional of an experience in cognition from the subsequent reaction, then it turns out that an adaptation (or unadaptedness) depends entirely on the nature of the subsequent reaction. The Affectional itself expresses only the condition of the system – the increase or decrease of its energy. In other words, the Affectional is the relationship of the system to the 'environment'; it is either a factor that takes energy from the system, or, just the opposite, it is a source of the growth of energy. If a child withdrew his hand from the fire reflexively, even if not in time to avoid pain, his adaptedness would not decrease but would rather increase because there would be less expense of energy of the psychical system.

Thus, the Affectional is not an adaptation, although it determines the direction and the production of adaptations. For an animal, an extremely warm or extremely cold climate determines the development of new adaptations in the organism of the animal in a completely analogous way, despite the fact that extreme warmth or cold, themselves, are not in any way adaptations. The Affectional means the same thing for psychical selection as a destructive or favourable action of the environment on an organism means for natural selection.

∴

Psychical selection is psychical causality just as natural selection is biological causality. But causality is not teleology, and if, in general, it leads to the appearance and development of balanced and harmonious systems, this far from always happens in particular cases. Psychical selection, just like natural selection, creates many things only for them to be destroyed. In the psychical system, selection always acts only partially and not integrally; it coordinates only 'parts of parts' and not the whole. Selection adapts some psychical experiences to others immediately when they meet together in a given specific coordination, but a *general* adaptedness for all the coordinations of the system very rarely results from this. The action of psychical selection is often contradictory. But over the course of centuries its organising tendency overcomes these contradictions, and the power of development prevails over them.

## 1.3  *The Model of Association*

I

The basic characteristic of the entire realm of psychical experience is a specific type of coordination of experience – the associative type, to be exact. Up until now we have employed the concept of the associative connection only in order to point out the boundaries of the realm of our investigation, but this does not at all mean that this concept has a cognitive 'a priori' meaning for us in the Kantian-epistemological meaning of this word. And as soon as we want to step away from the question of a universal psychological method in the direction of concretely-psychological cognition, then the task that arises is to 'explain' the fact of association of experiences in psychical experience from the point of view of this method.

First and foremost, what do psychologists have in mind when they speak of 'association'?

The indefinite, unorganised flow of experiences that is the real, vital 'a priori' of all experience and cognition, is still, of course, not an associative combination of elements just because experience and cognition crystallise precisely from that flow in the process of development. Instead, that primary chaos of life is only the potential material for the appearance an associative combination. But a stable, solidly organised complex of elements also does not in itself form an 'association' until it is broken down in experience and cognition into its constituent parts, which are then viewed as 'associated' among themselves. Two complexes, A and B, that invariably encounter one another together in the field of psychical experience would not constitute an association, because they would not at all be distinguished as two separate complexes but would be taken as one. Thus, if we speak of the associative connection of A, B, C, etc. then we thereby have in mind not only their mutual connection but also their separateness; we have in mind that sometimes they appear together and sometimes apart in combinations with other complexes. But, at the same time, we do not consider the confluences of A, B, C, etc. in the field of consciousness as 'random', but we recognise a certain regularity such that each of them 'drags' others behind – i.e. each is positive and not negative or neutral in regard to the condition for the appearance of other complexes in the sphere of immediate psychical experience. Sometimes this condition turns out to be sufficient in itself and sometimes it does not, but when this condition is present the manifestation of the experiences associated with it always requires a lesser sum of any other conditions than when it is absent.

The basic, most general and typical form of associative connection is association according to *contiguity*. Once two experiences enter into one field of consciousness, they subsequently reveal the tendency to mutually evoke one another – when encountering a horse that one has seen earlier, one remembers the rider who was sitting on it at the time, and vice versa. How can this connection be 'explained' from the point of view of psychical selection?

Two complexes, A and B, exist simultaneously in a field of consciousness. They are jointly 'subject to' psychical selection, positive or negative; in other words, they jointly undergo energetical changes in the sense of the strengthening or weakening of these complexes. But both complexes thereby form *one system of energetical equilibrium* in the given psyche. This results from the fact that the field of consciousness presents, as we have seen, a realm of coordinated changes of the psychical system (i.e. changes that are energetically connected at a given moment), and the energy of those changes is exchanged with their external environment but also among them, themselves.[13]

Thus, due to the process of psychical selection, what we now have are not two separate complexes of elements 'randomly' united for a while but a certain, specific system of equilibrium. It remains 'outside consciousness' as long as this equilibrium is not disrupted. If it is disrupted in a specific way for one part of this system – let us say for part A – then 'complex A' enters the field of consciousness, but then, as in any energetical system, the equilibrium is also disrupted for part B, and we can expect that B will also 'crop up' in consciousness. If after all the intervening time, the system of these two complexes remains absolutely unchanged then each of them inevitably must be summoned one after the other, but one cannot speak of such complete stability when dealing with an alive and alert psyche. The system, changing slowly and continuously in its tiniest parts, can be significantly transformed and even completely broken down. This is why the associative connection has only limited significance, and this is why it presents a multitude of various levels of steadiness from an imperceptible minimum of stability to a continuity bordering on the maximum.

This point of view explains all the distinctive features of the associative connection. For example, it is particularly durable if it arises under conditions of a strong *Affectional*; everything that is undergone at a moment of great joy or intense suffering is associated most durably so that each part of the field of con-

---

13   Such a connection is all the more strikingly expressed physiologically in that separate vital-differentials of cells and partial centres that correspond to the 'field of consciousness' merge together by means of conductors (associative and projective fibres) in one continuous, general vital-differential of the central system.

sciousness of that time, entering into consciousness again, resurrects the others with great strength and clarity. Many techniques of mnemonics and pedagogy are based on this well-known fact.[14] A strong Affectional signifies the energetic action of psychical selection, and since precisely this action also creates one system of equilibrium from two complexes that come together in consciousness, then it is understandable that more intense selection causes a greater relative unity and more stability of the new system – i.e. a more durable connection of its parts. In absolutely the same way, the association of experiences is also strengthened when they repeatedly enter the consciousness together. Only in this case the intensity of psychical selection is replaced by duration – its action, so to speak, accumulates.

On the other hand, the more intense psychical life is during this intervening time while the associated complexes remain 'below the threshold' of consciousness, the weaker the associative connection of these complexes becomes and the less the chance that one of them will enter the field of consciousness 'dragging' the other into appearing along with it. Intense psychical life means a great number of changes of the psychical system and, consequently, a great number of transforming influences, and these influences also act beyond the borders of the main coordination, transforming partial systems of energetical equilibrium, which were formerly bundled together, into associative groupings. And here, as in the preceding case, the duration of the transformative influences has the same significance as their intensity: associations become less durable if they are not resumed in consciousness.

All this relates to the simplest and most basic type of the associative connection – associations 'according to contiguity'. It is exactly the same, it goes without saying, also with associations 'according to temporal consecutiveness', since the latter *includes* in itself a moment of contiguity. If complex A *completely* disappears from consciousness at the moment that complex B appears, then the association according to consecutiveness does not form. It obtains only in the event that complex A – even if only partially and in a weak form – is still retained for a certain amount of time along with B. Thus, we are completely justified in viewing both primary types of association as the *result of psychical selection*. The issue of associations 'by similarity' and 'by contrast' –

---

14  In olden times, when the boundaries of landlords' estates were drawn, little boys were whipped on the boundary lines so that even in old age they could not forget where the boundary was. The same method is used by contemporary classical teachers when they make a pupil go without dinner while requiring them to learn the vocabulary, or by patriarchal parents when they beat children and repeat over and over again: 'do not do this, do not do that ...', etc.

associations of a 'higher' type – is a bit more complicated. In order to proceed to them, we need still one more intermediary link: the phenomenon of psychical 'habit'.

II

If any psychical reaction of a sensory nature (a perception, a psychical image) or of a motor nature (an act of will, a desire) repeatedly appears in consciousness, then the more this continues the more *habitual* it becomes. In so doing, it changes in precisely three regards. From one perspective, it is all the more easily reproduced in the psyche; the chances grow that it will be repeated again under other, equal conditions. From another perspective, as a complex of elements of experience, it acquires ever greater definiteness and conservatism; the mutual relationships of its elements become more durable and stable. And from a third perspective, the Affectional colouration of the reaction changes, generally speaking, in the direction of indifference; a high Affectional, positive or negative, decreases and becomes an ever less significant magnitude. But a negative Affectional is not limited in this way; a negative Affectional ultimately turns into a positive Affectional, although it usually also does not turn into a notably high magnitude.[15] The question is: what can the idea of psychical selection provide for clarifying these facts that play such a huge role in psychical life and development?

First and foremost, it is obvious that the question here has to do with the repeated and in general prolonged action of psychical selection; it is repeated over and over, and each time the reaction is subject to this action. If the selection is positive (if the reaction appears in the consciousness as something 'pleasant') then it immediately becomes understandable why the chances of a further repetition of the reaction grow – this is a general and basic trait of positive psychical selection. But how is it possible for the very same effect of 'habituation' also to obtain when selection is negative, when the reaction is directly 'unpleasant'? A priori, one would obviously expect the direct opposite result, that repetition of the reaction would be more and more difficult. It is true that *sometimes* this does happen, and the more often a given complex is repeated in consciousness, the stronger the internal resistance that it

---

15 'Folk wisdom' expresses this aspect of the process of habituation with the words 'you will like him when you get used to him'. Occupational habits even make it possible for people to find a certain satisfaction in what is downright unbearable for everyone who is not used to it. For example, many chemists who work with hydrogen sulphide, if only to analyse it, begin to positively like the odour of this gas.

thereby encounters and the stronger the tendency to suppress it and remove it from the psychical field.[16] But this happens in rather a minority of cases, and we will now take up the opposite type of phenomenon – when an 'unpleasant' reaction appears with an ever decreasing resistance from the psyche and that subsequently becomes even 'pleasant'. For example, when people, having begun to take up a certain kind of work that they loathe, gradually 'gets absorbed' in it and even begins to find a certain pleasure in it.

In any event, there is no doubt that such 'habituation' under the conditions of a reaction with a negative colouration occurs considerably more slowly and with a greater expenditure of energy than when the reaction is positive. It is considerably easier 'to get absorbed' in an immediately-pleasant occupation than one that is immediately-unpleasant. Thus here also, obviously, the typical *tendency* of negative selection is present, only it is paralysed and outweighed by some kind of other influences. What kind of influences? The question is easily answered if one keeps in mind that the field of psychical selection is the *entire field of consciousness* as one whole.

It is hard to imagine greater pain than that experienced by a ten-year-old schoolchild 'learning' to smoke. The unaccustomed tactile, olfactory, and taste sensations from tobacco smoke cause a large number of disharmonious, convulsive reactions – from the diaphragm and other muscles of the respiratory system (coughing), from the vascular system (palpitation of the heart, quickening of the pulse) the muscles of the face (grimacing), various glands (tears, salivation), etc. In total, this signifies a great expenditure of energy and consequently great pain. If this were all that the matter boiled down to, then it is unlikely that anyone would 'get used to' smoking. But the situation is considerably more complex, and, in addition to the presence of the complexes that have been indicated, there are still a great many more. The idea of the act of smoking is associated in the psyche of the child with the idea of a certain relative 'equality' with adults and, consequently, with a certain fundamental broadening and elevation of life. In the end, this combination boils down to association 'according to contiguity' – to the fact that the child saw only grownups as smokers and at the same time observed their mutual relationships, which, from the child's perspective, were extremely 'free'. While the act of smoking caused 'unpleasant' sensations, nevertheless consciousness of growing freedom was 'pleasant'.

---

16  For example, when people are forced to carry out a task that is unpleasant to them, it often happens that each time they do it, it becomes more difficult, their work becomes less energetic, and the coordination of willed actions that mentally determine it becomes ever more disharmonious and proceeds ever more listlessly. This is the typical picture of negative psychical selection.

One part of the association, taken separately, has a negative Affectional; the other part is positive. What is the colouration of the association as a whole? The feeling of pain that overshadows the first part of the association is very intense but is fleeting and has only an individual-physiological basis. On the contrary, the feeling of pleasure that characterises the second part of the association might perhaps not be especially intense, but it has a socio-psychological basis that is constantly maintained by the social environment that surrounds the child and that is therefore notable for its lingering action. For example, some children might smoke until they vomit one or two times and suffer for a few hours, but, looking at the people around them many times every day, the thought keeps recurring: 'Oh, how good adults have it, to do what they want and to smoke with such obvious pleasure'. If, in this continually renewed association, it is the lingering though less intense action of a positive Affectional that preponderates, then those children will again and again resume their attempts to smoke. If the intense though less prolonged influence of the negative Affectional wins, then attempts will become more seldom or will stop. In the first case the chances of a repetition of the reaction grow, as indeed happens in situations of 'habituation'; in the second case they decrease.

This particular example gives us an indication of the general path along which a 'habit' of repeating 'unpleasant' reactions is created. With every factual repetition of the reaction – a repetition conditioned by the totality of circumstances, even though they are only 'external' conditions – this reaction appears as a constituent part of a specific *field of consciousness* and psychical selection associates it 'according to contiguity' with the remaining content of that field. The more that such factual repetitions occur and the more that various 'fields of consciousness' accommodate the given reaction, the more will 'associative connections' according to contiguity be formed in it. And every associative connection, as we know, increases the chances of the repetition of the reaction. In so doing, the Affectional colouration *itself* becomes less important, since the action of psychical selection relates, as we have seen, not to separate parts of the field of consciousness but to its whole. And the special Affectional of the reaction enters as an *addend* in the general sum of conditions of psychical selection. If this addend has a 'minus' sign but the others have 'plus' signs, then depending on the magnitude of the vital sum, the chances that the reactions will be repeated will either grow or diminish. In the first case, the process of 'habituation to the unpleasant' results, and it is understandable that this process turns out to be, generally speaking, considerably slower and more difficult than 'habituation to the pleasant'.

Another aspect of this process is expressed in the increase of distinctness and conservation of the psychical reaction that 'turns into a habit'. This is explained simply by the general prolongation of the action of psychical selection that appears with every repetition of the reaction. *Like any energetical process*, psychical selection is directed toward a stable equilibrium, and, acting on a given complex of elements, it strives to make a balanced, conservative system of them, which is also a definition of 'habitual' complexes. But the distinctness that results is always, of course, not absolute but only relative, since psychical selection strives at the same time to form systems of equilibrium of a broader content. To be precise, this is an equilibrium of the given complex *together* with other associative systems that it encounters in the same field of consciousness.

The 'atrophy' of the Affectional to the extent that it becomes a habit is also explained by this latter circumstance. To the extent that associative systems of an energetical equilibrium are created, the equilibration of the various parts of each such system also occurs. Any significant 'plus' or 'minus' becomes diffuse, so to speak, by being distributed among all the parts of these systems. A certain average Affectional is obtained for the various associative complexes, and it is perfectly natural that this is usually a small *positive* Affectional, because the very 'habituation' occurs, as we have seen, only when the action of psychical selection on the various associations that include the *given* reaction is positive and not negative in the common sum. For example, if chemists gradually begin to find the smell of $H_2S$ rather pleasant, then this is first and foremost because the idea of many interesting and useful chemical reactions is associated with this sensation for them – an idea that has a positive Affectional that passes on to the perceived smell.[17]

In a great many cases, however, the change of an Affectional occurs along yet another path, for which that same 'habituation' to smoking can serve as a good example. To an unhabituated person, tobacco smoke, as a new intense external influence, causes, as we know, many convulsive reactions that are all 'unpleasant' since they represent a great expenditure of neural energy (coughing, heart palpitations, narrowing of peripheral blood vessels, etc.). Because of these convulsive reactions, an enormous Affectional obtains during the act of smoking, but if this act is repeated then they are gradually removed by psychical selection according to the general law of the action of psychical selection. And with the removal of these convulsive reactions, the negative Affectional of the person who is smoking decreases or even transforms into a positive Affectional if it is associatively joined together with 'pleasant' experiences.

---

17 At the same time, of course, an opposite phenomenon occurs: the positive Affectional of the idea of such interesting and useful chemical reactions *diminishes* due to the 'unpleasant' colouration of the smell that is realised or sensed in connection with these reactions.

As we see, the 'process of habituation' in all its basic manifestations fits entirely within the confines of 'psychical selection'. In other words, it is easily 'explained' by psychical selection.

III

The point of view of psychical selection has given us the ability to 'explain' various manifestations of the process that is signified by the word 'habituation' and that usually – but not always – accompanies psychical 'exercise' (*Übung*), i.e. repetition of similar psychical complexes in the flow of experience. But it indeed also has given us the ability to understand those cases when 'exercise' does not entail 'habituation' – cases in which the repetition of particularly 'unpleasant' experiences results in the decisive preponderance of a negative selection, thereby increasingly resisting further repetitions. Thus, the idea of psychical selection turns out to be broader and more general than the view that I would call 'psychological Lamarckism', a view that that stops only at the surface of the facts of 'exercise' and 'habituation', ascertaining them but not reducing them to unity with undoubted facts of a contrary nature.[18]

I obviously can now make both these and other facts – as already 'explained' and already reduced to the unity of the idea of psychical selection – as the basis of further 'explanation' of psychical facts of a more complex character. And I will do this first and foremost in relation to the higher types of the associative process – to associations according to similarity and contrast that constitute the basis of any cognitive 'generalisation' and 'discrimination'.

Any complex of elements that is singled out from the flow of experiences appears in experience first of all as a certain indefinite whole. Even to distinguish a complex from other complexes that are contiguous with it is possible only because that complex does not appear in association with exactly the same complexes. Rather, each time it is repeated it is associated – at least partly – with different and new complexes. This is completely analogous with the conditions that make possible the *decomposition* of a complex into its parts

---

18   For Avenarius in *Kritik der reinen Erfahrung*, such Lamarckism is one of the central ideas and is connected with an understanding of the principle of 'pure description' that is too superficially formal. The principle of pure description essentially requires that nothing *that fundamentally goes beyond the confines of given experience* is brought into cognition, so that any 'explanation' would only be a *simplified description*. But the principle of pure description should by no means reduce the methods of this simplified description to the mechanical summary of the facts – such a summary is only material for a unifying idea, but it is still not a unifying idea. Everything that Avenarius says about *Übung* is only a mechanical summary.

and elements. These parts and these elements are repeated in other, new combinations so that the former complex is reproduced – not only wholly but sometimes also partially – in *other* complexes. For example, if a child, having previously seen only one cat, encounters another cat, then the greater part of the combinations of the former cat – of the psychical image of the cat – is factually reproduced in his psyche, but in association with certain new combinations in place of certain old ones. Similar facts thereafter occur again and again, and, in so doing, the 'common' part of all corresponding complexes – perceptions or psychical images of 'cat' – is repeated and is subject to a more prolonged and systematic action of psychical selection than the remaining – 'individual' – parts of these complexes. In consequence, that common part becomes more of a 'habit'. Here 'habituation' also leads, it goes without saying, *to greater repeatability, to greater conservation, and to comparative Affectional indifference*. All these traits are also characteristic of a complex that is gradually isolated out in this way – the 'generalised conception' of a cat.[19]

The process of 'generalisation' that is accomplished is thus at the same time a process of *association according to similarity*. The fact of the matter is that the part of similar complexes that is most often repeated is naturally associated *according to contiguity* with each of the parts of its that are less often repeated and 'drags' them along with it into consciousness. If A, as a combination that is repeated more often, stands apart from B, as a more individual part of one complex, stands apart from C in another complex, and from D in a third complex, this standing apart is not absolute. Nevertheless, A remains associated with B because it is found together with B in one field of consciousness and along with B is subjected to the action of psychical selection, which, as we have seen, creates in this case an associative relationship. But A is also united in an associative connection with C, with D, etc. in exactly the same way. Consequently, no matter which of the associative combinations A appears in, A 'has a tendency' also to summon into consciousness its remaining combinations: A + B 'drags' behind it A + C and A + D, etc. One cat 'reminds' one of other cats; one bird reminds one of other birds … This is what association 'according to resemblance' is.

The development of psychical experience leads to the progressive 'generalisation' of experiences. The decomposition of the complexes of experi-

---

19  Properly speaking, the primary conception of such-and-such a given cat – for example the first that a given child has seen up to that time – is formed along the following path. A series of successive perceptions of one and the same cat does not present an exact repetition of one and the same complex but only an approximate repetition, and the conception of such-and-such a given cat is already a 'generalisation'.

ence goes further. The part of one series of complexes that is repeated and the part of another series of complexes that is repeated can contain common combinations that, in their turn, are isolated out by psychical selection as especially 'habitual' for the psyche. This is a 'generalisation of the second order' – etc. Generalisations of higher orders are associative centres for generalisations of lower orders, just as those generalisations are associative centres for even lower ones. This chain of generalisations is at the same time a chain of associations – more and less broad – according to similarity.

Since a 'generalisation' (i.e. the part of similar complexes that is repeated) is 'isolated out' to a certain degree only because it is repeated in the contents of these complexes, and since it forms their common associative centre, it is natural that it never appears *absolutely separate* from these complexes; it is never isolated out from them completely – even for a short time. As we know, an associative connection signifies a system of energetical equilibrium that has been worked out by psychical selection, and therefore a 'generalisation' – being only the central link of a broad system of this kind – can in no way be completely torn away from that system, even if only for one moment. If this were to happen then we would have an energetically out-of-balance combination that due to its imbalance would immediately remove the contiguous (associative) psychical groupings from equilibrium – i.e. it would draw the 'particular' complexes that it generalises into the 'field of consciousness'. In other words, generalisation is *always* manifested in the psyche as the central part of association by similarity, and it exists only in that association. People can never realise a 'pure' generalisation in their consciousness that would be 'abstracted' from everything that is individual in the generalised particular complexes.

Thus, a generalisation presents nothing other than association according to similarity in which the repeating part of associated complexes is to a certain degree isolated out – so to say 'underlined' – by psychical selection. It is understandable that the higher the degree or 'order' of generalisation, the broader the association according to similarity that it corresponds to and the more it connects a significant number of particular complexes. But the field of consciousness as a realm of coordinated changes of the psyche is always limited. Like any organised system, the psyche cannot simultaneously experience an indefinitely large number of changes without of its coherence and unity being disrupted. This is why a generalised complex never, or almost never, appears in consciousness together with *all* the particulars that it unifies. Only some of them are present, and, moreover, some are very distinct, some are less distinct, and still others are in a completely attenuated form, and psychical selection very quickly replaces some of them with others so that the whole generalised complex has a fluctuating character. This is the permanent psychological characteristic of 'generalisation'.

What is called an 'idea' in cognition is a durable, socially-conditioned association *according to contiguity* between a vaguely-unstable 'generalisation' of complexes in the consciousness and a completely defined, highly conservative complex – a 'word' – that has an insignificant sum of elements. Fundamentally, this association is 'explained' just like any other association, but its social origin, so far, lies outside the confines of our task.

As can be seen, our point of view, based on the facts of 'habituation', easily boils the basic processes of cognitive activity down to the principle of psychical selection. It thereby 'explains' the characteristic 'coldness' of cognition, the comparative inability of the Affectional to distinguish between 'generalisation' and 'idea'. The most 'general' is the most repeated – the most 'habitual' – and, as we have seen, 'habituation' leads to the atrophy of the Affectional. This 'coldness' of cognition is also the condition of that *conservation* of ideas that is expressed in the logical 'law of identity'. A high Affectional signifies, after all, the intense work of psychical selection, and it consequently signifies the transformation – the destruction of the identity – of complexes located in consciousness. A high Affectional is therefore not compatible with the strict conservation of complicated ideas.

IV

Before we move on to the third, most complex form of the associative connection, we must dwell a little on cases of *competition* between psychical complexes that are very important for explaining this third form.

The field of consciousness is a realm of coordinated changes of the psychical system. This realm is always inevitably limited due because to two circumstances. On the one hand, the psyche, presenting itself as an organised, very complex, and only relatively stable whole, cannot altogether sustain an indefinitely large number of simultaneous changes; once the number of changes goes beyond a certain threshold, the psyche begins to simply break down. On the other hand, the more the changes that simultaneously appear, the more the degree of coordination of those changes also diminishes, and beyond a certain boundary their coherence disappears, and a murky, indefinite mass of experiences ('*Verworrenheit*') results that is not psychical experience. What results is a huge expenditure of energy of the psychical system. Psychical selection is directed toward narrowing of the field of experiences, and when this point is reached consciousness 'enters its normal boundaries'.

Experimental psychologists – such as Wundt, for example – have made experiments with the goal of determining the maximum content of consciousness. The results of these experiments are hardly subject to exact expression because the units of measurement are far from worked out. One thing that is certain is that for every psyche there is a maximum content that serves as a certain natural boundary to the broadening of the flow of experiences.

The mutual competition of psychical complexes is contingent on this boundary. The more complexes there are in the field of consciousness, the more powerfully psychical selection strives to reduce their numbers. In so doing, the removal of some leads to the increase of the vividness and clarity of others and vice versa. This is what the competition of experiences consists in.

The degree and intensity of competition depends, of course, not only on the number of competing complexes but also on their content, their nature, and their mutual relationships. The more heterogeneous the complexes and the fewer the common, connective combinations they have, the more difficult their mutual coordination is, the less they are mutually coordinated, and the more intensely they compete with one another. This is well known by anyone who has had to think about several different matters at the same time. And there is one extremely important series of cases when competition becomes particularly powerful even when a small number of experiences are involved. This is when the issue has to do with contradictory volitional complexes.

If the life of the psyche is considered in its relations to the external environment then it is necessary to establish two basic types of psychical experiences: complexes that are *images* (sensations, perceptions, psychical images) and *volitional* complexes (desires, impulses). 'Images' are immediate reflections of influences of the environment on the psychical system, and 'will' is the reciprocal reaction of the system on these influences, reactions that modify them. Complexes of the 'environment' cause changes in the complexes of the 'psyche'. To the extent that these latter have a passive nature and are not reflected, in turn, in complexes of the environment, they are only 'images'. To the extent that they obtain an active colouration, being reflected, in turn, in the environment, they constitute 'will'.[20] The inseparable connection of

---

20  A 'conception' is an incomplete complex-image that does not spring up from the direct and immediate influence of complexes of the surroundings but all the same appears as an indirect reflection of them. A desire is an incomplete volitional complex that is not reflected in an immediate form on complexes of the surroundings but under sufficient conditions is immediately transformed into a volitional act that then is 'reflected' in the

both types of psychical experience – the impossibility of a sharp boundary between their realms – is self-evident.

The typical psychical reaction presents a continuous combination of complexes of the first series with complexes of the second series. A person 'perceives' a specific image, let us say 'loot' and this image immediately brings with it a volitional impulse of a specific nature – the act of 'seizing' the loot. At first this is one unbroken complex and only with the broadening and increasing complexity of experience is it divided into two mutually associated parts.

A volitional complex, taken in itself, always represents an *expenditure* of energy of the psychical system, that has an *energetically-negative* magnitude. In physiological terms, a volitional complex is also expressed in *innervation* – a flow of energy directed from the central nervous system to the periphery and, in the final analysis, to the external environment. Thus, for any complex in which 'volitional' combinations prevail, psychical selection must turn out to be negative, trying to remove this complex from consciousness. It is with good reason that many philosophers have considered desires and will as suffering. Such complexes would quickly disappear from consciousness if there were no continuing action of those conditions that are 'external' in relation to the field of consciousness that summoned these complexes and by which they, so to speak, are stirred up again and again. As long as the action of coldness continues to act on an organism, the desire to find shelter from the cold and wrap oneself up in something never ceases. And it never ceases despite the negative colouration of the field of consciousness in which the desire appears. But as soon as the conditions that cause and renew the desire are removed – the desire is 'gratified', for example – then it disappears very quickly from consciousness due to the action of negative selection. So, for example, after an excellent dinner it is difficult to even imagine how someone could want to eat.

It is completely understandable that volitional complexes compete among themselves more than image-complexes do when they come together in consciousness. A continual expenditure of energy in various directions results, and the negative Affectional is particularly significant. In so doing, none of the competing complexes usually attains the level of a full volitional act – precisely because of the competition of others – but remains at the stage of 'desire'. A struggle of various 'desires' results, and it continues until negative selection removes all of the competitors except for one. This is the most intense and

---

surroundings. (Regarding the relationships of these incomplete psychical reactions to complete psychical reactions, see my work *Poznanie s istoricheskoi tochki zreniia*, pp. 68–77.)

stable desire and therefore the one that displaces all other desires, fills the field of consciousness, and crosses over into action.

In reality, of course, it is not mere volitional complexes that compete but a whole association of images and desires. The action of psychical selection becomes more complex because images, in themselves, can also have a positive Affectional – frequently a very significant one. Consequently, a positive selection appears that strengthens not only the image itself but also the desire associated with it. Then a 'desire for what is pleasant' becomes active and crosses over into action. But what is important at that given moment for our analysis is something else: in every competing association the intensity of the image changes along with the intensity of the corresponding desire – increasing and decreasing approximately in parallel with the latter. Such a correspondence is inevitable due to the extremely close associative connection between image and desire.

v

Along with association 'according to similarity', association 'according to contrast' or, speaking more generally, 'according to difference', plays a huge role in people's cognitive life. This is a more complex type of associative connection.

When you see a black African, the concepts of a 'white' Caucasian, a 'copper coloured' Indian, a swarthy-yellow person of the Mongol race, etc. come to mind. In so doing, it is precisely the *differences*, and not the similarity, of their traits that come to the fore in your consciousness, that single themselves out with the greatest clarity and distinctness. In this case it is the colour of their skin. This is what association according to difference is. It is not difficult to see that it *presupposes* the association according to similarity. Seeing a black person, you do not recollect white down or white paper but a white person. The traits of similarity that are common to these two complexes of elements form a necessary and primary connection between them, and only those complexes that are already brought together by this connection can serve as material for the new combination that you signify as association according to difference.

The new combination itself presents a certain contradiction with the former combination. In association according to similarity the common parts of the associated complexes (the 'form of generalisation') are distinguished by the greatest intensity and the traits of difference remain in the background and are jumbled and merge together into a kind of murky mass of experiences, whereas in association according to difference the relationship is absolutely the other way around. In association according to difference common traits retreat into the background and are recognised only weakly and murkily, and it is as if 'differences' are underlined, appearing with all the greater clarity and distinctness (the 'form of differentiation'). Our task consists in figuring out the psychological genesis of such associations.

It is easiest to describe this genesis with a concrete example.

Let us suppose that there is a war on the Southern African steppes between 'white' people and 'black' people, and you by chance lag behind the European troops and are lost in a place that you are unfamiliar with. Looking around, you notice that in the distance on the horizon the silhouette of some kind of human figure stands out. You peer at it but you are completely unable to make out whether it is a Black African or a European in dark clothing. Two mutually competing psychical complexes appear in your consciousness, but this involves not only the images of a 'white' and a 'black' person but forms that are closely associated with *specific desires*. The conception of a European is inseparably connected with the desire to rush to meet him in order to obtain help from him or directions for the way to the troops. The conception of a Black African is connected with the desire to hide and to prepare for an attack. The 'external influences' that summon up both complexes do not cease – you continue to see the indistinct silhouette. The complexes compete intensely, mutually weakening one another and not allowing one instead of the other to be completed by a real act of volition. This 'vacillating' condition is accompanied, as we know, by a significant expenditure of energy, so that it is expressed in a strong negative Affectional; one's condition is undoubtedly 'unpleasant'. There is consequently an intense negative selection that embraces the entire field of consciousness, but what does it lead to? It is easy to figure out, if we analyse competing complexes.

The images of a 'white' and 'black' person have a common part A – the common traits of both types and therefore are traits already associated in the psyche according to similarity. But besides this common part the images also have 'differences' – part B in one and part C in the other. These differences are mainly elements of colour. A + B (a European) is associated with one volitional complex, and A + C (a Black African) is associated with another. It is clear that part A is not situated in a close and direct connection with either of the two 'desires' and that the parts that are differentiated from one another are proximally connected with one – combination B – and the other – combination C. A negative selection is directed against *all* the combinations that the consciousness is filled with, but as long as the 'external cause' continues, it cannot remove the volitional complexes that it has summoned up. They are renewed, so to speak, again and again. Since they are *inseparably associated* with B and C – the parts of both complexes that are differentiated – they are continually maintained in the consciousness as long as both 'desires' are maintained. And here psychical selection is powerless, so to speak, against the continuing action of an 'external cause'. But the common part of both complexes – part A – is connected with both desires considerably more weakly and only indirectly. Therefore negative selection in fact suppresses part A all the more strongly.

The result in regard to both image-complexes is that the following picture is obtained. Their *differences* appear in consciousness with the greatest clarity and their *common part* fades into the background and becomes pale. The common part does not disappear completely from consciousness only because of its connection with the parts that are differentiated. Such is the basic and primary structure of *association according to difference* or, what is the same thing, of the 'form of differentiation'. It appears when two images, mutually connected according to similarity turn out to be in competition with one another due to the difference between the volitional complexes associated with them.

After sufficient analysis it is possible to determine precisely such an origin and such a vital meaning for any 'form of differentiation'. A person does not 'differentiate' as long as there is no 'need to differentiate', and this means as long as given images are not associated with different volitional reactions. But since there are no conceptions that can be connected with *volitional complexes* and because, in essence, both present only two different phases of a complete psychical reaction, the realm of 'differentiation' is equalised with the realm of experience. 'To the extent that it is needed' the psyche creates all possible forms of differentiation on the basis of forms of generalisation that have already been composed. *All cognitive combinations* boil down to these two aspects.[21]

In the processes of so-called 'pure cognition', a person often creates forms of differentiation where no particular 'practical differences' are evident – i.e. connections of given similar images with different *volitional reactions* that would compete with one another. But, in reality, it is always possible to find such a connection. Even in 'scholastic amusements' when 'the distinction is made of splitting a hair into four equal parts' the essence of the matter is still the same. A 'word' represents mainly a *volitional* reaction in the psyche – the reaction of an utterance – and, to the extent that similar images are signified by different words, they are thereby connected with different volitional acts. But, apart from this, there are no such images – visual, auditory, tactile, etc. – that could be included in its makeup of 'innervational elements', and that includes volitional

---

21   I have written in greater detail about these two associative types that together form the 'monistic tendency of consciousness' in the work, *Poznanie s istoricheskoi tochki zreniia*, pp. 85–107.

elements.[22] All this is sufficient to explain to us how any association according to similarity can serve as the starting point for the appearance of many associations according to difference.

Any psychical association – according to contiguity, to similarity, or to difference – presents itself as a certain whole complicated psychical complex, and, like all other simpler complexes, it enters into associative connections with other similar associations. Associations of a higher order are obtained in which primary associations with the nature of generalisation and discrimination are 'generalised' or 'distinguished'.[23] They are further followed by associations of a still higher order, and this process continues toward the harmonious association of all the data of experience. In the progressive process of generalisation, all sorts of 'forms of generalisation' and 'forms of discrimination' are associated according to similarity, and the tendency toward the greatest harmony of cognition is realised. In the progressive process of discrimination, all combinations of both kinds are associated according to difference and a tendency toward the greatest completeness of cognition is realised. The meaning of both tendencies is the same: the maximum of life in the sphere of cognition.[24]

We explained earlier that the associative organisation of experience is *genetically-primary*, it is more general and less specific, and objective regularity is one of its particular and derivative forms – one of the results of its progressive harmonisation.[25] Having become familiar with those forces that create and develop the basic organisation of experience, we see that there is nothing that

---

22   In my above-mentioned work, *Poznanie s istoricheskoi tochki zreniia*, I dwelt in greater detail on the origin of 'forms of generalisation' and 'forms of discrimination' and on the phenomena of *attention* that play such a role in the development of these forms. I also indicated several experimental proofs found among several authors in support of the point of view of my presentation, and I considered psychical processes mainly from the aspect of their physiological expression or 'manifestation', pp. 78–107. This is not the place to present all of this again.

23   I do not touch here upon the role played in this process of progressive association by the powerful social tool – the word – that tool without which in fact 'cognition' is even impossible. This would take us too far from our main theme. (For specifics on this see *Poznanie s istoricheskoi tochki zreniia*, pp. 128–56.)

24   Image-complexes and volitional complexes in themselves essentially exhaust the entire content of psychical experience. It is usual also to distinguish complexes of 'experiences' in the mind. But to the extent that one has in mind pleasure and pain in general, the question has nothing to do with particular complexes but with their colouration that has, as I have shown, a specific energetical significance. In regard to emotions, in the proper meaning of the word, such as fear, anger, joy, love, they are undifferentiated complexes of indefinite 'sensations' with indefinite 'desires' – unformed combinations of image and will.

25   See Chapter 2, 'Life and the Psyche', in the present volume.

is either transcendent or transcendental, nothing that could be fundamentally distinguished from the contents of developing experience as absolute forms of it. From this point of view, psychology presents itself as the science of psychical (or associative) forms of experience *that are determined* by the variable content of experience.

## 2  Applications of the Method (Illustrations)

I consider it unnecessary to force the attention of the reader down the whole tiresome path of investigation – partly inductive, partly deductive – that led me to the idea of psychical selection as the universal method of understanding the origin of psychical phenomena. I have so far limited myself to outlining this idea concisely and schematically. I will now provide concrete examples of my idea, emphasising those that seem to be to be most typical and cognitively important. It is impossible to provide more within the limits of a chapter, but I believe that there will be enough so the reader will be able to judge the possible general significance that this idea has in regard to cognition that strives to be monist.

I am venturing here to leave the confines of the tasks of the old psychology and, with the help of the method I have developed, to subject to *explanation* and *criticism* what the old psychology only *described*. When encountering people, we find various levels of fullness and harmony of psychical life in them – from genius to extreme psychical retardation, from calm eventemperedness to wild insanity. Each type of organisation seems different: the majestic and severe monoideism of the 'Hebrew', the refined and mellow many-sidedness of the 'Hellene',[26] the dull and vacuous lack of principles of the 'Philistine' … Emotional, intellectual, wilful characters pass before us, people with clear consciousness and people with confused consciousness, people who are eternally striving and people who are invariably apathetic, and so on and so on. We are drawn together with them and we push away from them, we try to change them and are ourselves changed by them. And they apply to us, just as we apply to them, various methods of systematic or haphazard influ-

---

26  The use of 'Jew' or 'Hebrew' and 'Greek' or 'Hellene' to stand for two poles of being was common in nineteenth-century Europe and was employed by a diverse variety of writers, including Ernst Renan, Matthew Arnold, Friedrich Nietzsche, Heinrich Heine, etc. Bogdanov follows Heine's use of 'Hebrew' and 'Hellene' to refer not to racial characteristics but to personality types. Heine famously said that all people are either Hebrews (ascetic and spiritual) or Hellenes (cheerful and in love with the world) [trans.].

ence: people educate, corrupt, correct, reward, punish, support, and push away one another. Here lies a realm where psychological theory and practice closely impinge on one another, transforming from the one to the other. Here explanation and critique acquire an especially great significance for life. And here we hope by analysing several basic types of psyche – and partly also by analysing several basic methods of how one person affects another – to show how the idea of psychical selection can serve as a reliable basis for explaining and evaluating these types and methods.

The issues that I have marked out lie close to the boundary between psychology and social science, but they are still not socio-psychological issues. Although it is unquestionable that psyches take shape in social life, as long as we deal with one psyche or with two psyches in their mutual interaction and as long as we take their social origin only as *a given* and the results of that social origin only as *a constant* value in our analysis, we will not go beyond the limits of psychology. Questions of social science begin where two psyches are taken not only in their mutual relationship but in *their general relationship to external nature*, in their cooperation. This is not now a part of my task.

I

In the processes of psychical selection it makes the most sense to single out three different points for analysis – different, it goes without saying, only in the abstract but completely inseparable in a concrete phenomenon. First, the material of experiences that 'is subject to' psychical selection. This material can be considered from the perspective of its quantity (its profusion or dearth), from the perspective of its quality (diversity or homogeneity), and from the perspective of the intensity of separate experiences. Second, it can be considered from the perspective of the tendency of psychical selection (in a positive or negative direction) toward the preservation and strengthening of experiences or to the weakening and removal of experiences from experience. This tendency is expressed, as we know, in the Affectional – in the colouration of pleasure or pain that characterises various experiences. Third, it can be considered from the perspective of the intensity of psychical selection in its various moments. Intensity obviously serves as an index of that same Affectional. The interrelationships of these three 'sides' of psychical section are very diverse and, correspondingly, the *results* of selection (the psychical combinations and types of structure that selection produces) are extremely disparate.

The idea of psychical selection creates the possibility of certain deductive conclusions in relation to the nature of psychical development under one or another condition of selection. It goes without saying that such a deduction always has significance only to the extent that it is justified by experience itself and to the extent that its conclusions do not contradict the facts but permit them to be grouped with the greatest possible completeness and harmoniousness. If deduction turns out to be precisely this, and if its conclusions are *true* in relation to experience, or, what is the same thing, *cognitively useful*, then the very idea of psychical selection as the basis for deduction obtains reliable and completely convincing proof of its usefulness. Keeping all this in mind, I will now turn to certain typical combinations of conditions of psychical selection.

Let us imagine the following ideal combination. The sum of experiences that appear in the field of psychical experience presents the greatest maximum that is possible for the human psyche of a given era. A huge mass of impressions that are obtained 'from without' and that are clear and diversified to the highest degree continually broaden the field of experience of a given individual, leading him to directly or indirectly engage with everything that is alive in his era. All these experiences are not only intense, in themselves, but they also deeply affect the psychical system in its whole, powerfully changing its energetical equilibrium. In a word, the experiences possess a high Affectional, appearing as intense 'delights' and intense 'sufferings'. Let us suppose that both colourations maintain an approximate equilibrium in the general flow of experience. Acute delight alternates with acute suffering; periods of happiness are replaced by periods of grief and vice versa. Summarising all these conditions in terms of psychical selection, one would have to say that the material for selection is the maximum, the intensity of selection is the maximum, and the direction alternates without an especial preponderance of one or the other of the sides of psychical selection.

What kind of picture of psychical development results under such conditions?

A rapid change that results from the influences of the external environment now signifies, of itself, a rapidly changing field of consciousness. But this would be only the chaos of life if intense psychical selection did not cause other changes of that field, namely changes that are directed toward the growing organisation of experience. Intense psychical selection creates, as we know, more and more forms of energetical equilibrium between different complexes of elements, or, what is the same thing, creates more and more associative connections. Experiences are transformed by this process into psychical *experience*, but this also so far expresses only a certain minimum of psychical organisation. In order to figure out how the process of development proceeds further, we must dwell on the two different sides of psychical selection individually.

The intense action of negative selection is similar to the action of a hammer that crushes and destroys everything that is not solid and stable but that 'forges' what is really solid and, by eliminating other parts of it, gives it a pure and definite form. Negative selection *strives* to destroy everything that appears in the field of experience, but where life is rich and strong, negative selection in fact is successful in destroying only the least 'vital' and the least stable combinations. First, they are combinations that are weak and pale, that superficially affect the psychical system and that, at the same time, are not situated in a direct connection with frequently repeated influences of the external environment, influences that are capable again and again of causing the same psychical combination. In a word, these combinations are complexes that are 'not vitally important' – the fleeting products of fantasy, for example – and, in general, are 'trifles' of psychical experience. Second, they are combinations that are 'contradictory' and 'disharmonious' – those that are made up of 'competing' complexes that mutually weaken one another (especially those complexes that are associated with different volitional reactions). All these are combinations that have an 'eclectic' colouration and are a 'compromise' of contradictory vital tendencies.

Contrary to these two types, there are combinations of two opposite types that resist the action of negative selection the most. First, they are those complexes that are 'vitally important', i.e. either those that burst into the current of psychical experience with great strength or those that are subject to frequently repeated external influences which cause them to crop up again and again. Both of these types of combinations can be designated as being most closely connected with the 'objective world' – what is 'external' for 'subjective' experience.[27] Second, they are those combinations that are most 'harmonious' (in which the mutual interconnectedness of their parts is most durable and their mutual equilibrium most stable) and that are most harmoniously associated with the greatest quantity of other stable complexes. It is understandable that still greater resistance to negative selection will become apparent in the event that a complex or association corresponds to both characteristics – i.e. is both vitally important in its connection with repeating external effects and most harmonious in its organisation. Consequently, when there is a sufficient quantity of material in the sphere of psychical experience, negative selection – if it acts for long enough and is intense enough – must yield predominance to precisely such especially stable combinations. In so doing, a

---

27   The 'external' world means a world with a *different regularity*. And in actuality, as we have seen, the regularity of the 'objective world' for cognition is not the same as for the subjective world. This is the regularity of socially-organised – and not individually organised – experience. This is the 'physical' connection – and not the 'psychical' association – of phenomena.

person's psychical development obtains a dual colouration: on the one hand, a 'realistic' colouration (the predominance of complexes that most correspond to repeated influences of the environment) and, on the other hand, a 'monist' colouration (the predominance of harmonious and harmoniously united complexes).

What traits bring intense positive selection – moments and periods of 'happiness' – into the development of a psychical system? Positive selection strives to bring any experience that is located in the field of its action to the greatest fullness and clarity. And for each experience, it strives to arouse all of the associated complexes, and to arouse all the associations of those complexes, etc. In this way, positive selection constantly floods the field of consciousness with more and more rapidly appearing experiences; the flow of experience pours out more broadly and flows more rapidly. In so doing, some complexes do not have time to disappear from the field of consciousness, while other complexes crop up along with them, followed by a third set ever further away in the associative chain from the first complexes, which had not previously encountered them in consciousness. And when two complexes encounter one another in consciousness, it signifies their associative convergence – the formation of an associative connection between them that, although only weak, is *direct*, and that subsequently can develop further. In this way, the material of experience appears in all sorts of associative combinations, all sorts of means of unifying the experiences that have found their way into psychical experience. Everything is juxtaposed. Everything is compared. Everything serves as an object that can be formed into more and more groupings. This is called *the creative activity of fantasy*. Everyone knows from experience how broadly and richly this activity unfolds in moments of satisfaction, pleasure, and happiness and how it contracts and is suppressed in moments of pain, suffering, and grief.[28]

---

[28] Life that is full of suffering often gives rise to 'dreaminess'. But this does not at all mean that negative selection also encourages the work of the imagination. No, here the matter proceeds otherwise, and it is easy to see exactly how. Negative selection removes, little by little, all 'unpleasant' images and combinations from consciousness, and in the given case it *succeeds* in removing them completely, including also those in which 'real' relationships of the mind to the external world are expressed. The field of consciousness then remains for 'pleasant' images and combinations, the main deficiency of which is that they are 'unreal'. But since they nevertheless are 'pleasant', positive selection now enters the scene, but, combining them with the activity of imagination, in the given case, does not deserve to be called 'creative' because of the fragility of its material and results. In this way, as long as people really *suffer*, they do not dream, and they dream as long as the stimuli of suffering do not burst powerfully into their mind. At that point they return to 'agonising reality' and negative selection.

In its full development, any psychical complex transforms into a volitional reaction, as long as it either includes the reaction in its content or is more or less closely associated with the reaction. Positive selection, striving to bring any complex to the greatest fullness and clarity, obviously leads thereby to the development of the *activity of will*: intense 'pleasure' provides the strength for action. Only the overcrowding of the field of consciousness by different images and volitional reactions that are summoned up by that same positive selection can powerfully interfere with such an action. When this occurs, due to the competition of the other volitional complexes, no single volitional complex attains the greatest fullness and 'transforms into action'. But if negative selection also acts intensely in the psyche, then this overcrowding is easily removed and the conditions are obtained for the development of an active-volitional type.[29]

The general picture of the development of the psyche under ideal conditions that we have outlined turns out to be the following: a huge number of immediate experiences as the result of varied influences of the environment, all sorts of combinations of psychical complexes that are produced from the material of these experiences by positive psychical selection, and the preservation from these combinations – under the action of negative selection – only of those that are most stable by virtue of their connection with the most frequent effects of

---

29 Regarding the question of the meaning of pain and pleasure for active will, the facts of experience seem hopelessly contradictory. Pain is usually considered the *motive* for an active will and at the same time it is well known that powerful pain *suppresses* the will. Pleasure 'gives energy' for activity, and, at the same time, a happy life 'pampers' and 'weakens'. From the point of view of psychical selection, all these seeming contradictions are explained and eliminated. It is self-evident that long and powerful pain suppresses the will; negative selection weakens volitional complexes and does not let them cross over into action. But where the action of negative selection is not so strong or where a volitional complex possesses special intensity, then negative selection is able only to remove other complexes that compete with the given volitional complex and that are preventing it from crossing over into action, so that this transition is made easy. In the majority of cases the matter is actually even simpler. The very same external influence that 'causes pain' summons a volitional reaction directed toward the removal of this influence by means of the previous development of elaborated associative connections; the appearance of an enemy is not only 'unpleasant', but it is closely associated with the reactions of struggle, and so on. Finally, wherever a person consciously sets the goal of 'cutting pain short' and 'acts' to attain this, positive selection also plays an important role. The given volitional reaction is closely associated with a 'pleasant' conception of the removal of 'unpleasant' conditions that gave rise to the pain. In a word, all the contradictory relationships between pain and activity can be explained with the help of psychical selection. (It will be necessary to deal with the relationship between 'pleasure' and activity later on.)

the environment and by virtue of their harmoniousness. A psychical type is obtained that is characterised by *creativity, an active will, a realistic worldview, and a tendency toward monism.*

If, in so doing, a person is situated in broad communication with other people and if he intensely and fully apprehends their experience by means of their utterances, then all the general and important contradictions of the vital experience of contemporary society and all the essential needs and requirements of the era will find a place in the material of his psyche. Then his psychical development, by virtue of its monist tendency, will be directed toward the harmonious reconciliation of these general contradictions and toward the satisfaction of these general needs and requirements, and the resolution of these tasks in the given psyche will be, on the one hand, the most full and perfected due to powerful creativity and active will, and, on the other hand, the most reliable and stable due to its realistic bases. Here we behold the *encyclopaedic genius of his times*.[30]

As a 'normative' type, we will make it the starting point of our subsequent analysis. We will examine the ways in which this type is transformed or, better, what it is replaced with under one or another changes of conditions of psychical selection. We need not be hindered by the fact that it is perhaps in reality utterly impossible to find a psyche that corresponds the least bit to this norm. The given norm expresses the *progressive tendency of psychical development* and is the ultimate abstraction of cognition. Cognition necessarily operates with such ultimate abstractions in all sciences when it strives to establish *general laws* of phenomena. The task consists in passing, step by step, from an ultimate abstraction that expresses ideally simple conditions, bringing in complicating conditions, one by one, to an understanding of the concrete reality that we find in our experience.

II

Let us suppose that the all basic conditions of psychical selection remain the same as in our ideal case, except for one: negative psychical selection is comparatively weak, moments and periods of suffering are far fewer than moments and periods of enjoyment, and the latter decisively predominate. We would see a 'lucky guy' for whom everything turns out well, for whom pleasure does not come at a high price, and for whom external conditions – the 'environment' – is more favourable than hostile. What type of psychical development would result in this case?

---

30  In world literature, this type was represented (approximately) by Goethe's Faust.

From a crudely quantitative perspective, the general profusion of experiences here must seem to be no less than in the previous case if not even more. The sum of the original material of experiences that is obtained from the external environment does not change quantitatively, as we have posited, and positive selection, acting at large, maintains and creates anew all sorts of combinations from this material, and consequently the activity of negative selection, as destructive of these combinations, is relatively weak and limited. But from the qualitative perspective, it is now obvious that, from the very beginning, less is yielded. The diversity of impressions that are obtained from outside is less significant, since 'unpleasant' negative influences of the environment are represented weakly in the general sum of impressions. The basis of psychical life is relatively narrower but only relatively in comparison with the ideal type.

The creative, combining activity of the psyche is 'fantasy' that proximally depends, as we have seen, on positive psychical selection and must expand very widely and continually create a mass of more products of association, but their nature and vital significance are not the same. Their development is only weakly regulated by the selective action of negative selection that destroys all less stable combinations and allows more stable combinations to be preserved and to have a greater space for further development. Those combinations that would not be retained in a psyche of the 'normal' type are also retained here. A mass of 'unrealistic' combinations and 'non-monist' (eclectic, disharmonious) combinations also remain here. The general picture of psychical life presents itself in such a way that 'imagination' predominates over 'critique' and does not possess strict, harmonious orderliness in regard to the psychical whole. There is much 'glitter' and 'versatility' in this picture, but there is comparatively less monist 'order'.

The activity of will in this picture also obtains a distinctive imprint. As we have seen, positive selection is generally favourable for the quantitative development of this will; it maintains and strengthens a multitude of combinations that are accomplished by volitional acts. But precisely because such accomplishment appears so easily and because there is insufficient selective regulation of volitional reactions (the regulation that is realised in the 'normal' case by intense negative selection), volitional life acquires the colouration of impulsive disorderliness. There is much movement and much activity, but the transition from some desires and moods to others is accomplished comparatively easily and in reality is unstable. Volitional life is also insufficiently 'monist'.

If the preponderance of positive selection over negative selection becomes too great, then the volitional type is lowered to an even greater degree. There is a never-ending mass of weak psychical combinations that spring up again and again, that unfold in consciousness without constraint or delay, and that continually fill the field of consciousness to overflowing. And that mass of weak psychical combinations brings with it a similar mass of diverse volitional complexes, haphazardly packed into consciousness. It is understandable then that these volitional complexes – precisely by virtue of their numerical strength and basic instability – cannot be and are not transformed into 'actions' and remain at the stage of 'desires', which, moreover, are desires that are insufficiently elaborated and indefinite. External activity turns out to be insignificant: the will is 'weakened' and 'overprotected' and activity is replaced by 'dreaminess' and 'a sense of reverie'. This state of will is expressed all the more keenly and powerfully by the fact that it is, after all, only possible in the absence of 'unpleasant' external influences of great force. It is such external influences that, by deeply shaking the psychical system, cause it to expend its energy in various directions; some influences excite energetic volitional reactions (in physiological terms, a flow of innervation). Thus, there are considerably fewer stimuli of active will, the field of psychical experience is filled with too many unstable volitional complexes, and consequently the production of full volitional reactions is impossible.[31]

The action of many narcotic poisons, such as morphine, hashish, and alcohol – in their 'pleasant' phase – temporarily summon a psychical state that under conditions of constantly weak negative selection are transformed into a particular type of psychical development. The action of the poison removes all 'unpleasant' stimuli and gives full play to positive selection. This is quickly replaced by unstable psychical complexes that are accompanied by the beginning of a certain confused activity of will in the form of the manifestation of physical liveliness, talkativeness, etc. and then by a 'dreamy' mood and inactivity. Incidentally, the action of narcotics changes depending on different conditions, but in all cases when the action is most 'pleasant', it is precisely as I have just described.[32]

---

31  This is how one explains the seeming contradiction between joy as the source of energy for an active will and joy as the source of the effeteness that kills the activity of will. See the last note in the preceding section.

32  Manic excitement presents a pathological case where the predominance of positive selection in the mind is so extreme that negative selection disappears. Along with this, the harmonising tendency retreats, and one sees the incoherent and haphazard appearance in the psychical field of more experiences that flood the consciousness in a turbulent swirl and produce incoherent and haphazard activity in the form of a mass of useless movements, jabbering, etc. A 'pleasant' condition, indeed!

    In real 'mania' the matter is more complex. In mania, a profound general disorganisation of the system occurs on the basis of an abnormal current of psychical selection.

Thus, the predominance of positive over negative selection causes the divergence from the 'normal' type to a new one. The latter is characterised in general by the predominance of 'fantasy' over realism and complacent eclecticism over monism, by the relative instability of the tenor of the will, and, in more sharply expressed cases, by its outright weakness. This is the multi-faceted type – but less profound – that Heine designated as 'Hellenic'. In Ancient Greece it was really quite widespread (mainly, to be precise, in the era when the culture of Ancient Greece was at its vital maximum and beginning to decay). Heine, himself, was a quite typical representative of Hellenism in this sense.

In our time, it is predominantly those with 'artistic dispositions' who are representatives of such 'Hellenism'. This type is most favourable for the creative works and for involvement in art. But, nevertheless, its utmost representatives now display only high 'giftedness' but do not create anything vitally stable and of social value. The more that negative selection (suffering, poverty, and hard work) appears on the scene and accompanies periods of happiness and enjoyment of a cheerful life, the more likely the chance of harmonious, well-proportioned, truly artistic creativity and the greater will be the conditions for the vital reality of their works of art. 'Giftedness' will be replaced by 'talent'. And when the intensity of negative selection begins to correspond to the intensity of positive selection, then, given a great abundance of vital material, the conditions for the production of *artistic genius* will appear. The role of suffering in the development of really harmonious creativity is very well known and very frequently stressed by the great artists themselves, especially poets. It is not without reason that suffering marks strong people with a particular 'nobility' that expresses the fundamental unity of the tenor of their will. A great work that is produced by an artist of genius as a result of suffering is a vitally harmonious, monistically-idealised incarnation of that stormy flood of experiences that chaotically and uncontrollably weigh on the consciousness of the artist until the harmonising force of suffering changes the form and tenor of that flood consistent with *its* laws. These are the laws of a strong life that does not fear heavy blows, that overcomes pain, and that makes use of death itself. These laws produce the supreme realism that is called the 'objectification' of creativity and the supreme unity of what has been experienced, and they are worshipped in the name of harmony and beauty.

Thus, the destructive force of life is transformed into a creative force – wherever life overcomes it.

## III

Let us now take a look at another type of deviation from the 'norm': the predominance of *negative* selection under the same basic profusion of psychical life – a multiplicity of perceptions, 'profound impressionability' – along with very great suffering. In short, there is much more suffering than pleasure and happiness. Even though the pure type corresponding to this case is rarely encountered, such a combination of conditions is met with much more often than the opposite case (which I have just examined) in our world, full of struggle and contradictions as it is. This is why it is very easy to explain.

Suffering is a destructive force; it is the expression of the lowering of energy of the system and the diminishment of life. It is a partial death. Therefore, the systematic preponderance of pain over pleasure obviously must always lead to the decline, the degradation, and then the death of the system. This would be the case even if *all* changes of the psychical system flowed in the sphere of consciousness. In that case, immediate psychical experience would directly indicate to a person in what direction his vital process was heading – toward development or toward destruction. But consciousness corresponds only to the *main* coordination of changes of the psyche, while far from all 'immediate experiences' enter it – and even only a small part of them. As I have explained, beyond the limits of psychical experience, in a vital connection with the main coordination, there exists a great many other, more minor groupings in which a huge part of the immediate experiences of a given system flow. Beyond consciousness is hidden the 'unconscious', or, to be more exact, the 'extra-conscious', since the form of organisation of these groupings are the same – that is to say, associative organisation – and if there is no 'consciousness of them' then it is for the same reason that a person cannot immediately 'be conscious' of the experiences of another person, that is, because of the relative independence of these groupings.[33] Thus the psychical organism is considerably broader than the realm of consciousness; there are considerably more 'experiences' than the organism 'is conscious of'.

It is obvious that an accumulation of energy can occur 'beyond the confines of consciousness' at the same time that there is an expenditure of energy within the field of consciousness. And then, regardless of the fact that the colouration of negative selection (suffering) predominates in the consciousness, the psyche as a whole might not go into decline but might develop. It might even

---

33   I made an attempt to 'explain' this vital independence in Chapter 3, 'Universum', in the present volume.

not only develop qualitatively (in the sense of harmony and unity) but also quantitatively (in the sense of profusion of content). Then the type of psychical development of which I will now speak will result. But, naturally, this far from always happens, and it is even in a minority of cases. More often the expenditure of life, taking place in the sphere of consciousness, is not compensated for by elemental growth outside the limits of consciousness. Suffering exhausts the psyche and degrades it, and life breaks down.

Imagine a powerful disposition, full of the elemental forces of life, that is capable of developing through a great deal of suffering and that repeatedly draws from the dark depths of the extra-consciousness the energy that the harsh influences of the 'external world' take away from it. The heavy hammer of suffering crushes and destroys everything that is weak, insubstantial, and petty in the psyche. Into what form would the psyche then be forged?

Suffering brings into the 'ideal' psyche – whose fortune is to be equally full of happiness and grief, pleasure and pain – a tendency of life that is both realistic and monist. Demolishing all that is insubstantial and disharmonious, this suffering is unable to undermine either the vital combinations that are based on the repeating influences of the environment or the vital combinations that, being in themselves harmoniously-whole, are, at the same time, harmoniously interlaced with a multitude of other solid and stable combinations. But does the same thing result when conditions change, when life provides much more suffering, when a powerful psyche systematically resists its fate?

An evil fate – this refers to external forces, the environment, 'reality'. Realistic images, whose durability depends on their 'real' basis (the repeating influences of the environment), are coloured in the vast majority of cases with intensely sombre colours. Negative selection is much more intensely directed against those realistic images than when one's fate is more 'just', and it undermines their vital significance in the general system of the psyche. The realistic images are not removed. *This*, generally speaking, is something that negative selection is unable to do, since it has to do with images that reflect influences of the environment that are repeated again and again. But those images *fade out*, and the life of consciousness is not concentrated on them. Those few 'realistic' complexes that are coloured with a positive rather than a negative Affectional (hints of life itself toward happiness) play the greatest role in psychical creativity, and an even greater role is played by complexes that are derived from 'real' combinations that are themselves not 'real', i.e. *do not themselves have a direct basis in the external environment* but constantly accompany a positive Affectional (ideal pictures of happiness). This imprints the characteristic of 'utopianism' on the entire development of the psyche. Utopianism is not simple 'dreaminess' and not simple 'phantasy formation'. The dreamer and fantasist are distinguished in the profusion and instability of psychical combinations that spring up, whereby they are paler for the dreamer and clearer for the fantasist. There are few products of creativity for the utopian, but those products are very stable because the predominance of negative selection does not permit 'light dreams of fantasy' and destroys the greater part of the products of fantasy.

Thus, extreme predominance of negative selection does not engender a realistic tendency but, to a significant degree, the opposite – a *utopian* tendency in the development of the psyche.

But then a *monist* tendency is at the same time expressed in full measure. The destructive action of negative selection can tolerate only tightly cohesive, harmonious combinations that are devoid of any internal contradictions. All disharmonious connections and relationships are removed, and, as a result of such development, the psychical whole appears as a strictly holistic system.[34] All psychical content is consequently grouped in one trend, everything is tightly connected and embraces one powerful idea, on which all the energy of life is concentrated.

Activity of will, at the same time, cannot be extensive – negative selection does not permit many different volitional impulses to develop. But, on the other hand, that activity of will is distinguished by great intensity and steadfast logical consistency and by a strictly unified trend. This unity flows from the same 'monist' structure of the psychical organism according to which volitional reactions that are connected with basic groups of experiences that are tightly associated do not encounter any competition from other reactions, since those other reactions are quickly suppressed by negative selection. The intensity of volitional life depends in part on that very unity – on the weakness of competition of volitional complexes – and in part on the great energy of experiences of the given psyche in general. At any rate, powerful suffering signifies the energetic influence of the environment (profound shocks to the psychical system) and therefore also intense reciprocal influences on that same environment (great expenditure of energy on volitional impulses) ...

Thus, the basic traits of this third type of psychical development are the following: *utopianism*, strict *consistency* of thought and will, and steadfast *activity*

---

34   In the sphere of cognition, associations according to similarity (forms of generalisation) are based, in general, as we have seen, *more* on the harmony of unified experiences than are associations according to difference (forms of discrimination) in which the *competition* of experiences plays a certain role. And it is characteristic that in the psychical type that I have examined the first type of association decisively predominates over the second, and the greatest significance is attached to *what is common* in phenomena and *differences* are apprehended comparatively weakly.

in life's struggle. This is the type of 'Judea', as it was portrayed by Heine. In reality, this type is more often encountered in the Jewish race, with its striking vital capacity and its painful historical fate. This is the type of the Old Testament prophets, and also of the later narrow and severe teachers and leaders of this people. But many of the great fighters for an idea from other nations who are strong in their steadfast consistency also belong to this type. One of the purest and most perfect representatives of it is our own archpriest Avvakum.[35] His horrific biography presents us with the puzzle of how, from an uninterrupted chain of incredible suffering, there arose the gigantic force of his iron will that was absolutely incapable of allowing itself to be changed under any conditions whatever. My point of view can solve this mystery – the mystery of the life of all great ascetics and ardent fanatics of a single idea.

It is difficult to say who has contributed more to the progress and power of humanity – the bright, cheerful 'Hellenes', representatives of the fullness of life that overflows its brim, or the severe, single-minded 'Hebrews', representatives of that fundamental harmony of life that is expressed in its elemental wholeness, in all-conquering *belief in oneself*.[36]

IV

All three of the types of psychical development that I have examined up to this point represent *ultimate magnitudes* in the sense that they presuppose (1) the greatest material of experiences, both in quantity and in variety, that has been historically possible and (2) psychical selection that acts either evenly or unevenly but always with the *greatest intensity*. Now we must move on to more everyday, so to speak, types of psychical development, to types that stand further from the maximum of the life of consciousness.

So let us imagine that only one of the two maximum conditions applies – the greatest possible intensity of psychical selection, to be precise. This would be a person who 'feels' everything that he experiences deeply and powerfully, but whose material of experience is quantitatively less than the maximum. Here we can imagine a series of descending levels of general magnitudes of this material. Let us assume that this material of experience is qualitatively varied and

---

35 Avvakum (1620–82) was a Russian priest whose opposition to a series of reforms of the Russian Orthodox Church led to a schism in the church. Avvakum was one of the most outspoken leaders of the schismatic 'Old Believers', and because he would not recant his denunciation of the reforms, he was persecuted, imprisoned, exiled, and ultimately burned at the stake [trans.].
36 In literature this type is most clearly presented by Ibsen's *Brand*.

diverse (as in the previous examples) and embraces all the realms of immediately felt experience and indirect experience that is transmitted in social communication. This person's impressions are varied, and not only varied but also intense. Colours, sounds, smells, etc., are clearly perceived and appear vividly in his consciousness, except that the profusion of impressions is not so great as in the 'ideal' cases. In this case, intense psychical selection creates a series of types that are extremely similar to the three preceding ones – one might say paralleling them but lying on a different and lower plane. These types are more 'ordinary'.

Psychical creativity that organises the given material of experiences, because of its extremely narrow base in this case, cannot extend either as broadly or as far as in the three types. A representative of the harmoniously balanced activity of psychical selection in this case does not appear as a great monist organiser of the universal experience of his era, because his psyche does not embrace that experience. Nevertheless, all the basic tendencies of the 'normative' type find full expression in his psyche. He would be a realist with a clear view on life, someone who easily and freely applies the results of his experience and is able to make vitally valid conclusions from that experience and someone whose active will rationally and consistently acts on the external world, fully corresponding to the views that he worked out for himself or acquired from others. If he is an educated and cultivated person, then he could turn out to be talented and courageous, always free of one-sidedness and narrowness, a fighter for an idea that he has taken as the leading principle of his life. Or he could reveal himself to be merely invariably correct and noble in his relations with the other people with whom he comes in contact in his life. English novelists often portray this type of 'perfect gentleman'. If the level of his cultivation, according to the circumstances of his life, turns out to be jumble, then he will be one of those 'simple' men who impress us with the internal harmony of their psychical constitution and their philosophically clear and firm relationship to life. Such people, when they are close to the masses in conditions of life and material of experience, often turn out at critical moments in history to be 'heroes'. They attract the 'crowd', which finds in them the closest and most immediate spokesperson of their needs and desires and which involuntarily trusts the sound and powerful logic of their words and actions. It seems to me that George Washington, for example – a personal who was not in the least a 'genius' – belongs precisely to this type of person. The same, it seems to me, can be said of Gladstone and Abraham Lincoln ... In our times, one is more likely to find this type of person in the Anglo-Saxon race. In the ancient world, there were many of them among the leaders of the Roman people before the era of its decline.

The noble type of Heine's 'Hellene' loses a great amount of its beauty and greatness as soon as the primary material of his psychical life falls short of the maximum. The lustre of living, fiery creativity disappears; the bright, joyous play of imagination loses that broad vital significance that it had when maximal, universally human experience lay at its basis. Losing its breadth and depth, the play of imagination becomes 'superficial' and 'frivolous'; its typical form in this case is the so-called 'wit' of conversations in high society and friendly chats between good-natured alcohol abusers. Eclecticism in this case is generally even more significant than among representatives of the noble-Hellenic type, because experience is less broad and complete and is now more scattered and irregular in its content. It is therefore more difficult for it to be uplifted by an organising tendency, even when that tendency is stronger than in this series of cases. It goes without saying that one cannot speak of a definite and stable direction of will. In this case people live 'in the moment' and are usually constant only in their variability. The levels at which all these tendencies are manifested depend, of course, on the extent that positive selection predominates over negative selection, and the greater or lesser profusion of primary content provided by external impressions determines the various nuances of this type – from artistic dispositions (with dilettantism as the result of weak creativity) to banal bon vivants (usually libertine, like 'callow youth').

Representatives of such a type exist more often among the parasitic classes of society when they have just begun to degenerate, and it is understandable why. Parasitism provides a profusion of pleasant impressions but narrows the sphere of life in general, excluding from it useful labour and communication with other classes who are living fuller and more active lives. Thus, in regard to the Hellenic type the psyche turns out to be too meagre; it is too lacking in joyfulness. But it remains like this only at the first stages of degeneration. Further on, with the lowering of the general energy of the psyche, all experiences become less profound and psychical selection – both positive and negative – becomes weaker. The transition is made to a still lower type, which I will have to address later on.

Now, exactly how is the noble 'Hebraic' type transformed when there is the same depth and force of Affectional life but the broad basis of a large profusion of primary experiences is taken away? A 'Hebraic' type still results, but it is much narrower, limited, and conservative. The organising tendency in this case has too little material and the material is relatively uncoordinated, so that, generally speaking, this tendency is unable to independently create a harmonious monist system. However, representatives of the 'Hebraic' type often find ready-made systems through communication with other people that sufficiently harmonise with their personal experience, and then they profoundly and infallibly master these systems to the highest degree. This happens with fanatics who accept dogma, whose enthusiasm is uncontrollable, who are merciless towards themselves and others. They are excellent tools in the hands of organisers – people of the highest type.

The Catholic Church systematically prepared such tools in its monasteries, methodically creating all conditions for the production of this type. The walls of the monastery served as a means to narrow the realm of experience and the material of primary experiences. Fasting, obedience, punishment and all kinds of 'mortification of the flesh' guaranteed the predominance of negative over positive selection. It remained only to provide a dismal but integral dogma, and unquestioning zealots were prepared. The Inquisition could select from among them. In the Jewish nation, the prevalence of this type flowed from the historical lot of the Jewish people. Isolation from the encircling Christian environment caused a relative narrowness of experience, and all sorts of oppression and victimisation from that environment caused a comparative preponderance of suffering and grief over the joys of life.[37]

The second group of types that I examined, as I have already pointed out, parallels the first. It is like a diminished and underdeveloped variation of the first group. The relative narrowness of experience that causes this 'diminishment' and 'underdevelopment' can, of course, sometimes depend on so-called 'organic causes' such as, for example, a hereditary imperfection of the organs of perception, hereditary instincts, or even early-developing habits directed toward the narrowing and limiting of the sphere of what is perceived, etc. But, much more frequently, everything depends on the immediate environment – the 'technological' and 'social' environment, to be precise. Is it conceivable that

---

37   The psycho-neurosis of 'melancholy' presents an extreme case of the predominance of negative selection when there is an extremely small content of experiences. Terribly intense negative selection removes from consciousness or weakens to the extreme all experiences other than those that are repeatedly summoned by organic causes that are outside consciousness (a convulsive state of the vasomotor system). These agonising experiences fill the field of consciousness and bring with them associations – it is easy to imagine what kind. After all, those same states of the vasomotor system had previously appeared in the presence of distressing emotions – ennui, fear, shame – and in connection with corresponding images of something sad, horrible, shameful. Now these images appear in consciousness without competition and impose their imprint on the utterances of the melancholic person (sadness, contempt for himself, self-abnegation). Activity, in general, is extremely suppressed, except that sometimes tormenting emotion causes such a powerful volitional reaction that negative selection cannot suppress it, and it is then uncontrollable (*raptus melancholicus*). [The term *Raptus melancholicus* is obsolete. In Bogdanov's day, it referred to frenzy or extreme agitation in someone suffering from melancholia. Trans.]

the highest type of psychological life could develop from a peasant child, when all the material of his experience is limited to a few square miles of space and to the traditional thinking of those around him? And how many possible seeds of a higher life perish because of the fatal narrowness and poverty of the upbringing of girls? Here is something for humanity to fight against; here humanity can look forward to great victories.

V

Let us turn now to further variations in the nature and direction of psychical development. Imagine that the intensity of psychical selection is not the maximum, as in all previous cases, but a different, lesser magnitude. Affectional life is less profound, experiences do not affect the psyche as strongly, and joy and suffering are felt less vividly and energetically. This is a more 'everyday' disposition with a 'paler' existence.

At this point, we can begin by excluding from the number of logically conceivable combinations all those that include the maximum of primary, immediate experiences – the greatest possible profusion of 'impressions'. Such combinations are impossible for life; particular types of psychical development cannot result from them. The maximum of experiences only obtains any kind of organised, integral form when the organising process – psychical selection – is accomplished with great intensity, either maximal or close to the maximum. Otherwise something unorganised, contradictory, and on the order of psychical chaos would result, and that, of course, is not any kind of type of psychical development because it is not an organically viable whole. Thus the matter boils down to those variations that diverge from the maximum not only in the intensity of psychical selection but also in the amount of experiential material.

Thus, the variation we are considering now involves relatively little material of experience (though varied and diverse) and a relatively low Affectional of experiences. A few negative characteristics that proceed from these conditions are immediately self-evident. They include the absence of living creativity of imagination and the absence of a strong, steadfast will. The first, as we have seen, presupposes intense positive selection, and the second presupposes intense negative selection, neither of which is present. Further, in this case psychical development in general can be accomplished only slowly and sluggishly because the factors of this development are weak. The psyche as a whole is conservative, but this does not mean that the complexes and combinations that enter it are particularly durable. In psyches of the highest types, durability of psychical forms depends mainly on the breadth and continuity of their associative connections with other psychical forms that have been put together, and they additionally depend, at minimum, on a *direct* and *immediate* connection with the repeating influences of the environment.³⁸ Here the case is somewhat different. Associative connections are created by psychical selection, and where they are relatively weak they are limited in their development and do not attain either great breadth or especial stability. Therefore the majority of the most durable psychical complexes in such a psyche owe their durability not to associative connections but precisely to the repeating influences of the environment. This is stability that is produced by the adding up of the results of weak psychical selection in a long series of external repetitions that cause the complex. This is stability of habit. The predominant role of habitual psychical images and psychical acts is the basic feature of this type of development.

The weakness of positive selection and creative imagination combined with the special significance that the direct and immediate influences of the environment have for such a psyche cause *shallow realism*. And the weakness of negative selection and of destructive criticism combined with narrowness and emptiness of experience in general cause *shallow utopianism*. Commonplace temperance and a multitude of humble illusions, narrow practicality, and theoretical naïveté go together perfectly.

Here the monist tendency not only has adverse material by way of insufficient, incomplete, and therefore comparatively uncoordinated experience, but, in addition to that, because it is entirely the result of psychical selection, it is manifested to a weakened degree. Thus, *eclecticism* appears in the most obvious and naïve forms. The head of a philistine, in the words of Heine, contains a multitude of separate boxes that do not communicate with one another and each of which contains a particular department of cognitive materials and practical norms. Each box is unlocked as necessary and then is locked up as another one is unlocked. The morality of such a philistine is completely separate from the business rules that he follows in trade, familial virtues are separate from lecherous desires and habits, theory is separate from practice, etc.³⁹ This characteristic incoherence of psychical structure is particularly easy to observe when listening to an animated conversation among women of the philistine

---

38   *In the final analysis, any* psychical form is vitally durable precisely to the extent that it is situated in harmonious correlation with the most repeated influences of the surroundings (see Avenarius's chapter on *'Multiponiblen'* in *Kritik der reinen Erfahrung*). But this harmonious link in a mind of the highest type can be *indirect*, and it sometimes is indirect precisely for the highest, monistically-organising forms (for broad generalisations, for example).

39   I am not reproducing Heine's idea in his exact expressions, since I do not happen to have the book at hand, but I vouch for the essential faithfulness of my reproduction.

PSYCHICAL SELECTION 217

type. They rapidly switch from one subject to another, change their premises from one minute to the next, manifestly contradict themselves, but absolutely do not notice it.

Depending on which aspect of psychical selection – positive or negative – predominates and depending to what extent different nuances of the philistine type – more animated (in the case of extreme lack of character) or more austere (in the case of obtuse stubbornness) – they are caricatures that parallel the types of the 'Hellene' and the 'Hebrew'. But in general this type is very well known. It is either an expression of slow and spiritless processes of personal and class development or of decadence. The stagnant and degenerating parasitic groups of society deliver this in abundance. In stagnant groups, the type that predominates – the type that is more defined, more elaborated, and more even-tempered – is the 'petty-bourgeois', the 'philistine'. In groups that have degenerated, the picture is complicated by the disorganisation of the available psychical material, by instability, by disequilibrium, and by impulsiveness – only without energy. All this is the product of the fact that the material of life that is given by the previous phases turns out to be too great and heterogeneous for the weak organising tendency that is caused by weak selection. What we observe here is a vacuous type of decadent who is thrashing about in a 'search for something that does not exist'. But this is neither a type of development nor a type of equilibrium but a type of degradation. It is something close to those unviable combinations that I pointed out at the beginning of this paragraph.

The philistine and the decadent are the predominant figures of reactionary classes and trends.

VI

Let us now move on to those variations that are not based on material of experience that is uniform or diverse, profuse or scanty but that is *one-sidedly narrow*, such as especially exists for various forms of specialisation. I have in mind not only the specialisation of technical or scientific labour but, in general, all those cases where for whatever reason the realm of experiences does not unfold uniformly, being broadened especially in the direction of one particular group of mutually-connected and to a significant degree homogenous complexes of experience and being correspondingly narrowed in the other direction. In this sense, for example, the inhabitant of a polar land turns out to be developed one-sidedly in comparison with a person from a temperate zone, because experiences connected with 'winter', 'cold', etc. occupy a disproportionately large place in the material of life of the first person, while the realm of experiences related to 'summer', 'heat', etc. is correspondingly reduced. In pointing this out, I mean, once again, to emphasise the *relative* nature of the concepts that are employed in this analysis. We cannot as yet establish an absolute measure for the maximum or minimum of experiences, for the greatest and least intensity of psychical selection, or for the breadth or narrowness of experience, and when I employ these terms I have in mind only relative magnitudes and tendencies connected with their change in one or another direction.

So, what we are looking at is a psyche with a content that develops one-sidedly – the psyche, for example, of a specialised manufactory[40] worker or a trained, narrow specialist. Since psychical selection does not create anything fundamentally new but only processes material given to it, its work appears in a factually one-sided direction – to the greatest degree toward the organisation of those *specific* experiences that predominate in the given system of experience. These experiences, as I have pointed out, are comparatively homogenous and already, from the very start, are mutually close to the current of experience and, moreover, appear in the psyche with comparatively great fullness and are considerably less uncoordinated than other spheres of experience. Consequently, the process of organisation occurs here under the most favourable conditions and a comparatively harmonious and integral system of associations is easily created. At the lowest levels of development, these are mainly close associations according to contiguity in which the so-called 'immediate' acquaintance of the psyche with the given realm of experience is expressed. At higher levels, there is a progressive series of associations according to similarity and difference (of forms of generalisation and discrimination). This is the so-called 'systematic' cognition of the given realm, which can turn out to be 'monist' – i.e. regularly-associated – to a greater or lesser degree. But all this is only in the given 'specific' realm of experience and not in others.

In the other realms of experience, the content of experience is sparser and more fragmentary, and the organising tendency finds considerably less favourable conditions. Therefore, if the intensity of psychical selection – especially of negative selection – is in general not very great, then incoherence and eclecticism rule outside the confines of the 'speciality', and this type merges with the 'philistine' type. This trait stands out particularly clearly in the representatives of 'pedantry' and 'bookishness', who, though living quite an intense life in one narrow sphere, are striking in the paleness and insipidity of their psyches and by a childish form of thinking in all other spheres.

---

40   'Manufactory' refers to factories such as textile mills in which workers perform simple, repetitive, machine-like tasks, as opposed to 'machine production' in which workers are responsible for supervising the operation of largely self-regulating machines. Bogdanov spells out the significance of this difference in Chapter 9 of the present volume. [Trans.]

In those cases when psychical selection is especially intense, and, consequently, when the organising tendency is especially strong, things proceed differently: development proceeds in a monist direction, despite the fact that it is in a special form. In this case, experiences that relate to the sphere of 'specialisation' are, of course, well-organised and are coordinated into a harmonious system of associations. But, in playing a predominant role in a given realm, these experiences pass through a large part of the field of consciousness, and encounter experiences of other realms that are comparatively unsystematised. Under conditions of intense psychical selection, such encounters lead to the formation of more or less durable associative connections between them and other experiences. In the beginning, of course, they are associations only according to contiguity, but psychical selection, by removing disharmonious and contradictory elements from the complexes that have entered into such associations, transforms them in such a way that an ever greater correspondence appears among them until higher associations – associations according to similarity and subsequently associations according to difference – are obtained from them. At the same time, the more uncoordinated material from the most varied realms of experience is included, so to speak, in the well-established, organised forms of the vitally main realm of the 'special'. Psychical selection *adapts* it to those forms, since it, in general, adapts complexes of experience to one another. Naturally, in this case, it is predominantly the less elaborated and definite complexes that are adapted to the more elaborated and definite complexes rather than the other way around. Then all life and all experience is imagined and conceived of in the forms that are elaborated in the 'special' realm.

Examples of this kind of organisation of experience can be met at every step. A merchant absolutely automatically looks at all human life from his own specialised perspective of trade so that he sees an element of calculation of reward in a person's every action. He sees the purchase of gratitude in manifestations of altruism and the purchase of glory in heroic struggle, etc. And this is not at all just a metaphor.[41] Jeremy Bentham, having been brought up in the mercantile atmosphere of developing capitalism in England, even systematised this 'specialised' point of view and created an entire practical philosophy constructed, in essence, on the merchant's idea of possibly profitable transactions with the

---

41   The systematic use of metaphors from one's own 'special' realm, that is characteristic of all 'specialists', is already in itself an expression of the process of organisation of experience in forms of special experience, since words and concepts are inseparable and a metaphor brings in a new colouration to the concept to which it is applied. See *Philosophy of Thought* by M. Müller.

reality of life. In exactly the same way, workers who spend all their working time around machines are naturally inclined to a mechanically-materialistic worldview that packs all reality within the confines of relationships that are the same as relationships among parts of a mechanism. In many cases this is also true of the point of view of engineers, and even of capitalists who remain close to their factories and spend a significant part of their time among their machines. Jurists, whose specialised experience is organised in a system of compulsory norms, also typically conceive of the norms of actual scientific knowledge ('laws of nature') according to the form of compulsion and, for example, are inclined to understand the causal relationship as a special compulsory power and as a necessity that limits 'freedom'. Similar examples could be brought up ad infinitum. And, though it is rare for all the thinking of specialists to be organised in forms that are produced by their specialties, nevertheless, some of the 'imprints' of that specialty are always carried into all realms, and this imprint indeed expresses the elementary levels of the realisation of the tendency that I have pointed out.

The organisation of the whole sum of personal experience in the forms of specialised experience can sometimes turn out to be vitally-progressive in the highest degree, and in other cases, just the opposite, it can be a regressive phenomenon. But it is obvious in general that it cannot give the maximum organisation to experience but can serve only as a step toward that maximum. The class division of society signifies a well-known 'specialisation' of experience in our meaning, and therefore there is every reason to think that none of the contemporary class worldviews will be sufficiently broad for a future classless society. But, in any event, the worldview of the future must spring up from the psychology of the most progressive class of our times. That class must create forms of unifying experience for its rapidly broadening life – forms that are the most flexible, the most supple, and the most capable of development.

Regarding the nature of volitional life under conditions of specialisation, the conclusions here are self-evident. The more that 'specialised' experience is distinguished by organisation then – to the extent that volitional life is related to that realm of experience – the more that consistency and unity will be revealed in the tenor of the will. The intensity of the manifestations of the will depends here on the general conditions of psychical selection – its energy and tenor, either positive or negative. Beyond the boundaries of the 'specialised' sphere, the more that experience is uncoordinated and thinking is eclectic, the less also is the tenor of volitional life unified and interconnected. At the same time, the energy of volitional life in general cannot but be comparatively reduced. Thus, a person sometimes manifests the greatest wholeness of will in his specialised activities that is worthy of a true 'Hebrew'. Because of the narrow sphere and homogenous nature of 'specialised' experiences, such wholeness is attained here *especially* easily – it does not need an exceptionally powerful action of negative selection. But, at the same time, outside the realm of speciality, such a person turns out to be spiritless and weak, like a philistine. This is the case, as we know, of many great people who are petty in their family life and personal life in general. The traits of the 'Hebrew' and the traits of the 'philistine' are the characteristics toward which the life of the 'specialist' gravitates.

VII

Obviously, the illustrations that we have adduced far from exhaust the possible types of psychical development, but it is not my goal to exhaust them. I want only to clarify in these examples the application of the method that I am establishing. In order for this application to be scientific and cognitively useful, we must not forget for an instant that all types of development that are established through this method are only *ultimate abstractions* and express only *tendencies of adaptation* that are connected with one or another variations of the conditions of life. Thus, to be more precise, the depiction of the type of the 'Hellene' tells us the following: the greater the degree to which the profusion of psychical material is associated with an intense life of 'feeling' in which at the same time joy and happiness dominate over suffering and grief, the greater degree to which the development of the psyche produces certain specific traits in it – living creativity with the predominance of fantasy over 'realism', a worldview with an equable and eclectic colouration, a will that has an active but unstable direction, etc., etc. Utilising such formulas, we can analyse step by step the concrete living types as we find them in reality and in art, and their 'concreteness' alone guarantees that they do not exactly coincide with the 'pure' types that have been obtained by 'abstraction'.

In any concrete type, *different* tendencies of development that are expressed by abstract types meet and mutually overlap, since *ideally-simple conditions* are never found in 'reality' but only in the 'abstracted' and 'analysed' activity of the cogniser. The task of the psychoenergetical 'explanation' of one or another 'concrete' type consists precisely in establishing – by means of the analysis of the objective conditions of the development of that type – the interconnectedness and correlation of the different tendencies of psychical development that necessarily proceed from the given combination of conditions.

I need to illustrate my point of view, but the lack of space forces me to limit myself to only one or two examples, and I begin with the one whose content can substitute for a multitude of them: the psychology of Shakespeare's Hamlet.

What kind of a person was Hamlet? First and foremost, there is no doubt that he was an individual of an extremely lofty type. Fate gave Hamlet two basic conditions for attaining the maximum of life. First, he had a huge profusion of primary psychical material, in the form of huge numbers of varied impressions from a childhood that was spent in the glittering surroundings of the court and from a youth that was gay and rich in content spent as a student travelling in Germany studying science. At the same time, he had a sensitive and impressionable disposition that deeply apprehended everything that experience took in. He was intensely emotional and capable of the highest pleasures and the greatest suffering. But before the beginning of the tragedy, his suffering was very small and his happiness very great. He had the love of his parents, the love of a woman, vivacious friends, general respect and adoration – even a great deal of flattery – and, finally, complete freedom of development; he had a whole world of intellectual and aesthetic delights. It is clear that Hamlet was destined to become a real 'Hellene' – a subtle artistic disposition, full of creativity and brilliance, but with the inevitable deficiencies of an artistic disposition. We know what these deficiencies are; they issue from the weakness of negative selection. The powerful harmonising force, in the form of suffering, was too seldom mixed into his psychical development and did not fully regulate it. In Hamlet there was little severe realism – the products of his own psychical labour often screened reality from him. He lacked wholeness. There was a great deal of complacent eclecticism in him, and consequently his will lacked stability, steadfastness, and a unified tenor.

That Hamlet had all the positive traits of an artistic disposition hardly requires proof – there are so many lively images and so much brilliance in his speeches, even in the most unhappy circumstances. But it was essentially upon the negative traits of the 'Hellenic' type that the entire tragedy was built. Only the lack of a firm and sober realism can explain the doubts and vacillations of Hamlet in regard to the very fact of the crime, since, at the time, obvious proof was present. He could not believe that evidence when it directly and sharply entered the field of his consciousness, and the impression was smoothed over. Hamlet's lively imagination was drawn into the matter and obligingly created and acquired new images and combinations that were more comforting. With the help of various 'possibilities', his imagination obscured and subjected to doubt what was too gloomy but also, alas, too real. And the eclecticism of Hamlet, the lack of unity in his view of things was evidenced at each step in the rapid exchange of one point of view for another point of view that was essentially incompatible with the first. And, after all, the instability of the tenor of his will and his lack of practical consistency and steadiness are the traits that are signified by the common noun – 'a hamlet'.

Although there is insufficient monism in the Hellenic disposition, it is nevertheless not chaotic. The organising tendency in it is not as strong as the tendency toward a plenitude of life, but nevertheless the organising tendency is not insignificant. Negative selection is unavoidable in life. The happiest person experiences suffering – and quite a lot of it. The sufferings of organic development, of indistinct and discontented impulses, the pain of parting with one's nearest and dearest – Hamlet had all of these in his life. He also experienced physical suffering. After all, judging from the characterisation given by the queen regarding his physical organisation, although it was very strong it was still not completely harmonious. Finally, Hamlet worked a lot, and labour as an expenditure of energy is equivalent to suffering and causes negative selection.[42] Therefore, although the monist tendency did not bring Hamlet's psyche to full unity, it was nevertheless sufficient to organise it somewhat (albeit very little) into basic 'unities', monist associative groupings. As far as we can judge from Hamlet's utterances, there were two of these groupings; his disposition suffered from 'bifurcation'.

What was the content of these two competing groupings? Hamlet was first and foremost the son of a great soldier and a descendant of fierce Norse knights. A great many of the impressions of his childhood were connected with war and military glory. There is no doubt that his entire upbringing at home, beginning with countless stories of campaigns and heroic deeds and ending with continual exercise with all kinds of weapons, was directed precisely toward making him a warrior in the full meaning of the word. And as a youth he did not cease, of course, to be interested in military matters and everything related to it. He most likely studied strategy and the whole theory of war thoroughly, and from his fencing one can judge how familiar he was with its practice. Thus, Hamlet was a warrior; this was one aspect of his psychology, one systematic grouping of his experiences.

The other aspect was that Hamlet was an aesthete, an artist, and probably a poet. As a youth, Hamlet lived a full and joyous life in the sphere of art, beauty, and love. His conversations with actors and the subtle elegance of many of his satirical remarks reveal such a depth of aesthetic upbringing! The fresh, pure, and joyful love of Ophelia must have brought so much poetry into the spiritual life of his youth! Hamlet, the aesthete, lived for too long in an atmosphere of harmony, and this atmosphere became a vital necessity for him. But such harmony is a matter of happiness – of exclusive happiness in our

---

42  The relationship of *labour* to psychical selection has great theoretical and practical interest, and I hope yet in the future to specially take up the elucidation of this question.

harsh times – and the hothouse plants that grow under the influence of this harmony are too tender. When happiness ends, the tender plant faces a sad fate.

The two personalities of Hamlet – the warrior and the aesthete – could get along together satisfactorily as long as bloody and pitiless war existed for him only in imagination and in military amusements. In the conceptions of youth, war – as a majestic collision of awesome forces – is aesthetic, and Hamlet, the aesthete, could find pleasure in the martial dreams of Hamlet, the warrior, as long as the war was potential and not real. But when one must *experience* a severe struggle, things go badly for the aesthete. It is painful to receive blows, and it is even more painful for someone with an impressionable, delicate disposition to end the life of another. Plus, it would be easier for an aesthete if it were only pure blood that was flowing, but blood is mixed with dirt, and wounds are mostly repulsive and disgusting. In battle one must resort to guile, be stealthy, and deceive, and this is very un-aesthetic. It is agonising for a tender soul to be in an intense state all the time as struggle requires. Harmony of life is possible only when healing rest follows the expenditure of energy, and constant fatigue destroys any harmony. Things were even worse for Hamlet. Struggle brought him even more contradictions and intensified more strongly the discord between his martial and his aesthetic personalities. The people who were the closest to him – the mother whom he adored and the uncle whom he respected and loved – turned out to be enemies. What could cause a more agonising disharmony in his soul than the transformation of a beloved being into an object of hatred and loathing?

The spirit of his father continually awakened the warrior in Hamlet, while all the circumstances resurrected the aesthete in him. The warrior wanted to inflict blows; the aesthete drew back from blood and dirt. The thirst for vengeance conflicted with the thirst for harmony – this is the whole meaning of the tragedy. Hamlet's vacillation and his unceasing meditation are revealed in the long futile conversations between the one of his personalities that wanted struggle and the other that wanted love and happiness. The first personality was underdeveloped because Hamlet still did not have to *really* live the life of a soldier; the second is fully developed because he lived the life of an artist and an affectionate person in reality. But behind the first personality stands a *developing* reality – more and more influences of the 'environment' that awaken the soldier in Hamlet – and behind the second there are only memories and dreams. The 'objective' course of things advances the soldier; 'subjective' wishes and desires promote the aesthete. In any event, Hamlet, the aesthete, must perish or lose his self-determination; the question is whether Hamlet, the soldier, will escape destruction.

We see here the full expression of the great harmonising power of suffering. For a disposition like Hamlet's, spiritual torment is the heavy, though beneficial, hammer that forges the soul into new, higher forms. Negative selection that destroys or breaks down any flimsy, unreal, or disharmonious combination frees up a place for combinations that have solid, real bases, that are vitally-harmonious, and that it cannot destroy. Negative selection introduced into Hamlet's psyche what was lacking in it: a rigorous, really-monist tendency. After all, the lack of wholeness in the organisation of a Hellene and the extremely great role of imagination depends precisely on the fact that happiness and positive selection predominate too strongly over suffering and negative selection. The tragedy that flows through the soul of Hamlet removed *this* irregularity and thereby created conditions for the transformation of the Hellenic type to a still higher type – what we call 'ideal'. As one watches, the hero gradually becomes another person.

The destruction of the old coordinations in Hamlet's psyche proceeded so quickly, due to his terrible suffering, that the formation of new ones did not keep up with him and a period of temporary disorganisation ensued. This was Hamlet's spiritual sickness – considerably less 'pretended' than he himself, apparently, supposed. But a powerful soul survived and at the end of the play we see Hamlet, the soldier, straighten to his full height – calm and decisive, with clear vision and a firm will. What happened to Hamlet, the aesthete? He did not die but organically flowed together with the other soul of Hamlet. The thirst for harmony in life found a new outlet for itself; it was internally transformed. Having punished a crime and re-established justice, that thirst was transformed from a passive desire *to live* amid harmony into an active will *to create* harmony in life. A conscious soldier for truth and justice – this is the active aesthete who strives toward vital harmony in human relations. Now the psyche of Hamlet is devoid of any dualism, and his will is not weakened by internal struggle. Now he is not distressed about how exactly he must re-establish the 'broken interconnectedness of things'. He strides with a firm tread toward the resolution of this task that is worthy of a real warrior and a real aesthete.

Hamlet perishes, but he perishes as a victor who has accomplished his task. He perishes, of course, not by chance but precisely because, during his internal struggle (which did not allow him to expediently carry on an external struggle), objective conditions (conditions of the 'environment') took shape for him in a most unfavourable aspect. His enemies did not stand idly by but employed all their resources. All the same, even under these conditions, Hamlet was stronger, and he took his enemies with him in his death. While dying, he did not forget to renew the last link of the 'broken connection', and he carried it out with brilliant simplicity, naming as his successor the young hero of another country, a reliable and whole person – Prince Fortinbras.

This, then, is the essence of the tragedy: it is the story of the transformation of a Hellenic spirit into another more finished and whole form through the power of agonising struggle, through the power of deep suffering.

From our point of view, the tragedy of Hamlet does not present anything that is fundamentally mysterious. The tragedy develops entirely in correspondence to the laws of the action of psychical selection. It is a most authoritative testimony supporting the cognitive value of those laws.

VIII

I will now take up another illustration of my method that is of an incomparably less tragic nature – a phenomenon that is very widespread in contemporary Russian life that is called the 'growing wiser' of the spirit of the intelligentsia. It is the story of radical 'children' who in due course became moderate 'fathers'.

The material of experience that contemporary young people bring with them from school and student life, as we know, is not extremely large, but it is not particularly one-sided. It is true that our classical high school has been built, so far, mainly on the principle of specialisation, and moreover on a distinctive specialisation. Most of the cognitive material that is given to children comes from one very narrow realm that possesses, in the eyes of the organisers of the school, the huge advantage that it is 'dead', and, as such, does in itself not contain any objective possibility of progress.[43] But this material has a 'negative' Affectional colouration, and young psyches strive to reduce it to a minimum. This latter, generally speaking, succeeds because it is aided and abetted by their family and the milieu of their coevals. Thus, the content of experience of young people is in fact predominantly reduced to the following groups of experiences: what the family provides, what the milieu of coevals provides, what is provided by the 'class struggle' between young people and the administration and staff of schools, and, finally, what the school provides in regard to the cognitive material of 'learning'. Of all these groups it is precisely the last that is distinguished by the most relative lack of coordination and paucity of content, and it therefore has minimal significance in the development of the young soul.

---

43   The Russian *gimnaziia* (based on the German *Gymnasium*) – the high school that prepared students to enter the university – as opposed to the more practical *real'noe uchilishche* (based on the German *Realschule*) – emphasised the study of Greek and Latin precisely because the government believed it would be a conservative influence [trans.].

The totality of experience turns out to be a very diversely constituted grouping. What the family contributes to the psyche of children – 'cultivating' them – is not at all the same as what the milieu of their coevals contributes and cultivates in them. What coevals contribute is not at all what scholastic 'learning' contributes, and even this 'learning' is not at all the same as what its official transmitters (as objects of hatred and struggle)[44] contribute. The organising work of psychical selection over all these series of experiences proceeds with great intensity. The Affectional life of childhood and early youth is very turbulent and energetic. More and more complexes enter the field of experience of a psyche that is not fully formed, and they deeply captivate that psyche and at times strongly shock it. But positive selection – sensations of a pleasant nature – usually predominates. The psyche grows and develops. The energy of life increases, and although far from all of these changes pass through the field of consciousness, nevertheless a significant part of them are expressed in the field of consciousness in the form of 'pleasant' experiences. Thus, in those most particular cases that we have in mind here, all the conditions exist for the development of the psyche in eclectic forms – diversified but partial experience (in which there are very large gaps that stand in the way of the harmonious unification of that experience) and the relative weakness of negative selection (which is the main factor of development toward a rigorous monism).

And, in reality, the psychology of an adolescent is generally remarkably eclectic. The most heterogeneous ideas and norms that are highly incompatible with one another get along with one another with the greatest ease. The family with its patriarchal structure and blood ties instils some concepts. The milieu of coevals with its 'republican' relationships coloured by the aristocratism of intellect and strength instil other completely different concepts. And fragments of learning create the seeds of a third and also heterogeneous set of concepts, etc. The very same actions that are, one might say, 'rebellious' and 'wilful' are defined by the family as 'sinful' or 'indecent' but are considered by their coevals as manifestations of courage and boldness. In the struggle with teachers at school, actions such as self-defence or attack seem dangerous and, in practice, frequently harmful, while in history textbooks (even those that are thoroughly approved) deeds that are extremely similar are, in some instances, praised as heroic. Naturally, it is impossible for a single and whole point of view on life to be put together by a young being, and, under the great force of posit-

---

44  I have omitted those cases in which particular mentors have 'good', semi-friendly relationships with students. These mentors have approximately the same relationship to students as the ideologists of the proletarian movement have to the proletariat. That is, they come from the bourgeoisie – a distinctive variation of the milieu of coevals.

ive selection, the psyche moves from one series of associations to another with the greatest ease and without being restrained by the fact that they are mutually contradictory.

Subjected to severe repression by the authorities for his 'prank', the schoolboy thinks gloomily: 'What an idiot I was!' And, thinking about life, he completely involuntarily begins to evaluate all human actions by reducing them to the categories of 'advantageous – disadvantageous'. But the moment he is released from the punishment cell, friends express delight and praise, and he is proud and pleased: 'What a great guy I am!' The former categories are forgotten and they are replaced by the new categories of 'glorious – shameful'. At home there are parental reprimands, tender admonitions, rebukes, and the child feels: 'What an evil, bad boy I am!' This presents the categories of 'moral – immoral'. Each point of view temporarily pushes out the others that, it goes without saying, are incompatible with it, and the young eclectic does not feel the need to reduce them to a higher unity.

This unthinking eclecticism is so typical for adolescents that when we encounter a deviation from it we have the impression of something that is not normal or natural. There are children who seem 'precociously adult' – there is 'too much' definiteness and logic in their judgements and 'too much' consistency in their actions. In the great majority of cases the causes are the same and are very simple and understandable from our point of view. Not all children are 'happy' enough to be vivacious eclectics. Some children are forced to suffer too much as a result of illness or unfavourable surroundings. Negative selection predominates over positive selection and brings with it, as we have already seen many times, the predominance of a monist over an eclectic tendency. In addition, the experience of such children is often for the most part less diversified – one certain aspect of it preponderates. For example, among children who work in factories, the realm of experiences that are connected with obligatory labour and material worries predominates. Thus, both the effective forces of psychical development and the material of psychical development are considerably less favourable for the production of the eclectic type. The premature, comparative wholeness that impresses us so strikingly is imposed on the child's psyche by life itself. And we are not deceived by this. There is nothing good in this wholeness. It is inevitably narrow because it contains a very small stock of experiences. Meanwhile, like any completely assembled form, it prevents the production of a new unity of the psyche that would correspond to progressively broadening experience. In this regard, the indefiniteness and incompleteness of the typical eclecticism of youth is considerably more expedient for development. And this narrow unity is achieved at the cost of great early suffering and of a huge expenditure of energy in the period of life when energy should be stored up. Here conditions for the further progress of life are severely narrowed and the path toward the maximum of life is hindered.

But let us return to our vivacious, eclectic youth. Having finished high school, let us suppose that he enters university. His surroundings are changed, the stream of experience is immediately widened enormously, and, moreover, it is widened in some directions much more than in others. Experiences connected with the 'family' quickly recede to secondary or even tertiary importance. The youth is 'emancipated' from the family that had usually helped him to the greatest degree and extent, and direct communication with it is practically broken off. Just the opposite, the milieu of coevals takes an incomparably great place in his system of experience. It becomes considerably wider in quantitative terms and considerably fuller and more varied in qualitative terms. There is a great deal of dynamism and life in the circle of friends, and a great deal of sharp and powerful impressions are obtained from it. At the same time, another side of 'learning' turns itself toward the youth; it changes from disordered, incoherent training to systematic education – the broadening and harmonisation of certain aspects of his experience. War with those who have direct authority over him ceases to play its former role in the life of the young man (with the exception of a few cases of aggravation), but broadened experience brings wider contradictions of life that more than make up for this former antagonism. These are the contradictions of socially-transmitted economic and political experience. Finally, the young student is often forced to support himself by working, and then he becomes acquainted with these contradictions even more closely and immediately, experiencing them for himself directly or indirectly.

Life, as a whole, is incomparably more intense than before; both pleasure and pain are more intense, and the organising tendency is stronger. The youth's unfolding sexual life with its sharp Affectional colouration significantly increases the intensity of psychical selection. The systematisation of experience proceeds more extensively and more quickly. Nevertheless, eclecticism does not disappear, since positive selection usually predominates over negative selection, but, all the same, conditions become more favourable for development in the direction of monism. The material of experience is less uncoordinated; there are fewer gaps in it that deeply separate the various realms of experience. Negative selection takes hold of the psyche more profoundly; the agonies of youths are more serious and more prolonged than the agonies of children. A real 'elaboration of a worldview and life programme' takes place.

Of course those realms of experiences that fill the consciousness to the greatest extent – what is given by the milieu of coevals and what is given by general social conditions and their vital contradictions – play the greatest role in this elaboration. The systematisation of this material forms the well-known radical-democratic worldview that combines ideas of freedom, equality, and, in part, brotherhood. The milieu of coevals provides the basic *positive* content for those tendencies which these ideas express, and the contradictions of social conditions determine the negative content.[45] We see a youth who possesses, apparently, a quite harmonious system of views. The continuing accumulation of energy in the young organism guarantees that the immediate activity of will must be quite great. And although the predominance of positive selection does not allow *especial* steadfastness and consistency in manifestations of will, nevertheless, once the psyche as a whole is organised with sufficient harmony, a certain unity in the tenor of activity becomes completely possible.

In the exclusively favourable conditions in which we now see our hero, his utterances do not reveal any substantially important eclecticism. Two main spheres of experience (family and friends) are reduced to certain combined forms, and the third sphere – learning – does not contradict these forms. Learning, through its discipline, only assists the precise elaboration of these forms and places its imprint on them. But we already know that where positive selection comes to the fore and significantly preponderates over negative selection, eclecticism cannot be fundamentally removed. Positive selection *preserves* too much; what was created by past experience is not sufficiently destroyed. The psyche only seems monist, because its life manifests insufficient diversity.

Those special forms of thought and will that are created by the family with its special relationships have not disappeared or died – they are simply not revealed as long as there are no objective conditions for this to happen. They are terribly durable, and it requires a great deal of struggle and suffering to be done with them – considerably more than is factually the lot of a vivacious school-age youth. And meanwhile these forms are in profound vital contradiction with the foundations of the radical-democratic worldview.

---

45   The milieu of coevals realises the principles of freedom and equality to a significant degree in its very organisation, and closer circles of comrades provide a space for the principle of brotherhood. Contradictions of general social conditions, on the contrary, are closely connected in experience with sharp manifestations of the lack of freedom, inequality, and the struggle of all against all. The positive Affectional colouration of the first series of experiences and the negative Affectional colouration of the second make up the general psychological basis for the active idealism of life in its contemporary forms.

In matters of love, a young student stands on the point of view of the widest freedom. He expresses such views and often carries them out quite consistently himself. But if his sister should try to take this point of view – and not theoretically but in practice – what then? Our hero begins to behave in a completely contradictory way. We hear announcements from him and see actions on his part that we would really expect only on the part of his respectable father. What is going on? A 'family' event summons a 'family' point of view to the scene. Old associations of ideas and desires, peacefully slumbering in neutral equilibrium, once again are drawn into the field of consciousness, and it turns out that they have been marvellously preserved. And they are sometimes manifested with extremely great energy.

The influence of the family – in the given case, a petty bourgeois family that promotes purely philistine tendencies in the psyches of its children – is terribly profound both in its duration and in its intensity. Family influence covers quite a few years and is active at the ages when the psyche is most pliable and plastic, when it is still only taking shape. This is why a petty bourgeois is hidden in a radical youth, who only needs an event in order to tear away the shell of superficial layers of progressive idealism.

There are, of course, cases where this petty bourgeois manages to die out to a significant degree, but these cases are not typical for radical youths who from the bourgeoisie. Those young people who are forced in these years to undergo especially great labour and suffering – provided their psyche possesses sufficient vital stability in order for them to undergo it without great damage – attain considerably great wholeness in their worldview and considerably great consistency in their actions, since negative selection is the most powerful factor for monist development. But we are not dealing with these cases now.

We now return to our hero – to him who is fated to 'grow wiser'. The years of education have ended, and he embarks upon 'life'. For example, he goes to work somewhere in the provinces in private employment or for a *zemstvo*[46] in order not to restrict his 'freedom'. And now the material of experience that is provided to him by his surroundings changes abruptly. 'Comrades' and 'learn-

---

46   *Zemstva* (plural of *zemstvo*) were organs of local government – responsible for education, roads, public health and services, etc. – established in the Great Reforms of Alexander II (1855–81). They were elected institutions, so that, even though the franchise was allocated based on property and status, they still had a democratic component. *Zemstva* hired professionals of various sorts – teachers, surveyors, agronomists, administrators, etc. – to carry out their work. Thus, university graduates who went to work for the zemstva could feel that they had not been co-opted by the tsarist regime [trans.].

ing' retreat into the past (the recent, living past, for now). He is in the 'realm of the petty bourgeoisie'. What is the essential change that occurs?

The comradely milieu of school has disappeared, and it is replaced with a philistine environment. Formal learning also has receded into the distance; it is replaced by 'work'. New family relationships subsequently appear that differ from the former in that our hero now turns out to be the head of a family rather than a subordinate member of one. This is the basic content – the material – of his new phase of experience. This material is distinguished by comparatively weak variety and great conservatism. The flow of experience moves very slowly; the same complexes are repeated again and again – today is like yesterday and tomorrow is like today. Those complexes affect the psyche comparatively weakly and do not bring to it either significant elevation of energy or great expenditure of energy. Affectional life is diminished; psychical selection is not very intense.

What then is the result? Those psychical groupings that took shape during the years of being a student and that formed the system of a radical-democratic worldview are not supported in the new experiences and are less and less often brought up in the field of consciousness by an associative path. What is there to 'remind' a person in philistine surroundings of the principles and ideals that took shape in his soul under completely opposite conditions? Very, very little. Therefore, all that surrounds him repeatedly excites different, old associations and repeatedly draws back into the field of consciousness memories and desires that were established in childhood and the petty-bourgeois environment associated with childhood. The 'petty-bourgeois' person in our hero is inevitably awakened and rises little-by-little to his full height. If this 'petty-bourgeois' person were created from scratch, then the process of his development would be long and complicated, full of contradictions, inner struggle, and pain. But here the matter is considerably simpler and easier: a system of associations that already existed but that was left out of consciousness for a long time is drawn into his field of consciousness and fills it ever more often and ever longer.

And the 'worldview' of his youth? One cannot say that it was quickly destroyed. For this to happen, a more intense Affectional life would be necessary than what obtains in the given case. Under weak psychical selection a lot of time is needed for the destruction of well-established forms. The 'worldview' is preserved for still quite a long time and dies out only gradually due to its own incompatibility with the strengthening 'philistine' forms of psychical life. But to the extent that it is preserved it remains almost all the time on the threshold of consciousness just as in the previous period of life the 'petty-bourgeois' system of associations was preserved on the threshold of consciousness. The difference, by the way, is that during the time that the petty-bourgeois system was hidden it was rooted considerably more solidly in the psyche than the 'worldview' that temporarily supplanted it.

And here, as we saw in the previous phase, what is 'hidden' is manifested from time to time. Usually it is manifested not in the form of active, consistent influences directed toward changing the environment – in the philistine world such influences would need too great an expenditure of energy – but in the form of verbal utterances that issue forth when something 'is reminiscent' of the ideals of youth. This happens, for example, during encounters and conversations with old comrades. In such events an outside observer for the most part thinks: 'not only a renegade, but still a poser'. It seems, however, that such a point of view is not entirely accurate. More often than not there is no conscious lie but only a temporary appearance of old associations in the field of consciousness and the eclecticism of a philistine being replaced by the eclecticism of a youth.

There are, however, cases when peaceful and placid existence absolutely does not set in immediately after the exit from the milieu of student camaraderie. An example is when someone thrust harshly into a philistine environment is subject to a great deal of suffering from that environment but which is experienced not by the 'best' side of his psyche but by a less stable one. In this case, intense negative selection quickly destroys the 'citizen', leaving a place for the philistine, and 'betrayal' is accomplished without any beating about the bush. The same thing results when former comrades intrude into the everyday life of our hero, presenting him with demands that are beyond his strength and that contradict all his current habits and inclinations. This leads to a harsh conflict – to sharp competition between the two sides of his psyche that to this point have peacefully coexisted and hardly encountered one another in the field of consciousness.

I will not follow further the process of our hero's development into a 'pure' philistine – either the complacently-cheerful type full of trivial activity with a problem-free fate and the predominance of positive selection or the irritably-mistrustful type with a tendency to obsessive hypochondria and with an 'unhappy' career in life and the predominance of negative selection. I think that the illustrations that I have adduced are sufficient to show how the idea of psychical selection can be applied to the issue of the working out of psychical types. I now pass on to other possible applications of the idea.

## IX

I will now take several illustrations of our method from the realm of events where one psyche affects another, striving to cause one or another specific changes in it – when one person 'educates', 'rewards', 'punishes', 'corrects', etc. another person. These, as was shown above, are issues *on the border* between psychology and sociology and, in investigating them, it is more productive to move them precisely to psychology because it is here that a specifically psychological method is applicable.[47]

I have already noted in passing that all such means of influence are basically an unconscious application of the very same principle of psychical selection. The 'influencer' strives to undermine and weaken some complexes in the psyche of another by creating a direct associative connection between them and 'unpleasant' complexes (the condition for negative selection) or to strengthen and consolidate other psychical complexes by summoning an association of them with 'pleasant' complexes (the condition of positive selection). This occurs in all cases when the point is to 'reward' or 'punish' or when one person 'convinces' other people, appealing to their advantage or disadvantage (whether 'material', 'spiritual', or even 'moral'). Sometimes the method is somewhat different, and the psyche of another person is 'trained' to something, systematically causing a repetition in that psyche of a specific complex and making this latter 'habitual'. But we already know that 'habituation' itself boils down to the accumulation of actions of psychical selection. And I will not take up an analysis of these means of influence 'in general' but will dwell on their particular peculiarities, mainly from the point of view of the *critique* of these means of influence on the basis of the idea of psychical selection.

There are a great many cases where punishment, reward, 'habituation', etc. do not lead to the intended results no matter how energetically or systematically they are applied but lead to other sometimes unexpected and in any case unwanted results from the point of view of the 'influencer'. How can our principle serve to explain such cases and consequently – given sufficient data – also to the scientific prediction of them?

---

47   It would be natural to put the psychology of *imitation* in the first place in this series of illustrations as a fact that has fundamental significance for the psychical communication of people. But from the point of view of the question of psychical selection this example is less interesting than the others. The analysis of processes of imitation shows that in essence they entirely boil down to associations according to contiguity and to phenomena of 'habituation' that I have already examined. Besides, I do not want to repeat myself yet again; I analysed the question of imitation in my earlier work, *Poznanie s istoricheskoi tochki zreniia*, pp. 109–13.

Any 'punishment' intends to create in the psyche of the person who is being punished a close association between a certain complex that is 'undesirable' and another complex that is intensely 'unpleasant'. The result that is thereby attained is that the first complex acquires a negative Affectional as a part of the given association, and it is eliminated through negative selection. Here it is already immediately obvious that the result that is hoped for might not be obtained first and foremost because negative selection is not all-powerful and its action has limits in its objective conditions.

In reality, one must absolutely not imagine that any energetic punishment you like can succeed in training people not to gratify, let us say, a basic need that arises again and again from the cyclical process of the exchange of energy between their organism and the environment. This could only result in the destruction of the psyche. And, in general, the solidity and stability of one or another psychical form could be so great that it would be impossible to remove it with the help of that system of punishment that is at the disposal of the punisher or even with the help of any system of punishment whatsoever. Besides that, of course, the positive Affectional of the complex that is removed has huge significance both in the degree of its 'habituation' and in the breadth of the associative connections that interlace it with the rest of the psyche. No kind of punishment can undermine the conviction that God exists in the psyches of sincere believers or the striving to realise their ideals in the psyches of idealists.

From this it is obvious that punishment might not lead to the intended results. But how can they sometimes lead to other results – for example, to directly contradictory ones?

Here it is necessary to keep in mind that the phenomenon under discussion is considerably more complex than it seems to our 'pedagogue' who is bringing pressure to bear on someone by traditional measures. All the complexes that simultaneously fill the field of our consciousness are associated with one another, and, consequently, an association is created not only between conceptions of punishment and conceptions of what the punishment is for but with other complexes, as well. An image of the 'pedagogue' inevitably enters the association, as also, frequently, do conceptions of the pedagogue's motives, the goals he is pursuing, etc. It is from this associative connection that, under certain specific conditions, all the 'unintended' consequences can result.

In reality, an 'unpleasant' image not only is weakened by negative selection, but, just like other psychical complexes, it drags behind it certain *volitional complexes*. And psychical selection strives to create precisely such a combination so that a volitional act would be an *expedient adaptation*, so that it would eliminate the very conditions that summoned the given unpleasant image. Thus, for example, for an uncultured person with a spontaneously-violent will, an act of lawful 'punishment' might bring with it a volitional reaction that simply and directly brings that act to a halt: resistance to the one who is doing the punishing, killing that person, and so on. Under certain conditions the most cultured, the most highly organised, the noblest psyche could react in exactly the same way.

From this point of view, all those cases where punishment is still not successful in causing the results – in the sense of the negative selection that it intends – and instead causes an energetic struggle against the one who is doing the punishing are completely understandable. But since still other complexes enter into the association that arises, the result can be even more complex. Let us suppose that a person closely associates conceptions of his sufferings with conceptions of the ideas (views on 'morality', for example) that motivate his tormentor, and he begins an energetic struggle against these same ideas. Or let us suppose that he causally relates a conception of punishment to a conception of the *right* (in an objective sense) of another person to apply such a means of influence on him. Then a struggle against the corresponding legal institutions arises. In any political struggle for liberation, one has occasion to see a great many cases where penalties for political crimes transform those people who brought these punishments upon themselves more or less by chance into real, professional revolutionaries.

At the same time, one must keep the following in mind. Severe punishments, especially when they are prolonged, can essentially change the mutual relationship of positive and negative psychical selection in the life of a given person – obviously in the direction of negative selection – and then the very type of psychical development can change. In this way a severe 'Hebrew' can sometimes be created from a 'Hellene' and a gloomy fanatic from a 'happy-go-lucky fellow'. It is understandable how unfortunate such a result is from the point of view of the person carrying out the punishment. This is what happens: instead of an opponent with a comparatively unified will, who is rather scatter-brained or even vacillating, an enemy is produced who is terrible in his 'stubbornness', 'bitterness', and, more precisely, in his monistic steadfastness. And this relates, of course, not only to political fighters. At the other pole of social life, in the world of 'criminal offenders', penal servitude and long sentences in prison sometimes produce remarkably holistic types with an extremely harmonious and complete anti-social worldview and the greatest consistency in the struggle for narrowly personal, anti-social goals.

In essence, the method of 'punishment' provides any kind reliable results only in regard to those types of psychical development that we have designated as 'philistine'. Here, by virtue of the comparative instability of the existing psychical forms, one can consider it very probable that 'undesirable' combinations will be destroyed, even if they are very 'habitual', and the weakness of creative activity and of the psyche guarantees that other, still more 'undesirable' combinations are not created and do not develop instead of it. Where the matter concerns a psyche of a more noble type, one can often expect results of precisely the latter kind. But punishment cannot create anything particularly durable and reliable in the psyche of a 'philistine' due to its general vacuousness. And frequently even here the objective result of induced suffering is reduced to zero; negative selection for the most part removes from consciousness the 'unpleasant memory' of the punishment that was carried out. The person 'does not think' about the punishment, 'tries to forget' about it, and continues to indulge in 'undesirable' but 'pleasant' habits that are maintained by positive selection.

All the considerations that have been presented provide a sufficient basis for a fundamental critique of 'punishment' as an educative method in general and also for a critique of concrete forms of punishment. First and foremost, it is evident that it is an unreliable method even from the point of view of the immediate goal. Too often the results that are obtained are completely different from what one had in mind or are even directly contradictory to it. Familiarity with the psychical type of the person who is being 'put right' – given a sufficiently clear understanding of the principle of psychical causality (i.e. precisely psychical selection) – would permit one to anticipate these cases ahead of time and to realise ahead of time the inapplicability of the given method to them. But from the foregoing it is clear that this inapplicability relates precisely to the most noble types of the human psyche with the greatest intensity and fullness of life, and if culture progressively ennobles humanity, removing lower types of psychical development, then the realm in which 'punishment' is not an unconditionally harmful method of education must progressively be narrowed.

But even in those cases where a given method of 'correction' possesses a certain crude, immediate expediency, one must not lose sight of the real *complexity* of its results, of the great number of collateral effects that the method brings and that can constitute a negative magnitude that far exceeds its positive significance. In the psyche of the object of punishment an association is created that is 'desirable' to the one who is carrying out the punishment and which, according to his calculation, must impart a colouration of pain to the 'undesirable' psychical form. But this is not the only effect; still other associations arise. The conception of the suffering that is endured is inseparably connected with the conception of the person who caused them, and this undermines the *social connection* between both parties – a connection based precisely on the positive Affectional that the conception of one person possesses in the psyche of another. When people become 'unpleasant' to one another, the kinds of reactions that mutually divide and separate them become preponderant. And thereby the very possibility of expedient 'influence' on the person whom one has in mind to 'correct' diminishes ever more greatly, i.e. the given system itself then removes the basis of its own applicability.

According to the very essence of the matter, the goal of 'punishment' is attained only at the cost of the expenditure of energy of the psyche of the 'one being corrected'. This, of course, would not be the principal deficiency of the given method, if all the expenditure of energy were accomplished precisely at the expense of the psychical form that is 'undesirable' and that it is intended to weaken or eliminate. But in reality the suffering that is induced always embraces not only one definite psychical combination but at every given moment the whole field of consciousness (and in the total sum of a great many of different fields of consciousness) through which a multitude of other psychical complexes are passing in addition to the complex that is subject to eradication. Thus the destructive work spreads considerably wider and further than is required by the goal for which it is undertaken.

Punishment is very frequently viewed not so much as a means of immediately correcting the 'guilty' as it is a means of 'frightening' others who are not guilty yet but are capable of becoming guilty if the opportunity presents itself. Thus, the same associative connection between the 'undesirable' and the 'unpleasant' is created in the psyches of all members of society, only here the 'unpleasant' appears in a less living and concrete form and consequently with less intensity. In essence, this is nothing other than the spreading of the act of 'punishment' over all society with a significant corresponding lowering of the degree of punishment. Instead of real pain there is an intimidating association by means of an image that is distressful for every member of society and more distressful to the degree that the psyche is more impressionable and more social.

From this point of view the fundamental defects of this method are not less (and they may be even more) significant than from the 'corrective' point of view. First and foremost, it is obvious that the economic principle of life is being violated here; it is not the particular people, whom the 'intimidating' influence is needed to restrain, who undergo that influence but also a huge number of others – often in the millions – who are 'frightened', properly speaking, for nothing. Of course, a separate 'intimidating' association of an image in one or another psyche presents only an insignificant magnitude of a negative nature. Nevertheless, it is a 'minus' and not a 'plus', and when life is filled with such associations, the extent to which they distort the image and likeness of human development becomes completely clear.

Additionally, the immediate expediency of intimidation is comparatively small. It can hold back from 'undesirable' actions only those who have an inclination to these actions and in whom that inclination is quite weak. Wherever there are strong and deep motives for these actions, the 'intimidating' association of images appears, for the most part, to be too inadequate a method.

There is still one more point of view on the problem of punishment. It is considered as the restoration of absolute justice that has been violated, as the 'natural' law of the criminal and the 'obligation' of society toward him, and so on. But it is obvious that this point of view provides exactly nothing for the psychological critique of the principle of 'punishment' or for the explanation of its real vital significance. This is all that it is possible to say about it here.

In stating the fundamental defects of the very principle of 'punishment', our critique does not in the least provide the grounds for denying its *historical* necessity and its *relative* social usefulness under certain concrete conditions. But it does provide the grounds to assert that *the progressive development of the conditions of human life must lead to the limitation and elimination of the principle of 'punishment' from the sphere of the influence of people on other people.*

Any concrete form of punishment is subject to particular critique in regard to its specific expedience, and here the idea of psychical selection permits one to anticipate to a significant extent in advance the dimensions and nature of the real influence of a given form of 'punishment' on the psychical development of a person. For illustration, I will dwell on one extremely widespread method of 'correction' of criminals that has many adherents among criminalists – long-lasting solitary confinement.

The essence of this method consists in combining the deprivation of freedom with yet another source of suffering – cutting off of all living communication of the person with other people, taking away normal socially-conditioned experiences. As a result, so high a negative Affectional results that only a few strong natures can in general endure several years of such 'correction', and for average people only a few months will leave harsh traces of a general deterioration of life. In semi-civilised countries where physical torture is not yet formally abolished and freedom of the individual is still considered to be a certain *quantité négligeable*, solitary confinement is considered to be an excellent substitute for torture in preliminary investigations, especially for political crimes.

In this sense one must undoubtedly consider the immediate expedience of the method to be quite significant: the destruction of the psyche, the general collapse of vital energy, and along with this also the resistance to all external – for example, an interrogator's – influences, are usually attained to such a high degree that it is clearly manifested in a huge percentage of psychical illness among those who have been subjected to solitary confinement. But from the point of view of any kind of positive results of the method, the picture that results is absolute different.

Everything that is produced by psychical selection is produced from the material of immediate primary experiences, and psychical selection is limited to them. These are the experiences in which the closest relationship of the psychical system to its environment is expressed. Deprivation of freedom reduces these experiences to both a quantitative and qualitative minimum, limiting the whole realm of accessible perceptions of external environment to the insignificant space of imprisonment and its lifeless, monotonous conditions. The system of solitary confinement finds, however, even this minimum to be still too large and considers it necessary to further limit the influx of living perceptions. Everything is taken away from prisoners that could allow them to communicate with other people – fellow prisoners or guards. It is true that the possibility of working and also of reading is not thereby usually excluded, but simple mechanical work of the only sort that is compatible in the great majority of cases under the conditions of solitary confinement would, after a short period of time, cease to be a source of *new* impressions, and reading – delivering pale, abstract images by means of words – can never in any way replace the bright experiences of 'real' life.

Where, then, do the 'ones being corrected' remain? Obviously, in their *past*.

There is no present – or almost none – for these people, because the present has too insignificant a positive content. And if their psyches are remarkably strong and if the abnormal conditions of life have not caused their psyches to progressively collapse and decay, then it is not difficult to anticipate the tenor and direction of their development. A harsh prevalence of negative selection – a life full of suffering – will cause a *monist* tendency of particular force and intensity. The most rigorous systematisation of psychical content will occur around one specific organising idea that is connected with one specific direction of will. An integral and steadfast psyche will take shape, and a 'person of iron' will be produced – if not a 'Hebrew' then a 'fanatic' or, in any event, a being that does not know vacillation or pity in the struggle for life.

Meanwhile the same vital content that previously brought that person into conflict with public authorities serves as the material of this systematisation. One can consequently expect with great probability that the sum of vital content that psychical selection presents in solitary confinement will be reduced to an idea that will be profoundly hostile to the public authorities. And *if* these authorities at the given time are the actual organ and expression of the will of society then the governing idea worked out in the 'criminal' under the given conditions will be profoundly anti-social. And it is not difficult to see that such scanty vital material that solitary confinement provides could hardly be more in harmony with such an idea – could hardly accommodate it better. After all, the basic content this vital material consists of hostile and painful actions of social authorities on the person of the 'criminal'.

In this way, all the conditions are provided for that usually narrow and one-sided wholeness that is often so striking to us in people who 'successfully' undergo long solitary confinement. Normal members of the opposition are transformed into severe and formidable fighter who devotes their whole lives to the service of one idea; ordinary criminals become terrible and fierce 'enemies of society'. This, of course, is not what is desired by the system of 'correction' in question. But, in essence, no matter what 'correction' the system as a matter of fact aims for in the heads of trained criminalists, in reality it totally aims for something else – to break and weaken the psyche of 'those being corrected' so that they, due to lack of energy, cannot be especially harmful. And in the *majority* of cases this is attained; in the minority, however, what I have just described is attained. The task of the investigator who takes my point of view will consist in precisely stating the facts as they are in such cases. A critique of them will be immediately self-evident, once the basic regularity of their influence on psychical life is known.

The same considerations as I expressed in regard to solitary confinement relate, with insignificant reservations and changes, to any prolonged and severe deprivation of freedom. The types of characters and leaders of penal servitude, with their striking 'criminal' wholeness, can serve as a good illustration of the life we are talking about.

It goes without saying that both the fundamental and the particular shortcomings of the method of psychical influence on people that are based on 'punishment' objectively diminish to the extent that the concrete forms of punishment are alleviated – for example from physical maiming to deprivation of freedom, from deprivation of freedom to social censure. But the deficiencies are not absolutely eliminated as long as that method is maintained. Thus the question arises of whether there is another method of transforming the human spirit that would be more 'economical' in the sense of expenditure of energy and at the same time that that would lead more directly to the goal.[48]

---

48 G. Simmel, in his *Einleitung in die Moralwissenschaft* [*Introduction to Moral Science*] subjected the psychical effect of 'repentance' to fundamental criticism from a very similar point of view. 'Repentance' is a distinctive unhealthy condition of the mind that adds up to prolonged fixation in the field of consciousness of 'sinful' or 'criminal' complexes with the colouration of a strong negative Affectional. Historically, an elevated tendency toward 'repentance' was developed in humanity precisely by long training by means of a system of 'punishments' and is, so to speak, its 'subjective reflection'.

In order not to drag out this presentation with yet more illustrations of our method, we will not dwell on the principle of 'rewards' that naturally complements the principle of 'punishment'. The basic shortcoming here is the same: instead of a 'desirable' association of conceptions, a large number of other, mostly completely 'undesirable' conceptions are imposed on the psyche. But since this is attained through positive, and not negative, selection then another fundamental shortcoming that is characteristic of the principle of 'punishment' is avoided – excessive expenditure of energy of the psychical system ...[49]

In bringing my series of illustrations to an end, I will dwell on one group of phenomena that play a huge role in the processes of psychical life and psychical development – the phenomena of *labour*.

X

*Labour is consciously-expedient activity*, and I will make this generally-accepted definition the starting point of my necessarily cursory analysis.

The word 'activity' in this definition expresses volitional, or, what is the same thing, as we have seen, the *innervational* nature of labour-related complexes. Innervation is the expenditure of energy of the psychical system. Thus, labour, as activity, is the expenditure of energy, and the expenditure of energy corresponds to a negative Affectional of the psychical complex. Does this mean that labour is always 'unpleasant'?

This would be the case if an innervational complex filled the field of consciousness entirely and without exception. But other complexes are always present in this field. First, there is the psychical image of the goal of labour, which almost always has a positive, 'pleasant' colouration. Second, there are various feelings and perceptions obtained from the external environment during the process of labour and also psychical images that are associated with them, etc. All these accompanying complexes can possess such a high positive Affectional that the entire field of consciousness frequently acquires a 'pleasant' character. Labour then becomes 'delight'. But if the accompanying

---

49  The confines of this chapter require me to leave to one side a large number of other means by which people influence other people, like 'acclimatisation', 'suggestion' (with or without hypnosis), etc. But if readers, themselves, attempt to apply methods based on the idea of psychical selection to these phenomena, then I believe they will be easily convinced that this idea will not encounter real contradictions and will vividly illustrate the most varied facts from these as well as from other realms of psychical experience. Psycho-pathology is just as legitimate a field for the application of the idea of psychical selection as 'normal' psychology. The data of both fields must equally provide material for the scientifically-organised, practical application of this idea.

complexes are 'indifferent', i.e. the totality possesses an insignificant Affectional, then it is immediately evident that labour as such – as the expenditure of energy – possesses the colouration of 'suffering'. It is not for nothing that in many languages the ideas of 'labour' and 'suffering' are so close to one another that they are expressed by words with the same root or even by the very same word.

Here, by the way, is still one more complicating circumstance that is very important for us. During the process of labour, the expenditure of energy takes place in significant – if not the largest – part owing to 'extra-conscious' coordinations outside the confines of consciousness. The 'main coordination' participates in the general expenditure of energy of the system only to a certain extent – this becomes obvious if we consider the process of labour from its physiological side. The 'centres of consciousness' are, to the extent that we can judge, only the 'higher' centres of the nervous systems. The lower ones – of the spine-cerebrum, of ganglions, of the sub-cortex – serve entirely or in part as centres of 'unconscious' reactions. There is no need to repeat that from the empiriomonist point of view there is no such thing as the absolutely-unconscious and that the matter boils down to a certain real *separateness* of the lower associative coordinations from the main coordination. What is important for us is that during the processes of labour the lower centres of the nervous system are the immediate source of the innervation that leads to the movement of the muscular apparatus. In the sphere of 'wilful' actions, the higher centres play a role in regard to the lower motor centres that is approximately the same as discharging them with an electric battery – the higher centres give a shock that leads to the liberation of the built-up potential energy of the lower centres.

It is therefore possible to assume with complete justification that the greater part of the expenditure of energy during labour is not carried out at the expense of the main coordination of experiences and that the field of consciousness is coloured by a negative Affectional to a comparatively lesser degree than would be the case if the entire sum of innervation that occurs were 'acknowledged'.[50] It is understandable that such a relatively weak negative Affectional can fairly often be outweighed by the positive Affectional of accompanying experiences, and labour is then 'pleasant'. However, so far in the history of humanity this is not at all what occurs most often.

---

50  It is this factual prevalence of 'extra-conscious' innervation that also explains to a significant extent, as I have suggested, why the question of whether or not 'innervational sensations' actually exist remained unresolved for such a long time and even, until the very recent past, was often decided in the negative.

As has already been pointed out, labour is not simply innervation; its necessary point consists in the *consciousness of a goal*. I will not take up an analysis of the concept of a goal or an explication of the genesis of the real teleology of life here, since this has been done by others many times and to do so would be to present things that are sufficiently well known. For my task, the following is of the essence. A 'goal' is a complex-image that accompanies all volitional complexes that enter into a given process of labour with a greater or lesser degree of clarity and completeness. A goal is a 'psychical image' and not a 'perception', i.e. it is not an image that is located in immediate correlation with any influences of the environment that are proximally 'reflected' in it and that directly 'summon' it into the psychical field, but it is rather an *indirect* and *derivative* reflection of such influences. Generally speaking, a complex-'goal' possesses a positive Affectional or, at the very least, a minimally negative Affectional in comparison with all the complexes that it competes with in a given psyche. Precisely due to such an Affectional, a goal is registered, so to speak, in consciousness during the process of labour.

The psychical image of the goal 'defines' the acts of labour. Among the volitional complexes-desires in the psyche, the ones that are retained and developed to the level of 'actions' are those that are correlated with the complex-goal – i.e. united with them – and present the greatest positive or the least negative Affectional. Those that contradict these complexes – i.e. that provide the least favourable Affectional when combined with them – are removed in competition with the former. It is clear that all this is the direct result of psychical selection, a result that could have been theoretically predicted on the basis of the principle under discussion.

The 'goal' defines the process of labour in the form that it will be 'achieved'. This means that, as a result of labour, the *psychical image* of the goal (that will be realised) turns into the *perception* of the goal (as it is realised). The relationship of the psychical system to its 'environment' changes substantially in one specific point: the experience that did not have a directly correlating complex in that environment now has one. The experience becomes an *immediate* experience. Let us say that a settler builds a house. The house-goal is only a psychical image, a more or less pale derivative complex, formed by the psyche from the material of previous immediate experiences (perceptions of previously seen homes and such). The home that is constructed signifies a mass of immediate perceptions – primary experiences – that appear by turn as living material for a still greater mass of secondary, derivative experiences.[51]

---

51  I have chosen the most typical example – labour that changes the relationship of a sys-

Labour, as the process of attainment of a goal is a process of *adaptation*. In other words, by changing the relationships between the complexes of the 'psyche' and the complexes of the 'environment', labour changes them in the direction of greater mutual harmony of the two series. Thus, the construction of a home leads to a situation in which a mass of perceptions of an 'unpleasant' nature – cold, dampness, etc. – are removed from the psychical experience of the colonist and replaced by 'pleasant' perceptions. The result is the elevation of the vital capacity of the psychical system and the growth of its energy. Of course, sometimes labour gives completely different results. But for the problem of psychical development, of its means and paths, what is important is what relates to *useful* labour that is successful and that elevates the energy of the system.

Our analysis has now established a sufficient quantity of data so that, based on the idea of psychical selection, we can draw certain definite conclusions about the meaning of useful labour in regard to the transformation of the psychical system.

Labour signifies the expenditure of energy of a psychical system both from the perspective of its main ('conscious') coordination and also from the perspective of its subordinate, collateral ('extra-conscious') coordinations. The expenditure of energy leads to negative psychical selection, and this selection at that time does not occur only in the field of consciousness. As I have explained, *extra-conscious coordinations of experiences are organised according to the same associative type as the main coordination is organised, and consequently they are also subject to the same psychical selection*. This selection is not apprehended in the form of 'pleasure' and 'pain' for the same reason that the psychical selection that proceeds in *another person's* psyche is not apprehended in that form. Instead, it is because it occurs within the confines

---

tem to the 'external surroundings'. But it is also possible, as we know, for labour to directly change only the internal relationships of a psychical system. Examples include the labour of producing a worldview, instilling character in itself, and so on. But only the relativity of the idea of 'surroundings' is revealed in these (derivative, secondary) forms of labour. If a person sets himself the goal of producing a holistic worldview – a harmonious cognitive organisation of experience – then this means that certain realms or aspects of his psychical experience are unorganised and disharmonious and 'are perceived' by the mind in a negative colouration (i.e. when entering the field of consciousness, colour it with a negative Affectional). These realms and aspects of the psychical system also comprise that 'environment' for the more organised parts of that psychical system that is transformed by the process of labour. The unity of the mind does not at all have an absolute nature and the mutual inadaptability of one series of its complexes with another, of whatever sort, makes one of them 'the external environment' for the other. Of course, it is only comparatively external. Incidentally, the term 'environment' is applied to the *less* organised series.

of another coordination that is not the same as the one that constitutes the content of the psychical experience of a given individual. Nonetheless, it is necessarily accomplished, and in the case that I am analysing it is accomplished precisely as negative selection. Naturally, it also brings with it its typical tendency for the system to develop – a harmonising and 'monist' tendency. Incidentally, its action extends not only to the main coordination but also to no small degree – or even to a great degree – to subordinate, secondary coordinations.

This is what constitutes the essential distinction between the form of negative selection under discussion and all other forms of negative selection and its vital superiority over them. Various kinds of suffering that depend on the miseries of life (grief, sadness, pain, etc.) – to the extent that they do not destroy but rather develop the psyche – bring a monist, harmonising tendency into it. But it is not necessary that this tendency also includes lower coordinations; in many cases even the most probable action of negative selection is limited to the realm of 'consciousness'. In other cases that action probably extends also beyond the confines of that realm, but it is impossible to judge even approximately in what direction and to which precise separate coordinations it extends. In a word, in the case of grief, sadness, pain, etc., the action of psychical selections is either narrow and one-sided or comparatively unsystematic so that it must be less subject to regulation. In the processes of labour, the action of negative selection is altogether multi-faceted because it extends to a series of coordinations that are vitally interconnected by a relationship to a specific system of influences of the environment that the given process of labour is directed toward changing.

On the other hand, useful labour is characterised by the fact that in its final result there is an increase in the energy of the system so that the vital 'plus', which springs up from new relationships of the system to its environment, actually exceeds the general sum of expenditure of energy during labour. And this, of course, signifies positive psychical selection that in the extent of its action does not yield to negative selection in the given case and follows it in time. Positive selection brings a broadening of psychical life in regard to associative creativity and volitional activity. And, for all that, this broadening is not as indefinite and unsystematic as in the case of any 'joys' and 'pleasures' that randomly appear. Here it extends proximally to the same series of complexes that are subject to harmonisation by the action of negative selection that is caused by the given process of labour.

Such is the immediate influence of useful labour on psychical development. But there is still an indirect influence that might be even more significant and important, although also less definable. The relationships of the 'psyche' to its 'environment' change. The immediate content of the two series of complexes of experience changes. And the 'environment' becomes the source of more and more perceptions for the 'psyche'. The material of immediate experience that grows thereby becomes the source for further development.

A great sociologist placed the following idea at the basis of his theory of social development: human beings, in changing external nature in the process of labour, change their own nature.[52] Such a psycho-genetic analysis permits us to apply more concrete content to this formula: in the process of useful labour, human beings change their nature in regard to the growth of the harmony and fullness of their life and the variability of its forms.

The action of psychical selection is just as narrow and fortuitous as the field of psychical selection – a given field of consciousness. This action is partly contradictory. In bringing partial harmonisation of separate angles of the system, it sometimes thereby increases the general disharmony of the system, and in developing a separate realm of the psyche, it often does so at the expense of its other realms. This action creates habits that are harmful for the psyche, and it supports desires that are destructive of its life. It is a spontaneous phenomenon.

In the process of labour – useful labour – psychical selection attains a definite tenor, and this tenor is vitally-progressive. Here psychical selection loses its spontaneous nature – its narrowness and indefiniteness.

Labour transforms the psyche. This has long been well known, and it has served as the basis for countless applications, both rational and irrational.[53] But only useful labour changes the psyche in a direction that is vitally-progressive. And only that labour which has its source in the organisation of a separate individual and in the intrinsic and basic needs of that individual is useful for development from the point of view of that individual as a separate psychical organisation. This is labour in the full meaning of the word 'free'. It is labour whose goal is not 'imposed' on the individual by any 'external coercion', i.e.

---

52   Bogdanov is, of course, referring to Karl Marx, *Capital*, Chapter 7, Section 1. [trans.].
53   An example of a rational application of labour is 'interesting' and 'pleasant' labour as a means of education. An example of an irrational application is forced labour as a means of 'correction'. Forced labour is an expenditure of energy that, generally speaking, is not rewarded with a corresponding or a large growth of energy that appears as the result of this expenditure (the opposite case can only be an exception). Therefore, forced labour is nothing more than a particular case of 'punishment' and is subject to the same criticism as the principle of 'punishment'. Under certain circumstances, consequently, forced labour is 'useful' for psychical development, but only under certain conditions, and this usefulness is always a differential magnitude – the usefulness of 'the lesser of two evils'.

a complex that disharmoniously enters the individual's experience. It makes no difference if this is the violence of another person or the power of hunger.

History poses complex questions, and it simplifies them. In our time, history has transformed the issue of systematic, regular, continuous progressive development of the human psyche into the issue of free labour.

CHAPTER 6

# Two Theories of the Vital-Differential

I have placed a specific psychoenergetical idea at the basis of my theory of psychical selection: the continual correspondence between 'pleasure' and the elevation of the energy of the centres of consciousness, on the one hand, and between 'pain' and the diminishment of energy, on the other.

If the theory of psychical selections permits the 'explanation' – i.e. the harmonious systematisation into simplified models – of a great deal that is 'inexplicable' or 'less explicable' by other doctrines, then one must see in this theory the strongest proof of my energetics of pleasure and pain. Scientific critique must judge whether this is the case in reality.

But if one could show that this energetics is not valid, then the theory of psychical selection that it is based on could be rejected a priori without any detailed critique. I am therefore obligated to pay extremely close attention to objections to my understanding of the connection between the 'Affectional' and changes in the energy of the neural centres.

A. Lunacharskii has made such objections in his *Izlozhenie kritiki chistogo opyta* [*Exposition of the Critique of Pure Experience*] by Richard Avenarius.[1] A. Lunacharskii defends Avenarius's theory of the Affectional from my critique – a theory according to which pleasure is connected with the diminishment of the vital-differential and pain with its increase regardless of whether that vital-differential consists in a preponderance of 'nourishment' over 'work' or the other way around.

I am most anxious to review Lunacharskii's arguments, since this will give me the opportunity to introduce new evidence proving the validity of my point of view.

I began my critique of Avenarius by pointing out how unfortunate his choice of the concept of 'nourishment' was for characterising one side of the varying equilibrium of life and the concept of 'work' for characterising the other side. These concepts simply *do not correlate*. 'Nourishment' is the delivery of material to a given organ in order for it to be vitally assimilated, but it is not that assimilation, itself. 'Work' is the *direct disassimilation* of energy. To use a very contemporary comparison, these concepts are used in the same mutual relation as the recruitment of soldiers and the loss of life in battle. The first one

---

1 Lunacharskii 1905.

cannot be directly balanced by the second. The killed and wounded cannot be directly replaced by recruits; the army must 'assimilate' its 'nourishment'. Recruits must be trained and put in detachments in order to become a real 'plus' for the army to fully correspond to the 'minus' of the losses. On the contrary, a great number of recruits can require the diversion of a significance part of the forces of the army for their training, discipline, etc., so that it makes up an immediate 'minus' and not a 'plus' for the actual army. According to these considerations, based on evidence that is simple and clear, I propose to connect in the idea of 'vital-differential' the more rigorous and precise (and at the same time fully correlative) concepts of 'acquisition' and 'expenditure' of energy: assimilation and disassimilation.

I further pointed out that under such a logically complete understanding of the vital-differential the *reverse* vital significance of the two types of vital-differential appears completely obvious. The preponderance of acquisition over expenditure is the elevation of the energy of life, the possibility of great expenditure in the future, and the immediate elevation of vital-conservation. The preponderance of expenditure is the lowering of the energy of life and the decrease of vital-conservation. For Avenarius, any vital-differential is a decrease of vital-conservation and, the most that a vital system can attain in its struggle for existence is to 'maintain' itself 'amid decreases of vital-conservation', but not at all to increase vital-conservation.

Lunacharskii tries to overcome these considerations, and he draws on all the wealth of his critical imagination to vindicate his teacher's construction. Lunacharskii attempts at first to prove that I have not made an effort to 'embrace the general meaning' of Avenarius's theory, and I have therefore not completely understood him. He cites my argument (pp. 99–101 in the 1904 edition of *Empiriomonism*)[2] and he objects to it in the following way.

'First and foremost, the critic indirectly makes one think that Avenarius's phrase "either the decrease or the preservation of the system in the presence of decreases" means that the absolute decrease of vital capacity is stated as something that is inevitable. The meaning of the phrase, however, is different. Changes in System C are considered either as the *decrease* of vital-conservation or as its *maintenance*, which now obviously excludes the thought of decrease, but, since this preservation of vital-conservation must now be considered with the presence of preceding and forthcoming decreases (*unter solchen Verminderungen*), then it is obvious that it must be a *new type* of vital-conservation' (*Izlozhenie*, p. 60).

---

2  pp. 69–70 in the present volume [trans.].

Lunacharskii's ploy is fruitless, because it obviously evades the question. I pointed out that for Avenarius the idea of the *increase* of vital-conservation is missing, since for him the 'maintenance of the system'[3] is the opposite of the decrease of vital-conservation. Lunacharskii says that this 'maintenance' signifies a 'new type' of vital-conservation, that can be elevated – i.e. it is essentially a large vital-conservation – and it is illustrated by Avenarius's examples. At the same time, Lunacharskii is keen on proposing that 'maintenance of the system' should be taken into consideration not only with the 'preceding' but also with the 'following' decreases of vital-conservation. How he manages to derive this from the three words 'unter solchen Verminderungen' [under such decreases], it is a mystery to me, since it is perfectly obvious that System C as a *physical* complex cannot 'be taken into consideration' with anything that is 'following' and that 'maintenance' is definitely not an 'increase'. At any rate, this is unquestionable in regard to Avenarius with his classical precision of expression. The essence of the matter consists in the *absolute* nature of Avenarius's idea of vital-conservation; for him, any fluctuation of life is a 'decrease' in vital-conservation, and the removal of this fluctuation is only 'maintenance', i.e. cessation in decrease. To set off a qualitatively 'new type' against the quantitative 'decrease' as Lunacharskii does in his enthusiasm, was something that, it goes without saying, the rigorous formalist Avenarius was incapable of.

Lunacharskii is dimly aware that he, properly speaking, is substituting himself for Avenarius, and he exerts a special effort to eliminate such a suspicion. But here matters turn out even worse. Earlier he at least was re-working Avenarius, adapting Avenarius to himself – someone who came later and therefore, on the whole, has a more elevated worldview. But now, arguing that he is not making such a distortion, he involuntarily begins to adapt his own views to the formulas of Avenarius, distorting his own evolutionary worldview. This is what he says:

---

3 It is not completely missing. The idea of the increase in vital-conservation is not among his basic ideas or even in the entire work, with the exception of a chapter on 'congregated [social] systems'. There it unexpectedly – in contradiction to what precedes and follows – bursts to the surface, is maintained for several minutes without explanation, and then once again disappears without a trace. This chapter is completely unique; it does not flow together organically with the rest of the work, and was written under the obvious influence of the Darwinian idea when Avenarius was an altogether hopeless Lamarckian. The 'Index' of the book contains the term 'Verminderung des Vital-Erhaltungswertes [decrease of the vital-conservation value]' not the term 'Vermehrung des Vital-Erhaltungswertes [increase of the vital-conservation value]'.

It is in vain that A. Bogdanov would argue that I distort the meaning of Avenarius's teaching. If he would only recall the theory of 'absolute constants', then Avenarius's theory regarding development would present itself to Bogdanov in the following form. In a mother's womb – that sanctuary for the preservation of life – an organism exists in almost ideal conditions, i.e. nothing disturbs the current of life – small and narrow, to be sure – of the young organism. Then the organism is ejected into a new environment where it undergoes a thousand hostile influences. In order to continue life, it must develop a huge system of preservative forms, and it must broaden and enrich its life (and its consciousness along with it), striving to turn an infinitely different environment into the same almost ideal conditions. I.e. it must adapt itself to a variable and infinitely rich reality, and adapt that reality it to itself, in order that its life begins to flow harmoniously, so that nothing would seem to be a 'mystery', 'surprise', or 'danger' to it, and that nothing would threaten it with harm or be offensive to it. Through the growth and development of the brain, on the one hand, and the creative processing of reality, on the other hand, an individual moves to an ideal equilibrium between its needs and the environment. And in the future we must acquire anew an almost ideal relationship, such as we found in the mother's womb, and, in the meantime, we realise it only approximately and extremely imperfectly. The whole wide world will never become a 'sacred sanctuary of life', but life becomes infinitely complicated since it is adapted not to the mother's womb but to infinite nature.

This is a worthy ideal! It is a pity that A. Bogdanov does not wish to understand the superb ideas of our philosopher's theory and treats his theory in such a slipshod way.

pp. 61–2

I answer categorically: the ideal is *not* worthy; the ideas are *not* superb. I have no desire to live in a sanctuary – small or large – for the *preservation* of life and Lunacharskii, himself, if he gives it any thought, will of course reject this domicile.

The infinite *growth* of life is not at all the same as the ideal *preservation* of it in the womb of mother nature. The permanent *possibility of successful struggle* for the satisfaction of more and more needs engendered by the blows and caresses of mother nature is not at all the same as the 'ideal *equilibrium* between needs and the environment'. If Lunacharskii says that he means that among these needs is the need for development, growth, and broadening of life, then he is playing with words. How can one speak of the 'equilibrium of needs with the environment', when the need for development signifies precisely the absence of this equilibrium. The need is ruled out, unless it is mystically understood as an internal striving that is immanent in the human spirit. In the final analysis, the starting point of any possible development lies in the absence of an equilibrium.

So, I can only repeat my charge against Avenarius's theory:

'One senses in Avenarius's formulation the remnants of a conservative, static understanding of life, remnants that have gradually been removed as evolutionary thought has developed'.

And I now would even add a new charge:

'This formulation tends to entangle in the net of the remnants of conservative thinking even those thinkers who altogether do not incline toward stasis but who, being carried away by excessive piety in regard to their revered teacher, endeavour, no matter what, not to distance themselves from his whole construction'.

Further on, Lunacharskii attempts to defend Avenarius's idea of vital-differential from the perspective of its basis in logic:

> A. Bogdanov is up in arms against the term *nourishment*. He would like Avenarius to talk about the assimilation and discharge of energy. The critic asserts that if Avenarius had not obscured the problem with the term 'nourishment', then it would have been clear that the assimilation of energy in any quantity at all would never be superfluous and the discharge of energy would always lower vital-conservation.
>
> But in the case at hand A. Bogdanov is considering the matter completely abstractly. He has torn himself away from the facts, and so he begins to contradict himself.
>
> What are the conditions for the greatest possible assimilation of energy? Could this assimilation somehow occur all by itself?
>
> No! Nourishment, though not the only source, is by far the most important source of the material from which the assimilation of energy is drawn. Is it possible, however, to acknowledge that assimilation of energy depends directly on the quantity of nourishment? No! Just the opposite, under conditions of rest and the absence of work of a given organ, assimilation does not occur. Even Bogdanov acknowledges this. Thus, work is the necessary precondition for further assimilation, i.e. there are cases when work is a necessity, when the absence of work would unquestionably mean the *lowering* of vital-conservation. In these cases a vital-differential must be present that is reflected in consciousness as a need to move, to work – as *Arbeitsbedürfniss* [the need to work], *Mehrarbeitsbedürfniss*

> [the need to work more]. And in experience we encounter a corresponding feeling at each step. A. Bogdanov's theory leaves out a huge number of facts that are relevant here (play, creativity, schooling[4] – all the splendour of life as the result of a *surplus of powers*) as something that is absolutely inexplicable.
>
> But it is obvious that when there is insufficient nourishment the need for expenditure could never be felt ... etc.
>
> Op. cit., pp. 62–3

I will begin with by restating my ideas. I have never asserted that 'the assimilation of energy in any quantity at all would never be superfluous and the discharge of energy would always lower vital-conservation' as Lunacharskii – due to a misunderstanding – has ascribed to me.

I strictly distinguish between the *immediate* increase or decrease of vital-conservation (and the vital-differential that accompanies it) from its *indirect* results that can sometimes even be directly contradictory. I painstakingly explained that assimilation, if it is accomplished with insufficient harmony, can change the structure of the system so that the system becomes less stable and transforms into powerful fluctuations on the opposite side – on the side of the expenditure of energy. I pointed out examples of such a kind (depression as a result of long, free and easy living, etc.), and I compared such phenomena with crises of overproduction in economic life. The growth of productive forces of capitalist society is, of course, an immediate vital 'plus' for it; however, in certain conditions that same exact growth leads to still greater expenditure – to a certain economic degradation.

Avenarius, with Lunacharskii backing him up, by no means wants to distinguish *immediate* changes of vital-conservation from the *results that follow* those changes. And this confusion is exactly what Lunacharskii unjustly ascribes to me.

In addition, Avenarius and Lunacharskii persistently confuse the *source* or *conditions* of assimilation – nourishment – with the assimilation itself, and this is something I do not want to do.

Lunacharskii's arguments arise from these two confusions. He says: 'There are cases when work is a necessity, when its absence would mean the *lowering* of vital-conservation'. Fine! But what of it? There are cases when work – the expenditure of energy – is necessary for the appropriate assimilation or

---

4 Bogdanov's exact expression is 'results of *Scholī*', written in the Greek alphabet [trans.].

for the prevention of considerably greater expenditures of energy on internal rearrangement in the system itself. There are cases when it is necessary to spend excess capital in order to obtain considerably greater profits. Does it follow from this that the *expenditure* of capital immediately increases its size or that inordinate profits are a pathological vital-differential for capital – that it lowers the social vital-conservation of capital? The analogy is obviously complete.

Lunacharskii thinks that games, creative work, and similar useful expenditures of energy in the presence of 'abundance of strength' do not fit the theory. But what could be simpler? The 'abundance of strength' had built up from positive vital-differentials – from the preponderance of acquisitions over expenditures. The accumulation of that abundance was not accomplished in an ideally-harmonious way and led to a less stable equilibrium of the system; any further stimuli would now cause an increased expenditure of energy. But this expenditure could be accomplished along different paths – on the one hand, with the help of chemical and physical reactions that do not transfer across the boundaries of System C, and, on the other hand, with the help of innervational reactions leading to the exercise of various subordinate organs. In the first case – when System C 'boils in its own juice', so to speak – the expenditure of energy does not produce any 'plus' for life. It is only expenditure, a negative vital-differential. System C 'suffers' from an abundance of strength that is not used for external reactions but all the same is consumed within the system and in its immediate physiological environment. In the second case – when the 'abundance of strength' is expended in the external world – it leads to continuous changes in the relationships of the organism to its environment and, consequently, to more and more 'effects'. These effects can either themselves be a direct source of assimilation for System C (to the extent that the energy of stimuli is retained and built up in cells – a quite particular sort of 'nourishment'), or the effects can indirectly cause an increase of assimilation in System C as its 'physiological stimulus' (changing the chemical status of nerve cells, on the one hand, and changing the physical conditions of the circulation of blood in the brain, on the other hand). In both cases, a positive vital-differential can be established *for the centres of consciousness* – a preponderance of acquisition ('games and creative work are pleasant') – *even though the organism as a whole* expends more than it acquires (a preponderance of work of the lower motor centres, wear-and-tear of the muscles and other tissues). However, after a certain amount of time, the expenditure of other organs and tissues (as they grow and as their physiological state changes) begins also to be reflected on the centres of consciousness. And now, instead of effects that harmoniously stimulate assimilation, other disharmonious impressions are obtained that lead to an increase in the expenditure of energy of the centres of consciousness.[5] Then the preponderance of assimilation comes to an end, System C is 'fatigued', and 'games and creative work cease to be pleasant'.

Lunacharskii jumps to a rash conclusion when he declares that 'under conditions of insufficient nourishment, the need for expenditure can never be felt'. Insufficient nutrition, in decreasing the vital stability of the system, leads at each step to the intensified expenditure of energy, just as in any social system a deficiency of means usually leads to expenditures that would be needless under more normal conditions.[6] And the 'sensing of a need' for expenditure, consistent with contemporary psychophysiological theories, means precisely that this expenditure has already begun but still has not gone beyond the confines of the system – has not yet been manifested in the external world. 'It is obvious' that 'under conditions of insufficient nourishment, the need of expenditure' can – and frequently must – 'be felt'.

Allow me to follow my critic further:

> A. Bogdanov has rained down many blows on the theory of the Affectional, attempting to prove that pleasure accompanies the assimilation of energy and displeasure accompanies the disassimilation of energy. However, he thereby absolutely loses sight of the fact that, for example, a vigorous young man gets pleasure from running, jumping, and wrestling and from solving problems and riddles, etc. – things that would be total agony for a decrepit old man. This example obviously proves that the same process (whether it is the assimilation or expenditure of energy) can accompany various Affectionals – a fact that is explained with complete clarity by Avenarius and absolutely inexplicable from the point of view of A. Bogdanov.
>
> p. 63

I have already essentially answered this criticism. I cannot help, however, but turn the attention of the critic to how quickly and easily he – to speak in the language of Avenarius – asserts 'identicals'. It is the very same process! After all,

---

5  And apart from this, intensified assimilation in the highest centres is never accomplished completely harmoniously. The physiological state of the nerves becomes less stable, and beyond a certain boundary their energy begins to dissipate. And, finally, assimilation that is also completely harmonious can, beyond a certain boundary, cross over into the dissipation of energy if a given composition of cells and surrounding tissues permits a difference in the charge of energy between them that is no greater than a specific magnitude.

6  It is well known to physiologists that an insufficiency of nutrition is, in itself, a stimulation.

the fact of the matter is that in System C *completely different* processes occur in a vigorous person and a decrepit person when they are 'running about' that are far from completely identical. They have only one part in common – the innervation of a certain series of volitional muscles – and it does not have the same meaning for both. Is it possible that just using the same word, 'running about', is sufficient to prove that the processes are identical? It is a fine thing to have respect for one's teacher, but one need not get carried away.

I have pointed out, by the way, that the biological role of the Affectional, from the point of view that I am defending, is completely clear and understandable. In directly expressing the decrease or increase of the energy of System C, the Affectional is present in the first case as a vital stimulus for the struggle against unfavourable conditions, and it is present in the second case as a striving to maintain favourable conditions. On the contrary, from the point of view of Avenarius, the role of the Affectional is very questionable and even mysterious; he is not remarking on the growth or decrease of the energy of the system but only on the deviation from uniformity in that growth or decrease. System C can be uniformly exhausted or can uniformly grow and become stronger without any indication on the part of the Affectional. The Affectional must become negative (pain) when the system crosses over from slower to faster growth and strengthening, and it must become positive (pleasure) when the situation is the other way around. In all such cases, Avenarius's conception of the Affectional turns out to be biologically untenable, and it is quite inadequate for a modern theory of development.

To this, Lunacharskii answers:

> However, this is how it is in reality: a person becomes *used to* illness, degradation, and misery and sometimes almost does not notice the chronic physiological or social ailment that takes him to his death. The Affectional really provides far from a precise indication of the comparatively slow processes and is altogether not a very reliable guide. Thus, A. Bogdanov, himself, asserts on the following page that the way a patient with manic exaltation feels is pleasant, and he adduces other similar examples.
> p. 64

Lunacharskii does not see that 'getting used to illness, misery, and suffering' does not at all proceed in the same sense as would follow from Avenarius's conceptions. The person who 'gets used' to misery and 'does not feel it' any longer, simply has passed from a higher level of life with more significant expenditures of energy to a lower level where an insufficiency of nutrition is balanced by a lesser expenditure. The person who is 'habituated' to misery can live for many, many years in a way that would be inconceivable if the expenditures of energy still outweighed the assimilation of energy to any significant extent.

Those cases where a person 'does not feel' an illness – even a deathly illness – say nothing in favour of Avenarius. *System C* is far from being the same as the entire organism, and destructive processes in other organs and tissues often do not produce influences that are immediately destructive and that lower its energy. This can occur because of the absence of apperceptive neural apparatuses in these organs and tissues or because of a previous paralysis or destruction of these apparatuses or because of comparatively great resistance in the conductive pathways or, finally, simply because (simultaneously with the decrease in the energy of System C that reflects the processes of illness) an elevation of energy occurs that is no less than the decrease. With tuberculosis, for example, even the most specific poisoning of the system with its toxin apparently often stimulates the life of System C such that its energy in the course of the illness is elevated and not lowered for quite a long time.

These cases thus say nothing in favour of Avenarius. But other cases from the same realm speak directly *against* him.

You burn your hand. By reflex (stimulation, the constriction of blood vessels), a large *negative* vital-differential is established in System C; expenditures outweigh acquisition by, let us say, 1000 units of energy. Gradually your organism copes with the wound, and the negative vital-differential of System C decreases: 900 units, then 800 units, etc. According to Avenarius, suffering must be replaced by a pleasant feeling. But in reality, alas, it does not. Pain remains pain, it only weakens in conformity with the lowering of the vital-differential. From the point of view of my psychoenergetics, this is exactly how it must be ...[7]

But in the end the 'unreliability' of the Affectional, of which Lunacharskii speaks, cannot be conceded. Lunacharskii, evidently, concedes that the Affec-

---

7 It is true that in these circumstances there are such utterances as 'it is pleasant that the pain is diminishing'. But this secondary, reflected pleasure does not change the basic fact of pain. It proceeds in the following way. A large negative vital-differential of 1,000 units embraces a large number of particular systems of the brain, L, M, N, etc. Adapting to the situation, these systems *elevate* assimilation, although far from enough to make up for the vital-differential. When the vital-differential lessens, this elevated assimilation does not disappear immediately, and it temporarily attains a preponderance over disassimilation in certain of the systems. It is to these systems that the feeling of pleasure relates. Of course, these are precisely those systems that are affected most indirectly – usually the higher systems. The gladness in the event of the lessening of pain always has a certain *abstract* nature.

tional can *mistakenly* reflect the immediate state of System C, as his reference to my example of manic exaltation shows. This is a downright rejection of scientific cognition.

There is no third thing between the state of System C and a 'fact' of consciousness that could create a lack of correspondence between them. The Affectional must *absolutely truly* reflect the state of the system with which it is connected, but only its *immediate* state, of course. It cannot appraise the possible results of that state, since it is not a conscious spirit but an immediate function of an immediate physiological fact. The joy of a manic patient *truly* reflects the immediate elevation of the energy of his brain, and there it is not any kind of mistake on the part of the Affectional. Obviously, it is Lunacharskii, and not the Affectional, who is making a mistake.

To acknowledge that the Affectional is sometimes confused means to acknowledge that the connection of System C with the facts of consciousness is not uniformly consistent – that it is random. This is a disguised personification of consciousness and the assumption of a certain 'freedom of will' for the Affectional. This is where Lunacharskii has ended up in attempting to defend a hopeless cause.

But in essence all these premises are already contained in Avenarius's own theory of the Affectional. The theory's model goes like this: the deity of the Affectional sits on the centre line of the vital equilibrium and observes whether the passage of the vital process approaches that line or departs from it. In the first case, it is satisfied. In the second case it is dissatisfied, and it does not care about which direction the approach or the departure is headed – to the right or to the left, up or down. It evaluates two opposite cases identically. It has no concept of a strictly unequivocal connection. Lunacharskii stubbornly wants to believe in this unjustified divinity, and it is really not necessary.

I have shown that the appearance of a vital-differential itself – i.e. the departure from an ideal equilibrium – is sometimes undoubtedly accompanied by pleasure, and this happens precisely when the vital-differential is positive. I have provided the following example:

> One is in a calm, neutral mood, and suddenly the mail brings one news that one did not at all expect but that turns out to be excellent. Or, a chance combination of minor circumstances prompts one to discover something that one was not in the least looking for but that turns out to be valuable. In these cases, what vital-differentials are being removed? It is absolutely the opposite; vital-differentials spring up, but they are positive.
> p. 78

What does Lunacharskii answer to this?

> What does it mean that news *'seems excellent to someone'*? Obviously, it means that it is useful to him, i.e. it releases a certain underlying vital-differential. A person calls 'good' what, in one way or another, promotes the equilibrium of his brain. If a *revelation* or *news* has no relation to my *needs*, then it would be unhelpful and indifferent to me. But, of course, although a revelation satisfies my needs, it presents me at the same time with many separate vital-differentials – tasks with regard to its application. And from this it is obvious that a person who *enjoys labour* only enjoys it because that labour is a 'physiological stimulus' to further nourishment of certain parts of his brain. Someone who does not have an underlying vital-differential of overflow, even when obtaining an inheritance or acceptance of marriage by his beloved, thinks first and foremost of anxieties and troubles.
>
> *Izlozhenie*, p. 64

The dogmatic nature of this objection is obvious. 'People call "good" what, one way or another, promotes the equilibrium of their brain' – this would only occur in the event that the brain is constructed according to Avenarius. A rigorously evolutionary point of view can accept only the following proposition: people call 'good' whatever elevates the energy of their brain. A static ideal is present in one of these two points of view, and Lunacharskii can easily imagine which. But another important thing also becomes clear here.

Reading Avenarius, I often could not decide whether he meant that a 'vital-differential' is a *process* or an *object*. Sometimes it seems to me that it is a strictly dialectical correlation – the difference at any given moment between the inflowing and the outflowing energy. And sometimes it seems to me that it is a static fact – if an excess of nourishment built up and lies without movement, then there is a vital-differential, or, if a surplus expenditure is made and is not compensated for, then there is a vital-differential. Avenarius provides data for both of these interpretations. Lunacharskii, obviously, accepts the second: 'the vital-differential of overflow' and so on.

But such an understanding is scientifically useless. Surplus and deficit are accounting terms, and that is where they belong. Biology needs magnitudes that are continually flowing; it needs, speaking algebraically, *derivative magnitudes that express life as a process*.[8] The conceptions of built-up surplus and

---

[8] From the point of view of my theory, the Affectional with its value (+ or –) is directly deriv-

deficit can provisionally serve as very imprecise, auxiliary conceptions, but they must not be made into foundational concepts.

Lunacharskii supposes that the fact of 'sweet melancholy' contradicts my point of view: I myself pointed out that the emotion of sadness is connected, in its physiological conditions, with the preponderance of expenditure over acquisition of energy of the brain. But Lunacharskii thinks this only because he has taken the fact of 'sweet melancholy' without analysing it.

'Sweet melancholy' is composed of two elements: pleasant images and sad ideas. People with a pleasant pain recall near and dear beings from whom they have been separated by life or by death. The very image of this being is intensely pleasant and excites a series of other emotions – of a sensual nature, for example – and the pain from separation becomes dull and weakened and the emotion of sadness becomes less intense. If the first side of the psychical state preponderates over the second, then we see 'sweet melancholy', and if it does not, then the psyche really does suffer. But sadness in the first case remains sadness, i.e. the emotion of suffering; it *decreases* the magnitude of the pleasant emotion. If you remove this sadness, with the belief in an imminent meeting, for example, then the psychical state immediately becomes considerably more 'sweet'. All this is in complete agreement with the psychoenergetical point of view.

There remains one, final concrete argument that Lunacharskii directs against my theory:

> In order to show, once and for all, how easily it can happen that bringing in certain casuistic objections actually proves your opponent's propositions, I point out yet one more fact to A. Bogdanov. It is impossible for ascetics to gratify their need for an elevated life – a need that appears as the result of an overflow of energy (a longstanding absence of its expenditure) Ascetics are therefore recommended both to think sad thoughts (to think about death and the sorrows of life and to mourn the suffering of Christ on the cross) and also to devote themselves to pious exercises (vigils, fasting, genuflections, or even self-flagellation). What is this if not the desire to simultaneously increase the *expenditure* of energy and to artificially arouse the emotion of sadness – i.e. the contraction of blood vessels that

---

ative from the magnitude of the energy of System C over time. (If the magnitude of energy is q and time is t, then $dq/dt$ is the precise expression of the Affectional with its variable value.)

A. Bogdanov spoke of. However, both attain gratification and bring ascetics to the inner harmony they desire. Thus, 'the physiologically absurd' turns out to be reality.

op. cit., p. 66

Well, really! After years of sleepless nights, hunger, self-flagellation, and all sorts of atrocities that ascetics carry out on themselves, they obtain an 'overflow' of energy that they also try to use up by further atrocities that are pleasant to them in the highest degree ... It is a fine ascetic who pursues an 'overflow' in order later to enjoy delight according to the coaching of Avenarius. Permit me to stand up for the ascetic.

'Contraction of the blood vessels' does not provide ascetics any kind of pleasure, and all the self-torments are also by no means 'pleasant' to them in themselves but only to the extent that they are associated with the thought of higher delights – the idea of which is by no means connected with the narrowing of blood vessels in the corresponding parts of the brain. The 'heroic deeds' of the ascetic serve as the means to attain these higher delights that appear to the ascetic in the form of *rapture*. Rapture is an emotion that is closely related to joy on the one hand and sexual gratification on the other; it is an emotion that is directly contrary to pain and the 'contraction of blood vessels'. It is attained in the following way. Through torments and sad reflections, the ascetic maintains for a long time the nourishing arteries of the brain in a convulsively-narrowed state, and nerve cells are in such relative depletion that, as soon as sufficient nourishment is present, a very rapid and powerful assimilation becomes possible. Then, at a certain moment (perhaps as the result of the exhaustion of the vasomotor centres due to the long constrained state in which they exist while maintaining the narrowing of peripheral blood vessels, or perhaps by a different reflexive path), an extreme weakening results – an almost paralysed state of the small arteries and capillaries of the brain. A new increase of expenditure does not occur, except for certain convulsive contractions of voluntary muscles. The face becomes pale, similar to what is observed in many anaemic and exhausted people when they are extremely happy, and this can easily be explained in the following way. An extreme flood of blood to the brain allows the draining of blood vessels of the on the periphery of the head – the muscles and skin – because both the brain and this periphery obtain nourishment from the main jugular arteries. Thus, a huge positive vital-differential for System C arises that is expressed in the holy joy of the ascetic with the depth and poignancy that surpasses even sexual gratification.

By the way, Avenarius explains the pleasure of the sexual act by the fact that it restores the equilibrium of the neural-sexual centres that is destroyed in the period of abstinence. It is strange that Avenarius does not see that even if the equilibrium of these centres is restored by means of the expenditure of energy in the sexual act, the equilibrium for all of System C in its entirety is nevertheless profoundly destroyed. The terrific storm that is borne by the whole vasomotor and motor system is hardly similar to 'the restoration of equilibrium'. And, once again, from my point of view it is all simple: the strong overflooding of the brain with blood and the quickening of the pulse signifies a great positive vital-differential in which innervational expenditures of energy disappear in the convulsive movement of voluntary muscles.

∴

I will now summarise. The conception of the vital-differential and the Affectional that R. Avenarius accepts, following the majority of old physiologists must be rejected on the following grounds:

1. It is illogical at its foundation. Its initial concepts of 'nourishment' and 'work' do not correlate to one another, and the concept of the vital-differential sometimes appears to be dynamic and sometimes appears to be static.
2. It assumes an *ambiguous* and not an unequivocal interconnection of psychical processes with physiological processes.
3. It contradicts many facts.

Instead of this theory, I have provided another one, whose forefather I consider to be Spinoza, and whose basic material has been given, in my opinion, by the views of Meynert and in part the James-Lange theory of emotions.

It is perfectly obvious that my purely energetical theory of the vital-differential and the Affectional is absolutely free of both formal deficiencies of Avenarius's theory. As far as how my theory relates to the facts, I suggest that everything that I have presented previously[9] and the analysis of Lunacharskii's objections to it that I have just provided show that my theory has not – so far, at least – run into real contradictions.

So far, I have illustrated the heuristic and working significance of this theory with the theory of psychical selection. But this, of course, is only its most immediate application.

Everything that the critique of my theory has provided so far supports, in my opinion, the validity of the idea that *for our times, my theory is an integrally necessary part of an empiriomonist worldview.*

---

9  Chapter 2, 'Life and the Psyche', in the present volume.

***Book Three***

∴

CHAPTER 7

# Preface to Book Three

With this book, I conclude my presentation of the foundations of the philosophical worldview that has come to me over the course of many years as the necessary systematisation of all the material of science and life that I have had access to.

Amid the unprecedented historical whirlwind that is profoundly shaking the old world, philosophical interests pale and recede to a distant plane for the great majority of observers and participants in the struggle. Even among a great many people in the ranks of the only *essentially philosophical* political current of our time – Marxism – a naively-practical mood is revealed that is expressed in the usual phrase: 'this is not the time for philosophy!'

Comrade Bel'tov has come out very strongly against such theoretical indifference, and he was profoundly right to do so. It is necessary to see clearly in order to act properly, the further off the goal of the journey is and the more impetuous the movement of events, the more a wide horizon is necessary. The significance of a philosophically-supported worldview grows in proportion to the intensity of the life that surrounds us and the importance of the events that are unfolding and in which we must participate. Those comrades who consider the correlation between philosophical theory and political practice to be immaterial are making a serious theoretical mistake and risk making many serious practical mistakes in the future.

All this is unquestionable, except that it is not necessary to conclude from this that all comrades are obligated to be of one mind philosophically. As far as the development of the party is concerned, philosophical nuances within a common social worldview are just as necessary as tactical nuances within a general programme and as a critical stance toward that same programme. However, this is so elementary that it needs no proof – even if a reminder is sometimes necessary.

No matter how mistaken the formula 'this is not the time for philosophy' is, still, if it is considered not as a norm but as a simple statement of fact – and a very sad fact – then it turns out to be almost true. It is difficult for whomever lives in a whirlwind of events to find the place, time, or mood for calm and objective philosophical analysis. I, personally, for the last one-and a half to two years found that even with the greatest efforts I was not able to undertake systematically any of the work that is subjectively-necessary for me until imprisonment by His Majesty gave me the leisure time for it.[1] But in prison many sources became inaccessible to me, and it is very probable that as a result there are major flaws in the present work that in other circumstances could have been avoided.

During those same one-and-a-half years, the previously published parts of this work (which includes not only the first two volumes of *Empiriomonism* but also the books *Iz psikhologii obshchestva* [*On the Psychology of Society*][2] and *Novyi mir* [*New World*][3]) encountered an energetic polemic on behalf of certain comrades, although it is true that the polemic was not so much in the form of substantive critique as in the form of reiterated disapproval. To the extent that I have been able to clarify for myself the motives and the arguments (that are more implied than definitely expressed) of this polemic, I am now providing an answer to them. But in view of the fragmentary nature of this polemic, it would be awkward to limit myself to tracing them piece by piece, since my answer would turn into a tiresome series of polemical fragments. In order to avoid this, I have decided to systematise my answer in the form of a concise presentation of the path along which I arrived at my philosophical views.

I choose this form, of course, not because I view the history of my personal philosophical development to be of any particular interest, but simply because in such a form it will be all the easier to harmoniously and precisely depict the line of my departure from my esteemed opponents and to sort out their misunderstandings in an orderly fashion. It is possible, by the way, that certain features will be found in this presentation that are typical in general of the development of the generation of Marxists to which I belong.

1      Three Materialisms

At the time when life, in the form of comrade-workers, prompted me to become familiar with Marx's historical materialism, I was occupied principally with the natural sciences and was an enthusiastic supporter of the worldview that could be designated as the 'materialism of natural scientists'. This somewhat primitive philosophy was once, for good reason, the ideological banner of strict

---

1   Bogdanov had been a member of the Executive Committee of the St. Petersburg Soviet of Workers' Deputies during the Revolution of 1905. He was arrested when the Soviet was suppressed in December 1905, and he spent the next six months in Kresty Prison, St. Petersburg [trans].
2   Bogdanov 1906c.
3   Bogdanov 1905c.

democrats – the 'nihilists'. There was a great deal of distinctive radicalism in it and a great deal that was kindred to all 'extreme' ideologies.

Attempting to arrive at a strict *monism* in cognition, this worldview constructs its picture of the world entirely out of one material – out of 'matter' as the object of physical sciences. The whole content of the world and the essence of all experience – both physical and psychical – is formed by matter conceived in the form of atoms in their various combinations and continuous movement. The invariable laws of the movement of matter in space and time is the ultimate instantiation of all explanations that are possible. A strict tendency of *scientific objectivism* is thereby attached to monism and from this proceeds the extreme hostility of this philosophy to all the fetishes of religious and metaphysical-idealistic worldviews. It is difficult to truly give up this philosophy, and, even when you manage to do so, you involuntarily continue to preserve a certain sympathy for it and involuntarily single it out among all others.

But the social materialism of Marx made demands on my worldview that the old materialism could not satisfy. And, meanwhile, these were demands whose validity could not be denied and which, in addition, completely correspond to the objective and monist tendency of the old materialism itself, except that those demands took that tendency even further. It was necessary to *cognise one's own cognition*, to explain one's own worldview. And, according to the idea of Marxism, it was possible and obligatory to do this on the ground of social-genetic investigation. It was obvious that the fundamental concepts of the old materialism – both 'matter' and 'invariable laws' – were worked out in the course of the *social* development of humanity, and it was necessary to find the 'material basis' for those concepts as 'ideological forms'. But since the 'material basis' changes as society develops, it becomes clear that all given ideological forms can only have historically-transient and not objectively-suprahistorical meaning; they can be 'true for their times' (*objectively* true, but only within a certain era) and in no way 'true for eternity' ('objective' in the absolute meaning of the word). The old materialism is not compatible with such a proposition. The bases of the old materialism – 'invariable laws' of the movement of matter, 'matter' itself as a fundamental concept, and 'space' and 'time' as the theatre for the action of these invariable laws and of the movement of matter – is taken to be absolute and without them the entire worldview loses its meaning. The old materialism aspires to be absolutely *objective cognition of the essence of things*, and it is incompatible with the historical conditionality of any ideology.

I said that for me Marxism implies the rejection of the absolute objectivity of any truth whatsoever, the rejection of any eternal truths. But, as is well known, far from all Marxists (and most likely the minority) hold this 'extreme' opinion. In this regard it is curious to note the sharp difference – extending almost to contradiction – between the views of F. Engels and the views of his authoritative pupil, N. Bel'tov. In the *Anti-Dühring*, Engels expresses himself *almost* in the same sense in which I have just now characterised the relativity of truth. Engels devotes several pages to an analysis, full of irony, of Dühring's *endgültige, ewige Wahrheiten* (eternal, final, absolute truths)[4] with conclusions that are very unfavourable for these truths.[5] Engels divides the entire realm of knowledge into three parts and summarises his position regarding each of them separately. I will present a summary according to his text.

In the realm of 'exact' sciences – mathematics, astronomy, mechanics, physics, chemistry – 'absolute truth becomes remarkably rare with the passage of time' (p. 82). 'With geology, it is even worse' (p. 82).

In the realm of the sciences of living organisms – 'whoever wants to establish truly unchanging truths, must be satisfied with such banal truths (*Plattheiten*) as, for example, all people must die, all female mammals have milk-producing glands, and so on. One does not even have the right to say that the higher animals carry out digestion with their stomach and intestines, since the activity of the nervous system, which is centralised in the head, is necessary for digestion' (p. 83).

In the third, socio-historical group of sciences that study the development of material culture, law, morality, religion, art, etc., the situation is even less comforting.

> Here cognition is relative in its essence, since it is limited to the explanation of the interconnectedness and consecutiveness of specific social and political forms that exist only at a given time and for given peoples. The hunter of eternal, unchanging truth will find very little to bag here. It includes the most trivial banalities, the most vapid platitudes – for example, that people generally speaking cannot live without work, that so far people are for the most part divided into rulers and ruled, that Napoleon died on 5 May 1821, etc.
>
> p. 84

Comrade Bel'tov looks at the matter absolutely differently. It is true that he uses high-flown expressions such as '*ewige Wahrheiten letzter Instanz*' [eternal truths of the last instance], but he completely accepts the existence of 'objective

---

4　I have translated Bogdanov's translation. The literal English translation of Engels's phrase is 'final, enduring truths' [trans.].

5　Bogdanov is referring to Chapter IX, 'Morality and Law. Eternal Truths' [trans.].

truths' that, once having been established, now *cannot be changed* by the further development of knowledge, other than merely being 'supplemented and affirmed'. And Bel'tov considers such truths to exist even in the 'socio-historical' group of sciences, adducing as an example Marx's theory of the circulation of money. Clearly, the question is not at all about 'the most trivial banalities and platitudes', but about the most real scientific theories that, from the perspective of the view expounded by Engels, can in no way be accepted as unchanging for future times. Who exactly is correct,[6] Engels or Bel'tov?

*Relatively*, it goes without saying that Engels is correct, and it requires a very great tendency toward dogmatism to assert that in such a complex, involved issue like the theory of the circulation of money in contemporary society a supra-historical, objective truth has been attained that will not undergo essential changes in the future. Of course, I completely accept Marx's theory of the circulation of money as 'objective' truth for *our* times, i.e. I accept the 'social validity' of this theory for *contemporary* humanity. When we rely on it in practice and in cognition, we do not arrive at contradictions and absurdities, but, on the contrary, we reach the goals whose realisation depends on the correct understanding of a given issue. But we do not know if this will be absolutely the same for subsequent generations with broader experience. *But who gets to decide?* The sole authority of comrade Bel'tov is not sufficient, and the *persuasiveness* and even the *obviousness* of a theory still do not prove anything.

In fact, what could have been more persuasive for people of earlier times than the idea that the sun travels across the blue heavenly vault from the east to the west? As far as complete 'obviousness' is concerned, one could not wish for anything better than this. No one in those times would arrive at any contradictions or absurdities in making this 'truth' the starting point for their practice (and further knowledge). Clearly, this was the 'objective truth' of those times,

---

6   By the way, if memory serves, it is possible to encounter individual expressions in other works by Engels that are close in meaning to Bel'tov's point of view. (I cannot immediately point them out exactly, since I do not have these books to hand.) But if Engels is occasionally inconsistent in this question, the essence of the matter does not change. Moreover, the *Anti-Dühring* is one of his *basic works* of philosophy.

   I will add still one more decisive pronouncement of Engels's that directly concurs, in essence, with the point of view that I am defending: 'But to the extent that the history of humanity so far still young, and to the extent that it would be ludicrous to ascribe any kind of absolute meaning to our modern views, the fact is already evident that all history up to the present time can be characterised as the history of the period from the practical discovery of how to convert mechanical movement into heat (making fire through friction – A.B.) to the discovery of how to turn heat into mechanical movement (steam-engines – A.B.)'. This was also written in the *Anti-Dühring*, pp. 113–14.

and it was considerably more unquestionable and indisputable than the theory of money of our times. But what became of that inviolable and obvious objective truth? The idea of the movement of the sun has been completely overturned by science, and the blue vault of the sky has been determined to be an optical illusion. Who can guarantee that the same thing will not happen to comrade Bel'tov's *less* convincing and *less* obvious truths?

There are no criteria in our 'historical' world for *suprahistorical* objective truth, and therefore not only is comrade Bel'tov wrong, but Engels is also wrong to be indecisive in that through all his irony he does accept some – albeit measly – 'eternal truths'. First, can *'Plattheiten'* really be called *'Wahrheiten'*? Are 'platitudes' really truths? Truth is the living organising form of experience; it *leads* us somewhere in our activities and provides a point of support in life's struggle. Can 'banalities', inasmuch as they are trivial, approach such a characterisation? The equation, '$2 \times 2 = 4$', is not a truth but a tautology – two designations of one and the same thing. And to the extent that familiarity with different designations of this combination can provide us with something new, the same old relativity appears. For example, according to the 'ternary' system of calculation $2 \times 2$ is not 4 – no such symbol exists in that system – instead $2 \times 2 = 11$. And, meanwhile, what is impossible about the 'ternary' system? After all, the duodecimal system exists alongside the decimal system, and among certain primitive tribes it seems that there is a quinary system, etc. $A = A$ is an eternal truth of logic, but what is that worth? What does it give us? How can it direct our actions? It either leads us nowhere or it even leads us to an error, sometimes forcing us to confuse the identity of symbols with the identity of the phenomena that they signify.

'All people must die ...'. Yes, we do not see exceptions. But far from all protists die. Does a cell die that joins with another in the act of conjugation or that splits in two in mitosis? And yet that cell does not exist anymore. Who can guarantee that future generations will not find another means of the 'resolution' of life other than what we now observe in the crude crisis of death? I am not even speaking about the fact that psychiatry often has occasion to observe two deaths of the same person that changes and modifies the *'Plattheit'*.[7] And what about 'dual personality'? Did the personality of Felida that ultimately disappeared 'die', giving up its place to another of her personalities?

'All female mammals have milk-producing glands'. As is well known, milk-producing glands are only a particular development of fatty glandules of the

---

7 I have in mind, for example, those cases of progressive paralysis, when a doctor cannot succeed in detecting anything remaining from the former personality of the patient and in general from a 'human being', but nevertheless the 'patient' is still 'alive'.

skin. Therefore there is nothing inconceivable about an individual – or even a generic – deviation in which 'milk-producing' glands do not appear but only common fatty glands, except that the observation of such a case *so far has not happened*.

'Napoleon died on 5 May 1821'. What kind of 'truth' is this? And what is 'eternal' about it? The statement of a single correlation that is probably of no real significance for our generation cannot serve as the starting point for any kind of activity; it leads nowhere. To call such things 'eternal truths' means to mock the idea of 'eternal truth' – something that Engels, properly speaking, does but, unfortunately, does not follow to its conclusion.

The criterion of 'objective truth' in Bel'tov's meaning does not exist. Truth is an ideological form – an organising form for human experience. And if we know this with certainty, and if we know that the material bases of ideology changes and the content of experience broadens, can we have any kind of right to assert that just this ideological form will never be transformed by the development of its objective bases and that just this form of experience will not be burst asunder by its growing content? *Consistent Marxism does not permit such a dogmatic and static outlook.* It is only inconsistency here that permits eclectic exceptions, as with Engels (a few 'eternal truths', and they become ever fewer although very unfortunate, etc.) or as with Bel'tov ('No "fate" can move us any more from the discovery of the correct point of view once it has finally been discovered'). (*On the Development of a Monist View of History*, p. 176).

Thus, it is necessary to reject the old 'materialism of the natural scientists' and seek something better in the realm of philosophy, and this was not easy. It became somehow accepted to speak contemptuously of this materialism, and perhaps in Germany it really was as 'vulgar and debased' as Engels suggests, but in Russia materialism was far different. The far from debased models of Turgenev's Bazarov or Chernyshevskii's heroes testify to this, as do the living figures of the calibre of, I would suggest, Professor Kliment Timiriazev.[8] This materialism, like Marxism, was all the more powerful because it was not satisfied with words and empty models but required substantive monist explanations. In this respect it often turned out to be even higher than, for example, empiriocriticism. I cannot help but recall, regarding this topic, a conversation with Timiriazev – a chance conversation that he probably has forgotten. We were talking about the inheritance of acquired characteristics. Timiriazev said that inheritance of such a kind was proven in certain cases, but that it *still had not been explained*. He added that 'those "barbules"

---

8  Kliment Timiriazev (1843–1920) was a botanist and one of Russia's leading proponents of Darwinism. [trans.].

and "sprockets" that mesh together to produce this inheritance and how, precisely, they mesh together still remain to be found'. This is what a natural-scientist and materialist said. And, Avenarius, for example, would be completely satisfied by the bare statement of such heredity, since after all in his *Kritik der reinen Erfahrung* he constantly reduces the development of adaptations to some kind of '*Übung*', to 'exercise', and considers the exact path along which this Lamarckian '*Übung*' acts to be a completely superfluous question. How much greater is the cognitive exactingness and rigorousness in the picturesque expression of the materialist about 'barbules' and 'sprockets'!

This very exactingness prevented me from accepting the other refined and diluted philosophical materialism that comrade Bel'tov propounds in the name of Marx with the help of quotations from Holbach.

In the words of comrade Bel'tov, the idea of the primacy of 'nature' in relation to 'spirit' is the basis and essence of materialism. This definition is very broad, and in this case it has its disadvantages. What is designated 'nature', and what is designated 'spirit'? If one understands the inorganic world and lower stages of the development of life as 'nature' and the higher stages of life – human consciousness, for example – as 'spirit', then for anyone who has been freed from the swaddling clothes of crude mythology – for anyone familiar with the contemporary situation of natural sciences – 'materialism' is unavoidable. But then a great many people who have not attained this honour must be counted among the 'materialists'. Comrade Bel'tov has already managed to bring the pantheist Spinoza into this firm, and it seems that he is also inclined to recruit Ostwald's energetics into it, as well – and with complete justice, at that. Comrade Bel'tov has a stubborn misunderstanding of Mach and the empiriocriticists; he counts them as idealists, whereas from the perspective of his definition they are rigorous materialists. All of them say that 'spirit' – i.e. the highest manifestations of human consciousness – is the result of long evolution from lower forms that correspond to comrade Bel'tov's conception of 'nature'. It is true that these lower forms are also complexes of 'elements' exactly the same as elements of the 'psychical series', but since they are to an identical degree also elements of 'physical complexes' then there is nothing specifically 'spiritual' in them – they are elements and only elements.[9] Finally, there is the

---

9   Incidentally, regarding empiriocriticism, comrade Bel'tov himself in one place admits that in certain conditions it could be spared from the general anathema and be accepted as not contradicting materialism. The conditions are not formulated completely clearly and consist in that for empiriocriticist school *experience* would be only a 'subject of investigation and not a means of cognition' (Preface to the Russian translation of Engels's *Ludwig*

mysterious 'empiriomonists' of whom comrade Bel'tov often speaks ... I personally know only one in the literature – a certain A. Bogdanov – but, on the other hand, I know him very well and can guarantee that his views completely satisfy the sacramental formula of the primacy of 'nature' over 'spirit'. It is precisely he who views all that exists as a continual chain of development, the lowest links of which are lost in the 'chaos of elements' and the highest known links represent *people's experience*[10] – first 'psychical' experience and even higher 'physical experience' – and this experience and the cognition that arises from it correspond to what is usually called 'spirit'.

I would not even guarantee that panpsychists like Max Fervorn[11] would not get into the heavenly kingdom of materialism. The fact of the matter is that, in accepting the 'psychicalness' of everything that exists, panpsychists can, however, counterpose their lower forms – unorganised or weakly organised – as 'nature' against higher forms like 'spirit' proper. If they say to me that 'psychical' and 'spirit' are in general the same thing, then I would observe that this is a question of terminology; after all, they call the higher needs of a person 'spiritual' in contrast with the lower 'material' needs, even though both of them are 'psychical' to the extent that they are 'felt'.

In general, the very weakest aspect of the criterion that comrade Bel'tov considers to be sufficient for determining the 'materialist-ness' of philosophical views consists in its vagueness and fuzziness. The concepts of 'nature' and 'spirit' are so indefinite, and the antithesis between them can be taken in such different meanings, that it is completely impossible to found a worldview on the basis of them. Or else it is necessary first to give clear and precise definitions of both concepts, something that comrade Bel'tov does not do and that would be extremely difficult to carry out in reality.

But excuse me! I did not express myself with complete precision. Comrade Bel'tov *provides* a definition of 'spirit' and 'matter' (or 'nature') ... But let us see what kind of definition it is and whether it can even be designated by such a term.

---

*Feuerbach*, p. 6). The task of the empiriocriticists is to figure out whether to accept this condition or not.

10   The 'nature' that comrade Bel'tov is speaking of should not be confused with physical experience as the result of the long social processing of human experiences that are constantly changing in their content and forms, depending on the development of science. In the empiriomonistic picture of the world, this 'nature' corresponds to those lower 'immediate complexes' that must be 'substituted' in place of 'inorganic complexes' and lower 'organic' complexes of experience ('things in themselves', to employ the terms of Kant and comrade Bel'tov).

11   Max Fervorn (1863–1921) was a German botanist and philosopher [trans.].

> In contrast to 'spirit', one calls 'matter' that which, *when acting on our organs of feeling evokes one or another sensations in us*. What precisely acts on our senses? To this question, along with Kant, I answer: *things-in-themselves*. Therefore, *matter is nothing other than the totality of things-in-themselves, to the extent that these things are the source of our sensations*.
>
> Kritika nashikh kritikov, a collection of essays, p. 233

So, 'matter' (or 'nature' in its antithesis to 'spirit') is defined through 'things-in-themselves' and through their ability to 'evoke sensations by acting on our organs of feeling'. But what exactly are these 'things-in-themselves'? That which 'acting on our senses, evokes sensations in us'. This *is all*. You will not find any other definition from comrade Bel'tov, unless you consider what is assumed by the negative characterisations: *not* 'sensation', *not* 'phenomena', *not* 'experience'.

What is actually being said here? Pretty much nothing. If one sets aside the 'senses' that have fetched up absolutely inopportunely and about which I will make special mention, then one obtains 'matter', 'nature', 'things-in-themselves'. These are unknown things through which is evoked everything that is known, and we do not know any more about this unknown thing. Have we gone far enough? 'The sleep-inducing force' is what causes sleep. What we have here, obviously, is one of the 'eternal truths' in the most pitiful meaning of that word.

Comrade Bel'tov objects, as follows:

> Please! We know a great deal about 'things-in-themselves'. First, they exist, and, moreover, they exist outside our experience. Second, they are subordinate to the law of causality – they can 'have an effect' ... Third, *the forms and relationships of phenomena correspond to the forms and relationships between things-in-themselves* just like 'hieroglyphs' correspond to the things they signify.
>
> op. cit., p. 234

We can frankly set aside the first two points – they embody all the lack of content of the basic definition: let the 'sleep-inducing force' exist and act upon us according to the laws of nature, and it will cause sleep. Since this 'force' lies outside experience, what does it add to the fact that we happen to fall asleep? The third point is important, however, and that is why I was particularly careful to formulate it in the authentic expressions of comrade Bel'tov. I will dwell on it.

# PREFACE TO BOOK THREE

First and foremost, how substantive is this proposition? Let us say that we know that the nature and duration of sleep 'corresponds' to the form and degree of action on us by the 'sleep-inducing force', that it is impossible for us to compose any kind of concrete conceptions either of that form or of that degree because all of it is outside experience, and that we can only make inferences about them both, again on the basis of those facts that we already have – the 'empirical' nature and 'empirical' duration of sleep. Can we know any more? We can know exactly nothing more. We only add to the 'empirical' sleep an imaginary sleep that is inaccessible to us, with what is called a 'sleep-inducing force' as its cause. There is nothing more than this.

But from this 'nothing' we subsequently obtain a 'something' and something strange, at that. Here the 'form' and 'relationships' of things-in-themselves are spoken of. This means, one can conjecture, that things-in-themselves possess them both. Excellent! And do they have an 'appearance'? An absurd question, the reader says! How is it possible to have a form if it does not have an *appearance*? After all, these two expressions are the same. I think this, too. But we read the following in comrade Plekhanov's[12] notes to the Russian translation of Engels's *Ludwig Feuerbach*:

> But, after all, 'appearance' is precisely the result of action on us by things-in-themselves; *aside from this action, they have no appearance*. Therefore to contrast their 'appearance' as it exists in our consciousness to the 'appearance' that they would have in reality means not to realise what concept is connected with the word 'appearance' ... Thus, things-in-themselves have no appearance. Their 'appearance' exists only in the consciousness of those subjects on which they act ...
> 
>     p. 112 of the 1906 edition – the same year in which the previously cited collection *Kritika nashikh kritikov* was published

Wherever the word 'appearance' appears in this citation, replace it with the word 'form' (its synonym), and in every case the meaning will completely coincide. Comrade Plekhanov brilliantly disproves comrade Bel'tov.

But a minute later, comrade Plekhanov sharply avenges comrade Bel'tov:

> What is a snail *for me*? It is part of the external world that acts on me in a certain way, conditioned by my organisation. Therefore, if I grant that the

---

12   Because Plekhanov published some works under his own name and others under the pseudonym, N. Bel'tov, Bogdanov is able to ironically point out Plekhanov's contradictions by treating him as two different authors [trans.].

snail somehow or other 'sees' the external world, then I must acknowledge that the 'appearance' in which the external world presents itself to the snail is itself conditioned by the *properties* of this really existing world ...

op. cit., p. 113; the italics are mine

Properties! But 'properties' of objects are the same as the 'form' and in general the 'appearance' of objects, and these 'properties', obviously, 'are precisely the result of action on us by things-in-themselves, and, aside from this action, they have no "qualities"'! After all, the concept of 'property' has absolutely the same *empirical* origin as the concept of 'appearance' or 'form'. It is the same kind of concept; it is taken from experience in the same way as these concepts and is made an abstraction by the same process. Where did the properties of things-in-themselves come from? 'Their "properties" exist only in the consciousness of the subjects on which they act'!

So, truly, the snail cannot crawl from one page to the next before comrade Plekhanov renounces 'eternal truth'.

Thus a tangle of non-dialectical contradictions is engendered from a formally empty concept.

In the end, what kind of definition results for 'matter' and 'spirit' as antitheses? Only one: matter is what, acting on the sense organs, produces sensations (i.e. 'spirit'). As regards the 'sense organs', they obviously are taken here not as phenomena but as a corresponding 'thing-in-itself', otherwise, they are also the result of action of some kind of thing-in-itself on some other kind of thing-in-itself. This means that matter is what, acting on matter, engenders 'spirit', or matter is the cause and spirit the effect, or matter is something that is primary in relation to spirit which is secondary. We have happily returned to the same formula that it was necessary to elucidate with the aid of definitions of 'matter' and 'spirit', and the definitions turn out to be plain contradictions of that formula.

And are we to accept this collection of 'eternal truths' as the philosophy of Marxism? Never!

It is necessary to seek further.

## 2     Energetics and Empiriocriticism

In any event, materialistic atomic theory is obviously incompatible with the extreme dynamism of the Marxist worldview – with Marxism's 'dialecticalness'.

Therefore, Ostwald's 'energetics' – hostile to atomism but in all other respects of a kindred spirit with the old materialism – attracted my warmest sympathies. I soon noticed, however, an important contradiction in its 'philosophy of nature'. In repeatedly emphasising the *purely methodological* significance of the concept of 'energy', it was unable to sustain that significance in a great number of cases. 'Energy' is transformed from a pure symbol of the correlation between facts of experience into the *substance* of experience, into the 'matter of the world'. I tried to clarify to myself the causes of the contradiction which I often was guilty of when I examined various problems of philosophy from the point of view of energetics.[13]

The essence of the matter is that energetics really does provide monism, but only *monism of method* – monism of our means of investigation. It does not in fact provide a *picture of the world*. It is agnostic regarding the 'matter' of the world, and it is completely compatible both with the old materialism and with panpsychism. When 'energy' is represented as a substance, then it is the same thing as the old materialism minus absolute atoms – materialism with a correction in the sense of the *continuity* of what exists. Obviously, by itself, energetics turned out to be insufficient for a worldview, even if it is absolutely necessary to accept it. It is necessary to search further ...

At approximately the same time, I became acquainted with Kantian criticism, old and new. But there was almost nothing to take from it. I very quickly understood the scholastic nature of this philosophy – it has scientific pretensions but lacks a scientific foundation – and I could not seriously apply its countless – and useless – 'theories of cognition'. At each step I encountered a naïve faith in the possibility of deriving something important from the pure analysis of concepts – the faith of Anselm of Canterbury and even of such semi-positivist thinkers as A. Riehl. I felt an involuntary indignation when I read, for example, Riehl's truly ignorant argument that the sum of energy in nature must be limited, because it is unchanging, and what is unchanging can only be a finite quantity.

Of course, like any scholasticism, neo-Kantianism provides a great deal of practice in logical analysis, and one cannot deny its usefulness in this specifically gymnastic sense. In exactly the same way it is possible to sometimes find sensible thoughts in writers of this school. Unfortunately, such thoughts are not directly connected with the inner logic of Kantianism but are simply brought in

---

13   This comes through with particular emphasis in my first philosophical work, *Osnovnye elementy istoricheskogo vzgliada na prirodu* and partly also in *Poznanie s istoricheskoi tochki zreniia*.

by the scientific knowledge of the authors. Essentially, Kantianism has nothing to teach regarding the problem I have taken up.

Acquaintance with empiriocriticism helped me to make a step forward.

Empiriocriticism reduces the entire construction of the picture of the world down to the systematisation of experience through a continual critique of its content. It emphasises the identity of the psychical and the physical elements of *experience* (elements of light, sound, and innervation or elements of form, elements of hardness, warmth, cold, etc.), and the identity even of whole *complexes* of these elements in both realms (for example, 'bodies' and 'perceptions' of them) and finds that the entire difference is reducible to the nature of the connection between complexes or between elements. The task of cognition, in the opinion of the empiriocriticists, consists in the description of the connection between elements and complexes – a description that is as simple, precise, and systematic as possible and that is useful for *predicting* the course of events in the greatest number of cases possible. For this goal it is necessary that the description contains the most possible material of experience and that it removes from that description all that is 'subjective and accidental' – all that is *individual* both in the sense of the peculiarities of one or another person and also in the sense of the circumstances at the moment of observation. The critique provided by empiriocriticism consists in this 'cleansing' of experience.

It is necessary here to attend to still one more circumstance that is characteristic of this school. In its 'critique' of experience, it considers communication among people as a previously given point, as its own kind of 'a priori'. Moreover, in striving to create as simple and precise picture of the world as possible, empiriocriticism also has in mind the universal applicability of this picture, its practical satisfactoriness for the greatest possible number of 'fellow humans' for the longest possible time. From this it is already obvious how mistaken comrade Plekhanov was to accuse this school of a tendency to *solipsism* – the acceptance of only the individual experience of a cognising person and the acceptance of this individual experience as the Universe (as 'everything' that exists for the cognising person). It is characteristic of empiriocriticism precisely to assume the *equivalence* of 'my' experience and the experience of my 'fellow human beings', to the extent that they are accessible to me through their 'utterances'. What we have here is a sort of 'epistemological democracy' (although not yet an epistemological 'social democracy'. I will speak of this further on).

Of the entire school of empiriocriticism, the person who is most suspected of 'idealism' and 'solipsism' by our domestic philosophers is its real founder, Ernst Mach (who, by the way, did not call himself an empiriocriticist). Let us see how he drew the picture of the world.

For him the universe is an endless net of complexes consisting of elements that are identical with elements of sensation. These complexes change, unite, and separate; they enter into various combinations according to different types of connection. In this net, it is as if there are 'nodal points' (my expression) – places where elements are connected with one another more closely and densely (Mach's formulation). These places are called the human 'I'. There are less complex combinations that are similar to them – the psyches of other living beings. Some of these complexes appear in a connection with these complex combinations – and then they appear as the 'experiences' of various beings. Subsequently the connection is broken, and the complex disappears from the system of experiences of the given being; then it can appear in it again, perhaps in a changed form, etc. But, as Mach emphasises, in every case this or that complex nevertheless does not cease to exist; if it disappears from the 'consciousness' of one or another individual, it appears in other combinations, perhaps in a connection with another 'nodal point', with another 'I' ...

It is clearly extremely rash to see 'solipsism' in this picture. And in regard to 'idealism', is it really possible to call this is 'idealism' just because elements of 'physical experience' are considered to be identical to elements of 'psychical' experience (elements of sensation) when this is simply an indubitable fact? The negation of 'things-in-themselves' ... But we have seen in comrade Bel'tov's picture of the world what kind of sense the assumption of things-in-themselves results in. And comrade Bel'tov, himself – through his witty and superficial critique – has shown (as was done before him by some positivists, by the way) that Kant's assumption of 'things-in-themselves' leads to still more unfortunate results.

In any case, because empiriocriticism is the most rigorous of the existing forms of positivism, I have borrowed from it for my worldview. Its 'critique of experience' was the most suitable starting point for further work. I need be as little embarrassed by the origin of this intellectual current in the 'bourgeois-intelligentsia' as comrade Bel'tov is embarrassed by the even more bourgeois tenor of Holbach. Bourgeois philosophy is not a 'Cretan' who always lies ... But what exactly should be taken from empiriocriticism?

Without even speaking of the huge *scientifically-critical* work that was carried out by individual representatives of this school (particularly Mach in the realm of physics and the physiology of external sensations), it is also possible to completely agree with certain of the basic propositions that relate directly to a general picture of the world. The first and foremost of these is the proposition that the elements of experience in themselves are *neither physical nor psychical* and that one or the other of these two characterisations depends entirely on the *connection* – on the type of *combination* – of the elements. One can also assume that the physical and psychical types of connection of elements are the very antithesis of one another. But doubt immediately arises. And the questions also arise: are these types really absolutely irreducible either one to the another or both to some third and from whence does their difference come? For the empiriocriticist, it is sufficient to state this difference and to systematically describe it as an 'independent' or a 'dependent' difference. The question of 'why?' is done away with by this form of positivism; it is not concerned with any kind of thorough-going monism. It is at this point that a parting of the ways between empiriocriticist and Marxist thinking must begin. The latter is not satisfied with stating the two types, but definitely seeks a monist – or, what is the same thing, causal – explanation of them.

Subsequently, in looking into the content and structure of 'physical' complexes and the 'psychical' complexes that *correlate* to them (a 'body' and the 'perception' or 'psychical image' of that body), it was easy to see that their correlation was far from as simple as Mach, for example, formulated it. It is far from a simple equality or identity or complete parallelism. No, the physical complex 'body' – the 'human organism', for example – is of considerably richer content than a simple 'perception' or 'psychical image' of a human organism. A 'physical' complex *totalises in itself* the content of countless separate perceptions and unites this fluctuating content into a considerably more stable whole. The 'physical' complex – the 'human body' – includes, so to speak, all the anatomy, all the histology, all the physiology of a person; and the 'perception' of the human body gives only an almost insignificant part of all this. And even a 'psychical image', although it might have considerably more content than a perception, all the same never contains anything close to a significant part of the material that belongs to a 'physical body'.

In a word, it is necessary to radically reconsider the relationship of the 'physical' and the 'psychical' – not only because it is impossible to be reconciled to the *dualism of the interconnectedness of experience* that the empiriocriticists are content with, but also because conditions are revealed in the very nature of that interconnectedness that are not appropriate for physical and psychical forms and that resist investigation.

Thus the task of 'empiriomonism' was posed.[14]

---

14   I have not touched on the 'immanent school' at all, because it is only an intermediary form between Kantianism and empiriocriticism. That school also was not relevant when I was working out my worldview because I became familiar with it only after I had encountered the school of Mach and Avenarius. [The 'immanent school' was based on the concept of 'conscious immanence', which treats the mind and object as a unity. Proponents of this

## 3   The Path of Empiriomonism

Even at the time when I was not particularly familiar with the Marxist worldview, it always struck me as amusing when the so-called critical Marxists of the day argued that Marxism still 'was not philosophically grounded' and, it goes without saying, that they would ground it. These worthy scholastics with their characteristic acumen did not understand that first and foremost a philosophy – as the completion of a system of knowledge – *must itself be based* on the entire sum of experience and science. And if Marxism presented itself as a true scientific theory, and no philosophy was organically connected to it, then it is necessary *to ground philosophy in a Marxian way* (having elaborated philosophy in a Marxian way, of course) but in no way to ground Marxism on some sort of philosophy. The old materialism, having based itself on the natural sciences, correctly understood the relationship of science and philosophy.

Therefore, after I became a Marxist, I always carefully verified from the point of view of Marx's social philosophy everything that remained with me from previous views and everything that seemed correct to me in new ideas, until I mastered it enough to be able *directly* to apply it to issues of general philosophical significance.

I found that I had no reason to give up my previous desire to seek the basis for philosophy in the natural sciences. It was absolutely the opposite: Marxist philosophy must first and foremost be precisely *scientific*. After all, because they are based on technological experience and technological sciences, the natural sciences are the *ideology of the productive forces of society*, and, according to the basic idea of historical materialism, the productive forces of society present the basis of society's general development. But it was also clear that Marxist philosophy must also reflect the *social form* of productive forces, being based, obviously, on sciences that are properly 'social'.

In regard to the ideas of 'matter' and 'spirit', it is necessary to reject them not only because they are vague and indefinite. In investigating their social origin beginning with the era of universal animism, I came to the conclusion that they completely reflect a specific, historically transient form of relationships of social labour – the authoritarian form of the division between organisational and implementational functions. The organisational function was abstracted into the idea of an active 'spirit', and the implementational

---

school include the German philosophers Wilhelm Schuppe (1863–1913) and Richard von Schubert-Soldern (1852–1924). Trans.]

function was abstracted into the idea of passive 'matter'. The idea of 'things-in-themselves' turned out to be the idea of 'spirit' or 'soul' metaphysically-transformed on the basis of new (mercantile) relationships. It was only the long process of this transformation that made it possible for materialists to make such quid pro quos as identifying 'matter' with a 'thing-in-itself', with a hidden 'soul' of phenomena, with a real 'noumenon'.[15] It is hopeless to seek for monism along this path.

Further, it was obvious that 'energetics' is in complete harmony with the basic tendencies of Marxism not only in its monist form but even more in its very content. The principle of the transformation and conservation of energy is the ideological expression of the essence of *machine production*, consisting as it does precisely in the application of a *quantitatively-given* supply of energy for the goal of labour through the *transformation* of that energy into new forms. But this could only be *methodological monism* in precisely the same way that the practical energetics of machine production expresses only the *unity of methods of social labour*.

Very little results from this for the construction of a holistic picture of the world. Empiriocriticism proposes specific material for this picture – elements of *experience* that are in themselves completely free of the colouration of the primordial dualism of a 'physical' and a 'psychical' world. Is this suitable and adequate material for a Marxist philosopher?

In order to answer this question, it would be necessary to know what requirements this picture of the world would be obliged to satisfy – what its vital significance is. And since the picture of the world appears in an *ideological form*, it is necessary to resolve a more general question – what is the vital significance of the ideology which determines how the picture of the world develops and what are the conditions for its greatest viability.

In investigating these questions by the methods of historical materialism, I arrived at the following conclusions: (1) ideological forms are *organising adaptations of social life* and, in the final analysis, organisational adaptations *of the technological process* (by direct and indirect paths). (2) Therefore, the development of ideology is determined by the *need* for organising adaptations of the social process and *available material* for them. (3) The vital capacity of the organising adaptations consequently depends on how harmoniously and orderly they organise content of social labour in reality.[16]

---

15   Regarding this, see the article '*Aftoritarnoe myshlenie* [Authoritarian Thinking]' in the collection *Iz psikhologii obshchestva* [*Essays on the Psychology of Society*] and Chapter 4, 'The Thing-in-Itself', in the present volume.

16   The article '*Razvitie zhizni v prirode i obshchestve* [Development of Life in Nature and Soci-

But at this point I cannot but take into consideration the theory of ideological development that has been proposed by comrade Bel'tov. It is a theory of 'reactions' that, in his opinion, effectively augments the basic conception of historical materialism. Let us examine this theory.

According to comrade Bel'tov's view, it is the change in classes and social groups that provides the basis of changing ideological forms. This, of course, is absolutely true for class society and coincides both with the basic propositions of historical monism, in general, and also specifically with my point of view. As the 'organised' content of social-class life changes, the 'organising' forms also change accordingly. But later on comrade Bel'tov's 'supplementation' begins. In their struggle with the preceding ideology, the ideologists of the new class or group inevitably strive to relate as negatively as possible toward it. They strive to 'do the opposite' of the previous ideologists, and they go mad with extreme opposition. In their reaction against the one-sided former ideology, they create a new, opposite one-sidedness. Only after such vacillation between 'extremes' (or even several vacillations) some kind of new ideology, finding itself in more favourable conditions, can establish 'objective truth' that will remain forever.

Examples. The school of mercantilism, the ideologists of undeveloped forms of capital, considered money to be the *sole, true value*. Hume, an ideologist of more developed, manufacturing capitalism, in his desire to 'do the opposite' of the mercantilists came to reject the value of money and to treat it simply as a *relative* sign that expresses the value of other commodities. Subsequently, Marx, who by then had not gone mad with the desire to 'do the opposite' of Hume, eliminated both extremes and created the 'objectively true' theory of money and commodities. In France, the materialism of members of the Enlightenment was a reaction against the religiosity of the old aristocracy, and the idealism of the utopians of the nineteenth century was a reaction against the materialism of the Enlightenment. In England in the seventeenth century, the attraction of aristocrats toward materialism was a reaction against the religiosity of the petty bourgeois revolutionaries ...

If one examines comrade Bel'tov's theory from a purely formal point of view, then at the outset one obtains an impression of inadequacy and lack of distinctness on one very important point. It is unclear precisely which aspects and parts of the former ideology must cause the reaction against itself (the extremeness of the new ideology) and how far this reaction (this extremeness) can go. If the matter had to do only with those aspects and parts of both ideo-

---

ety]' in the book *Iz psikhologii obshchestva* and almost all of the present volume (especially Chapter 9, 'Historical Monism') are devoted to these questions.

logies in which the direct vital contradiction of the corresponding classes or groups was expressed, and if the extent of 'reaction' was determined entirely by the forms and degree of these actual contradictions, then in theory *there would be exactly nothing new* in comparison with the basic historical-materialist conception. Therefore, one must think that the 'reaction' goes *beyond* these bounds and the desire to 'do the opposite' of former ideologists acts on the development of the new ideology as a *special, independent force* that is tacked on to the force of the practical class and group contradictions. Comrade Bel'tov's illustrations completely support this idea; one could even draw the conclusion from them that this special force of 'reaction' could also go against class thinking, against class interests, and in general against the 'basis' of ideology. In reality, did materialism correspond to the class psychology of the English aristocracy? Obviously not. Materialism was endowed too strongly with *Enlightenment* qualities – hateful to a class that ruled with the aid of brute force plus the ignorance of the masses – and materialism was too weakly endowed with that *authoritarian* spirit, which expressed what was most dear to this class. And from the point of view of the *interests* of the aristocracy, the spread of materialism was extremely disadvantageous. But, nevertheless, the English aristocracy, in order to 'do the opposite' of the pious revolutionaries, sank into materialism ...

Here we see that this theory does not simply 'supplement' Marx's historical materialism, it *limits* it. In their influence on ideology, class forms of life and class interest run up against the counteracting force of ideological 'reaction' and retreat in the face of it. Of course, those forms retreat only to a certain limit. The problem is resolved by a compromise of *two* principles. Theories of this type are conventionally called 'eclectic'.

It would be permissible for us to accept such a theory only in the event that it was impossible to explain the facts without it. Do we have such an extreme case here? Let us examine the illustrations that comrade Bel'tov has provided.

The theory of money. What caused the one-sidedness of the mercantilists, and what led Hume to the opposite one-sidedness? In one place (*The History of Socialism*) Kautsky says: 'The pursuit of gold and silver was particularly strong in the sixteenth century, when the source of power that lay behind the natural economy began to dry up, and the power of the credit system had not yet attained sufficient development'. These few words, which state the undoubted facts in passing, provide sufficient material to explain both 'extremes'. It is necessary only to keep in mind that what appeared with the greatest force and clarity in the new ideological theories was not that they 'remained as before' but rather that they 'moved forward'; they became stronger and developed. And the simple cause of all this was that the need for organising (i.e. ideological) forms was particularly strong in regard to new and volatile content that could not be packed within the confines of the old forms. The intensified, aggravated thirst for money found itself a 'one-sided' expression in the declaration that money was the sole, true value – a one-sidedness that proceeded from the fact that this 'value' grew quickly while other values stayed the same or decreased. The system of credit and banknotes with 'arbitrary denotations' that rapidly developed in the eighteenth century caused a one-sided declaration – including by a few theorists – of the value of 'arbitrary denotations', or, more accurately, the arbitrary meaning of the value of money, because, as the practical importance of credit and banknotes grew, the immediate vital significance of gold and silver grew slowly or decreased. But this phenomenon did not develop very abruptly and therefore the majority of bourgeois theorists did not fall into the 'onesidedness' of Hume's abstract psyche.

The materialism of the French Enlightenment and the idealism of the later utopians ... But materialism, with its scientific-positivist tendencies, was the natural ideology for the rising industrial bourgeoisie, with its 'earthly' interests and growing 'material' power. 'Idealism' – a subdued form of religious worldview – was a characteristic of the petty bourgeoisie, which still had not broken its ties with the authoritarian order. The authoritarian class proper – feudal aristocrats – were inclined simply to stick with religion, since, on the one hand, it sanctioned the rule of the ruling class, and, on the other hand, it completely corresponded to the authoritarian type of thinking (the antitheses of 'God – world', 'spirit – body', and so on, ideologically reflect the antitheses that appeared in reality as 'power – subordination' and organisational – implementational functions). At first, as long as it was still an estate in the feudal world, the petty bourgeoisie was straightforwardly religious, and it preserved this characteristic long after it had ceased to be a feudal estate, partly because of the general *conservatism of its ideology* and partly because of the *authoritarian structure of each separate petty bourgeois enterprise* (the family). But in so doing the religious worldview gradually became empty and colourless, transforming into 'idealism'. The French utopians no sooner had been turned into idealists by this process than they wanted to 'do the opposite' of the Enlightenment, all the more so precisely because they were imbued with petty bourgeois tendencies (90 per cent of the proletariat of that time also retained petty bourgeois thinking). The strengthening of the authoritarian (and therefore 'idealistic') element in the thinking of the French utopians was also facilitated by the circumstance that, because of their real powerlessness, the utopians strove to rely on organised authoritarian forces – the state and, in part, the church – to achieve their goals. All these were considerably more serious causes for 'idealistic' sentiment than the wish by to absolutely 'do the opposite' of the Enlightenment.

The English aristocrat-materialists of the seventeenth century ... Were they, properly, ideologists of the aristocracy? In those days, the aristocracy marched under the banner of *Catholicism* – and partly of the Church of England – as they were obliged to do in accordance with the authoritarian position and authoritarian thinking of the aristocracy. But the aristocracy, both before and after that time, have frequently provided ideologists to other classes of society. The materialists of the seventeenth century were precisely ideologists of the big industrial bourgeoisie that was being born. In England, the seventeenth century was an era of rapid technological progress and the development of manufacturing. The industrial bourgeoisie grew, and its interests and its type of thinking – with its tendency toward *materialism* that predominated in this era – embraced elements of other classes that stood close to it. The aristocrat-materialists were *bourgeois* ideologists, as also were many aristocrats in France in the eighteenth century – notably, Baron Holbach. These English materialists were for the most part scientific researchers who worked with absolutely non-feudal diligence in laboratories with the instruments of chemistry and physics. There was nothing of an aristocratic-class nature in their materialism; the 'papists' were the true and most numerous representatives of aristocratic-class tendencies. It is true that there were monarchist-absolutist tendencies among the aristocrat-materialists, but they also corresponded to the mood and interests of the big industrial bourgeoisie who more easily obtained all kinds of privileges, monopolies, and useful patronage for themselves under the bureaucratic system. Centralised, absolute monarchy was not at all the class ideal of the aristocracy; this form was bourgeois-aristocratic and to a great extent precisely bourgeois. The ideals of the aristocracy lie in the feudal past.

In a word, in those cases when comrade Bel'tov brings the theory of 'reaction' into his explanation of ideological facts, it turns out either to be completely superfluous or patently false. His theory is both formally eclectic and essentially unsound. And, as a matter of act, comrade Bel'tov's theory has as its premise the idea of a polemical mood that is so sharp that it could not be held for decades in the psychology of whole generations. For an explanation of the polemical enthusiasm of separate people, this theory might perhaps sometimes be satisfactory, and it altogether depicts comrade Bel'tov's own martial temperament much better than it does the laws of ideological development.[17]

---

17   Here is a characteristic quotation from Bel'tov's book. 'How can you think that Chateaubriand sympathised with an old aesthetic theory when Voltaire – hateful, malignant Voltaire! – was one of its representatives' (*On the Question of the Development of a Monistic View of History*, p. 172). Of course, it happens that some ideologists can become extremely angry at others, but can one make a historico-philosophical theory out of this?

We can thus continue to investigate the issue of ideological development in general and of the development of a picture of the world in particular without being constrained by either a theory of 'reaction' or the desire to 'do the opposite' of our predecessors.

The vital significance of a philosophical picture of the world consists in that it is the most recent and highest *universally-organising* cognitive form. Embracing all possible content, it must obviously be constructed from material that would be *universal*. Combinations that are produced in the course of *social* development – those that are designated by the terms 'spirit' and 'matter', for example – cannot have a universal nature. As is well known, such concepts are absent at the lowest level of social development. It is obvious that it is necessary to take as a starting point material that was characteristic of the most primitive *concrete* thinking, since all *abstract* thinking is undoubtedly the product of further social development. Consequently, the *immediate elements of experience* turn out to be the sole appropriate material, and on this point we can with good conscience accept what is proposed by the semi-bourgeois positivist philosophy of the empiriocriticists, just as previously we were earlier able to take the dialectic from bourgeois Hegelianism and the theory of the value of labour from bourgeois classics.

Then there is the issue of the method of grouping these elements. The empiriocritical school finds it sufficient to state the dualism of this interconnectedness: the 'subjective' interconnectedness or the 'dependent' (on the cognising organism) series of psychical experience and the 'objective' interconnectedness or the 'independent' of series of physical experience. For us, such a position is obvious dualism, and it is here that a radical divergence from the empiriocriticists begins. It is necessary to examine both types of interconnectedness.

It becomes clear that the difference between them is essentially caused by *communication* among people and also among other living organisms. *Physical interconnectedness has an identical meaning for everything that is situated in communication; psychical interconnectedness has meaning only for a separate living being.* If I see a 'physical body' – a large stone – on the road, then from the utterances, the actions, and the gestures of other people, I am convinced that this stone also exists for them and that it has the same qualities for them as it does for me. People walking down the road say, 'Oh, that stone should not be there!', and they walk around it. Those who do not see it, for some reason, stumble over it, are bruised, and cry out ... But if *I imagine* a stone on the road, then it does not serve as an impediment to anyone, and from the actions and utterances of other people I am easily convinced that no matter how clearly I imagine it, it has no real meaning for them. My psychical image of the stone on the road can attain such force and clarity that I 'see' it, as in the first case, but when other people tell me that I am mistaken and there is no stone or when they freely walk through it, then I understand that this complex is only 'psychical' – only 'subjective' – and that this is a 'perception' and not a 'body'. Only communication with other people reduces my hallucination to the level of 'psychical' fact that has immediate meaning for me alone.

And meanwhile the stone-psychical-image or stone-hallucination occupies a definite place in the series of my experiences. It affects the further course of my experience. And, in the case of a hallucination, the degree of its subjective meaning for me can extend to the point where it closes me off from other people, so that I can go up to it and feel it with my hand or even stumble over it, but all this is *only for me*.

Thus, in regard to 'physical' complexes, their 'objectivity' – i.e. the *social validity* of these complexes and their correlations – consists in the content of the experience that is *coordinated* with 'fellow-humans'. Just the opposite, in regard to 'psychical' complexes, their 'subjectivity' – i.e. only the *individual meaningfulness* of psychical complexes and their interconnectedness – consists in experience that is coordinated only for each person separately and not coordinated among different people.

Thus two different characterisations are obtained: 'the physical' is *socially-organised experience* (i.e. socially-coordinated in the communication of people) and 'the psychical' is *individually organised experience* (i.e. coordinated only in the confines of individual experience).

The question now automatically arises: what is the source of the interrelationship of both forms?

It was easy to establish that the discrimination between 'subjective' and 'objective' experience was accomplished gradually and sequentially on the basis of broadening communication among people. Much of what was 'objective' and 'physically existing' for preceding generations has passed into historical memory as being 'subjective', or *only psychical*. The movement of the sun across the sky has turned from 'actual' to 'apparent'. The world of 'souls' and 'spirits' has lost its 'objectivity' (that also was originally purely 'physical' objectivity). 'The objective' *has been distinguished* from 'the subjective' through social processing in communication among people. The very *forms of objectivity* – time, space, causality – have undergone a long historical development.

'Pure' or 'geometrical' space is produced from 'visual' or 'tangible' space through continual verifications introduced by communication with other people, and certain important stages of this development happened comparatively recently – for example, the transition from the limited space of the ancients to the infinite space of contemporary people and from the heterogeneous space of people of the ancient and medieval eras (Democritus and Epicurus thought that pure space has an 'up' and a 'down') to the homogeneous space of contemporary people (who consider the existence of antipodes to be absurd). The conception of time went through a similar evolution, and the evolution of the idea of causality was even more complex. All these forms on which the 'objectivity' of the content of experience depends attained their contemporary state through what is essentially social evolution.

Through its communication, the collective work of humanity not only transformed the forms of physical experience and not only removed a mass of weak complexes (false forms) from it but also broadened the realm of physical experience, enriching its content to an extent that people of the past could not have dreamt of. Progress of the organisation of psychical experience also occurred simultaneously with this work and depended on it; people learned to rationally control the chain of their conceptions and, by means of 'attention', even to regulate their perceptions. The world of experience was crystallised, and continues to be crystallised, out of chaos.[18]

Communication among people is the force through which the forms of this crystallisation are determined. Properly speaking, there is no *experience* outside these forms, because the unorganised mass of experiences is not experience. Thus, experience is social at its very foundation, and experience progresses through the *socio-psychological process of its being organised* to which the individual-psychological organising process is entirely adapted. If for the empiriocriticist the experience of all fellow human beings is of equal value – something I have previously designated as a certain cognitive 'democracy' – then for the empiriomonist this experience is moreover the result of the collectively organised work of all people, of a kind of cognitive 'socialism'.

From this it is evident how truly capricious it is, philosophically, to accuse the 'empiriomonists' of solipsism and scepticism.

But, having reduced two types of interconnectedness of experience to two phases of the organising process, we have made only one step toward the establishment of monism. We still need to explain how appropriate material – i.e. *material that is common to different people to a sufficient degree* – turns out to be available for collectively-organised work.

Like the previous question, this is a question that empiriocriticism absolutely cannot answer.

We must not limit ourselves to thinking that the same complexes fall one after another into the interconnectedness of experience now for one, now for

---

18  All this is explained and substantiated in Chapter 1, 'The Ideal of Cognition' in the present volume.

'fellow human beings' and thus attain a certain 'social validity'. It remains completely incomprehensible why 'physical' complexes possess this quality and such 'psychical' qualities as, let us say, 'emotions', 'fantasies', etc., are not socially valid – why 'they' see the very same tree that 'I' do, but they do not experience the same sadness, the same memories, or the same daydreams that I do. Next, why do the very same 'physical bodies' appear in the interconnectedness of the experience of different people (or of the same person under different circumstances) with such a substantially different form and content that the elements they have in common actually disappear compared with their differences. For example, a 'person' in the form of a black dot on the horizon and 'the same person' in the form of someone I am having a conversation with, or a drop of stagnant water seen with the naked eye and the 'same' drop of water – a world of infusoria and bacteria – seen with a microscope. And all this relates precisely to 'physical', 'objective' complexes. Where is the logic of such transformations to be found?

Further, that same 'communication' among people that serves as the basis of the forms of experience presupposes, evidently, some kind of distinctive duality of 'living' complexes. To be precise, we attach the 'experiences' of these beings (their perceptions, feelings, psychical images, etc. that are not immediately accessible to us) to 'physical bodies' – organisms which move and make sounds. Where is the logic of this duality to be found?

The way out of these difficulties is the idea of *universal substitution*.

The easiest path toward it goes through comrade Bel'tov's 'things-in-themselves'.

Let us assume for a moment that Holbach and comrade Bel'tov are correct and that any 'phenomenon' springs from the action of external 'things-in-themselves' on the 'thing-in-itself' that constitutes the essence of a given 'person'.

Consistent with the *law of causality*, a 'thing-in-itself' that acts on another 'thing-in-itself' can do only one thing, and that is to cause some kind of *change* in this latter. Consequently, all 'phenomena', all 'impressions', all 'experience' represent only *the change of a thing-in-itself*.

But from the point of view of a *dialectical* (i.e. dynamic) worldview, those very 'things-in-themselves' cannot be anything other than *processes*. Consequently, any 'impression', any 'phenomenon', and any 'experience' is only a specific change in the course of some kind of process – of a 'thing-in-itself' called a 'living being'.

Changes of such a kind are known to us as 'experience'. They are broken down into specific *elements* – colours, tones, elements of form, hardness, etc. To be even more accurate, they are not elements of *experience, but elements that appear and disappear* in experience – elements that form experience not statically but dynamically, by means of changes of their groupings. *Where do these elements come from?*

From the point of view of causality, which does not assume that something can be created out of nothing, it is absolutely inconceivable that these elements do not belong to the order of 'things-in-themselves' – either something that 'acts' or something that 'experiences action'. But we now have the facts necessary to judge regarding the order and 'form' of these mysterious 'things'. It turns out that they *contain elements that are identical with the elements of experience.*

All this already exists in a hidden form in the assumption of causality in regard to 'things-in-themselves' that comrade Bel'tov emphasises.

But perhaps there are still some other kinds of elements contained in 'things' that are not accessible to us, that do not appear in the 'changes' that are called 'experience'. If there are such elements then they obviously lie quietly and have no relation to experience and therefore it is impossible to come to any conclusions about them. That is, in a cognitive sense, *they simply do not exist.*[19]

Thus, 'things-in-themselves' consist in those elements that appear and disappear in 'phenomena'. This conclusion can hardly be pleasing to comrade Bel'tov, but according to his own premises, it cannot be escaped except at the cost of *eclecticism.*

In order to proceed further, it is necessary to recall the origin of these 'things'. They are the metaphysically transformed 'souls' of objects and phenomena of experience. And 'souls', in turn, represent a distinctive development of 'substitution'. To be precise, people 'understand' one another by means of recognising feelings, perceptions, and other 'experiences' behind the physical phenomena of the living body. In the era of authoritarian relationships, these 'substituted' experiences were recognised as a kind of 'power' governing over the body and located inside the body as a 'soul' – i.e. an organisational force. This means that if we take a 'thing-in-itself' and cleanse it of the social fetishism of metaphysics, then we obtain an authoritarian 'soul'; and if the 'soul' is then cleansed of authoritarian fetishism, then a 'substitution' appears – the means of commu-

---

19   From the point of view of the ideas that I am presenting, the relationship between a 'thing-in-itself' and a 'phenomenon' is the same as between velocity and acceleration, or, to take a more concrete example, as between a constant electric current in a nerve and a negative oscillation of that current forming a 'neural current' (a stimulus conducted by the nerve).

nication among people, the source of all cognition, the substitution of psychical 'experiences' for the physical processes of the actions and utterances of other people.

At this point everything becomes clear.

The 'thing-in-itself' of any living being turns out to be simply the sum total of its experiences ('conscious' and 'extra-conscious'), and its body is nothing other than the 'manifestation' of this 'thing' in the experience of other living beings and in the living being, itself. 'Psychical complexes' are substituted for 'physiological' processes and communication among people appears simply as the action of one complex of experiences on another and back again, according to the law of causality. The 'body' of a living being (or, more precisely, the 'perception' of the body) is the reflection of the sum of its experiences in other living beings and back again. It only gradually adopts the *objective* character of an actual 'physical body' through, as we have seen, the social organisation of experience.

But if this is so, then a 'substitution' is needed not only for living bodies but also for inanimate ones. Here one also must assume similar 'things-in-themselves' – i.e. complexes of elements that are accessible to us only indirectly, through their action on us. It goes without saying that these complexes cannot be imagined as being organised according to the highest (associative) type according to which the psyche of a 'living being' is organised. 'Unorganised' (i.e. organised only very weakly and at a very low level, of course) 'immediate complexes' correspond to 'unorganised' bodies of physical experience. Thus the idea of *universal substitution* is obtained.

In the era of animism, humanity already possessed 'universal substitution' but in an erroneous, fetishistic form, as the *animation* of all of nature – as the population of unorganised bodies by highly-organised 'souls'. Critically verified substitution, first, does not now consider the 'body' as the dwelling place of the 'soul' and, second, in assuming that the 'bodies' of physical experience are reflections of immediate complexes, ascribe to these latter only the kind of level of organisation that corresponds to the level of organisation of the 'bodies' themselves.

Now our picture of the world has attained a certain wholeness. Before us are endless, unbroken series of complexes, whose material is identical with elements of experience and whose form is characterised by the most varied levels of organisation that progressively move up from the 'chaos of elements' to the complexity and harmoniousness of 'human experience'. All these complexes, acting on one another, cause changes in one another and are mutually reflected in one another. Reflections of this kind, appearing in the highest, psychical complexes, form the 'impressions' of living beings; communication that arises among living beings through these 'impressions' leads to their *social systematisation* – to their organisation into 'experience' in the precise meaning of that word.[20]

From the point of view of this picture of the world, it is absolutely understandable why the exact same 'objects of nature' can appear in experience in a very different form; the exact same immediate complex 'is reflected' in another complex under different conditions in a very different manner. This proceeds directly from the law of causality. The psychophysiological duality of life is also explained: a single life, taken in its immediate content or in its 'reflections', does not cease being a single life because of it.

The universal parallelism of 'immediate' complexes and their 'reflections in physical experience' confirms the universal applicability of the law of conservation of energy. After all, this law has nothing to do with whether we take a 'complex' in its immediate aspect or in its 'reflection' – the point is that there is the exact same energetical magnitude. Therefore, the 'psyche' is energetical just as the corresponding physiological processes are.

Discriminating between 'phenomenon' and 'thing-in-itself' turns out to be superfluous. We face a world of *direct* experience and a world of *indirect* experience – a world of what is immediately sensed and a world of supplemental 'substitutions' of it. The realm of 'substitution' coincides with the realm of 'physical phenomena'; nothing need be substituted for 'psychical' phenomena since they are 'immediate complexes'. Substitution is based *on them* and it develops along a social path *from them*; 'immediate complexes' are the primary material of substitution in 'communication' among people.

Such is the picture of the world that can be considered 'empiriomonist' *for our times* – i.e. the most harmoniously united experience.[21]

## 4   Regarding Eclecticism and Monism

I have shown how the views on life and the world (in which I see the path toward 'empiriomonism' – toward the ideal of integral and rigorous cognition)

---

20   All this is thoroughly expounded in Chapter 2, 'Life and the Psyche', in the present volume.
21   The resolution of still one more question is necessary for a full and complete picture. This is the question of the discontinuities in experience, of why the 'consciousness' of different people is disconnected, why all 'immediate complexes' do not flow together into one solid whole, and why the universe does not form in this way a single universal, chaotic 'consciousness'. This question will be discussed in the next chapter 'Universum'; I do not want to drag out and complicate this presentation here.

took shape from my critique of the content of various worldviews that I am familiar with and from the results of my own work that have supplemented what I was not able to find in those worldviews. These views did not take shape at all quickly, and it is only in the present work (Book Three of *Empiriomonism*) together with the simultaneously written works *Iz psikhologii obshchestva* and *Novyi mir* that a more or less finished expression of my views appears. I mention in passing that I frequently use the same word to designate my final philosophical goal (empiriomonism as the ideal of cognition) and the path that seems to me to lead to that goal (empiriomonism as an attempt to provide as harmonious a picture of the world as possible for our times and for that social class to whose cause I have dedicated myself). I believe that these different meanings of the word 'empiriomonism' will not confuse the reader. From all that has just been explained, the reader can see that I have the right to consider this endeavour *mine* and not to consider myself as a member of one of those *philosophical* schools proper, whose ideas I have made use of as material for my own construction.

Only the social philosophy of Marx has served as more than just material for me – it was simultaneously the governor and the method of my work.

In view of this, I have the right – and in the interests of clarity I consider it necessary – to make special mention of the grave error that comrade Bel'tov and comrade Plekhanov have made in systematically confusing my views with one of the 'schools I have passed through'.

Comrade Bel'tov stubbornly considers me to be a 'Machist' and an empiriocriticist.[22] Comrade Plekhanov, on the contrary, counts all the empiriocriticists as 'empiriomonists'.[23] And both of them are misunderstandings.

I have learned a great deal from Mach, and I think that comrade Bel'tov could also learn a lot of interesting things from this outstanding scholar and thinker, from this great destroyer of scientific fetishes. I advise young comrades not to be dismayed by the thought that Mach is not a Marxist. They should follow the example of comrade Bel'tov, who has learned so much from Hegel and Holbach, who, if I am not mistaken, also were not Marxists.

However, I cannot consider myself to be a 'Machist' in philosophy. In my general philosophical conception, I have taken only one thing from Mach: the idea of the neutrality of the elements of experience in regard to the 'physical'

---

22  See, for example, the preface to the book *Kritika nashikh kritikov* [*A Critique of Our Critics*]. [Bogdanov implies that he is addressed by name in the preface, but this is not the case. Plekhanov refers only to 'critical' opponents of Marxism who 'bow down to Kant or to Avenarius or to Mach' as 'eclectics'. (trans.)]

23  See the comments on page 121 of his translation of Engels's *Ludwig Feuerbach*.

and the 'psychical', the idea of the dependence of these characteristics only on how they are *connected* in experience. Subsequently, in all that follows – in the theory of the genesis of psychical and physical experience, in the theory of substitution, in the theory of 'interference' of complexes-processes, in the general picture of the world that is based on these premises – I have nothing in common with Mach. In a word, I am considerably less a 'Machist' than comrade Bel'tov is a 'Holbachian', and I hope that this will not prevent both of us from being good Marxists.

As far as the empiriocriticists are concerned, I can assure comrade Bel'tov that the western European representatives of that school do not even know what 'empiriomonism' is, and it is therefore particularly unjust to call them empiriomonists. I am personally prepared to bear all the punishment for my 'empiriomonist' tendencies and deeds, so why should they have to answer for them? It is all the more unjust, since any of them who became familiar with my views would consider me as an inveterate metaphysician ... It must be noted that some of them are also counted among the metaphysicians by their teachers, Mach and Avenarius. In general, they often are almost as deserving of the title 'metaphysician' as comrade Bel'tov is of the title 'eclectic'.

There would be nothing strange about this if comrade Bel'tov had no time to familiarise himself with my works. But in that case, it would not be appropriate for him to express decisive and specific judgements of my views. If he read my works, then he could not but know that I take the very idea of empiriomonism to be the antithesis of the *dualism* of the empiriocriticist school and that I have devoted a lot of work to the critique of the ideas of that school. At the same time, however, I do recognise that the demands that their 'critique of experience' place on cognition is a great merit of this school, and I consider its views to be just as suitable a *starting point* for the development of Marxist philosophy as, let us say, democracy is a suitable starting point for the development of the idea of socialism.

I admit that for an absolutely inexperienced reader, who, moreover, has not read even to the end of the first volume of *Empiriomonism*, my very sympathetic testimonial regarding empiriocriticism might serve as the occasion for laughter. But for a person who is versed in philosophy – who knows the difference between the starting point of investigation and the summation of its results, the difference between an introduction and a philosophical worldview in the large – such a misunderstanding is impossible. At the same time, I more than once emphasised the basic difference between my views and the views of the empiriocriticists, pointing out, for example, that 'an empiriocriticist will be correct from his point of view to reject the very posing' of the problems of monism that I outlined, that the 'empiriocriticist conception is a passing stage' in the development of the picture of the world, and so on (see p. 129). A professional philosopher like comrade Bel'tov or comrade Plekhanov, it would seem, could not be mistaken about this.[24]

---

24   It is doubly wrong for comrade Plekhanov to introduce this patent confusion into a popular pamphlet that is aimed at completely non-specialist readers (the notes to the Russian translation of Engels's pamphlet on L. Feuerbach).

Comrade N. Valentinov in the journal *Pravda* has reproached me more than once (also without argumentation) because I *am not* an empiriocriticist. The rebuke is just, and in my justification, I offer only one argument, and that is that empiriocriticism does not satisfy me.

In the newspaper *Iskra* (no. 77), comrade Ortodoks undertakes a polemic with me from comrade Bel'tov's perspective. What comrade Ortodoks introduced *of his own* into this polemic can be boiled down to three points:

[Note: Ortodoks was the pseudonym of Liubov Akselrod (1868–1946). She was a close associate of G. Plekhanov and was second only to Plekhanov among Menshevik philosophers of Marxism. Because she wrote under a masculine pseudonym, Bogdanov refers to her with the masculine personal pronoun. (Trans.)]

1. Comrade Ortodoks does not know the difference between 'psychology' and 'ideology', naively considering them to be the same. He protested against my acceptance of a necessary link between the development of *social instinct* and the emergence of society. Ortodoks proposes that social instinct is a 'psychological factor' and therefore cannot be considered a cause of social development. It did not occur to me to say that social instinct is the 'primary cause' of social organisation, but it is undoubtedly an initially-necessary and *universal form* of social organisation. Comrade Ortodoks does not know that in biological development manifestations of social instinct exist in places where there is still no 'society' – i.e. systems of social collaboration – in the precise meaning of the word. And comrade Ortodoks evidently does not understand that without this link, which is initially created *biologically* precisely in the form of this instinct, society could not spring up.

2. Of the three chapters in the first book of *Empiriomonism* that he criticises, comrade Ortodoks read only one chapter – the first – about the development of *forms* of experience and therefore triumphantly attacks me with questions ('Where did the wolf come from?') that relate to the *material* organised by these forms and that find a definite answer in the *second* and *third* chapters. [In her critique, Akselrod/Ortodoks interprets Bogdanov as taking the position that reality is created by social communication: for example, two people communicating about a wolf. Asking 'where did the wolf come from?' implies that there is a reality of 'things' outside of experiences and communication of those experiences. (Trans.)]

3. Comrade Ortodoks inaccurately cites and distorts my thoughts. He ascribes to me the words: 'social being and social consciousness are identical in a full sense', while what I said was that they are identical *'in the precise meaning of these words'*, the meaning of which I had carefully explained before this. I pointed out there that everything that is social in *psychical terms* – i.e. in the precise usage of the terms (as accepted, for example, in psychology) – must be attributed to the realm of 'consciousness', which, as I pointed out, incidentally, is considerably broader than the realm of what is properly social. Comrade Ortodoks, himself, in another place calls this idea a 'banal and obvious truth'. And here,

But perhaps these 'minor misunderstandings' do not prevent the fundamental accusation of comrade Bel'tov and Comrade Plekhanov against the 'empiriomonists' – the accusation of eclecticism that has been pointed out – from being just. In reality, is it possible to create something integral and harmonious – something non-eclectic – from such varied combinations as Marxism, the materialism of natural sciences, energetics, empiriocriticism, the theory of universal substitution, etc.?

First and foremost, I note that our time – an era of specialisation – is also, naturally, an era of *one-sidedness*. Therefore, any attempt to work out an integral – i.e. monist – worldview must unavoidably utilise a multitude of diverse philosophical combinations that are one-sided. The only way it is possible to arrive at *monism* is to separate out the 'truth' from each of them and, with the aid of one governing principle, to harmoniously connect together the material that is thereby obtained. This is what I have tried to do. The governing principle of my work was the idea that *knowledge is social*, and I regarded knowledge as *an ideology* – which I suggest is a Marxist idea.

Consequently, the problem of the eclecticism or monism of a worldview is not resolved by pointing out the sources from which its various elements emerged, otherwise it would be necessary to accept *Karl Marx* – who combined elements of materialism, Hegelianism, socialism, bourgeois classical economics and many others that existed prior to him in a completely separate and even contradictory state – as the greatest eclectic of the nineteenth century. The problem of eclecticism or monism of a doctrine is resolved by *evidential argument*. This is exactly what comrade Bel'tov *does not provide*. He polemicises with Conrad Schlacht, with solipsists (among whom he mistakenly counts Mach), with N.G. from *Russkoe bogatstvo*, etc. None of this has any direct relationship to 'empiriomonism'. Here Bel'tov confines himself to declarations of the following sort:

> substituting one word, he then ascribes to me the point of view that 'being is a product of consciousness, i.e. of ideology'. Leaving aside the ignorant confusion of consciousness with ideology, it is absolutely clear that comrade Ortodoks himself has invented this nonsense for me.
>
> For my part, regarding all three points, I will express myself briefly and give comrade Ortodoks three useful pieces of advice:
>
> 1. 'Ignorance is not an argument'. In order to discuss philosophy, it is necessary to be familiar with the discipline. You need to study.
>
> 2. You must read what you criticise. Otherwise your critique will not attain its goal.
>
> 3. It is improper to distort the words and ideas of your opponent, even if it makes the task of refuting him extremely easy, since such a distortion will be revealed when your opponent wants to do so and has the time to do so.

'Eclectic people who love "colourful thoughts" skilfully "unite" the most contradictory theories. However, eclecticism "non est argumentum"' (*Kritika nashikh kritikov*, Preface, p. iv).

True, comrade Bel'tov, eclecticism is not an argument ... But what is also not an argument is the word 'eclecticism' as a groundless characterisation of views you are not sympathetic with. Arguments would be welcome, comrade Plekhanov!

And until you present them, it would take a truly naïve conviction in one's infallible authoritativeness to pass such verdicts as ... But forgive me, reader. I cannot deny myself the sorrowful pleasure of introducing and analysing the harsh verdict pronounced on me by comrade Bel'tov in the form of a witty comparison:

> The relationship of our 'practicals'[25] to philosophy always reminds me of the relationship of Prussian King Frederick William I to philosophy. As is well known, this wise monarch remained absolutely indifferent to the philosophical exhortations of Christian Wolf until it was explained to him that Wolf's principle of sufficient reason must cause soldiers to flee from service. Then the soldiers' king ordered the philosopher to leave Prussian soil within 24 hours or be put to death by hanging. Our practicals, of course, do not ever want to put anyone to death for their philosophical convictions. It could not be otherwise. But our 'practicals' are prepared to accept any given philosophy until it is pointed out to them that it interferes with the realisation of their immediate practical goals. Thus very recently they accepted Kantianism. Then Mr P. Struve and Mr S. Bulgakov showed them that Kantianism is not just an abstract theoretical speculation,[26] and now they are prepared to rise in revolt against the 'uniting' of Kant and Marx. But no one has brought such argumentation, for example, regarding *empiriomonism*, and our 'practicals' are prepared to accept *Machists* as *Marxists*. In time they will regret it, but then, perhaps, it may be too late ...
> 
> *Kritika nashikh kritikov*, pp. iv–v

---

25   The term *praktiki* – 'practicals' – refers to Social-Democratic Party activists who are involved in the revolutionary struggle and who tended to ignore philosophical issues [trans.].

26   In the 1890s, Petr Struve and Sergei Bulgakov were 'legal Marxists' who had attempted to found Marxism on a neo-Kantian basis but who ultimately realised that Marxism and Kantianism were incompatible and left the Social-Democratic camp. Apparently Plekhanov is suggesting here that this is what 'showed' the practicals that 'abstract speculation' can harm the movement [trans.].

Thus, here is a verdict that is harsh not only in regard to me ... Comrade 'practicals' are similar to Frederick William I. The difference – perhaps of no consequence? – consists in that they will not 'put anyone to death by hanging' for their philosophical convictions. Comforting! Comrade Bel'tov finds that they are correct in this, and this does honour to his leniency. But who in this comparison plays the role of the accused philosopher? Obviously, 'for example', I do, since later on empiriomonism is directly pointed out. Properly speaking, this is not so insulting – the role of Wolf in all his history with Frederick William was far from the worst. In comrade Bel'tov's comparison, 'empiriomonism' corresponds to the 'law of sufficient reason'. Well, this also is not insulting: if all the arguments that can be brought against my views are as just as the accusation brought against the 'law of sufficient reason', then 'empiriomonists' have nothing particular to be concerned about ... Now, who in this case fulfils the modest function of those people who 'explained to the wise monarch', etc.? According to the precise meaning of the comparison – comrade Bel'tov ...

Further, what is awaiting the offender, i.e. me? So influential a theorist as comrade Bel'tov guarantees me a direct promise not to be 'put to death by hanging'. There remains ... expulsion within 24 hours, about which he makes no reservations. Think of it, reader: expulsion beyond the borders of Marxism! ...

Irritation with the 'empiriomonists' started so long ago for comrade Bel'tov that he not only forgets to present argumentation in support of his severe sentence but also makes obvious errors against the technical principles of the art of polemics that he knows so well ...

But enough of this tragicomic incident. Speaking briefly and clearly, I do not recognise either comrade Bel'tov or anyone else to be a competent discretionary authority to judge the problem of the eclecticism or monism of my views. I recognise comrade Bel'tov even less than anyone else, since I have had the honour, through the analysis of his views, to show that in actuality eclecticism is not so alien and odious to him, personally, as he seems to think.[27] Would you not care to present arguments, comrade Bel'tov!

I, however, have no doubt whatever that from the point of view of *monists of the future* sufficient dissonances and 'eclectic' combinations will be found in

---

27   In this sense, it is possible to encounter surprising oversights on the part of comrade Bel'tov, such as the remark (on page 152 of the book *On the Question of the Development of a Monistic View* ...) that the psychology of workers 'will adapt itself to future relations of production'. If this is not, as I suggest, simply an oversight, then this is a crude deviation toward *historical idealism* ('future relations' in the present can exist only *ideally* and at the same time they suddenly turn out to be a really-determining force for the development of proletarian psychology).

my views. The measure of eclecticism and monism is historically relative, and as humanity develops, so the rigorousness of demands for monism will grow ... But I am concerned with the *present*, and I have no pretensions at all of establishing 'objective truth' or such supra-historical, objective monism for all times.

I know how difficult the task is that I have taken on myself; I know how short the ten-year span of my life has been that I have dedicated to it. But it is impossible for me to shirk it, and I have never seen anything personal in this task that life has set for me. I gladly meet any critique within the surroundings of the movement that I am a part of, as long as it is a *critique* and as long as it contributes material for the elucidation of the truth. If the result is that the truth is elucidated even at the cost of the destruction of my ideas, I will gladly welcome what will be a new truth for me ...

30 April 1906, Kresty Prison

CHAPTER 8

# Social Selection (Foundations of the Method)

I

The term 'social selection' can easily summon up false comparisons and preconceptions: it is reminiscent of the theories of sociologist-Darwinists that science long ago outlived, of the eclectic 'socio-biological' endeavours of F.A. Lange, E. Ferri, L. Woltmann,[1] and many others, and of old, half-forgotten meanderings of socio-scientific thought. My task is not at all to resurrect these dead ideas or to correct them. The very concept of 'social selection' in our investigation has a different meaning and different content.

In my previous works, I have already pointed out more than once that the concept of 'selection' in the case of the study of the processes of life and development cannot and must not be connected only with the conception of *individual* organisms, of their reproduction and competition, of their individual death or preservation. 'Selection' only becomes completely appropriate for investigating any living phenomena whatever – in all realms of life – when it expresses *biological causality in general*. In this most general form, the law of 'selection' boils down to this proposition: forms that are adapted to their environment are preserved and forms that are not adapted are destroyed, or, employing a more precise and scientific formula, the preservation and destruction of living forms is strictly determined by their environment.[2]

All living complexes and all living combinations are subject to this principle. This applies to the preservation or death of a specific *species* in its geograph-

---

1 Friedrich A. Lange (1828–75) was a German philosopher and sociologist. Enrico Ferri (1856–1929) was an Italian criminologist. Ludwig Woltmann (1871–1907) was a German anthropologist. Lange developed what he called 'socialist Darwinism', while the latter two propounded varieties of social Darwinism [trans.].
2 The first of these two expressions can easily be taken as a simple tautology. After all, the very 'fitness' or 'unfitness' of living forms boils down precisely to the fact of whether they are preserved or destroyed. 'Fit forms are preserved' – this, consequently, is the same thing as 'preserved forms are preserved' ... The second expression directly indicates the essence of the matter – the role of the environment in the preservation or destruction of life. This expression is free of tautology and directly indicates the path of biological investigation; the *causes* of the preservation or destruction of life must be found in its environment. This, by the way, excludes *absolute internal causality* of life ('vitalistic' causality) that is not reducible to external causes.

ical environment, of a specific *organism* in its access to the means of life and its struggle with enemies, and of a specific *cell* (or group of cells) of an organism in its environment (presented first and foremost by the internal relationships of this organism). And this principle also applies to the preservation or disappearance of a specific *reflex* in a general system of vital functions of an organism, of a specific *association of conceptions* in an associative-psychical environment, etc. The 'unit' of selection is not at all only what is called an 'individual' in the narrow meaning of the word but rather *any vital unity*.

As far as the selection of social forms is concerned, such selection does not at all boil down to the preservation or perishing of the human individuals of which society is composed. The 'unit' of selection in this case can, of course, be an individual, but it can also be a social group, a class, or some kind of a technological technique, a word, an idea, a norm, etc. Any social norm – moral or legal, for example – does not have separate physical existence; it presents a system of psychical groupings in a large number of human individuals belonging to a given society. But this does not in the least prevent it, on the one hand, from forming a specific vital unity – a 'social form' – or, on the other hand, from being 'adapted' or 'unadapted' to its environment. A social norm is subject to positive or negative 'selection' – i.e. to preservation (or development) in the first case or destruction in the second – and this does not at all occur only through the survival or the early death of the individuals in which it is embodied. It can strengthen, weaken, or disappear even when all the individuals who bear it survive. The psychical world of these individuals is the essential part of that environment on which the fate of a given form depends, and its contradiction with this psychical world – with the system of 'experience' of these people – leads for the most part to the death only of the norm itself, and the people in whom it lived continue to exist without it (or they preserve certain remnants of it in the form, for example, of 'recollection' of it).

The same applies to any technological technique that people apply to their work, to any word that they use in mutual communication, to any idea that serves to unify their experience, etc. Because these social forms are 'supra-individual', their paths of 'selection' are different and are not limited to the reproduction or death of individuals. 'Imitation' plays a huge role in the mechanism of positive selection of these forms, and various forms of 'struggle' between people play a huge role in the mechanism of negative selection (and, by the way, also of positive selection, at least indirectly, by removing elements of the social environment that are unfavourable to one or another form).

Even such social forms as a 'social group' or 'class' that are *apparently* made up of a multitude of individual people can be subject to selection in one direction or another independently of the life or death of the individuals of which it is composed. For example, the 'destruction of the petty bourgeoisie' occurs not at all only through the eradication and extinction of all members of the 'petty bourgeoisie' and perhaps even less by this route. The petty bourgeois who 'perish' often still live for a long time after they 'perish' in the form of members of the lumpenproletariat or the working proletariat, and they sometimes find their new existence more pleasant than before. The fact of the matter is that a 'social group' and 'class' represent not so much a totality of individuals as a *system of relationships among people*, and these relationships exist, it goes without saying, not in the air and not in scientific abstractions but are embodied in definite, mutually connected, psychophysiological adaptations of people. This system of relationships can be destroyed and the corresponding adaptations of people can atrophy, and then the 'class' disappears, even though the people who made it up continue to live.

The 'selection' of social forms is dependent on their *entire* environment, both social and extra-social (social nature and external nature). But the influence of the extra-social environment is extremely slow in comparison with the speed of the development of social processes and is transformed at almost a constant magnitude – this is the 'natural selection' that needs tens and hundreds of thousands of years to produce any significant change in living forms. Social development, however, passes through major stages in centuries and even in decades, and such speed of selection depends, obviously, on *another* part of the environment, on social nature. In the first societies, where the social environment was comparatively insignificant, its role in human development was also insignificant, and the speed of development could hardly be distinguished from 'natural selection'. The colossal growth in the speed of progress, which has occurred since that time, belongs properly to 'social selection' – i.e. selection of social forms *by the action of their social environment*. This social selection will be the main subject of my investigation.³

Due to its extremely *general* and consequently also *abstract* nature, the model of 'social selection' needs further analysis and a certain concrete instan-

---

3  I do not touch here on the question of the 'variability' of forms that provide the material for any selection, because all that it is possible to say in the confines of its most general definition boils down to one point: 'variability' is identical with 'causality', in general, and is considerably broader than specifically biological causation – the selection of forms that can, if desired, be viewed as a particular case of the 'change' of those forms in one direction or the other. In the final analysis, consistent with the idea of causality, the starting point of any change of forms always lies in their environment, and the task of more concrete investigation is to explain both the particular regularity in the change of forms due to their environment and also the regularity in the selection of changes. Some of these particular regularities will come up further on in this presentation.

tiation in order to apply it successfully. I will now turn to this, except, however, I must call the attention of the reader in advance to the fact that the task I have set for myself here is not a *systematic application* of the method in question to socio-scientific investigation but only the *clarification of the method itself*. I will touch on concrete historical issues only in order to illustrate this method.[4]

II

Society constitutes not a mechanical grouping of elements but a living *system* whose parts are situated in an organic interconnectedness among themselves. Each social form that appears as one of these parts is, in its turn, made up of a large number of elements that are organically interconnected among themselves but also possess a certain living independence. There is neither absolute unity nor absolute separateness. Each 'unit of selection' has only a *relative* nature. And very important consequences for an understanding of the processes of selection ensue from this.

When sociologists who have a poor knowledge of biology – and even some biologists – present the idea of 'natural selection' too simplistically and try to apply it to the life of society, they usually arrive at a conclusion that is highly deplorable from a philosophical point of view. They say that the law of selection in social life is 'subject to considerable limitations', 'allows many exceptions', and that its action is often 'distorted'. Philosophers cannot construct their worldview like Latin grammar; scientific laws have the right to be called laws only when they *have no exceptions*. If the principle of selection is really a biological law – a formula that is useful for investigating and understanding the *processes of life in general* – then it cannot 'be subject to limitation' and be 'distorted' in the sphere of processes of social life that is also *life*. Either a 'law' expresses a *constant tendency* of the entire cycle of phenomena that it embraces or it is not a 'law', but a temporary empirical generalisation, that poses to cognition the task of 'explanation' by seeking real laws.

In reality, the law of selection has no exceptions in the social realm, just as it has none in other realms of life. Seeming exceptions result when the mat-

---

4 Several times I have already found it necessary to write in greater detail than here about the principle of 'selection' in its more general and more particular applications ('natural selection', 'psychical selection', 'social selection'). I wrote about it for the first time in my youthful work, *Osnovnye elementy istoricheskogo vzgliada na prirodu*, then in the book *Poznanie s istoricheskoi tochki zreniia*, and then in Chapter 5, 'Psychical Selection', in the present volume. I will therefore attempt to repeat myself here as little as possible and will dwell only on what has the closest and most immediate relationship to the task of this work.

# SOCIAL SELECTION (FOUNDATIONS OF THE METHOD) 307

ter is examined from a perspective that treats an individual organism for the most part as an *absolute unit of selection*. It is necessary to keep in mind that units of selection are *relative* and that they are mutually connected within more complicated complexes. Then we obtain the concept of 'system selection' that is very important for our analysis. In order to explain it, let us examine a few seeming 'exceptions' to the law of selection.

'In social life it is often not the most adapted but the least adapted – dull-witted and puny folk who have the good luck to possess capital – who survive'. 'Medicine facilitates the preservation of organisms with the least viability and supports the existence of pitiful, sick people'. 'War perverts the action of selection, destroying the most healthy and strong organisms – the best youth of the country – while the worst elements who are not suitable for military service, continue to live, far from the theatre of fighting'. Etc.

At first glance it already becomes clear that in regard to the formulation of the law *that we have adopted* all these cases are not 'exceptions' at all. If weak and puny parasite-rentiers survive, while at the same time strong, richly-gifted proletarians die, this is not because the first *are really* adapted to their environment while the second are not. The parasites' relations to other people and to their labour – the relationships of 'capital' – create a special, exceptionally favourable environment to which they are completely sufficiently adapted, while for the proletarians the social environment is absolutely different and in this case their powerful organisation cannot adapt to it. In exactly the same way, a special environment – the significant parts of which are medical technology and nursing care – is created for the ill person. The environment is exceptionally unfavourable for soldiers, containing as it does conditions of insufficient food, uncomfortable shelter, and powerful mechanical effects in the form of bullets, shrapnel, etc.

But it is obvious that if we are satisfied that this formula, due to its great generality, does indeed include the given cases, then we would not move forward by even one step. We achieve a rather new point of view if we consider the 'adaptedness' or 'unadaptedness' of the individuals in these cases not as completely separate living units but in their connection with other living units as elements of a more complex 'system'. Then the matter presents itself in the following form.

If the given parasite-rentiers – dull-witted and vacuous people who do no work – are placed in the *average* conditions of the social and extra-social environment, then one can confidently expect to see the profound unadaptedness and death of their organisms. But due to their connection with the broader living whole and due to their specific position in a specific system that is highly favourable for their viability (in this case, for example, in the economic grouping known as a capitalist enterprise), they survive along with that system *on account* of the system's viability. This is positive selection *according to interconnectedness*. The fate of the soldier can serve as an example of negative selection according to interconnectedness. The hundreds of thousands of Russian peasants who died in the war with Japan[5] would, in the usual conditions of the process of social labour, have possessed sufficient adaptedness to live through middle age and leave descendants. But by virtue of their connection with the complex social organisation of the 'bureaucratic-state mechanism' ('bureaucracy' being part of the broad social apparatus), they perished. As peripheral elements of that mechanism, as 'working tools' of that machine, they were subject – earlier than the other parts of the mechanism – to the destructive influences of the present world environment in which this apparatus, as a whole, is absolutely unviable.

Selection according to interconnectedness or 'systemic' selection is important for understanding not only social phenomena but also a huge amount of other biological phenomena, and the 'psychical selection' that elucidates all processes of psychical development directly presents a particular case of systemic selection. The preservation of rudimentary organs without an organic function – that is, conditions that should cause cells to atrophy and die – is entirely explained by the systemic relationship of these elements to the viable whole – to the organism. The development of so called 'accompanying changes' – changes that are not vitally useful in themselves or even harmful for the living system but that inevitably appear together with other useful changes – are also a result of positive selection according to interconnectedness. In 'colonial' organisms the role of systemic selection naturally must turn out to predominate. The separate differentiated individuals of any siphonophore can live for a long time despite significant weakness if the colony as a whole is healthy and well nourished, and, on the contrary, individuals that are highly viable in themselves die prematurely if the colony as a whole is weak and undernourished. The same holds in regard to the forming elements of all complex organisms that must be considered as essentially a colony of cells. In the realm of psychical selection, it happens that the same 'desire' – the same 'form' – is subject sometimes to positive selection (expressed in the feeling of pleasure) and sometimes to negative selection (expressed in the feeling of pain) depending on what associative connection appears in the field of consciousness. When combined with some psychical complexes, a given complex obtains a 'pleasant' colouration that leads to its consolidation in psychical life,

---

5   The Russo-Japanese War, 1904–05 [trans.].

and, when combined with others, it obtains an 'unpleasant' colouration that signifies a tendency for it to be weakened and removed from the psychical system.[6]

It is obvious that in the sphere of social life the wider and deeper that social interconnectedness becomes, the more significant the role of 'systemic selection' must be. 'Systemic social selection' has much more important significance for understanding the life of contemporary cultured society with its huge dimensions and endless complexity of relationships than it does for understanding the life of small primitive societies with simple internal relationships, although even there systemic selection must be kept in mind.

For now I will limit myself to one illustration. In studying the history of past centuries, it is easy to see that eras of economic prosperity are unfavourable in the highest degree for any kind of substantive reforms in governing or legal organisations. In times of prosperity, forms that are obviously obsolete, that obviously contradict the general level of development of the collective and hinder its development and that do not have vitally important significance even for the most powerful classes of society continue to be stubbornly preserved and do not cause wide, active protest and energetic struggle even from the most progressive classes. In such a case, the mood of society as a whole is characterised by some kind of elemental conservatism of political and juridical norms. This continues until a crisis occurs. In the course of the crisis, this mood quickly disappears and reforms burst upon the scene. If the outmoded forms have a broad and general nature (for example, the entire political structure) and are connected with the interests of sufficiently wealthy groups of society, then, in the era of crisis, partial reforms are followed by revolution – precisely when society has already begun to recover from the economic crisis. From the point of view of systemic selection all this consists in the following form. As long as *positive* selection governs the life of society and as long as the vital capacity of the entire system grows, the decrepit forms are preserved due to their interconnectedness with the whole, *on account*, of course, of the system's vital capacity. But when this latter begins rapidly to decline, as happens during crises of production that represent a particular, acute illness of society (and also sometimes during 'military' crises, and so on), then various parts of the social system are not destroyed to the same degree but corresponding to their, so to say, individual vital capacity. The decrepit and parasitic forms turn out, naturally, to be the weakest and least capable of resisting the destructive influ-

---

6  Everything related to the selection of psychical forms is discussed in detail in Chapter 5, 'Psychical selection', in the present volume.

ences. However, if an energetic reaction of the whole social system – 'struggle' against what is obsolete and the creation of new forms to replace it – is needed in order to conclusively destroy and exterminate these decrepit and parasitic forms, then the lowered energy of society (i.e. of its progressive and vital elements) can be insufficient for such a task. In this case, the 'revolution' breaks out *only after* the crisis, in the phase of a new increase of energy of society – an increase that is now transmitted in the least degree to the parasitically decrepit elements and in the highest degree to the vital and progressive elements that are less exhausted by the storm they have been through.[7]

But another outcome is possible. If the decrepit and dying forms are too tightly interwoven with all the other contents of the social process, and too strongly preserved in it, then the action of systemic selection that occurs during the crisis can turn out to be fatal for the entire system. Everything in it that is viable, uncompromising, and fit can perish or degrade *due to its interconnectedness* with unfit, vitally useless combinations. This is what happened, for example, with Spain in the seventeenth to eighteenth centuries, in which, during a long period of economic prosperity, the moribund feudal-Catholic elements became too strongly entrenched in the living fabric of the productive organism. Then, when the favourable environment for the entire system was exhausted and when it became no longer possible to exploit America by plundering it and to exploit Europe by means of American gold and silver, then the old vampire did not itself die of starvation but sucked all the blood from the living body of the Spanish nation and brought it to an extreme level of degradation. This was the result of systemic selection. The same thing would have happened in contemporary Russia if it had turned out that the mechanism of the old bureaucracy has grown too deeply into its fabric. The result of social selection, in general, far from always appears as *progress*.

III

Social selection is not characterised by any specific, concrete manifestations that would distinguish it from other aspects of selection. The processes of social selection proceed in the form of the usual physiological and psychological facts of preservation or growth, on the one hand, and decline or destruction, on the other. Death from disease or the physiological growth of an organism have exact analogues in social selection. A norm can perish as the result of being

---

7 Bogdanov clearly has in mind the Revolution of 1905, which he did not think was complete. In 1906, he was looking forward to a new socialist revolutionary upsurge [trans.].

displaced by another, or ideas can spread widely as a result of social communication among people. Statisticians and anthropologists can adequately explain the extent to which illness and mortality of people as well as the possibility of their good or bad physical development is determined by their social environment and their position in the system of production and distribution, and the fate of *ideas* or *norms* depends in exactly the same way on their relationship to the social environment, even though the manifestation of their adaptedness or unadaptedness would be far from so sharp and clear as when the fate of *people* is at issue.

The human psyche is, in any event, the basic implement of social development, and 'psychical selection' therefore presents the main form of the embodiment of 'social selection' – the most constant and usual form. The development of each psychical individual – of which all of society is composed – is accomplished through psychical selection, and even the most *specifically social* processes – such as 'imitative behaviour' and 'communication' and 'social collaboration' among people – are realised by means of psychical selection that proceeds in separate psyches. When a psychical organism acts as a part of a social whole, it does not cease at that time to be a psychical organism and does not cease to be subject to all psychological laws. One or another form of social collaboration presupposes the mastery of his special role in the complex of collective labour by each person taking part in it. This mastery is a *psychical* change in the given individual, and it is produced by psychical selection. The social origin of the material that underlies the action of psychical selection in this case does not change the fact that it is psychical, just as the social meaning of the psychical adaptation that is produced also does not change its psychical nature. From the point of view of origin and vital significance, the individual, with all its psychical content, is after all also a *social form* ...

The role of psychical selection as an implement of social selection is not only huge in all phases of the development of humanity, it is also one that grows along with the course of social progress. For example, in primitive societies the role of psychical selection is significantly less than in contemporary societies. In the former, due to the dominance of the elemental conservatism of the psyche, the crude selection of individuals that is directly expressed in the death and reproduction of individuals is comparatively more significant.

In general, social selection should be considered not only as a particular aspect of 'natural selection' (considering, of course, *every* process of selection to be 'natural'), but also the *most particular* aspect of selection. It does not have manifestations that are specific to it and are unique to it; each of its cases relate at the same time to some more general form of selection. This, it goes without saying, does not at all diminish its fundamental, decisive significance for human life and cognition.

IV

If social selection represents a particular *social* form of causality, like general selection expresses a specifically biological causality, then the question naturally arises of how the principle of social selection relates to the law of causality in its broadest and most universal meaning, i.e. in the present state of knowledge, to the law of *conservation and transformation of energy*.

At first glance the application of the idea of 'energy' to social processes might seem completely hopeless and pointless. One cannot speak of any kind of exact measurement of energy here, and we cannot even completely establish the specific form of energy that is characteristic of social life. More accurately, we have every reason to assume that the most varied forms of physical and chemical energy enter into social phenomena.[8] And if energetics were cognitively useful only where it is altogether possible to attain a *direct* and *exact* application of energetics on the basis of *immediate* measurements, then, with present methods of social observation and experience, it would of course be pointless to try to use the idea of energy in the sphere of social science. But *indirect* and *approximate* applications of energetics are possible. Such applications exist and have great significance even in the realms of physics and chemistry, where, after all, direct and accurate measurement is also not always possible. Applications of energetics have even greater significance in the realm of physiology, and in studies of psychical selection we have seen that in principle they can be useful for psychology. Therefore, the attempt to also utilise energetics in socio-scientific investigation is also completely appropriate.

All applications of energetics of this kind have a predominantly *deductive* nature, and, it goes without saying, this is especially so where one deals with the most complex phenomena that we know of – social phenomena. But comparison of the conclusions one arrives at with the data of direct observation

---

8  I am not speaking here about the energy of *psychical processes* that undoubtedly are part of social processes because, consistent with what I have explained previously (Section VIII of Chapter 1 and Section II of Chapter 5 in the present volume), psychical phenomena present *the same* sum of energy that is presented by the physiological phenomena that correspond to them. The difference is only in the means of perception (more direct or more indirect), but the means of perception does not change the quantitative relationships of energy.

always can and must serve as a sufficient verification of the validity of one's deductions and the basic premises from which those deductions proceed.

In considering an entire given social form as an energetical complex – as a certain sum of energy in a qualitatively specific combination – the basic connection between energetics and social selection can be formulated in the following manner:

*Every act of social selection represents the growth or diminishment of energy of the social complex to which it relates. In the first case we see 'positive selection', and in the second case we see 'negative selection'.*

The case of a complete energetical equilibrium is, it goes without saying, only an ideal combination, a product of abstract thought. This is a case of the 'absolute conservation of a system' that Avenarius mistakenly identified as one of the ideal norms of life and a point of view that he, himself, also departed from when he analysed social combinations. Such an equilibrium would essentially be the 'absence of selection', and in the complex environment of life in which resistances inevitably grow, the equilibrium would transform into negative selection – into the degradation of living forms.[9]

Leaving the fiction of absolute equilibrium to one side, it is possible to subject the general formula to doubt in another sense. First, is it possible to speak specifically about the growth and diminishment of energy of one or another social form when in the majority of cases we cannot even distinguish it in space as an individual complex, and, second, is there sufficient reason to be confident that every case in which energy increases corresponds precisely to positive selection (i.e. the elevation of vital capacity) or that every case in which energy decreases corresponds to negative selection (i.e. the lowering of vital capacity)? Both objections issue from the most valid and obligatory demands of scientific thought, which prefers to leave the question open rather than be satisfied with an arbitrary answer.

The first objection is easily disposed of. Because a 'social' form represents a specific coordination of psychophysiological complexes belonging to separate organisms, it is *entirely* decomposable into those psychophysiological com-

---

9   This growth of resistances of the external surroundings proceeds from the fact that in order to survive a form of life *exhausts* the 'means of life' that it finds in the external surroundings. And even if the sum of these means turns out to be relatively unlimited (as, for example, the sum of sunlight, carbon dioxide, and water for plants in the atmosphere and soil), then, all the same, the general development and growth of life in the surrounding environment would lead to the displacement and death of a form that *only* was preserved but did not develop (for example, other plants growing around it that would deprive it of sunlight by their shade and of water by their roots, etc.).

plexes, and it does not include anything that entered when those complexes came together. Therefore, a social form is energetically the same as psychophysiological complexes it is composed of. And the concepts of growth and diminishment of energy are undoubtedly applicable to those complexes. They apply to their 'physiological' aspect because a social form is entirely made up of physical and chemical processes, and they apply to their 'psychological' aspect because a social form is *identical* to the 'physiological' aspect from the point of view of energetics – being distinguished only by the means by which it is perceived. In practice, in a great many cases, it is impossible to spatially isolate – in the sense of anatomy and histology – even physiological complexes that have a completely definite significance for life. An example is the difficulties and failures of theories of the localisation of neural centres. This, however, does not lead contemporary researchers to deny the applicability of energetical ideas to all realms of physiology. Obviously the same must apply also to social complexes.

The problem regarding the connection between positive social selection and the elevation of the sum of energy that is presented by one or another social form and the connection of negative selection with the decrease of energy is somewhat more complex. But it is easy to apply an argument here that is just the same as the one I applied regarding the problem of positive and negative vital-differentials.[10]

Any living complex, no matter what its specific 'form', represents a dynamic equilibrium – approximate, it goes without saying – of two opposed energetical processes: the assimilation of energy from the surrounding environment and disassimilation – 'acquisition' and 'expenditure'. Assimilation is the transfer of energy of the external environment in those aspects and combinations that are characteristic of the given living form. Assimilation expresses the *power* of life over dead nature, the *victory* of organisation over unorganisedness. Disassimilation is the transfer of energy of a living complex to lower forms and combinations that are characteristic of the unorganised environment. Disassimilation is the *price* that is paid for this power and this victory. Life *overcomes the resistance* of the external environment, and it is for this that energy is expended. If the sum of the energy that is embodied in a living form grows, then the possibility also grows of expending energy and overcoming the resistance of the external environment: 'vital capacity' grows. This relates to each of the elements that make up a 'social form', and it consequently also relates to the social

---

10  See Part I of Section 1, 'Psychoenergetics' in Chapter 2, 'Life and the Psyche' in the present volume.

form as a whole. Just the opposite, the lowering of energy signifies great weakness in regard to the resistances of the external environment and the lowering of 'vital capacity'.

It remains to be pointed out that in all this the matter has to do only with the *immediate* elevation or decrease of vital-capacity and the degree of vital-capacity *at a given moment*. Any growth or diminishment of energy of a living complex necessarily changes its emerging equilibrium – the relationship of its parts with one another and with the external environment. This change can have absolutely new results in the future that are different from the changes of the beginning phase. The temporary growth of energy can be connected with such a disadvantageous transformation of internal relationships of forms that it leads to a considerably greater lowering of energy later – even to death. A temporary decrease of energy might indirectly have the opposite results. It is precisely social life that provides the clearest examples of such 'oscillations of selection'. It is unquestionable that the rapid growth of the productive forces of capitalistic society means an increase of energy of the social whole; but the disharmonious nature of this process leads to its undergoing a 'crisis' – a huge waste of productive forces and a sharp decrease in energy. 'Positive selection' is replaced by 'negative selection'. In the course of the crisis, on the other hand, because the weaker or disproportionally developed elements of the social system perish, healthier interrelationships of its parts are established, the possibility of new development is created, and there is a still more significant growth of energy than before. 'Negative selection' is replaced by 'positive selection'. In this sense, a bloody, agonising revolution, an unfortunate war, etc. very frequently turn out to be analogous to crises of production.

All of this does not in the least change, first, the *immediate* living significance of energetical 'pluses' and 'minuses' for the social complex, and, second, their *ultimate and general* significance (if one keeps in mind the great number of cases of selection). The immediate energetical significance of the process of selection is important for the analysis of social development in the very same sense in which infinitely small differences are important for mathematical analysis in general; in order to understand the process as a whole, it is necessary to trace its trend in its elements. The ultimate and general (aggregate) meaning of the processes of selection for a certain period corresponds to their energetical integral. The preponderance of immediate elementary 'pluses' over 'minuses' will also yield a 'plus' in the final sum – in the integral of life. The preponderance of elementary minuses will also yield a 'minus' in the final sum.[11]

This is the basic correlation of social selection with energetics.

---

11   I must note that the application of terms of mathematical analysis here is not at all a

V

The contrast of energetical meaning of the positive and negative selection of social forms corresponds to the fundamental difference between the two *tendencies of development* that cause them both. This difference is perfectly analogous to what is observed in the realm of psychical selection. However, the greater complexity and breadth of social phenomena also give both tendencies of social selection completely distinctive characteristics.

The social process always includes in its huge profusion of content a great many carry-overs from the past and germs of the future. Even after the conditions that brought one or another form into life have disappeared from the social environment, the form continues to be preserved, sometimes for a very long time, due to its 'systemic' interconnectedness with a large number of other adaptations that have not yet become outmoded. When a new combination of conditions of the social environment is created that needs a new social adaptation, it is not created quickly, by any means, and sometimes very slowly, due to inner resistances of the social process. Depending on the facts of the matter, the degree of harmoniousness and orderliness of the social whole – the degree of its organic unity – can turn out to be extremely different.

It is precisely here that the basic difference between the tendencies of positive and negative social selection is revealed.

Imagine a vast social complex that includes a multitude of varied social adaptations. Some are completely developed, some are obsolete, and some are undeveloped. This could be, for example, a whole society or a whole social class or a whole ideological realm of the life of a specific class, and so on. Imagine that this complex is at a phase of 'positive selection', i.e. its sum of energy is generally growing. Of course its growth is usually the result of a high adaptedness of only certain parts of the complex, but due to its vital unity – due to the systemic interconnectedness of its parts – this elevation of energy extends to the other parts. Energy is, so to speak, 'allocated' in the complex like a living whole. Only *to the extent* that such an energetical 'allocation' occurs in the social complex and that the social complex represents one whole from the point of view of positive selection, *to that extent* it also forms a 'general field' for the distinctive tendency of positive selection that we must find.

---

simple 'analogy'. The laws of mathematical analysis are applicable wherever there are 'magnitudes', and if it is *very difficult* to measure the processes of life in the great majority of cases, this still does not mean that one can deny that their magnitudes are capable, in principle, of being measured.

I will begin by elucidating this 'to the extent that', which is blocking the path of my analysis.

Social complexes can have very different forms and content, but a trait they usually have in common is the *absence of spatial continuity*. The human organism appears as the bearer of social life, and the elements of one or another social form usually enter the composition of various human individuals as their psychophysiological adaptations or they directly coincide with these individuals. Despite all its living unity, a social complex – whether it is a 'technological adaptation', a 'norm', an 'idea', a 'class', or a 'group' – is spatially scattered and disconnected.[12]

Given the limits of the contemporary state of science, we must assume that the immediate transmission of the elevation or lowering of energy from some parts of a social complex to others only occurs when spatial continuity *exists* – where elements that undergo the given change in energy are consequently located in a physiological connection with other elements that belong, along with them, *to one organism*. Where there is no *such* connection, we cannot, generally speaking, assume the possibility of direct 'allocation' of energy among parts of the complex – from some of them to others. In order not to cause misunderstandings, I will explain both cases with examples.

Let us suppose that we are dealing with a specific class in society that plays a specific technological role in the system of production, that occupies a specific place in the economic structure of society, and that has a specific ideology. This class represents a complicated social complex made up of a multitude of individual people who, unlike the tissue of an organism, are not connected in spatial continuity. But *in the confines* of each individual, all elements of class life *are* united by such a continuity; the technological, economic, and ideological adaptations that are present in a given individual are connected by the physiological wholeness of the organism.[13] Now let us suppose that certain parts of the complex-class undergoes 'positive selection' – the growth of energy.

---

12  In order to be precise, I note that this *is not a universal and necessary trait* of social complexes. Taken from the aspect of their social origin and their historical role, human individuals *are also social forms*, and spatial continuity is present in this aspect. In exactly the same way, we can also consider a certain part of the psychophysiological individual to be a 'social complex' – the part that appears as an element of a broader social complex, for example, the system of ideological elements of a separate mind that belongs to the 'ideology' of a group or class. A person is *a social being* to a much greater degree than is usually thought and remarked on.

13  I intentionally speak here only of the 'physiological' aspect of phenomena, because I have already acknowledged that their 'psychical' side is distinguished from the 'physiological' side only by the means of perception, and, from the point of view of energetics and selec-

If these parts are only a few of the individuals who make up the class, then we do not have any basis to expect that 'positive selection' has also been directly spread to the other members of the class, i.e. that they experience this elevation of energy – the growth in the sum of energy that is embodied in them. If there are no special conditions, then the class as a whole is not the object of positive selection.

But let us suppose another case in which it is not separate individuals who undergo immediate 'positive selection' but a whole specific realm of class life, elements of which exist in the psychophysical organisation of each of the members of the class. For example, suppose that in the realm of the 'technological' life of the class – of its 'productive labour' – conditions arise that are favourable for the life of the class that elevate the sum of its energy (the shortening of the working day, the application of instruments that make work easier, etc.). An immediate growth of energy then occurs in the sphere of technological adaptations of the given class. But in the human individual these adaptations are connected with a large number of others – so called 'economic' and 'ideological' adaptations – and are connected by the concrete psychophysiological unity of life. Because of this connection, we must acknowledge that 'positive selection' in each member of the class spreads from some elements of the member's organisation to others, from technological elements to specifically 'economic' and 'ideological' elements, and, to a certain degree, the existent growth of energy *is spread* among them. The class as a whole is now the object of 'positive selection'.[14]

Now we can return to the basic line of our analysis. Imagine a complicated social complex that is subject to the action of positive selection, and this action, found in certain separate parts of the complex, also crosses over to the remaining ones. In what direction will the general change of the complex occur?

First and foremost, one should expect that the content of the complex will *become richer*. The developing combinations will appear with great force and completeness, and the combinations that are just now born develop and take their place in the general interconnectedness of the whole. These and other combinations, becoming vitally stronger, turn out to be greater than before, and

---

tion, the 'psychical' and 'physiological' aspects are identical. Thus, we can always take the one of them that is most convenient for us as the basis for our investigation.

14  I direct the reader's attention to the fact that the conditions I have indicated relate only to the *immediate and direct* spreading of selection from some parts of a social complex to others. And in this case the spreading is inevitable only in the event of sufficient force of selection (growth or reduction of energy) and in the event of sufficient vital coherence of the organisms. This does not deny the possibility of the *indirect* spreading of processes of selection the 'spatial continuity' that I have been discussing is not present.

the influence on the life of the remaining elements of the whole also causes new changes in them, in part becoming germs for further development, etc. Here, as in all processes of life, quantitative progress transforms into qualitative complexification. A simple, so to say geometrically-proportional magnification of the complex is impossible. Any given form of life is the expression of a specific equilibrium of that form. In leaving that equilibrium, life changes its 'form', and the more complexly it changes the more complicated it becomes in this change (as long as the change has a creative and not a destructive nature, which is exactly what positive selection is).

But positive selection has another aspect. In preserving, strengthening, and developing *everything* that turns up in the sphere of its action, positive selection simultaneously preserves and strengthens *too much*; it simultaneously develops *too much that is heterogeneous*. In any social complex, as in any complex form of life, there are elements of various formations of life. There are remnants of past conditions, developed adaptations that fully correspond to past conditions, and, finally, embryonic combinations that are due to develop in the future. In general there can never be full harmony among these three formations. In particular, the remnants of the past can even easily turn out to be direct vital contradictions of the remaining elements of the complex that destroy its wholeness and reduce its stability in regard to the influences of the hostile forces of nature. Meanwhile, positive selection not only supports but temporarily even intensifies these outmoded elements of the complex, while also developing all the remaining ones at the same time. This obviously leads to the growth of internal heterogeneousness of the whole complex and the strengthening of internal contradictions in its structure, but the vital contradiction is manifested only when the action of positive selection ceases. In its very essence, positive selection does not allow the vital incompatibility of those or other forms to be revealed because, by supporting and increasing them at the same time, it makes them vitally compatible as long as it lasts. The contradiction can really appear only in the form of a reciprocal – partial or complete – destruction of complexes, i.e. it must necessarily be in the form of negative selection. In this way, positive selection creates and increases *hidden contradictions*.

Thus, the influence of positive selection in the process of the development of social forms is characterised by two general tendencies: the growth of living content and, at the same time, the growth of its hidden contradictions.

English trade unionism in the era of England's domination of the world market can serve as an illustration of this. The part of the English working class that united in trade unions represented a special social group – a group of skilled labour with comparatively high pay and limited competition until the market for production broadened. If we do not consider individual vacillations of the market (especially in periods of sharp crises), this group lived in exceptionally favourable economic conditions and was able to elevate its standard of living quite rapidly. It unquestionably found itself predominantly subject to the action of positive selection. But at the same time as the duties, the sum of technological experience and professional skill, and the quantity of knowledge and mental development rapidly grew in this group, its ideology preserved with stubborn and striking conservatism a large number of remnants that did not correspond either to the general tendencies of the class or to the level of culture they had attained – that is, the ideology of moderate political liberalism, Manchester-school economics, Anglican religiosity, petty bourgeois morality, etc. This peculiar living eclecticism was retained over decades, but it inevitably had to come to an end when the exceptional conditions that had provided the predominance of positive selection in the life of that group for such a long time disappeared. To the extent that England's monopoly on the world market disappeared in the face of growing competition on the part of young capitalist countries, the position of English skilled workers worsened, unemployment among them increased, their pay was subjected to ever greater pressure from entrepreneurs who were forced to do so, and ever greater negative selection appeared on the scene. The contradiction between the progressive and conservative elements of the proletariat's trade-union psychology that had previously been concealed then really began to be revealed. At this point, the ideological anachronisms turned out to be obviously incompatible with the needs of life and the development of the social group, and they began to be rapidly destroyed.

VI

The role of negative selection in social development is altogether the opposite of the role of positive selection and can be formulated in this way: the narrowing of the field of life along with the removal of its contradictions and the 'harmonisation' of it.

The first is self-evident. Negative selection is a destructive process. In energetical terms, it boils down to a decrease of the energy of the complexes it affects; if negative selection does not destroy the whole then it always diminishes the sum of its elements and its vital manifestations. This is the purely 'negative' side of its work.

The 'positive' side of negative selection is that it utterly destroys what has the least vital capacity and what is most contradictory. Negative selection, as we have seen, reveals hidden contradictions of life, and it achieves this by *intensi-*

*fying* the decline of life that was caused by these contradictions. If 'obsolete' elements are preserved in a complicated complex under the action of positive selection, then they, of course, continually *lower* the sum of energy of the whole, even though that lowering is not noticeable, since it disappears in the more significant *elevation* of life caused by the favourable correlations of the environment. But if such an elevation of life ceases, the conditions of the environment become unfavourable and cause the lowering of energy of the complex, and now the constantly deleterious influence of 'obsolete' elements on life is no longer masked by anything and clearly appears, being added to the action of the unfavourable external conditions.

The vital incompatibility between what is obsolete and what is developing most frequently takes the form of 'parasitism' or, even better, 'vampirism'. As long as great wealth flowed into Spain because of monopolistic exploitation and robbery of newly-discovered countries and without any particularly significant expenditure of social labour, feudal nobles and monks could safely be parasitic on the organism of the Spanish people without exhausting it to the point of making development impossible. But, as their monopoly was lost and their robbery was curtailed, the nobles and monks of the obsolete world began to extract from their immediate social environment – Spanish peasants and artisans – *the same sum* of energy necessary to preserve the level of life that they had attained. This is the simplest form of vampirism. The vampirism of ideological norms that have outlived their basis in life is manifested in different and more complex ways. When difficult times befell English trade-unionists, their out-of-date worldview did not harm the trade-unionists by depriving them of the means and the energy for their immediate preservation. Rather, it prevented the success of their struggle for life because it did not allow new adaptations that corresponded to their changing conditions of life to develop and to be manifested in reality. The old worldview did not allow any methods of the struggle for life other than the old ones that were already far from sufficient and often led to a fruitless expenditure of effort, such as going on strike against the worsening conditions of labour that had resulted from the general narrowing of the market, giving political support to one or another bourgeois parties depending on the promises of their candidates – promises that they partly could not and partly did not want to carry out. All this was now unable to seriously improve the situation, but it nevertheless prevented organised workers from joining together in an independent party and defending their vital interests through a systematic political-class struggle. New adaptations were engendered, but for a long time they ran up against the conservatism of traditional worldviews and methods of struggle that were inconsistent with them. *For these adaptations, tradition was a fatally-hostile part of their social envir-*

*onment*. Only when negative selection finally undermined and destroyed tradition, could these new adaptations – also repeatedly weakened by negative selection and often even destroyed by them but brought back to life again and again by those same conditions – grow and develop and increase the vital capacity of the whole. Here the 'vampiric' forms did not so much 'drink the blood' of the progressive elements of life as 'gnaw their throats' for as long as they could.

It stands to reason that, in its action on a complicated social complex, negative selection inhibits the life of the complex along all lines, but under normal conditions negative selection that is not too intense only kills some parts of the complex, those that are least durable and least adapted to the present conditions of the environment. The influence of negative selection is deeper and stronger wherever there is a vital contradiction that itself is now a source of negative selection, and its tendency is directed toward the destruction of the least vital of the two sides of the contradiction, whereby the *contradiction itself is eliminated*. Life is 'harmonised' due precisely to this negative selection.

Under favourable conditions, the diminishment of life that is immediately caused by negative selection turns out, in the final analysis, to be gain for life. A complicated social complex, having undergone a temporary shock that is not enough to destroy or radically weaken it, turns out, as a result of this shock, to be liberated and cleansed of its least viable elements – mainly from the carry-overs of the past and also, in general, from the least successful, weakest, and unadapted forms and combinations that have entered its content. Although the sum of its content immediately diminishes and although its 'static' vital capacity (i.e. relating to the given moment) declines, nevertheless, its 'dynamic' vital capacity – its possibility for further development – grows. It becomes more integral and more harmonious; all of the better, more durable and stable elements of development can unfold without encountering a greater obstacle on the part of obsolete or unfit elements. This is why so frequently a period of negative selection, like a crisis or revolution, becomes the starting point of new development that is considerable more luxuriant.

Thus, the tendency of negative selection in social development is to quantitatively diminish and narrow life, but, at the same time, to harmonise life and 'improve its health' by removing what is contradictory and unviable.

∴

I shall sum up my conclusions.

Social selection expresses the fact that the preservation, development, and destruction of social complexes are dependent on their social environment.

Social selection represents a particular form of biological causality-selection, in general. It does not even have any specific manifestations that are peculiar to it, and it appears sometimes in the form of 'natural' selection – physiological preservation, growth, and destruction – and sometimes in the form of 'psychical' selection (and the latter is its most usual form).

In energetical terms, it appears in the form of the growth of the energy of the social complex (positive social selection) or the diminishment of energy (negative selection).

In applying the point of view of social selection in a concrete investigation, it is necessary to constantly take into account the systemic interconnectedness of social complexes and to choose the 'unit of selection' appropriately (i.e. to determine precisely the scope and boundaries of the complex, as a whole, that in one or another given case is subject to the action of selection).

The tendency of positive selection in social development is a dual process: the growth of life and, at the same time, the growth of contradictions hidden within life.

The tendency of negative selection is the narrowing of life but, at the same time, the harmonisation of life – the revealing and removal of its internal contradictions.

These tendencies mutually supplement one another, jointly conditioning movement toward the harmonious maximum of life. Positive selection is the elemental creative work of life; negative selection is its elemental regulator.

To the extent that the progress of life has not only a qualitative but also a quantitative nature, it presupposes a certain level of predominance of positive over negative selection. If this *predominance* is too significant, it is as if positive selection overloads life with an excessive profusion of forms that spring up and develop, and life becomes disharmonious. If there is no such predominance at all, then it is impossible for life to grow, and it stagnates.

It is therefore impossible to consider positive and negative selection as completely equivalent occasions in the development of life. The essence of the difference between them in this sense can be expressed in this way: positive selection is *life itself*, and negative selection is *the supervisory mechanism* of the movement of life.

CHAPTER 9

# Historical Monism

1    Main Lines of Development

The principle of 'social selection' is nothing that is essentially new to the social sciences. In their investigation of economic life, the classical economists without doubt already relied on this principle, although, of course, they did not specifically formulate it. Their abstract method possessed precisely this idea, their concept of 'economic benefits' expressed precisely the conditions of positive social selection, and their 'competition of enterprises' is one particular case of social selection in general. The adaptedness or unadaptedness of specific forms in a given social environment (for the classical economists it was usually precisely a bourgeois environment) is what they were constantly trying to explain by their abstract analysis.

Marx liberated this principle of investigation from its bourgeois, static limitedness and studied the causal relationship of the development and degradation of social forms in *changing* and *diverse* social environments. He broadened the method to all of social life, having established that the development of ideological forms necessarily depends on social selection on the part of fundamental social formations lying deeper beneath them. But he did not provide a special, distinct formulation of the method, and he did not establish its connection with the contemporary methods of the life sciences in general. It could not have been otherwise, since Marx carried out his radical transformation of social sciences at just the same time that analogous reforms were being carried out in the natural sciences.

Let us now examine what the basic interconnectedness and correlations of social development will look like if they are investigated from the point of view of the principle of social selection that I have explained in detail. After all that has been presented, it is easy to anticipate that there will no *essential* changes in Marx's historical-philosophical conception, but it will be possible to attain greater precision and distinctness both in its basic formulation as well as in its particular applications.

I

We have agreed that the term 'social selection' means the basic vital dependence of social forms on their *social* environment. If this is so, then as far as society as a whole – as a living unity – is concerned, this concept is inappropriate. Society, itself, is not subject to 'social selection' because society is the very environment – taken in its whole scope – that conditions social selection. The environment that conditions the development and degradation of society as a whole and within which society as a whole is an object of selection is what lies beneath it – *external nature*.[1]

The relationships of society to this external nature are expressed – just the same as for any other living form – in the acquisition and expenditure of energy, in 'assimilation' and 'disassimilation'. If the acquisition of energy from external nature predominates over expenditures, then the strength of society grows; it is in a state of 'positive selection'. If expenditure preponderates over acquisition, then the sum of energy decreases; society is subject to the action of 'negative selection'. In essence, everything that has been said about the growth of the 'power of society over nature' or the 'power of nature over society' and of the increase or decrease of the 'productive forces of society' – all this serves as a descriptive designation of these two occasions of selection for the social whole.

Society consists of human individuals, but it would be a big mistake to consider social 'exchange of energy' with the environment as a simple sum of the physiological exchange of energy of individual organisms. Far from all functions in the life of the human organism are social, and for cognition (that unites what is *homogenous*) the concept of the 'social system' has meaning and value only when it embraces the system of social – and only social – functions. In breathing, in the circulation of blood, and in the digestion of an individual person, there is nothing that is exactly social, yet these processes play a huge role in the *individual* balance of acquisition and expenditure of energy. The *social* struggle for existence is completely different; it lies entirely within the confines of the *labour and thought* of people, or, since thought can with full justification be considered as a particular form of work, the social struggle for life can be included entirely within the confines of labour – and of social labour, at that. The social process is a *process of the social collaboration of people*.[2]

---

[1] This summary concept includes not only inorganic and organic 'extra-social' nature, but for any given society it also includes other *societies* that exist separately from it.

[2] I will not dwell here on the development of this methodologically very important idea, which many people have violated – for example, certain economists who include the section 'on consumption' (in the sense of private consumption) in a course of political economy, a social science. All that follows indirectly serves to explain and elucidate this idea. In my first philosophical work, *Osnovnye elementy istoricheskogo vzgliada na prirodu*, I devoted a significant

In any complex living system, and especially in one as maximally complex as a social system, it is necessary to distinguish functions that relate to the *immediate* struggle with external nature from functions that are indirectly and obliquely related to that struggle. For example, the collective procurement of food in the form of hunting is an act of the immediate struggle for life. Collective deliberation on the means to procure food – putting a plan together for hunting, and so forth – is an act that only indirectly enters the system of the struggle for life. The difference is not at all in the degree of sociality of some functions or others (they are equally social) and the difference is not in their vital importance (they can be equally important for life). The difference is only in the direction of their functions. In the first case their object is *external nature* and in the second the object is *other social functions*. In the act of hunting the object of the action consists of birds, beasts, etc.; in the act of putting together a plan the object consists of the conceptions of people regarding this process of labour. The function of the first kind is designated as socially-technical; the function of the second kind so far remains without a special designation.

This distinction is of *fundamental* significance for social energetics. The social 'assimilation' of energy from the external environment only occurs in the realm of the immediate struggle with nature – only in the socio-technological process – while the 'expenditure' of energy occurs *not only* there but in the other realms of social life. Therefore, the very possibility of extra-technological social functions and the real boundaries of those functions *are entirely determined* by the 'excess' of energy (the preponderance of acquisition over expenditure) that is provided in the sphere of socio-technological life. The entire social process as a whole is accomplished through technology.

This elementary proposition, which is utterly inaccessible to the theorists of 'historical idealism' (inaccessible, at any rate, in its necessary conclusions if not in its stark formulation), is the actual basis of the doctrine of *historical monism*.

Before I turn from the basic proposition to its necessary conclusions, I must pay attention to – and eliminate – one very natural misunderstanding that my formulation might evoke in the reader.

The socio-technical process is the process of labour. In this process, it is self-evident what energy of the social whole is *expended*, but where is the *acquisition* of energy here? Since we do not recognise individual-physiological

---

part of the fourth section (Ch. IV, 'Society') to it, in which I developed a fundamentally valid idea in a youthfully immature and awkward form. I believe I removed these deficiencies in the chapter '*Razvitie zhizni v prirode i obshchestve*' in my book *Iz psikhologii obshchestva*.

processes of acquisition – such as individual consumption, digestion, circulation of the blood, etc. – as social functions, then when we are dealing with the social system is it possible to speak of the 'assimilation' of energy from external nature? The social system obviously does not have its own organs and functions of acquisition, and it is pointless to look for them. The system of social collaboration is not an organism at all, and all discussions of social digestion or circulation of the blood, etc., boil down to poor metaphors and analogies that are capable of satisfying only the obsolete school of sociologists who treat society as an organism.

This objection comes entirely from a hazy and naively-materialistic understanding of energetics. Besides, the 'assimilation' of energy is a not completely felicitous term, since it allows a certain level of obscurity. It is necessary to establish the concept precisely.

'Energy' does not contain anything absolute; it is not a 'substance' of things but a correlation of things. The 'sum of energy' is always a relative magnitude; it is a measure of the changes that one 'thing' can excite in another 'thing'. When we speak of the sum of energy of a living system, it is always to be understood that it is 'in relation to its environment'. If the 'assimilation' or 'accumulation' of energy is accomplished, this means that the potential energy of the system grows in relation to its environment, and the energy of the environment is reduced in relation to it. Both can occur by various means.

For the human organism, the taking in and 'digestion' of substances that are located in the surrounding environment is one of the technical means of 'assimilation' of energy. It is along this path that, in actuality, the potential energy of the organism in relation to its environment is increased and the energy of the environment in relation to the organism is decreased. But the relative magnitude of the energy of the organism and the environment is also changed when people 'clothe' themselves in a specific covering, taken, of course, from that very environment. Then the capability of the environment to harmfully change the organisms (by means of chilling, mechanical injury, etc.) also is diminished and the capability of those organisms to change the environment to correspond with their vital functions increases. A significant part of the energy that would have gone toward maintaining the temperature of a naked body is now retained for new influences on the environment.

From this point of view, there is nothing strange or difficult in the issue of the 'assimilation' of energy from the external environment in the technological process of labour. The social labour of people, in changing external nature, transforms it in the sense that the energy of the social system in relation to its environment increases, and the energy of the environment in relation to the social system decreases. This relative change is the magnitude of the vital 'plus' of the social system, its 'assimilation'.

All 'production' – i.e. the transformation of objects of nature into a 'product of human labour' – is nothing other than the progressive creation of an environment in relation to which the energy of the social system would be at a maximum.³

But, in itself, social labour is the *expenditure* of energy – the lowering of energy of the social system in relation to its environment. We are looking at two variable magnitudes with 'plus' and 'minus' marks. Their difference represents the living balance of the socio-technological process. All the rest of the extra-technological life of the social whole runs at the expense of this balance. Consequently, that life is possible only when the difference between assimilation and expenditure in the technological process represents a sufficiently *positive* magnitude.

I will now move on to the other realm of social life and examine what constitutes its content and real meaning.

II

From all that has just been presented, it undoubtedly follows that the technological process is the *genetically primary* realm of social life and that all social development can issue only from it. In nature, in general, nothing develops 'itself from itself'. Changes of any form – organised or unorganised – are conditioned, in the final analysis, by influences *from outside*, and, since the realm of technology is the 'frontier' realm of social life for the social system, that is precisely where these influences are immediately apprehended. As long as one accepts that the law of causality fully applies to society – and without causality one cannot speak of social science – one cannot but conclude that technology is of primary significance in the social process.⁴

---

3  It is most imprecise to apply the term 'social environment of people' to the means of production and its products. These are objects of *external* nature, the environment that is transformed by social labour but is not at all 'social'. The 'social environment of people' corresponds only to an environment that is made up of *social forms* that are really inseparable from *social beings*. From my approach, what is 'social' lies within the confines of the 'human', and not what is outside of humankind.

4  In any event, if proof were still required for this proposition, then all the literature of the historical-materialist school that explains the dependence of all social development on the 'growth of productive forces' of society – i.e. on its *technological* progress – provides a great deal of proof. Important evidence is also provided by the growing preponderance of the tech-

Primary technological forms of social life seem extremely simple in relative terms, but, of course, this is only relative in comparison, for example, with many ideological adaptations. The entire socio-technological system as a whole is extremely complex even for the least developed societies and is made up of a huge amount of separate socio-technological adaptations. To the extent that society develops, the quantity and complexity of these adaptations grow.

But where a huge number of vital forms are united into a complex system, particular and partial *vital contradictions* must inevitably arise among them. The harmony of life is not provided initially; it can be attained only as a result of development. The more complicated a living complex and the more intense its life, the more it will inevitably have 'internal contradictions'.

The removal of internal contradictions of a living system can occur along several routes. Sometimes it is simply through negative selection, arising out of the contradiction itself, that one or even both of its sides are destroyed – either one of the adaptations that contradicts the other or both of them together. For example, a whole group of reptiles developed a special type of movement (and travel) that is expressed in a wavelike and spiral flexing of the body, and, as a result of this, all of its limbs, which were not only useless for that kind of movement but were extremely inconvenient encumbrances, gradually atrophied. It is clear that this means of removing contradictions between vital adaptations is extremely uneconomical from the point of view of *development*.

In other cases, the mutually contradictory correlation of different functions or parts of a complicated complex are levelled out by the change of one of the two sides or of both. This route is very common in the lives of separate organisms and whole species. For example, instincts can change in the sense of switching from a diurnal to a nocturnal way of life, from eating plants to eating animals, etc. This type of harmonisation can be connected with a certain increasing complexity of life, although this is far from necessarily the case.

The third type of harmonisation – at the present time most important for us – is *always* connected with the increasing complexity and broadening of life. This is the development of *organising adaptations*.

Experience shows that it is not uncommon for two vital combinations that would appear to be mutually contradictory if directly joined together to be easily connected without contradiction by means of a third combination – an 'organising' combination. For example, any complex organism would, in general, be impossible without such combinations. Functions of the neural centres

---

nological process over the rest of social life as one looks back toward the primitive, embryonic forms of social life. See *'Razvitie zhizni v prirode i obshchestve'*, pp. 53–6.

are of this type. If opposing muscles – for example, the flexors and extensors of the limbs – were in any way independent of one another in their contractions (more precisely, if they were stimulated to contract by separate and independent centres), then in a huge number of cases their movements would only be mutually paralysing. The connection of the two by means of a *common neural centre* removes this vital contradiction. In regard to nutrition, all organs and tissues would turn out to be mutually unadapted or 'contradictory' if there was no nourishment of the organising function of the vasculomotor and trophic nervous system. The hypertrophy of some parts and the atrophy of other parts of the organism would occur – to the detriment of the organism, needless to say. In regard to the struggle with external nature, if they all were not regulated by the 'inhibiting' functions of the central nervous system, various reflexes and automatic movements would continually create contradictions to other expedient reactions and would subject the living whole to danger.

The term 'removal of contradictions' is, in essence, an extremely insufficient definition of the organising function. 'Removal of contradictions' designates only the saving of the vital system from a certain *expenditure* of energy; the role of organising adaptations, however, often has a considerably more positive nature. Experience shows that in the struggle for life, two mutually coordinated magnitudes can give a more significant *real* sum than would be obtained by simple addition. Thus, the combined contraction of thousands of muscle fibres provides a positive effect for the struggle for life that is not one thousand but incomparably more than one thousand times more than would be obtained from the isolated contraction of one fibre. The coordinated movement of two hands achieves not twice, but four or five times more useful work than the movement of one hand.

Of course, this function of organising adaptations (the creation of 'active harmony') is not essentially distinguishable from the first (removal of contradictions). And here the matter has to do not at all with the creation of new energy from nothing but only with the distribution of energy that is more favourable for life. It all boils down to the fact that in the general expenditure of energy of a living system, a more significant portion goes to 'useful work' and a less significant portion goes to 'harmful contradictions' – in this case these terms of applied mechanics express the meaning of adaptation with complete precision. With the 'removal of contradictions', the harmful resistances that arise from the relationship of one part of the complex with another are diminished. With the creation of 'active harmony' of parts of the complex that do not represent such a 'harmful contradiction', the coefficient of 'useful work' increases and the coefficient of 'harmful resistance' on the part of the *external environment* decreases. In mechanics, the coefficient of useful work can sometimes increase by improving the fit of parts of the machine to one another, removing internal friction, and sometimes by coordinating two or more mechanisms.

In social life, with its huge complexity, organising adaptations play a role of the greatest importance, one that grows according to the scope of social development. *These organising adaptations include the entire realm that rises over the 'technological process' and that gives form to the ideological process as it springs up, develops, and disintegrates.* They can be grouped in three basic types:

1. *Forms of immediate communication* – a cry, speech, body language. They serve for the *immediate unification and coordination of human actions*, and subsequently also psychical images and emotions – psychical reactions that are inseparably connected with actions and are themselves determined by them.[5]

   The way that 'forms of communication' – direct or indirect (through summons, orders, directions, requests, etc. or through the transmission of motives for actions such as the report of facts, explanation of facts, expression of moods, etc.) serve to coordinate human actions is something that I will not dwell on here, especially since all this is quite familiar to everyone from personal experience.

2. *Cognitive forms* – concepts, judgements, and their complex combinations in the form of religious doctrines, scientific and philosophical theories, and so on. They serve to *systematically coordinate labour on the basis of lived experience*. This is a coordination of a less immediate and more complex character. It has the tendency to create the maximum harmony not only among actions that are carried out in the present but also between them and actions carried out in the past and actions that are still due to take place in the future. And here the coordination of conceptions serves as a means of coordinating acts of labour. There is also no need here to specifically give an account of how cognitive forms factually fulfil this function. In regard to knowledge and theories of natural science it is sufficiently obvious. In regard to ideas and 'knowledge' of a technical nature, it also becomes obvious if one keeps in mind that they are connected with technical knowledge, for which they serve as a means of systematisation and regulation by providing unifying and regulating formulas. And, finally, in regard to other cognitive combinations (religious, scientific,

---

5   These, properly, are 'incomplete psychical-motor reactions'. They represent the beginning phases of a 'full psychical reaction' that completes a volitional act and is expressed in 'action'. A detailed analysis of their vital significance and their occurrence in 'full psychical-motor reactions' is provided in *Poznanie s istoricheskoi tochki zreniia*, Part II, Ch. 2.

philosophical), their coordinating significance for human actions is less obvious because it is realised along a more indirect route; it can, however, always be explained after sufficient investigation.[6]

3. *Normative forms* – custom, law, morality, propriety, practical rules of experience for human behaviour. Their role consists in *removing contradictions of social life through the limitation of one or another function* that would result in disharmonious conflict within social life if they were not removed. In order to be convinced of the precise significance of these social norms it is sufficient to conceive of them clearly *in their action*.[7] The vital inseparability of the coordination of conceptions and the coordination of actions stands out here with special clarity.

If one draws a parallel between the three types of organising adaptations of the social process and the organising functions of the nervous system in an individual organism, then the forms of immediate communication are probably comparable with the simple transmission of a stimulus through nerve cells and fibres from some parts of the organism to others (for example, the 'transmission of a reflex'). Cognitive forms would then correspond to the accumulation of stimuli in nerve cells and the production of complex associative connections among various psychomotor reactions in which the very form of these reactions changes and is refined. Finally, 'norms' then appear as analogues of the 'impeding' functions of the central nervous system. The imperfection of this analogy issues from the fact that society is not an organism; the analogy itself arises from the basic similarity that connects all complex and highly organised forms of life. Here, in particular, the analogy arises from the similarity among forms (an organism, a society) that are actually related to one another as a part and a whole.

Along with these three types of ideological adaptations that we have noted, *forms of art* are usually given as a separate type. From the point of view of our

---

6  The 'truth' of one or another cognitive form is expressed precisely in the possibility of basing 'practice' on it without running into a contradiction – i.e. in the final analysis, in its suitability for the coordination of actions. Marx clearly and energetically formulated this vital meaning of all cognition. Among later thinkers, E. Mach explained with great clarity the real significance and genesis of cognitive functions – the role of cognition as a tool in the struggle for life and the origin of cognition in technology. I have continually noted and emphasised the organising and coordinating nature of cognitive forms in regard to human labour in all my works, beginning with *Kratkii kurs ekonomicheskoi nauki*. For a fuller resume of these considerations, see my work *Iz psikhologii obshchestva*, Chapter III, '*Razvitie zhizni v prirode i obshchestve*'.

7  Regarding the meaning of 'norms' in the social process see my article '*Normy I tseli zhizni*' ['Goals and Norms of Life'], in my book *Novyi Mir*, which is devoted specifically to this question. See also *Iz psikhologii obshchestva*, Ch. III, '*Razvitie zhizni v prirode i obshchestve*'.

socio-philosophical task, there is no need to single out this group of forms; they do not represent a special type of adaptation. To briefly justify such an attitude, I will permit myself to cite a few lines from another of my works:

> The social content of art boils down partly to the transmission of immediate feelings from one person to another and partly to the communication to others of acquired experience (i.e. partly to the first type of organising adaptations and partly to the second). Singing, music, and the rhythmic movement of dance serve, like speech and body language, as means of 'expression', i.e. the transmission to others of an experienced mood, only in a less specific form. Many pre-civilised peoples use music and especially dancing for attaining a unity of feeling when they are preparing to carry out some important matter together – a conference of tribes, setting off for war or hunting, and so on. Singing and music have a similar meaning even among cultured peoples in certain life events – in military parades, for example. Songs and drawings are, in addition, a means of transmitting accumulated experience, especially at the early stages of development; one need only recall the huge cognitive significance that the songs of Homer and Hesiod and the works of art and sculpture in temples and on squares, etc., had for the education of the ancient Greeks. There can be no doubt that singing and poetry have a common origin with speech, dances and the plastic arts have a common origin with body language, and music has a common origin with body language and speech. In a word, art is a series of ideological adaptations of a quite varied sort; it also contains many technological elements, especially architecture, for example.[8]

Now I will only add that the sphere of art contains elements of a third ideological type – socio-normative elements. At the dawn of history many manifestations of art were amalgamated together with customs (and also with religion), and, the other way around, at the highest levels of culture there appeared the striving to transform all of people's life into artistic works of art. Thus, the principle of art – beauty – became a norm of human behaviour.

Thus, the three types of organising adaptations of social life that have been pointed out encompass *the entire ideological process*. And the ideological process forms the entire realm of the social process that lies outside the technolo-

---

8  See the note on pp. 73–4 of *Iz psikhologii obshchestva*.

gical process, outside the immediate relationships of the struggle of the social person with external nature.

III

In order to recognise technological social adaptations as genetically primary and ideological adaptations as derivative, the correlations of their functions in life that I have elucidated will be quite sufficient for people who have thoroughly mastered scientific, or, to be more precise, dynamic thinking. But dynamic thinking is far from universal, and therefore it is quite possible to expect still further objections due to the idea that 'the ideological' cannot be genetically secondary and derivative in relation to 'the technological', because of the *qualitative difference* of the two – a difference that precludes a genetic connection. This objection can be eliminated through an analysis that is not particularly complicated.

Not only is there no absolute qualitative difference between 'organising' adaptations and adaptations for the 'immediate struggle for life' in all of living nature, but it is frequently difficult even to tell the difference. The nervous system is an organising apparatus of an individual organism, but genetically, a nerve cell belongs to the group of 'epithelial' cells like glandular or ceratoid cells of the epidermis. The nerve cell develops in the direction of an 'organising' function; the glandular and ceratoid cells develop in the direction of 'technological' functions. Their common origin is masked by this, but it is not in the least eliminated. At any rate, nevertheless, the organising and the technological functions are quite sharply distinguishable here. And what about, for example, the vital role of the 'sensory-motor' neural node of lower animal organisms? It simultaneously both *causes* the muscle contractions that are necessary for the defensive and offensive movement of the organism and also *regulates* the interconnectedness of various muscle reflexes in order that their energy not be expended fruitlessly; the same adaptation turns out to be a tool for the immediate struggle with the surrounding environment and an organising form for a great number of such immediate adaptations.

Socially-organising forms are not exceptions. They also have a common origin with socio-technological forms, frequently arising through a simple modification of them or even simply *coinciding* with them. For example, the same cry by herd animals and also by people can serve as the means of frightening away attacking enemies – i.e. a tool of immediate struggle – and also as a signal for summoning other members of the group – i.e. an organising adaptation of the first type, a means of immediate communication.

In general, 'ideological adaptations' represent combinations (for the most part more complex) of the same elements that are present in 'technological forms', in adaptations for the immediate struggle with external nature. Body language, a cry, or a word springs up as the result of the distinctive development of certain elements of immediate reactions during labour. In the language of gestures of primitive tribes (and of children of a lively temperament) many 'designations' boil down simply to the abbreviated, incomplete reproduction of acts of labour. The language of sounds was initially created mainly from 'sympathetic movements' connected with the 'socio-technological' acts of people that, even more precisely, constitute an inseparable, if not immediately useful, part of complexes of labour (the 'irradiation' of neural excitation due to the physiological interconnectedness of neural centres). The brilliant theory of the origin of word roots, proposed by L. Noiré and adopted and popularised by Max Müller – scientists whose basic worldview has nothing in common with historical materialism – has superbly explained how primitive language arose directly from the processes of people's collective labour. In this way, the simplest ideological forms – forms of direct communication – are entirely reducible to a 'technological' origin. And, since 'word' and 'concept' are genetically identical and are distinguishable only at the higher levels of development, as was shown by the same Max Müller, then there is no need even to search specifically for 'technological' roots of cognitive forms, the element of which is a 'concept'. Finally, normative forms also do not contain any elements other than the concepts themselves (and the combinations of concepts – judgements) plus elements of actions that are connected with them (or 'desires' – the initial psychical phase of 'actions'). Consequently, the idea of a common genesis of 'ideology' and 'technology' – given that the development of the latter is of a *primary* nature – does not encounter empirically grounded objections.

And, by the way, the fact that both technological adaptations and ideological adaptations are made up of psychophysiological complexes would be sufficient, in essence, for the acknowledgement of the truth of this view. Meanwhile, both physiology (with its development of the organism from one undifferentiated cell) and psychology (with its comprehensive associative interconnectedness of all possible psychical complexes) do not leave any space for fundamental differences in their origin.[9]

---

9   More concrete coverage of the genetic connection of the two realms of the social process can be read in my work *Iz psikhologii obshchestva*, Ch. III, '*Razvitie zhizni v prirode i obshchestve*'.
    In these chapters, the reader may find wearisome the extremely concise and cursory references to vast and important groups of facts and, along with them, citations of my own works. But as much as I would like to, I cannot provide a different kind of presentation. To substant-

IV

Thus, the premises that I have at my disposal for my analysis are as follows. The entire ideological process derives from the 'energetical balance' of the technological process (from the preponderance in the technological process of 'assimilation' over 'expenditure' of energy), all ideological adaptations are of a genetically secondary nature, and they have an organising function in the life of social labour.

Because 'ideology' has a derivative origin, it follows that the starting point of any ideological change lies in the sphere of the 'technological process' – the same basic proposition that historical materialism formulated in other terms – 'the growth of productive forces'.[10] This is only a somewhat abstract expression of the progress of social technology, and it is what is designated by the name 'economics' – the borderline realm of the technological and ideological process. But, of course, there would be no point in undertaking this work if all its meaning boiled down to the simple recognition of what has already been recognised by the most progressive scientific school and supported by concrete material in a huge number of its works.

It is now necessary to dwell on the 'organising function of ideological forms'. The first question is: what do they 'organise'? The answer is obvious: they organise social life, existing social adaptations. Which adaptations, exactly? If technological forms are primary, then they come first and organise ideological forms. In reality, it is easy to see that this is the case. The primary roots of human language serve to designate *actions* that are immediately related to the process of social labour. The realm of *concepts* corresponds to early levels of development of the realm of words, i.e. the two essentially coincide. And *customary norms* also spring up first and foremost in the realm of relationships with a society's immediate struggle for life in its labour. But all this is in the initial phases of development; further on, the picture becomes more complex.

If organising adaptations form the 'superstructure' over the adaptations of the immediate struggle for life, then in all the more complex forms of life the superstructure is multi-storeyed, and the more complex the living whole, the

---

ively repeat what I wrote earlier would be extremely inappropriate and even disadvantageous for a systematic presentation because of the proportion of a short work it would take up. The unpleasant necessity for me to cite my own words proceeds from the circumstance that no matter how little is probably new in the ideas that I am propounding, still in *this* connection and in *this* elucidation, into which I must bring these ideas, I have not encountered or hardly encountered them in literature I am familiar with – even in the literature most related to my topic.

10   The reference is to Marx's 'Preface to a Critique of Political Economy' [trans.].

more levels there are. For example, the organising apparatus of the human body – the nervous system – presents a certain series of neural centres (three or four series for the majority of functions) that are arranged one *over* another, in the sense that the centres of the 'lower' series *are subordinate to* the centres of the 'higher' ones – i.e. lower centres are regulated, supervised, and connected by higher ones. The higher centres consequently serve as 'organisers' for the 'organised'. Relationships in a social system are absolutely analogous, except that in a social system the stairway of organising adaptations has even more levels. Two ascending ideological series of the greatest importance for life will serve as examples.

In the realm of cognition the stairway of *concepts* has many steps. The primary, simplest concepts have the greatest amount of elementary empirical content and are the closest to concrete reality – i.e. to the immediate struggle for life. Historically, such concepts are about common actions during labour, elements of the technological process. These concepts 'organise' the experience of labour most immediately. Concepts of 'objects' – even of such objects as the materials and tools of labour – are already derivative and of a second order, 'doing the organising' for the primary concepts. An 'object' is a complex connected with many different actions that are repeated in many different occasions of the experience of labour. Therefore, a concept of one or another 'object' is an organising centre for a large number of concepts that express the activity of labour. For example, the concept of an 'axe' (a *given*, specific axe) serves as the centre for conceptions of the most varied actions that are performed with the help of an axe and also, of course, for all impressions (perceptions) that are inseparably connected with these actions.[11] The concept of such-and-such a 'tree' associatively connects all psychical-motor reactions that are related to the given tree, etc. Different concepts of a more partial nature are united by a generalising concept with greater volume and less specific content: the related concepts of 'axe', 'tree', etc. (not *given*, specific objects but objects of a given kind in general). In science and in philosophy the chain of generalising concepts runs systematically, link by link, higher and higher, ascending to the most general, 'universally-organising' concepts for human experience. Such a chain is created even earlier in 'everyday thinking', only considerably less

---

11 Only in cognitively-scientific abstractions is a distinction made between perceptions (or conceptions) and actions (or desires). These are different phases of psychical reactions in general; they are inseparable in life to the extent that even in *incomplete* psychical reactions it is impossible for elements of both kinds to be completely absent. Of course, in the mind of every person, social-technological complexes are made up of both elements. See *Poznanie s istoricheskoi tochki zreniia*, pp. 67–77 and *Iz psikhologii obshchestva*, pp. 78–81.

harmoniously and completely, with significantly tangled links that are connected to complexes that are often far from homogenous from the point of view of 'scientific cognition' (for instance 'edible' and 'inedible' things, 'expensive' or 'cheap' objects, etc.). But the means of forming the tangled system of concepts of everyday thinking and the harmonious system of scientific thinking are the same: it involves the unification of combinations that 'organise' experience by means of others that, in turn, 'organise' the first. The difference is that the material of the scientific system of concepts is broader and that more socio-ideological work is applied to this material. The scientific system of concepts contains countless elements that in everyday thinking are scattered among different, separate psyches, whereby the action of social selection from all this mass of material preserves and organises only those with the greatest vital capacity and stability.

If we keep in mind that 'everyday thinking' and its system of concepts usually continues to be preserved along with 'scientific thinking' and that in a great number of cases people use concepts of the first type and switch over from them to concepts of the second type only when they run into contradictions or when the first type is completely inadequate. It thus becomes clear to us that we are fully justified in considering 'scientific' concepts to be organising adaptations in regard to concepts of everyday thinking that stand on the same level of generalisation as them.

Thus the chain of cognitive forms doubles itself and becomes more complex, transforming into a complex ideological tissue. But with sufficient investigation it is always possible to determine the relationships of certain elements of this tissue as 'organising adaptations' of a higher and lower order.

The realm of relationships of 'property' serves as another example of the ideological stairway as a series of levels of the social organising process.

Here the primary-organising forms are those whose sum forms the 'factual distribution of property' in a given society. Initially, 'property' is only a *fact* and not a 'law'. It is nothing other than the continuing relationship of a particular individual or group to particular objects of external nature in the process of social labour. The development of 'organising norms' can be represented in a model of the following form. A given person or group or tribal commune works a given expanse of land, occupying it without any 'juridical' basis, simply because it must extract the means of life, the land is there, and no one is occupying it. There is nothing 'ideological' here but only a technological process. The actor in this process is humanity, and the object is nature. But the multiplication of people leads to absolute overpopulation and overcrowding of the land, and it is no longer possible for everyone to find an unoccupied plot of land sufficient to feed himself. At this point, 'contradictions of labour' appear, theft – the seizure of land that is already being worked by other people (or communes) – occurs, and so on. There then arises the 'law' of property of a given person or commune for a given plot of land as an organising form that removes these contradictions. The socio-psychological content of this law consists in the *recognition* by other people of the exclusive relationship of labour of a given individual or commune to a given plot of land and the readiness to prevent the action of anyone else from contradicting this exclusive relationship. We can see that this is already an 'ideological' fact, and its 'organising' significance for a system of labour is clear without the need for argument.

The extent to which the model just introduced corresponds to the historical beginning of the law of property is absolutely not important for us – in all likelihood property in weapons, tools, flocks of animals, and such developed earlier than property in land – but this model draws a completely precise living meaning of the beginning of property and its connection with the technological, social process.

The appearance of the initial organising relationships of property in this way did not in any way represent a 'legal principle'; they were so far still only ideological elements of property. Such and such an expanse of land 'appertained' to commune A, such and such a flock of animals to family B, such and such a tool to the one who made it, person C, and so on. But with the increasing complexity of social life, these elementary forms turned out to be insufficient and even came into conflict with one another in newly arising vital contradictions. For example, a flock belonging to B turns out to be grazing on a field that belongs to A who tries to take possession of the flock, himself, just like everything else located in his field. A tool belonging to C turns out to have been made from a horn broken off a bull that belongs to B's flock, which again is the occasion of conflict, etc. There then appears customary legal 'property norms' – organising adaptations now of a higher order that regulate the primary elements of property. These norms are also far from universal and very far from a 'sacred principle of property' that embraces the entire social organisation. They are approximately of this nature: 'land belongs to him who first began to work it and so does everything that is grown on it but not what accidentally happens to get on it', 'a tool belongs to him who made it, but a tool that is knowingly made from material of someone else that is improperly acquired must be returned to the owner of this material', etc.

Further development creates the need for organising norms of a yet higher order that are indeed worked out over the course of time. And the chain continues right up to some kind of final, all-embracing principle. In 'customary' law this process does not attain full completeness and its norms are not distinguished by a high degree of elaboration and precision. But in a system of 'formal law' – in written laws, for example – all these features are attained. To a certain degree, the relationship of both systems of law is analogous to the relationship of everyday thinking with scientific cognition – but only to a certain degree and not completely. However, it is not necessary to analyse their connection any further here; enough has been said to explain the basic idea behind our illustrations.[12]

Thus, to the extent that adaptations of a different type emerge, by virtue of their mutual contradictions or insufficient interconnectedness among them, there also emerges the need of organising forms of a higher order that are produced by social selection. As a result, ascending ideological chains are obtained that are usually intertwined with one another.

V

In the majority of cases, the common origin of ideological and technological forms has its starting point so far back in the past that we are obliged to look for it not in historical data, even of the most distant past, but indirectly in deductive-analytic investigation. This remoteness of their common origin also explains the dominance in everyday thinking – and also in the formal science and philosophy that is closer to it – of the contraposition of 'material' and 'ideal' elements of social life, as utterly separate, as qualitatively different.

When we said that contradictions between technological complexes – their mutual unadaptedness – engenders the need for organising ideological forms and that development creates such forms, then the question of *what* immediate, concrete material those forms were made acquired particular significance regarding whether the empiriomonist conception was convincing. We

---

12   As regards the last example, I will only make one remark of a terminological nature. The factual distribution of property that is adopted usually relates to 'economics' as opposed to 'ideology'. We have seen, however, that we are dealing with *ideological* adaptations. 'Economics' is, in general, a *borderline realm*. The term 'economics' unites relationships of social collaboration (in production), on the one hand, with relationships of property (in distribution), on the other. The first represent the social characteristics of the immediate *technological process* isolated out through abstraction, and the second represent the group of primarily organising *ideological* combinations that are immediate to the technical process. For the tasks of the economist with his specific research, the uniting of the two is not problematic *at any rate in the investigation of modern, exchange and capitalist societies*. For our philosophical goals, the precise distinction between technological and ideological elements in the borderline realm is much more important. See also the note on p. 36 of *Iz psikhologii obshchestva*.

could, it is true, limit ourselves to the *general* evidence provided above that there are no qualitative differences in the content of technological and ideological forms. But this consideration does not possess the graphic clarity that would overcome doubt more quickly and precisely. It would be ludicrous, for example, to argue that there is an absolute difference between the organising apparatus of the nervous system and other organs since embryology permits one to follow the development of the nervous system from cells of the ectoderm, from which many organs with the most 'technological' functions originate. But social development, unfortunately, is not as clearly reproduced in the individual as biological-species development is, and therefore a greater space remains here for a 'higher' and even a 'transcendental' origin of ideology.

I am attempting to represent more concretely the very emergence of 'ideological tissue' from 'technological tissue' in those same illustrations that we have utilised for a graphic depiction of the ideological stairway.

In primitive language, according to the conclusions of comparative philology, a word expresses action. And according to the brilliant theory of Noiré, these very words are a *physiological part* of the actions that they designate (or, more precisely, of those psychophysiological complexes that correspond to 'actions'). The technological act of labour, as an indivisible whole, includes not only those muscle contractions that immediately change external relationships in a useful way but also all the involuntary muscle contractions which accompany the volitional contractions (due to constant neural irradiation), and, needless to say, it also includes the processes in the central nervous system (or, *what is the same thing*, in 'consciousness') that condition all these muscular contractions. Now, what is the primarily generated concept of which the act of labour serves as the content? Why, only the *contraction of this act of labour*. This concept is the inseparable unification of a word with the conception of a given action. But a word, itself, as we have seen, is originally an inseparable part of the complex of labour – to be precise, a word is the involuntary muscle contraction of the vocal apparatus that enters the content of the complex of labour. The conception of the action (that also includes the desire to reproduce it) – this, according to the views of contemporary psychophysiology, is the beginning phase of a volitional complex of 'action', the psychical basis of action itself.[13] Thus, the primary cognitive-ideological element – the concept – turns out in the given case simply as an abbreviated form of the technological element – the act of labour.

---

13   The same is true of a 'word' when it is not pronounced but only thought.

But a 'concept' is an *organising* adaptation. Why can an abbreviated act of labour play an organising role for a complete act of labour? Precisely due to its 'abbreviated' nature. A concept is a tool for organising experience, a tool for uniting lived experience and for regulating subsequent experience – i.e. in the final analysis, a concept is a tool of living labour. But to unite lived experience in organisms with psyches is possible, of course, only in an abbreviated form, since the psyche is limited. The map of a city is an extremely reduced reproduction of the city's form and can be an excellent guide to travel around the city, but if the map were a precise and equal reproduction of the city itself, it would be absolutely useless. The system of concepts is precisely a 'map' of the experience of social labour.

It goes without saying that in the subsequent development of humanity the forms of cognition become more complex, and it is not only concepts of the highest levels of generalisation but also concepts of more particular content that are not so simply reducible to the 'technological' basis that become more complex. But once we see that the basis of ideology lies not in the sky but on the ground and that its first source proceeds immediately from 'technology', then we do not need a detailed investigation regarding whether somewhere in the highest levels of ideology there is something somewhat supernatural that is in part not reducible to the 'material' basis of social life – the technological process.

Let us move on to a second illustration – elements of legal life.

The initial element of legal life is the law of property of a given person (of a given tribal group, to be factually more accurate). The essence of this law consists, as we have seen, in an active acknowledgement by all members of society of the fact that the possession and use of a given thing by a given person is connected with the *desire to oppose* anyone who would contradict this possession and use by attempting to take it away or seize it. As regards the very *fact* of possession and use, there is nothing originally 'ideological' in it; it is a phenomenon from the realm of technology. And it is only when the fact of possession is transformed (by 'abbreviation') that we can see an ideological fact – of a cognitive but not a legal nature – alongside the technological fact. The legal element consists in the desire of all members of society to oppose the theft of things by anyone at all. But 'desire' is an abbreviated form of the volitional complex of 'action'; in this case it is the generalisation of various actions of struggle against the seizure of things belonging to strangers. And these actions present nothing ideological in themselves; they are *technological acts* of struggle against forces that are hostile to a given society, against what are, in relation to society, forces of external nature. Thus, the initial elements of legal life turn out, under closer analysis, to be genetically derivative elements of 'technology', the result of simultaneous 'abbreviation' and unification of a series of complexes that belong to a technological type.

The progressive and increasing complexity of 'organising' forms, as far as social development is concerned, leads to a situation in which it is extremely difficult, at the highest steps of the ideological stairway, to detect the traits of the original 'low-lying' source of ideology in the technological process of labour, just as it is difficult to directly find in a nerve fibre the traits of the undifferentiated embryonic cells from which it originated. But these difficulties change nothing in the fundamental resolution of the issue which is of sole importance in our *philosophical* investigation of social life. This fundamental resolution, as we see, is completely monist.

VI

Society is the most complex form of life that we know of, and even in the earliest phases of its existence it possesses a colossal profusion of elements of development, the greatest in the whole biological world. In the continual and multi-faceted relations with external nature that are necessary in the struggle for life, individuals in society become – spontaneously or consciously – creators of a countless quantity of embryonic combinations that are striving to develop into new social forms. But here, as everywhere in nature, only a negligible number of the most viable of that mass of embryos develop to full maturity. Their fate is decided by the law of 'selection'.

There is nothing mysterious for us in the appearance of embryos of new forms; they are only modified combinations of existing social elements – modified by various effects of the social and extra-social environment. What is important for us now is to investigate the occasion of 'selection', the conditions of preservation and development or weakening and destruction of the groupings that spring up.

We begin with the first groupings to develop – technological adaptations. The technological process is a *borderline realm* between social life and external nature. Therefore, the new forms that spring up here are subject to the immediate influences of the 'environment' from two aspects – from the aspect of extra-social forces and from the aspect of social forces – and can exist and develop only if the sum of these and other influences turns out to be favourable and has the sign of 'positive selection'. And the direction of both actors of selection on the same 'technological forms' can be, and often are, very different and even directly contradictory.

Let us suppose that a new technological method appears. For example, a hunting tribe uses stone instead of bone for arrowheads, or an agricultural tribe changes the rotation of crops, and so on.[14] The first condition for the preservation and development of a new form is its immediate correlation with the external conditions of the environment. Obsidian arrowheads can be much better than bone, but the use of them will not develop into a general technological form in a given country if obsidian is very seldom encountered or is only brought in randomly. To replace plant A with plant B in crop rotation could be very beneficial for production, but this innovation will not spread in a given society as long as plant B rarely appears in its system of production or as long as its fruits and seeds are obtained entirely from another land in a quantity that is barely sufficient for immediate use. In general, the first actor in the selection of technological adaptations is external nature and the first occasion of the selection of technological adaptations is actual 'natural selection'. In our era of global interaction among peoples and of countless technological trials, the action of this selection frequently occurs in a very striking form – with the failure of experiments in acclimatisation, of attempts to produce certain minerals, etc.[15]

Let us go further. Imagine that the extra-social development of a new technological form does not encounter any obstacles on the part of nature. Then the entire problem boils down to the influence of the social environment, to 'social' selection in the proper meaning of the word.

---

14   Social labour, as an adaptation, does not in the least consist in the tool but in the *production and application* of the tool. The elements of such an adaptation are psychophysiological complexes in the human organism and are not inanimate objects, plants, animals ... There is nothing social in the tool itself; it is simply a complex from external nature. The social world, indeed, is the highest form of biological organisation. I will not here further develop and once again substantiate this very simple idea (see *Iz psikhologii obshchestva*, pp. 53–4). I only request that, to avoid any misunderstanding, the reader does not forget in the future that the question of technological development – like the question of ideological development – is a matter of *forms of human life* and not of something else, and that therefore the concepts of 'psychical selection', 'natural selection', etc. as means of manifestation of 'social selection' are completely appropriate here. The expressions 'the development of tools' and 'the development of the means of production' are only *metaphors*.

15   This also includes all those 'unsuccessful inventions' that appear in people's heads but cannot be realised in reality because they contain miscalculations: *perpetuum mobile*, people flying with wings, construction of machines that do not work, and so forth. Here, by the way, for conceptual clarification, I direct the attention of the reader to the fact that inventive activity in the sphere of the creation and improvement of the immediate means of struggle with nature relates to the technological process to the extent that the 'inventor' deals only with external nature. 'Ideology' begins where the results of this activity are socialised through *transmission* or socially regulated by means of *norms*.

The 'immediate social usefulness' of a new social form is the first condition of its social preservation and development. This usefulness consists in that the given adaptation promotes the preponderance of the assimilation of energy from the external environment over expenditures of energy. As economists would say, 'the productivity of labour increases'. This increase provides the basis for positive selection, and it is not difficult to see exactly how.

Society is made up of people, and social selection, as I have already shown, takes on the form of 'psychical selection' in a great many cases. The social preponderance of assimilation over expenditure of energy appears as the growth of the energy of the psychical apparatus of the members of society themselves. For example, an independent petty producer, due to technological development, attains same results as before but with less labour and so his labouring energy accumulates and contributes to the growth of the vital capacity of his organism. Or, for example, the organiser of an enterprise who has the same sum of means at his disposal obtains more products than before, which increases his power over people and over nature. In all such cases, there are conditions for positive psychical selection that strives to strengthen and solidify complexes in the psychical organisation of the members of society that make up *the given technological form* in its social totality. It is 'pleasant' for hunters that because they utilise new weapons they can kill game easier and more often. It is 'pleasant' for agriculturalists that because they change the rotation of crops they obtain an enhanced quantity of products. And this 'pleasant' (and its generalised forms – 'useful', 'profitable') signifies the positive psychical selection that underpins a new adaptation.

But the *immediate usefulness* of a new adaptation is far from enough to determine its social fate, even though a definite tendency in a favourable direction is created. A new occasion arrives on the scene that I would call, borrowing a term from mechanics, the 'parasitic drag of the social system'.

Now, due solely to the fact that a new technological form is joined to old ones – even though it is *immediately* useful – the previous, historically established equilibrium of the social process ceases to exist. To one degree or another it is 'disturbed' by the new combinations, and in many cases – in practice, in the great majority of them – the 'disturbance' has the nature of a certain living contradiction connected with a known expenditure of energy of the whole.

It might be that obsidian arrowheads are excellent, but they contradict the customs and precepts of ancestors that taught people to make arrowheads from fish bones, and, in addition, those fish bones now go to waste, since there is nothing to use them for. It may be that the change in crop rotation promises an increase in yield but the ancestors did not do it that way. The ancestors, after all, were wise and honest and knew what was pleasing to God, and God should not be provoked with this mischief. And, at the same time, there is still strip farming or communal agriculture with the customary three-field or other system that requires individually-worked strips to be turned into common pasture at a specific time, and thus almost any change in crop rotation introduced by one member of the commune would make farming by those who live according to the old ways either extremely difficult or simply impossible.

All this prepares the ground for another, negative tendency in social selection; and if it outweighs the first (positive) tendency that sprang from the 'immediate usefulness' of a given form, then social selection removes this form. This is something that is often observed in reality.

It is clear that two variable magnitudes are involved here. One of them is the level of 'immediate usefulness' of a new technological combination and the other is the level of 'disharmony' – the vital contradiction – that it brings into the social whole. The first magnitude is determined comparatively simply. In the majority of cases, at any rate, no particular doubts arise as to whether or not a new technological techniques increases the 'productivity of labour' and whether it does so to a significant or insignificant extent. The second magnitude – 'social resistance' – is considerably more complex, and it is more difficult to express by a simple formula. Nevertheless, it is possible to point out two basic conditions on which the increase or decrease of social resistance depends.

The first condition is the level of 'novelty' of a given technological form, or, what is the same thing, the degree of its *difference* from the previous, already existing technological forms with which the new form is combined in the system as a whole. The greater the difference and the 'more unaccustomed' the new combination, then, generally speaking, the more significant is the immediate resistance that it encounters in the social environment. The invention of the steamboat encountered the widest incomprehension by ordinary and enlightened people alike right down to Napoleon, and the difficulties that its inventor had to contend with were huge.[16]

But the steam locomotive, invented later, presented something less unusual; its similarity with the steamboat made it closer to the technology that now existed and it achieved social success more easily. Of two similar inventions possessing 'immediate usefulness' to the same degree, it is the one that is least 'new' in its content and that has more points of contiguity with the old technology that has the greatest chances of being preserved and of developing.

---

16   The first steamboat, invented one hundred years before Fulton, was simply smashed by the crowd, and its inventor, Papin, was forbidden by the enlightened authorities to employ such a criminal means of travel. Napoleon called Fulton's steamboat a 'child's plaything'.

Even socio-psychological moments of 'inquisitiveness' and 'interest in the new' include *distrust* and *fear* of these new things and hence the striving to relate to them more cognitively than practically, i.e. not to bring them into everyday life.

In other words, the level of *plasticity* of the social system depends on the strength of the tendency of negative selection. The structure of society itself determines the greater or lesser possibility of new combinations being introduced into it. Because of the basic construction of its organisation, stagnant primitive-tribal society is a hundred or a thousand times less capable of *survival by changing its forms*, than contemporary, capitalist society. The cause of such immobility is first and foremost the poverty of general vital content, and therefore anything 'new' has very little chance of finding any elements that harmonise with it. Anything new appears as if in the role of a 'foreign body' that has entered the living organism. Especially important in this regard is the absence of organising forms and the weak development of speech and knowledge. It would be difficult to find a place in its fragmentary, embryonic thinking – limited due to insufficient words and concepts – for anything out of the ordinary. Elemental conservatism governs there.[17]

The poverty of vital content is not the sole condition, but, generally speaking, it is the main condition that gives rise to the insufficient plasticity of social systems. There is no need to investigate other conditions here, since it would distract us with particulars. In any case, it is obvious that the same new adaptation, depending on the given level of its 'novelty', survives and develops with considerably more difficulty in a more stagnant social system than in a more plastic one. The tendency toward negative selection is stronger in the first case.

Thus, a new technological form enters social life and survives in the social environment only when its 'immediate usefulness' – the energetical 'plus' of life

---

17  Usually, when semi-civilised people must unwillingly assimilate elements of civilisation too quickly, they gradually begin to go extinct. It would be a mistake to ascribe this process exclusively to the alcohol and syphilis that are brought in by 'cultured guests'. Extinction is also observed where the action of these factors is comparatively limited. Neither can one say that pre-civilised people are in general distinguished by poor health. The rapid breakdown of forms of life, thinking, and customs, and the intense adoption of 'newness' imposed from outside – all this leads to a huge expenditure of nervous energy and to excessive work for the psychical system that is given the task of removing countless contradictions that arise from the inadaptability of the old, conservative organisation to the new, fluid content. This excessive neural-psychical work must, due to the inevitable antagonism between the intensity of psychical life and generative activity, slow down reproduction and lower the viability of new generations. The insufficiently plastic system *perishes* beneath the flood of new content to which it cannot exert sufficient resistance.

connected with it – outweighs the negative tendencies of selection that arise from its destruction of the historically given equilibrium of social life. Therefore, by the way, new forms of life clear a road for themselves more easily when this same equilibrium becomes less stable and is shaken by the powerful blows of crises, revolutions, wars, etc.

## VII

'Ideology' is one of the constitutive parts – and a very important part – of the social environment on which the fate of a new technological or ideological form depends. The conservative and retarding influence of ideology can be huge. History knows examples where a whole culture has become incapable of developing because it developed an ideology that ruled out social progress. This is what happened with the slave-owning culture of the ancient world, and it was almost this way with the feudal-Catholic culture of Spain in modern times and with the feudal-bureaucratic culture of China.

On the other hand, a broad and supple ideology is extremely conducive to the development of new forms and to their organic merging into the social whole; its organising forms can play the role of a connective link between the 'new' and 'unusual' and the 'old' and 'accustomed'. The main role in this sense is played by forms of cognition; they help the 'understanding' and assimilation of the new. Many inventions and improvements have perished because they were 'incomprehensible' to the people of their times due to insufficient knowledge.

One thing that no ideology can do is *to cause* development, to serve as its *primary motive power*. Ideology cannot do this because it has an indirect and not a direct relationship to the source of any development – to the immediate struggle of humanity with nature. If it is sometimes assumed that this is not so, that 'ideology' itself can be a real starting point for development, then this is usually due to the lack of clarity in the use of the term 'ideology'. Since people attribute all *scientific activity* to 'ideology', and, since jolts to technological progress sometimes issue from scientific activity, people conclude that ideology is capable of being an independent stimulus to development. The mistake here is that 'scientific activity' does not at all boil down entirely to 'ideology'.

Any 'scientific' progress has its basis in the sphere of the *immediate relationships of humanity with nature* in the sphere of 'technological experience'. Such 'technological experience' appears in equal measure as experience of work in workshops, factories, and fields and as experience in laboratories, physics offices, observatories, geological excavations, and the collection of plants and capturing of birds by natural scientists. Equally, the difference of immediate goals does not change the *type* of activity that is identical in both cases –

the immediate struggle with nature, to be precise. Therefore 'scientific-technological' experience is not at all 'ideological' experience. 'Ideology' begins with the *concepts* that are created on the basis of 'technological' experience. And if, for example, in their 'scientific' work the Curies discovered radium – the application of which probably transformed whole, vast realms of social technology – then they achieved this not by the 'ideological' route of pure thinking but by the 'technological' route of the analysis of things. Neither chemical analysis nor spectroscopic analysis present themselves as 'ideological' processes; they are 'technological' processes. And even where the object of scientific investigation is the living human body and its functions, the essence of the matter remains the same. As an object of investigation, the human organism is a complex of 'external nature', the very same as the instruments and machines that are used for this.

Scientific-technological experience is distinguished from everyday-technological experience only by the systematic and planned selection of the conditions under which it proceeds. Because of this particular trait, scientific-technological experience is more easily and completely organised with the help of 'concepts' than everyday-technological experience is, and the immediate goal of 'scientific work' is connected with this particular trait. It is in this precise meaning that one can, using Engels's formula, designate scientific-technological experience as the 'production of ideas', but one must not forget that in practice this is, nevertheless, first and foremost the production of certain combinations *in external nature*, and consequently, at the same time, it is the 'production of things'. When Engels proposed that in socialist society the 'production of ideas' will be the motor of social development and will attain predominance over the 'production of things', he was absolutely correct. But this must not at all be understood to mean that the role of the motor of social development switches over to 'ideology'; it only means that one realm of the technological process (the production of ideas) therefore comes to the fore compared with its other realm (the production of things), without, however, at all detracting from the decisive significance of the production of things as a motor of social development. *Everywhere* humanity stands face to face with nature, the stimulus for social development is generated from that encounter.

I will illustrate the relationship of the two realms of technological experience with one example that reveals not only their fundamental similarity but also the possibility that they directly coincide. It is well known that in seafaring technology the determination of longitude has huge practical significance. The main instrument for such a determination is the chronometer, set according to the prime meridian, and the method of using the chronometer is to observe the eclipses of the moons of Jupiter and to relate this to corresponding tables. When the captain aims his telescope at Jupiter, he is repeating exactly what Galileo did for the first time 300 years ago, and although one of them has the 'everyday-technological goal' of finding his way and avoiding reefs and the other one had the 'scientific-philosophical' goal of getting to the heart of the nature of things, the *immediately-technological* content of their actions are identical. In both cases a change is introduced into the immediate relationships of humanity and nature with the help of specific methods and tools. Is there any essential difference between the delivery of the light of a planet to a human eye in an increased quantity and with a changed reciprocal deviation by means of a telescope and the delivery of chemical energy for human organisms in a changed combination for better digestion by means tools for acquiring food and by kitchen implements? If this comparison makes the reader smile because of its novelty, this does not make it less true, just like the old idea of the conversion of the energy of solar rays into the chemical energy of a cucumber.

The transformation of everyday-technological experience into scientific-technological experience, and vice versa, is a particularly characteristic and constant trait of machine production.[18]

I considered it necessary to dwell on this issue in order to explain the concepts precisely and to eliminate any possibility of confusing 'ideology' with *scientific technology* in the following analysis. There is scarcely any other concept that has had to undergo such confusion as the concept of 'ideology'. So far many even quite scholarly 'critics' of historical monism stubbornly confuse 'ideological' with 'psychical'. It is even more likely that there will be misunderstandings in regard to more subtle distinctions.

VIII

Turning to the selection of ideological forms, it is necessary first and foremost to note the exclusive role of the social environment in this selection. In regard to technological forms, we have seen that the prime immediate factor of selection is the extra-social environment. For the development of ideological forms, the extra-social environment does not have such an immediate significance; it influences ideological forms only *through the technological process*.

This proposition proceeds from the fact that ideology stands in an indirect – not a direct – relationship to the struggle of society with nature, which is the struggle that lies at the basis of the 'natural' selection of forms of life. 'Organ-

---

18   Several more considerations relevant to this can be read in my work *Iz psikhologii obshchestva*, pp. 83–5, where the entire question is dealt with in a more popular form.

ised' adaptations stand between nature and socially-organising adaptations. As a result of this, the selection of ideological forms has a narrower – I would say, more one-sided – nature; it is only social selection.

It is not difficult to determine the basic direction of the line along which the action of social selection proceeds in the realm of ideology. In the multi-storied superstructure of ideology, this direction is from lower to higher, from technological life to higher, all-embracing organising forms. In knowledge it is directed toward 'ultimate generalisations', in legal life it is directed toward the 'bases of the constitution', in ethical life it is directed toward the 'moral ideal', etc. If the stimuli of development issue from the technological process, then they must first of all act on the primary-organising adaptations that are immediately connected with them. Only when the primary-organising adaptations are changed must the forms that *they* organise – the ideological complexes of a second order – turn out to be unadapted to them and to undergo change and the action of selection, etc. Such, as we have said, is the *basic* line of social selection. A direct result from this is the *growth of conservatism of ideological forms directed from below to above, form organising adaptations of a lower order to a higher order.*

All this completely corresponds to what is observed in reality. In regard to the realm of knowledge, the entire history of science can serve as an illustration. Reform of the concepts that make up the system of science always comes from the bottom up. First, there is an accumulation of particular facts that do not fit within the bounds of the system, but this incompatibility is simply not noticed at first. Subsequently, when generalisations are formed from the new facts that are patently inconsistent with the particular generalisations existing in the system, people begin to express bewilderment and pose questions, but the system, as a whole, nevertheless continues to be preserved. Its particular propositions are improved and touched up in order to smooth over the contradictions, but the highest principles of the system remain inviolable. It is only when the lack of correspondence between the highest principles and the transformed basis of the system becomes too sharp that those principles become 'debatable'. They begin to be questioned, and this indicates the beginning of 'negative selection'. But the decisive moment for negative selection is the appearance of new 'highest principles' of the same level of breadth and generality as the old ones that at the same time completely harmonise with the entire sum of facts and particular generalisations that the system contains. An era of hopeless contention begins for those old high forms, and they finally perish.

An analogous procedure is observable in the sphere of property relationships. The matter begins with a change of factual property relationships. The concrete distribution of property among people and groups changes, and the concrete 'economic' content of the connection between those people and groups and the 'things' that their property consists of also changes. Subsequently, the particular norms of custom and law that immediately systematise and regulate these relationships are reformed. For example, separate laws are issued that correspond to the changing economic conditions. It is only later that the 'constitution' of society, the basic principles of its legal organisation, is drawn into the process of transformation.

If in both illustrations I outline the interconnectedness and consecutiveness of social development very superficially and in the most general terms, this is because, as we come closer to the issue, we inevitably encounter increasing complexity in it that is very important for us and that issues from the fact that the social system is far from being a complete unity. Both modern and ancient civilised societies are subdivided into classes, and this leads to the simultaneous existence of different ideological systems, to a struggle between them, and to their development in different directions. We will return to the problem of the selection of ideological forms later on, after our analysis has been broadened by introducing the concepts of 'classes' and 'class development'.

But now I must dwell on another complication of the problem.

IX

The 'multi-storeyed nature' of the ideological superstructure, the direction of its basic line of development from below to above, and the growth of the conservatism of forms in that development explain one of the remarkable paradoxes of life that is encountered by a theory of social development. To be precise, at the same time that the real bases of a complex ideological system are already disappearing – and have even, for the most part, disappeared – the development of the ideological forms that correspond to them continue to be refined at the highest levels of ideology. Thus the religious dogmatics of Catholicism completed their development and Catholicism's highest principle (authoritarianism) obtained its fullest and purest formulation only when the feudal basis of Catholicism was already 99 per cent destroyed and new forms of the struggle for life had engendered new concepts. In governments of modern times, the bureaucratic-absolutist constitution and its theory are attaining their maximum development – in a system that is formally identical with Asiatic despotism – when the relations of production are already in need of completely different governing forms. And so on. At the lower levels of ideology a new line of development begins, but at the higher levels the old line continues to move progressively forward. The role of social selection turns out to be sharply bifurcated, and this is because the immediate social environment is different for different layers of ideology.

For the lowest layers of the superstructure this environment is formed, on the one hand, by technological forms and, on the other hand, by the next higher ideological forms. For the higher layers of the superstructure, the environment is formed by the next lower and the higher ideological forms. When the immediate environment of the lower levels has already been transformed and is significantly transforming those lower levels from one direction ('from below'), the environment of the higher layers remains as before and causes them to be elaborated in the former direction.

All this naturally flows from the regularity that we have designated as the 'basic line of ideological development'. But on the basis of social selection there arises *from this regularity* yet another, derivative regularity – a 'derivative line of ideological development' with a direction opposite to the first.

As I have just now pointed out, the proximal and immediate social environment of each given layer of the ideological superstructure – the environment on which the development of that layer must most directly depend – is made up of the layer that lies lower and the one that lies higher, of the forms that organise *it* and of the forms that *it* organises. In the process of selection, each given layer must adapt to both parts of its environment.

In consequence of this we have reason to expect that a given ideological form or a given group of ideological forms that belong to one or another layer must change not only in the event that the layer located *below it* is transformed but also in the event that due to some cause or other the layer located *above it* is changed. Under what conditions does this happen?

As society develops, the technological process, broadening and proliferating in various directions, is transformed into an extremely complex, branched system; its various realms are so differentiated from one another that to a certain extent they carry on an independent existence. For example, in our times, with the strongly developed social division of labour, agriculture lives a life that is significantly different from that of the manufacturing industry, commerce lives a different life from that of the scholarly world, etc. In the Middle Ages, feudal forms of existence in the countryside existed side-by-side with the petty bourgeois development in cities, and so forth. It is completely natural that each such realm of a socio-technological system also produces to a certain extent a separate ideology – as is easy to see in all the examples we have cited. The distinctness of the 'organising' storeys of the superstructure that appear in this way is revealed in all their dimensions, from the very lowest to the very highest links. Thus, even the last 'universally-organising' link of this chain can include traces of its origin in a specific realm of the social process.

It is completely natural that the development of the ideological series is accomplished with different energy and completeness in different realms of social life. The realm in which development proceeds more quickly and intensely acquires *finished* ideological systems – cognitive or normative – earlier than all other realms. In other realms, similar systems turn out, at the same time, to be not yet complete and to lack higher organising forms. But, since the vital singularity of all these realms is thoroughly relative, and, at the same time, a more or less close vital interconnectedness exists among them, and since any organising form, if it becomes firmly established and develops, has a tendency to contain indefinitely broad content, then in many cases a direct unification of unfinished ideological series with finished ones occurs. The higher organising forms of the perfected series also become organisers for the unfinished series; they substitute themselves functionally for the missing links of the unfinished series – a phenomenon for which there are many analogies in the biological world.

But at the same time a mutual adaptation must inevitably occur between the higher unifying forms and the lower forms that have now fallen into the sphere of the organising function of the higher forms. Keeping in mind the especially significant conservatism of higher forms, it is easy to think that this adaptation boils down in the majority of cases to a change precisely of the lower, more particular forms, and in so doing they will be changed in direction such that full harmony between them and the higher organising forms is created. It is obvious that this process of adaptation of lower layers of ideology to higher layers in a given realm can also continue *all the way down to the technological forms* of this realm. Thus, there appears a second, derivative line of ideological development – from the top down.

One can point out as many illustrations of this process as one likes. The first time I found it necessary to touch on this process, I cited examples exclusively from the realm of forms of thinking. First, the authoritarian *dualism of the organisational and the implementational functions*, the ideology of which was created in the sphere of the basic fields of collective labour and then spread out to all realms of technological and ideological experience so that any phenomenon of reality began to be known in a two-fold form – as a 'bodily' and 'spiritual' combination or as 'appearance' and 'essence', and so forth. This is the metaphysical formalism of empty abstractions that verbally combines contradictory content. It begins in the social interconnectedness and social contradictions of the market, and it puts its stamp on all the everyday, scientific, and philosophical thinking of the bourgeois world. Second the energetical monism, that springs up from the technological experience of machine production and that, in our times, strives to transform all realms of scientific thinking and then, of course, everyday thinking, as well. And so on.[19] But the same it can be observed just as often in the sphere of 'normative' ideology – custom, law, morality.

Thus, the strict law of property of modern times – based on the Roman law of property – unquestionably took shape in the sphere of exchange, trade, merchant capital, and embryonic industrial capital. In the countryside, during the first centuries of modern times, however, the relationships of a natural economy existed, and completely different customary-legal property relationships and unsystematised norms of property prevailed. The closer the economic connection between the trading-industrial world and the agricultural world became and the broader and deeper the interaction between them, the more the agricultural world was penetrated by new legal forms that transformed property relations from the top down, powerfully speeding up radical reform of the entire sphere of social life right down to its technological forms. In an analogous way the moral ideal of the petty bourgeoisie (the ideal of 'absolute justice' under which is hidden no more than an exact exchange of equivalents), having sprung up from the relationships of petty exchange, subsequently brought all other life relationships of the petty bourgeoisie into the sphere of its influence – relations of family, friendship, love, and ideological interaction among people. The evaluation of human feelings and actions from the point of view of one ultimate principle – 'everything must be paid for; nothing is free!' – penetrated everywhere.

It would be possible to bring in still other illustrations, but a theory of classes and class psychology, without which even the examples I have cited cannot be fully understood, is their real domain. I will return to this problem later, but in the meantime I will make special mention of one interesting and important 'transformation' of two lines of ideological development – a fundamental line and a derivative line.

Those two lines are the general scientific methods of induction and deduction.

X

Science has all technological experience as its basis ('everyday-technological' experience and specialised 'scientific-technological' experience, alike) and strives to systematically organise that experience into harmonious and orderly

---

19   See the entire article 'Aftoritarnoe myshlenie' in *Iz psikhologii obshchestva*, and even earlier Part III, Sections 7–11 in *Poznanie s istoricheskoi tochki zreniia*.

forms of knowledge. Consequently, science consciously and systematically carries out the process of producing specific ideological series. But the conscious creativity of organising forms has no other methods and paths than spontaneous creativity, and conscious creativity finds it necessary to reproduce spontaneous creativity, only in a more harmonious and abbreviated form. *Induction* represents such an 'idealised' reproduction of the *fundamental* line of spontaneous ideological development, a line running from the 'more particular' to the 'more general', from organising combinations that are of narrower meaning to combinations of a broader meaning – in a word, from 'lower' to 'higher' forms. This meaning of induction is too obvious for it to be necessary to especially dwell on it. And *deduction* stands in exactly the same relationship to the *derivative* line of ideological development that runs from the 'general' to the 'particular' or 'from top to bottom'. Both the conditions and means of the application of deduction immediately reveal this basic identity.

Deduction is applied when there are insufficient general forms for harmoniously uniting a certain sum of empirical content or a certain quantity of the particular forms that organise the empirical content – when, for example, it is unknown according to what 'law' the given 'phenomena' are occurring. Then one attempts to apply, in the capacity of this general form, a form that has already been produced in some other related realm of experience, to find out whether this produces a cognitive contradiction or, on the contrary, cognitive harmony and the growth of the ability to embrace experience with organising forms. In the latter case, deduction is successful, the cognitive connection is established, and partial cognitive forms that need to be organised are re-formed and adapted to those higher and more general forms with which they have been thus united.

The essence of the matter is best explained with an example. Suppose that in the realm of observations of inorganic nature we have arrived, through long and difficult induction, at one of the ultimate generalisations of chemistry and physics – the idea of the 'eternity of matter', to be specific. Let us suppose that this issue has still not been investigated in regard to living matter in physiological processes, and a general law of its quantitative changes has still not been obtained. The desire then arises to apply an idea to this realm of experience that has already been worked out in a related field by subjecting to it the observations and particular generalisations that we already have. But in so doing the very generalisations must be transformed under the influence of a new 'organising' idea. For example, the empirical generalisation – 'when an animal goes without food, the weight of its body decreases' – attains this new form: 'when an animal goes without food, its weight decreases at exactly the same magnitude as the weight of the surrounding environment grows'. This transformation is the result of 'deduction'. But the question consists in whether the generalisations that have been transformed in this way are viable, and this means whether they actually 'organise' the experience that they embrace and do not turn out to contradict it. In the first case, 'deduction is confirmed by experience', and in the second case 'deduction is disproven by experience'. This is the so-called 'verification of deduction', and when it is carried out consciously and systematically, verification quickly decides the question of the vital connection of a given 'general law' with a given 'particular realm of experience'. In our example this verification boils down to a technologically simple experiment – the placement of a starving animal in an environment that is enclosed and easy to weigh, in some kind of hermetically sealed box with contrivances that guarantee the possibility of breathing. This verification leads to the 'confirmation of deduction' and the entire theory of the organic world is transformed to the extent made necessary by its subjection to the law of the 'eternity of matter'.

While such verification occurs *consciously* and *systematically* in scientific deduction, it is accomplished spontaneously in spontaneously flowing ideological creativity, but here it is also unavoidable and vitally necessary in all respective cases. When, consistent with the law of the 'derivative line of ideological development', any kind of higher organising form – cognitive, legal, moral, etc. – is 'spread out' over one or another realm of social life, then the social fate of these transformations appears as a *living verification* of the given higher forms in a given realm. For example, if the principle of property in its big bourgeois form extends to life in a countryside that has not yet left the phase of feudal-communal structure with a small admixture of petty-bourgeois elements, then it can easily happen that the transformative tendency of the new form of property causes a strong negative selection due to its contradiction of the technological and economic content that it must organise. Then it is not 'inculcated' in the given realm until sufficient changes favourable to it occur in the very basis of country life and negative selection is replaced by positive selection.

Although higher ideological adaptations are distinguished by more significant conservatism than lower ones, they are not, needless to say, absolutely conservative. Therefore, wherever they are transferred from the realm in which they appeared to another realm, thus engendering a 'derivative line of ideological development', they do only always only *transform* lower forms, but it is not uncommon for them to be *themselves transformed* by the influence of the lower forms to a greater or lesser degree. The same is also the case in 'deduction'. The *verification* of the deductive applications of any law often leads to a change in its formulation, usually in the sense of greater breadth and precision. Thus the principle 'for every action there is an equal and opposite reaction' that Newton established for mechanics was spread to other realms of physical experience in the nineteenth century and was transformed into the principle of the conservation of energy, which, because of the rigour and limitlessness of its application, became a universal form of thinking.[20]

The derivative line of ideological development and its particular case as well – the deductive spread of cognitive norms beyond the bounds of the realm in which they appeared – are observed *not only when* there are insufficient higher organising norms in a certain realm of labour-related experience, but also when the available norms of this type turn out to be in contradiction with the changing vital content that it must organise. In this case, those norms might be 'ousted' by norms that were formed in another similar realm but at the same time are more in harmony with the transformed basis of the given realm. This is what often occurs in the contemporary era with its headlong development, intensified by the discrepancy between 'lower' and 'higher' ideological formations. The religious worldview of the Russian countryside corresponds well enough to the technology and economics of the era of serfdom, but it now no longer fits the contemporary content of country life with its strongly developed money economy and internal struggle. The religious worldview is therefore forced out by the 'city' worldview – the cult of reason and knowledge.

It still remains to add that the derivative line of ideological development can begin, of course, not only with the very highest organising forms but also with the underlying and more particular forms, just as 'deduction' need not take only higher laws or final generalisations as its starting point.

XI

Although the derivative line of ideological development is directed from higher organising forms to lower ones and can even impart a modifying influence on the technological forms that are 'the last to be organised', this does not, however, make ideas the *primary* social motor of development under such conditions. A 'basic' line is always concealed behind a derivative line; those ideological adaptations that transform a certain realm of social life 'from the top down' – giving impetus even to its technology – are themselves the result of development that goes 'from the bottom up' and that has its starting point in the technological process. This means that here, 'in the final analysis', 'techno-

---

20   In order not to dwell on a particular example, I will not explain here why the two principles are identical. For a popular treatment of this question see the chapter devoted to 'the third stage of the development of causality' in my work, *Osnovnye elementy istoricheskogo vzgliada na prirodu*.

logical' changes indeed provide the basis for everything. And if we encounter a process of social development going in the opposite direction, from ideological to technological forms, then we cannot consider the social-genetic investigation of this process to be completed until we explain the origin of the ideological changes that arise in that process of social development – until we trace this origin right down to its 'technological basis', to its starting point.

Thus, in investigating the 'social environment' as the condition for the development (or degradation) of social forms, we must make a distinction between two parts of this environment. This distinction is more precisely formulated in the following way: in regard to the development of forms of human life, socially-dynamic conditions are situated in the technological process while socially-static conditions are situated in the ideological process. The term 'dynamic conditions' of any phenomenon means those conditions that constitute its 'energetical cause', i.e. the processes – the energy – that serve as the *source* of the given phenomenon, and this is precisely the significance of the technological process in social life. The term 'static conditions' refers to everything else. Static conditions influence the course of a phenomenon, and they influence its 'form'. Static conditions 'define' the course of a phenomenon in the sense of defining the boundaries of its development, but they do not 'cause' it; they do not provide its origin. This is the role played by ideology in relation to new social forms and their changes.

The 'defining' significance of ideology in the social process is precisely that it *limits* and *gives form* to that process. It turns out to be a powerful agent of social selection in the social process. Let us suppose that a new social form appears in embryonic form. Imagine that it will be a technological contrivance – a new 'machine' (i.e. the production and application of the machine, of course; the machine itself, as we know, is not a *social* complex at all). There is no need to explain and prove that this new form arose from the technological process, from its requirements and from its material. What will be the influence of existing ideology? In order to clearly conceive the *limiting* aspect of this influence, it is sufficient to compare the fate of a new machine under handicraft, capitalistic, and socialistic systems.

In a handicraft system with guild norms, in the majority of cases, *the more technologically advantageous a new form is, the more inevitable it is that the form will perish*. The greater that a machine raises the productivity of labour, the more 'harmful' it is from the point of view of a guild organisation. The entire system of normative adaptations of this organisation is aimed at the precise definition of the forms and boundaries of the process of labour; it is in this way that the stable equilibrium of petty-bourgeois handicraft enterprises is achieved and that they are preserved from the destructive forces of the struggle and spontaneity of the market. A machine threatens this stability. It destroys the equilibrium of petty enterprises, and it provides a space for the power of the market over them. Because of this power, the machine is capable of destroying the majority of petty enterprises, while elevating only a few instead. Therefore, the entire ideology of the handicraft system is harshly hostile to the machine and to rapid technological progress, in general, and *limits* it. If the ideology does not destroy a newly appearing invention, then it imparts a *distinctive social form* to it. Handicraft ideology transforms that invention into the *privilege* of a particular group of enterprises – of some kind of 'guild' – and establishes limits and conditions for its application in production.

In the world in which capital rules, however, the ideological environment does not have this kind of social selection. Under capitalism, a machine does not encounter the kind of resistance that would increase in parallel with its immediate usefulness for production. On the contrary, resistance *decreases* with the growth of a machine's usefulness, and the chances of success of the new form increases. Nevertheless, resistance also does exist here. A machine that raises the productivity of labour will not find a place in production if it is not *profitable*, i. e., if its market price is not lower than the price of the labour power that it replaces. The fetishistic idea of 'profit' entirely governs the thinking of entrepreneurs – the organisers of production – and itself determines their actions. Everything that stands in contradiction to the idea of profit is rapidly and inevitably removed by negative selection. As a result, as is well known, there is a significant limitation of the application of machines, particularly at the lower stages of the development of capital when labour power is cheap. And the same ultimate capitalist ideal regulates – although in an entirely different way from guild norms – all production and applications of a machine and determines the concrete *form* of a given technological implement. It determines the material for construction of the machine, the extent of its use, the quantity and quality of those who work with it, supplemental implements such as controls, enclosures, etc.

In socialist society, all limitations that result from privileges or because of subjection to the fetish of profit disappear. In the conscious and systematic organisation of production under socialism, the question of any new machine is decided from the point of view of its direct 'usefulness'. But even there, although to an incomparably less extent than in our society, the relative conservatism of ideology will have a limiting influence on the application of new technological devices, and this influence will become perceptible – and sometimes even decisive – in regard to those machines, for example, that achieve only a negligible increase in the productivity of labour and to those machines whose usefulness, though probable, has not yet been completely established.

As far as the forms of realisation and application of new technological combinations, one can expect that a large role will be played by the *aesthetic norms* of social consciousness ...

Consequently, even then 'ideology' will remain a limiting and formative force but not an independent motive power of social development; it will be a 'static' but not a 'dynamic' condition of development.

∵

Summarising the connection and correlation between 'ideology' and 'technology' in the process of social development, we arrive at the following formulations:

1. The technological process is the realm of the immediate struggle of society with nature; ideology is the realm of organising forms of social life. In the final analysis, the technological process presents precisely the content that is organised by ideological forms.
2. Consistent with such a correlation, the technological process represents the fundamental realm of social life and social development, and ideology represents a derivative realm of social life and development. Ideology is energetically conditioned by the technological process in the sense that it arises and develops on account of the inherent preponderance of assimilation over disassimilation in it. From the qualitative aspect, the material of ideological forms also has its basis in the technological realm.
3. The development of technological forms is accomplished under the immediate action both of 'extra-social' selection (the influence of external nature) and also of social selection. Development of ideology is directly subject only to social selection.
4. The starting point of any social development lies in the technological process. The basic line of development goes from technological forms through the lower organising forms of ideology to higher ones. Correspondingly, the growth of conservatism of social forms goes in the same direction.
5. The derivative line of social development, directed from higher organising forms to lower ones and from ideology to technology, is always only a continuation and reflection of the fundamental line. It not only does not change the relatively large magnitude of conservatism of the higher forms of ideology but it even depends on this conservatism as a necessary condition.
6. Thus, the dynamic conditions of social development and degradation – the motive forces of these processes – lie in the technological process;

static conditions of social development and degradation – limiting, regulating, formative conditions – lie in ideology.

## 2  Classes and Groups

I

In the preceding part of my analysis, I consistently treated society as one living whole, with a single direction of selection of its elements – its social forms. But such a point of view is only permissible up to a certain point; it expresses only an *abstraction* from a few traits that really appear in the life of society sometimes to a greater and sometimes to a lesser degree. At further stages of analysis, these traits must be taken into account, and they boil down to the *relative vital separateness* of specific parts of society, and, corresponding to this separateness, to a *relatively different direction* of the selection of social forms within the confines of these parts.

Primitive society, small and tightly cohesive, is not divided into classes. The level of its vital unity is characteristic of a living organism – not, of course, of an organism of a higher type but one of the lower multi-celled organisms such as coelenterates (cnidaria or ctenophora). The beginning of the division of society into classes and social groups lies in the same place that any social development in general lies – in the technological process. As it expands and grows in different directions in the external environment, the socio-technological process undergoes powerful *differentiation* that is expressed in the 'division of labour'. As we have seen, the development of technological forms is dependent not only on 'social selection' but also – and first and foremost – on 'extra-social' selection, on the immediate influences of external nature. As the social whole grows and expands ever more widely, the diversity of the conditions of external nature, in which the various members and groups of that social whole must carry out their labour, provides the starting point for the development of the 'social division of labour' – for the separation of agriculture from manufacturing and from mining and, subsequently, for the further disintegration of these sectors into even smaller ones.

There was another subdivision of society that paralleled this subdivision and that also was caused by the broadening and increasing complexity of technology, except that it emerged from society along a different path. It was precisely the division of labour that lowered the level of immediate coordination of separate labour-related functions and increased the immediate contradictions of the technical process. From this arose the necessity for an adaptation directed at the immediate and systematic harmonisation of the parts of the process of labour – to the immediate and systematic removal of the particular contradictions that arose in it. These adaptations were worked out in the form of the separation of the organisational function from the implementational function.

The 'organiser' of the process of labour represents a personal form of the 'organising adaptation', just as 'ideology' represented an impersonal form. In the development of life it often occurs that similar functions are carried out by organs that are extremely dissimilar in their origin and in the type of their structure. Nevertheless, there is, of course, a difference in the nature of the 'organising' function of a human organiser and any 'idea' or 'norm'. In the first case this function has a more immediate and more lively and fluid nature. Each 'instruction' of the organiser is like a 'norm' that the organiser creates for that *given, particular* case. While even the most modest ideological norm – in terms of vital significance – embraces a whole indefinite series of particular cases. But then the activity of the organiser embraces each particular case of organisation incomparably more completely, and the organiser can entirely define it, whereas the impersonal, ideological form always defines one or another social fact only partially and captures only any one of its 'aspects' or particularities. The basic similarity of both types of 'organising social adaptations' is expressed also in their chain of development. In both cases an ascending series is formed that narrows as it rises upward, such as any feudal chain of organisers, going from the head of a peasant family through a multitude of lord-vassal links to the emperor or pope, or a bureaucratic chain, going from the lowest police officer to the absolute monarch. Such a chain is completely analogous to any ideological chain of concepts or norms from the most particular to the most general.

The differentiation of an implementer and an organiser and also of organisers of different levels can similarly – and to an even greater degree – serve as the basis for *different* directions of social selection, just like the form of the division of labour that I first pointed out. In order not to confuse these genetically different and vitally dissimilar means of dividing up society, I will designate a division of the first kind with the term 'social groups' (farmers, artisans, traders, etc.) and the division of the second kind with the term 'classes' (slave-owners and slaves, entrepreneurs and workers, etc.). Thus, in my terms, the typical relationship between social groups will be *specialisation* and the typical relationship between classes will be *domination* and *subordination*.[21]

---

21  I have provided a schematic overview of the development and the ultimate forms of both of these social relationships in a popular form in the article 'Sobiranie cheloveka' ['The Reintegration of Humankind'] in my book *Novyi mir*. The concept of 'estate' (a juridically singled-out part of society) is not useful here for our analysis. An 'estate' can be either a

II

*Of itself*, the division of labour in society still far from equates to the division of society into groups and classes. As long as the differences or even the specific contradictions do not go beyond the confines of the technical process, they are no more than differences and contradictions among parts of one whole – something that is inevitable, it goes without saying, in any complex form of life. And social selection strives to harmonise the relationships of these parts through the production of *organising forms*. Only when these differences and contradictions *are organised as such*, only when they cross over into the realm of organising forms so that separate 'ideologies' are created, only then can we speak of the division of society into groups and classes.

Quite significant specialisation unquestionably existed in the ancient Indian commune, even if it was of a primitive nature. But this still did not signify the division of the commune into social groups, because the entire realm of thinking and norms in everything important remained identical for all members of the collectivity. The setting off of 'elders' also did not signify division into classes for exactly the same reason. The elder of the commune, as an organiser of labour, was only the person with the most experience in comparison with other members of the commune, but he was no different from the others as far as the entire method of 'understanding' this experience was concerned. Just the opposite, in a city commune of the Middle Ages, each craft was organised in a special social group that lived an independent life in the sphere of technology. Each social group consolidated this separateness, on the one hand, by a system of handicraft instruction that was inaccessible to representatives of other crafts, and, on the other hand, by a particular system of norms in the form of a guild statute that regulated the internal life of the craft and in the form of special privileges of the guild in regard to external life. Ideological conservatism strengthened this separateness so that when a new division occurred within a handicraft (a class division) and 'journeymen'[22] with an independent ideology organised against 'masters', the union of journeymen expanded and not infrequently went beyond the limits of a separate town and even a separate nation, but it never left the confines of an individual handicraft. Inter-town

---

class or a social group. [Bogdanov addresses this point because Imperial Russia defined the categories of its social structure as 'estates' – *sosloviia*. While the noble estate would more or less correspond to a class, the estates of clergy or of Cossacks or of various categories of city-dwellers would not. (Trans.)]

22  The Russian word *podmaster'e* can mean either 'apprentice' or 'journeyman'. I believe that Bogdanov is referring to associations of journeymen [trans.].

and international unions of journeymen of a single handicraft appeared, but no inter-handicraft unions of journeymen appeared even in a single town.

This class division of a handicraft became realised in fact only when journeymen, having ceased to be simple 'grubs' of the master, were forced by their economic position to look on life and on their interests as being *different* from their 'masters' and to create different norms of behaviour for themselves than the norms that corresponded to the views and desires of their masters. In sum, class division occurred when an 'ideology' of journeymen arose.

In general one can say that the real separateness of social groups and classes begins where the division of labour gives rise to *mutual lack of understanding* among people.

Thus, the *basis* of these social divisions lies in the technological process, in 'production'; but their *formational* point is ideology or, more accurately, 'ideologies'.

III

The specialisation of labour essentially creates a partial *qualitative* heterogeneity of people's life experience. The material of life that is organised in ideological forms is not the same for a cobbler as for a farmer and is not the same for a farmer as for a sailor, etc. At first, when socialisation itself was still only taking shape and workers in a tribal commune *predominantly* devoted themselves to a specific field of labour, while occupying themselves from time to time with other fields and possessing a certain 'facility' in almost all of them, this difference between the technological experience of individual workers compared with the life content that they all had in common was so insignificant that it could be reflected – and even then reflected weakly – on only the most 'particular' concepts, only on the very lowest links of the ideological series, and it disappeared without a trace in the levels that lay above it. To the extent that specialisation developed, the realm of ideological differences broadened at the bottom of the series, on the one hand, and rose from lower links ever higher, on the other. Now each difference that appeared became a condition for social selection and intensified the difference in the *direction* of social selection. At each step it was easier and easier for new differences to be created. Thus the tendency for differentiation, if it could manifest itself in a pure, isolated form, had to progressively intensify, and the magnitude of differentiation that it expresses would then, mathematically speaking, be something like an exponential function.[23]

---

23   i.e. functions for which the basic variable (in the given case, time) serves as a *logarithm*, as an exponential power (for example $y = a^x$).

But along with differentiation another, contrary tendency exists – an 'integrating' tendency or simply an organising tendency. The *common* content of the life of social groups not only does not disappear but grows in its turn, especially due to the mutual communication of people. And in the presence of specialisation communication continues and even progresses because it is stimulated by specialisation. The further that specialisation proceeds, the less separate groups are able to manage without one another, the more necessary and frequent are their 'economic' dealings and, on the basis of these dealings, the more necessary and frequent is their mutual exchange of experience and ideas. When the mutual 'incomprehension' of social groups (always partial incomprehension, needless to say) becomes a palpable obstacle to communication and the source of real 'misunderstandings', then social selection strives to work out common ideological forms of mutual 'comprehension' for these groups. Vital necessity forces the 'familiarisation' of social groups with one another, and the parts of their worldviews that contradict one another are mutually acted on and smoothed over. This second tendency can, in its turn, progressively strengthen, finding support in each success that is achieved – in each success that increases the homogeneity of the environment of social selection for different groups.

We thus observe two progressively developing antagonistic tendencies, and in the whole sum of concrete conditions the balance between the two tendencies always preponderates on one side or the other. As the differentiation of the technological process progresses, it is in general possible to ascertain in the series of vacillations a preponderance of the first, differentiating tendency in the life of various social groups. But at a specific level of development, coinciding with the beginning of machine production, a turnabout occurs.

From the colossal material of technological experience, systematised by science, common technological techniques are worked out. They are technological forms that are applied, with insignificant variations of particulars, in various aspects of social labour. The essence of this transformation consists in that a new link – a mechanised apparatus – appears between people's bodies and the tools that act directly on the material of labour. And the relationship of human beings to external nature is condensed in their relationship to this apparatus, to the machine. Machines reflect in their construction the results of the most multi-faceted experience accumulated over centuries that have been reduced by scientific cognition to the simplest forms. Machines are considerably more homogenous and substantially more similar to one another than the materials and products of their work, and the content of the technological experience of people who work with machines is considerably more similar and homogenous than it was for old specialist-artisans or workers in textile mills. The improvement of machines, which gradually leads to the transformation of all of them into 'automatic mechanisms', reinforces this tendency toward a limit that is yet unknown. It is as if 'specialisation' is transferred from people to machines, and it is not only that a convergence of 'specialties' occurs in the basic content of people's technological experience, but, in addition, the connection between individuals and their 'specialities' weakens. Switching from one occupation to another becomes ever easier. Thus, in the final analysis, social development undermines the division of social groups, and a path to a higher social unity takes shape.[24]

IV

The division of society into classes – in its foundation, in its development, and in its final results – is deeper than its division into social groups. In its final phase, class division does not smooth over and subside without being noticed, as the division of society into groups does, but is overcome by force in harsh struggle and violent crises.

The difference in the content of experience for the 'organiser' and the 'implementer' is, from the very beginning of the distinction between these functions, both qualitative and quantitative. But the qualitative difference of experience here is not the same type as normal 'specialisation' but is absolutely different. A cobbler, a blacksmith, a farmer carry out their various acts of labour, but all these acts lie on one plane of life – in the sphere of the immediate influence of the human organism on nature that is external to society. It is the immediate struggle with nature, and, in a word, it is the realm of the *technological* process in the fullest and strictest meaning of the word. The role of the 'organiser' who directs and coordinates the labour of such workers – whether it is the patriarch of a tribal commune, a Medieval lord, a slave-owner of the ancient world, or an entrepreneur in the era of capitalism – is different. They act on nature *through* the implementers, but – *to the extent* that they are indeed organisers and not implementers – they do not enter into the immediate struggle with nature. Their labour does not pertain to the technological process to the same extent and in the same sense as the labour of implementers. For the organiser, the immediate object of activity is not nature that is external to society; it is other people. And the tool of this activity is not the means of production but

---

24  A more thorough and detailed description of this tendency is provided in Section VII, *'Promyshlennyi kapitalizm'* ['Industrial Capitalism'] in *Kratkii kurs ekonomonicheskoi nauki*, and also in *'Sobiranie cheloveka' Novyi mir.*

the means of communication. I have already compared organisational functions with ideological adaptations and, in reality, the hugely important role in social labour of the organiser 'indirectly' related to external nature. It is located in the realm of the 'ideological process'.

Organisers 'deliberate', creating the most expedient plan for organised processes of labour, and 'give orders' that inform each of the implementer what they must do. Organisers then 'supervise' the work, stopping and limiting the implementers wherever they deviate from the plan. We see, therefore, that the work of organisers reproduces in an embryonic form and in a fluid state all three of the basic types of ideological forms I have pointed out above. All this profoundly distinguishes their function – and, consequently, the content of his experience – from the implementational function with its 'immediate-technological' experience.

From a quantitative perspective, the experience of the organiser is also distinguished from the experience of the implementer by greater breadth and completeness, and this difference is more significant than the strong specialisation of implementational labour.

Finally, for the successful execution of his function, the level of *organisation* of experience in the psyche of the organiser must be significantly higher than what is needed by the implementer. This is a difference which, together with the preceding, is usually expressed in one word: 'education'. And in reality 'education' at all times has been the specific distinction of the organisational classes.

Thus, the specific features of organisational life is its greater breadth, diversification, and organisation of experience, but, at the same time, it is experience that is less immediately related to labour and is not based on the direct struggle with external nature.

Of itself, the breadth and diversification of experience is, of course, a highly favourable condition for the *plasticity* and *progressiveness* of a social type; the rich material of life provides many elements and stimuli for development. The organisation of experience can sometimes be a favourable condition and sometimes be an unfavourable condition in this regard – everything depends on the *form* into which experience is organised. But here a third characteristic of the organisational type has a decisively unfavourable significance. Organisers are not *directly* related to the struggle with nature through labour; they are more or less separated from the immediate struggle, which is the starting point of any social progress. From this feature a deep *conservative* tendency is born, and in the majority of cases it stamps its imprint on organisational life so that the opposite, progressive tendency pales and disappears in its presence.

But this occurs only when the entire ideology of a given organisational class is already completely organised and has expanded into a definite system. As long as this has not happened, as long as the ideology of the class is not finalised and systematised from the very lowest to the very highest links, the work of ideological creativity proceeds intensively and the conservatism of the class, lacking a basis in a stable grouping of norms and ideas, remains hidden. This is why, no matter what era you pick, so much of life and movement of the young organisational class is the direct opposite of what is observed in the final phase, when that class has already 'organised' life within the limits of its worldview and interests.[25]

In any case, the very direction of the development of the organisational class cannot be identical with the direction of the class that is subordinate to it. The difference between the basic social function of the two classes is too significant, and the difference in the content of their experience and the difference in the desires and interests that flow from that experience is too significant.

V

However, before moving on to an explanation of the essence of the difference between the two directions of class development and the consequences that result from it, it is necessary to define the concept of 'organisational class' more concretely.

I have already pointed out that the organisational function in itself still does not cause 'class being' and class cleavage and that 'class' appears only in conjunction with the ideological isolation of organisers and implementers. I now add that the organisational class usually takes shape and becomes a class earlier than the 'implementational' class does. It is not infrequent that the organisational class already has a definite worldview and elaborated system of norms that organise its life and protect its interests at the same time that the implementational class remains an amorphous social mass for which the organisational ideology is an external, oppressive force. The implementational class either does not have its own ideology or has only embryonic combinations of one. The slave-owners of the ancient world were a real class, but it still never turned out that slaves were raised to the level of a class.

---

25   The conceptual nature of this entire work does not permit me to dwell at all either on the basic manifestations of the conservatism of the organisers' social consciousness or even on those influences by which that consciousness is limited and often masked. I have written about both in the chapter 'Aftoritarnoe myshlenie' in my book *Iz psikhologii obshchestva*.

But in such cases as this, a deep differentiation that sharply differentiates the organisational class from the rest of society can nevertheless be observed. But often not even this happens, and the organisational function is isolated in an individual. Differentiation does not result since two altogether different directions of development do not result. This occurs in those cases when organisers are far more closely tied in the process of labour with their 'implementers' than with other, similar organisers. I will dwell on two combinations of this type that have special significance for my analysis.

The petty-bourgeois household economy contains one organiser – the head of the family – and several subordinates – the wife, children, and domestic slaves (known in contemporary society as 'servants'). Although in society the those subordinates can be singled out as hired labour that possesses the characteristics of a proletarian class, nevertheless, within the confines of the 'family' proper, the interrelationships remain extremely close. The head of the petty-bourgeois family is too sharply separated from the other similar independent members of the petty-bourgeoisie by the contradictions of competition and exchange and too closely united with his wife and children by the relationships of life. In addition, in a typical petty-bourgeois enterprise, the head is not only a 'organiser' but also an 'implementer'; in handicraft, farming, and petty-mercantile labour, other members of the family only 'help' him and are subordinate to his directions. As a result, such an enterprise can represent one solid collectivity with a common line of development.

But if, as has been observed in the majority of cases in recent centuries, the household economy of kitchen and children is separated sufficiently sharply from the economy of the workshop, store, or office and becomes the exclusive specialty of women, as a subordinate function in this system of relationships, then no kind of living closeness of men and women in the family can prevent their social types from beginning to develop in different directions, so that a differentiating tendency comes to the fore. Here differentiation has a dual nature – that of both a social group and a class simultaneously. Both subordination to the husband and specialisation in the domestic household makes women into the socially-lower type that they are still today in the middle layers and partially in the lower layers of society.

In the petty-bourgeois and middle-bourgeois family, the woman tends predominantly toward a religious-authoritarian ideology with a conservatism that, even amid the general progress of life, crosses over to an outright reactionary character. The man, although not immune from these tendencies, is, in comparison to the woman, the bearer of positivism and progressiveness. Compared with the narrowness and ignorance of the middle-class woman, the worldview of the man seems broad and enlightened. Why is this so? Religious and conservative ideology is the expression of relationships of domination and subordination. The woman in a bourgeois family revolves exclusively within the confines of these relationships because the other side of the bourgeois world – its anarchistic relationships among enterprises, its competition – is hidden from her by the person of her husband, and direct participation in that side of life is inaccessible to women. Things are different for the man. For him, in addition to the authoritarian organisation of the household economy, the social struggle – the *anarchistic* form of social organisation – is close and immediately palpable. Therefore, the corresponding ideology – metaphysical or bourgeois-positivist, with its progressive tendency that is expressed in the desire to hold one's ground in the fierce struggle for existence – assumes a major place in his ideological world.[26] And if the profound ideological heterogeneity that is obtained in this way nevertheless does not create broad and deep class contradictions that are capable of sharply separating the man and woman in the family, this is mainly because the man – the organiser – is considerably more governed by authoritarian ideology within the confines of the family than outside of it. Ideological adaptations appear, corresponding to the inner relationships of the family that express and support an authoritarian organisation. It is here that we find a full explanation the common, flagrant paradox of hypocrisy in which an atheist man values the religiosity of his wife and finds it necessary to bring up his children in religion. But for the very same reason, the man is also a *conservative* in his family, and he is especially anxious to preserve that narrow specialisation that limits the experience of the woman to such a negligible scope and guarantees that it is impossible for her to escape from the confines of family and subordination.

I have not at all dwelt on all this in order to criticise one social relationship or another but only to illustrate the relativity of the concept of 'class' and the necessity of a large number of specific conditions in order for a simple division of organisational and implementational functions to turn into class demarcation. The fate of bourgeois women is a case of incomplete development along these lines that is closest to our times; hence the distinctive nature of the women's movement of our time that has much that is reminiscent of a class, but is not a class movement.[27]

---

26  Bourgeois positivism with its empty, pure abstractions is only the highest form of bourgeois metaphysics in which such abstractions are still not devoid of the remnants of fetishistic forms. The interconversion of these forms can easily be seen in such thinkers as Spinoza, Kant, Spencer.
27  A brief explanation regarding the petty bourgeoisie, which is usually called a 'class', is appropriate here. From the point of view of the criterion that I have adopted (according to

## VI

Another example of the separation of the organisational and implementational function that that is not a class division is an example that is also very important for our goal, and that is the relationship of 'ideologists' and the 'masses'.

It is not necessary to specifically analyse these relationships here.[28] The organisational function of ideologists, no matter who they are (writer, philosopher, religious teacher, political leader), cannot be doubted since ideology is always the realm of organising adaptations. Ideologists 'manage' the vital relationships and the experience of people, both creating 'forms' for them and making these forms 'social' by means of communication. The degree of the breadth and significance of this work can be very different, from the ephemeral and trivial role of any minor work of poetry that systematises a certain quantity of impressions experienced by a few people to the worldwide transformative activity of a great religious reformer. But the very method of the organising work of ideologists is, in substance, the same, and it is significantly different from the usual organisational method that boils down to 'directions' and 'orders'. Here we see the type of organising process that makes the role of ideologists something like an intermediary link between the role of a typical personal organiser and the role of impersonal ideological forms. Ideologists individually produce organising forms, but they do not directly and immediately organise the life and experience of people (as 'directions' and 'orders' do). They only take place through social selection and acquire the character of impersonal norms and ideas similar to norms and ideas that are produced spontaneously. For example, a religious teacher proposes such-and-such a religious doctrine to the masses, but this doctrine only really becomes the

---

which a class division is based on the differentiation of the organisational and implementational roles), the petty bourgeoisie is not a class, but an undifferentiated social type, an embryo of two classes simultaneously, the bourgeoisie and the proletariat. It is an amorphous mass from which classes crystallise. Therefore it would be possible for there to be a society that consists of only members of the petty bourgeoisie, while a society made up only of capitalists or only of hired workers would be impossible. This also explains the instability of ideological type that is characteristic of the petty bourgeoisie but that is not characteristic of real 'classes', with the long-term tendency of social selection. But in capitalistic society the petty bourgeoisie obtain certain features of a 'class' to the extent that they are politically and economically forced to experience 'subordination' to capital.

28  I have done this, in part, in Section XIII of *'Razvitie zhizni v prirode I obshchestve'* in *Iz psikhologii obshchestva*.

organising form for experience and activity of these masses when the masses adopted it as 'truth' – i.e. when it takes on the impersonal form of a socially created cognitive system. Bosses are 'obeyed' because they are the boss (i.e. the organiser) but the teaching of leaders is followed not because they are ideologists but because their teaching is 'true'. Because of this truth (i.e. the social adaptedness of their teaching), they can become 'leaders' (i.e. organisers to whom everyone now immediately and blindly subordinate themselves). But they are a 'leader', a 'tsar', an 'incarnated God', and in general the representatives of *authority* precisely to the extent that they are no longer simply ideologists.

Of course, there exist all sorts of transitional forms between the pure 'ideologist' and the immediately practical 'organiser' who acts by virtue of authority. A 'legislator' represents a typical overlapping of these forms. A leader of a political party is closer to the type of an 'ideologist' proper. And the highest representatives of an ascending chain of organisers who possess authority, within certain limits, to create 'norms' that are obligatory not only for the given moment but also for the future are closer to the opposite type.

At the present, however, the details, peculiarities, and transitional forms of these types are not important; what is essential for us now is only the question of whether the relationship of 'ideologists' to the 'masses' can become a class distinction, and if not, why? Now it must be clear to us that to the extent that 'ideologists' remain ideologists, such a transformation is impossible. 'Ideologists' create organising forms for the experience of labour of the 'masses' but these forms acquire a meaning for life only to the extent that they turn out to be and become in reality the 'ideology' of these masses, i.e. that it expresses their actual experience and actual desires. Thus, 'ideologists' fulfil their role only under conditions where their experience and tendencies of development correspond with the experience and tendencies of development of the *masses* that they serve. Consequently, it is impossible for there to be an essential difference of direction of social selection in the environment of 'ideologists' and in the environment of their masses.

Of course, under certain conditions an organisational *class* might also be created out of 'ideologists', except that it would no longer be a class of ideologists for the masses that it ruled.

I think that what I have presented is sufficient to explain the concept of 'class differences', and I believe it would be superfluous to dwell on particular correlations of 'classes' and 'social groups' – for example, on the 'sociallygrouped' division of any organisational class that arises from the specialisation of organisers or on the 'class' division of any social group that arises from a distinction within it between 'organisers' and 'implementers'. I therefore turn to questions that are of essential importance for us: how are classes replaced, what is their social fate, and under what conditions do social class systems decay?

## VII

To simplify the question, let us imagine a society that consists of only two classes, a ruling class and a subject class. For now let us leave to one side the question of the form of rule – slave-owners and slaves, feudal lords and their peasants, capitalists and proletarians ... Imagine that all or nearly all the immediate technological process is carried out by the subject class and that the ruling class also is strictly specialised in carrying out the organisational function in society. Let us examine how the development of both classes must then occur.

The primary and basic content of experience that 'ideology' must organise is that same immediate technological process. In the beginning, while the division of the two parts of society is still only being generated, and subsequently while it develops toward its completion, the 'organisers' still preserve a certain direct connection with immediate technological labour. And, even when the organisers themselves completely cease to be even partly 'implementers', as long as they directly and continuously manage the labour of the implementers, their 'experience' and the direction of social selection in their environment, which produces ideological forms, still cannot essentially part ways with the 'experience' of the implementers and the direction of selection in the workers' environment. Within these confines, the content that is 'organised' by ideology for both organisers and workers is still the same; it is only unequally and unevenly distributed between the two parts of society. Due to this uneven distribution of experience and due to the fact that the 'organisational' psyche contains that experience in broader dimensions (even though in less vivid, less intense manifestations),[29] an uneven distribution of ideological, creative work results that occurs for the most part in the organisational environment. In the implementers' environment there appears, generally speaking, only or almost only the lowest inks of the ideological chain – those links that organise technological experience in the most immediate way and in the narrowest dimensions. Those who embrace experience more broadly – i.e. the organisers – are able far more easily and quickly to create forms that are more broadly organ-

---

29   The conception and idea of any labour action is, needless to say, a less vivid and intense psychophysiological reaction than the actual execution of the action.

ising. Thus it is precisely the organisers who produce all or approximately all the higher links of each chain.

But this does not at all signify an ideological *divergence* between the organisational and implementational parts of the social whole. Absolutely not. As yet, the entire 'organisational' (in origin) ideology, in the final analysis, entirely organises the same content that belongs (if only partly and in different proportions) to the immediate experience of the 'implementers'. It is one, common ideology. Of course, it is accessible in full measure only to the highest layer of society and is acquired by the lowest layer in a comparatively fragmentary way. Nevertheless, in neither case does it run up against contradictions in life – and it really fulfils its organising function for both organisers and implementers. Such, for example, was the general religious worldview of feudal lords and peasants at the beginning of the feudal development of society. It satisfied them both; it corresponded to the basic content of experience of both lords and peasants that still had not diverged.

However, things could not stop at this idyllic phase, and the divisive point was the growth of the social system and a change in the means of production. The realm of immediate struggle with nature inevitably underwent changes, and these changes provided an impetus to a real 'class' differentiation.

Let us imagine a patriarchal commune of the *preclassical* ancient world, of the era when the children of the kings (i.e. the patriarchs and tribal leaders) personally herded cattle and when the king, addressing his own 'slave', Eumaeus, called him a 'swineherd the equal of the gods'. In this era one cannot speak of two 'classes', of ideological division, etc. There was a natural economy, hardly extending beyond the boundaries of the plot of land worked by the commune – for example, one of the islands of the Greek archipelago. Although 'kings' and other patriarchs carried out almost exclusively 'organisational' functions, they lived absolutely the same life as their relatives and 'slaves' – in general the 'implementers' in the system of labour – whose work the 'kings' organised *directly*. But then barter gradually began to complicate the natural economy. Exchange developed among patriarchal kinship communes and among tribal 'tsars', and the communes were continually and increasingly transformed from independent economic collectivities into cells of an incomparably wider whole – a social system with a growing division of labour among its parts. This momentous transformation affected the two different parts of each such commune – organisers and implementers – far from equally. Of course, the representatives of the kinship commune appeared in trade and in external dealings, in general, as organisers, but for everything else life was focused as before inside the commune, in its daily labour, and in the part of the communal economy that still remained 'natural'.

Two results of tremendous importance flowed from this. On the one hand, a vital convergence sprang up among the organisers of different communes, engendered by their common affairs and interests, by inter-communal dealings, by exchange,[30] and by all the political and religious forms that were produced by these connections. On the other hand, the former vital closeness between the heads of communes and their subordinates gradually weakened, because the content of the experience of labour now turned out to be increasingly more different both qualitatively and quantitatively. The experience of the organiser included new, expanding content that extended far beyond the borders of the immediate life of labour of the commune and that belonged to the experience of labour of a more complex collectivity of which the given commune became only a part. The experience of the implementers did not include this new content or did so only to an insignificant degree. From this point on, the organising ideological activity of both parts of society was based on different material – and the starting point of 'class' division is obvious.

From this point on, the ideology of the ruling class had to include both the life of a natural economy and the life of trade, both the intra-communal division of labour and the inter-communal division of labour, both the labour experience of separate households and the experience of the social whole ('polis', city, state). All this is easily revealed in the ideology of the free people of the classical world. There were 'customs' (norms of the world of the natural economy), formal law along with 'morality' (norms of exchange society), a living concrete polytheistic religion (a system of knowledge of the natural world), and science and philosophy (abstract knowledge that appeared for the first time in exchange society). Ancient art drew from both sources of life and gave forms to ideal, superhuman, or, what is the same thing, collectively-human content – forms that in their directness and simplicity are related to the naïve realism of primeval art. Such was the ruling ideology of the classical era.

Now what was the other side of the coin? The narrower and predominantly 'natural-economic' content of the labour experience of slaves[31] had no need of

---

30   Even earlier, the requirement of exchange dealings for the common defence against attacking enemies created more or less broad alliances and agreements among communes. But these combinations did not exert a differentiating effect to any powerful degree, since the common struggle directly drew together both organisers and implementers.

31   All the members of the patriarchal commune who were not connected to it by blood kinship were called 'slaves', and they included non-tribal members adopted by the commune, prisoners captured in war, etc. Their position was not much different from the position of the other members of the commune who were subordinate to its head and absolutely did not correspond to our usual idea of 'slavery'. As a result, when the commune underwent

this complex ruling ideology and did not conform to it. The old, naïve-religious worldview that in many aspects had already been reduced to 'superstition' for the rulers continued to predominate among slaves (let us note that even the women of 'ruling' families, whose subjection to the husband and father represented an ameliorated form of slavery, also preserved both naïve religiosity and a tendency to 'superstition' in a much greater degree than free men). The mutual relationships of slaves, their relationships with masters, and the relationships of members of the slave-owning family among themselves – in a word, the internal structure of the slave-owning enterprise – was nevertheless determined predominantly according to 'custom', i.e. according to normative adaptations of the old type and not according to the formal law that governed inter-enterprise, exchange, political, etc. relationships. Science, philosophy, and higher forms of art were not for slaves – not only in the sense that slave-owning exploitation did not leave any energy or possibility for all this, but also because all these things did not coincide with everyday existence. They did not harmonise a slave's experience.[32]

But there is still more to ideology than this. First, one must keep in mind the fact that, in general, ideological creativity was predominantly the affair of the organisers and that even in the early stages of the era of slavery it was able to occur in the psyche of the implementer to the most insignificant degree. Ideological creativity, as we know, is born from a social surplus of energy, from the preponderance of the assimilation over the expenditure of energy, and this surplus or preponderance is concentrated at first almost entirely and subsequently, as we shall see, entirely and wholly in the 'organisational' part of the social whole. Second, one must also keep in mind the circumstance that the organisational function of the 'masters' is not limited only to the technological process but is also included the 'ideological' realm, so that the 'masters' dictated specific norms to the slaves and instilled specific concepts in them. For these reasons, the ideology of slaves could not take shape independently; its blank spaces were filled up with material of the ruling ideology. And not only the blank spaces: in many cases ideological forms could be 'foisted off' on slaves in direct contradiction to the content of their experience ...

---

    class differentiation, everyone except the head of the family, himself, turned out to be 'slaves' (now in the new, more rigorous meaning of the word).

32  In this regard, the reader may perhaps recall 'educated slaves' who were familiar with art, literature, philosophy, and who sometimes, although rarely, worked independently in these fields. But such slaves were on the whole exceptions, and their education in the great majority of cases had the nature of vocational training. This situation changed only in the last phases of the development of slavery when lords transferred the organisational role in production increasingly to slaves, so that the psychology of the slaves changed.

Under these conditions, what did the ideological life of slaves look like?

Its largest part consisted of norms and concepts preserved from past norms and concepts connected with the natural-economic aspect of the life of the slave-owning organisation and that was slowly transformed by the slave class's own development (or degradation) in accord with the immediate changes of the technology of slave labour.

Slaves obtained the other – now the smallest – part of their ideology from the ideological creativity of the lords, and this part, in turn, must be divided into two. Some ideological adaptations were acquired by slaves from lords 'integrally', i.e. in such a way that they become a continual and indivisible part of slave ideology. These are the ideological adaptations that were in harmony with the experience and desires of slaves and that harmonised their existence. Other ideological adaptations entered the life of slaves as a continual contradiction that was imposed on them 'by force', through 'coercion'. These are the ideological adaptations that did not correspond to the experience or desires of slaves, even though they fully corresponded to the interests of the lords.

Thus, for example, certain technical skills or religious beliefs, and even certain especially broad moral norms that were worked out in the lords' milieu, could suit the content of the slaves' life so much that they would sooner or later have sprung up among them independently even if they had not already been ready-made for a long time. It is clear that such ideological forms in the slaves' milieu immediately found only positive selection and took root in the slave psyche like plants in favourable soil. Just the opposite, it is doubtful that many legal norms that were created by lords in their relations with slaves could ever become a positive and inseparable part of the slaves' worldview, such as the absolute power of lords over slaves' mating, the right of the lord to enjoy all his female slaves, or the custom of chaining slaves together on plantations in order to prevent them from running away. These norms must have encountered negative selection in the slave psyche, and they therefore could not at all become *norms of the slave ideology*. Nevertheless, were they not in one way or another imposed on slaves, adopted by slaves, and did they not govern slaves' behaviour? Yes, but not as *their norms* and absolutely in a different sense and in a different form. We have arrived here at the central point of class separation, and we must specifically dwell on this point.

VIII

A society that is divided into classes is still a society, i.e. a certain *vital whole*. When the direction of social selection splits in two, as in the case we have just encountered, it still does not just boil down to a situation where norms that are created by the slave-owners in their own interests and that are hateful to slaves remain only in the slave-owners' milieu. No. If the content of these norms also relates to the lives of slaves, then the question is decided by a certain *resultant of social selection*, of two trends of social selection appearing in two realms of the social environment. This resultant sometimes turns out to benefit the subordinate class when the 'norm' that is connected with it disappears from life. For example, an oppressive law becomes a dead letter, as happened with certain English laws regarding agricultural workers in the fourteenth to sixteenth centuries. But more often the resultant inclines in favour of the ruling classes. This is completely understandable if we keep in mind that the entire surplus of social energy – its entire 'plus' – that remains from the struggle with nature is concentrated in the sphere of the ruling classes. To express the same basic fact in the usual terms of economists, all 'surplus labour' of society – all 'surplus value' – 'belongs' to them. And then, regardless of the negative tendency of selection in the environment of the 'subordinate' class, the given ideological form is preserved and 'organises' its living relationships, or, more accurately, limits and defines them.

This ideological form enters the life of the subordinate classes not as a harmonising form but as a form that creates a contradiction. It is an external fact, just like the hostile forces of external nature, to which it is necessary to adapt. And at the same time – to the extent that such a relationship arises – *part of the social milieu* (the ruling class) *is transformed in relation to the other part* (the subordinate class) into an extra-social phenomenon, into a new realm of the extra-social environment. This is the *basic class contradiction* in its most general form.

It is possible to relate to the hostile force of external nature in two ways: either *passively*, submitting to its power, or *actively*, struggling against it. In the era of the power of nature over humanity, in most cases the relationship of the first kind was unavoidable. In an encounter with any kind of cave lion, which it would be unthinkable to fight and from which it would be necessary to flee, people fatalistically give themselves up to the will of fate. Even only two centuries ago this was the relationship of humanity to the action of lightning, for example. With the development of power and experience, with the passage from the power of nature over humanity to the rule of humanity over nature, the remnants of such a relationship disappear and passivity yields to struggle. The exact same thing is also true in the realm of the internal relationships of society and specifically of class society.

In the era of slavery, the social power of the social whole still ruled so absolutely over the subordinate class (whose labour created that power), that any relationship toward norms that were imposed from without (other than a passive relationship) did not exist – except for insignificant exceptions. Class contradiction was present, but class struggle was not.

How did class society develop *under such* conditions?

IX

As long as slave-owners directly organise the labour of their slaves, the internal interconnectedness of their enterprise far outweighs the divisive tendency of class differences and budding class contradictions. For slave-owners at this time workers are subordinate members of *the very same social whole* to which the slave-owners belongs; they are the slave-owners' workers but not their tools. The slave-owner is still not the *owner* of slaves, but their *master*.

In this phase of development, the class of masters is the bearer of technological progress. A master who has a small number of slaves often not only directs their labour but works with them himself. If the participation of the master in the technological process of labour is not always direct, it is always *close*. The productive labour of slaves appears in the lord's thinking as a necessary *social* process.

The organisational function can be differentiated and divided just like any other function, and this is what happens to it as the slave-owning economy developed historically.[33]

Lacking the factual possibility of personally and immediately directing all the labour of his slaves, the slave-owner begins to provisionally entrust and in some respects to completely transfer the supervision of slaves to other people – in part to members of his own family, of course, and in part (and more and more as time goes on) to certain of the most experienced and knowledgeable slaves. This is the beginning of the process that separates the class of masters from productive labour.

As time goes on, this process accelerates. For the lord, personally, the transfer of the immediate organising function to slaves who are trained for it represents a huge gain in time and energy so that it is easy to understand how powerfully psychical social selection must act in this direction. Together with the expansion of the slave-owning economy that now brings together hundreds and thousands of slaves, instead of individuals and dozens, not only does the immediate organisational function transfer entirely to individual slaves but, with the passage of time, the supervision of that function is also entrusted to

---

[33] I remind the reader that I am not writing a work of economics, and therefore I cannot dwell on the question of the causes of the growth of the scale of slave-owning enterprises, the decline of the smallest of them, and so forth.

other slaves, and a *chain of organisers* appears in which the master represents the highest link. In this way, a chasm opens up between the technological process and the social existence of the class of masters, and, at the same time, between slaves and masters.

This chasm does not become any less profound because some of the slaves fulfil organisational functions. It is rather the opposite. Since it is entirely and exclusively the master's will that gives to and takes from individual slaves power over other slaves, the organisational role of the master has a universal and absolute nature that is *qualitatively* different from the partial, limited, and, moreover, fortuitous role of slaves who are placed above other slaves. The will of the master within the confines of his own enterprise contains all the power and creates all lower powers and is limited by nothing, whereas everything else is limited by his will. In the eyes of the master, the slave-administrator is equal to the lowest of his slaves and can at any moment be turned into the lowest of his slaves. *Therefore*, the greater the distance between the function of the master and the technological process – expressed in the ideological distance between the master and the lowliest of his slave-implementers – the greater the distance between the lord and the highest of his slaves also becomes.

The ideological leap that the thought of the ancient world made in the devolution from lord to slave is easier to conceive if we take its direct reflection in the Christian religion. Christianity – a religion of slaves and all oppressed people – originally appeared at the end of the ancient world, when the slave-owning economy arrived at the ultimate form of its type and clearly and vividly reflected this type in its construction of the universe. There was a hierarchy of people, and a hierarchy of angels and saints above it. But the saint who is the closest to God is as absolute a nonentity in relation to God as the lowest nobody. With a single word, God can exalt the lowest of the low to the highest heights (to the first after Himself) and cast down the highest of the high (the first after Himself) to the depths of insignificance.[34] The same construction was also repeated

---

34   In the subsequent, feudal version of Christianity – in Catholicism – this ideological leap was somewhat ameliorated. For Catholicism the saints possessed more or less independent rights to interfere in the course of natural phenomena and transfer part of their power by means of their relics, images, clothing, and so forth. They could be prayed to like lesser gods, and the Mother of God represented a directly intermediary link between the highest God and these lower ones. Such a construction completely corresponds to the very nature of the feudal relationship, significantly ameliorated in comparison with the relationship of the slave-owning world. In the chain of lords and vassals, the transitions from one link to the next were not as sharp, and the highest lord – a king or even the pope – was not so sharply set off from the next one down.

in the political structure of the Roman state – in the absolute power of the emperor, who stood outside the laws and made the laws.

The chasm that separated the master from the immediate technological process substantively changed the line of development of the class of masters.

The change was that the connection between lord and slaves altogether ceased being a *social* connection. At the basis of any social connection lies the *unity of the process of labour* as a social struggle for existence. Such a unity no longer existed for slaves and masters. Correspondingly, a slave did not appear to a master as a member of the social whole to which the master, himself, belonged. The real connection was not destroyed, however, but what did it turn into?

**It turned into a relationship between a person and a tool of production.**

In reality, the technological process, implemented by slaves, no longer possessed the meaning of a socio-technological process in general for the collectivity of the masters – for the society that consisted of slave-owners. It had the same meaning for them as the world of extra-social forces has for us – livestock or machines, for example. A slave then became no more than an *instrumentum vocale*, a 'talking tool'. This is an ancient expression.

But no social whole can exist without its own special technological process, the process of the immediate struggle of this whole for its collective life. Where was such a 'technological process' for a slave-owning society that slaves could not be members of?

For the class of lords as a social whole, the technological process consisted in the *process of exploitation of slaves* (and also the acquisition of slaves). And this fact was recognised and enunciated with complete clarity by the ideologists (the philosophers) of the slave-owners: 'All the skill of the master boils down to the craft of utilising his slaves'. All the striking declarations of ancient writers, which expressed utter aversion and contempt for productive labour, proceeded from this one fact. 'Slave' work was the equivalent of extra-social processes, and to do slave work meant to descend to the same level as a tool or a brute beast. Only someone who lived entirely by exploitation could be considered a full member of society, as expressed in the full rights of citizenship. The rights of artisans and peasants were usually limited – these people were considered to be intermediary beings between a human being – 'a political animal' – and a slave – 'a tool with the gift of speech'.

The basis of all social development consists in technological progress. What kind of technological progress was possible in a society based on owning slaves?

Since the organisational class had earlier been the bearer of technological progress, technological progress now became impossible as progress of the *technology of productive labour*. It now took on the form of the *progress of exploitation*, or, let us say, it was replaced by the progress of exploitation. In the ideology of the slave-owners, this fact was reflected in such a way that even for science (which had originally sprung up from technology, it goes without saying) technological applications were considered to be 'shameful' and to lower its 'dignity', and the entire development of science, and philosophy as well, occurred in a direction that was partly absolutely alien to the idea of technological progress and partly directly hostile to it.

But is it possible that the role of the bearer of technological progress passed from lords to slaves? This did not happen in reality, and again it is because the development of the class of lords went in the direction of progressive exploitation. The slave-implementers were brought by progressively increasing exploitation to such vital exhaustion that, for their part, there was absolutely no surplus energy to expend on improving tools and techniques of labour or even thinking about possible steps in this direction. And the slave-organisers? Their position, of course, was somewhat better, but the direction of their organisational activity was determined by the absolute will of the lord, and since this will presented one, and only one, demand – maximum exploitation – all the 'progressive' work of the psyche of the slave-organiser went toward carrying out exactly that task. This explains the horrifying cruelty of slave-supervisors toward those who were subject to them and the utter lack of thinking about improving the conditions and means of labour of the latter.

Thus an inescapable contradiction was created – progressive exploitation in the absence of technological progress – that led to the death of the classical world and its culture. This type of development itself undermined its own roots and condemned itself to death. It was only a quirk of fate that the execution of the death sentence fell to the lot of newcomers from the north. All the same, the decline and collapse was inevitable. The *parasitic development* of the ruling class went side-by-side with the *degradation due to exhaustion* of the subordinate class. The entire surplus of the energy that arose from the technological process was expended outside the confines of that process and above, and beyond this surplus even the basic fund of social energy embodied in the agents of the technological process – productive workers – gradually began to be squandered.

This is one type of class development of society, with degradation as the inevitable outcome.[35]

---

35   In order not to complicate the question, I have not touched on the course of development and the fate of other classes of ancient society, since they did not play the defining role in the life and death of the ancient world. The peasantry and artisans were suppressed by

X

Another type of class development of society lies considerably closer to us. This is capitalism.

The starting point of ancient class development consisted in patriarchally organised natural-economy communes that were joined together to a certain extent by the weak and superficial connection of the social division of labour and of the exchange relationships that expressed that division of labour. The starting point of *contemporary* class development consists of petty-bourgeois economic units that were profoundly and tightly connected by the social division of labour that were absolutely incapable of maintaining their existence outside exchange relationships. These are the city artisan and merchant enterprises of the Middle Ages.

By all appearances, these starting points *predetermined* both types of class development. Everywhere class development was based predominantly on a natural economy, it headed down the inevitable path toward slavery, but where it was based predominantly on exchange, it developed on the path toward capitalism. This is corroborated not only by the history of those peoples of the East who did not know petty-bourgeois city organisation and whose fate turned out to be hardly worse that the fate of the classical world, and it is corroborated by the course of development of European peoples for the last millennium. Precisely to the extent that the development of classes originated on the basis of a natural economy, it lapsed into the slave-owning type. This was the fate in the majority of cases of countries that obtained a class foundation while they were still in the phase of a natural economy. The system of serfdom, developing from a feudal foundation, is highly reminiscent of a slave-owning system and leads in essential traits to the same results. The parasitic type of modern agrarian aristocracy is distinguished from the ancient slave-owning aristocracy perhaps only by less nobility and the absence of aesthetic colouration. But the degeneration of bonded peasantry because it was exhausted by excessive exploitation is similar to the degeneration of slavery, and down to the present it can be sensed in the 'idiocy of rural life' that is retarding the general course of development of the contemporary world.

---

the competition of major slave-owning enterprises. They were brought to ruin by wars that were fought to acquire slaves (who were, of course, ultimately obtained by the great slave-owners), they were impoverished by usury on the part of the latter, and, in any event, they were unable to serve as a support for the collapsing structure. A proletariat of parasites only hastened the exhaustion of the social whole.

The reason why the difference between these two fundamental points of class differentiation acquires such a decisive significance for what follows consists first and foremost, I would suggest, in precisely the following. In small, natural-economic organisations, the organisational function that had been separated out (embodied, for example, in the patriarch) extended its influence and impact on the *entire* life and activity of the organisation, and specifically on all the members of the organisation that carry out the implementational function. And this is the necessary result of the 'self-sufficient', economically-closed nature of such organisations. The organiser regulates *everything*, because this 'everything' is a complete organic whole from which it is impossible to isolate any part. When class discrimination was born from petty-bourgeois relationships, in which each economic unit is a fraction of the economic whole, then the organisational function (and the expression of that function, the 'authority') of the entrepreneur (first in the form of a merchant capitalist and then of an industrial capitalist) extends only to the specific, specialised sphere of activity of implementer-workers – to their occupational labour. In the other part of their existence, implementers are 'independent', i.e. are 'organisers' of their own actions and even of their own 'personal economy'. In the first case, worker-implementers absolutely lack the possibility of independent development – they are entirely 'determined' and limited by an external, organising power; in the second case, this possibility exists and moreover the smaller the portion of the existence of workers that their occupational function takes up (in which they are 'subordinate' to an organiser), the greater is the possibility of independent development.[36]

Another cause, essentially inseparable from the first, consists in that petty-bourgeois society, due to its profound division of labour (and the complex socially-grouped composition that expresses this division) forms a considerably broader basis for technological progress than patriarchal or feudal society with its weak social division of labour (in which the entire social whole boils down to a large number of *almost exactly identical* natural-economic units).

Let us now turn to the issue of the fundamental tendencies and ultimate results of capitalist class development.

XI

Already at its very beginning, the capitalist type of class development was characterised by a sharply salient vital separation between the 'organisational' or

---

36   This is why, by the way, the shortening of the work day has such huge significance for social development.

entrepreneurial class and the 'implementational' or working class. From the very beginning of the splitting off of these parts of society, their 'desires' and 'interests' turned out to be the opposite of one another, and this means that the direction of social selection in them is essentially different. The initial harmony and the fundamental ideological unity that is observed in the patriarchal-kinship group and even in the feudal group are completely absent. The genetic continuity and stability of structure of the separate economic unit-collectivity such as those organisations possess is also absent from the very beginning of capitalism. Workers are not attached to the 'organiser' of the enterprise – to the capitalist – either by a connection of blood or the connection of unavoidable patronage and hereditary personal subordination. All these conditions make class development under capitalism incomparably more rapid than under any other type of class division.[37]

Capitalist class development, like all class development in general, has two poles. We will begin with the upper pole – with tendencies characteristic of the 'organisational' class.

In essence, a picture that we are already familiar with is repeated here. In the beginning the entrepreneur had a comparatively close, 'directly-organising' relationship with the technological process. Later the organisational function was partially transferred to special 'implementers' – hired directors, supervisors, trained technicians, etc. – that was the inevitable result of the very growth and increased complexity of the enterprise. Subsequently, through the further transfer of organisational work onto the shoulders of non-entrepreneurs, organisers completely lost the primary role in production. The organisational class, which was transformed in this way into a class of only rulers, 'acquired' (or appropriated – in this case it is the same thing) all the excess energy that was obtained by the technological process (in this case in the form of 'surplus value'). Thus, the evolution of the organisational class means that it is reduced to a purely exploitative function – to naked parasitism. The final result of this process is represented in the type of a 'rentier' – a landowner, a shareholder, or someone with large investments in banks. This is a type of person who is a parasite living off the surplus labour of enterprises that they know only by name, *if they even know that* (as happens with investors in banks that provide credit to industrial enterprises).

---

37   It goes without saying that in order for this class development to be accomplished, specific conditions in regard to technological progress are necessary, but once these conditions exist, this development does not encounter those *retarding obstacles* that were pointed out in our comparison.

But there is an important difference between this form of parasitic degeneration of the 'organisational' class and the parasitic degeneration of the slave-owners of classical antiquity. For both the capitalist and the slave-owner the basic tendency of life is, of course, progressive exploitation. But this tendency entirely *replaced and removed* the tendency of technological progress for the slave-owners, while, for the capitalist, parasitic degeneration *merged* with technological progress.

Such is the influence of the different social environment into which these two exploitative types were placed. Slave-owning enterprises, affected by exchange only at their tops, hardly competed with one another, and therefore in those times when slave-owners were still immediate organisers of slave labour, the stimulus of technological progress was insignificant. In later times, when exchange intensified and competition became perceptible, the social type of the slave-owner had already *completely* taken shape and *completely* separated off from any positive role in production and therefore could not now find new paths of adaptation to this competition other than the same limitless squeezing of slaves. Just the opposite, the capitalist was already socially born amid competition – one might even say *from* competition. After all, the authority of the capitalist did not have a hereditary-estate nature like the authority of the slave-owner. The capitalist's authority was won in the bitter, always vaguely criminal struggle that is called 'primary accumulation', and it can expand further only through a new struggle – capitalist competition. Thus, the capitalist as the organiser of an enterprise constantly experiences the pressure of this social struggle in which the one who wins is the one who is best armed and in which the best weapon is the highest technology. And, to the extent that the desire for maximum exploitation encounters resistance from the working class, concern regarding technological progress comes all the more to the fore. When one weapon in the struggle for life becomes blunt, the more important it becomes to sharpen another. This stimulus did not exist for the slave-owner, because slaves do not present resistance; at the most, they die of exhaustion.

To the extent that slave-owners moved away from the primary role in production and to the extent that they transferred that role to slave proxies, they also transferred to those proxies only their fundamental relationship to the enterprise – i.e. they required their proxies only to exploit slaves mercilessly but not at all to improve the means of production. Capitalists, removing themselves from direct organisational activity in their enterprises, did not cease to still sense the action of competition, and they therefore did not become indifferent to technological progress. They therefore also required from their hired employee proxies – directors and engineers – not only energy in squeezing the surplus labour out of workers but also technological initiative, the ability to improve the organisation of work, the timely introduction of newly invented machines. Capitalists especially valued initiative in the improvement of the enterprise and technological ingenuity in these employees. Thus, technological progress did not suffer material loss because capitalists evolved into parasites; it was simply transferred into other hands – into the hands of a broader and more vital class of capitalist 'employees', i.e. hired organisers.

In regard to the production of the ideological forms of the capitalist class, the direction of social selection in the environment of that class changed in correspondence to the changes in its social function.

In the realm of cognitive adaptations, the technological-progressive role of the big bourgeoisie at the first stages of its development is marked by a *scientific* and *materialist* tendency. The growing systematic nature of the struggle with nature and the power of society over nature is expressed in the rapidly expanding sum of technological knowledge and in the development of the *natural sciences* that 'organise' this knowledge. All classes of society participate in the creation of this part of ideology, of course, but the big bourgeoisie and its ideologists (who come both from the milieu of the big bourgeoisie and also from the milieu of the hired-organiser intelligentsia that adjoin it) are pre-eminently creators of a *system, a worldview*, that has this ideological material as its basis and content.

However, the technological progressiveness of the big bourgeoisie is at the same time connected with competition – with the spontaneous chaos and contradictoriness of the socially-productive whole. This progressiveness, consequently, is born from the power of social forms over people, and therefore subordination to socially-spontaneous forces is the specific form for the entire socio-technological experience of the big bourgeoisie. It is natural that social selection, in correspondence with his form, also produces the entire worldview of the big bourgeoisie. This worldview turns out, despite the real, technological basis of its content, to be thoroughly imbued with *social fetishism*.

People apprehend the way they are dominated by their social relationships as the constant active interference in their life by some kind of impersonal forces that are not perceptible in their real form and that cannot be overcome by any kind of attempt at resistance. 'Exchange value' is the *first* and most typical of these 'social fetishes'. It rules over people in the market, often destroying them pitilessly, but the fetishist of the market is unable to understand that it is a fetish. The labour-related essence of exchange value is hidden from the fetishist by an impenetrable shell; this is the shell of contradiction and struggle that shrouds the real social collaboration of people in the social whole. Such a social fetish, because its content is not perceptible, takes the form of *empty abstraction*, and at the same time, as a uniting point of a broad series of phenomena.

It serves as an 'organising' cognitive form, as an 'explanation' of those phenomena. 'Goods are bought and sold in such-and-such a ratio because that is their value' – this is the wording of the social-fetishistic understanding of the facts.

I will not undertake here to point out other illustrations of how all realms of social life in their bourgeois-fetishistic reflection obtain a social-fetishistic shell. I have already touched on this issue more than once and, although I have never been able to dwell on it with the fullness that it deserves,[38] nevertheless it would be especially awkward here, since it would divert us far from the basic thread of our presentation. What is sufficient here is the general consideration that if the *basic* conditions of life for the class of capitalists are necessarily connected with social-fetishistic forms of thinking, then social selection in this class milieu will inevitably display the tendency of *all* ideological forms to agree – to be brought into harmony – with this fetishism. As a result, the scientific-philosophical bourgeois worldview is imbued with a 'metaphysicalness' that groups the data of experience around empty abstractions – 'forces' and 'substances' – and that takes the laws of phenomena to be *impersonal forces* that rule over nature. Such forces *are not perceptible in their real form* but are *active* and *irresistible*, just like the mysterious forces of the market. Such is the 'materialism' of the bourgeoisie. 'Matter' appears as a universal substance, defined, in the final analysis, only as an unknowable cause of sensations. As a universal form, bourgeois materialism appears as a law of nature so empty that it boils down to the idea that, once the totality of conditions are given, what is caused must inevitably occur. The law, itself, plays the role of an active force that summons the transition from conditions to what is conditioned.[39]

Finally, a third trait of the bourgeois worldview in the era when the bourgeoisie plays a positive social role is a *dynamic* or *evolutionary* tendency that still issues, of course, from that same technological progressiveness.

---

38  See, for example, in *Iz psikhologii obshchestva*, the chapters '*Aftoritarnoe myshlenie*' and '*Razvitie zhizni v prirode i v obshchestve*', and also the books *Poznanie s istoricheskoi tochki zreniia* (a somewhat different method of analysis), Section III, Ch. 9, '*Obshchie tipy formy sotrudnichestva i form myshlenie*' ['General types of the form of collaboration and forms of thought'], and *Novyi Mir*, Sections VIII–IX.

39  In the realm of one of the most exact sciences – physics – Ernst Mach brilliantly showed how almost every scientific concept, as it becomes crystallised, acquires the nature of a fetish. That is, it is transformed from the simple designation of a series of facts into a 'quality' that 'explains' them or a 'force' or 'essence' of things. Especially instructive in this regard, in my opinion, is the analysis of 'temperature' in *Wärmelehre* and 'mass' in *Mechanik* (the analysis of 'energy' is wrongly complicated by certain 'roots', and, of course, the basic, social 'root' is lost). But, it goes without saying, Mach did not adopt the only worldview that, having explained the objective, extra-cognitive bases of fetishism, is able to radically destroy the very *fetishism* of concepts.

Thus, the worldview that proceeds from positive scientific-technological content is evolutionary, but at the same time it is invested in socially-fetishistic forms. This is the direction in which the cognitive ideology of the capitalists is elaborated in the first phase of the development of this class before it degenerates into parasitism.[40]

In regard to normative ideology, it was here that the big bourgeoisie was naturally obliged to systematise into juridical and 'moral forms' – and thereby to solidly organise – the basic social conditions of its 'organisational' position in society, its class rule. This part of the bourgeois-ideological system boils down to two principles: *property* and *legitimacy*. Property is predominantly 'legal', and legitimacy is predominantly 'moral'. I will explain this characterisation since it might cause a certain misunderstanding.

We have already seen that the real relationships of production take the normative form of relationships of property, that the factual relationships of property are subsequently systematised in a series of norms of a more general nature, and that, in the final analysis, this ideological chain is completed in a universal, pervasive principle of 'property'. The content of this principle, which is changed into various social formations, is determined by the basic type of relationship of production. Thus, the petty-bourgeois principle of property in its pure form consists in the idea of the immediate relationship of the small producer to the means and the product of his labour – what Russian Populists call the 'basis of labour'. Fully consistent with this principle, the ideologists of the petty bourgeoisie, beginning from the times of classical antiquity and down to our own times, display a tendency to limit non-labour-related private property and promote a utopia of 'petty-bourgeois socialism' that boils down to the creation of property of petty labourers at the expense of the property of the non-labouring big bourgeoisie. The big-bourgeois principle of property now naturally has a different content that is expressed in the word 'capital' – i.e. property as a tool of domination over labour and the exploitation of labour, property as a 'self-increasing value'. At a superficial glance, the capitalist conception of private property seems (due to the absence of a labour-related com-

---

40   In general, a materialistic colouration is characteristic of the big bourgeoisie due, of course, to the technologically-progressive role of this class. 'Idealism', which is genetically tied to religious worldviews and combined with them, is more characteristic of the estate-authoritarian classes – feudal lords, for example – that are further removed from technology and science. The petty bourgeoisie – standing out from the relationships of the feudal system by virtue of a conservatism that was maintained by the struggle to preserve its social position – preserved religious and idealistic tendencies for a long time. The big bourgeoisie, in its turn, as we have seen, displayed these tendencies in the era of its decline and degeneration when it became authoritarian and conservative.

ponent) simply empty. It is private property and that is all. But in practice the content of the principle is revealed in the universal fact that is basic to the capitalist system, that *the product of labour belongs entirely and exclusively to the owner of the means of production and not in any degree to the labourer.*

All sorts of legal norms of capitalist society are generalised in this principle and are particular applications of it. All civil legislation, to the extent that it is created precisely by the big bourgeoisie, serves as the organised embodiment of this principle. All criminal legislation and the entire state constitution, to the extent that they depend on capitalists, serve as the organised guarding of this principle.

But the entire existence of the class of capitalists is surrounded by struggle – both internal struggle in the form of competition and also in external struggle in the form of constant conflict with the 'implementational' class, the proletariat. And the consequent repeated intensification of this struggle has the tendency to disturb the stability of capital and the durability of its social domination. Because of all this, the *struggle against social struggle* in some cases is only against its extremeness (in regard to competition) and in other cases is against it in general (in regard to class actions by the proletariat and petty bourgeoisie). The organising forms for this struggle are produced in the shape of various norms of 'social and political behaviour' that the big bourgeoisie strive to disseminate and consolidate in all society. The final link of all such norms that expresses their fundamental and general tendency is the law of 'legality'.

The seeming emptiness of this principle, which is characteristic of all the intellectual fetishes of bourgeois society, conceals a very real content. It is as if 'legality' requires subordination to norms established in society without regard to what they include, but since this is the principle of the class that rules over production, it really signifies the subordination of society to the class rule of the big bourgeoisie. Therefore the principle of legality fully takes shape as soon as this rule becomes a widely accomplished fact.

I called the principle of legality 'predominantly moral' on the basis that, playing a subordinate role in relation to the principle of property, it obtains real force only to the extent that it coincides with the principle of property and then is realised by way of compulsory actions, and, to the extent that the tendency of the principle of law does not agree with the tendency of the 'sacred basis of property', it has only 'ideal' influence, i.e. is not accompanied in life by the force of compulsion. For example, the 'legality' of behaviour of the lower classes of society is strictly supervised by courts and other authorities and is ensured by severe punishments. 'Legality' in the relationship of the bourgeoisie itself to these lower classes constantly serves as the subject of promises and assurances of bourgeois politicians and is sanctioned by bourgeois social opinion. But the matter does not go any further than this as long as the real power of the other classes does not step in.

Regardless of this subordinate role in practice, the principle of 'legality' appears as a real 'form of normative thinking' for the bourgeoisie and its ideologists, and even where a revolution happens to arise against the norms established in society (by other classes), they unintentionally clothe their *anti-legal* struggle entirely in the same form of 'legality' – for example, the defence of the 'natural rights' of an individual, a citizen, an entrepreneur ...

Such are the basic ideological tendencies of the organisational class of capitalists in the phase of its development when capitalists are actually organisers.

XII

The working class gradually evolved from the petty bourgeoisie of the town and country over the course of approximately the same period as the capitalist class evolved. They were artisans and peasants who lost their independent functions – simultaneously organisational and implementational – in petty production. In the beginning, the working class simply retained the ideology that had been created earlier by the petty bourgeoisie. It was only the unhealthy contradictions that arose from the incompatibility of that petty-bourgeois ideology with the new social position of the proletariat and with changing technology that led to the progressive removal of this ideology by new tendencies and that created a distinctive ideology that was the proletariat's own. I will speak here, of course, only of these tendencies and not of the petty-bourgeois remnants.

The cognitive side of the ideology of the proletariat, naturally, developed in a scientific-materialist direction. This proceeds directly from the fact that the worker is the immediate actor in the unfolding technological process. In particular, the *technology of machine production* – in its cognitive expression – inevitably forms a materialist world-understanding.[41] In exactly the same way, a dynamic tendency is necessarily characteristic of the ideology that is born

---

41  In my presentation, in the interests of brevity and unity, I do not touch at all upon the first stage of development of the labouring proletariat – workers in textile mills. At this stage, the worker, due to the extreme narrowness of experience that proceeds from the petty specialisation of labour and due to the significant conservatism that proceeds from the (comparative) immobility of technology in each given narrow specialty, stands considerably closer to the slaves of the ancient world and only to an insignificant degree manifests the capability of ideological development in an *independent* direction (and also toward the class struggle).

in the activity of labour that continuously implements technological progress and continually changes its content in full dependence on that progress.

In these relationships, proletarian ideology coincided at first with the ideology of the big bourgeoisie, and, generally speaking, it simply borrowed the material of the latter. At the same time, social fetishism also at first presented the general colouration of proletarian ideology. This, by the way, occurred not so much because of the influence of the ideology of the capitalists as because the proletariat preserved the fetishism of its petty-bourgeois phase. But the further the development of machine technology and the class struggle proceeded, the more significantly the proletariat parted ways with the capitalist class in its worldview.

However, this parting of the ways did not begin here in the realm of normative ideology. The capitalist principle of property signified, as we have seen, the subordination of the producer-proletarian in general. To be specific, the capitalists' ownership of the labour power that they *have purchased* signifies the subordination of the proletarian to a degree of exploitation that is arbitrarily established by the capitalists, and all the specific legal norms that are pushed by the big bourgeoisie are directed toward this subordination. But proletarians, as we have seen, are not slaves who are absolutely and completely constrained by the necessity and habit of subordination. Outside the confines of their 'working day', proletarian are their own 'organisers' and the organiser of their personal economy – a male proletarian is the 'head' of his family, for example. More than this, in the very act of selling their labour power – at the starting point of their slavery – proletarians appears to be the absolute owners of that labour power who are 'able' to dispose of it, even if, in practice, they only have the ability – and not always and within very limited confines – to choose their masters. On the grounds of such elements of social independence that originally appeared only as remnants of the petty-bourgeois form of existence, workers did not at all display a slave-like relationship to those norms that were created for them by the capitalists.

This was the origin of the class struggle. It began – corresponding to the petty-bourgeois origin of the worker – in the petty-bourgeois form of the individual seller of labour power and the individual capitalist purchaser of it in the market for labour power, and it progressed because of concrete norms of subordination – the amount of pay for work, the duration of the working day, etc. They were particular norms for a given worker. Subsequently, struggle gradually became collective within the confines of the enterprise due to cooperation within the capitalist enterprise, due to the norms that were made general because of that cooperation, and due also, of course, to the individual powerlessness of the worker. Further, the collectivisation of this struggle beyond the confines of the individual enterprise occurred due to the commonality of the conditions of labour in the various enterprises in one field and to the fact that the conditions of labour depended on successes in that struggle. Finally, two factors – the general dependence of the workers of various fields on the labour market with its army of unemployed and the progress of technology that, as we have seen, *draws together* the labour-related functions of workers with different specialties – burst the bounds of the separate fields of production and made the workers' movement the most class-inclusive that the world has ever seen.

But in this process the struggle is not only 'collectivised', it is also 'generalised' – i.e. it is directed against *all the more general* norms created by the big bourgeoisie. Even as an 'economic struggle', this struggle strives in increasingly broad dimensions to change and replace the concrete norms of subordination and exploitation with new norms, but, *all the same*, only norms of a kind that are more favourable for workers. Subsequently, when the struggle is elevated to the 'political' level, its object becomes legal 'norms of the norms' of economic subordination that embrace the realm of production as a whole. But in doing so, the struggle now affects the highest, all-embracing normative principle of bourgeois being – capitalist private property, the principle of bourgeois rule. That is, to be more accurate, the tendency of the whole proletarian struggle – the tendency that is hostile to this principle and that had already been hidden like an embryo in the lower forms of struggle – *is revealed*.

In this struggle, the working class, in pushing its own norms forward from the more concrete and particular to the most general and fundamental, gradually creates an *entire normative ideology of its own* that makes it a *class* in the fullest and strictest meaning of the world. What kind of ideology is it?

The *labour principle of property* inherited from the petty-bourgeois phase provides the primary material for the development of the proletarian normative ideology, but not the only material. At the beginning, only concrete norms of the 'just' valuation of labour power – i.e. norms that 'correspond' to the expenditure of labour – are promoted. But subsequently, as the struggle grows broader and deeper, the idea of a 'just' valuation of labour power gives way to the tendency to value labour at the maximum that can be achieved in practice. This tendency is then generalised into the idea that, since *the entire product of each enterprise is produced by workers, all of it* (or all its value) *must consequently belong to the workers*.[42] When the struggle becomes a general class

---

42  This phase of development of proletarian ideology finds its principal expression in the idea of *productive associations of workers*.

struggle, these more particular normative conceptions give way to the broad, all-embracing principle of the social ownership of all the means of production – to the principle of *socialism*. The principle of socialism is the highest link in the chain of the development and generalisation of the normative proletarian ideology.

This principle stands, of course, in sharp contradiction with the principle of capitalist property, but it is not at all simply a negation of the latter. We already know that social selection – in this case, social-class selection in the proletarian milieu – preserves and develops only those ideological forms that *organise* the real content of life, which, in the final analysis, is precisely technological progress. This is the meaning of all norms that are put forward by the proletariat in its struggle. Norms of a concrete nature that relate to wages, the working day, and so on have a tendency to organise the process of labour so that labour power can develop to the maximum under conditions of continually changing technology, and this is realised precisely through the elevation of the level of the life of the worker. The more general norms of proletarian ideology that are in general aimed at limiting and ultimately eliminating capitalist property have the tendency to transfer to the working class the general organisational function in the system of production that so far belongs to the capitalists. Both tendencies are real tendencies of the development of production itself. The highest type of worker is really being created in progressing machine technology; it is a type that is characterised by the highest level of life both in workers' labour energy and in their intelligence. And the capitalists are forced to retreat from them in the struggle and to agree to the changes in the norms of exploitation that the worker needs, because production itself – the very possibility of the progress of production – requires it. At the same time, workers actually acquire organisational functions in the technological process. They acquire them individually because work on a machine has features not only of implementational labour but also of organisational labour. Moreover, the further this goes, the more these organisational functions are acquired collectively, since in the economic struggle workers really do limit the organisational role of the capitalists in their enterprises and in the political struggle they limit the organisational role of the class of capitalists in the entire life of society.[43] In this way,

---

43   It is not necessary to speak in detail about all these here, but I have quite thoroughly presented the basic features of these processes a number of times, first of all in *Kratkii kurs ekonomicheskoi nauki* (in the paragraphs on technology and cooperation in the sections 'Mashinnyi kapitalizm [Machine Capitalism]' and 'Sotsialisticheskoe obshchestvo [Socialist Society]'), and subsequently in the books *Iz psikhologii Obshchestva*, (in the chapter '*Aftoritarnoe myshlenie*') and *Novyi mir*, Sections xiii–xvi.

proletarian normative ideology expresses the actual relationships of labour of the proletariat and serves as the completely real organising form of their development.

However, proletarian normative ideology does not rule capitalist society, and the proletariat is forced in many cases to adapt to the external force of norms that are imposed by the ruling class. In the struggle with this external force, the proletariat elaborates norms of behaviour that have nothing in common with the bourgeois principle of 'legality' and in many cases directly contradict it. These proletarian norms find a perfected, generalised expression in the principle of *comradely class solidarity*. The principle of 'legality' requires universal subordination to norms established from the outside behind which is hidden the class rule of the bourgeoisie; the principle of class solidarity of proletarians requires subordination to the *conscious collective interests* of the working class – i.e. to the extent that, in practice, the matter has to do with the common struggle and is in the interests of developing this struggle. Therefore, everywhere that established norms only immobilise the development of the general-proletarian struggle, workers display the tendency to destroy these norms in revolution, and the principle of their behaviour, in contradiction to bourgeois 'legality' and 'loyalty', turns out to be revolutionary.

Following behind normative ideology, the cognitive ideology of the proletariat is gradually isolated from bourgeois cognitive ideology and turns into its opposite. On the one hand, the proletarian worldview is liberated from social fetishism, and on the other hand, its dynamic tendency acquires a *revolutionary* nature in contradiction to the *evolutionary* dynamism of bourgeois ideology.[44] As a result, the scientific-materialist tendency of proletarian ideology essentially breaks away from bourgeois-materialist ideology, so that even the designation of the two by the word 'materialist' is, properly speaking, a relic of the past.

Social fetishism, as we have seen, is the expression of the general unorganisedness of the social system of production and originally takes shape in the sphere of exchange and competition, where it is immediately sufficient to cognitively organise the contradictory content of experience. Participating both in exchange and in competition, the proletariat is unable to avoid the phase of social fetishism and, consequently, a metaphysically-coloured worldview with abstractly-empty ultimate generalisations, and in this phase the proletariat still makes use of bourgeois knowledge and bourgeois philosophy. But as

---

44   I use the word 'evolution' here in the original, narrower meaning of this word as is retained, for example, in embryology: the development of like from like, development that is very different from the *qualitative* transformation of forms.

competition is replaced by solidarity in the internal relationships of the working class, as the individual sale of its labour power by the proletariat is replaced by collective struggle with the capitalist class for better conditions of labour, and as the real relations of exploitation and subordination that are masked by the form of the sale of labour power are revealed, the basis for social fetishism in the working class disappears. Forms of knowledge that are adapted to the internal contradictions of collective being become insufficient and unsuitable when these inner contradictions in the class existence of the proletariat are eliminated, on the one hand, by internal unity and, on the other hand, by external contradictions (struggle with the capitalist class). A new type of cognitive form expresses new relationships.

In the realm of social life, the principle of the new knowledge is that the socially directed labour of people is the real basis of value – not only economic value but every other value as well. The technological value of products that takes the place of the fetish of exchange value is the quantity of the energy of social labour of people that is crystallised in them. The cognitive value of an idea is its capability to elevate the sum of the energy of social labour that systematically determines – that organises – the techniques and means of human activities. The 'moral' value[45] of human behaviour has as its content the elevation of the energy of social labour through harmoniously uniting and consolidating the activity of people – through 'organising' that activity in the direction of maximum solidarity.

Corresponding to the changed forms of understanding of social life, the forms of knowledge in all other realms of experience become insufficient and inadequate. The previous empty abstractions, such as 'substance', 'force', and 'the absolute', lose their fetishistic properties and also lose their vitality. Thought, as it advances, becomes aware of their naked emptiness, and it can no longer be organised by them. If such empty abstractions continue to be temporarily retained, they only serve as designations of known gaps in cognition. New forms are worked out from new technology – from the general, uniform procedures and methods that are presented by the system of machine production. At this point in time, the completion of these forms and their highest link is the law of transformation and conservation of energy. *This universal expression of machine technology* spreads along a 'derivative' line of ideological development to all other realms of experience, and, acquiring in this way the nature

---

45   The word 'morality' that relates to the realm of *norms of compulsion* here is not *completely* appropriate. The psychology of freedom is alien to what is properly 'moral', i.e. a categorically-imperative element.

of a universal monist principle, turns out so far to be capable of organising the entire experience of people to the last instance without contradiction.

Energetics became known to bourgeois science before it was known to the proletarian worldview. But in bourgeois thinking this principle acquired a metaphysical, i.e. a social-fetishistic colouration; the conservation of energy was understood as some kind of eternal 'substance'. Now contemporary scientists and philosophers of the bourgeois world – representatives not so much of the bourgeoisie as of the hired intelligentsia with its intermediary class nature – are gradually liberating the energetical monism of science from elements of metaphysics and fetishism, revealing its *methodological* content. But they can neither complete the work of eliminating fetishism nor develop and broaden the positive content of this principle to the highest limits. By relating this principle only to physical experience and not resolving to extend it to psychical experience, they not only narrow its meaning and significance, but they also reveal remnants of a substantial, i.e. metaphysical, understanding of energy – an understanding that makes energy a substance of the physical world.[46] Only in proletarian thinking is this principle capable of monistically permeating all knowledge and harmoniously organising all experience.

The *dynamic* tendency in the proletarian worldview diverges from the dynamic tendency in the bourgeois worldview due to the different roles that the two classes play in the process of social development. Both classes participate actively in technological progress, but for the bourgeoisie this progress is vitally useful only to the extent that it broadens the possibility for exploitation, i.e. to the extent that the organisation of social labour changes only quantitatively while remaining qualitatively as before, preserving its class form. On the contrary, for the proletariat, technological progress is transformed into the path toward social revolution, toward a qualitative change of the form of society and to the destruction of its class structure. In both cases, this different relationship to progress in the basic realm of experience carries over to all experience and all cognition. The result is a contradiction between the 'evolutionary' dynamism of bourgeois philosophy and the 'revolutionary' dynamism of proletarian philosophy.

From this perspective, the 'scientific-materialist' nature of the proletarian worldview turns out to be far from identical with the 'scientific-materialist'

---

46   Energy, as an organising methodological concept, obviously can also find a place in relation to psychical experience, and attempts to apply its monistic tendency to cognition, as well, are necessary and unavoidable. But energy as a physical 'substance' cannot also be simultaneously a 'psychical' substance (i.e. 'spirit').

nature of the bourgeois worldview.[47] The cognitive ideologies of the two classes diverge on all fundamental lines.

The contradiction between normative and cognitive ideologies continually grows and leads to the progressive division of the classes into two separate societies that relate to each other in the same way that they relate to the forces of external nature.

This division attains its maximum when the capitalist class finally loses its real organising function in production and transforms into a parasitic class.

The normative principles of the capitalist class then become reactionary, and its worldview becomes openly disorganised.

Capitalist property, already freed from *any* productive content, is transformed into the principle of pure exploitation, similar to the slave-owning principle, and finds its ultimate embodiment in stock market gambling and credit and bond speculation as well, verging on outright robbery.

The capitalist class has already ceased to conform to the principle of legality in regard to class interest and even more often in regard to personal interest, and the principle of legality is thus systematically and more or less manifestly destroyed. At the same time, it is formally accepted and aggressively imposed on the rest of society everywhere its preservation remains profitable for the capitalists. This contradictory relationship of the capitalist class to its own principle naturally undermines at its root the remnants of the influence which that same principle is used to promote, and other classes consider this to be 'blatant hypocrisy'.

In the realm of knowledge, the scientific-materialist tendency disappears, since its base – technological experience – becomes distant and alien from the parasitic class. The very same fate befalls the dynamic tendency both because of the same estrangement from technological experience and also because, in the atmosphere of conservatism and reaction that characterises the obsolete bourgeoisie, the elements of dynamism in their worldview encounter intense contradictions and undergo negative selection. Only social fetishism remains – limited and ameliorated by nothing – as the organising form for the content that continually shrinks.

However, once the bourgeoisie is no longer able to hold on to economic power, its efforts to consolidate its rule in *authoritarian class* and state forms lead to the resurrection within the bourgeoisie of elements of authoritarian ideology similar to feudal tendencies. The break-down of bourgeois thinking is complicated by manifestations of religiosity, sanctimoniousness, and so on.

---

47   The word 'materialism' when applied to proletarian ideology can be permitted only in in the broadest sense – in the sense of being the antithesis of 'idealism' and any metaphysics.

But at the same time the proletariat, having been organised into a force that is capable of harmoniously organising all production and having completed the elaboration of a new ideology, eliminates the anarchy of production and all norms of rule of the big bourgeoisie and replaces it all with new forms of life *of its own*. The sources of parasitism disappear, the class of parasites disintegrates, and a single society with a single ideology remains. Class development is completed, and a new phase of the history of humanity – a phase of united, harmonious development – begins. This moment still lies in the future, but the tendencies of the present that are leading toward it are so powerful and obvious that its necessity is unquestionable.

∴

Let us summarise the main conclusions that are relevant to the division of society into groups and classes:

1. The division of society into groups and classes is the result of the quantitative and the qualitative progress of technology. 'Social groups' spring up on the basis of the development of specialisation; 'classes' spring up on the basis of the progressive splitting off of the organisational and the implementational functions in society. Separation into social groups and social classes boils down to vitally important differences in the direction of social selection.
2. Social groups or classes acquire the properties of definite and stable social complexes when specifically-different ideologies take shape in them that are caused by a persistently-different direction of social selection in the milieu of these collectivities.
3. The splitting off of a social group is (according to its degree) a function of two variable tendencies – a tendency that *differentiates* technology and exacerbates the difference between specialties, and an *integrating* tendency that creates affinity and unity in the specialised functions of production. The predominance of the first of these tendencies has been historically observable in the progress of technology from the beginning right down to the era of machine production. The boundaries of social groups strengthen and attain the high degree of solidity that is characteristic, for example, of guild demarcations. Subsequently, the accumulation and organisation of socio-technological experience leads to a situation where the preponderance inclines toward the integrating tendency. Common methods of struggle with nature – methods principally of machine production – are worked out in the most varied sectors and the boundaries of specialisation burst. When the socially-grouped division of society

absolutely disappears in the unity of the methods of labour, the ideologies of social groups come together and merge.

4. In regard to class division, in the earlier stages of differentiation it is retarded by the particular relationship that exists between the functions of the organiser and of social ideology. The organiser is the personal form of the organising adaptation and ideology is the impersonal form. The organiser exists and works and the ideology develops owing to *the very same* socio-energetical magnitude – owing to the preponderance of assimilation over the expenditure of energy in the immediate process of labour, in the technological process. Due to this correlation, the organisational elements of society appear as the primary creators of ideology, and the ideology that they create is then common to the entire social whole.

5. The ideology that is elaborated by the organisational part of society retains complete vital significance for both parts of society as long as the content that it organises remains actually common to them both. When this condition is destroyed and the vital content of the two parts of society becomes essentially different – for example, in the beginning of the era of slavery, when the upper part of society was drawn into trade and the lower part continued to live within the confines of a natural economy – the ideological separation of the classes begins and the ideology of the upper class begins to contradict the vital experience and desires of the lower class, and this contradiction continues to grow.

6. The organisational function of the 'higher' class permits it to organise the life of the 'lower' class by means even of the kind of norms that do not correspond to the vital conditions of the lower class. These kinds of norms take on the nature of an external force for the subordinate class that is similar to the forces of extra-social nature – to forces that are hostile but that must be adapted to. This is the initial and fundamental class contradiction, the starting point of the development of any class struggle.

7. There are several types of class development, but there are two extreme types: classical slavery and capitalism. Other types – feudalism, for example – are essentially reducible to these two, and transform into them at certain stages of their development (all this applies, of course, not to the ideally possible but only to the historically known types of class development).

8. Both types of class development coincide in that over the course of time the organisational class, becoming progressively distant from the technologically-productive process, loses its actual organisational function. It is transformed into a parasitic class and inevitably degenerates, and it thereby loses its social power.

9. The two types differ in their starting point and in their final social results. The ancient type of class development originated in patriarchal slavery and a natural economy. Later on it was made complex by exchange, something that only the top circles of society were involved in. The organisational influence of the master extended to include the entire existence of the slaves. The tie between master and slave was fixed (it could not be broken by the will of the slave but only by the will of the master). This type of class development quickly led to the transformation of the immediate worker into a tool of production. Unlimited exploitation caused the complete degradation of the worker. Technological progress ceased. Slave ideology was unable to take shape and did not advance beyond an embryonic stage. Class struggle was absent. The degradation of both classes ended in the disintegration and collapse of the entire society.

10. The capitalist type of class development has its origin in the organisation of petty-bourgeois exchange. The organisational role of the entrepreneur was limited to a specific part of the existence of the workers – the working day. The tie between entrepreneur and worker was variable (subject to agreement). This type of class development led to the progressive transformation of the mass of individual worker-implementers into a solid collectivity that is suitable for an organisational role on a scale that expands limitlessly. The rapid technological progress that is characteristic of this type of development stimulates the rapid development of contradictory class ideologies and class struggle. It will all come to an end with the downfall of the former organisational class and the transition of society from a society that develops through class contradictions to a society that develops integrally and harmoniously. Extra-social and social spontaneity are equally overcome by the systematically organised power of humanity, and humanity's power over nature grows without limit ...

CHAPTER 10

# Self-Awareness of Philosophy (The Origin of Empiriomonism)

I

The domain of the phenomena that are subject to cognition concludes with the phenomenon of cognition, itself. Here cognition appears as one of the social processes; it is the most complex of all, but in principle it is totally cognisable. Neither in its forms nor in its dynamics is there anything that is essentially inaccessible to the organising experience of the activity of labour that cognition, itself, represents. All forms of cognition – from the most particular to the most general – must be investigated from the perspective of their origin, their vital significance, their development, and their ultimate fate.

This is what I have done in the entire preceding presentation. In so doing, I systematically made use of specific methods and techniques that express a specific point of view regarding the object under investigation. In part, I analysed everything from the same point of view and with the same methods of investigation, but only in part. For example, I showed that induction and deduction present an abbreviated reproduction of the processes of ideological development in general, as those processes flow through social life. I made special mention of the connection of the law of conservation of energy with machine production, etc. It is obviously impossible to provide any exhaustive analysis of such correlations here, but I must fully analyse at least one correlation. I must determine the foundations of *my own worldview* from the perspective of its social origin – to understand them as ideological derivatives of deeper-lying social conditions. This is what I shall now attempt to do.

When we see a specific type of worldview – religious-dualist or, let us say, metaphysical-monist, for example – it is necessary to use inductive methods in order to accurately explain its objective foundations. First and foremost, it is possible to establish precisely the social milieu – class, social group – which this type of worldview governs. Then it is necessary to explain the main relationships of social labour that are characteristic of this milieu – of the given class, the given group. We can propose a priori that the main features of the worldview that define its type depend precisely on the main vital relationships of that milieu that engender and maintain this worldview. Through a simple comparison of the model of a worldview with the model of the relationships of labour of its social milieu, we can usually obtain enough material for a *hypothesis* that such-and-such traits of the worldview are the result of such-and-such technological relationships, forms of social collaboration, or forms of internal struggle, etc. We then arrive at a 'method of discrimination', and the systematic application of this method is the decisive moment in the verification of the hypothesis. To be exact, it is necessary by means of discriminative observations to establish what occurs with such-and-such traits of a worldview when such-and-such a relationship of social labour – the hypothesised basis of those traits – develops, solidifies, and becomes widespread, and what occurs when that relationship degrades, weakens, and disappears. Either the given traits of the worldview (or the tendency for those traits to develop) are revealed in all social complexes where the given relationship of social labour is present (and also the other way around), or those traits are absent (or are eliminated) everywhere the hypothesised basis for them does not exist, etc.[1] If in all such comparisons an underlying parallelism between the forms of cognition and the forms of production is revealed, then the hypothesis has solid ground beneath it and, as a scientific theory, it can now serve as the basis for new conclusions and further investigations.

Operating on these methods, I have explained in my earlier works the origin of the dualist type of thinking in the dualism of the organisational and implementational functions in labour, the origin of the metaphysical monism of empty abstractions in the anarchistic, contradiction-filled forms of the social division of labour that is characteristic of 'commodity' society, and finally also, in part, the origin of modern monist ideas in the comradely forms of social collaboration that are characteristic of the working class. It is easy to see that an investigation of such a kind becomes more difficult the *newer* the worldview with which it is dealing. There is less data for comparison, less material for verification, and the elements of hypothesis are inevitably stronger. For the same reason, investigation is more difficult the less widespread the worldview being examined and the more 'individually' it is coloured, etc.

All these difficulties with the social-genetic analysis of my basic ('empiriomonist') positions stand out very forcefully. But if the worldview itself is true to life, if it is not the result of individual peculiarities but is an expression of

---

1 In all such comparisons it is necessary, of course, to keep in mind the inevitable *delay* in the development and degradation of ideological forms (which are derivative and more conservative) in comparison with the corresponding forms of social labour (which are primary and more flexible).

a definite and progressive social tendency, and if, in general, it really merits investigation, then there is no reason to consider the difficulties to be insurmountable. Like it or not, it will be easier to attempt to resolve this question by figuring it out in practice.

II

I must begin with a clear formulation of where my point of view stands in relation to the customary antithesis between materialist and idealist systems. If I find that it belongs to the first or second of these series, I will immediately be able to apply to it the conclusions that can be made in regard to that series in general.

In formal terms, the difference between the materialist and the idealist point of view is usually reduced to the question of the correlation between 'matter' and 'spirit': what is considered primary and what is considered derivative?[2] For me, obviously, the antithesis itself is absolutely unnecessary. It is unnecessary not only because both of those concepts are vague and indefinite but also because, as the investigation of their origin makes them more definite, they turn out to be vestiges of authoritarian dualism – a reflection of the lowest social formation. In this sense, my position can be designated as equally alien to both materialism and idealism. But such a formulation is absolutely insufficient for the goal that is posed at the moment – an explanation of the *genetic* correlations of 'empiriomonism' with other points of view.

There is an especially close connection between the natural sciences and materialist systems. The material of the natural sciences always lies at the foundation of materialist systems, and they raise the methods of the natural sciences to the level of the highest, universal forms of cognition. But the natural sciences themselves represent the highest systematisation of *technological experience*, 'the ideology of productive forces'. Consequently, in the final analysis, a materialist worldview appears as just such an ideology in all (or, perhaps, in almost all) of its historical forms.

Idealist systems correlate with the ideological process in precisely the same way that materialist systems correlate with the technological process. As a rule, 'moral' phenomena serve as the basis for the various forms of 'idealism' and so

---

2   In science the concept of 'matter' boils down to the coefficient of 'mass' that appears in the equations of mechanics, and this latter, under precise analysis, turns out to be the 'contrary magnitude of acceleration' in the presence of the mutual interaction of two physical complexes-bodies (see E. Mach, *Die Mechanik in ihrer Entwicklung* [*The History of the Science of Mechanics*]).

do the most abstract cognitive forms – laws of logic, pure categories of cognition, and so forth. Idealism is consequently an 'ideology of ideology' (predominantly).³

My point of view eliminates the concepts of 'matter' and 'spirit' because they are imprecise and they muddle up analysis. But it does make use of the contrast between 'physical' and 'psychical' experience and, in investigating the correlation of the two, it leads to the conclusion that of these two realms of experience the 'physical' represents a *higher* stage of organisation, and consequently also a *derivative* stage. Psychical experience is organised individually; physical experience is organised socially, i.e. they are *different phases* of the organising process from which the 'psychical' is the *relatively-primary*. But is this not idealism in the shell of a modified terminology? Is it not the acceptance of 'spirit' for what is relatively primary and from which 'nature' develops? To think this would be mistaken to the highest degree.

The 'psychical' and the 'physical' as forms of *experience* do not at all correspond to the concepts of 'nature' and 'spirit'. These latter concepts have a metaphysical meaning and have to do with 'things-in-themselves'. We have removed metaphysical 'things-in-themselves' from our analysis as empty fetishes and replaced them with the 'empirical substitution'. This substitution – the starting point of which lies in the recognition by each person of the psyches of other people – assumes that the 'basis' of phenomena of physical experience consists in *immediate complexes of different levels of organisation*, to which 'psychical' complexes also relate. Recognising that physiological processes of the highest neural centres – as phenomena of physical experience – are a reflection of psychical complexes that also can be 'substituted' for them, I found that altogether all of the physiological processes of life permit the substitution of complexes of an 'associative' type, i.e. a psychical type. But the lower the complexity and organisation of physiological phenomena, the less complex and the lower the organisation of the substituted complexes. Further, I recognised that beyond the confines of physiological life, in the 'inorganic world', the empirical substitution also does not cease, but those 'immediate complexes' that must be substituted for inorganic phenomena now possess not an associative form of organisation but a different, lower one. These are not 'psychical' combinations

---

3   Except for a few exceptions, authoritarian and religious tendencies are considerably more characteristic of idealism than materialism. This becomes clear if we recall the basic similarity between ideological forms and the organisational function in society: the organising adaptations of social life in the first case is impersonal and in the second case is personal. The forms of idealism that are based on 'moral consciousness' – i.e. on normative ideology in the purest form – especially gravitate toward authority and religion.

but less definite combinations – less complex and also of different degrees of organisation that in their lowest, ultimate phase appear simply as a chaos of elements.

And it is here among the *immediate* complexes that are substituted for physical experience that we must seek analogues of 'nature' and 'spirit' in order to establish their mutual relationship.

But the answer to the question is obviously already contained in this substitution, itself. 'Nature' – i.e. the lowest inorganic and simplest organic combinations – is *genetically primary*, and 'spirit' – i.e. the highest organic combinations, associative combinations, and especially those that form 'experience' – is *genetically derivative*.

Thus, my point of view, while not being 'materialist' in the narrow sense of this word, belongs to the same order as 'materialist' systems, and it is consequently the ideology of the 'productive forces' of the technological process.

A worldview that strives to connect the methods of the natural sciences with the 'social materialism' of Marx and that is essentially a continuation of these methods in the sphere of socio-historical cognition could not, of course, be anything different.

III

In a class society, any worldview is either the ideology of some specific class or a specific combination of various class ideologies. Because individuals are created and defined by their social milieu (and in a class society by their class milieu), even what is most individual in their worldview can only be a distinctive combination of the elements of collective, class thinking.

The ideology of the technological process in such a case is inevitably the ideology of the class that stands in a close relationship to the technological process, i.e. the 'productive' class in the *broad* meaning of the word. But in contemporary society such a characterisation applies to the proletariat (the class of 'implementational' labour), to the petty bourgeoisie (the class of independent small producers), and even to a certain part of the big bourgeoisie (the ones who still continue to retain an *immediately organisational* function in their enterprises). Thus, the relationship of my worldview to the realm of technological experience still does not resolve the question of the class content of my worldview's philosophical foundations.

I must therefore turn to a more concrete examination of these foundations. It is necessary to begin with the more general philosophical question about the relationship of the psychical and physical world. Here my point of view is that I recognise, first, that both realms of experience are *fundamentally homogen-*

*ous* and, second, that *psychical experience is necessarily subordinate to cognitive forms that arise on the ground of physical experience*. The fundamental homogeneity of the two realms of experience consists in that their elements are identical and that the difference between their two regularities is the difference between the individual and the social organisation of experience – the two stages of the organising process. The subordination of psychical experience to norms of physical experience is expressed in the various particular applications of psychoenergetics.

It is obvious that such a conception absolutely does not correspond to the habits of thinking of the bourgeoisie and the petty bourgeoisie – to the habits that issue from all of its social experience. These classes are *individualistic* in all their tendencies in life, because the bases of their existence are *private property* and the market with its constant *struggle*. This individualism also finds a place in their conception of experience and cognition. In their theories of cognition, the cognising subject is always the individual, and the basic questions of philosophy are posed and resolved from the point of view of individual cognitive activity.[4]

On the other hand, it is precisely the material for the idea that the 'psychical' and the 'physical' are fundamentally homogenous and the idea that 'physical' laws predominate over 'psychical' laws (and not the other way around) that is constantly given to workers in machine production in their daily experience of labour. At each step they encounter the practical replacement of elements of psychical work – volitional effort, attention, and even imagination – with combinations of physical elements. *Automatic mechanisms* with their self-actuating regulators especially display in reality the equivalence of mechanical forces with the work of the intellect. They eliminate to a significant degree even the labour of observation and the supervision of productive processes; the machine even undertakes what previously could be done only by the most intelligent worker-mechanic and what a less educated worker could not do at all. At the same time it turns out that the replacement occurs with a certain proportionality. In a given system of mechanisms, a greater quantity of psychical work is replaced by a greater quantity of mechanical work; in a more complex 'apparatus', more complex psychical work is replaced by more complex physical combinations. At the same time, workers see in the regularity and systematic

---

4   The conception of the social nature of experience and knowledge is already familiar to ideologists of intermediary groups – to be precise, the hired intelligentsia who work for capital and the bourgeois state (i.e. the bourgeoisie *as a class*), especially as professional philosophers, beginning with L. Feuerbach, at least. But they do not bring this conception into their worldview at all completely. (This is true even of the 'empiriocriticists').

nature of the operation of these machines the results of the accumulated experience of other workers and the ideas and accomplishments of the experience of humanity. In the process of their labour, workers must also constantly adapt their psychical work to this iron regularity and systematic nature. But they cannot transform *this latter* to adapt it to the processes of their psyche, or, more precisely, they can do so only to a comparatively insignificant degree. And they can realise this in practice only if in their psychical work (for example, the work of invention) they continually keep their full attention on that same regularity that is collectively crystallised in existing machine technology. I.e. here also they must yet again adapt their individual creativity to organised, collective creativity.

Thus, in the experience of social labour of worker in machine production, there is material that has basic vital significance both for the recognition of the fundamental homogeneity of the 'psychical' and the 'physical' and also for the tendency to cognitively subordinate the 'psychical' to collectively elaborated forms of cognition of the 'physical'. In organising this material in perfectly-pure forms and making these forms universal, this philosophy must be considered to be the ideology of the class in question – precisely to the extent, of course, that it in reality does not admix alien tendencies that contradict the tendencies of the proletariat.

It goes without saying that it does not at all follow from the proletarian-class nature of the tendencies of a given philosophy by itself that this philosophy can and must be accepted by the proletariat and its ideologists. For this to occur, it would be necessary that this philosophy really organised social experience successfully, with sufficient completeness and harmony, in forms that correspond to the thinking of the proletariat. It would be necessary that there be no mistakes and contradictions in it. Any attempt, conscious or unconscious, to formulate the ideology of one or another class philosophically must first and foremost be subject to critique from the perspective of its 'truth', i.e. its correspondence with facts and the absence of internal contradictions. Unsuccessful attempts must be mercilessly condemned and rejected. 'Benign intentions' in this case would aggravate and not ameliorate the fault. Therefore 'self-awareness' of philosophy must appear on the scene only after its scientific-factual substantiation, and it is precisely such a sequence that I hold myself to.

IV

The second basic proposition that, in my opinion, expresses the empiriomonist tendency is the doctrine of 'substitution'. Here my task presented two aspects. First, it was necessary to purify 'substitution' of elements of authoritarian dualism and metaphysical social fetishism that complicate it and obscure its vital meaning. This was a negative and 'critical' task. Second, it was necessary to generalise 'substitution' and, on the basis of a valid analogy, to extend it from the separate physiological processes of the life of neural centres to all processes of life in general and then also to the processes of inorganic nature, and, in so doing, to change its content correspondingly. This was a positive and 'monist' task. Finally, it was necessary to obtain an understanding of the fact that substitution constitutes the basis of the social nature of cognition, and thereby of cognition in general – an understanding that corresponds to experience and is internally coherent, in a word, that is 'empiriomonist'.

The critique of 'substitution' is mainly directed against the concept of 'spirit' or 'soul' that is created by authoritarian thinking and against the 'thing-in-itself' that is derivative of this concept and is produced by the social fetishism of exchange society. The erroneous and superfluous form of substitution that considers psychical experience to be a 'manifestation' of some kind of 'thing-in-itself' that is lying deeper than it is also eliminated. Because it is the starting point of any substitution, psychical experience itself does not require any substitution in its turn.[5] At the same time that substitution is abbreviated in this sphere, it is extended in another direction – from the higher physiological processes to the entire realm of physical experience. This extension is necessary for monism, and, in reality, scientific thinking – just like everyday thinking – always practises this but for the most part is not clear in its own mind about it. Philosophy always displayed the greatest inclination for this (the countless theories of 'parallelism'). This extension alone provides the possibility of understanding all that exists to be a really unbroken series – to present the whole line of development *without any absolute* discontinuity (i.e. a point where 'consciousness appears for the first time').

In this unbroken series, nothing is stationary, and we must view the very *forms of experience* (time, space, causality) as developing forms of coordinations of elements and complexes and as types of how they are grouped in the process of the growth of organisation and mutual interconnectedness of the experiences that make up experience.

In such a view, the entire doctrine is characterised by a tendency that is strictly positive, monist, and relentlessly dynamic. All these traits are characteristic only of ideologies of progressive and progressing classes. The *growing profusion of living content that is real and that is close to the immediate struggle*

---

5 In psychophysiological research it is often necessary, as we have seen, to take the corresponding physiological process instead of the psychical process; but this is not at all the 'substitution' that is under discussion. Rather, it is an *action* that is the *opposite* of substitution.

*with nature* is expressed in this positive tendency that eliminates all spectres and fetishes and makes them superfluous to life. Monism is the cognitive reflection of the *growing organisation* of life. The progress of the practical unity of the living social forces of a class increases and intensifies the need for the cognitive unity of conceptions, and the foundation of the content of these conceptions is, as we know, only the abbreviation of complexes of the practical vital content. Finally, the connection between the dynamism of the worldview and the vital progressiveness of class is so simple and obvious that there is no need to explain it. The maximum dynamism in cognition corresponds to the maximum revolutionary character in life.

All these traits, in totality, state the ideology of the proletariat.

V

Let us now look at the general picture of the world as it appears from the point of view of my basic positions.

Our universe is first and foremost a *world of experience*. But it is not only a world of *immediate* experience. No, it is much broader. As a world of *possible immediate experience* it stretches out to infinity, i.e. it has the tendency to expand indefinitely. But, besides that, the universe is supplemented by a 'substitution', and it now appears here as a world of 'indirect experience'. The psychical life of another person and our own 'subconscious' experiences can never become objects of direct, immediate experience for us; however they do not lie outside our experience in general. If that were the case, one could neither think nor talk about them. My investigation led to the conclusion that such an expansion of the universe through substitution necessarily parallels the entire line of 'physical experience' but in such a way that the content of the 'substitution' was changed corresponding to the level of *organisation* of those physiological and simply physical processes in relation to which the 'substitution' is carried out.

As a result the whole universe presents itself in the following form:

The endless sum of elements that are identical to the elements of our experience are grouped together in endless series of complexes of different levels of organisation, from the very lowest to the very highest, from the indefinite 'chaos of elements' to the complexes of human experience and, perhaps, to even much more perfected forms.

These complexes become intertwined in more complex combinations. They 'act' on one another, and they 'change' one another. They are 'reflected' in one another, as we see in the complexes of our immediate experience. The 'consciousness' of a human being is a complex, variable, and steadily changing combination in which other combinations are 'reflected' in the form of 'perceptions', 'external impressions', etc., and it is from these 'reflections' that the vast material of psychical experience is formed. In that material there appear (through the action of some 'complexes-reflections' on other complexes-reflections) complexes-reflections of a *second order*. This is 'indirect experience', the world of 'substitution'. The interrelationship of *communication* between different 'consciousnesses' is created by means of 'substitution' and through this communication the *general types of organisation of experience* (time, space, causality) are produced, and part of collective experience (that exists piecemeal in different psyches) acquires the 'social organisation' that characterises *physical experience*. All this complex process of development, from the chaos of elements to the objective regularity of physical experience, is essentially homogenous. It is a change of complexes in which some unite with others and in which they mutually influence one another; it is change that leads to their ever greater organisation and coherence.

In this endlessly unfolding fabric of the universe, its separate 'cells' – complexes and combinations of complexes – do not flow together in one continuous field like the field of consciousness, but remain divided among countless independent 'fields of complexes'. In order to envisage this separateness in the same universal forms of experience it is necessary to assume a specific type of change: *the interference* of immediate complexes-processes.[6] If two complexes are connected by means of a third, and a complex that is contradictory to that third complex is attached to it (the removal of elements that appear in it and the appearance of elements that disappear in it) then this intermediary, connecting complex 'is destroyed' for experience, and the connection of the two others is interrupted. Thus, through the application of the idea of causality (since 'interference' is one of its forms) *discontinuities boil down to continuity*.

Consequently, here is our conception of the world whole: an endless series of complexes, broken down by cognition into elements that are identical with the elements of experience and situated at different levels of organisation. The fabric in which these series are interwoven is assumed by cognition to be continuous, and its apparent discontinuities are accepted as the result of interference, i.e. the mutual destruction of contradictory complexes that serve as a connection between others.

---

6   There is no harm in reminding the reader that 'complexes' must be understood to be *dynamic* and not static. It is the continuous appearance and disappearance of elements, similar to the elements of experience, in specific combinations. I often also employ a static conception of a complex but in that case the matter has to do, of course, with nothing more than a *stable equilibrium*.

*From a social-genetic* point of view, from where did this entire picture arise? This question must be posed, since any picture of the world must *first and foremost* correspond to the immediate picture of the *social* relationships among which humans live that are the most important for them and the most constant in their experience. The answer to this question appears automatically if, in this same picture, we replace complexes, in general, with *social complexes*, the highest and most complicated form of complexes.

What we then obtain is a precise depiction of contemporary society in which the labour-related groupings of the most varied levels of organisation are united together – from small peasant households to colossal capitalist trusts, from individual families to great political parties. All these combinations mutually influence one another, mutually change one another, and, in one way or another, 'reflect' one another. But, at the same time, they do not directly flow together into one whole; they exist separately, regardless of the real living interconnectedness (complex cooperation) that makes *one* society out of them. The 'principle' of separateness is the *struggle* that springs up where these complexes come into contact (for example in the 'market' that connects all the different economic enterprises). This struggle is a process in which contradictory tendencies are united, striving to mutually destroy one another and partially succeeding. From the social-genetic point of view, this struggle is the prototype of that 'interference of immediate complexes' that itself causes the discontinuities of complexes in our general picture of the world.

In thus establishing a connection between our picture of the world and the social structure of our era (as a 'reflection' is connected with a 'prototype'), we can draw two further conclusions from it. The first conclusion is that this connection satisfies one of the essential conditions that are required of a worldview, and that is that it must be *historically true*. The second conclusion is that, if this picture is to be considered true for contemporary cognition, then, since the given structure of society must create the tendency to preserve this basic cognitive model, one can hardly expect *radical* changes to occur in it before social life is *radically* reconstructed.

∴

On this point I end my attempt to carry out 'self-awareness' in regard to my worldview. I had to utilise more the method of analogy than the comparatively precise abstract-historical method that I outlined at the beginning of this chapter. This, of course, imparted a more hypothetical character to the entire attempt, but at the same time (also at the beginning of the chapter) I pointed out the difficulties of investigation that made this unavoidable. And if my readers take the trouble to intently examine my attempt, they perhaps will find in it a more immediate persuasiveness than could be provided by the method of its construction in itself. In historical-philosophical explanations of ideology – due to complexity but at the same time also to the closeness of cognisers to their own organisation – the role of lively intuition (necessarily very significant) can, in practice, turn out to have very successful results, as has been noted more than once by materialist historians.

We have arrived at the following characterisation of the philosophical worldview that has been outlined: the cognitive ideology of the technological process – proletarian in its tendencies – reproduces in its general model the basic features of the structure of contemporary society.

All processes of life are cyclical and one cycle of life, as it develops, turns into the beginning of another, higher cycle. Cognition, which is also one of the vital processes of life, is also cyclical. And when cognition arrives at the *cognition of cognition itself*, when, passing through a series of objects of ascending complexity, it finds its own self at the end of this series and thus returns to itself, it thereby completes one of the cycles of its development. This completion is at the same time a higher form of verification, and if it finds confirmation of itself in that form, then it begins a new cycle of its development with all the more confidence and clarity ...

# Bibliography

Bazarov, V.A. 2002, 'A.A. Bogdanov (Malinovskii) kak myslitel'', *Vestnik Mezhdunarodnogo Instituta Aleksandra Bogdanova*, 4.

Berdiaev, N. 1902, 'Zametka o knige Bogdanova', *Voprosy filosofii i psikhologii*, 4, part 2: 839–53.

Biggart, John, Georgii Gloveli and Avraham Yassour 1998, *Bogdanov and His Work: A Guide to the Published and Unpublished Works of Alexander A. Bogdanov (Malinovsky) 1873–1928*, Aldershot: Ashgate.

Bogdanoff, A. 1905, 'Psychical Selection (Empiriomonism in the Study of Psychics)', *Journal of Philosophy, Psychology, and Scientific Methods*, 2: 301–6.

Bogdanov, Alexander 1897, *Kratkii kurs ekonomicheskoi nauki* [*A Short Course of Economic Science*], Moscow: A.M. Murinovoi.

Bogdanov, Alexander 1899, *Osnovnye elementy istoricheskogo vzgliada na prirodu* [*Basic Elements of an Historical View of Nature*], St. Petersburg: Izdatel'.

Bogdanov, Alexander 1901, *Poznanie s istoricheskoi tochki zreniia* [*Cognition from an Historical Point of View*], St. Petersburg: A. Leifert.

Bogdanov, Alexander 1903a, 'Ideal poznaniia (Empiriokrititsizm i empiriomonism)' ['The Ideal of Cognition (Empiriocriticism and Empiriomonism)'], *Voprosy filosofii i psikhologii*, 2, part 2: 186–233.

Bogdanov, Alexander 1903b, 'Zhizn' i psikhika (Empiriomonizm v uchenii o zhizni) I–V' ['Life and the Psyche (Empiriomonism in the Theory of Life) I–V'], *Voprosy filosofii I psikhologii*, 4, part 2: 682–708.

Bogdanov, Alexander 1903c, 'Zhizn' i psikhika (Empiriomonizm v uchenii o zhizni) (Okonchanie)' ['Life and the Psyche (Empiriomonism in the Theory of Life) (Conclusion)'], *Voprosy filosofii I psikhologii*, 5, part 2: 824–66.

Bogdanov, Alexander 1904a, 'Psikhicheskii podbor (Empiriomonizm v uchenii o psikhiki)' ['Psychical selection (Empiriomonism in the Theory of the Psyche)'], *Voprosy filosofii i psikhologii*, 3, part 2: 335–79.

Bogdanov, Alexander 1904b, *Empiriomonizm. Stat'i po filosofii* [*Empiriomonism. Essays on Philosophy*], Moscow: Izdanie S. Dorovatovskogo i Charushnikova.

Bogdanov, Alexander 1904c, *Ocherki realisticheskogo mirovozzreniia* [*Outlines of a Realist Worldview*], St. Petersburg: Izdanie S. Dorovatovskogo i Charushnikova.

Bogdanov, Alexander 1905a, *Empiriomonizm. Stat'i po filosofii. Kniga I* [*Empiriomonism. Essays on Philosophy. Book I*], 2nd edn, Moscow: Izdanie S. Dorovatovskogo i Charushnikova.

Bogdanov, Alexander 1905b, *Empiriomonizm. Stat'i po filosofii. Kniga II* [*Empiriomonism. Essays on Philosophy. Book II*], Moscow: Izdanie S. Dorovatovskogo i Charushnikova.

Bogdanov, Alexander 1905c, *Novyi mir* [*New World*], Moscow: Izdanie S. Dorovatovskogo i Charushnikova.

Bogdanov, Alexander 1906a, *Empiriomonizm. Stat'i po filosofii. Kniga II* [*Empiriomonism. Essays on Philosophy. Book II*], 2nd edn, Moscow: Izdanie S. Dorovatovskogo i Charushnikova.

Bogdanov, Alexander 1906b, *Empiriomonizm. Stat'i po filosofii. Kniga III* [*Empiriomonism. Essays on Philosophy. Book III*], Moscow: Izdanie S. Dorovatovskogo i Charushnikova.

Bogdanov, Alexander 1906c, *Iz psikhologii obshchestva* [*On the Psychology of Society*], St. Petersburg: 'Pallada'.

Bogdanov, Alexander 1908, *Empiriomonizm. Stat'i po filosofii. Kniga I.* [*Empiriomonism. Essays on Philosophy. Book I*], 3rd edn, Moscow: Izdanie S. Dorovatovskogo i Charushnikova.

Bordiugov, G.A. (ed.) 1995, *Neizvestnyi Bogdanov v 3-kh knigax. Kniga 1. Stat'i, doklady, i vospominaniia, 1901–1928* [*The Unknown Bogdanov in 3 Books. Book 1. Articles, Reports, and Recollections, 1901–1928*], Moscow: AIRO-XX.

Dudley, Peter (ed.) 1996, *Bogdanov's Tektology: Book One*, Hull: Centre for Systems Studies Press.

G–d [P.B. Struve] 1899, *Nachalo*, 5, part 2: 121–3.

Gorelik, George 1980, *Essays in Tektology: The General Science of Organization*, Seaside, CA: Intersystems Publications Limited.

Jasny, Naum 1972, *Soviet Economists of the Twenties: Names to be Remembered*, Cambridge: Cambridge University Press.

Kant, Immanuel 1922, *Critique of Pure Reason*, translated by F. Max Muller, London: Macmillan.

Krementsov, Nikolai 2011, *A Martian Stranded on Earth: Alexander Bogdanov, Blood Transfusion, and Proletarian Science*, Chicago: University of Chicago Press.

Lenin, Vladimir Il'ich 1927, *Materialism and Empirio-Criticism: Critical Notes Concerning a Reactionary Philosophy*, Moscow: International Publishers.

Lunacharskii, A. 1905, *Rikhard Avenarius. Kritika chistogo opyta v populiarnom izlozhenii* [*Richard Avenarius's Critique of Pure Experience in a Popular Exposition*], Moscow: Izdanie S. Dorovatovskogo i Charushnikova.

Nevskii, V.I. (ed.) 1931, *Deiateli revoliutsionnogo dvizheniia v Rossii, Bio-bibliograficheskii Slovar', Tom piatyi, Sotsial-demokraty, 1889–1904, Vypusk I, A–B* [*Actors of the Revolutionary Movement in Russia, A Bio-Bibliographical Dictionary, Volume Five, Social-Democrats, 1889–1904, Issue 1, A–B*], Moscow: Vsesoiuznoe obshchestvo politicheskikh katorzhan i ssyl'no-poselentsev.

Pavlov, Evgeni V. 2013, 'Nikolai Bukharin on the Life of A.A. Bogdanov', *Platypus Review*, 57, http://platypus1917.org/2013/06/01/bukharin-on-bogdanov/ accessed October 8 2016.

Pavlov, Evgeni V. 2017, '"When was Caesar Born?" Theory and Practice of Truth in Plekhanov and Bogdanov', *Stasis*, 5, no. 2: 50–79.

Plekhanov, Georgii V. 1906, *Kritika nashikh kritikov* [*A Critique of My Critics*], St. Petersburg: *Obshchestvennaia pol'za*.

Poole, Randall A. (ed.) 2003 [1902], *Problems of Idealism: Essays in Russian Social Philosophy*, New Haven: Yale University Press.

White, James D. 2018, *Red Hamlet: The Life and Ideas of Alexander Bogdanov*, Leiden: Brill.

# Name Index

Aristotle 20
Avenarius, Richard 5, 5n, 6n1, 6n2, 7n, 9, 12, 14, 14n1, 14n2, 15, 29, 29n1, 29n2, 35, 35n, 36, 48, 48n3, 49, 53, 66–68, 67n, 70–75, 77–79, 79n1, 79n2, 105–106, 105n, 106n, 122n1, 129, 129n1, 134, 134n2, 137, 188, 188n, 216, 216n1, 249–261, 251n, 261n, 262–263, 274, 282, 282n, 296–297, 296n1, 313
Avvakum 211
Azam, Étienne Eugène 56, 61

Babinski, Jules François Félix 57
Bentham, Jeremy 219
Binet, Alfred 57

Democritus 157, 291

Engels, Friedrich xxxi, 159, 270–273, 271n, 274n, 277, 349
Epicurus 20, 157, 291

Ferri, Enrico 303
Fervorn, Max 275
Feuerbach, Ludwig 408

Hegel, G.W.F. 9n, 296
Heine, Heinrich 198, 207n, 211, 213, 216, 216n
Herbart, Johann 168n1
Hering, Karl 18n2
Holbach, Paul-Henri baron 157, 274, 281, 288, 292, 296
Hume, David 26n, 285–287

James, William 13, 13n, 263
James-Lange theory of emotions 13, 363
Janet, Pierre-Marie-Félix 57

Kant, Immanuel xxiv, xxvi, xxxii, 3, 26n, 133, 136, 137, 159, 159n, 275n, 281, 296n, 300, 371n1
Korsakov, S. 17n

Lange, Carl 13, 13n, 88n1, 263, 303
Le Dantec Felix 179n

Lenin, V.I. xxi
Lunacharskii, A.V. 249, 250–261, 263

Mach, Ernst 5–9, 5n, 6n1, 6n2, 7n, 8n, 11, 14–15, 14n2, 18, 21n1, 21n2, 29, 36, 36n, 48n4, 88n, 91, 141, 274, 280–282, 282n, 296–297, 296n1, 299, 332n, 389n, 405n
MacNish, Robert 56
Marx, Karl xix–xx, xxxvi–xxxvii, 269, 274, 283, 285, 296, 299, 300, 324, 407
Mayer, Robert 88n1
Meynert, Theodor 80, 84, 168n, 263
Müller, Max 6n2, 219n, 335

Newton, Isaac xxiii, xxiv, 357
Noiré, Ludwig 6n2, 48n3, 335, 341

Ortodoks (Liubov Akselrod) 298n
Ostwald, Wilhelm 26n, 88n1, 274, 279

Plekhanov, G.V. (N. Beltov) xx, xxi, xxvi, xxvii, xxix, xxxi, xxxii, xxxiii, xl, 159, 267, 270–277, 278, 271n, 274n, 275n, 280–281, 285–286, 288, 288n, 292–293, 296–301, 298n, 301n

Reymond, Emil du Bois 64
Riehl, Alois 6, 6n2, 88n1, 164n, 279

Schopenhauer, Arthur 42
Schubert-Soldern, Richard von 282
Schuppe, Wilhelm 282
Simmel, Georg 14n1, 24n1
Spencer, Herbert 157, 159, 371n
Spinoza, Baruch 16, 79, 168n, 263, 274, 371n1

Timiriazev, Kliment 273

Valentinov, Nikolai 298n

Woltmann, Ludwig 303
Willy, Rudolph 21n2
Wundt, Wilhelm 75n2, 127, 156, 192

# Subject Index

a priori   xxxvi, 24, 84, 86, 120, 141, 169, 170, 181, 184, 249, 280, 403
abstraction (verb)   28, 64, 221
abstractions   xl, 66, 72, 278, 362
   cognitive   xxx, 28
   empty   15, 123, 136, 354, 388–389, 397, 404
   metaphysical   xxvi
   pure   135
   scientific   305
   ultimate   204, 221
adaptations   xviii, 6–7, 33–34, 38, 42, 51, 171–172, 179–80, 221, 235, 274, 305, 316–319, 321–322, 329–330, 333–336, 340, 344–345, 347, 354, 362–363, 387
   called 'I', the   42
   cognitive   6, 388
   economic   317, 318
   environment, to the   72
   ideological   317, 318, 329, 332–358, 368, 371–372, 378
   labour, a process of   245
   normative   359, 377
   organising   284, 329–324, 336–339, 342, 351, 363, 372, 401
   psychical   172–173, 179, 311
   psychological   179
   psychophysiological   305, 317
   social   6–7, 316, 334, 336
   socially-organising   351
   technological   317–318, 329, 334–335, 343–344
adaptedness   61, 69, 74, 75, 180, 307, 308, 311, 316, 324, 373
Affectional, the   75–80, 92, 168, 169n, 170–177, 173n, 179–180, 182–184, 186–187, 187n, 189, 191–195, 199–200, 209, 213, 215, 226–227, 229, 230n, 232, 235, 237, 239, 241n, 242–244, 244n, 249, 256–259, 261n, 263
animism   33, 135, 137, 157, 283, 294
animists   13, 23, 98, 134, 157, 167
apriorism
   absolute   116, 160
   socially evolved   25

aristocracy   285–286, 288
   modern agrarian   384
   slave-owning   384
aristocrats   285, 287, 288
Aristotle   20
assimilation   49, 211
   energy in labour, of   401
   nourishment, of   73, 74, 253, 254, 262
   social, of energy   326, 328
   technological process, in the   328, 336, 361
associations   12, 111, 122, 139, 151, 181, 186–189, 194, 197, 197n, 201n, 202, 205, 214n, 228, 231–239
   chain of   190
   conceptions, of   242, 304
   contiguity, according to   182–183, 185, 191, 219, 234n
   difference, according to   183, 188, 194, 196–197, 210n, 218–219
   experiences, of   63, 95, 181, 183
   habitual   53
   images, of   238–239
   interconnection of   52, 63
   model of   181
   psychical   201n
   similarity, according to   183, 188–190, 194, 197, 210n, 218–219
   temporal consecutiveness, according to   183
associative
   activity of consciousness   97, 166
   centre   190
   chain   111–112, 115, 117, 120, 122, 125, 202
   combinations   28, 125, 152, 181, 189, 202, 408
   complexes   98, 150, 166–167, 187
   connection   52, 57, 57n2, 59, 111–113, 122, 122n2, 171, 175–177, 175n, 181–183, 186, 189, 190–191, 194, 197, 200, 202–203, 203n, 215–216, 219, 234–235, 238, 308, 332, 337
   convergence   202
   coordination   171, 177, 181, 243
   creativity   246
   fibres   182, 182n

grouping   183, 223
interconnectedness   54, 56, 110, 150, 335
link   59, 115–117
organization of experience   97
organization   151–152, 208, 407
path   232
process   188
psychical environment   304
regularity   65
relationship   189
series   111–113, 111n, 120
system   110, 120–121, 150–151, 187
authoritarian   3, 134n3, 283, 286–288, 293, 354, 371, 390n, 399, 405, 406n, 409, 410
Avenarius, Richard   5, 5n, 6n1, 6n2, 7n, 9, 12, 14, 14n1, 14n2, 15, 29, 29n1, 29n2, 35, 35n, 36, 48, 48n3, 49, 53, 66–68, 67n, 70–75, 77–79, 79n1, 79n2, 105–106, 105n, 106n, 122n1, 129, 129n1, 134, 134n2, 137, 188, 188n, 216, 216n1, 249–260, 251n, 262–263, 274, 282, 282n, 296–297, 296n1, 313
   Der menschliche Weltbegriff   122n1, 129n1, 134n2
   Kritik der reinen Erfahrung   6, 14n1, 14n2, 48, 48n3, 70–72, 72n, 79, 79n1, 106n, 129, 129n1, 188, 188n, 216, 216n1, 274
   System C   29, 29n1, 67, 67n, 68, 70, 71, 250, 251, 255, 256, 257, 258, 259, 261, 261n, 262, 263
   Series E   36
Avvakum   211
Azam, Étienne Eugène   56, 61

Babinski, Jules François Félix   57
Bentham, Jeremy   219
Binet, Alfred   57
Bogdanov, A.
   correlation between thought and being   xxv
   debt of, to Mach
   empiriocriticist, not one   298n
   empiriomonist, the only one   275
   Engels
      in relation to   xxxi
      Engels, similarity to   270
   idealism, accused of   xl
   ideology, analysis of   xxxi
   *Iz psikhologii obshchestva*   122n1, 268, 284n1, 284n2, 296, 325n2, 332n1, 332n2, 333n, 335n, 337n, 340n, 344n1, 350n, 355n, 369n, 372n, 389n
   *Kratkii kurs ekonomonicheskoi nauki*   332n1, 367n, 395n
   Machist, not a   296
   Marxism
      conception of   xxxi
      expulsion from   301
      adoption of   283
   Marxist generation
      his own   268
      education by him   xviii
   nature, point of view on   153, 158
   *Novyi mir*   268, 296, 332n2, 363n, 367n, 389n, 395n
   *Osnovnye elementy istoricheskogo vzgliada na prirodu*   xx, xxii, xxv, xxvi, 26n, 87n2, 176n, 279n, 306n, 325n2, 358n
   philosophical
      development of   268
      foundations of his worldview   407
      starting point   xxvii
   Plekhanov, feud with   xxi
   *Poznanie s istoricheskoi tochki zreniia*   26n, 69n, 71n, 75n1, 76n, 113n, 168n2, 172n, 176n, 192n, 196n, 197n1, 197n2, 234n, 279n, 306n, 331n, 337n, 355n, 389n1
   reception of, in Russian Social-Democracy   xx
   scepticism regarding philosophy   xxii
   view of philosophy of   xxxii
   value of philosophy for   xxxi
   worldview of   267, 269, 281, 403, 407, 413–414
bourgeois/bourgeoisie   227n, 231, 321, 389, 391, 394, 398–399, 408
class rule   396
fetishism   389, 391
habits of thinking   408
Hegelianism   289
ideologists, ideology   288, 371, 390, 396
industrial   287, 288
intelligentsia   281
materialism   389
metaphysics of the   371n
philosophy   281, 371n1, 398, 408n

SUBJECT INDEX  421

politicians   392
positivism   371n1
principle of legality   392, 396
scholars   xxxvi
science, scientists and philosophers   398
social environment   324
social opinion   392
state   408n
theorists   287
thinking   354, 398
universities   xxxvii
woman   370
world   371
worldview   389
bourgeois/bourgeoisie, big   388, 390–391,
    393–394, 407
  materialistic colouration   390n
  norms of rule   400
  principle of property   357, 390
bourgeois/bourgeoisie, petty   231–233, 285,
    287, 305, 353, 355, 370, 390n, 391, 392,
    407, 408
  city organisation   384
  economic units   384
  elements of life   357
  embryo of two classes   371n2
  enterprise   370
  family   231, 287, 370
  fetishism   393
  form of existence   393
  handicraft enterprises   359
  household economy   370
  ideologists, ideology   390
  morality   320
  organisation of exchange   402
  principle of property   390
  relationships   385
  socialism   390
  society   385
  thinking in the proletariat   287
  type of psyche   217
bourgeois-aristocratic form of monarchy
    288

capital   307, 408n
  self-increasing value, as a   390
  tool of domination, as a   390
  development of   360
  durability of social domination   391

  excess   255
  industrial   355
  merchant   355
  relationships of   307
  rule of   360
  subordination to   371n2
  vital conservation of   255
  profits of, a pathological vital differential
    255
capitalism   219, 285, 360, 367, 384, 386, 401
capitalist
  class   320, 388, 389, 391, 392, 393, 397,
    399
  class development   385, 386, 402
  competition   387
  conception of private property   390
  enterprise   308, 393
  ideology   285, 390, 393
  legal norms   391
  normative principles   393–394
  ownership of labour power   393
  principle of property   393, 395
  private property   394
  production   75n1
  property   395, 399
  society   254, 315, 340n, 347, 371n2, 396
  system   359, 391
  trusts   413
  ultimate ideal   360
capitalists   220, 371n2, 374, 386–388, 391,
    393, 395, 399
  industrial   385
  merchant   385
  organisers   392
causal
  chain   30
  cognition   144
  connection   xxiv, xxxii, 141, 143
  explanation   143
  interconnectedness of phenomena   xxiii
  monist explanation   282
  nature   145
  relationship   xxvii, 26, 26n, 34, 103, 104,
    110, 130, 135, 142, 144, 146, 147, 220, 324
  series   26n, 135
causality   26n, 32n, 34, 95, 110, 119, 127, 134,
    139, 142, 147, 160, 180, 293, 303n2, 305n,
    358n
  biological   180, 303, 312, 323

category of   30, 134
chain of   135
chain-like   xxxix
cognition, contemporary, in   xxiv
consecutiveness, and   148
form of experience   159, 410
form of objectivity   290
functional correlation, and   142
idea of   142, 291
law of   xxiv, xxviii, 30, 130, 276, 292, 294, 295, 312, 328
Mach's attack on   141
model of, general   145
modern positivism, and   142
organisation of experience, a type of   412
parallelism, and   144
phenomena, of   93
principle of   xxiv
psychical   180, 237
scientific   144
social science, in   328
social selection a form of   312
surrogates of   143
universal objective relationships of   96
universal   141
class   41, 213, 220, 285–288, 304–305, 309, 316–321, 317n1, 352, 355, 364–5, 363n, 369–371, 373–376, 378, 385–404, 390n, 407, 408n, 411
  aristocratic   288
  authoritarian   287, 399
  being   369
  bourgeoisie, big, the   390
  capitalist   390, 395
  cleavage   369
  concept of, relativity of the   371
  contemporary   40, 384
  contradictions   286, 371, 379–380, 401, 402
  development   217, 352, 369, 383–386, 386n, 401–402
  differentiation   373, 375, 376n2, 380, 385
  division   220, 364–365, 367, 372–373, 376–378, 386, 401
  English working   319, 320
  entrepreneurial   386
  ideology   376, 401, 402, 407, 409
  implementational   369, 386, 391, 407
  intelligentsia   398
  interest   286, 399
  life   285
  lower   391, 401
  organisational   368–370, 373, 382, 386–387, 392, 401–402
  parasitic   213, 399, 400–401
  productive   407
  progressive   410
  proletarian   370, 391, 407, 409
  psychology   286
  reactionary   217
  ruling   287, 374, 379, 383, 396
  selection   395
  slave and slave-owning   369, 378, 380–382, 383n
  social   296, 316
  society   285, 379, 380, 407
  solidarity, comradely   396
  structure   398
  struggle   3, 226, 321, 380, 392n, 393–394, 401–402
  subordinate   374, 379, 383, 401
  systems   374
  technological life   318
  theory of   355
  thinking   286, 407
  working   296, 371n2, 386–387, 392, 394–397, 404
cognition   xix–xx, xii–xvi, xxix–xxxv, xl, 4–7, 8n, 10, 15–16, 22, 30–31, 33–35, 37–40, 43–44, 47–48, 89–92, 94, 96–98, 103, 116, 117, 126, 137–142, 153–154, 156–159, 161–171, 177, 191, 196–198, 275, 297, 312, 325, 403–414
  abstract   139
  abstraction, ultimate, of   204
  Affectional, the, and   170, 180, 191
  animists, of   157
  associations according to similarity   210n
  categories, pure, of   406
  causal relationship, and   110
  class   398
  cognition, of   xx, 269, 403, 414
  communication, the source of all   294
  continuity in   152
  critique of   6, 47
  discontinuities in experience, and   104
  dualism in   15, 16, 33, 81, 142, 144

SUBJECT INDEX 423

empirical substitution, in   161
empiriomonist   128
energetics, and   39, 162, 163, 398n
Engels, according to   270
evolutionary theory of   6
experience, and   33, 38, 164, 181, 408
explanation, the task of   306
forms of   128, 342, 348, 403–405, 409
gaps in   397
harmony and unity in   16
hypothesis, the soul of   123
ideal of   4, 5, 16, 43
Kantian theory of   xxxii
labour, and   6, 403
Mach and Avenarius, according to   5, 6n1, 48n2, 332n1
Marx, according to   332n1
maximum dynamism in   411
metaphysical   128
methodology of, universal   xxxv
methods of   xxiii, 90
monist   xix, xxv, xxxiii, 38, 138, 142, 158, 165, 198, 218, 269
naturalistic   40, 140, 141
objective   48, 54, 269
philosophical, the soul of   89
philosophy, need for   137
practice as the foundation of   43, 141
prediction of the future, as   141
principles of   xxiii, 152, 178
psychological   44, 181
pure description, and   7, 188
regularity in   xxiii
Riehl, Alois, view of   6n2
Scientific   xxii, xxxi, 7, 65, 98, 153, 167, 259, 338, 340, 366
social adaptation, as   6, 7
social genesis of   6
social nature of   138, 410
social   128
socio-historical   407
stairway of concepts of   337
substitution, and   138–139, 157–158, 169
task of   170, 280
technology and   48n2, 332n1
tendency, unifying and generalizing   30
theories of   xxxii, xxxiii, 279, 408
things-in-themselves, of   161
tools of   xxv
unity of practice and   5
collaboration
  cognitive   xxx
  social   298n, 311, 325, 327, 340n, 388, 404
commensurability of
  cause and effect   xxiv
  changes in a psychical system   171
  changes in nature   xxvi
  experiences, all   168
  phenomena, all   62
  pleasure and pain   76
  psychical processes   163
commune, patriarchal   375–376n2
consciousness   xxvi, 35–37, 57n2, 82, 83, 99, 100, 100n, 107, 110–117, 119–120, 128, 144–146, 149, 152, 162, 163, 170–177, 181–187, 189–196, 202n, 206n2, 209, 237, 242–249, 252, 274, 281, 341, 410–412
  act of, xxviii   35
  associative activity of   97, 166, 202
  associative system, and   151
  centres of   63, 84, 243, 249, 255–256
  chain of   115
  characteristic, fundamental, of   171
  continuity of   410
  definition of   171
  development of   4
  discontinuities in   117
  dualism in   16, 39
  empiriomonist   view of, xxix
  energetical aspect of   88n1, 208
  experiences outside of   105, 112
  experiences, the main grouping of   114
  facts of   35, 105n, 142, 144, 163, 259
  field of   53, 57n, 60–61, 63–64, 92, 99, 105, 110, 111, 114n, 119n, 122n, 170–173, 175, 181–183, 182n, 185–187, 189–195, 200, 202–203, 202n, 206, 208, 214n, 219, 222, 227, 231–233, 235, 238, 241n, 242–243, 244n, 245, 247, 308, 412
  gaps in   130
  'I' in the field of   42
  ideology, confusion with   298n
  immediate   xxxix, 76n, 171, 176
  individual   xxix, 43, 57–58
  labour and   244
  life of   211
  main   58, 208

maximum content of   192
monism and   92
multiplicity of   56
naïve   42
negative selection, and   214n
nervous system, and   36
organ of   175
other people's   xxxix, 96, 103, 122, 155, 166, 295n, 412
outside of   105, 111, 182, 243
panpsychism, and   64, 137
phenomena of   xxvii
physiological time, of   21
Plekhanov's idea of   277
practical   136
psychical combinations in   206
psychical experience, of   171
realm of   208, 246, 298n
social   xix, 298n, 361
sphere of   46, 59, 177, 208, 209
split   61
stimuli, imperceptible, of   60
subconscious, and   58
threshold of   183, 232
unconscious, and   77n, 104, 208
utterances in   57
vital differentials in   105n, 253
consecutiveness   54, 109, 139, 270
  causal connection of facts, of the   141
  causality, of   148
  experience, of   26n
  functional correlation of   142, 146
  phenomena, of   96
  physical world, of the   26
  social development, of   352
  temporal   26, 183
continuity   23, 26n, 94, 117, 182, 279, 386, 412
  abstract time, of   23
  associative connections, of   215
  causal relationship, of the   104
  cognition strives for   103
  cognition, disruption of, in   104
  idea of   44
  necessity, and   150
  physical experience, of   164, 164n
  physiological space, of   19, 22
  principle of   130, 152
  rupture of   116
  spatial   317, 317n1, 318n

time and space, of   95
universal premise of cognition, the   44
universal, of phenomena   164
correlation   xxx, xxxii, xxxvii, 10, 12, 46, 63, 108, 170, 344
  Affectional and vital-differentials, of   76
  causality, and   103, 141
  causality, and   148
  consciousness and change in nervous system, of   35
  experience, of   102, 279
  experiences and vital differentials, of   87
  external stimuli and vital differentials   83
  functional   93, 93n, 99, 101
    causal   145
    complexes, of   92
    consecutiveness   146
    experience, facts of   141–142
    forms of   144
    physiology and psyche, of   37, 101
    psychical series, the, and the nervous system, of   15
    pure description, of   155
    reflection, the, and the reflected, of   93, 98, 146–147
    simultaneous, of the   142–144
  ideology and technology, of   361
  law of conservation of energy and machine production, of   403
  life and its environment, of   178
  matter and spirit, of   405
  organisation, types of, of   33
  organisational elements and ideology, of   401
  parallelism, and   46, 147
  philosophical theory and political practice, of   267
  physical complexes, of   150, 290
  physical, the, and the psychical, of   406
  physiology and experience, of   88
  physiology and the psyche, of   82
  psyche, the, and physiology, of   35, 46, 47, 83, 141, 142, 144, 164, 282
  psychical form and its surroundings, of   216n1
  psychical phenomena and physiology, of   35
  quantitative   xxvii

SUBJECT INDEX                                                                                          425

social development, of   324
social selection and energetics, of   315
sphere of utterances and sphere of experiences, of   49
stimulus and sensation, of   51, 81
technological and ideological adaptations, of   334
tendencies of psychical development, of   221
thought and being, of   xxv
uniformity of   xxxvii
vital differentials, of   174
*See also* functional correlation

Darwinian
    idea   251n
    point of view   72n
Darwinism   72, 179n
Darwinists   303
deduction
    confirmed or disproven by experience   357
    derivative line of ideological development, the   356
    formal   107
    psychical selection as the basis for   200
    scientific   357
deductive
    analytic investigation   340
    investigation, path of   198
    nature of energetics   312
Democritus   157, 291
description, pure   7, 141, 144, 155, 157, 188n
disassimilation
    energy, of   66–68, 79, 249–250, 256, 258n, 325
    nourishment, of   74
    technological process, in the   361
discontinuities
    apparent, caused by interference   412
    complexes in our picture of the world, in   413
    consciousness, in   116
    continuity, boils down to   412
    continuity, transformation into   117
    empiriomonism free from   161
    experience, in   104, 106, 295n2
    nature, processes of, in   23
    organism and psyche, between   104

reactions, motor, in   116
retina and brain, between   118
dreams   13, 25, 31, 44, 54, 55n, 61, 62, 202n
dualism   98, 103–104, 128, 134, 138, 142
    animistic   137
    animists, of   134
    authoritarian   405
    cognition, duality in, and   16
    consciousness, in   92
    empiriocriticism, and   15, 29, 289
    empiriomonism, the antithesis of   297
    experience, of   33, 38, 81
    method, of   164
    organisational and implementational functions, of the   354, 404
    physical and psychical series, of the   30
    physical and psychical, of   282, 284
    spirit and body, of   137
    religious   403
dynamic equilibrium
    *See* equilibrium, dynamic

economists   299, 324
empiriocriticism   xxvii, 5–6, 5n, 6n1, 7, 14, 129n1, 273, 280, 282, 282n, 291, 297, 299
    Mach's, suspected of idealism   280
    Philosophical foundation of   5
    philosophical thought, main currents of, in   15
    Plekhanov's view of   274n
    positivism, a form of   15, 281
    task of   74n
empiriocriticists   xxvii, 16, 280, 282, 291, 296, 297, 408n
    Bogdanov is not one   298n
Empiriomonism   xxii, xxxi, xxxiv, xxxix, 39–40, 96, 106, 156, 164, 268, 296, 298n, 295–301, 343, 403–405, 409–410
    Affectional, the, view of   170
    cognition, the task of   91
    cognitive life, and   128
    cognitive 'socialism', a kind of   291
    correlations of, with other points of view   405
    decisive test of   104
    empiriocriticists, European, unknown to   297
    experiences and physiological life in, universal parallelism of   165

first basic principle of   407
goal of and path toward   296
ideal of integral and rigorous cognition   295
immanent realism of   xxxiii
monist worldview of, still incomplete   40
objections to   153
origin of   403
philosophical
   aspect   xxxiii
   goal of   296
philosophy of *Basic Elements of the Historical View of Nature*, and   xx
physical, the, and the psychical, and   xxxi, 39, 407
physiological life, definition of   101
picture of the world   xxx, 158, 275
Plekhanov's and Lenin's materialism, contrast with   xxix
Plekhanov's view of   xl, 296, 300
point of view of   106, 103
psychical selection, and   170
psychology, view of   169
scientific aspect, of   xxxiii
solipsism and scepticism, accusation of   291
substitution, and   161, 409
task of, the   282
truth of our times, the   129
worldview   263
empiriomonists
   Bogdanov the only one   275
energetical
   complex   313
   continuity of physical experience   164
   equivalence   164
   pleasure and pain, significance of   197n2
   point of view   xxv, 88, 163
   psychical experience, nature of   88
   psychical phenomena, method applied to   88
   psychical processes, conception of   163
   vital processes, magnitude of   106
energetics   26n, 80, 165, 168n, 299, 312, 317n2, 327
   applications of   312
   bourgeois society, and   398
   cognitive methods of   165
   experiences, of   88
   harmony with Marxism   284
   machine production, of   284
   materialist understanding of   327
   method of   39, 279
   natural sciences, and   163
   Ostwald's   88n1, 274, 279
   pleasure and pain, of   249
   point of view of   279, 314
   principle of   130, 162, 167
   proletarian worldview, and   398
   social selection, and   313
   social   326
   technical process, of the   336
   worldview, insufficient for a   279
energy   xxvi5in, 66–70, 74–75, 75n, 77–80, 83–87, 163, 168–174, 168n, 210, 227–233, 256n1, 279, 312–318, 318n, 320–23, 350, 389n2, 401
   Affectional, the, and   172, 180, 242
   assimilation of   50, 67–69, 78–79, 104, 106, 249–250, 253–258, 377
   assimilation of, from the environment   49, 66, 314, 325, 327, 345
   brain, the, of   259, 260, 261
   cells, of   177
   centres of consciousness, of   249
   concept of   162, 279
   disassimilation of   314
   environment, of the   327
   equilibrium of, at the basis of life   66
   exchange of, between organism and environment   235
   expenditure of   xxv, 7, 66, 69, 73, 78, 104, 106, 113, 113n, 139, 185, 191, 193, 195, 206, 208, 210, 223–224, 228, 232–233, 238, 241–246, 247n2, 254–258, 261, 263, 325, 330, 345, 377, 401
   expenditure to the environment, of   49, 66, 325, 328, 345
   experiences of   210
   flow, of   45, 67, 193
   labour   75n1, 345, 395, 397
   labour, of   243, 284
   law of conservation of   xxiv, 38, 88n1, 164n, 165, 284, 295, 312, 358, 397, 398, 403
   law of transformation of   312, 397
   life, of   227, 250

SUBJECT INDEX 427

living complex, of a   314, 315
living system, of a   67, 68, 69, 79, 327
mechanical understanding of   88n1
metaphysical understanding of   398
muscle reflexes, of   334
natural selection, and   178
nervous system, central, of the   75n1
neural   49, 60, 62, 73, 75, 77n, 84–85, 84n, 88n1, 89, 174, 187, 249, 347n
organising methodological concept, as an   398n
psychical adaptations, of   172, 173
psychical experience, of a   169
psychical selection, and   174, 220, 245
psychical system, of a   168, 170–173, 177–178, 180, 182, 208, 242, 245–246
psychical   88n, 213, 312n, 345
social class   318
social exchange of, with the environment   325
social forms, of   314, 315
social processes, of   312
social surplus of   377, 379
social system, of a   327, 328
social   310, 383
society, of a   310, 315, 326
stimuli, of   83–84, 152
substance, not a   279, 327
System C, of   257–258, 261n
technological process, from   383, 386
vital-differentials, and   49, 59, 60, 77, 80, 87–88
Engels, Friedrich   xxxi, 159, 270–273, 271n, 274n, 277, 349
   absolute truths, Engels's rejection of   270
   *Anti-Dühring*   270, 271n
   Bogdanov, and   xxxi
   Bogdanov's similarity to   270
   *Ludwig Feuerbach*   274n, 277, 296n, 298n
   materialism, Engels's point of view regarding   159
   Plekhanov's difference from   270
entrepreneurs   320, 360, 363, 387
Epicurus   20, 157, 291
Epistemology   24, 26, 156, 181, 280
equilibrium   xxxvii–xxxviii, 50, 128, 201, 217, 249, 412n
   absolute, a fiction   313

associations, of   231
associative connections, of   190
associative systems, of   187
associatively adjacent complexes, of   113
brain, of the   260
dynamic   xxxiv, xxxvii, 110, 112, 115, 314
economic enterprises, of   359, 360
energy between a living system and its environment, of   66, 179n
environment and needs   252
experiences, opposing, of   112
life, of   66–67, 69, 314, 315, 319
motor centres, of   59
natural selection, in   178
needs and the environment, of   253
nervous system, of the   49, 51, 59, 78, 79
neural sexual centres, of   262, 263
organising and disorganising processes, of   xxxiv
organism, and its environment, of   45
psyche, in the   110, 182–183, 200
psychical images, of   115
psychical selection, in   182, 187, 200
social complex, of a   313
social life, of   348
social process, of the   345
vital differentials, of   106, 109, 114, 259
vital   106
experience, experiences
   abstract   24
   actual   123
   Affectional, positive, of   168
   analysis of   123
   aspects of   90
   association, harmonious, of   22, 34, 35, 38, 39–40, 48, 97, 109, 122, 170, 295
   associative relations of   149, 166, 179, 181, 197–198, 245
   basis and boundary of cognition, the   5
   beings', other   102–103, 166–167, 294
   bifurcation of   42
   biological   126
   body, one's own, of   95
   chain of psychical   171
   classes and groups, of   41
   cleansing of   280
   cognitive decomposition, of   8n
   cognitive processing, of   xxx

coherence of   45
collective   17, 18, 24–25, 27, 30, 32n, 43, 100, 144–145, 412
colouration, sensory, of   79n1
communication of, to others   333
competition of   192, 210n
complex, organised, of   99
complexes of   10, 95–96, 101, 117, 147, 149–151, 188, 197n3, 275n1
complexity, increasing, of   193
conception, monist, of   110
conception, orderly and harmonious, of   166
conscious, extra   112
content of   396
content, entire, of   134
contradictions in   43, 108
coordination, correlation of   18, 26, 142, 290
critique of   5, 15, 16, 129n, 280, 281, 297
data of   12, 18, 34, 41, 86–87, 90, 124, 142, 144, 154, 197, 389
development of   24, 91, 198, 379
direct   155, 295
discontinuity of   104, 106, 295n2
disharmony in   42
diversification of   368
dualism of   33, 81, 282
elements of   7–9, 29, 38, 63, 65, 91, 94, 123, 147, 149, 153, 155, 158–159, 164, 184, 280–281, 284, 289, 292–294, 296, 411–412, 412n
emotional   21n2
energetical commensurability of   168
external   7, 35n
facts of   xxxiii, 119, 123, 144, 147, 279
field of   108, 120, 122n2, 191, 200–201
flow of   7, 21n2, 188, 202, 232
flow, unorganised, of   181
forms of   44, 159, 292, 298n, 410
forms, universal, of   412
gaps in   111n2, 130
ground of   91
Hamlet's   222, 224
harmonisation of   34n
higher animals, of   97, 167
human   29, 125, 158, 273, 294, 275n1
human, universally   213
ideological   349, 354

immediate   xxx, 11, 18, 21n1, 28, 44, 47–49, 55n, 58–59, 64, 75, 89–91, 93, 97–98, 101, 103–107, 110–112, 117, 126, 130, 140, 145, 148, 152, 158, 165, 166, 175, 177–178, 203, 208, 212, 215, 244, 247, 375, 411
indirect   212, 295, 411–412
individual   18, 23–24, 27–28, 31, 32n, 41–43, 46, 91, 95–96, 98, 100, 155–156, 160, 248, 280, 290
individual, but socially organised or objective   96n1
intelligentsia's   226–228, 230–232
interaction among   92
interconnectedness of   9, 98, 150, 154, 291
interference of   107, 108, 110–113, 117
internal   27, 35n
labour, of   134, 337, 376, 358, 368, 373, 376, 408–409
life of   365
lived   331, 342
living beings'   124, 130, 281
lower classes'   401
main system, chain, coordination of   62, 118, 243
material of   211, 212, 215, 217
motor reactions, and   49
null   106, 107
objective   17, 26, 31, 32, 32n, 34, 42, 58, 95, 96, 101, 110, 141, 154, 290, 291
ordered   44
orders of   16
organisation of   xxx, 30, 91, 127, 130, 166, 197, 200, 219, 219n, 244n, 338, 342, 357, 368, 398, 412
organisation, monist, of   35, 41
organised
  by ideology   374
  collectively   xxx, xxxi, 39, 95
  individually   xxix, xxx, xxxi, xxxii, xxxiii, 27–28, 31, 33, 39, 130, 290, 406
  socially   xxx, xxxi, xxxiii, 24–25, 27–28, 27n, 30–31, 32n, 33–34, 41, 96, 100–103, 124, 130, 150n, 165, 175, 201n, 290, 294, 406
organising forms for   272–373
organising   403
outside of   276–277
pain and pleasure, of   77, 203n

parallelism of series of   37
people's   25, 53, 96–97, 275, 398
people's, other   23, 33, 41–42, 47–48, 55, 90, 93, 97, 166, 208
personal   95, 155, 213, 220, 331
phases of   108
phenomena of   26n, 139, 159, 293
physical   xix, 8, 13, 25, 27, 31, 34, 36, 38, 42, 63, 81, 110, 116, 119n, 150, 158, 160, 164–165, 164n, 176, 269, 275, 275n1, 281, 289, 291, 294–295, 297, 358, 398, 406–408, 410–412
physiological   151, 356
picture of   104
point of view of   144
possible   48, 98, 122, 123, 138, 411
practical rules of   332
primary   240, 244
profusion, increasing, of   7
progress of   139, 189
psychical interconnectedness of   149
psychical   xix, xxviii, 13, 27–28, 31, 34, 36, 38, 41, 44, 46–48, 51–64, 55n, 76, 77n, 81, 88–90, 93, 96–97, 96n2, 99–100, 105, 107–108, 100n, 110, 115–116, 122, 124, 138, 140–141, 145–146, 150, 152, 154, 160, 162–166, 167–171, 175–177, 179–181, 189, 191–193, 200–202, 206, 206n, 208, 242n, 244, 244n, 246, 269, 275, 281, 289, 291, 294, 298, 398, 398n, 406, 408, 410, 412
   critique of   52, 58
   flow of   xxviii
   forms of   198
   individually organised   27, 290
   interconnectedness of   149
psychical, extra   63
psychological   99
psychophysical   13
reality, as   150
realm of   xxx, 12, 15, 90, 130, 170, 196, 214, 217–220, 356, 397–398, 406–408
regularity of   15n, 41, 65
relationships of   92–93, 123
scientific relationship to   142
scientific   100, 349
secondary, derivative   244
selection of, psychical   169
selection, and   202
series of   10, 12–13, 15, 39, 247
slaves'   377, 378
social class   369
social   6, 24–27, 27n, 32n, 48, 291, 312, 408–409, 408n
socially conditioned   239
socio-technological   388
space, of   21
specialised   220, 221
sphere of   14
stream of   229
subconscious   411
subjective   17, 18, 32, 32n, 34, 201, 290
substance of   279
substituted   293
sum total of   45, 283, 294
system of   14, 18, 34, 44–45, 52, 117, 218, 229, 281, 304
systematisation of   5, 6, 38, 229, 280
technological   135, 283, 320, 348–350, 354–355, 365–368, 374, 399–400, 405, 407
Tektology and   xl
temporal measure of   23
time, and   21, 21n
unconscious   103
uncoordinated   216, 220
unification of   117, 210n, 304
unity of   xxxiii, 162
universe, a world of   411
utterances, given by   47
utterances, without   50
visual field of   108
visual series of   118n
widening of   161
women's   371
workers'   392n, 409
world of   xxxi, xxxiv, 5, 44, 45

*Faust* Goethe's   204
Ferri, Enrico   303
Fervorn, Max   275
fetishism   3, 398, 411
   animation of all nature, of   294
   causality, of   142
   idea of profit, of the   360
   market, of the   388
   matter, of   24
   metaphysics, bourgeois, of   371n

properties of empty abstractions, of the 397
religious and metaphysical   269, 406
scientific   296, 389n2
substitution, old, of the   139
thought, of   43
fetishism, social   388, 393, 396, 397, 399
   bourgeois   398
   exchange society, of   410
   exchange value, of   388
   capitalist ideology, of   390
   forms of thinking, of   389
   metaphysical   293, 410
   market, of the   389
Feuerbach, Ludwig   408
Fortinbras   226
functional correlation
   *See* correlation, functional

hallucination   10, 13, 25–26, 30–31, 57n2, 116n, 290
Hamlet   221–226
happiness   7, 7n, 42, 78, 200, 202, 207–209, 221–225
'Hebrew' (personality type)   198, 211, 217, 221, 236, 240
Hegel, G.W.F.   9n, 296
Hegelianism   299
Heine, Heinrich   198, 207n, 211, 213, 216, 216n
'Hellene' (personality type)   198, 211, 213, 217, 221–222, 225, 236
Herbart, Johann   168n1
Hering, Karl   18n2
Historical Materialism   xix, xxi–xxii, xxiv, 7, 328n, 268, 283–286, 328n2, 335–336
historical monism   6, 285, 326, 350
historical point of view   133
Holbach, Paul-Henri baron   157, 274, 281, 288, 292, 296
Hume, David   26n, 285–287
hypothesis, metaphysical   119n, 284, 293

'I', the   13–14, 27–28, 42–43, 53, 104, 281, 292
Ibsen's *Brand*   211n
idealism, xxxiii   14, 230n, 280, 281, 390n, 399n, 405–406, 406n
   Bogdanov accused of   xl
   historical   301n, 326
   ideology of ideology, an   406
   immanent   14
   Mach's first position   7n1
   metaphysical   269
   nineteenth-century utopians, of   285
   progressive   231
   refined   134, 135
   transcendental   14
   utopians, of the   287
idealist
   interpretation of Mach   8n
   philosophy   xxix, xxxix
   point of view   405
   systems   405
   tendencies   390n
   worldview   269
idealists   235, 274, 287
ideological
   activity, organisational   376
   adaptations   317–318, 329, 332–333, 340n, 357–358, 368, 378
      derivative of technological adaptations   334
      genetically secondary   336
      in relation to technological adaptations   335
   anachronisms   320
   banner of the strict democrats   xix, 268
   categories   xxiv
   chain   390
      of concepts or norms   363
      lowest links of   374
      ascending   340
   change lies in the technological process   336
   conservatism   364
   creativity   357, 377, 369
      of slave masters   378
      of the work of organisers   377
   development   289, 344n1, 354–358, 392n, 403
      basic line of   353
      derivative   353, 397
      laws of   288
      Plekhanov's theory of   285
   differences, the realm of   365
   forms   xx, xxiv, 269, 273, 284, 286, 348, 353, 361, 363, 372, 377–379, 389, 406n
      capitalist class, of the   388
      common   366

SUBJECT INDEX 431

　　development and degradation of
　　　404n
　　development of   324, 352
　　direct communication, of   335
　　growth of conservatism of   351
　　material life, of   365
　　material of   361
　　organising   284, 336, 340, 395
　　origin of   340
　　Plekhanov's view of   285
　　production by social selection   374
　　psychical forms, confusion with   350
　　selection of   350–352
　　technological forms, and   341
　　three basic types of   368
　elements
　　distinction from technological elements   340n
　　property, of   339
　environment   7, 360
　essence of empiriomonism   xl
　fact   288, 339, 3442
　heterogeneity   371
　isolation of organisers and implementers
　　369
　life of slaves   378
　machine production, expression of   284
　norms   321, 363
　process   331, 333, 336, 349, 359, 368,
　　405
　realm   377
　　of class life   316
　separation of classes   401
　series   337, 354, 356
　　lowest links of   365
　stairway   338, 341, 343
　superstructure   352–353
　system, bourgeois   390
　systems   352, 354
　tendencies of the organisational class
　　392
　theories   286
　tissue   338, 341
　type, socio-normative elements of   333
　unity, of the patriarchal kinship group
　　86
ideologists   227n, 285–286, 288n, 372–373,
　408n
　aristocracy, of the   288

　bourgeois   392
　bourgeoisie, big, of the   388
　bourgeoisie, petty, of the   390
　class   288
　Hume as   285
　industrial bourgeoisie, of the   288
　mercantilism, of   285
　organisational function of   372
　practical   373
　proletariat, of the   409
　pure   373
　relationship to the masses   373
　slave owners, of   382
ideology   284–286, 298n, 320, 344n1, 348–
　　351, 353–355, 359–362, 377, 390, 400–
　　402
　authoritarian, of the family   371
　basis of   342
　Bogdanov's analysis of   xxxi
　bourgeois women, of   370
　bourgeois, authoritarian elements in
　　399
　bourgeoisie, big, of the   393
　bourgeoisie, industrial, of   287
　bourgeoisie, petty, of the   371n2, 392
　bourgeois-materialist   396
　class   317, 317n, 407, 409
　class, capitalists, of the   393
　class, organisational, of the   369
　class, ruling, of the   376
　class, upper, of the   401
　classes, progressive, of the   410
　classical era, of the   376, 377
　cognitive   399
　　bourgeois   396
　　capitalist   390
　　proletarian   396
　　technological process, of the   414
　cognitive and normative, contradiction
　　between   399
　concept of   350
　conditioned by the technological process
　　361
　conservativism of higher forms   361
　creation of   364
　derivative   336, 361
　development of   284, 361
　economics, as opposed to   340n
　extreme   xix, 269

formational point of social divisions, the 365
genesis of   335, 341
highest levels of   342, 352
historical conditionality   269
historical-philosophical explanations of 414
ideology, of   406
journeymen, of   364, 365
knowledge as   299
layers of   353
liberalism, political, of   320
lower levels of   352
machine production, of workers in   409
masses, of the   373
material bases of   273
normative   390, 393, 406n
  bourgeoisie, of   390
  capitalist   393
  proletariat, of the   394, 395, 396
organisation of the technological process, of the   374
organisational   369, 375, 401
organising adaptation, an impersonal form of   363
organising forms of   361
productive forces of society, of   283
productive forces, of the   405, 407
proletariat, of the   392, 393, 394n, 396, 399n, 400, 411
realm of organising adaptations, the   372
religious and conservative   371
scientific technology, confusion with 350
religious   370
slave owners, of   383
slaves, of   378, 402
social development, cannot cause   348
social environment, a constitutive part of 348
social   401
source of   343
technological experience, begins with 349
technological process, of the   407
working class, of the   392
implementational
  class   369
  function   284, 287, 363, 368, 385

labour   368, 395
proletariat   407
implementers   363, 367–368, 396, 370, 374–375, 376n1
  experience of   368, 374–376
  organisers and, differentiation of   363, 367, 371n2
  proletarian   385, 402
  psyche of   377
  slaves as   381, 383
  technical specialists as   386
induction   355–356, 403
innervation   13–14, 37, 49, 50, 59, 67, 75, 78–79, 85, 108, 193, 196, 206, 242–244, 255, 257, 263, 280
innervational theory of volition   14n1
intelligentsia   226, 281, 388, 398, 408n
introjection   6, 6n1, 35–36, 35n, 91, 122n, 137, 141

James, William   13, 13n, 263
James-Lange theory of emotions   13, 363
Janet, Pierre-Marie-Félix   57

Kant, Immanuel   xxiv, xxvi, xxxii, 3, 26n, 133, 136, 137, 159, 159n, 275n, 281, 296n, 300, 371n1
  idea of absolute space   20
  Plekhanov's agreement with   xxxii, 276
Kantian
  categories   150
  criticism   279
  epistemology   26n, 156, 181
Kantianism   279, 280, 282n, 300
Kantians   157
Knowledge   xxvi, xxxv, xl, 3, 4, 7, 24, 133, 271, 320, 347, 348, 358, 398
  abstract   376
  bourgeois   396
  development of   271
  faith, and   138
  forms of   356, 397
  ideology, as   299
  immediate   xxvi
  indirect   xxvi
  naturalistic   139
  new   397
  realm of   270, 351, 399
  scientific   156, 220, 280

SUBJECT INDEX 433

social   28, 299
social selection in   351
supra-experiential   14
system of   283, 376
technical   331
technological   388
Korsakov, S.   17n

labour   48, 223n, 228, 231, 244n, 246, 247n2, 325, 328, 332n1, 335, 337, 345, 362, 367, 370, 374n, 375–376, 379–380, 385, 404, 408–409
  activity of   242, 337, 393, 403
  acts of   244, 331, 335, 341, 342, 367
  adaptation, a process of   245
  complexes of   242, 341, 335
  conditions of   321, 394, 397
  contradictions of   338
  coordination of   331
  division of   40–41, 353, 362–365, 375–376, 384–385, 404
  energy, expenditure of, and   223
  enjoyment of   260
  exchange value of   388
  exchange society, in   27n
  expenditure of energy in   242–243, 245
  expenditure of   394
  experience of   134, 337, 358, 373, 376, 408
  exploitation of   390
  field of   365
  forced   247n2
  free   247, 248
  goal of   242, 284
  groupings   413
  hired   370
  implementational   367–368, 407
  market   394
  material of   11, 366
  methods of   401
  organiser of   364
  organisational   395
  collectively organised   43
  parasites, in relation to   307
  power   360, 393, 394, 395, 397
  practical   43
  principle of property   394
  processes of   33, 242–244, 246–247, 326, 327, 343, 359, 363, 368, 370, 380, 382, 395, 401

product of   391
productive   318, 380, 382–383
productivity of   345–346, 359–360
proletarian   392n
psychical   222
relationships of   339, 396, 404
scientific   217
skilled   319
slave   378, 380, 383, 387
small producers, of   390
social   48, 75n1, 283–284, 321, 325, 327–328, 328n1, 336, 342, 344n1, 366, 368, 397–398, 403–404, 404n, 409
socially directed   397
socially-necessary   xxxvii
socially-organised   27n
specialisation of   365
struggle for life, in the   336
struggle with nature, as   368
'suffering', and   243
surplus   379, 386, 387
system of   339, 375
technical   217
techniques of   383
technological   341, 374
theory of value   289
transforms the psyche   247
useful   213, 245–247
Lamarckism, psychological   188
Lamarckian   274
Lange, Carl   13, 13n, 88n1, 263, 303
Le Dantec Felix   179n
Lenin, V.I.
  *Materialism and Empirio-criticism*   xxi
laws (juridical)   239, 270, 332, 338–340, 352, 355, 376, 379, 382, 391
laws (natural)   30, 80, 84, 123, 127, 207, 269, 306, 356–358
  cognitive abstractions, as   28
  entropy, of   128
  'eternity of matter', of the   357
  experience, and   28
  identity, of   191
  ideological development, of   357
  inorganic world, of   125
  Le Chatelier's   xxxviii, xxxix
  mathematical analysis, of   315n
  minimum, of the   xxxix
  motion, of   xx, xxiii, xxiv, 269

nature, of   xx, xxx, 88, 220, 276, 389
phenomena, of   204, 389
physical   xxx, 28, 33, 408
progress, of   128
psychical selection, of   187, 226
psychical   408
psychological   xxx, 28, 311
psychophysical   85
scientific   xxxi, 306
selection, of   xxv, 303, 306–307, 343
sufficient reason, of   301
uniformity of nature, of the   64
Weber-Fechner   81, 82, 83, 87n2
Lunacharskii, A.V.   249, 250–261, 263
*Izlozhenie kritiki chistogo opyta*   249

Mach, Ernst   5–9, 5n, 6n1, 6n2, 7n, 8n, 11, 14–15, 14n2, 18, 21n1, 21n2, 29, 36, 36n, 48n4, 88n, 91, 141, 274, 280–282, 282n, 296–297, 296n1, 299, 332n, 389n, 405n
*Analyse der Erfahrung*   14n2
*Der Wärmelehre*   6, 7, 389n
*Die Analyse der Empfindungen*   6, 21n1
*Die Mechanik in ihrer Entwicklung*   389n, 405n
machines   220, 308, 331, 344n2, 349, 359, 360, 366, 367, 382, 395, 408, 409
automatic mechanisms of   367
improvement of   367
new   359, 360, 388
production   284, 350, 354, 366, 392, 397, 400, 403, 408, 409
self-operating   138
technology   393, 395, 397, 409
MacNish, Robert   56
Marx, Karl   xx, 274, 285, 299, 300, 324
Mach's coincidence of views with   6
Marx's
abstract method   xxxvii
historical-philosophical conception   324
idea   xix
labour theory of value   xxxvii
social materialism   xx, 269, 407
social philosophy of   296, 283
social theory of   xxxiii
worldview   xix

Marxism   xxxiii, 267, 273, 283, 299
basic tendencies of   284
Bogdanov's conception of   xxi
Bogdanov's expulsion from   301
Bogdanov's study of   xviii
idea of   xx, 269
objective truth for our times, the   271
rejection of absolute objectivity of truth   269
Marxist (adjective)
'dialecticalness'   278
knowledge is social, idea that   299
philosophy   283, 284, 297
thinking   282
truth based on practice, idea of   32n1
worldview   278, 283
Marxist (people)   xxi, 269, 300
Bogdanov's generation of   268
Bogdanov's becoming a   283
critical, so-called   283
Russian revolutionary   xx
several generations of, educated by Bogdanov   xviii
masses, the   212, 286, 372–373
material   xix, 64, 67, 152, 157, 269, 287, 340, 342
basis of ideological forms   xx, 269
experience, of   41
nature, of   64
processes   xxx
productive forces   xxiv
materialism   xxxiii, 14, 65, 157, 159, 274–275, 274n, 279, 286, 288, 299, 399n, 405, 406n
Enlightenment, of the   285, 287
historical
   See historical materialism
natural sciences/scientists, of   xix, xxii, 268, 273, 299
Plekhanov, of   274
Plekhanov and Lenin, of   xxix
bourgeoisie, of   389, 390n
old, the   xx, 269, 273, 279, 283
pan-   159
Marx's social   xx, 269, 407
Plekhanov's   xxxiii
materialist (adjective)
Bogdanov's point of view   407
hypothesis   159

monism 31
scientific-
    direction of the proletariat 392
    nature of the bourgeois worldview 399
    nature of the proletariat worldview 398
    tendency in the realm of knowledge 399
    tendency of proletarian ideology 396
    systems 405
    tendency 399
    worldview 220, 405
materialists (people) 157, 159, 274, 284, 414
    aristocratic 288
    philosophers xxvi, 274
    dialectical 160
    seventeenth and eighteenth centuries 136
    seventeenth-century English 288
matter xix, xx, xxvi, xxxiii, 14, 64–65, 130, 269, 276, 278–279, 283–284, 289, 356, 389, 405n
    Plekhanov's definition 275
    thing-in-itself, as xxvi, xxxii, 284
Mayer, Robert 88n1
Meynert, Theodor 80, 84, 168n, 263
metaphysicians 64, 122, 297
metaphysics 14, 33, 94, 122–123, 153, 157, 161–2, 293, 389, 398, 399n
    bourgeois 371m1
Middle Ages 353, 364, 384
    era of 291
    lord of the 367
monism xix, xxvii, 15–16, 38, 90, 92, 94, 128, 204, 207, 223, 227, 229, 282, 284, 291, 299, 301–302, 324, 410–411
    cognitional method, of 38
    cognitive, 40 142
    empiriocritical 29
    method, of 279
    metaphysical 403–404
    methodological 284
    modern 404
    objective 302
    problems of 297
    psychical 149
    scientific 269

spiritualist 31
tendency toward 40, 89
monist
    associative groupings 223
    cognition 142, 158, 165, 198, 218
        physical world, of the 38
    colouration of a person's psychical development 202
    conception
        experience, of 110
        life, of 87, 101
        social process, of the 48n3
    depiction of life 52
    development 231
    explanations 273, 282
    form of energetics 284
    future, of the 301
    Marxist form 284
    methodology xxxiii, xxxvi
    methods of investigating the psyche 176
    methods of cognition xxiii, xxv
    organisation of experience 35, 41, 91
    organising tendency 219
    panpsychism 149
    picture
        experience, of 104
        world, of the xxii
    point of view xxviii
    principle, universal 398
    science xxii, xxx
    tendency xx, 204, 209, 210, 216, 223, 225, 228, 240, 246, 269, 398n, 410
    thinking 38, 97, 138, 166
    worldview 35, 40, 299
Müller, Max 6n2, 219n, 335

natural sciences, the xix, xxx, 5, 157, 142–143, 162, 268, 324, 405
    knowledge and theories of 331
    materialist systems, and 405
    development of 388
    ideology of productive forces of society, the 283
    materialism of 274, 283, 299
    methods of 405, 407
    philosophy in 283
    systematisation of technological experience, and the 405

natural scientists   41, 348
  materialism of   273
natural selection
  *See* selection, natural
nature   xxiii, xxvi, 64–65, 71, 98, 137, 140,
    147–149, 156–157, 167, 177, 252, 276, 279,
    328, 338, 345, 351, 367, 389, 406
  animation of   294
  Bogdanov's point of view of   153, 158
  continuous flow of transformations, a
    xxiii
  dead, power of life over   314
  external   199, 247, 305, 325–330, 334–335,
    338, 342–344, 349, 361–362, 366–368,
    379, 399
  forces of   319
  genetically primary   407
  historical view of   xxii
  inorganic   xxiii, xxv, xxviii, 64, 94, 97,
    125, 134–135, 137, 139, 143, 148, 152, 153,
    156, 161, 166, 356, 410
  mastery of   xl
  objects of   295, 328
  organic   xxiii, 64, 94, 97, 134, 141, 143, 161,
    166, 334
  physical   103, 124
  Plekhanov's conception of   274
  power of, over humanity   379
  power of, over society   325
  power over, of humanity   167, 379, 402
  power over, of society   325, 388
  primacy of, in relation to spirit   274
  processes of   xxiii, 23, 154
  realm of   xxxiii
  regularities of   xxx
  relationship with, of humanity   348, 350
  social   305
  spirit, relationship to   276
  spiritualised   134
  static view of   xxii
  struggle with, and social class   379
  struggle with, immediate   326, 349, 367,
    375, 410–411
  struggle with, of humanity   4, 135, 139,
    326, 348, 388
  struggle with, of life   69
  struggle with, of organisers   368
  struggle with, of society   350, 361
  struggle with, through labour
  struggle with, through machine produc-
    tion   400
  uniformity of   64
neo-Kantian
  philosophers   35
  philosophy   279
Newton, Isaac   xxiii, xxiv, 357
Noiré, Ludwig   6n2, 48n3, 335, 341

objective
  bases of fetishism   389n2
  causality   96
  character of the physical world   18
  conception of life   95, 96
  correlation   150
  critique of 'thing-in-itself'   137
  data of experience   18, 34, 141
  existence   156
  experience   xxxiii, 31–32, 32n, 34, 42, 58,
    95–96, 101, 110, 290
    elements of   65
    organisation of   31
    realm of   26
  facts   17, 156, 157
  forces   151
  foundation for substitution   158
  foundations of a worldview   403
  meaning   5
  monism   302
  observation   51
  parallelism of life   97, 166
  person   91
  phenomena   178
  philosophical analysis   267
  physical body   294
  physical complexes   292
  physical world   63
  physiological coordinations   100
  physiological process   101
  processes   160
  properties of things   136
  psychical experience   52, 289
  reality   xxvii, 150, 154
  reflection of immediate experience   101
  regularity   63, 65, 91, 95, 150, 154–155, 177,
    197, 412
  right   236
  space and time   22, 26n
  subjective, distinction from   290

SUBJECT INDEX 437

tendency of the old materialism xx, 269
things-in-themselves 136
truth xx, 47, 269–273, 285, 302
world 26, 95, 156, 201, 201n
objectivity
  absolute 156, 269
  forms of 290
  functional correlation, of a 155
  experience, of 96n1, 291
    collective 18
    immediate 158
    socially organised 27n, 32n, 96n1, 100
  external objects, of 25
  phenomena, of 161
  physical complexes, of 290
  physical interconnectedness, of 150
  psychical interconnectedness, of 150
  physical, of the 16, 41
  physical series, of 18
  physical world, of the xxx, 25, 95
  science, of xxvi
  space and time, of 24
  universal validity, or xxxi
organisational (*organizatorskii*)
  activity 387
  class 368–370, 373, 382, 386–387, 392, 401–402
  elements of society 401
  function 283, 287, 354, 363, 368–369, 371, 374–375, 380–381, 383, 385, 392, 395, 400–401, 404, 407
  influence 402
  life 368
  part of society 375, 377, 401
  position in society 390
  principle 293
  psyche 374
  role 402
  type 368
organisers 212, 214, 226, 337, 345, 354, 360, 363–364, 367–377, 381, 383, 385–388, 392–393, 401
organising (*organizuiushchii*)
  adaptations 332, 401, 406
  apparatus 337, 341
  centre 42
  cognitive form 389
  combination 329
  experience 398, 403

forms 32, 216, 273, 285–286, 289, 334, 338–340, 343, 347–348, 351, 354, 356–358, 361, 364, 372–373, 391, 396, 399
forms of ideology 361
function 330, 336, 354, 375, 380, 399
idea 240, 356
ideological activity 376
ideological forms 340, 361
norms 339, 358
principal series 39
process 91, 125, 158, 215, 291, 406, 408
relationships 339
role 11
storeys 353
tendency 29, 43, 180, 213, 217–219, 223, 229, 366
unity of the world of experience 44
work of psychical selection 227
Ortodoks (Liubov Akselrod) 298n
Ostwald, Wilhelm 26n, 88n1, 274, 279
  *Naturphilosophie* 26n, 88n1

pain 177, 185, 186, 202, 207, 232, 237–8, 246, 258n, 262
  Affectional, the, and 75, 172, 173, 175, 257
  diminishment of life, and the 76
  energy of the psychical system, and 180
  energy, expenditure of, and 50, 77n, 170, 171, 185
  experience of 50
  negative vital differential, and 77
  'pleasant' 261
  quantitative nature of 76
  vital capacity, and 179
  vital-differential, and the 258
  what an organism avoids 76
panpsychism 64–65, 127, 137, 148–149, 151, 153, 157, 159, 275, 279
pleasure and pain 169, 197n3, 209
  Affectional, the, and 92, 168, 170, 176, 179, 199, 249
  central nervous system, the, and 76
  energetics of 249
  energy
    of psychical system, and 178
    of centres of consciousness, and 249
    of psychical experience, and 169
    of the psychical system, and 171
  evolutionary point of view, and the 76

life, development of, and the 179
  magnitudes, as 76, 88n2
  nervous system, and the 77, 77n
  organising tendency of 229
  physiological change, and 178
  psychical selection, and 169, 245, 308
  qualitative tones of 76
  quantitative nature of 76
  will, the, and 203n
  Wundt's 'Indifferenzpunkt', and 75n2
parallelism 11, 107, 130
  boils down to causality 143
  causality, and 147
  cognition and labour, of 43
  cognitive 96
  correlation of consecutiveness, and 148
  correlation of simultaneity, and 147
  experience, immediate, and physiological life, of 165
  experiences and vital differentials, of 85, 112
  forms of cognition and forms of production, of 404
  functional correlation, of 144
  functional correlation of simultaneity, of the, 142
  methodological idea of 35
  natural sciences, in the 142–143
  neo-Kantian 35
  objective and subjective manifestations of life, of 97, 166
  panpsychism, and 148
  physical processes and immediate experiences, of 104
  physical, the, and the psychical, of 282
  physiological and psychical processes, of 145, 148, 151
  psyche and physiology, of the 46
  psychical and physical phenomena, of 164
  psychical and physiological processes, of 147
  psychical and physiological series, of the xxviii, 37
  psychophysical 35, 36, 37, 47, 295
  psychophysiological 101, 145
  'reflection' and 'reflected', of 165
  series of experience that form bodies, of 37
  series that form a body, of the 10
  theories of 35, 410
parasitic class 213, 383n, 399–401
parasitism 321, 386, 390, 400
peasants 17, 32n, 215, 308, 383n, 392
  lords, and 374
  bonded 384
  rights of 382
  Spanish 321
  experience of 375
  household 413
  worldview of 375
perception xxx, 7–8, 13, 17, 19–20, 32, 36–37, 42, 47–48, 60, 62–63, 98, 102, 108–109, 119, 145, 148, 153, 155, 169, 173n, 184, 189, 189n, 192, 240, 244–245, 290, 337
  attached to an utterance 48
  beings, living, of a 94, 96, 137, 100, 122, 125n, 148, 292
  bodies 280
  body, of a 11, 12, 148
  body of a living being, of a 48, 294
  body, one's own, of 144
  body, physical, of a 36n, 152
  complex, vital, of a 121
  coordination of 95
  direct 175, 312n
  elements in 37
  environment, of the 53, 94, 240, 247
  environment, external, from the 242
  experiences, immediate, of 244
  external 94–96, 100, 102, 119
  external and internal 35
  external objects, of 136
  formation of 12
  forms of xxviii
  grouping of 27
  human body, of a 282
  immediate 27, 31, 38, 172, 244
  indirect 175, 312n
  makeup of 14
  means of 39, 88, 178, 312n, 317n2
  organisation, homogenous, of 149
  organism human, of a 282
  organs of 214
  person, another, of 116n, 144
  person, of a 90, 91, 93, 95, 99
  person, pre-civilised, of a 23
  physical phenomena, behind 293

SUBJECT INDEX 439

process, physiological, of a   148
process, vital, of a   93
reflected in consciousness   412
regulation of   291
social agreement of   96
space, of   18
substitution of   140, 147
system of psychical experience, in   168
'thing-in-itself', corresponding to a   30
things in space and time, of   136
utterances, of   96
visual   12, 51, 94, 109, 140, 172–173
world, external, of the   158
philosophers
   domestic   280
   metaphysical
philosophy   xix–xxii, xxix, xxxi, xxxiii, xl, 23, 31, 40, 133, 135, 137, 219, 267, 269, 281, 283, 289, 296, 298n, 300, 340, 376–377, 377n, 383, 398, 408–409
   Bogdanov's, starting point of   xxvii
   bourgeois   354, 396
   chain of generalising concepts in   337
   criticism in, has led to consistent positivism   3
   development of   158
   dualism in   164
   empiriocriticists, of the   289
   energetics, from the point of view of   279
   experience, harmonisation of, in   34n
   Greek   21
   historical point of view, the, based on   133
   'I' and 'not-I', the fatal question of   104
   idea of the absolute in   9n
   Kantian   279
   Marxian way, elaborated in a   83
   Marxism, of   278
   Marxism, revolutionary, within   xxi
   natural sciences, basis in the   283
   natural scientists, of   xix
   origin of   134
   Ostwald's, of nature   279
   Plekhanov's evaluation of   xxxii
   Plekhanov's feud with Bogdanov in   xxi
   Plekhanov's, bases of   xxxii
   positive   63
   proletarian   398
   'self-awareness' of   409
   task of   xxxiii
physical
   bodies   xxvii, 11, 12, 16, 37, 39, 65, 91, 100, 119, 126, 149, 165, 282, 289, 292, 294
      coincidence with psychical image of   30
      objective measurement of   162
      objectivity of   17, 25
      systematisation of perception of   145
   characteristics of the soul   135
   complexes   38, 39, 146, 150, 152, 156, 251, 274, 282, 292, 405n
   connection of phenomena   201n
   development   311
   elements   409
   energy   xxxiv, 312
   environment   124–125
   experience   27, 31, 36, 38, 42, 110, 116, 150, 158, 160, 164, 275, 275n1, 294–295, 358, 398, 406–407, 409, 412
      elements of   281
      forms of   291
      continuity of   164n
      objective regularity of   413
      organized socially   130, 406
      realm of   291, 410
      realm outside of   165
      social organization of   413
      subordination of psychical experience to   409
   health   74
   independent series   289
   interconnectedness   150
   objectivity   290
      phenomena of   406
   phenomena   32, 38, 160, 164, 293, 295
      perception of   xxix
   point of view   127
   process corresponds to a psychical process   137
   processes   88n1, 82, 294, 314, 412
      parallelism of   104
   reality   31, 134
   realm of experience   8, 13, 25, 38
   science, method of   39
   sciences   xix, 269
   series   26, 29, 42
      complexes in   13

inclusion of the psychical series  31
interconnectedness of  15
psychical series must adapt to the  32
socially organised experience  290
sphere of experience  13
suffering  223
things in place of immediate complexes  126
torture  239
universe  103
word  8n, 12, 13, 16, 35n, 37, 42, 91, 92, 95, 153, 398
  picture drawn by natural science  xxx
  bodies and processes of  150
  bodies or processes of  37
  connection with human consciousness  xxix
  regularities of  26
  socially organised experience  25, 27
  See also physical, the, and the psychical
physical, the, and the psychical  xxx, 36, 42, 65, 92, 164, 269, 282
  antithesis of, ceases  42
  association of  139
  combination of  31
  complexes  155
  connection of  35
    types of  282
  contradiction between  30, 31
  contraposition of, will lose its meaning  39
  correlation of  83
  difference between  12, 28, 30
    formulated by Mach and Avenarius  29
    origin of  16
  elements of experience are identical  15, 63–64, 280
  experience  xix, 63, 176, 297, 406
  fundamental homogeneity of  409–410
  interconnectedness of  289
    types of  130
  manifestations of life  52
  mutual correspondence and harmony of  30
  neo-Kantian view of  35
  parallel aspects of one reality  90
  parallelism of  164
  processes, interconnection of  263
  regularity of, different types of  83
  relationship of  83, 146, 282, 407
  two forms of the same process  xxviii
  under the same generalising forms  30
  unifying forms, of  xxxi
  world  25
    philosophical investigation of
physiological
  actions  79
  analysis  104
  change  178
  complex  117, 151, 153, 314
  conditions  261
  connections, derivative system of  61
  correlates of the experiences of others  xxviii
  environment  255
  fact, immediate  259
  facts  259, 310
  growth  310
  individual  55
  interconnectedness of neural centres  335
  life  44, 46, 50–51, 58, 61n, 64, 77, 90, 96, 101–102, 118, 119n, 151, 160, 165, 406
    organisation of  97, 166
  manifestation  46, 73, 78, 79, 197n1
  organisation  97, 101, 152
  organism  35n, 48n1, 91, 99, 100n
  phenomena  88, 118, 312n, 317n2, 406
  point of view  59, 104
  process  xxviii, 37, 39, 47, 56, 58, 82, 84n, 88, 91, 96–97, 96n2, 100, 101, 119n, 124, 130, 144–145, 147, 148, 151–152, 165–166, 175, 177, 263, 295, 327, 356, 406, 410n, 411–412
    of the nervous system  35
    connected with the act of consciousness  xxviii
  psychical complexes, substitution for  294
  psychical process, parallelism with  151
  psychical processes, and  82, 148, xxvii
  reflection  112, 165
  relationships  83, 87
  series  37, 39, 141
  space  18, 19, 22, 31, 95

SUBJECT INDEX                                                               441

contradictions of   20
geometrical space, and   18
result of development   19
states   114, 255, 256n1
stimulus   74, 255, 260
substitution of, for the psychical   97
system   105
time   21, 21n2, 95
   abstract time, relationship with   21
wholeness   317
physiology (a science)   104
physiology (a process)   50, 130, 182n, 282, 323, 325, 335, 341
   central nervous system, of the   29n1, 35
   nervous system, of the   37, 83, 157, 174–175
   psyche, relationship to   142, 144
   realm of   312, 314
   sensations, external, of   281
plasticity
   forms, of   43
   psyche, of the   231
   social systems, of   347
   social type, of a   368
pleasure   75n2, 76, 77, 76n, 77n, 88n2, 169, 174, 185, 186, 202, 203, 204, 208, 222, 224, 246, 256, 258n, 259, 262, 308
   Affectional, and the   75, 168, 257
   Avenarius' view of   77
   enhancement of life   76
   increase of energy   77, 170, 171, 200
   quantitative nature   75–6
   sexual act, of the   262
   vital differential, positive, corresponds to   77
   what living beings strive for   76, 179
pleasure and pain   169, 197n3, 203n, 209
   Affectional, and the   92, 168, 170, 176, 179, 199, 249
   central nervous system, and the   76
   energetics of   249
   energy
      of a psychical system, and   178
      of centres of consciousness, and   249
      of psychical experience, and   169
      of the psychical system, and   171
   evolutionary point of view regarding   76
   life, development of, and   179
   magnitudes, as   76

nervous system, and   77
organising tendency, and the   229
physiological change, and   178
psychical selection, and   169, 245, 308
qualitative tones   76
quantitative nature of   76
Plekhanov, G.V. (N. Beltov)   xx, xxi, xxvi, xxvii, xxix, xxxi, xxxii, xxxiii, xl, 159, 267, 270–277, 278, 271n, 274n, 275n, 280–281, 285–286, 288, 288n, 292–293, 296–301, 298n, 301n
   *Kritika nashikh kritikov*   276–277, 296, 300
   *On the Question of the Development of the Monistic View of History*   301n
positivism   3, 5, 15, 122, 124, 130, 138, 142, 144, 158–159, 279, 281–282, 287, 289, 370, 371n1
primitive society
   *See* society, primitive
production   xxxvii, 328, 344, 344n1, 365, 387, 391–392
   anarchy of   400
   collaboration in   340n
   crises of   75n, 309, 315
   development of   395
   exchange society, in   27n
   fields of   394
   forms of   404
   handicraft   360
   machine   284, 350, 354, 359–360, 366, 392, 397, 403, 408
   market for   320
   means of   328n1, 367, 375, 387, 391, 395
   of objects   11
   of ideas   349
   of organising forms   364
   of things   349
   organisation of   400
   organisation of under socialism   360
   organisers of   360, 386
   organising function in   377n, 399
   progress of   395
   realm of, as a whole   394
   relations of   301n, 352
   relationships of   390
   specialised functions of   400
   sphere of   4

system of   311, 317, 344, 395–396
tool of   382, 402
proletariat   287, 296, 305, 307, 374, 386, 393, 400, 409
   class   370
   class actions   391
   conscious collective interests of   396
   contradiction within   320
   English, skilled   319
   evolution from the petty bourgeoisie   392
   fetishism, petty bourgeois, of   393
   ideology of   392, 395–396, 400, 411
      bourgeois   393
      bourgeois, petty   392
      cognitive   392, 396
      new   400
      normative   394–396
   labour power, sale of   397
   labour relationships of   396
   not slaves   393
   organizational function, transfer, to   395
   resistance to exploitation   387
   social collaboration, comradely forms of   404
   social position of   392
   solidarity of   396–397
   struggle of   394–396
   subordination of   393
   tendencies of   409
   thinking of   398, 409
   worldview of   396, 398–399
psyche   xxviii, xxix, xxx, 14, 31–33, 43, 44, 46, 56, 61, 92, 95–97, 99, 100, 103–104, 111, 116, 119n, 122, 124–125, 127–128, 134, 137–139, 142, 145–148, 153–158, 162–164, 166, 167, 169, 172–176, 179, 182, 184–185, 189–192, 195–196, 199–200, 203–205, 208–210, 212–213, 215–216, 218, 223, 225–242, 244–248, 261, 281, 294–295, 311, 338, 342, 368, 374, 377, 378, 383, 406, 409, 412
   another being's   145, 167
   another person's   xxix, xxviii, 94, 99, 120, 125, 147, 148, 152, 234, 245
   development of the   16, 203, 209–10, 221, 227
   energetical knowledge of the   164
   Hume's abstract   287

individual   43
   principle of selection of   xxv
   individually organised experience of   xxix, xxx
   life of the   192
   nature, inanimate, distinguished from   156
   one, reflected in another   120
   one's own   xxviii, 161
   perceiving and perceived   xxix
   perceptions of   12
   physiology, and   151
   realm of the   27, 247
   whole, as a   208, 215, 230
psychiatry   113, 272
psychical   335
   activity   39, 51, 163
   adaptations   172–173, 179, 311
   apparatus, the   345
   association   201n2
   basis of action   341
   beings   125
   category of freedom   30
   centres   85
   chaos   44, 215
   combinations   17, 63, 150, 173, 201, 205–206, 210, 238
   communication   234n
   complexes   14, 37, 65, 110, 137, 146, 151–153, 173, 188, 191–192, 195, 197, 203, 206, 216, 234–235, 238, 242, 290, 294, 308, 335
      another psyche, of   xxviii
      emotional   29
      substitution of   xxix
      volitional   29
   coordinations   58, 103, 114
   creativity   209, 212
   development   101, 199–200, 202, 204, 206, 209–211, 215, 221–222, 228, 236–237, 239, 242, 245–246, 247n2, 308
   elements   15
   energy   88n1
   environment   97, 154, 167, 304
   exercise   188
   experience
      *See* experience, psychical
   facts   32, 169, 188, 290

SUBJECT INDEX                                                          443

field   111, 117, 185, 206n2, 244
form   90, 147, 174, 215, 216n1, 235–238
groupings   57, 62, 122, 125, 152, 190, 232, 304
habit   184, 186
illness   54, 239
images   7, 8, 11–15, 27, 30–31, 34, 42, 47, 48, 51, 59, 63, 95, 96, 100, 115, 119, 137, 169, 184, 189, 192, 216, 242, 244, 282, 292, 289–290, 331
indifference   50
individual, a   311
individuality   28
influence   241
insensibility   49
insertion into the physical, the   149
interconnectedness   150–152, 289
life   xxx, 44–45, 47, 50, 53–54, 59, 62, 106, 110, 144, 147, 158, 183–184, 198, 205, 208, 213, 232, 241–242, 246, 308, 347n, 411
material   217, 221–222
motor reactions   331n, 337
nature is not   64
order, the   164
organisation   24, 126, 200, 247, 345
organism, the   46, 208, 210, 311
phenomena   xxix, 35, 37, 88, 158, 160, 162–165, 198, 295, 312n
physiological conception of the   175
point of view   104
phase of actions   335
processes   11, 13, 91, 137, 144, 145, 147, 148, 151, 163, 165, 197n1, 263, 312n, 410n
   organized complex of neutral elements, as an   xxviii
   another psyche, of   xxviii
   physiological process, substitution for   xxviii
reactions   173–175, 184, 186, 192n, 193, 196, 331, 337n
reality   150
realm   xxxi, 38
   relationship to nervous system   xxvii
retardation   198
selection
   See selection, psychical
series   13, 15, 29–32, 37, 39, 42, 141, 274
state   41, 206, 261

solipsists   138
substance   398n
system   78, 103–104, 115, 120, 149, 167–173, 177, 180, 183, 191–193, 200–202, 206, 208–210, 240, 242, 244–245, 244n, 309, 347n
types   151, 166, 204–205, 210n, 233, 237, 406
whole   167–168, 205, 210
work   46, 408–409
world   8, 12, 13, 17, 25, 35, 35n, 42, 44, 63, 167, 284, 304
   See also physical, the, and the psychical
psychoenergetical
   explanation   221
   idea   249
   method   162
   point of view   261
psychoenergetics   66, 87–88, 96, 162, 164, 164n, 258, 408
psychogenetic analysis   247
psychological
   experience   99
   'miracles'   113
   adaptation   179
   genesis of associations   195
   investigation   170
   Lamarckism   188
   life   215
   method   181, 234
   organising process   291
   point of view   8n
   theory   199
      of parallelism   35
psychologists   23, 35, 101, 181, 192
psychology (condition of mind)   95, 220–223, 227, 286
   class   355
   freedom, of   397n
   imitation, of   234n
   scientific specialisation, of   xxxv
   trade union   320
   workers, of   301n, 320
psychology (science)   xxxvi, 28, 35n, 50–53, 168–169, 198–199, 234, 288, 298n, 312, 335
   applied   169
   laws of   28
   old, the   198

psychomotor reactions   173, 332
psychopathology   55, 242n
psychophysical
   combinations   13
   conceptions of life   96n2
   experiences   13
   law   85
   organisation   318
   parallelism   35, 36, 37, 47
   principle of   35
psychophysics   81, 87
psychophysiological
   absurdity   79
   adaptations   305, 317
   complexes   38, 313–314, 335, 341, 344n1
   data   59
   individual, the   317n1
   life
      duality of   295
      parallelism of   101
      unity of   318
   organism   64
   parallelism   145
   process   39
   reaction   374n
   research   410n
   series   38
   theory   256
psychophysiologists   75, 179
psychophysiology   xxxiv, 49, 80, 341
punishment   169, 214, 228, 234–239, 241–242, 241n, 247, 347n2, 297
pure description   7, 141, 144, 155, 157, 188n

realism   14, 135, 207, 216, 221–222, 376
reality   xxxv, 7n, 31, 133, 136, 202, 209, 221–222, 252, 298
   actual   xxxiii
   analysis of   65
   authentic   xxix
   beyond the bounds of direct experience   155
   cognitive
      continuity of   104
      relationship to   5
   concrete   337
   dualism of   15, 90, 134, 354
   experience of   154
   higher   14
   individual experience of   155
   Kantian categories of   150
   Metaphysical   155
   monism of   38, 101
   objective   xxvii
   physical bodies, of   17, 134
   relationship of empiriocriticism to   14
   supra-individual   156
   system of experience, a   14
   two aspects of   35, 126
regularity   41, 94, 110, 170, 181, 201n, 241, 305n
   abstract time, of   21
   associative   65
   basic line of ideological development, of the   353
   bodies, of   12
   derivative   353
   dynamic   xxxvii
   experience, of   5, 7, 15n, 41, 47, 65, 150
   functional correlation of simultaneity, of the   142
   labour on machines, of   409
   machines, of the operation of   409
   non-objective   65
   objective experience, of   95
   physical experience, in   81
   processes of nature, of the   xxiii
   psychical experience, in   81
   quantitative   xxxviii
   relationships, of   94
   socially valid   41, 65
   two types of   15
relativity   9n, 20, 139, 244, 270, 272, 371
   concept of class, of the   371
   movement, of all   20
   truth, of   270
religion   270, 287, 333, 406n
   Anglican   320
   Catholic   352
   Christian   381
   polytheistic   376
religiosity   399
   wife, of a   371
   slaves, of   377
   old aristocracy, the, of   285
   petty bourgeoisie, the, of   285, 287
Reymond, Emil du Bois   64
Riehl, Alois   6, 6n2, 88n1, 164n, 279
   *Der philosophische Kritizismus*   6n2

SUBJECT INDEX  445

ruling class
  *See* class, ruling

Schopenhauer, Arthur  42
Schubert-Soldern, Richard von  282
Schuppe, Wilhelm  282
selection
  negative  185, 188, 193, 195–196, 200–201, 202n, 203, 203n, 205–210, 206n2, 213, 214n, 215–216, 218, 221–223, 225, 227, 229–231, 233–237, 240, 246, 304, 308, 313–316, 319–320, 322–323, 325, 329, 347, 351, 357, 360, 378, 399
  positive  172, 178, 194, 202–203, 202n, 203n, 205–207, 206n2, 213–216, 225, 227–230, 233–234, 237, 304, 308–309, 313, 315–321, 323, 325, 343, 345, 357, 378
  psychical  167, 169, 169n, 170–180, 176n, 182–194, 185n, 196, 198, 199–200, 203–205, 203n, 206n2, 211–213, 215–220, 223n, 227, 229, 232–237, 234n, 239–240, 242n, 244–247, 249, 263, 306n, 308, 311–312, 316, 323, 344n1, 345, 380
  natural  xxv, 169n, 178–180, 179n, 305–306, 311, 344
  social  303, 305, 306n, 309–316, 318n, 323–325, 338, 340, 344n1, 345–346, 351–353, 359–366, 371n2, 372–374, 378–380, 386, 388–389, 395, 400
sensations  xxvi, xxvii, xxxii, 6n1, 7, 8, 8n, 10–13, 21n1, 45, 51, 53, 60, 64, 77n, 81–83, 85–87, 109, 140, 168, 179, 185, 187, 192, 197n3, 227, 243n, 276, 278, 281, 389
sensory
  colouration  75n1, 79n1
  nerve  87n1
  perception  18
  psychical reaction  184
  properties  136
  surface  82
  tone  75, 76, 77, 179
serfdom  358, 384
Shakespeare  221
Simmel, Georg  14n1, 241n
  *Einleitung in die Moralwissenschaft*  241n
slaves  363, 369–370, 374–383, 387, 392–393, 402
slave class  378

slave-owners  363, 367, 369, 374, 379–383, 387
social
  social complexes  313–317, 317n1, 318n, 319, 322–323, 359, 413
  consciousness  369n
  fetishism  398, 410
  energetics  326
  environment  186, 304–305, 307, 311, 316, 321–322, 324, 328n1, 343–344, 346–348, 350, 353, 359, 379, 387
  form  304–305, 316, 317n1, 319, 324, 328n1, 343, 359, 361–362, 388
  group  304–305, 319–320, 363n, 364, 370, 373, 400, 403
  life  40, 199, 236, 284, 306–307, 309, 312, 315, 317, 324, 326, 328n2, 329, 331–333, 336, 339, 340, 342–343, 347–348, 354–359, 361, 389, 397, 403, 406n, 413
  norm  304
  superstructure  336, 351–353
  validity  18, 22, 24–25, 26n, 27, 32, 41–42, 65, 95, 100–101, 150, 150n1, 154, 156, 271, 290, 292
social-genetic  6, 26, 269, 359, 404, 413
  point of view  6n2, 26, 413
socialist system  359
society  72, 122, 217, 220, 238, 240–241, 268–269, 288, 304, 306, 309, 311, 317, 325, 329, 342–343, 345, 352–353, 362, 367, 370, 376, 395
  advanced  43
  classless, future  220
  contemporary  40, 41, 42, 204, 271, 360, 370, 407, 413, 414
  cultured  309
  distribution of property in  338
  division of  362, 363, 364, 367, 374, 400
  economic structure of  317
  energy of  310
  exchange  27, 27n, 376, 410
  feudal  375
  high  213
  immediate struggle for life, and the  336
  individualistic  42
  law of causality applies to  328
  layers
    highest  375
    lower  370

life of   309, 362
living whole, as a   362
organism, as an   327
organism, not an   332
primitive   347
productive forces of   283
socialist   349, 360
structure of   347
subdivision of   362
surplus labour of   379
unity, living, as a   325
solipsism   xxxiii, 280, 281, 291
soul   22, 26n, 35n, 44, 54, 91, 133–137, 154, 157, 224, 225–226, 232, 284, 293–294, 410
space   xxvii, 20–24, 26, 171, 290–291, 313
  absolute   20
  abstract   xxx, 18, 19, 20, 21
  classical views of   20, 20n, 291
  contemporary view of   291
  elements of   8, 10, 11
  form of experience, of   159
  forms of   21
  geometrical   18, 31, 95, 290
  outer   97
  physiological   18–22, 31
  psychical   xxx
  sensory   18
  tactile   11
  theory of   18
  visual   11, 290
space and time   xx, 22n, 26n, 94, 269
  abstract   22, 25, 26n
  abstract forms of   23, 24
  forms of   18, 160
  forms of experience of   410
  Kantian   xxxii, 136
  movement in   xx
  objective   24, 26n, 290
  organisation of experience, of   412
  perceptions of   23
  physiological   22, 95
  sensations of   7
  social coordination of   24
  subjectivity of   xxxii
specialisation   134n3, 219–220, 363–364, 366–367, 370–371, 400
  era of   299
  experience, of   220

  forms of   217
  labour, of   217, 368, 392n
  organisers, of   373
  principle of   226
  scientific   xxxv
Spencer, Herbert   157, 159, 371n
Spinoza, Baruch   16, 79, 168n, 263, 274, 371n1
  *The Ethics*   79
spirit   13–14, 130, 135, 274–276, 278, 284, 287, 289, 290, 398n, 406, 410
  'spirit' and 'nature'   275, 406, 407
  'spirit' and 'matter'   130, 275, 278, 283, 289, 405–406
spiritualism   14, 65
subconscious   58, 114
  experiences   58, 411
subjective   16–17, 31, 41, 108, 136, 267, 290
  interconnectedness   289
  meaning   290
  parallelism of life   97, 166
  pleasure and pain   178
  reflection   241n
  truth   138
  world   201n
  experience   32
  forms   xxxii, 156
  interconnectedness   65
  experience   xxxiii, 17, 18, 25, 27, 32n, 34, 110, 141, 154, 201, 280, 290
  colouration   22, 31
subjectivity   xxxii, 290
substance   xxiv, xxvi, 9n, 64, 101, 155, 327, 389, 397–398, 398n
  abstraction, empty, an   389
  fetishes of   24
  'old materialism', of the   279
  being, of   xxvi
  energy, and   3xxvi, 279, 327, 398n
  experience, of   279
  Kant's position regarding   xxvi
  Plekhanov's position regarding   xxvi
  Spinoza's position regarding   16
substitution   139–142, 144–145, 154–162, 164, 294–296, 408, 410–412
  animistic   142
  associative complexes for nonorganic phenomena, of   98
  basis of the social nature of cognition, the   411

SUBJECT INDEX 447

causality, and 145
cognition, necessary for 153
critique of 411
empirical 161–162, 407
empirical, meta- 161
empirically indefinite for physical and unorganised processes, of the 158
experience, indirect, of 159
feelings and thoughts for utterances, of 139
'matter' for 'experience', of 65
mechanical complexes for complexes of energy, of 155
metaphysical 160
metaphysically indefinite for the physical and psychical, of the 158
old, the 145
one aspect of life for another 104
physical for the physical 155, 158
physiological for the psychical 168
psychical 177
psychical complexes for physical experience 407
psychical experiences for physical processes 295
psychical for inorganic phenomena 157
psychical, the, for the physical 145, 153, 154, 158, 159
psychical, the, for the physiological 139, 161
psychical process, a, for its physiological reflection 166
reflected for the reflection, of the 127
relative and conditional 140
scientific 145, 154, 158
theories of 154, 298
'thing-in-itself' for a 'phenomenon' 154, 159
'things-in-themselves' 161
universal xxviii, xxix, 293, 295, 300
world of 413
suffering 7n, 77, 77n, 168, 175, 182, 193, 200, 202, 202n, 204, 207–211, 214–215, 221–223, 225–226, 228, 230–231, 233, 237–240, 243, 246, 257–258, 261
surplus value 379, 386
series E 36

technological
act 341
adaptation 317, 318, 335, 343, 344
 social 334
basis of ideology 342
combinations 346, 361
complexes 340
development 344n1, 345
elements 318, 333
environment 214
experience 349, 353–355, 368
fact 342
forms 329, 335–336, 340–348, 350, 353–355, 357–359, 361–362, 366
functions 334, 341
ingenuity 388
initiative 387
knowledge 388
labour 374
life of a class 318
life 328, 351
method 343
process 284, 327, 328n2, 331, 336–339, 340n, 342–343, 344n2, 349–351, 353, 358–359, 361–362, 365–367, 374, 377, 380–383, 392, 395, 401, 405, 407
 proletarian cognitive ideology, of 414
 slave-owning society, of 382
 process, ideology of the 407
progress 288, 328, 348, 360, 380, 382, 383, 385–388, 386n, 393, 395, 398, 402
progressiveness 388–389
relationships 404
role
 production, in 317
 big bourgeoisie, of the 388, 390n
roots of cognitive forms 335
technique 304, 346, 366
tissue 341
type 343
value 397
technology xxv, 7, 48, 326, 328, 335, 342, 346, 358, 361, 364, 387, 390n, 392n, 395n
 cognition, and 332n1
 continually changing 395
 correlation with ideology 361
 differentiation of 400

increasing complexity of  362
machine   393, 395, 397, 409
medical   307
new   397
machine production, of   392
productive labour, of   383
slave labour, of   378
progress of   394, 400
realm of   328, 342
scientific   350, 390
social   336, 349
things-in-themselves   135, 158–160, 278, 284, 292, 410
  animists, for   134
  anthropomorphic, not   137
  called a 'living being'   292
  cause of a phenomenon   157
  cleansed of metaphysics   293
  cognitive uselessness of   136
  derivative from the 'soul'   137
  development of   135
  difference from phenomenon   136, 295
  empirical substitution, as an   160
  final causes, and   135
  initial   161
  irrelevant to tektology   xl
  Kant's view of   133, 136
  living being, of a   294
  metaphysical   406
  obsolete philosophical idea, an   161
  Plekhanov's view of   xxvi, xxxii, 292
  product of animist dualism, a   137
  product of substitution, a   159
  substitution for a phenomenon   153
  substitution of the psychical for the physiological   160
time
  absolute meaning of   160
  abstract   xxx, 21, 23
  arithmetical   95
  evolution of the conception of   291
  flow of   xxx
  form of experience, a   159
  individual experience of   21n1, 23
  infinity of   20
  physiological   21n2, 95
  Plekhanov's view   xxxii
  pure   95
  uniform flow of   23
  uniform time   23
  unity of   11
Timiriazev, Kliment   273

unadaptedness   31, 68, 73, 307, 311
  vital differential, and   74, 77
  cognitive   39
  forms of the social environment, of   324
  technological complexes, of   340
  psychical system, of   180
unconscious (adjective)
  experiences   63, 103
  reactions   63
  states   50
  utterances   58, 112, 166
  reactions   63, 243
unconscious, the   77n, 104, 208
unconsciousness, absolute, no such thing as   243
utterances   22n, 23–28, 30, 42, 47–50, 48n1, 48n3, 52, 54–59, 62–63, 89, 91, 95–98, 100, 112, 114–115, 138–139, 144, 163, 166–167, 176, 177, 204, 214n, 223, 230, 233, 258n, 280, 289, 294

Valentinov, Nikolai   298n
vital-capacity   250, 314, 315
vital-conservation   67–72, 250, 251n, 253–255
vital-differential   49–52, 59–63, 51n, 65–66, 68–70, 69n, 73–85, 75n1, 79n1, 87–90, 104–107, 105n, 109–110, 112, 114–115, 117, 174–175, 176n, 177, 182n, 249–250, 253, 255, 258–260, 258n, 262–263, 314

Weber-Fechner law   81–83, 87n2
Woltmann, Ludwig   303
workers   xviii, xix, xxxix, 218, 218n, 220, 268, 301n, 320–321, 363, 365–367, 371n2, 374, 379–380, 383, 385, 387, 392–396, 392n, 394n, 402, 408, 409
working class
  See proletariat
worldview   xix, xx, xxii, xl, 4, 38, 92, 147, 221, 229, 231, 233, 267, 275, 279, 296, 306, 403–404, 411, 413
  anti-social   236
  big bourgeoisie, of the   388, 390

## SUBJECT INDEX

Bogdanov's   267, 269, 281, 403, 407, 413–414
bourgeois   389, 398–399
capitalist class, of the   393, 399
class   220
class society, of a   407
contemporary   139
dialectical   292
dualist   128
eclectic   299
empiriomonist   263
English trade unionists, of   321
future, of the   220
general questions of   xix
holistic   161
idealist   269
Lunacharskii's   251
Marxian   xix, 407
Marxist   278, 283
materialism of natural scientists   268
materialist   220, 405
metaphysical   396
middle class man, of the   370
monist   35, 40, 269, 299
organisational class, of the   369
philosophical   297
philosophically-supported   267
proletarian   396, 398, 399
radical-democratic   230, 232
realistic   204
religious   287, 358, 375, 377
scientific   14, 65
slaves, of   378
social   267
teleological   127
Willy, Rudolph   21n2
Wundt, Wilhelm   75n2, 127, 156, 192